A HISTORY

OF

Judaism

VOLUME II

EUROPE *and*

the NEW WORLD

BERNARD MARTIN

Basic Books, Inc., Publishers

NEW YORK

Copyright © 1974 by Basic Books, Inc.
Library of Congress Catalog Card Number: 73-90131
Volume I ISBN: 0–465–03006–8 Cloth
Volume II ISBN: 0–465–03007–6 Cloth
Set ISBN: 0–465–03008–4 Cloth
Volume I ISBN: 0–465–03009–2 Paper
Volume II ISBN: 0–465–03010–6 Paper
Printed in the United States of America
Designed by Vincent Torre
79 80   10 9 8 7 6 5 4

A HISTORY OF

JUDAISM

IN TWO VOLUMES

DANIEL JEREMY SILVER

BERNARD MARTIN

FOR

Nancy, Rachel, and Joseph,

WITH LOVE

CONTENTS

Contents

INTRODUCTION

$\mathbb{B}$Y THE BEGINNING of the thirteenth century the great age of the Jews in the Moslem world, which was the major locus of Jewish religious and cultural creativity in the post-Talmudic era, had already passed its peak and was moving toward its end. The old Jewish communities of Europe, many of them first planted in the days of the Roman Empire, had awakened from their apparent spiritual and intellectual somnolence and were preparing to assume their role as the new fortresses of Judaism. Some of them already had substantial achievements to their credit. Henceforth, they were to be—and to remain for centuries—the chief centers of Jewish life and thought. European Judaism, including its later offshoots in America, Israel, and throughout the world, is largely the subject of this volume.

Maimonides, a brilliant product of the Judeo-Islamic synthesis, undoubtedly represents the zenith of medieval Jewish philosophy. But Christian Europe in the Middle Ages also produced eminent Jewish philosophers and religious thinkers who contributed importantly to the progressive development of Judaism. And it was in Christian Europe that the mystical tradition known as Kabbalah had its fullest flowering, although its roots are to be found centuries earlier in Palestine and Babylonia. Both the rationalistically oriented philosophy of Maimonides' successors in medieval Europe and the imaginative theosophy of Kabbalah are discussed here.

Jewish life in Christian Europe first burgeoned creatively in the western parts of the continent, especially in the communities of the Rhineland and of Italy. It was not until after the first Crusades that there began a steady migration of Jews eastward into Poland, a migration which continued until the seventeenth century, when a reversal of the tide's direction was inaugurated. As a result of a century of bloody persecution culminating in total expulsion from their homeland in 1492, many of the exiled Jews of Spain established themselves in settlements all along the Mediterranean littoral, obtaining an especially cordial welcome in the domains of the Ottoman sultans. Jewish life and thought in the medieval and premodern communities of both the Ashkenazim of Europe and the Sephardim of the Ottoman Empire will engage our attention.

After living through two miserable centuries in which their fortunes reached a nadir that was not again approximated until the Holocaust of a generation ago, the Jews of western and central Europe began in the eighteenth century to witness the emergence of a new social and political order in the larger world that was ultimately to break down their ghettoized existence and precipitate them into the mainstream of European life. At the same time that these Jews were first being exposed to the winds of modernity that have ever since continued to buffet traditional Judaism, their still isolated and oppressed brethren in eastern Europe were swept by the powerful movement of Ḥasidism which attempted, for a time with great success, to introduce new vitality and spontaneity into the rigidified tradition. We shall consider both of these phenomena in some detail.

It seemed at the beginning of the nineteenth century that the political emancipation of the Jews in western and central Europe might prove a fatal blow to Jewish life in these areas. Judaism, however, demonstrated its capacity for adapting to new conditions in not only surviving the radical challenges posed by emancipation but also in producing, under its impact, new movements of great consequence. The general ideology of Haskalah, or enlightenment, already widely accepted in Germany and the West, was developed further and penetrated eastward into the bastions of tradition. In addition, the new interpretations of Judaism generally known as Reform, Conservatism, and Neo-Orthodoxy emerged, as did a new mode of Jewish scholarship—the so-called *Wissenschaft des Judentums*, or Science of Judaism—and fresh philosophical attempts at effecting a synthesis between Judaism and the dominant intellectual currents of the age. All these developments will be surveyed here.

Special attention will be devoted in the present volume to the evolution of the American-Jewish community from its beginnings to the present day, the origin and growth of the Zionist movement, the tragedies and triumphs of European Jewry in the twentieth century, and the establishment of the State of Israel and its achievements during the first quarter century of its existence. These—especially the destruction of east European Jewry in the Nazi Holocaust and the rebirth of a Jewish commonwealth in Israel—are no doubt the developments of the greatest immediate interest to the contemporary English-speaking reader, but he will find that to understand them adequately he must reach back centuries and grasp the forces and events that preceded them and out of which they were born.

To some, the amount of detail presented here will seem over-whelming; to others it will be quite insufficient in view of the com-plexity of the historical phenomena and ideas dealt with. I have given only so much as I think essential to an adequate understanding of how Judaism and Jewish life in their major centers in the modern world came to be what they presently are, and why I believe (as the attentive reader will easily infer that I do) that *lo alman Yisrael,* Israel is not orphaned, and that *am Yisrael hai,* the Jewish people lives—and will continue to live.

BERNARD MARTIN

ACKNOWLEDGMENTS

THANKS are due to the following for permission to quote from their material:

The Jewish Publication Society of America, Philadelphia, for quotations from Joseph Albo's *Sefer Ha-Ikkarim*, ed. and trans. Isaac Husik, copyright 1929; and *Hebrew Ethical Wills*, ed. and trans. Israel Abrahams, copyright 1926.

Schocken Books, Inc., New York, for excerpts from *A Jewish Reader: In Time and Eternity*, edited by Nahum N. Glatzer, copyright © 1946, 1961 by Schocken Books, Inc.; *Jerusalem and Other Jewish Writings* by Moses Mendelssohn, copyright © 1969 by Schocken Books, Inc.; and *Modern Hebrew Literature* by Simon Halkin, copyright © 1950, 1970 by Schocken Books, Inc. Reprinted by permission of Schocken Books, Inc.

Holt, Rinehart and Winston, Inc., New York, for excerpts from *The Golden Tradition*, edited by Lucy S. Dawidowicz, copyright © 1967 by Lucy S. Dawidowicz. Reprinted by permission of Holt, Rinehart and Winston, Inc.

The Soncino Press, Ltd., London, and Dayan Dr. I. Grunfeld, for quotations from *Judaism Eternal: Selected Essays from the Writings of Rabbi Samson Raphael Hirsch*, translated from the German original and annotated by Dayan Dr. I. Grunfeld, © 1959; and from Samson Raphael Hirsch's *Horeb*, translated from the German original, with introduction and annotations by Dayan Dr. I. Grunfeld, © 1962.

The Herzl Press, New York, for excerpts from *The Diaries of Theodor Herzl*, trans. H. Zohn (New York: Herzl Press, 1960), © 1960.

Rabbi Arthur Hertzberg, Englewood, New Jersey, for excerpts from *The Zionist Idea: A Historical Analysis and Reader*, edited and with an introduction and biographical notes by Arthur Hertzberg (Philadelphia: Jewish Publication Society, 1959), © 1959.

The Zionist Organization of America, New York, for quotations from Leo Pinsker, *Auto-Emancipation*, trans. D. S. Blondheim (New

Acknowledgments

York: Zionist Organization of America, 1948), copyright 1948.

A. S. Barnes & Company, Inc. for a quotation from *The Life of Glückel of Hameln: 1646–1724, Written by Herself*, translated from the original Yiddish and edited by Beth-Zion Abrahams, © 1963.

❧❧❧

Thanks are also due to the following sources for permission to reproduce photographic material:

The Photographic Archive of the Jewish Theological Seminary of America, New York, Frank J. Darmstaedter, Curator, for the photographs of the eight historic synagogues included in this volume, and for the portraits of Solomon Schechter and Mordecai Kaplan. Photograph of Mordecai Kaplan by John H. Popper.

Collection, The Jewish Museum, New York, for the painting *Interior of the Livorno Synagogue on Simhat Torah*.

The YIVO Institute for Jewish Research, New York, for the two photographs dealing with the Warsaw Ghetto and the Nazi Holocaust, and for the portraits of Abraham Isaac Kook and A. D. Gordon.

The American Jewish Archives on the Cincinnati Campus of the Hebrew Union College, Jewish Institute of Religion, for the portraits of Isaac Mayer Wise and Kaufmann Kohler.

Photograph of Abba Hillel Silver courtesy of Abba Hillel Silver Memorial Archives, The Temple, Cleveland, Ohio.

TRANSLITERATION OF
HEBREW TERMS

א is not
   transliterated

בּ = b

ב = v

ג‎,גּ = g

ד‎,דּ = d

ה = h

ו = v (where
   not a
   vowel)

ז = z

ח = ḥ

ט = t

י = y

כּ = k

כ = ch

ל = l

מ = m

נ = n

ס = s

ע is not
   transliterated

פּ = p

פ = f

צ = tz

ק = k

ר = r

שׁ = sh

שׂ = s

ת‎,תּ = t

ָ = a

ַ = a

ֳ‎,וֹ = o

ֻ‎,וּ = u

short ָ = o

יֵ = ei

ֶ = e

ִ = i

ֵ = ei

ֱ = e

ָ: = o

ֲ = a

vocal *sheva* = e

silent *sheva* is not transliterated

VOLUME II

EUROPE *and* *the* NEW WORLD

CHAPTER

❧ I ❧

Jewish Religious Thought after Maimonides

T HE CLIMATE of the thirteenth century, in whose first decade Moses Maimonides died, was hardly conducive to universal acceptance by the Jews of Europe of the rationalist version of Judaism which the great philosopher had elaborated. The power and privilege enjoyed by the social and intellectual elite of Spanish Jewry during the centuries of Moslem hegemony over the Iberian peninsula were curtailed as the rulers of the Christian kingdoms of Castile and Aragon intensified their efforts to drive out the Arabs and gain control of the entire land. In France also the position of the Jews deteriorated progressively under the growing hostility of the Christian church; in 1242 the *Talmud* was burned in Paris, and by the end of the century the French Jews were on the verge of total expulsion from the country. In Italy the Fourth Lateran Council, meeting in 1215 during the papacy of Innocent III, renewed the anti-Jewish legislation of previous church councils and decreed the hated "Jew badge," to be worn on the outer garment to make Jews easily distin-

[3]

guishable from Christians. In Germany and Austria charges of ritual murder and the blood libel led to wholesale massacres of Jews, and pitched battles between Jews and Christians were fought in various cities. As the favorable social and economic conditions which had helped give rise to rationalism and the critical spirit and had promoted receptivity toward these forces in certain Jewish circles everywhere declined, Jews tended increasingly to cloak themselves in the mantle of traditional piety and to find solace and strength in simple, unquestioning faith and obedience to the precepts of the Torah. Mystical tendencies grew more prominent, and the proud flight of critical speculative thought came to appear to many in the Jewish world not only arrogant and impious but dangerous and seditious.

Maimonides' philosophical works—his *Sefer Ha-Madda* (*Book of Knowledge*) and *Moreh Nevuchim* (*Guide of the Perplexed*)—became the focus of an intense controversy that lasted throughout the thirteenth century and into the fourteenth. The philosopher's attempt totally to deanthropomorphize the concept of God, his search for rational and utilitarian reasons for the commandments (*taamei ha-mitzvot*), and his ambiguous attitude toward the dogma of the resurrection of the dead particularly irritated his orthodox opponents. The bitterness of the controversy between the Maimonideans and anti-Maimonideans reached such a degree that the two parties excommunicated each other, and some disputants apparently invited intervention on the part of Church authorities. But even most of the anti-Maimonideans were shocked when the Dominican monks, who specialized in ferreting out heresy, confiscated and burned the *Guide* and *Sefer Ha-Madda* in southern France in 1233. The ideological struggle continued, reaching a new pitch of fervor seventy years later and culminating in the issuance in 1305 of a ban by the leading Spanish rabbinic authority, Solomon ben Abraham Adret, and a number of other rabbis, proscribing the study of philosophy and the sciences (except medicine) by anyone before he had attained the age of twenty-five. (For more on the Maimonidean controversy, see pp. 73–77.)

It is not surprising that the thirteenth century produced few distinguished or original Jewish thinkers. A considerable part of the philosophic effort of the century was devoted to the writing of commentaries and glosses on Maimonides' *Guide;* such works were composed by Samuel ibn Tibbon (ca. 1150–ca. 1230), Shem Tov ben Joseph Falaquera (ca. 1225–ca. 1295), and Joseph ibn Kaspi (ca. 1279–ca. 1340). These men were all staunch advocates of rationalism. So also was Jacob ben Abba Mari Anatoli, who, in the first half of the thirteenth century, presented highly allegorical interpretations of the Bible and preached philosophical sermons inspired by Maimonides from synagogue pulpits in southern France and Naples, to the extreme annoyance of the anti-Maimonideans.

In addition to expounding the philosophy of Maimonides, the thinkers of the thirteenth century applied themselves to the essential task of translating into Hebrew the works of the Spanish-Jewish philosophers who had written in Arabic, as well as the works of ancient Greek and of recent Moslem philosophers and scientists, thus making them accessible to non-Arabic speaking Jewry. This was no simple undertaking, since Hebrew at that time lacked a philosophical and scientific vocabulary. Largely responsible for supplying the defect was the famous family of translators in southern France, the Tibbonids. The founder, Judah ben Saul ibn Tibbon, began the work in the twelfth century by translating the major philosophical treatises of Saadiah, Baḥya ibn Pakuda, and Judah ha Levi. His son Samuel, in addition to writing a work on physical and metaphysical questions entitled *Maamar Yikkavu Ha-Mayyim* (*Essay on "Let the Waters Be Gathered"*) and philosophical commentaries on Ecclesiastes and the Song of Songs, produced the classic Hebrew version of Maimonides' *Guide of the Perplexed*, obtaining aid from the author himself in the course of his work. Later in the thirteenth century Samuel's son Moses translated Joseph ibn Zaddik's *Olam Katan* (*Microcosm*), Averroes' versions of Aristotle, and some of Maimonides' writings. (For more on the Tibbonids, see pp. 71–73.) Others besides the Tibbonids furthered the translating work. Shem Tov ben Joseph Falaquera abridged and translated Solomon ibn Gabirol's philosophic masterpiece, *Mekor Ḥayyim* (*The Fountain of Life*), from Arabic into Hebrew. Jacob Anatoli translated Averroes' Intermediate Commentary on the first five books of Aristotle's *Logic*, the *Almagest* of Ptolemy, and the astronomical work of al-Farghani. Kalonymus ben Kalonymus (1286–d. after 1328), one of the most eminent and assiduous of the medieval Jewish translators, rendered into Hebrew numerous works by Galen, Euclid, Averroes, al-Kindi, and al-Farabi. Thus the wealth of Jewish, Moslem, and Greek philosophical and scientific thought became available to Jewish (and non-Jewish) readers in Christian Europe.

The thirteenth century was not altogether lacking in Jewish philosophers with some measure of originality. The Italian Hillel ben Samuel of Verona (ca. 1220–1295) wrote a psychological work entitled *Tagmulei Ha-Nefesh* (*The Rewards of the Soul*) in which various and contradictory influences—Thomas Aquinas and other Christian scholastics, Avicenna and the neo-Platonists, and the greatest of the Arabic rationalists, Averroes—are discernible, but in which the moral demands of traditional Judaism regarding reward and punishment in the afterlife prevail. Hillel accepted the notions of "material intellect" and "active intellect" that had become commonplace among the Moslem and Jewish Aristotelians of his age. The material intellect was the capacity for acquiring rational knowledge resident in the soul, while the active intellect was the lowest of the heavenly "intelligences." The ultimate bliss of immortality for the soul consisted in the union of its rational element with the active intellect. However, while Averroes had maintained that there is only one universal soul from which the souls of particular persons emanate like the rays of the sun, and that there is no individual immortality, since after death particular souls are reabsorbed without differentiation into their source, Hillel insisted upon individual immortality.

Somewhat more original as a religious thinker was Isaac Albalag, who lived in the second half of the thirteenth century, probably in Spain. An extreme rationalist and a disciple of Averroes, whose works had been translated into Hebrew and had become popular in Jewish philosophical circles, he, unlike Maimonides, who did not believe that reason obliged him to do so, accepted the Aristotelian and Averroistic doctrine of the eternity of the universe. Albalag appears also to have adopted the theory of the "double truth" that was then being propounded by Christian Averroists, especially at the University of Paris, who wished to pursue their philosophical inquiries unhindered by theological dogmas and yet avoid conflict with Church authorities and accusation of heresy. In any case, the Jewish thinker distinguished two independent types of truths—philosophical and prophetic—and insisted that, although these may be inconsistent with each other, each is equally valid in its own realm. Considering the Bible, with its numerous anthropomorphic expressions and tales of wonders and miracles, Albalag generally (not always) disdained the method of allegorical and metaphorical explanation employed by his predecessors to render Scripture philosophically acceptable. Instead, he argued that the Torah sets forth no philosophical or speculative truths; its function is simply moral and practical, to guide and govern the behavior of the unenlightened masses. Albalag, not surprisingly, was condemned by later orthodox writers as a dangerous and depraved heretic.

In the first decades of the fourteenth century a phenomenon began to appear in Spanish Jewry that was to assume major proportions by the end of the century: the conversion of Jews to Christianity. One of the early apostates, Abner of Burgos (ca. 1270–1340), precipitated a philosophical debate over a fundamental religious issue that had never been resolved: whether man's will is free or predetermined. Following his conversion to Christianity, Abner wrote a work entitled *Iggeret Ha-Gezerah* (*Epistle on Fate*) in which he argued that his apostasy, like every other human act, was foreordained. Although he conceded that the will may choose alternative acts, its choice, he insisted, is in fact determined by antecedent causes that affect it, including astrological influences. Only on the assumption of causal determination of the will, according to Abner, could both the omniscience and omnipotence of God be maintained. The convert declared that such had been his view even when he was still a Jew, and that this in fact is the view of Judaism itself, properly understood; statements in the Bible and the *Talmud* affirming free will are merely for the ignorant masses who cannot grasp and accept philosophical truth. In addition to defending predetermination, Abner of Burgos set forth an apology for Pauline and Augustinian Christology and attempted to show that the central Christian doctrines of the Incarnation and the Trinity are supported by the aggadic *midrashim*. Later apostates, notably Solomon Ha-Levi of Burgos (after his conversion he was known as Pablo de Santa Maria and became a bishop of the Church) and Joshua Lorki (Geronimo de Santa Fé), employed many of Abner's arguments in their polemics against Judaism.

Isaac ben Joseph Ibn Polegar, a Spanish scholar and philosopher who was personally acquainted with Abner, replied to the convert in his *Iggeret Ha-Ḥarifot* (*Epistle of Blasphemies*) and his major work, *Ezer Ha-Dat* (*Support of Religion*). Polegar disposed of Abner's Christological interpretation of the *aggadot* by arguing that these are not to be interpreted literally and that they are not, in any case, normative for Judaism. Against Abner's contention that God's omniscience denies the reality of man's freedom, he developed a theory of the mutual and simultaneous coworking of the divine and human wills. At the moment a human action takes place, its completion is intended by God's will, which is the source of every action; but it becomes at the same moment the object of man's will, which thus replicates the divine will. Since God's foreknowledge of the action in question and His will as well as the human will in regard to it all arise at the same moment, according to Polegar, both divine omniscience and human freedom are maintained. It was an ingenious solution, but later Jewish philosophers who considered the issue found it inadequate. As we shall see, Gersonides, who was intent on defending human freedom, restricted God's knowledge to the species and to universals and held that He does not know individuals and particularities, including man's actions, and Ḥasdai Crescas, who was concerned with affirming divine omniscience and omnipotence, radically limited human freedom.

The first front-rank philosopher to appear in the Jewish world after Maimonides was the polymath Levi ben Gershom (1288–1344), known as Ralbag or Gersonides. Probably the most learned Jew of the fourteenth century, Gersonides, who lived in southern France and wrote his works in Hebrew, was not only an extremely subtle metaphysician but also a superb mathematician, astronomer, and Bible exegete. His reputation penetrated into Christian society, where he was known as Maestre Leo de Bagnols or Magister Leo Hebraeus. A number of his works were translated into Latin, one of them by direct order of no less a personage than Pope Clement VI.

Gersonides' major philosophical work, *Milḥamot Adonai* (*Wars of the Lord*), completed in 1329, begins where Maimonides' *Guide of the Perplexed*, written a century and a half earlier, leaves off. In it he discusses with great critical acumen a number of important issues which he believed his predecessor had treated inadequately or to which he had offered unsatisfactory solutions. A more thoroughgoing rationalist than Maimonides, Gersonides recognized the possibility of conflict between the revelation of the Torah and philosophy, and appears in some cases to have preferred Aristotle to the Torah. He was not, however, a slavish adherent of the Stagirite; in his work there is much trenchant criticism of Aristotelian views. *Milḥamot Adonai* is a comprehensive work divided into six sections, dealing with the major problems that agitated the medieval Jewish mind. The first section is concerned with the question of the immortality of the soul; the second with prophecy, divination, and dreams; the third with God's knowledge; the fourth with His providence; the fifth with the celestial spheres and separate intelligences of the Aristotelian system and their relationship to God; and the last with the creation of the world, miracles, and the signs whereby the true prophet may be recognized. Almost always Gersonides, in discussing any problem, begins with the views of his predecessors—Aristotle, Alexander of Aphrodisias, Themistius, al-Farabi, Averroes, and Maimonides. After criticizing their opinions, he develops his own view.

[8]

In dealing with the problem of the immortality of the soul, Gersonides begins with a discussion of the intellect in its various forms as conceived by the Aristotelian philosophers—the material or passive intellect, the active intellect, and the acquired intellect. Following the view of the second-century Aristotelian commentator Alexander of Aphrodisias, Gersonides takes the position that the material intellect is not a substance but a simple disposition or possibility (*hachanah*) whose substratum is the power of imagination (*ha-tzurah ha-dimyonit*), which is itself part of the sensitive soul (*ha-nefesh ha-margeshet*). Through the sensations which it receives from the outside world, the material intellect, under the influence of the active intellect (the lowest of the celestial "intelligences"), obtains abstract concepts (*muskalot*). Thereby the material or passive intellect is actualized and becomes the acquired intellect. It is this acquired intellect, with its comprehension of intelligible forms which are imperishable and eternal, that enjoys immortality, according to Gersonides, while the passive or material intellect dies with the body. Against Averroes, the Jewish philosopher maintains that the acquired intellect in its immortal state retains its individual character; it is not absorbed into the active intellect.

With regard to the phenomenon of prophecy, Gersonides follows Maimonides' view that the prophet is, first and foremost, a wise man or philosopher. The prophet's highly developed mind gives him the ability to understand the laws of nature (in Gersonides' own universe of discourse, the principles of causation resident in the active intellect) that govern events in the terrestrial world; he extrapolates from his general knowledge of the operation of these laws to predict how they will operate in the realm of human affairs. Gersonides appears to believe that the sublunar world is entirely ruled by celestial influences; yet he seeks to avoid determinism by insisting that man has been especially endowed by God with freedom to choose alternative courses of action, and that an understanding of the working of the laws of the celestial spheres provides the possibility of avoiding or mitigating their undesirable effects.

Faithful to classical Jewish tradition, Gersonides regards Moses as the greatest of all the prophets. It was through his mediation that God gave Israel the Torah, which, with its commandments and philosophical truths, makes possible achievement of the moral and intellectual perfection that leads to immortality. Like Maimonides, Gersonides cannot regard the *mitzvot*, or religious commandments, as arbitrary "decrees of the King"; he seeks to provide ethical and ratio-

[9]

nal grounds for them. Furthermore, he maintains that the Torah proclaims certain speculative truths, such as the immortality of the soul and the creation of the universe, which the philosophers would never have been able to attain with their unaided reason.

When Gersonides comes to deal with the question of God's knowledge of individuals and particular events in the terrestrial world, he dissents sharply from the position of Maimonides. Despite the objection that for God to know particulars implies change in the divine nature, Maimonides had affirmed such knowledge and dismissed the objection by asserting that the character of God's knowledge is totally different from man's. Gersonides does not believe that the objection can be so disposed of. The divine immutability, which he joins Maimonides and virtually all other medieval philosophers in insisting upon (the Greek conception of God as the impassive, eternally unchanging Being had triumphed over the biblical vision of God, even among theologians and philosophic exponents of biblical revelation), necessitates, according to Gersonides, the restriction of God's knowledge to universal laws and to species. Through His nontemporal and unchanging cognition, God knows the laws of the universe that regulate the movements of the heavenly bodies and thereby all the beings in the sublunar world; He also knows the fate destined for all individuals as members of the species to which they belong. But God does not and cannot know how individual men will make use of the freedom He has granted them. The actions of individuals are, in principle, unpredictable, and it therefore implies no defect in God's eternal and immutable knowledge to exclude them from its purview. So Gersonides, acting on his conviction that human freedom must be affirmed, responded to the question so forcefully placed on the philosophical agenda by Abner of Burgos and others.

Intimately associated with the problem of God's knowledge of individuals is the question Gersonides deals with in the fourth section of his *Milḥamot Adonai,* namely, divine providence. Here he is inclined to adopt the view of his twelfth-century predecessor. Although God bestows good on all through the regular motions of the heavenly bodies, His specific providence is not exercised in equal measure, Gersonides follows Maimonides in declaring, toward all men without distinction. Only those who have fully developed their minds and attained intellectual perfection are completely under the power of divine providence; the degree of providence is strictly correlated with the degree of mental development.

Diverging from both the Jewish and non-Jewish Aristotelians of the Middle Ages, Gersonides rejected their favored form of the cosmological argument for the existence of God, according to which the postulation of an unmoved mover is required to account for the system of motions in the universe. He also rejected the neo-Platonic doctrine of emanation. Instead, Gersonides offers a version of the teleological argument, or argument from design. The creation of the universe in time, he further maintains against Maimonides, is rationally demonstrable. One of his arguments in this connection is the relatively primitive state of the sciences; had the world existed eternally, the great astronomer and mathematician contends, the sciences would be far more highly developed than they presently are. But while Gersonides stoutly defended the idea of creation at a definite moment, he could not accept the notion of *creatio ex nihilo*. To his mind the principle *ex nihilo nihil fit* seemed indubitable. Hence he adopted the Platonic theory that the universe was created out of a "formless matter" that is coeternal with God. This is the meaning of the terms *tohu* (without form) and *bohu* (void) in Genesis 1:2. But the primal matter of creation does not have the same ontological status as God; indeed, strictly speaking, it cannot be said to have had "existence" at all, for all real existence is made possible only through the union of matter with form.

Gersonides also categorically denies one of the major theses propounded by Maimonides—that it is impermissible to ascribe positive attributes to God, since His absolute unity and simplicity are thereby endangered. This is not so. All the predicates in any proposition dealing with a totally spiritual, nonmaterial entity such as God are analytic; they are implicit in an understanding of the subject and do not introduce any multiplicity into it. It is also untrue that we can know only what God is not. From His actions in the world we may deduce some positive knowledge of God, and there is an essential analogy between the attributes of man and those of God. Qualities such as life, power, and wisdom have the same signification with regard to both the human and divine natures, although they inhere in God eminently and in man only derivatively. On the question of divine attributes Gersonides follows the Arabic Aristotelian Averroes rather than the Jewish Aristotelian Maimonides.

A word must be said about Gersonides' view of the "last things." In his version of Jewish messianism there are two redeemer figures— Messiah son of Joseph and Messiah son of David. After the assassination of the first, the second will appear in glory. Messiah son of

David will bring about the resurrection of the dead, and as a result of this stupendous miracle all the peoples of the earth will acknowledge the God of Israel and accept Judaism as their faith. Gersonides even calculates the time of the advent of the Messiah; he will come, according to his reckoning, in the year 1358. The "days of the Messiah" will not be characterized by a completely new world order. Human beings will still be mortal, but the earth will be "full of the knowledge of God" and men will use their God-given freedom for moral purposes.

In certain respects Gersonides, as we have suggested, is more radically rationalist than the author of *A Guide of the Perplexed*. In others, however, he remains more faithful to the categories of biblical-rabbinic theology and closer to the conceptions of popular Jewish piety than Maimonides. To be sure, Gersonides did not escape charges of heresy at the hands of later Jewish thinkers. Ḥasdai Crescas found some of his views deeply repugnant, and Shemtov ibn Shemtov did not hesitate to brand his *Milḥamot Adonai* (*Wars of the Lord*) as *Milḥamot Im Adonai* (Wars against the Lord). The pious leader of the Jews expelled from Spain in 1492, Isaac Abravanel, also sharply criticized the Provençal thinker who had died a century and a half earlier. But Gersonides did not become the center around which a long and acrimonious controversy raged, as was the case with Maimonides. He was not read and studied in later generations nearly as intensively as his predecessor. His *Milḥamot Adonai* was generally neglected in the centuries after his death, and it was not Gersonides the trenchant philosopher but Gersonides the pious Bible exegete who derived useful moral and practical lessons (*toaliyyot*) from his study of scriptural texts who was widely remembered and admired in the Jewish world.

The disorders of Gersonides' generation and the tragic experiences of the Jews of Europe in subsequent decades provided an environment that was not at all favorable for the reception of his critical, rationalist views. The philosopher himself witnessed the expulsion of the Jews from France and the massacres of his people that took place at the time of the Crusade of the Pastoureaux. Four years after he died the Black Death broke over Europe, and the Jews, accused by the credulous populace of poisoning the wells and rivers, were murdered by the tens of thousands all over the continent, from Spain to

Poland. German Jewry suffered most in the terrible years of the plague, but the Jews of Provence were not spared either; they were never fully to recover from the social, economic, and intellectual devastation of this period. Although Spanish Jewry was relatively little directly affected by the horrors of the epidemic, it too came increasingly to be dominated by more somber, pietistic moods, and the self-confident rationalism of earlier generations receded. The ban of Rabbi Solomon ben Adret against the study of philosophy and science, although certainly not universally observed, had its effect in discouraging metaphysical speculation and scientific inquiry. In addition, the narrow Talmudism and antirationalism which the great German rabbinic authority, Rabbi Asher ben Yeḥiel, had imported into Castile when he became chief rabbi of Toledo continued to exercise a strong influence.

The mediocre level to which speculative thought in Spanish Jewry had declined in the middle of the fourteenth century is illustrated by the work of Meir ben Isaac Aldabi (ca. 1310–ca. 1360), perhaps the philosophical writer most representative of his era. Aldabi's book *Shevilei Emunah* (*Paths of Faith*) is an eclectic mixture of the most varied and mutually inconsistent theories—borrowed from such diverse thinkers as Maimonides, Baḥya ibn Pakuda, Naḥmanides, Joseph ibn Zaddik, and Hillel ben Samuel of Verona. Many long passages are simply verbatim quotations from the works of his predecessors, and the author makes virtually no attempt to reconcile the contradictory views he presents. A firm believer in the divinely revealed character of the Oral Torah, Aldabi inveighs against the "erring spirits," the deluded "philosophizers," who neglect the subtleties of Abbaye and Rava in the Gemara in favor of the books of gentile sages dealing with philosophy and science, and are cavalier in their observance of the commandments. He is convinced that Aristotle derived all his knowledge and wisdom from King Solomon, and that all scientific truth may be found in the *Talmud*. Furthermore, Aldabi is a fervent protagonist of the Kabbalah; he speaks of the "mystery of the letters of the alphabet," believes in transmigration of souls, and deplores those who deny the reality of demons and evil spirits.

Aldabi was by no means alone in his enthusiasm for the Kabbalah. Many others in his age developed an intense fondness for mystical theosophy. Indeed, the attempt was even made to transform Maimonides, to whom everything that smacked of mysticism and antirationalism was so deeply repugnant, into a Kabbalist. The story was

[13]

spread abroad that the philosopher repented his rationalism in his old age and immersed himself in the "secrets of the chariot"; a number of Kabbalist tracts were attributed to his authorship.

The condition of Spanish Jewry deteriorated still further in the second half of the fourteenth century as Christian armies gained control of larger areas of the country and steadily pushed the Arabs back. In the Christian kingdoms of Castile and Aragon Jews still played prominent roles at court as tax-farmers and fiscal agents. But this very prominence contributed to the eventual undoing of Spanish Jewry. More than a few of the Jewish courtiers or *hatzranim*, as they are called in the contemporary Hebrew literature, were men of inferior moral character, concerned only with increasing their own wealth and power and imitating the way of life of the Christian princes and nobles with whom they associated. Many documents of the age testify to the prevalence of intrigue, gossip, and slander among the *hatzranim*, and to their attempts to diminish the authority of the rabbis and win complete control over the Jewish communities. The foremost Spanish rabbi of the time, Isaac bar Sheshet (1326–1408), frequently bewails the decline of moral standards in his responsa: "Righteousness and justice are trodden underfoot, liars insult the most honorable men, debauched and vile persons go about with arrogantly raised heads; and for this our grandees and princes are responsible." [1]

Even more accusatory is Solomon Alami, who witnessed the massacres of the Jews of Catalonia, Castile, and Aragon in 1391. In his *Iggeret Musar (Epistle of Reproof)*, written many years later, he charged not only the wealthy courtiers but the rabbis and "philosophizers" with responsibility for the massacres. He declares:

Let us search for the source of all these trials and sufferings, and we shall find that a state of dissolution prevails in the midst of us; that an evil spirit pervades our camp, which has split us into two parties. There are those of our brethren who expend all their energies in solving Talmudic problems and in writing numberless commentaries and novellae dealing in minute distinctions and interpretations, full of useless subtleties as thin as cobwebs. They diffuse darkness instead of light, and lower respect for the Law. Others, again, clothe the Torah in strange garments, deck it with Grecian and other anti-Jewish ornaments, and endeavor to harmonize it with philosophy, which can only be detrimental to religion and lead ultimately to its decay. Worse than these, however, are the frivolous persons who have not acquired substantial knowledge, but, relying upon the smattering of Greek that they possess, venture to ridicule tradition and to condemn the commandments of the Holy Law. Such frivolity prevails, above all, among the wealthy. We find these evil qualities among the proud representatives of the congregations, who have grown rich through dealing in money. They cast off everything that reminds them of their Judaism; they seek to dazzle by princely luxury; their wives and daughters array themselves in jewels like princesses; and swelled with pride, they deem themselves the princes of the land. Therefore the great punishment came: it was inevitable. How much our rich coreligionists could learn from their Christian neighbors! The Christian princes and grandees rival one another in efforts to promote and uphold their religion and to train their youth in the pious sentiments of their ancestors. Our Jewish rich despise their faith, and permit the teachers of religion to eat the bread of sorrow and poverty.[2]

The decadence of the *hatzranim*, the wealthy tax-farmers and officers of the royal exchequers, contributed not only to the internal corruption of the Jewish community, but also to the growth of rabid anti-Jewish sentiment on the part of the Spanish nobility as well as the masses of the people. Both strata despised the Jewish officials for their influence at court and held them chiefly responsible for their heavy burden of taxation. The Catholic clergy, whose power in Spain grew apace, were not at all averse to fanning the popular hatred of the Jewish financial aristocracy into intense animosity toward all Jews. Their aim, at first tentative but later pursued with fierce and single-minded determination, was to convert the Jews, or, if that was not possible, to kill or expel them. In their missionary zeal they forced the Jews to engage in public disputations on religion and to listen to conversionist sermons in their own synagogues. The fanatical priest of Seville, Fernando Martinez, denounced the "enemies of Christ" with flaming fury, urging that Jewish children be taken away from their parents so that their souls might be saved through baptism, and that synagogues be seized and turned into churches. The inevitable result of the venomous anti-Jewish propaganda of Martinez and his accomplices came in 1391, when a Christian mob rioted in Seville and slaughtered several thousand Jews. From Seville the riots quickly spread throughout Christian Spain—to Toledo, Cordova, Valencia, Barcelona, and other cities. In all more than seventy Jewish communities were destroyed. It was the beginning of the end for Spanish Jewry.

Unlike virtually all of their Franco-German brethren in the era of the Crusades, the Jews of Spain did not universally choose martyrdom when confronted with the alternative of baptism or death. Thousands, particularly among the wealthy and cultured, elected to save their lives and fortunes by conversion. Among these new Christians were many who converted only ostensibly, continuing to cherish their Jewish faith and to practice the rites of Judaism in secret, and hoping to revert openly to their ancestral religion as soon as the storm passed. These were the *Anusim*, or Marranos, whose tragic history we cannot here pursue. Not a few of the converts, however, took to their new faith with intense zeal. To prove their devotion to the church, they denounced their former coreligionists and joined the Christian missionary preachers in their attempt to persuade the Jews to abandon the error of their stubborn ways and receive the salvation promised in Christ. These men soon appeared in public religious disputations with the rabbis and wrote calumnious tracts exposing the "false rabbinic teaching." Jewish scholars in Spain responded by creating an extensive polemical and apologetic literature that is among the most interesting phenomena of Jewish religious history in the late fourteenth and early fifteenth centuries.

Perhaps the most talented and effective of the polemicists was Profiat Duran (d. ca. 1414), who became a Marrano during the catastrophe of 1391 but some years later decided to throw off his Christian mask and return to Judaism. Duran was the author of a satirical tract entitled *Al Tehi Ka-Avotecha (Be Not Like Your Fathers)*, in which he scathingly mocks the tenets of Christianity and those Jews who had been attracted to them, contrasting the irrationality of Christian dogma with the "reasonableness" and philosophical character of Judaism. The satire was written in such a cleverly ambiguous fashion that some of the Catholic clergy actually believed the author was quite serious when he said repeatedly, "Be not like your fathers," and lauded the doctrines of Christianity. It was cited by a number of Christian authors as *Alteca Boteca*, a corruption of its opening Hebrew words. When they were disabused of their naivete, the satire was publicly burned. Later Duran, at the request of his friend, the great philosopher and Talmudist Ḥasdai Crescas, wrote another work called *Kelimmat Ha-Goyyim (The Shame of the Gentiles)*, in which he sharply criticized the Church Fathers and later Christian theologians and showed how they frequently mistranslated and distorted Jewish writings for polemical purposes. This work, which comes close to reflecting a modern critical-historical approach to the problem of the development of Christianity, was extensively employed by later Jewish apologists.

The conversion of so many among the "philosophizers," the educated and enlightened, during the disasters of 1391 contributed greatly to the discrediting of philosophy and science among those who remained faithful to Judaism. Rabbi Isaac bar Sheshet is characteristic of the rabbinic attitudes of his time when he attacks the wisdom of the Greeks as destructive of the foundations of the Torah. It is so pernicious, in his view, that it even seduced such illustrious scholars as Maimonides and Gersonides into expressing grossly heretical ideas "to which it is forbidden to listen." Even greater rage against the Aristotelian rationalists is manifested by the popular Kabbalist writer Shemtov ibn Shemtov (d. 1430). In his widely read *Sefer Ha-Emunot* (*Book of Beliefs*) he praises the Kabbalah as the authentic interpretation of Jewish tradition and denounces Maimonides and other rationalist philosophers as directly responsible for the prevalent abandonment of Judaism.

When I penetrated as far as possible into their ideas the flame of indignation flared up within me. I realized that their doctrine is a dreadful misfortune for Israel and leads to apostasy and atheism. We have seen that when the great catastrophe occurred and the wrath of persecutions and apostasies was poured out upon us, our learned men and experts in speculation at once denied their faith and became converts. There is no doubt that because of their guilt, our communities were destroyed.[3]

❧§❧

The revolt against Aristotelian rationalism reached its climax in the work of Ḥasdai Crescas (1340?–1412?). This great philosopher and statesman lived through the convulsions suffered by the Jews of Spain at the end of the fourteenth century and experienced their anguish in full measure when his son—"my only one, a bridegroom, a lamb without blemish"—died as a martyr at Barcelona in the anti-Jewish riots of 1391. Influential at the court of King John I of Aragon and the wielder of extensive power among Spanish Jewry, Crescas devoted intense effort to salvaging the wreckage of the massacres and trying to rehabilitate Judaism and Jewish life in his native land. His literary works, written mainly in the last fifteen years of his life, were directed toward the same end.

In response to the intensive proselytizing campaign of the Catholic Church among Jews, Crescas wrote his *Tratado* in Catalan in 1398. The original was lost, but a Hebrew translation by Joseph ibn Shemtov entitled *Bittul Ikkerei Ha-Notzerim* (*Refutation of the Cardinal Principles of the Christians*) survived. In it he attempts to set forth the reasons why Jews cling so tenaciously to their faith. This he does indirectly by contrasting the rationality and intelligibility of Jewish teaching with the illogicality and unintelligibility of such central Christian dogmas as the Trinity, the Incarnation, the virgin birth, transubstantiation, original sin, and the existence of demons. In this apology for Judaism, which is written in a noninflammatory and dignified style, Crescas may also have been replying to the numerous Jewish apostates of his era who attempted to prove their devotion to Christianity by scurrilous attacks on their erstwhile religion and people.

Apologetic motives also lay behind Crescas' great philosophic treatise *Or Adonai* (*Light of the Lord*). This work is a sustained polemic against Aristotelianism, which Crescas came to perceive as a serious threat to the survival of Judaism, since Aristotelian arguments were being employed by so many learned Jews of his time to justify their defection from their ancestral faith. If the Torah, as Maimonides, Gersonides, and a host of lesser Jewish Aristotelians generally maintained, teaches basically the same truths as Aristotle, what is significantly distinctive about Judaism, and why should one remain loyal to it? Crescas believed that it was essential to investigate carefully the arguments of "the Greek [Aristotle] who darkens the eyes of Israel in these days" and to demonstrate that they are not at all infallible guides to truth. Having shown the weakness and, indeed, the groundlessness of the Aristotelian arguments, he would proceed to establish the "roots and cornerstones upon which the Torah is based and the pivots upon which it revolves." Crescas realized that the denunciations and excommunications that had been hurled by many orthodox "defenders of the faith" against the Aristotelians had not accomplished their purpose; the hold of Aristotelian notions upon the minds of considerable numbers of Jews could be broken only if they could be shown to be logically untenable. The chief target of *Or Adonai* is Maimonides' *Guide of the Perplexed*, the "Bible" of the Jewish Aristotelians. Crescas protests that he has the profoundest admiration for Maimonides' Talmudic scholarship; he also has no doubt of the sincerity of Maimonides' desire to demonstrate the compatibility of the Torah and Aristotle, and that Maimonides really intended thereby to defend the former. But the venture, he is persuaded, was deeply misguided, and, as the *Talmud* declares, "where the name of God is desecrated, no respect is to be shown to one's master."

Written in a difficult, unadorned style but using precise Hebrew philosophical terminology, Crescas' *Or Adonai* is divided into four books (*maamarim*), which are again subdivided into principles (*kelalim*) and chapters (*perakim*). The first book deals with the roots (*shorashim*) of Torah, which Crescas understands as God's existence, absolute unity, and incorporeality; the second with the foundations (*pinnot*) of Torah; the third with other doctrines which, although not fundamental, are obligatory on every faithful Israelite; and the last with speculative opinions that are traditional but nevertheless optional for the believer and susceptible of diverse philosophical interpretation.

Crescas begins his first book with a rigorous critique of the twenty-six Aristotelian physical and metaphysical propositions that Maimonides had regarded as axiomatically true and employed as premises for the proofs of God's existence, unity, and incorporeality. Showing with remarkable dialectical ingenuity the groundlessness and untenability of these propositions and their implications—among them, that the existence of a vacuum is impossible, that every element moves by an inward propulsion to its supposedly natural place, that the universe must be finite in magnitude, that an infinite number of causes and effects is impossible—Crescas proceeds to destroy Maimonides' proofs for God. To be sure, he believes the existence of God is rationally demonstrable (Crescas offers an argument based on the contingent or possible nature of all effects and the necessity of an ultimate cause as an explanatory principle for the actual rather than possible existence of effects), but God's unity and incorporeality are beyond the power of philosophy to demonstrate. Only the Torah, with its proclamation "Hear, O Israel, the Lord our God, the Lord is One," instructs us about the divine unity, of which the divine incorporeality is a necessary corollary. Philosophy agrees with these "roots" of the Torah, but cannot itself demonstrate them.

Crescas' arguments not only established the independence of the Torah, but helped liberate science from the choking bonds in which Aristotle's *Physics* and *Metaphysics* had shackled it for centuries. In breaking out of the finite and closed Aristotelian universe, in proclaiming the infinity of space, and in suggesting the possibility of a plurality of worlds, Crescas was one of the major harbingers of the new scientific spirit that emerged at the end of the Middle Ages.

Expounding his concept of God, Crescas finds the Talmudic term *Ha-Makom* (the Place) frequently used as a designation for God in rabbinic literature, an extremely suggestive metaphor, for just as space permeates the whole universe and everything in it, so does the glory and grandeur of God. Most of the medieval Jewish philosophers who preceded Crescas had regarded the divine essence and the supreme joy of God as consisting in knowledge. The author of *Or Adonai*, however, insists that the true essence of God is love and goodness, which are everywhere present and concerned with communicating themselves and bestowing benefits on His creatures. Against Maimonides and his doctrine of negative attributes, Crescas believes that positive attributes may properly be ascribed to God. Though attributes such as power and knowledge have the same general meaning when applied to God and man, they are different in God, since He has them in infinite degree. But a plurality of attributes implies no multiplicity in God; He remains the One, the Absolutely Good.

In the twelfth century Maimonides, apparently in response to a felt need to delineate Judaism's theology against Islam and Christianity, had listed thirteen fundamental principles or dogmas of the Jewish faith. His enumeration achieved widespread acceptance as a summary of Jewish belief and was even incorporated into the synagogue service in the popular hymn *Yigdal Elohim Hai* (*Praise to the Living God*). Crescas, however, conceived the dogmatic structure of Judaism otherwise than Maimonides. In his *Or Adonai* he declares that, besides the existence, unity, and incorporeality of God (which, as we have noted, Crescas defines as the *shorashim*, or roots, of Judaism), there are only six *pinnot*, foundations or cornerstones, without which Judaism is inconceivable. These are: 1) God's omniscience, which means a knowledge of all existents, both universals and particulars, throughout all time—past, present, and future; 2) providence, which is bestowed not, as Maimonides and Gersonides had held, according to a man's intellectual perfection, but in the measure of his moral perfection and love of God; 3) God's omnipotence, the dependence of all things upon His will; 4) prophecy, which is the fruit not of knowledge but of love and reverence for God; 5) man's freedom of choice; and 6) the purposefulness of the world and of the Torah. In Crescas' view, all these foundations are necessarily implied in the conception of Torah as divine command.

The powerful tensions in Crescas' thought are particularly evident in his discussion of divine omniscience and human freedom. Man's freedom of choice is explicitly taught by the Torah as well as presupposed by its commandments; hence, Crescas had to affirm it. But human freedom is obviously incompatible with divine omniscience if the latter is taken with thoroughgoing seriousness, as it is by our philosopher. Crescas therefore feels compelled to restrict radically the scope of free will. When considered by itself, in isolation from the entire chain of causes and effects in which it is imbedded, an action may be said to be free; but regarded from within the causal nexus and from the perspective of God's knowledge, every action is necessary or determined. However, this does not remove man's responsibility for his actions or the justice of reward and punishment; man feels himself free and the sentiment accompanying his action (e.g., eagerness or reluctance to fulfill a commandment, joy or indifference in the moment of its observance) makes it his own, one for which he is morally answerable and may properly be rewarded or punished. Crescas, rather interestingly, exempts matters of belief from responsibility. Belief, he asserts, is not subject to the control of the individual's will. Thus, the Israelites at Mount Sinai who, according to an ancient *aggadah*, were coerced into acceptance of the Torah by God's suspension of the mountain over their heads, were not rewarded for their belief but for the voluntary joy that accompanied it. In his discussion of the problem of freedom and determinism, Crescas does not advance much beyond the antinomy stated by Rabbi Akiva in the second century: "All is foreseen, but freedom of choice is given." [4] No other medieval Jewish philosopher, however, went as far as he in affirming the determinist position.

In including among the foundations of Judaism the idea that the creation of the universe was a purposeful act on the part of God, Crescas is again in sharp disagreement with Maimonides. The earlier philosopher had rejected the stock theological notion that the world was created for man, and man so that he might serve God, and asked sarcastically whether God's greatness and glory was magnified by man's service of Him. He found the whole question of purpose meaningless and unanswerable; creation was simply an arbitrary act of God. Not so, Crescas maintained. The purpose of creation is the happiness of the human soul, the fulfillment of man's yearning for union with the divine; the direct means to this end is loving observance of the commandments of the Torah. Man is made for immortality, a higher mode of existence in which his soul will discover still larger possibilities of love. The achievement of immortality is not dependent upon knowledge and the acquisition of true metaphysical ideas alone, as the Aristotelians believed, but principally on love of God, made manifest by obedience to His laws. That God revealed the Torah is an expression of His infinite love for His creatures and His concern for their eternal bliss.

[21]

In the third book of *Or Adonai* Crescas discusses the beliefs that, though not fundamental, must nevertheless be accepted by every Jew, and the denial of which is heresy. They differ from the six fundamental principles in that the Torah is conceivable without them, but since they are proclaimed by the Torah, they are equally obligatory as items of faith. In this category Crescas includes creation, the immortality of the soul (not the acquired intellect), resurrection, reward and punishment, the eternal validity and irrevocability of the Torah, the superiority of Moses to the other prophets, the coming of the Messiah, the efficacy of prayer and of the priestly benediction, God's acceptance of the repentant sinner, the value of the High Holy Days and festivals, and—rather oddly—the efficacy of the Urim and Tummim in predicting the future.

As we have noted, Crescas polemicized against Christianity in his *Tratado*. But he did not himself altogether escape the influence of Christian thought. This is particularly evident in his view of man, where he comes close to espousing the classical Christian doctrines of original sin and vicarious atonement. The sin of Adam in disobeying God's word and eating the forbidden fruit left in all human hearts a predisposition toward evil. This predisposition prevents non-Jews from achieving the full moral stature for which man is intended. Jews, however, are the children of Abraham, who is the complete antithesis of Adam. When Abraham was circumcised he became a "new being," and whenever the rite of circumcision is repeated by his descendants, the "sacrifice of blood and flesh" effectuates an atonement of Adam's sin and a restoration of the individual's original, uncorrupted nature. Furthermore, Abraham's sacrifice of Isaac (it appears that Crescas may have accepted an old *aggadah* according to which Isaac was actually sacrificed, burned, and later resurrected) constitutes, according to Crescas, a full atonement for all the children of Abraham and all who enter the covenant throughout all time.

In Crescas, the keen dialectician and critic, the man of faith finally triumphs over the detached thinker. A first-rate philosopher, he was acutely aware of the limits of philosophy as well as the dangers it posed to the religious life. From the arrogance of Aristotelian rationalism, which presumed to have unraveled all the mysteries of the universe and explained everything in clear-cut, self-evident categories, he summoned men to a renewed sense of the infinity and the indomitable enigma of the world, and proclaimed that salvation was to be found not in knowledge but in love of God and obedience to His commandments. Crescas' antiintellectualism and antirationalism were particularly appealing under the conditions of his tragic time, when Jews had become chastened and penitent under the blows of disaster; not only pride of intellect but all other human pretensions and ambitions had revealed their illusoriness. A thoroughgoing, self-confident rationalism was not to reappear in the Jewish religious world for centuries. Yet so devious and unpredictable is the fate of ideas that Crescas' critique of Aristotelian rationalism became one of the chief inspirations of Baruch Spinoza, the most rigorous of rationalist philosophers and the most iconoclastic of battlers against biblical faith, who heralded the dawn of the new age that emerged in the seventeenth century.

The primary aim pursued by Ḥasdai Crescas was to strengthen loyalty to Judaism among his brethren in the wake of the catastrophe of 1391, which marked the beginning of the hundred-year-long agony of the Jews of Spain, culminating in their total expulsion from the country in 1492. This was also the goal of his pupil Joseph Albo (d. 1444?), whose *Sefer Ha-Ikkarim* (*Book of Principles*) achieved great renown and was widely read both in his own time and in later centuries. Perhaps it was the fact that Albo himself played a prominent role in the long and arduous disputation at Tortosa and San Mateo (February 1413–November 1414), in which the Jews of Aragon and Catalonia were forced by the Antipope Benedict XIII to defend the *Talmud* as well as their refusal as Jews to acknowledge the messiahship of Jesus, that led him to compose his reasoned apologetic exposition of the principles of Judaism. Albo witnessed the intensification of conversionist activity by the clergy in Spain and the defection of thousands of Jews to the Catholic Church; apparently he believed that his work might help stem the tide of apostasy and give support to the vast majority of his brethren who were determined to hold on to their faith.

Both in the Middle Ages and in modern times charges of plagiarism were lodged against the author of *Sefer Ha-Ikkarim*. Much of the work is derivative, and for many of his ideas and formulations Joseph Albo is indebted to Ḥasdai Crescas and to his own contemporary, the philosopher and rabbinic codifier Simeon ben Tzemaḥ Duran (1361–1444). However, Albo also set forth some original ideas of his own. Furthermore, the very popularity of his book (it was one of the most intensively studied of medieval Jewish philosophical works) makes it of importance in the history of Jewish thought.

Central in Albo's exposition of Judaism is the concept of a religious faith in general, or, to use his own term, "divine law" (*dat elohit*), which, following Thomas Aquinas, he distinguishes from "natural law" and "conventional law." A religious faith, or divine law, is characterized by three fundamental principles (*ikkarim*): the existence of God, divine revelation, and reward and punishment. All the religions with which Albo was familiar—Judaism, Christianity, and Islam—were based on these foundations. Albo makes the point that while revelation, or God's disclosure of His will, is essential, the content of revelation may differ. Apparently against the exclusivist claim of the Church that it possesses the only way to salvation, Albo sets forth the idea (adumbrated in older rabbinic teaching) that more than one revelation may be authentic and God-given.

While the Mosaic law existed in Israel, all the other nations had the Noachian law, and the difference was due to geographical diversity, Palestine being different from the other lands, and to national diversity, due to difference in ancestry. And there is no doubt that the other nations attained human happiness through the Noachian law, since it is divine; though they could not reach the same degree of happiness as that attained by Israel through the Torah. The Rabbis say, "The pious men of other nations have a share in the world to come." This shows that there may be two divine laws existing at the same time among different nations, and that each one leads those who live by it to attain human happiness, though there is a difference in the degree of happiness attainable by the two laws.[5]

Albo could not believe that God in His goodness revealed himself only to one segment of mankind, thus insuring its salvation, while leaving the rest to eternal damnation.

But if, as Albo suggests, such religions as Christianity and Islam, although yielding different degrees of "human happiness," are just as God-given as Judaism, why should Jews, despite all the obvious worldly advantages of conversion, persist in loyalty to Judaism? First of all, Albo replies, because "eternal life" or salvation is more readily attainable in Judaism than in other religions. Despite the fact that the Torah ordains so many *mitzvot* or commandments, fulfillment of *even a single one of them* assures the Jew's spiritual perfection and consequent salvation. This idea, to which little more than passing reference is made in rabbinic literature and which is mentioned only once by Maimonides (in his commentary on the Mishnah, *Makkot* 3:16), is raised by Albo to the status of one of the six central "dogmas" of Judaism. It is very likely that the author of *Sefer Ha-Ikkarim* was impelled to it because of the repetition ad nauseam by Christian polemicists against Judaism of the Pauline argument about the human impossibility of fulfilling all the commandments of the Torah, and the further contention of Paul that God, in His grace, had replaced the Torah with Christ as the instrument of redemption. For Albo the Torah is the eternally enduring manifestation of divine grace toward Israel, making salvation easily attainable by the Jew.

But there is another reason for unswerving fidelity to Judaism: If the authenticity of other religions is open to question and doubt, that of Judaism is not. How, asks Albo, could the six hundred thousand adult persons present when God gave the Torah at Mount Sinai have been mistaken? This is utterly inconceivable, for all of these witnesses to the Sinaitic revelation, our pious author dogmatically asserts, "were prophets at that time and heard the voice of God speaking the Ten Commandments." [6] Albo finds no difficulty in the notion that all the Israelites at Sinai were elevated to the rank of prophet. He explicitly rejects Maimonides' contention that the divine gift of prophecy is restricted to the elect few, and that its essential prerequisite is philosophical understanding. Finally, our author observes in support of the superior status of Judaism that even its opponents, Christianity and Islam, acknowledge the authenticity of Judaism, contending only that its validity was restricted to a definite term.

It is interesting to note that Albo dissents from Maimonides' dogmatic assertion that the eternal unchangeability of the Torah is an essential item of Jewish faith. (Maimonides himself, in his *Mishneh Torah*, had noted evolutionary changes in regard to certain rituals.) He had sufficient historical sense, in reading the Bible and *Talmud*, to recognize that Jewish law and usage had changed considerably over the centuries. Thus, the *matzevah* or stone pillar permitted in the days of the patriarchs was later proscribed, the consumption of meat which was forbidden before Noah was legitimized in his time, and the rules governing consanguineous marriages were changed. Far from seeing such changes as a challenge to the validity of the Torah, Albo regarded them as evidence of its truth, for "though divine laws are not completely repealed, they may change in their permissions and prohibitions as the character of the recipients changes." [7] He also clearly envisages the possibility of further modifications in Jewish law, e.g., in dietary regulations, in the Messianic age.

There is nothing therefore to prevent us from supposing that the divine law may in the future permit some things which are forbidden now, like fat or blood or the slaughter of animals outside of the Temple. These things were originally forbidden when the Israelites left Egypt because they were addicted to the worship of evil spirits, and ate the flesh with the blood and also ate fat and blood, as we read in relation to the killing of animals outside of the Temple, "And they shall no more sacrifice their sacrifices unto the satyrs, after whom they go astray." But when this form of worship has been forgotten, and all people shall worship God, and the reason of the prohibition will cease, it may be that God will again permit it. And some of our Rabbis have the same opinion.[8]

Even now, however, Albo notes, the scholars of each generation are vested with the power to interpret the Torah and to adapt it to shifting circumstances.

For Albo the central value and chief requirement of Judaism is faith or trust in God. Philosophical reflection may lead those capable of it to the joy of communion with God, as Maimonides urged, and so may love, as Crescas maintained. But a more widely available pathway to this goal is simple faith, uncomplicated by speculative considerations and logical reasons. "Divine righteousness decrees that those who believe should obtain that degree of eternal life which is promised in the Torah, because they trust in God and believe in His Torah, though they are not able to acquire an intellectual comprehension. Thus the prophet says, 'But the righteous shall live by his faith,' which shows that the promise of eternal life is made as compensation for faith." [9] The major instrumentality for the strengthening of reverence for God or faith is the observance of the *mitzvot*. Indeed, the essential purpose of the *mitzvot* is to promote these sentiments. As Albo puts it, "The aim which the soul is capable of attaining while in the body by performing the commandments of the Torah is nothing else than the permanent acquisition of a disposition to revere God. And when it acquires this attribute of revering God, the soul is elevated and is prepared to attain eternal life, which is the good reserved for the righteous and is the happiness of the soul." [10]

God, according to Joseph Albo, singled out Israel to receive the Torah as an act of love. The divine love for Israel, he further follows Deuteronomy in maintaining, was essentially unmotivated, not dependent on any merit of Israel's but simply an expression of God's inscrutable will. Israel was chosen not only that it might be saved, but as the vehicle of universal redemption. Despite the clerical fanaticism and persecutions which embittered the life of Spanish Jewry in his day, Albo did not follow the natural tendency to seek solace and compensation for the sufferings of his faith-community by projecting it as the sole object of ultimate redemption. His universalist vision remained unclouded in this respect. The advent of the Messiah, according to Albo, will result in the perfection and salvation of all mankind. It must be so, for if God "will not fulfill the merciful promise He made to David that the Messiah will come in order that through him the human race may be perfected, and attain its purpose, the whole race will have been created in vain, since it will not attain its destiny." [11]

A question that agitated Albo's mind as well as that of many of his contemporaries was: If Israel is indeed the chosen people of God, why are its present sufferings so vast? He could offer only two suggestions toward the solution of this enigma, both intended to mitigate the sense of present horror and offer consolation to his grieving brethren. First, nothing in this world is unalloyedly good, without any trace of evil; such a thing would be impossible, for good and evil are strictly correlated and inconceivable without each other. Thus, the sufferings of the Jewish people are simply the admixture of evil in the fate of the nation that has the supreme privilege of being peculiarly God's own and serving as the instrument for the ultimate redemption of mankind. Second, the miseries of the Jews are temporary, and their very intensity is a sure sign that the messianic age is close at hand. As the night is darkest just before dawn, so the greatest sufferings come just before redemption.

✥

In Joseph Albo's time Jews whose interests focused on the terrestrial world could still maintain some hope that there was a future for them on the Iberian peninsula, although the more clearsightedly realistic must have understood how extremely precarious that hope was. Less than half a century after Albo's death, all the Jews of Spain were presented by Ferdinand and Isabella with the bitter alternatives: conversion or expulsion. In the last years of their millennial residence on Spanish soil, the Jews were the captives of mental and spiritual moods far removed from those of earlier and happier times. Science and philosophy were still studied, but the old zest for them had diminished greatly. The self-confidence and optimism that had nurtured speculative thought and the intellectual pride that had sustained the rationalist world outlook were now shattered and vir-

[27]

tually gone. In their place moods of penitence, self-accusation, and disillusionment with the possibilities of reason now came to the fore. Perhaps the most representative figure of the generation of the expulsion was the gifted preacher and theologian Isaac ben Moses Arama (ca. 1420–1494).

Like Albo, Isaac Arama had occasion to engage in public disputations on matters of faith with Christian scholars. As rabbi of several Spanish communities, he preached sermons on the teachings of Judaism in an attempt to undo the effects of the conversionist harangues to which the Jews of his day were frequently forced to listen. These sermons became the foundation of his literary works—notably *Akedat Yitzḥak* (*Binding of Isaac*), a collection of philosophical addresses and allegorical commentaries on the Torah which came to be regarded as a homiletic classic and influenced the form and substance of Jewish preaching for centuries, and *Ḥazut Kashah* (*Grievous Vision*), a polemic tract on the relationship of philosophy and religion. Arama's works contain interesting material on Jewish life in Spain in the last decades before its tragic end. In 1492 the author left his homeland along with the thousands of other exiles and settled in Naples, where he died two years later.

Though Arama was well versed in Judeo-Arabic philosophical literature, he had scant use for philosophy and much preferred the esoteric wisdom of the Kabbalah. He complains bitterly of the fact that science and philosophy are still cultivated in the Jewish academies of Spain, while the Torah and *Talmud* are neglected.

I consider it the greatest misfortune that at the very time we are oppressed and persecuted in exile and fall ever deeper into the abysses of sorrow as recompense for ancient sins, our own protectors and champions deceive us. Like traitors, they lead us astray into alien paths filled with snares and nets. . . . Now, in a time of distress, when misfortune increases so fearfully in the house of Jacob, a new infectious disease is spreading ever more widely among the leaders and elders of our people. Ever larger grows the number of those who devote themselves to foreign sciences, which are the most dangerous enemies of our Torah and religion. It is not enough that they study all these things in their original languages, but the majority of our youth are raised on strange tongues, and this is presently the major concern in our *yeshivot*. The Torah and the *Talmud* are forgotten there, and no one is interested in them.[12]

Employing the colorful imagery of the skilled preacher, Arama wrote his *Ḥazut Kashah* in the form of a report on a dream or vision revolving around the biblical story of Sarah and Hagar. In Arama's allegory, Sarah represents revealed religion and her maidservant Hagar is philosophy. The duty of the maid is obviously to serve her mistress. But the arrogant and cunning servant is not content with her subordinate position; she seeks to displace her mistress in her husband's affections and to usurp her place. In the eyes of the orthodox preacher the rationalist philosophers were usurpers and traitors who, wittingly or not, were undermining the faith and tradition of Judaism and distorting the meaning of the Torah.

Interestingly, Arama, who himself had to fight against the missionary zeal of the Catholic clergy, suggests that the attitude of the Christian theologians of his day toward philosophy ought to be emulated by Jews. The Christians make it clear that they regard their revealed faith as superior to philosophy, and that the latter can be no more than the handmaiden of theology. They make no concessions to philosophy, unlike the Jewish rationalists, those "deceivers of Judah" (*bogdei Yehudah*), who sacrifice the Torah for Aristotle. Arama finds particularly offensive and dangerous the *pashranim* or compromisers in the Jewish world who attempt to reconcile philosophy and religion and, in the process, interpret all the miracles and prophecies of the Bible in naturalistic terms. They reduce the Torah to parables and allegories and give their approval only to those commandments that recommend themselves to human reason. Arama himself did not disdain the allegorical method in his own exegesis of Scripture, but the intent of his interpretations was to exalt unquestioning faith and implicit obedience of even the least of the commandments.

Against the philosophers, who had transformed the living, anthropomorphic, and anthropopathic God (of the Bible) into an abstraction, the First Cause or Pure Being, Arama championed the biblical envisagement of God. He was enough of a philosopher to reject in principle the attribution of any material quality, changeability, or multiplicity to the divine. Nevertheless, in his view, the "error" of the masses who conceive God in physical terms is far less pernicious than the tendency of the philosophers to restrict His knowledge, His power, and His concern with the affairs of men. No limits to God's might are to be imagined. Of course, nature operates according to a regular and predictable order, but this in no way precludes divine intervention in the form of miracles whenever God wishes to effectuate one of His special purposes. The universe and human life are controlled not only by an impersonal, natural order but by a personal, providential order as well. Hence, Jews must not despair, even in the deepest abysses of trouble. God's hand is not foreshortened.

In reaction to the growing miseries of his people in the years just before their final expulsion from Spain, Isaac Arama stressed the election of Israel and its special relationship to God. Israel is the pinnacle of creation; all else was brought into being only for its sake. Israel is the people of prophecy, a phenomenon unknown and impossible in any other nation. The bond between God and Israel is like that between a man and his beloved wife. Why, then, does Israel suffer so? This question had become even more painful and insistent than in the generation of Joseph Albo half a century earlier. Arama's answer was that whom God loves, He especially chastens. Israel is not forsaken; its ultimate vindication is assured. The day will surely come, Arama consoled his heartbroken listeners, when, as a result of the travail and agony of the Jews, all the nations will turn to Israel's God and accept the saving faith of Judaism.

But the vindication which he fervently expected did not come in Isaac Arama's lifetime. In 1492 the Inquisitor General of Spain, the fanatical Thomas de Torquemada, blessed Ferdinand and Isabella with his cross in the Alhambra of Granada as they signed the decree of expulsion ordering all Jews who refused baptism to leave their realm within four months. The aged rabbi departed from his native land with myriads of his crushed and bewildered people and died in exile. Thousands of others, however, did not accompany him; to save their homes and fortunes, they meekly trotted off to the baptismal font. Among the converts was Abraham Senior, the wealthy tax-farmer and government-appointed chief rabbi of Castile.

It was in the circles of the rich and learned, especially the intellectuals who had been attracted to science and rationalist philosophy, that the alternative of conversion was most commonly chosen. The historian of that era, Abraham ben Solomon of Torrutiel, writes:

In the year 1492 God's wrath was poured out over His people Israel . . . for our sins had become fearfully great and our guilt reached to the heavens. . . . For the sake of the secular sciences the Torah was virtually forgotten, and only the poor and needy occupied themselves with the Oral Law. . . . And when the great catastrophe came, the majority of the Jewish nobles, leaders, and judges did not stand the ordeal and, to save themselves from expulsion, forsook the true faith and exchanged it for idols. Leading the apostates was the chief rabbi of all of Spain, Don Abraham Senior—he, his son, and all his family. Thousands upon thousands imitated him. May their names be blotted out from the book of life, for they not only sinned themselves but caused others, who looked to them as their leaders and followed their ways, to sin. Of all the prominent leaders and heads of the communities, only a few decided to sacrifice themselves for the sanctification of God's name. Chief among these was Rabbi Don Isaac Abravanel.[13]

The same profound indignation at the Jewish intellectuals who chose conversion rather than exile and misery is expressed by the noted preacher Joseph ben Ḥayyim Yaabetz (d. 1507), who settled in Mantua after the expulsion and gave addresses in various cities on the causes and meaning of the great disaster. Joseph Yaabetz had no doubt that the exile from Spain was God's just punishment for the neglect of the Torah by the "philosophizers," and he inveighs bitterly against them. "With what arrogance, mockery, and ridicule," he writes, "they regarded the pious, God-fearing women in whose conceptions and understanding God took on human forms. But it was precisely these simple women who sacrificed themselves for the sanctification of God's name and also demanded the same of their husbands, while all the educated, who so gloried in their wisdom and philosophical speculation, did not stand the test and became apostates." [14] Philosophy had proven to be a snare and a delusion; it had brought not salvation but destruction. Jews must now repent and seek redemption through simple faith, humble fulfillment of the *mitzvot*, and—Yaabetz added—immersion in the mysteries of the Kabbalah. The secrets of the "esoteric wisdom" had long exercised a powerful attraction on certain segments of Spanish Jewry. In the tragic years before and following the expulsion, Kabbalah became for many a veritable obsession, and it was among the Spanish exiles and their descendants who settled in the Ottoman Empire, especially in Palestine, that a great revival of mysticism took place in the sixteenth and seventeenth centuries.

The expulsion from Spain also intensified messianic moods and expectations among the Jewish masses. Those who survived the horrors of its aftermath (the majority perished from hunger, disease, and murderous pirates) were convinced that these horrors could be nothing but the "pangs of the Messiah." Through them the day of redemption was coming to birth, and soon the redeemer would appear in all his glory and put an end to the unbearable sufferings of God's chosen people. The chief spokesman of these messianic yearnings was Don Isaac Abravanel (1437–1508), the noble statesman and financier who led the Spanish Jews on their weary trek into exile. Finally settling in Italy after much trouble and misfortune, Abravanel wrote one work after another to "strengthen despairing hearts and offer consolation to those who languish in homelessness." Their substance is that Israel is not orphaned, the day of redemption is at hand. After a long and arduous exploration of the mysteries that he was convinced lay hidden in the Book of Daniel under veiled allusions and *gematriot*, Abravanel announced that in 1503 the "times of the Messiah" will begin, and not later than 1535 the complete redemption will take place.

Both years came and went, and the Messiah did not appear. But hope in his ultimate advent did not waver. Indeed, as the horizon in the Jewish world grew darker, messianic expectations grew ever stronger and provided the chief solace for the beleaguered and exiled people.

CHAPTER

❧ II ❧

Jewish Mysticism: The Kabbalah

WHILE the attempt to reconcile revealed religion and rational philosophy engrossed many of the best minds in medieval Jewry, it was not philosophy or rational inquiry as such that completely dominated its intellectual and spiritual life—certainly not in the last centuries of the Jewish Middle Ages. As early as the ninth century, the unique structure of mysticism which later came to be called Kabbalah was introduced into Europe. As time went on Kabbalah developed increasingly complex forms, reaching maturity with the appearance of the *Zohar* in the late thirteenth century, and came to play an ever more prominent role in Jewish religious life and thought. By the sixteenth century it came close to dominating the mentality of the Jewries of Europe and the Near East, and its hegemony was broken only in the eighteenth century. Before losing most of its power in the face of the new rationalism fostered by the Enlightenment, Kabbalah helped give rise to Ḥasidism. Even today it is not altogether dead, although its present-day devotees number in the thousands rather than in the hundreds of thousands, as was the case in the late Middle Ages.

Leaving aside the numerous theurgic, magical, and superstitious practices which clustered around it (particularly in its so-called "practical" version, the *Kabbalah Maasit*) and formed a large part of its appeal to the Jewish masses, one can distinguish three elements of major importance in the edifice of Kabbalah: 1) its exaltation of ecstatic religious feeling and of the search for the closest possible communion with God; 2) its development of a vast structure of theosophical doctrine or "hidden wisdom" concerning the ultimate mysteries of the universe, the higher reality beyond "common" or "external" reality; and 3) its eschatological emphasis which, as we shall see, gave rise, particularly after the triumph of the Lurianic Kabbalah, to messianic pretenders and movements.

The first element, which is of the essence not only of Kabbalah but of all mysticism, was a significant factor in biblical Judaism and in Rabbinic Judaism as well. Adherents of Kabbalah in the Middle Ages, however, raised it to a position of supreme importance. To "know" God, that is, to achieve a sense of communion with Him or some vision of His glory, was their central goal. To attain it they elaborated complicated systems of *exercitia spiritualia*, ascetic disciplines, and meditational techniques. These, however, were generally supplemental and subsidiary to what the Kabbalists, as well as pious Talmudists, considered the essential means for obtaining communion with God—scrupulous and dedicated observance of all the commandments of the divine law. Against rationalist philosophies of Judaism, such as those of Maimonides and Gersonides, which implicitly devalued ritual observance and even moral conduct by declaring cultivation of the mind and achievement of intellectual perfection to be the highest goal of life, the medieval Jewish mystics stressed simple, intense faith and devout obedience of the will of God as revealed in the *mitzvot* of the Torah. Piety or saintliness (*ḥasidut*) is the central ideal of the *Sefer Ḥasidim* (*Book of the Pious*), the major work emanating from the school of Rabbi Judah the Pious, the foremost teacher of the Ḥasidei Ashkenaz, the German pietists and mystics of the twelfth century. This emphasis on saintliness and piety was continued in the subsequent development of Kabbalah. Indeed, it was the conviction of many later Kabbalists that loving fulfillment of the commandments was not only the demand of God and the way to His presence, but also had vast consequences of a cosmic nature. Every *mitzvah* performed with devotion and "concentration" of the heart and mind (*kavvanah*) by a Jew, they believed, helped to bring about an "improvement" in the "upper spheres," while every sin or violation of a commandment produced a "blemish" in the "realms of purity." Thus, by his deeds, the Jew was not only advancing or retarding the salvation of his own soul but affecting, to a significant degree, the destiny of the whole world.

The theosophical strand of Kabbalah also had ancient roots in Judaism, constituting a continuous and important tradition from fairly early times. The biblical books of Ezekiel and Daniel, and even more the later apocryphal literature, notably the Book of Enoch and IV Ezra, contain many esoteric teachings and "revelations" of hidden things. These were apparently cultivated in small conventicles and transmitted to initiates as early as the second century B.C.E. by such groups as the Essenes and the Qumran community or Dead Sea sect (which many scholars are inclined to identify with the Essenes).

❧❦❧

The rabbis of the Talmudic age, as a class, were generally averse to apocalyptic visions and gnostic fantasies. A famous Talmudic passage tells of four teachers "who entered *Pardes* [Paradise, the esoteric realm]—Ben Azzai, Ben Zoma, Aḥer, and Akiva. Ben Azzai looked and died; ben Zoma looked and became insane; Aḥer became an apostate; only Akiva entered in peace and came out in peace." [1] Despite the disapproval reflected here and elsewhere in the *Talmud*, some of its outstanding figures were strongly attracted to theosophical speculation. Joḥanan ben Zakkai seems to have been the father of the branch of mystical lore known in Talmudic literature as *maaseh merkavah*, "the work of the Chariot," which derived its inspiration from the description in the Book of Ezekiel of the divine throne and the angelic hosts of heaven, but which broadened into speculation about the mysteries and attributes of the Godhead and into disciplines whereby the soul would be enabled to ascend to the heavenly spheres, there to enjoy a vision of the divine majesty. Rabbi Akiva is the major figure associated with the other great branch of mysticism in the Tannaitic era, *maaseh bereshit*, "the work of Creation," which based itself on the opening chapters of Genesis but developed into a wide range of cosmological and cosmogonic theorizing.

In the late Talmudic and post-Talmudic period mystical tendencies continued to manifest themselves both in Palestine and Babylonia, giving rise to a number of esoteric literary works. Among the major mystical texts of this era are the "palace" books—*Heichalot Rabbati, Heichalot Zutrati*, and *Sefer Heichalot* (which has been published as the Third Book of Enoch, or the Hebrew Enoch). In these works we find elaborate accounts of the celestial world of the Chariot and of the magical and theurgic techniques whereby the soul is enabled to rise to this world with its various "palaces" or "halls." Those who ascended to the Chariot—in the literature they are called *yordei merkavah*, "descenders to the Chariot"—could do so only after performing ascetic exercises of great difficulty and reciting ecstatic hymns, many of which end with the *trisagion* ("Holy, holy, holy is the Lord of hosts . . .") of Isaiah 6:3. These numinous poems have left their imprint on the classical *Siddur* and strongly influenced the worship of the synagogue.

The mystics of the *Heichalot* literature conceived God as utterly transcendent, mysterious, "wholly other." He was not for them, as for many later Jewish mystics, a loving father with whom intimate communion was possible, but the "holy King," surrounded in the "palaces of silence" by "majesty, dread, and awe." Although the *merkavah* mystics dwell on the physical features of the upper world, which extends through the seven palaces (*heichalot*) in the firmament of *aravot* (the highest of the seven firmaments), on the hosts of angels in the palaces, and on the rivers of fire flowing before the Chariot, the ultimate goal of their ascents was to behold, in fear and trembling, the One who is seated on the Throne of Glory, "a likeness as the appearance of a man upon it above" (Ezek. 1:26). The physical description of the divine Glory or *guf ha-Shechinah* ("body of the divine Presence") constitutes the heart of the extremely esoteric and grossly anthropomorphic work of the *merkavah* mystics known as *Shiur Komah* (*Measure of the Height*).

While the *merkavah* mystics concentrated on the Chariot and the divine Glory, speculation on cosmogony, or *maaseh bereshit*, was the focus of a little book that had an enormous influence throughout the centuries of Kabbalist ascendancy and even fascinated many of the great figures of the rabbinic tradition, from Saadiah Gaon in the tenth century to Elijah the Gaon of Vilna in the eighteenth, impelling them to write commentaries on it. This is the *Sefer Yetzirah* (*Book of Creation*), composed perhaps as early as the third century C.E., in which is described the work of the "thirty-two mysterious paths of Wisdom" whereby God created the world. These paths turn out to be the twenty-two letters of the Hebrew alphabet, plus the ten *sefirot*, which here make their first appearance in Jewish mysticism. In the *Sefer Yetzirah*, the *sefirot*, according to Professor Gershom Scholem, are "merely the primordial numbers of the later Pythagoreans"; [2] they are not envisaged, as they were in the subsequent development of Kabbalah, as emanations from within the divine, or as aspects of God's self-revelation, but simply as created powers employed by God in the construction of the universe. In the further evolution of Kabbalah, the number- and letter-mysticism adumbrated in the *Sefer Yetzirah* came to play a major role. It led to the belief among many Kabbalists that, through various combinations of the letters of the Hebrew alphabet (*tzerufei otiot*), miracles could be performed, and that tremendous mysteries and marvels were discoverable through applying the techniques of operating with letters and numbers known as *gematria, notrikon,* and *temurah* to the sacred texts of the Bible and the Jewish liturgy.

The ancient Jewish mysticism of the Near East seems to have been imported into Italy as early as the ninth century and from there transported to the Rhineland, where in the twelfth century it was cultivated by small groups calling themselves Ḥasidei Ashkenaz, "the pious of Germany." The chief literary memorial of these groups, *Sefer Ḥasidim*, whose authors were Samuel ben Kalonymos, his son Judah the Pious (d. 1217), and Judah's relative, Eleazar of Worms (d. ca. 1225), is not, strictly speaking, a mystical work. Although its authors were men of great religious fervor who longed for ecstatic communion with God, *Sefer Ḥasidim* is essentially a book of *musar* or "morality," inculcating lofty ideals of ethical conduct and a stringent asceticism. The Ḥasidei Ashkenaz, however, were intensely interested in number- and letter-mysticism. Eleazar of Worms was particularly infatuated with the mystery of the "names" of God; the masters of this mystery, he believed, commanded vast magical powers. Also characteristic of the medieval German pietists was their prayer mysticism, which involved a concentration of spiritual energy (*kavvanah*) and the search for the esoteric meaning and power in the liturgical texts through the application of the number and letter techniques mentioned above.

◆◆◆

Kabbalah in the strict sense may be said to have been inaugurated with the appearance in twelfth century Provence of a work entitled *Bahir* (*Brightness*). This treatise, which contains material from Oriental Jewish mysticism, sets forth a view of the nature of divinity and divine power that moves beyond the *Sefer Yetzirah* and prepares the way for the mature *sefirot*-doctrine of the later *Zohar*. Though *Bahir* does not employ the term *sefirah*, it speaks of ten emanations. The first three of these are called "words," and the last seven "voices," of

God; all are elements in the divine "body." *Bahir* also draws analogies between the spiritual universe, or macrocosm, which it calls *Adam Kadmon* (Primordial Man), and man, or the microcosm, termed *Adam Taḥton* (Lower Man), and points to affinities between the members of the divine and human bodies. It further envisions the *Shechinah*, a term which had earlier been used either as a circumlocution for God or to denote the divine presence in places, events, or persons, as an independent entity, the feminine counterpart of God. It is also in *Bahir* that the notion of metempsychosis, or transmigration of souls, first appears in Kabbalist literature.

The ideas of *Bahir* were cultivated by the mystics belonging to the circle of Isaac the Blind, son of the renowned French Talmudist Abraham ben David of Posquiéres, who took up the cudgel against Maimonides' *Mishneh Torah* shortly after its appearance because he was afraid that such a code would supplant study of the Torah itself. Isaac, who is frequently called the "father" of Kabbalah, was a firm believer in transmigration of souls. He is credited with writing a commentary on the *Sefer Yetzirah* and probably contributed to the ongoing refinement of the doctrine of the *sefirot*. Of his two foremost disciples, the Spaniards Ezra and Azriel, the latter established a mystical school in Gerona and energetically disseminated Kabbalist notions throughout Spain. The author of commentaries on the ten *sefirot* and on the Song of Songs, Azriel seems to have been familiar with the neo-Platonist philosophy of Solomon ibn Gabirol. He regards the creation of the universe as a process of emanation from God or the *Ein Sof* (Infinite), and conceives the *sefirot* as transitional stages in the emanation process whereby pure spirituality is transformed into corporeality.

The most influential of Azriel's disciples was the famous Talmudist and Bible commentator Moses ben Naḥman or Naḥmanides (ca. 1190–ca. 1270). While not sharing all the views of his teacher, Naḥmanides did espouse some Kabbalist doctrines, and his sponsorship of them gave prestige and legitimacy to Kabbalah generally because of his own immense reputation as a rabbinic scholar. In his commentary on the Torah Naḥmanides perceives esoteric meanings in the words and letters of the text. The Torah for him is filled with profound mysteries which the diligent seeker may fathom. Indeed, with his essentially mystical vision of the world and of life, Naḥmanides regarded the whole universe, including even its most common phenomena, as pregnant with marvelous secrets and reflecting the divine glory.

In the generation after Naḥmanides a Kabbalist "prophet" and "messiah" arose in the person of Abraham ben Samuel Abulafia (ca. 1240–ca. 1291). In this exotic figure, who made the most fantastic claims for himself and even conceived the bizarre idea of converting Pope Nicholas III to Judaism, and who was strongly persecuted by the rabbis of his day, against whom he wrote some bitter tracts, number- and letter-mysticism is carried to extraordinary lengths. Abulafia elaborated meditative exercises in which concentration on various combinations of Hebrew letters is regarded as the path leading to the unveiling of the deepest mysteries and the possibility of an ecstatic vision of God Himself. Considering the numerous analogies between Abulafia's "prophetic Kabbalah" and Hindu Yoga, Professor Scholem has termed the former a "Judaized version" of Yoga.[3]

Abulafia's disciple, Joseph ben Abraham Gikatilla (ca. 1247–1305), continued to develop his master's number- and letter-mysticism in his *Ginnat Egoz* (*Nut Garden*): the word *Ginnat* in the title is itself an acronym referring to *gematria, notrikon,* and *temurah*. But more important is the doctrine of the *sefirot* elaborated in Gikatilla's *Shaarei Orah* (*Gates of Light*), composed in 1293 after the *Zohar*, written by his friend and contemporary Moses de Leon, had already appeared. In *Shaarei Orah* Gikatilla describes how God, the *Ein Sof* or Infinite, manifests Himself, through deliberate self-limitation, in the first of the *sefirot*, which is called *Keter Elyon* (High Crown) and is emanated from Him. From *Keter Elyon* in turn are emanated the nine other *sefirot* in which the *Ein Sof* becomes manifest: *Ḥochmah* (Wisdom); *Binah* (Intelligence); *Ḥesed* (Loving Kindness); *Din* (Judgment) or *Gevurah* (Power); *Raḥamim* (Mercy) or *Tiferet* (Beauty); *Netzaḥ* (Eternity); *Hod* (Majesty); *Yesod* (Foundation); and *Malchut* (Kingdom). These *sefirot*, which are, of course, the standard attributes of divinity in the theology of classical Judaism, are here conceived as stages in God's self-revelation. Through them the mysterious, transcendent, and "wholly other" God becomes the loving friend and father. By meditation on the *sefirot* with the aid of *shemot* (divine names), and with *kavvanah* or intense spiritual concentration, the initiate in Kabbalah may rise from the lowest of them up to the *Ein Sof* Himself.

Joseph Gikatilla's *Shaarei Orah* did not become the "Bible" of Kabbalah. That distinction was reserved for the *Sefer Ha-Zohar* (*Book of Splendor*). In form the *Zohar* is a *midrash* on the Pentateuch. Written in Aramaic, it was brought forward in the 1280s by the mystic Moses de Leon (1250–1305) of Guadalajara and Granada, who declared it an ancient work written by the second-century *Tanna* Rabbi Simeon ben Yoḥai, renowned for his asceticism and withdrawal from the world. Even in de Leon's lifetime there were those who contended that he was not the discoverer of the *Zohar* but its author, and throughout the centuries antagonists of Kabbalah have generally branded him as a forger and fraud. Modern scholarship has established with virtual certainty that de Leon was indeed the author of the work (although he borrowed extensively from many older sources), but it is unjustifiable to assume, as did Heinrich Graetz and other nineteenth-century Jewish scholars inimical to mysticism, that he was motivated by desire for financial gain or similarly sordid reasons in attributing it to Rabbi Simeon ben Yoḥai. He appears to have wished simply to give his work greater credibility and authority by ascribing it, in the fashion of the authors of the intertestamental apocryphal and pseudepigraphical works, to a renowned figure of antiquity. In any case, within several generations after de Leon's death the *Zohar* was the object of supreme devotion among the Kabbalists as well as the majority of all Jews, who accorded to it no lesser reverence than to the Bible and the *Talmud*.

In the various parts of the *Zohar* most of the themes of earlier Jewish mysticism are given attention. Thus, for example, the *Sifra Di-Tzeniuta* (Book of Veiled Mystery) deals with the secrets of creation; *Raya Mehemna* (The True Shepherd) includes precepts and rules of behavior; *Midrash Ha-Ne'elam* (Esoteric Exposition) contains scriptural exegesis through the application of *gematria;* the section called *Sitrei Torah* (Secrets of the Torah) is concerned with angelology and the mysteries associated with the divine name and the divine unity; and *Heichalot* (Palaces) portrays the halls of paradise and hell.

The fundamental theme of the *Zohar*, as of Kabbalah in its entirety, is that the ordinary material world of everyday experience is only a reflection of an invisible spiritual world. These worlds are interconnected and sustain each other. "The earthly world is created precisely after the model of the supernal world; everything that exists above has its reflection on earth, and everything is one." [4] Not only is the "lower" world affected by the "upper," but the influence also operates in the reverse direction. "No influence descends from above unless it is preceded by a stimulus from below," declares the *Zohar*, and "there is never any stirring of the attribute of mercy from above without a stirring of the heart below." [5] The master of the

"mystery or hidden wisdom" (*hochmat ha-nistar*) is one who understands the secret of the interrelationship between the worlds and
strives, through his deeds and prayer, to realize a greater harmony
and union between them.

The connecting link as well as the major symbol of the correspondence between the material and spiritual worlds is, according to
the *Zohar*, man. The image of man is the pattern of everything in
heaven and on earth. "When the Holy One created man, He set in
Him all the images of the supernal mysteries of the world above, and
all the images of the lower mysteries of the world below, and all are
designed in man, who stands in the image of God." [6] The statement
of the Book of Genesis that God created man according to His own
image is to be understood as meaning that nothing could exist as long
as man's image was not present. Man's soul is the pattern of universal being. "Before everything else God created the soul of man. It is
written in the Torah, 'And the earth was waste and void and the
spirit of God hovered over the face of the waters.' Everything was
waste because man's eye was still closed. As soon as his eye opened,
God said 'Let there be light,' and there was light." [7]

In the view of the *Zohar* man is exalted to a position of supreme
importance. What he does or fails to do has consequences of universal import. Since his task is to effect a greater harmony between the
"lower" and "upper" worlds, God has given him the Torah, which
contains not only prescriptions for the proper conduct of life requisite to this end but also, in veiled and esoteric forms through which
the initiate in Kabbalah may penetrate, some information about the
interrelationships of the worlds and the mysteries of the hidden
divine life. The *Zohar* vehemently rejects the notion that the Torah is
to be construed literally:

> Woe unto those who see in the Torah nothing but simple narratives and
> ordinary words! Were this the case, then could we, even today, compose a
> Torah equally worthy of admiration. But it is all quite otherwise. . . .
> Every word of the Torah contains an elevated sense and a sublime mystery.
> . . . The narratives of the Torah are but the garment in which it is clothed.
> Woe unto him who mistakes the garment for the Torah itself! It was to
> avert such a calamity that David prayed, "Open mine eyes that I may
> behold wondrous things out of thy Torah." [8]

According to the *Zohar*, God in His transcendent nature is the *Ein
Sof*, the infinite, absolute, unconditional Unity which is beyond
human comprehension. He is also the *Ayin*, the ultimate Nothing-

ness, for in Him there is no actual differentiation of forms or individualities. But though He is a *deus absconditus*, He is also the source of all the forms of being and becoming. The link between the transcendent *Ein Sof*, or Infinite, and finite being is the ten *sefirot* or *middot* (attributes), which are, in one sense, merely different reflections of the single, concentrated light emanating out of Him. The first and supreme emanation is variously denoted in the *Zohar* by the terms *Keter* or *Kitra Ilaah* (Crown or High Crown), *Resha Ḥivvra* (White Head), and *Nekudah Rishonah* or *Nekudah Peshitah* (First Point or Simple Point). Out of *Keter*, in which the remaining *sefirot* are all potentially present, emanate the masculine *sefirah* called *Hochmah* (Wisdom) or *Abba* (Father) and the feminine *sefirah* known as *Binah* (Intelligence) or *Imma Ilaah* (Primal Mother). This triad of *sefirot* comprehends the highest spiritual realm, the *olam ha-sechel* or *olam ha-muskal* (intelligible world). Next comes a triad which embraces the moral world, or *olam ha-nefesh* (world of the soul), symbolized corporeally by the heart; here the masculine *sefirah* called *Gedulah* (Greatness) or *Ḥesed* (Loving Kindness) and the feminine *Gevurah* (Power) are united in a third *sefirah* known as *Tiferet* (Beauty). The last triad comprehends the *olam ha-teva* or *olam ha-murgash* (natural world); in it the masculine *Netzaḥ* (Eternity) and the feminine *Hod* (Majesty) are merged in their unifying *sefirah*, called *Yesod* (Foundation). The tenth *sefirah*, known as *Malchut* (Kingdom), links the three triads of *sefirot* which constitute the *olam ha-atzilut* (world of emanation) with three further "worlds" in which the *sefirot* first reveal themselves in concrete, limited forms. In the *Zohar* these are called *olam ha-beriah*, the world of creative ideas; *olam ha-yetzirah*, the world of created forms; and *olam ha-asiyyah*, the world of creative matter, or of action and creation. Through the "world of emanation" and the further "worlds" there is a constant flow of grace (*shefa*) from "above" to "below," ultimately reaching men on earth.

In the mature system of Kabbalist theosophy the category of emanation is central. While it is undoubtedly borrowed from neo-Platonist modes of thought, it does not function here, as in the philosophy of Plotinus and his successors, primarily as an explanation of the process whereby the wholly spiritual One is linked through a series of intermediaries to the multiplicity of the material world. Emanation in Kabbalah is intended rather to describe the emergence of God out of his hidden state as *Ayin*, or Nothingness, into the *pleroma* or plenitude of divine being. The *olam ha-atzilut*, or "world of emanation," is divinity itself, conceived as an organism consisting of the ten interrelated *sefirot*, which are aspects or manifestations of God's self-revelation of His moral and intellectual character. Although the Kabbalists insisted that the *sefirot* are not "persons" or "gods," as time went on they did come occasionally to be personified, especially in the imagination of the masses attracted to mysticism. The philosophical rationalists, who objected to the positive ascription of any abstract attributes or qualities to God, could not but regard the *sefirot* doctrine as a blasphemous repudiation of classical monotheism. They attacked it as both religiously and intellectually scandalous.

Equally, if not more, repugnant to the rationalist mentality was the prominent erotic motif in Kabbalah, a motif which assumed highly mythical forms. We have noted that the *sefirot* are characterized in the *Zohar* as masculine or feminine, and that their "unions" are spoken of. Especially stressed in fully developed Kabbalah is the "holy union" or "sacred marriage" between the sixth *sefirah*, known as *Tiferet*, and the tenth, *Malchut* (also frequently called *Shechinah*). *Tiferet* is regarded as receiving and concentrating the power of the *sefirot* above it and transmitting it to those below. In Kabbalist literature it is symbolized by such masculine terms as King, Sun, and Bridegroom. *Malchut* or *Shechinah* is the receptive terminus of the system of *sefirot* and is symbolized in feminine terms such as Queen, Moon, and Bride. For God to be One and Whole, these masculine and feminine aspects of His, *Tiferet* and *Shechinah*, must be joined, a process which the Kabbalists frequently described in unabashedly sexual terms. They further maintained that the divine unity was in fact disrupted by the sin of Adam; the *Shechinah* was separated from her "Husband" and had to go "into exile." The great task of man now, according to the Kabbalah, is to restore, through deeds, prayers, and mystical meditations, the divine integrity, the union of the masculine and feminine aspects in God's life. The mythical and erotic terminology employed by the Kabbalists in setting forth their doctrine of the need for union of the male and female principles within the divine life, as well as in human life (which they regarded as a mirror image of the divine), could not but enrage the nonmystical adherents of the rabbinic tradition, with its rationalist and puritan tendencies.

However, the Jewish masses, throughout a large part of the Middle Ages and beyond, were not shaken in their devotion to Kabbalah. A major part of its appeal no doubt derived from its teaching about man. We have already referred to the exalted place accorded to man and the human soul in the *Zohar*, but something more needs to be said on this subject.

The rather somber view of man that generally permeates rabbinic

Judaism is reflected in the Mishnaic statement: "Know whence you came: from a putrefying drop; and whither you are going: to a place of dust, worms, and maggots." [9] In the *Zohar* man's origin and end are conceived in vastly different fashion. Man is the crown of creation, the link that binds the "upper" and "lower" worlds together; he is a *Shechinta Tataa*, the divine presence on earth. The physical image of every person has a heavenly preexistence, as does his soul. "At the moment when the body is united with the soul, God sends the person's image [*deyokna*] bearing the divine impress down to earth. It is this image that stands by at the moment of conjugal union between man and wife. It has a human face, and the child that is to be born will carry its form. . . . This form is a heavenly phenomenon." [10] As for man's soul, according to the *Zohar* it is a reflection of the divine *sefirot* and in unbroken connection with them. Its descent to the lower world and union with an earthly body enables it to fulfill its mission of illumining a human life with divine light, and raising everything with which it comes into contact to a higher level. Having fulfilled its mission, it returns to the upper worlds, there to be united with the eternal source of light. But if it has not completed its assigned task during its association with one body, or is still stained by some impurity, it will be transmigrated to another body and have to wander further in the terrestrial world. The righteous and pure soul, however, rises freely and without hindrance to the upper worlds where, the *Zohar* teaches, "in one of the hidden corners of the loftiest celestial regions there is a palace called the Temple of Love." [11] There God Himself unites with all the holy souls "in a kiss of love."

After the appearance of the *Zohar*, Kabbalah continued to develop in Spain throughout the fourteenth and fifteenth centuries and gained ever larger numbers of adherents. It achieved renewed vigor and even greater popular appeal in the century following the expulsion of the Jews from Spain, for not only the exiles but Jews everywhere yearned for some explanation of the tragedy that might invest it with deeper significance and provide some hope that it would ultimately be redeemed—an explanation that neither the rabbinic tradition nor rationalist philosophy seemed able to yield convincingly. The new communities in the Ottoman Empire populated by the Spanish exiles became centers in which Kabbalist ideas and practices were intensively cultivated. In the sixteenth century the town of Safed in Upper Galilee became the major center of Kabbalah, boasting such renowned figures as Joseph Karo, author of the legal codes *Beit Yosef* and *Shulḥan Aruch*, who was also an ardent devotee of the "hidden wisdom"; Solomon Alkabetz, composer of the beloved synagogal hymn "Lecha Dodi"; and Moses Cordovero, the most systematic of all Kabbalist thinkers, who provided an exhaustive and, at times, philosophic discussion of Kabbalist theosophy in his *Pardes Rimmonim* (*Pomegranate Orchard*). More influential, however, than all the other mystics of Safed was Isaac Luria (1534–1572), also known as the *Ari*, the "holy lion." Although Luria himself wrote nothing in his brief lifetime, his views were energetically propagated by his pupil Ḥayyim Vital and by the school of the Italian Kabbalist Israel Sarug.

In Luria's mystical teaching the view of the relationship between God and the universe presented in the *Zohar* underwent significant modification, and novel mythical and messianic ideas were introduced into Kabbalah. Briefly, according to Luria's theosophical doctrine, God, or the *Ein Sof*, was originally the infinite All, with nothing outside Himself. In order to provide a space empty of His presence in which creation could take place, the *Ein Sof* "withdrew," so to speak, "from Himself into Himself." From this voluntary retraction or concentration (*tzimtzum*) came the infinite light. When this light in turn concentrated, an empty space encompassed by ten circles or dynamic vessels (*kelim*), which Luria also called *sefirot*, appeared. Some of the vessels, however, were unable to bear the stupendous light which thereupon rushed into them, and they burst. The "breaking of the vessels" (*shevirat ha-kelim*), this cosmic catastrophe at the time of creation, is the primary cause of the evil and chaos in the world. Instead of radiating with uniform intensity throughout creation, the light was fragmentized into sparks (*nitzotzim*) scattered here and there. The result was the world as we know it, a world in which light and darkness, good and evil, are everywhere commingled.

The sin of Adam, Luria further taught, added to the chaos wrought by the "breaking of the vessels." According to Lurianic doctrine, all the souls of all the human beings destined to be born throughout all time were created with Adam; each, in fact, is a "spark" from Adam. Originally these souls were separated according to their different grades of excellence and power. But Adam's disobedience caused a disruption in the realm of souls. The higher became intermingled with the lower, the good with the evil. As a consequence, not even the worst soul embodied in a human being is altogether devoid of good, and not even the best and purest soul is without some admixture of evil, or what Luria called the element of the "husks" or "shells" (*kelippot*).

The chaos and evil introduced into the universe by the "breaking of the vessels" and the intermingling of souls will be finally ended, in the view of the Lurianic Kabbalah, with the coming of the Messiah. Then the *Shechinah*, which is now in exile (as Luria, following the *Zohar*, taught), will be reunited with her "Husband," the Holy One Blessed Be He, and the original harmony and unity intended by God will be established. The Messiah's advent depends on God's pleasure, but man must prepare the redeemer's coming by doing everything he can to purify his own soul through gathering the "sparks of holiness" embedded in the realms of uncleanness. For this purpose, which he called *tikkun* (correction or repair), Luria urged upon his followers all kinds of ascetic exercises, including frequent fasting, midnight vigils, mortification of the flesh, and ablutions, in addition to prayer and punctilious observance of the precepts of the Torah, to be accompanied by the recitation of mystical formulas of concentration (*kavvanot*) that were elaborated in his circle.

Before the coming of the Messiah, the souls of men, Luria taught, will not be able to purify themselves or obtain *tikkun* in one lifetime and return upon death to their divine source; they will be compelled to undergo numerous reincarnations, not only in the bodies of other men but in animals and even in inanimate objects such as rivers and stones. To the doctrine of metempsychosis, which had already been expressed in the *Zohar* and *Bahir*, Luria added an idea of his own, namely, "impregnation" (*ibbur*), by which he meant that if a soul were too weak to fulfill its designated task on earth, God in His mercy might impregnate it with another soul or two, so that the conjoined souls might succeed where the single one would have failed.

In the Lurianic Kabbalah the third element which we noted at the beginning of this chapter as being of major importance in the Jewish mystical tradition, its eschatological emphasis, became more pronounced and powerful than ever before. Hunger for the final redemption, for the advent of the Messiah, dominated the lives of many Kabbalists. The exile of the Jewish people from its land, they believed, was a reflection of the exile of the *Shechinah* from the Holy One Blessed Be He, and the longing for the end of both exiles became ever more ardent and insistent. Expectation of the coming of the Messiah was shared by all Jews, but it took on special immediacy and fervor wherever Lurianic mysticism took root. And in the century after Luria's death his doctrines were widely disseminated by his disciples, finding enthusiastic adherents in Italy, Germany, Holland, and Poland—indeed, throughout the entire Jewish Diaspora.

That the spiritual and intellectual climate produced by the spread of Isaac Luria's Kabbalah should have contributed to calling forth claimants to messiahship, in answer to the intense popular yearning for redemption, is hardly surprising. Of the messianic pretenders who appeared in the seventeenth century, none inspired greater hopes and none dashed them with more disastrous consequences than Shabbetai Tzevi (1626–1676). Born in the Turkish city of Smyrna, Shabbetai Tzevi was early attracted to the Lurianic Kabbalah and began to practice its ascetic disciplines with extraordinary fervor. Soon he attracted a band of enthusiastic disciples who studied the mystical texts with him and become convinced that their teacher possessed supernatural powers. In 1648, which, according to an opinion cherished in many Kabbalist circles, was to be the year of the Messiah's arrival, Shabbetai Tzevi astonished his followers by pronouncing the Ineffable Name of God, thus putting forth, at least implicitly, a claim to messiahship. The terrible massacres that year of Jewish communities in Poland by Cossack hordes under the leadership of Bogdan Chmielnitzki appeared to give support to the widely held belief that the *ḥevlei ha-mashiaḥ*—the agonies that, according to tradition, were to precede the coming of the Messiah—were indeed manifesting themselves.

Driven out of Smyrna by the more conservative and rationally minded Jewish leaders, Shabbetai Tzevi traveled in the years that followed throughout the Near East, everywhere winning adherents. In Salonika he celebrated his marriage as Son of God with the Torah, outraging the rabbis of the city, who promptly banished him. In Cairo a few years thereafter he wedded a human wife named Sarah, a beautiful Polish Jewess with a questionable past who had become persuaded that she was destined to be the bride of the Messiah. Still later in Palestine, in the summer of 1665, he acquired a right-hand man, Nathan of Gaza, who advanced his master's claims far and wide, professing himself to be the risen prophet Elijah, the forerunner of the Messiah, Shabbetai Tzevi.

Returning to Smyrna in the fall of 1665, Shabbetai Tzevi publicly proclaimed himself the redeemer in the synagogue, while the assembled multitude shouted "Long live our King, our Messiah!"

Thereupon a wave of messianic hysteria, in which even some of the most learned rabbis and saner lay leaders were caught up, engulfed Jewish communities all over Europe and the Levant. In scores of synagogues prayers were inserted in the service under the formula "Bless our Lord and King, the holy and righteous Shabbetai Tzevi, the Messiah of the God of Jacob." Thousands of Jews sold their homes and disposed of their property, making ready to follow the proclaimed Messiah in what they believed would be his imminent triumphal return to the Holy Land.

But all the fervent hopes suffered a shattering blow less than a year later. At the beginning of 1666 Shabbetai Tzevi set out with a splendid retinue for Constantinople. On his arrival there he was immediately detained by the sultan's officers. For some months the Turkish authorities vacillated, keeping Shabbetai in confinement in the state prison in the castle of Abydos but permitting his followers to visit him and maintain him in royal style, with the result that his imprisonment did not affect his messianic claims in the eyes of his adherents. But in September, after Shabbetai Tzevi had been denounced as a traitor by another pretender to messiahship, a Polish Jew named Nehemiah Cohen, his position became extremely precarious. To save his life, Shabbetai, at the advice of the sultan's physician, an apostate Jew, put off his Jewish garments and donned the Turkish turban, thus signifying his adherence to the Moslem faith. The delighted sultan rewarded the would-be Messiah by bestowing upon him the title Effendi and appointing him a palace doorkeeper.

Shabbetai's conversion threw Jewish communities everywhere into consternation. The shame of the many thousands who had given full credit to his pretensions and who now had to admit their error weighed heavily upon them, aggravated by the jeers of Christians and Mohammedans at their credulity. But a considerable number of the pseudo-Messiah's followers refused to believe that they had been duped, insisting that Shabbetai's conversion was actually part of the messianic scheme. He had merely gone over to the Moslem faith for a time in order to gather up the "sparks of holiness" residing in Islam, for it was essential, according to Lurianic doctrine, that all the sparks everywhere be collected before the final redemption could occur. When he had completed his task he would return, perhaps in another incarnation. Some of Shabbetai's fanatical adherents formed a half-Jewish, half-Moslem sect in Turkey, called the Dönmeh, small remnants of which exist to the present day. Others, particularly in Poland, remained within Judaism but formed secret Shabbatian societies which clung firmly to belief in their master's messiahship and his ultimate reappearance in glory. The members of these societies practiced an odd combination of strict asceticism and licentious indulgence, the latter justified as a way of serving God by liberating the "sparks of holiness" from the realm of impurity. (For more about the Shabbetai Tzevi movement and its aftermath, see Chapter Six, pp. 164–167.)

❦

In the decades after the collapse of the Shabbetai Tzevi movement, vehement attacks were launched on what had obviously been its matrix, the world of Kabbalah. These attacks were not unprecedented. From its inception Kabbalah had been the object of profound suspicion and resentment on the part of some sober rationalists and traditional Talmudists, but opposition to it now became more widespread and insistent. It was charged with primary responsibility for the messianic debacle that had just occurred, and for the antinomian excesses in the Shabbatian circles. In addition, the older charges that had long been hurled at Kabbalah by rationalists were now taken up by many who had become disillusioned with mysticism and messianism. It was maintained that its *sefirot* doctrine tended to undermine strict Jewish monotheism; that it encouraged magic and theurgy, both of which are contrary to the essential spirit of Judaism; that it stimulated the luxuriant development of a pernicious angelology; that its exegesis of sacred texts through the techniques of *gematria, notrikon,* and *temurah* was preposterous; and, more generally and most vociferously, that its entire theosophy was wildly irrational and utterly incredible.

Kabbalah could not but weaken in the face of the onslaughts specifically directed against it, as well as the generalized rationalism of the European Enlightenment which gradually began to penetrate the Jewish world in the second half of the eighteenth century. It was further discredited by the unseemly controversy between two of the foremost rabbis of the age, Jacob Emden and Jonathan Eybeschütz, centering around Kabbalist amulets and charges of Shabbatian heresy. For fourteen years (1750–1764) this dispute agitated Jewish communities all over Europe, and led many to contempt not only for the whole fabric of Kabbalah but for the institution of the rabbinate as well. Although many outstanding scholars of the late eighteenth century, including the Gaon of Vilna, Elijah ben Solomon Zalman, continued to cherish the *Sefer Yetzirah*, the *Sefer Ha-Bahir*, the *Zohar*, and other mystical works, by the end of the century the force of Kabbalah as a popular movement in Jewry was largely spent. Nevertheless, it still had sufficient vitality in the middle of the century to give birth to the last and perhaps greatest of all mystical movements in the history of Judaism, Ḥasidism, of which we shall speak in a later chapter.

In the fifteenth and sixteenth centuries, in the age of the Renaissance and the Protestant Reformation, Kabbalah was greatly admired and ardently explored by many non-Jewish savants who undertook the study of Hebrew chiefly in order to obtain the key that would unlock its mysteries. Among them were the great Italian humanist Pico della Mirandola and the German scholar Johannes von Reuchlin. To be sure, some of the Christian students of Kabbalah were motivated by religious and apologetic reasons (they believed it possible to show that the doctrine of the *sefirot* and other Kabbalist notions were congruent with the central dogmas of Christianity), but they were also persuaded that the texts of Jewish mysticism were filled with priceless treasures of wisdom. That view was not generally shared by nineteenth-century Jewish historians of culture and literature. Such scholars as the German Heinrich Graetz and the Russian David Kahana, as well as many others nurtured on the ideology of the *Wissenschaft des Judentums* and Haskalah, regarded Kabbalah as an unfortunate, corruption-filled excrescence on the body of Judaism which for centuries distorted its pristine rational spirit and fostered the growth of nefarious superstition and obscurantism among the Jewish masses. Its parent, in their view, was deception and credulity, and its child, moral and intellectual bastardy.

This verdict of nineteenth-century Jewish scholarship can hardly be sustained by an objective examination of the evidence. It is difficult to believe that Kabbalah could have obtained such a widespread following among the Jewish masses and retained its hold for so many generations unless it enshrined some perennial values and answered some deeply felt religious needs.

What were these? First and perhaps foremost, Kabbalah set forth, as we have suggested, a vision of man and his destiny that was considerably more attractive than the standard anthropology of Biblical-Rabbinic Judaism. It linked man and God in a far more intimate bond than that conceived by the orthodox tradition. Kabbalah dared to affirm, in the words of a modern interpreter of Judaism, Abraham

Joshua Heschel, who was himself a product of the world of mystical Jewish piety, that "God is in need of man." God requires man not only as a "partner" in the work of creation, as a rabbinic phrase has it, or as a free moral agent who can respond to the divine command, but for a far more fundamental purpose: to help unite the life of divinity itself, to restore the disrupted union of the *Ein Sof* and His *Shechinah*. What larger goal and greater dignity could human life have? It is little wonder that this view was so powerfully attractive.

The Kabbalist conception of man's role and purpose in the universe also produced an enormously revitalized attitude toward the *mitzvot*. These were not simply "decrees of the king," commandments laid by God upon the Jew which he was obliged under the Sinaitic covenant to fulfill whether or not he understood their "reason," and for whose observance he might rightfully anticipate a reward, as he might expect punishment for their nonobservance. In Kabbalah the *mitzvot* were raised to a cosmic level; they were regarded as redemptive activities whose performance or nonperformance could hasten or retard nothing less than the salvation of the whole world. Here clearly was a far more powerful and compelling stimulus for ordering one's life according to the precepts of the Torah than that provided by the standard rabbinic view that they were the expression of God's will, or by the philosophers' search for their practical, utilitarian value in promoting man's happiness and moral progress. Obviously, too, the Kabbalist was likely to find far richer significance and personal joy in performing the *mitzvot* than the sober, earthbound rationalist.

Kabbalah also suggested a conception of Israel or the Jewish people that proved deeply meaningful to many. Israel, the beloved and chosen of God, was the terrestrial counterpart of the last of the *sefirot*, the *Shechinah*. The fate of Israel is related to the fate of the *Shechinah*. Its exile from its land and its travail among the nations in the Diaspora are a reflection of a tragedy that has occurred in the divine life itself—the exile of the *Shechinah* and her separation from the Holy One Blessed Be He. And the acts of *tikkun* (in the Lurianic Kabbalah, the gathering of the "divine sparks") that are the necessary preparation for the coming of the Messiah and the consequent restoration of Israel to its land also prepare the way for a cosmic restoration—the reunion of God, the divine Husband, with His beloved Bride, the *Shechinah*.

The designation by Kabbalah of a feminine element in the divine life, and its tendency to regard the human sexual act as a symbol of the union between aspects of God Himself, although deeply repugnant to the antimythical mentality of the rationalist philosophers and the "puritanism" which they shared with the orthodox Talmudists, also contributed significantly to the appeal of Kabbalah. The official Judaism of the Talmudic era and the Middle Ages had moved far away from the joyous celebration of erotic life in biblical times that is reflected in the Song of Songs. While affirming the legitimacy of sexuality and of conjugal relations in marriage, and maintaining that perfection is achievable only in the married state, the rabbis generally were deeply fearful of the explosive power of the libido. When they speak of the *yetzer ra*, or "evil impulse," it is very often the sexual drive they have in mind. Talmudic Judaism in general had no exalted vision of sexuality; it sought to curb it and channel its elemental force into socially constructive outlets. The representatives of scholastic Jewish philosophy in the Middle Ages by and large exalted man's mind and deprecated his body. Maimonides typifies their attitude when he speaks of sex as low, animal, a physical necessity in which the enlightened and virtuous will indulge as infrequently as possible.

Furthermore, both in the rabbinic tradition and in medieval Jewish philosophy, womanhood is frequently portrayed in negative terms, as a prime source of evil and corruption. All this was altered in the world view of Kabbalah. Femininity came to be regarded as an integral aspect of the Godhead and the sexual act as the symbol of the unification of the masculine and feminine elements in God Himself. No longer was the human sexual drive perceived as something essentially vile and bestial; on the contrary, it was invested with supreme holiness. *Iggeret Ha-Kodesh*, a tract attributed to Naḥmanides (though probably not by him), expresses the Kabbalist view clearly. It explicitly rejects the Maimonidean view that there is something shameful in sexual intercourse, and declares: "Sexual union is holy and pure. . . . Let no man dare say there is anything disgraceful or ugly in it. . . . God created everything as His wisdom decreed, and He created nothing in which there is disgrace or ugliness. . . . When sexual union is for the sake of God there is nothing purer than it. . . . When a man unites with his wife in holiness and purity, the *Shechinah* is with them." [12] This revaluation of sexuality and *das ewig Weibliche* on the part of the Kabbalists must have been experienced as a profound liberation by many men as well as women, and greatly intensified their devotion to Kabbalah.

Another factor in the popular appeal of Kabbalah no doubt was the fact that it seems to have been more successful in combining the ideas of God's immanence and transcendence in a unified conceptual system than either rabbinic orthodoxy or scholastic philosophy. For this purpose, Rabbinic Judaism had little more to operate with than the ancient concept of the *Shechinah*, understood as the "indwelling" of God, who is alleged to be present in holy places and holy events. As for philosophy, in its attempt to purify the idea of God, it tended to weaken greatly the notion of divine immanence and to conceive of God as utterly transcendent, the Supreme Being who does indeed act as Creator, Lawgiver, and Redeemer, but who is in His essence totally inaccessible to human comprehension and to whom we can ascribe only negative attributes. Kabbalah, on the other hand, while it maintained the strongest sense of divine transcendence and otherness (God, according to the *Zohar*, is "the most ancient of the ancient, the mystery of mysteries, the unknown of the unknown"), also held that, in another sense, God is quite knowable. His power and His love are reflected both in the macrocosm, the universe, and in the microcosm, man. Both the human body and the "body" of the universe are images of the divine "body." In the tree and in the human form, which Kabbalah employed to represent the *sefirot* and their interrelationships, it found vivid symbols that brought home the idea of divine immanence in a compelling and dramatic fashion. Thus the *deus absconditus* became the *deus revelatus*. To be sure, to accept the *sefirot* doctrine required allowing the imagination untrammeled flight, but that was not too difficult for the medieval mind, unencumbered by the sobrieties and restraints of modern scientific methodology. In any case, Kabbalah appears to have managed to hold in tension the idea of God's transcendence, without losing a living relationship to Him, and of His immanence, without allowing this to lapse into a pantheist identification of divinity with nature.

One final point must be cited in any attempt to explain the centuries-long hold of Kabbalah on the Jewish masses. In the stock platitudes of rabbinic wisdom and scholastic philosophy there was too little genuinely satisfying discussion of the core enigmas of human life—the problem of pain and suffering, the prosperity of the wicked and the torments of the righteous, the relationship of this life to existence in the "great beyond." Kabbalah, however, developed a mythological structure which, if it did not totally resolve these enigmas, at least gave its adherents the possibility of enduring them with a greater measure of hope and confidence than was provided by the "official Judaism" of the rabbinic teachers.

CHAPTER

❦ III ❧

Franco-German Judaism in the Middle Ages

THE HIGH ACHIEVEMENTS in philosophical theology, poetry, and science of the Jews of Spain and other Moslem territories in the Middle Ages were not generally duplicated by the Jewries of lands under Christian control. Perhaps the major reason for this is that the Christian civilization of medieval Europe attained its zenith only several hundred years after the Arabic. It is probably fair to say that in the ninth through the twelfth centuries the Jews of Christian Europe, largely concentrated in the lands today known as France and Germany (the Jewish community of Italy was relatively small), were considerably superior in cultural respects to the people among whom they lived; at least most of them had the ability to read and write, whereas in Christian society literacy was largely restricted to the monastic clergy. The stimulus to creativity provided by the highly developed Arabic civilization was thus lacking in the medieval Christian world. To be sure, the Jews who lived in that world were not unaffected religiously by its civilization and culture, but the effect appears to have been lesser than in the lands under Arabic dominion.

Furthermore, the Jews of medieval Europe seem to have resisted Christian influence more than Moslem. This difference in attitude is no doubt to be accounted for mainly by the difference in treatment they received from adherents of the two faiths. While the oppression suffered by Jews at the hands of Moslem fanatics was neither slight nor sporadic, it cannot be compared to the massive and sustained persecutions visited on them by Christian zealots, particularly in the era of the Crusades and the centuries that followed. It must also be noted that the theological and ritual differences dividing Judaism from Christianity are far more substantial than those distinguishing it from Islam. Moreover, the ideological attitude of Islam toward Judaism was considerably more benign than that of Christianity; there was nothing in it like the deicide charge, with its potential for murderous explosion, or the compulsion to engage in systematic inculcation of contempt for the Jews. For many reasons, then, the distance in the medieval world between Jew and Christian was far greater than the distance between Jew and Moslem. However, even though Christian civilization did not provide the Jews of France and Germany with the same powerful catalyst for religious and cultural creativity that Moslem civilization gave their brethren in Spain, Franco-German Jewry developed a style of religious life and thought that had its own special values and strengths and proved more durable than that of Spanish Jewry.

Jews first came to the Rhineland in small numbers with the armies of imperial Rome and lived peaceably among the Romans, Gauls, and Franks. After the conversion of the pagan tribes to Christianity, their position seems to have deteriorated somewhat; we hear of discriminatory measures by the Merovingians and other early dynasties. Charlemagne, the great king of the Franks from 768 and Emperor of the West from 800 to his death in 814, however, encouraged Jewish immigration. In an expanding economy Jews, with their mercantile skills and connections, came to be regarded as a valuable asset. Despite occasional banishments from one locality or another and various restrictions and indignities inflicted upon them at the instigation of the clergy, Jews lived in relative tranquility and amicable relations with their Christian neighbors in southern and northeastern France and in the major commercial cities along the Rhine from the ninth century to the commencement of the Crusades at the end of the eleventh.

We know little about the religious life or culture of Franco-German Jewry before the beginning of the eleventh century, when Rabbi Gershom ben Judah (ca. 960–1028), who was given the encomium "the Light of the Exile," established a *yeshivah* in Mainz. The rever-

ence which this great scholar was accorded in his own and later generations is reflected in Rashi's reference to him: "Rabbenu Gershom,
may the memory of the righteous and holy be for a blessing, who
enlightened the eyes of the exile, and upon whom we are all dependent, and of whom all the Jews of Ashkenaz are the pupils of his
pupils." [1] In authority the German scholar was the rival of the last
Gaon of stature in Babylonia, Hai, who served as the spiritual head
of eastern Jewry for forty years until his death in 1038. Gershom not
only founded an academy which attracted hundreds of students from
all over France and Germany and thus laid the foundations of Talmudic scholarship in these lands; he also attempted to correct the
corrupted text of the Talmudic manuscripts extant in his day, and
wrote an extensive commentary on the *Talmud*. He further managed,
as a result of his vast authority, to institute a number of *takkanot* or
special ordinances in Jewish life and practice which were universally
accepted by European Jewry. The most important of these are the
ḥerem or ban forbidding polygamy (in Christian Europe, unlike the
Moslem world, monogamy was the rule, and having more than one
wife was considered immoral) and the prohibition against divorcing a
wife against her will, except in the case of her adultery. Also attributed to Gershom is a *ḥerem* proscribing the reading of private letters without the addressee's permission, and a prohibition against
reminding a forcibly converted Jew who has repented and returned
to Judaism of his defection. Many other *takkanot*, not all of which
may in fact be his, were ascribed to Rabbenu Gershom in later times
to lend them the weight of his authority.

Shortly after the time of Rabbenu Gershom a notable school of
biblical exegesis began to develop in northern France. Its founder
was Menaḥem bar Ḥelbo. Although Menaḥem's work has survived
only in fragments quoted by later Bible commentators, these suffice
to provide a picture of his methodology. Largely eschewing the way
of *derash*, the fanciful, homiletic interpretation of Scripture favored
by the authors of the rabbinic *midrashim*, the eleventh-century
scholar sought to expound the *peshat*, the plain or literal meaning of
the biblical text. This was no easy task in view of the fact that the
epoch-making work of the great Spanish-Jewish philologists and
writers on Hebrew grammar, Jannaḥ and Ḥayyuj, who wrote in Arabic, was sealed to him; he was familiar only with the Hebrew compositions of Menaḥem ibn Saruk and Dunash ben Labrat. Nevertheless, Menaḥem bar Ḥelbo contributed much to giving his
contemporaries a clearer understanding of the literal meaning of the

Bible. His work was continued by his nephew and chief disciple, Joseph ben Shimeon Kara (born ca. 1060), who deplored the confusion of *derash* with *peshat* that was so prevalent in his age and insisted that "Holy Scripture is written clearly and precisely, without allusions at which one must guess, and it is not necessary to employ proofs and arguments from the *midrash*." Joseph Kara, who was also a student and colleague of Rashi, contended that one "who does not understand the literal meaning of the Torah and attempts to grasp its content with the aid of the *midrash* is like a man who is carried along by a powerful sea and struggles with the waves, trying to catch hold of anything he touches with his hands." In pursuit of his goal of explicating the plain meaning of the text (he was not always successful, lapsing occasionally into *derash*), the pious commentator, who probably had not the least idea that he was suggesting anything heterodox, made a number of comments that adumbrate the free, "scientific" biblical criticism which emerged with Baruch Spinoza in the seventeenth century.

❦

It was in Joseph Kara's home city of Troyes in the province of Champagne that the greatest of medieval commentators on the *Talmud*, the most popular and widely read exegete of Scripture among European Jews, and undoubtedly the major figure produced by Franco-German Jewry in the Middle Ages spent most of his life. This was Rabbi Shelomoh ben Yitzḥak (1040–1105), universally known in the Jewish world by the acronym Rashi.

Troyes was not noted for Jewish scholarship when Rashi was born there. Hence, he spent his youth in the *yeshivot* of Mainz, Speyer, and Worms established by Rabbenu Gershom and his disciples. It was then customary for students to wander from one *yeshivah* to another in pursuit of learning. Rashi himself refers to this when he writes that like "doves that roam from dovecote to dovecote in search of food, so they go from the academy of one scholar to that of another in quest of explanations of Torah." He also describes the hardships of his own itinerant *Lehrjahre:* "In want of bread and proper clothing, with a millstone hanging around my neck [apparently a reference to the burdens of his early marriage and family responsibilities] I served before them [his teachers]." After spending almost a decade in the Talmudic academies of Germany, Rabbi Shelomoh ben Yitzḥak returned at the age of twenty-five to his native city, where he spent the remaining forty years of his life surrounded by a group of admiring disciples and writing his great commentaries on the Bible and the *Talmud*.

For the Jews of Rashi's environment the *Gemara* of the *Babylonian Talmud*, written as it was in Aramaic, a language that was not their vernacular and which few of them understood thoroughly, was becoming increasingly unintelligible. Had Rashi not undertaken to explain and illuminate its subtleties and difficult points in his monumental running commentary, it is possible that substantive knowledge of the *Talmud* would eventually have been lost to European Jewry. The judgment of the Spanish rabbi of the fourteenth century, Menaḥem ben Zeraḥ, on the significance of Rashi's work is not much of an exaggeration: "Without him the *Talmud* would have been forgotten in Israel." That this would have happened is more than probable, for the oral tradition of interpreting the *Talmud* that had been maintained for centuries in the great academies of Babylonia was now coming to its end. Rashi, it would seem, had no desire to fixate the law of the *Talmud* by reducing it to a code, as did Maimonides, Alfasi, and other codifiers. By writing a running commentary instead of a code, he made it possible—perhaps without deliberate intention—for the *Talmud* to function as a storehouse of various legal possibilities and to yield, at the hands of later scholars skilled in the art of applying dialectical reasoning to its text, the rules and regulations required by their particular time and place.

There is little attempt at profundity or sophisticated speculation in Rashi's explanations. The author never forgets that his function is to clarify and interpret the meaning of the text, and he does this with admirable simplicity and directness, avoiding unnecessary verbiage as well as the temptation to discuss tangential and extraneous questions. When he suspected that a certain Hebrew or Aramaic term was not familiar to his readers (and he wrote not only for scholars but for the generality of Jews), Rashi provided, in his commentaries on both the *Talmud* and the Bible, the French equivalent. Scholars have found some three thousand *leazim*, or French expressions, in the great commentator's writings, and these have become a major source for contemporary knowledge of the vocabulary of the French language of the eleventh century. When Rashi himself was uncertain about the meaning of some enigmatic statement in the *Talmud*, he did not hesitate to acknowledge it; his candor and intellectual integrity are manifested in his readiness to admit, "I do not understand," "I do not know," "This is not clear to me."

Franco-German Judaism in the Middle Ages

An indefatigable scholar and teacher, Rashi did not live in an ivory tower, sequestered from all non-Jewish and worldly interests. His colloquial language was French and he was involved in practical affairs, earning his livelihood—like many of his fellow Jews in Champagne—through grape growing and wine making. In explaining passages from the Bible and the *Talmud* he makes reference to contemporary practices, instruments, and terms. His commentaries reflect more than a passing acquaintance with such technical matters as engraving, falconry, glasswork, ship repairing, and military affairs. The close association of Jews and Christians in Rashi's age, as well as his own liberal and practical attitude in halachic questions, is attested by his ruling that Christians may be employed by Jews in the making and sale of wine, and that wine handled by the former is not *yayin nesech*, the wine of idolators (which, according to the Talmudic rabbis, may not be used or profited from), since Christians are not idol worshippers.

Rashi acquired renown not only as an expositor of the *Talmud* but equally as an exegete of the Bible. His biblical commentaries, especially on the Pentateuch, manifest the same virtues as his *Talmud* commentary—clarity, conciseness, precision, simplicity, and directness. But while following the method of *peshat*, Rashi did not disdain the way of *derash*; in fact, his biblical exegesis is an interweaving of the two. Among clear and precise lexicographical explanations of the text are braided poetic tales and fanciful legends from the *Talmud* and *midrashim*. This gave his work a special charm and enhanced its enormous popularity among the Jews of his own time and subsequent centuries. Indeed, for European Jewry the Pentateuch and Rashi's commentary on it became inextricably intertwined, serving together as the foundation of instruction in the Jewish school. It is no mere accident of history that Rashi's Torah commentary was among the first Hebrew books to be printed, in the Italian city of Reggio in 1475.

Rashi did not have anything approaching the originality or profundity of a Maimonides or even a Saadiah Gaon, but his influence on Jewish life was undoubtedly greater and of more far-reaching consequence than theirs. His massive importance for the history of European Judaism is twofold. First, he brought the world of the Bible and the *Talmud* effectively into the life of the people and made them a significant element of everyday existence. Even the common Jew, without any pretension to higher learning, could until quite recent times quote Scripture and fragments of the *Talmud* with Rashi's commentaries, for they became a curricular staple of the Jewish school. The world of the *midrash* also became a part of his mental furniture through the interpretive use made of it by the French scholar. Rashi was the channel through which the major sources of ancient Judaism entered the mind of the medieval and, to a large extent, even the modern Jew.

Second, Rashi, as Solomon Zeitlin has noted, was "the founder of the rabbinate in western and central Europe" and "responsible for the institution of the rabbinate." [2] If he was not the absolute origina- tor of the style of learning and life characteristic of the post- Talmudic European rabbi, it was he who consolidated it, best ex- emplified it, and served as its chief inspiration in his own and later centuries. It should also be noted that Rashi exercised a definite in- fluence on Christian exegesis of the Bible. His commentaries were extensively utilized by Nicholas de Lyra, who taught at the Univer- sity of Paris some two hundred years after Rashi's death and whose Latin commentaries were in turn carefully studied by Martin Luther. The influence is apparent in Luther's great German transla- tion of the Bible. Other Christian exegetes and translators also made use of Rashi's work, including the translators of the King James ver- sion of the Bible.

Rashi's last years were deeply shadowed by the catastrophe of the First Crusade, which suddenly struck Franco-German Jewry and especially the communities of the Rhineland with barbaric fury. He wrote a series of heartbreaking elegies and laments after receiving word of the massacres of Jews in Metz, Worms, Cologne, Mainz, Speyer, and other cities by the rabble which, marching to Palestine to liberate the tomb of its crucified savior from the infidel Turks, was incited to take vengeance on the descendants of those who had al- legedly killed him. The decimation of these communities brought about the eclipse of the *yeshivot* in the Rhineland that had been founded by Rabbenu Gershom and his disciples, and the rise of others established by the sons-in-law and pupils of Rashi in Ra- merupt, Dampierre, Sens, Paris, and other cities of France. In these academies the heads and teachers were the brilliant dialecticians who came to be known as the Tosafists.

The task which the Talmudic scholars of the eleventh century from Gershom to Rashi set themselves was to render the difficulties of the *Talmud* clear and comprehensible to all, and it had been mar- velously consummated by the master of Troyes. The successors of Rashi in the twelfth century felt that it was now supererogatory further to explain the Talmudic text; instead they undertook to explore it analytically and dialectically. Men of extraordinary mental ability but with their interest focused entirely on the rather limited world of Talmudic scholarship, they exercised their skill on collating and contrasting all the passages and discussions in the *Gemara* that have the slightest relationship or analogy to one another, discovering hidden contradictions in them, and then reconciling the contradictions in the most subtle and ingenious dialectical fashion. Referring to their investigations as *tosafot* (supplements or additions) to the *Talmud*, they came to be called *baalei ha-tosafot*, or Tosafists. It is difficult to escape the conviction that the Tosafists not only sought to fathom the deeper meaning of the *Talmud*, but reveled in their stunning display of intellectual pyrotechnics as an end in itself. There is more than a little justification for the suggestion that just as the Christian knights of that age gloried in jousting with each other on the tournament fields and displaying their physical prowess, so the Jewish scholars exulted in jousting with the complexities of the Talmudic text and exhibiting their mental keenness.

The earliest Tosafists were Rashi's disciple Rabbi Isaac ben Asher (11th cent.) and his son-in-law and pupil Rabbi Meir ben Samuel (ca. 1060–after 1135) of Ramerupt. But the school reached its heights in the persons of the latter's sons and Rashi's grandsons, Rabbi Samuel ben Meir (ca. 1085–after 1158), or Rashbam, and Rabbi Jacob ben Meir Tam (ca. 1100–1171). Besides attaining fame as one of the most acute of Tosafists, Rabbi Samuel ben Meir wrote a commentary on the Pentateuch in which he rigorously pursued the way of *peshat* and polemicized against *derash*. It appears that he even argued with his grandfather about the latter's introduction of midrashic homilies and legends into his commentary on the Torah, and he claims that Rashi finally conceded that, had he the necessary leisure, he would write a new commentary following the method of *peshat* exclusively. Excellent as Rashbam's commentary was, it did not, under the melancholy and pietistic moods induced by the terrors of the Crusades, have the appeal of Rashi's legendary embellishments and frequently tender and touching explanations. It was completely forgotten, to be rediscovered and published only in the eighteenth century. Even more renowned as a Tosafist was Samuel ben Meir's younger brother Jacob, better known as Rabbenu Tam. Jacob Tam not only carried the Tosafist method of dialectic to its highest level; he also employed it practically for the derivation of new principles and laws to regulate Jewish life. In his own lifetime he achieved widespread recognition as a halachist, and for medieval Franco-German Jewry he was the supreme authority in all matters of religious law and practice.

It is interesting to note that the keen intelligence of Rashi and the Tosafists was not at all troubled by the philosophical and theological problems posed by the Bible and the *Talmud*. Unlike the great Spanish and Provençal scholars, they were unburdened by any knowledge of Greek-Arabic philosophy, and had no desire whatever to assume the burden. For them the words of the prophets and rabbis were self-evidently true and sufficient for all purposes; they felt no compulsion to question their truth or to reconcile them with the metaphysical speculations of Aristotle or Averroes. Whether deliberate or unconscious, the wisdom of their course can hardly be questioned. Philosophy might have saved them from some of their superstitions, but it probably would not have saved them, as it did not Maimonides, from whatever intellectual fanaticism and intolerance they had.

Despite the Crusades, the twelfth century was, as a result of the activity of the Tosafists, a great age of Jewish scholarship. But the "holy wars," in which the unholiest of atrocities were perpetrated and which continued on into the fourteenth century to the Crusade of the Pastoureaux (1320), had in general and in the long run extremely destructive effects on European Jewish life. The relationships between Jews and Christians, tense and problematic from the beginning as a result of the profound theological differences and the mutual animosities dividing the two faiths, deteriorated greatly. In the highly charged atmosphere generated by the Crusades, the blood libel made its appearance and soon became widespread. Starting in the twelfth century, the accusation was frequently made that Jews sacrificed a Christian victim each year to use his blood in their Passover rites. At Blois thirty-one Jews were burned at the stake on charges of ritual murder on the twentieth of Sivan 1171. That charge, although repeatedly denounced as false by Popes and Church Councils, was never to be completely suppressed in the years that followed, and it resurfaced as late as the twentieth century in Russia. In the thirteenth century, after the Fourth Lateran Council proclaimed the dogma of transubstantiation, the accusation was put forward that Jews maliciously desecrated the Host to make the body of Christ bleed. And during the Black Death of the fourteenth century, as we have noted, Jews were charged with poisoning the wells and rivers of Europe out of their implacable hatred of Christians. Rivers of blood were shed in consequence of these horrible libels, and more Jewish victims perished because of them than from the massacres of the Crusaders themselves.

The effect of the Crusades on the economic life of European Jewry was also disastrous. Before the Crusades Jews had a virtual monopoly of the international trade between East and West; the Crusades brought this to an end. Christian merchants now traversed the trade routes between the two worlds, and Jews were progressively forced to abandon them. Having lost their livelihood as international traders, barred from the craft and artisans' guilds, denied the right to own land, and with no place in the feudal order, Jews were compelled to turn to petty trade and the despised occupation of moneylender. Henceforth, the Jewish moneylender becomes the prototype of the Jew in Europe. It is an image that has not completely disappeared even in the twentieth century.

After each Crusade, the Jewish communities buried their massacred dead and lovingly cherished their memories as martyrs, for almost all the Jews of Germany and France had preferred death, often at their own hands, to saving their lives through baptism. The names of the victims and their dates of death were inscribed in *Memorbücher* kept in the synagogues, and their deeds were recalled on the anniversary of their sacrifice. (Out of this custom, probably inspired by the Catholic requiem mass, grew the practice of *Jahrzeit*, or memorializing all the dead on the anniversary of their passing.) Those who perished at the hands of the Crusaders were remembered by their powerless survivors not so much as victims of inhuman cruelty who must be avenged if the demands of justice are to be satisfied (although cries for vengeance are not altogether absent from the many moving elegies and laments composed in their memory, some of which found their way into the synagogue service), but as exemplars of supreme sacrificial devotion. They were *kedoshim*, "holy ones" or "saints," who died willingly for the sanctification of God's name, and their place in Paradise was assured.

❧

The Crusades shook but did not shatter the foundations of community life in Franco-German Jewry, for these foundations were old and firmly established. Something must be said about the organization and structure of the communities in which the Jews of France and Germany lived for centuries in the Middle Ages and later, and which proved a remarkably effective instrument for the promotion of their survival and sanity.

Already in the Talmudic era in Babylonia Jews lived as a largely autonomous or, at least, semiautonomous group, with their own civil administration and judicial system. In the Geonic period the exilarch of Babylonian Jewry was vested with extensive power over all the Jews in his realm by his Persian or Arab sovereign. Administration was centralized, with local officials responsible to the exilarch. A similar organization of Jewish life, but with lesser power, was generally maintained in the emirates and kingdoms of Spain under both Moslem and Christian rule; a *nagid* or chief rabbi appointed by the government wielded considerable authority. The Franco-German Jews, however, sought to avoid this system and to maintain the independence of their *kehillot* or communities, apparently out of their apprehension that an official, nationwide Jewish authority would facilitate imposition by the government of oppressive taxes and other forms of discrimination. Furthermore, there was rarely in the early centuries an effective national government to which a national Jewish authority could relate.

Every town in the feudal structure of Christian Europe at that time had its own overlord, and every Jewish community obtained its charter of rights and responsibilities from this overlord. As the towns were autonomous and independent of one another, so their Jewries constituted a network of largely autonomous and independent communities.

Each *kehillah*, which embraced all the Jews living in a particular town and its environs, was in fact an *imperium in imperio*. Although it was generally heavily taxed as a body by the secular government, its officials were authorized to allocate and collect the amount of the taxes to be paid by each Jewish householder. The officials were also empowered to impose assessments on members of the *kehillah* for maintenance of its own institutions. These included not only a synagogue and school for the young (in the larger communities, several synagogues and schools), but also a communal sick-care facility, a charity fund, a fund for dowering poor brides, a ritual bath, a burial society, a cemetery, a *matzah* bakery, and occasionally a *Tanzhaus* or social hall in which wedding banquets and other celebrations were held. In a very real sense, the Jewish community was a miniature "welfare state" in which responsibility for caring for the needs of sick, indigent, and distressed members was assumed by the group as a whole. Community officials appointed the professional functionaries of the *kehillah*—the rabbis, teachers, *hazzanim* or cantors, and *shohetim* or ritual slaughterers. The officials themselves were generally elected, either by direct ballot in which all householders or those who met certain property qualifications participated, by lot, or by special electors chosen for the purpose.

Democracy was hardly prevalent; frequently the wealthy constituted an oligarchy who ran the affairs of the community much as they pleased. Oppression and exploitation, however, were discouraged by the custom of "delaying the prayers" that was deeply rooted in many of the communities: anyone who felt aggrieved against the officials or leaders, or against another member of the *kehillah*, had the privilege of rising in the synagogue on the Sabbath and forbidding the reading of the Torah to continue until he stated his complaint and obtained some assurance that it would be rectified. Besides this, the rabbis, although occasionally neglectful of their responsibilities and in some places joining the rich and powerful in oppressive or unjust acts, were usually men of high moral stature who could be counted on to raise their voices in protest against injustice, and to insist that the affairs of the community be conducted according to the ethical standards of the Torah.

The position of the rabbi in the medieval Franco-German community was an important and powerful one. He was the official religious head of the *kehillah*, not the preacher in the synagogue or the "pastor" of the congregation. Together with his assistants he constituted the *bet din* or court which adjudicated all civil cases, including marriage, divorce, inheritance, and disputes over contracts, sales, and property. He was also the authority on all questions of religious law and practice, and supervisor of the community's religious and educational institutions. Quite often he conducted a *yeshivah* for advanced students of the *Talmud*. Until the fifteenth century the functions of the rabbi were generally unsalaried; he derived his livelihood from business or a trade (Rashi, as we have noted, engaged in vinticulture) and his rabbinic activities were a labor "for the sake of Heaven." Ordinarily the local rabbi had virtually absolute authority; he was the *mara de-atra*, the "master of the place," and his decisions were not to be questioned. However, each generation had one or two outstanding rabbis who achieved national or international recognition as halachic authorities, and these served, by tacit agreement, as decisors of difficult questions submitted to them by local rabbis or communities and as appeals judges. Such were Rabbenu Tam in France and Rabbi Meir of Rothenburg in Germany.

In the era of the Crusades Franco-German Jewry came increasingly under the domination of pietistic, otherworldly moods. Testimony to this is borne by the vast influence of the twelfth-century Ḥasidei Ashkenaz, the "pious of Germany," and their *Sefer Ḥasidim* (*Book of the Pious*), with its somber, elegiac tone and deprecation of the vanities of the world. But it is not to be imagined that Jews in this period or throughout the Middle Ages were concerned only with the world to come and the bliss of the afterlife. In the present world, too, though life was often grim and precarious, there were opportunities for enjoyment and good cheer. The weekly Sabbath and the festivals of the sacred calendar provided islands of peace and joy in the troubled sea of the everyday world. Happy occasions in the lives of families—circumcision feasts for newborn boys, *bar mitzvah* celebrations (these first emerged among the Franco-German Jews in the late Middle Ages), and engagement and wedding celebrations—were shared by broad circles of the community.

Among the Jews of medieval France and Germany books of *musar*, moral and religious edification, were especially popular. Perhaps the most widely read was the *Sefer Ḥasidim*, with its mystical overtones, which came, as we have noted, from the school of Rabbi Judah the Pious. These works were rarely of an original or deeply philosophical character; they sought simply to inculcate the elementary virtues of faith, hope, and morality. The custom of leaving "ethical wills" was also practiced by many Jews. Legal wills prescribing the disposition of property were rare, since Jewish law governing inheritance was quite fixed and allowed little discretionary freedom; so a father would frequently leave his children a moral testament, summarizing his own life experience and admonishing them to follow the ways of righteousness and justice. The following extracts from the will of Eleazar of Mainz, a fourteenth-century Jew about whom virtually nothing is known but who was probably not untypical of his age in his attitudes toward life, reflect the common values cherished by the medieval Jew:

These are the things which my sons and daughters shall do at my request. They shall go to the house of prayer morning and evening, and shall pay special regard to the Tephillah and the Shema. So soon as the service is over, they shall occupy themselves a little with the Torah, the Psalms, or with works of charity. Their business must be conducted honestly, in their dealings both with Jew and Gentile. They must be gentle in their manners, and prompt to accede to every honorable request. They must not talk more than is necessary; by this will they be saved from slander, falsehood, and frivolity. They shall give an exact tithe of all their possessions; they shall never turn away a poor man empty-handed, but must give him what they can, be it much or little. If he beg a lodging over night, and they know him not, let them provide him with the wherewithal to pay an inn-keeper. Thus shall they satisfy the needs of the poor in every possible way.

My daughters must obey scrupulously the rules applying to women; modesty, sanctity, reverence, should mark their married lives. They should carefully watch for the signs of the beginning of their periods and keep separate from their husbands at such times. Marital intercourse must be modest and holy, with a spirit of restraint and delicacy, in reverence and silence. They shall be very punctilious and careful with their ritual bathing, taking with them women friends of worthy character. They shall cover their eyes until they reach their home, on returning from the bath, in order not to behold anything of an unclean nature. They must respect their husbands, and must be invariably amiable to them. Husbands, on their part, must honor their wives more than themselves, and treat them with tender consideration. . . .

I earnestly beg my children to be tolerant and humble to all, as I was throughout my life. Should cause for dissension present itself, be slow to accept the quarrel; seek peace and pursue it with all the vigor at your command. Even if you suffer loss thereby, forebear and forgive, for God has many ways of feeding and sustaining His creatures. To the slanderer do not retaliate with counter-attack; and though it be proper to rebut false accusations, yet is it most desirable to set an example of reticence. You yourselves must avoid uttering any slander, for so will you win affection. In trade be true, never grasping at what belongs to another. For by avoiding these wrongs—scandal, falsehood, money-grubbing,—men will surely find tranquillity and affection. And against all evils, silence is the best safeguard.

Now, my sons and daughters, eat and drink only what is necessary, as our good parents did, refraining from heavy meals, and holding the gross liver in detestation. The regular adoption of such economy in food leads to economy in expenditure generally, with a consequent reluctance to pursue after wealth, but the acquisition of a contented spirit, simplicity in diet, and many good results. Concerning such a well-ordered life the text says: "The righteous eateth to the satisfaction of his desire." Our teachers have said: "Method in expenditure is half a sufficiency." Nevertheless, accustom yourselves and your wives, your sons and your daughters, to wear nice and clean clothes, that God and man may love and honor you. In this direction do not exercise too strict a parsimony. But on no account adopt foreign fashions in dress. After the manner of your fathers order your attire, and let your cloaks be broad with buckles attached. . . .

On holidays and festivals and Sabbaths seek to make happy the poor, the unfortunate, widows and orphans, who should always be guests at your tables; their joyous entertainment is a religious duty. Let me repeat my warning against gossip and scandal. And as ye speak no scandal, so listen to none, for if there were no receivers there would be no bearers of slanderous tales; therefore the reception and credit of slander is as serious an offence as the originating of it. The less you say, the less cause you give for animosity, while "in the multitude of words there wanteth not transgression." Always be of those who see and are not seen, who hear and are not heard. Accept no invitations to banquets, except to such as are held for religious reasons: at weddings and at meals prepared for mourners, at gatherings to celebrate entry into the covenant of Abraham, or at assemblies in honor of the wise. Games of chance for money stakes, such as dicing, must be avoided. And as I have again warned you on that head, again let me urge you to show forbearance and humility to all men, to ignore abuses levelled at you, but the indignant refutation of charges against your moral character is fully justifiable.

I beg of you, my sons and daughters, my wife, and all the congregation, that no funeral oration be spoken in my honor. Do not carry my body on a bier but in a coach. Wash me clean, comb my hair, trim my nails, as I was wont to do in my life-time, so that I may go clean to my eternal rest, as I went clean to Synagogue every Sabbath day. If the ordinary officials dislike the duty, let adequate payment be made to some poor man who shall render this service carefully and not perfunctorily. At a distance of thirty cubits from the grave, they shall set my coffin on the ground, and drag me to the grave by a rope attached to the coffin. Every four cubits they shall stand and wait awhile, doing this in all seven times, so that I may find atonement for my sins. Put me in the ground at the right hand of my father, and if the space be a little narrow, I am sure that he loves me well enough to make room for me by his side. If this be altogether impossible, put me on his left, or near my grandmother, Yuta. Should this also be impractical, let me be buried by the side of my daughter.[3]

While the Jews of the Rhineland and northern France were little influenced by Spanish Jewry, in whose midst philosophy and poetry bloomed so magnificently under the impact of Arabic civilization, this was not the case with the Jews of southeastern France, or Provence, who lived in proximity to Spain. There remnants of the ancient Roman culture and institutions persisted in the Middle Ages. In addition, an intensive urban life, as well as commerce and artisanry, flourished there earlier than in the other lands of Christian

Europe. Furthermore, the nobility and upper classes of Provence developed a liberal and tolerant attitude in matters of religion; more than a few of them were religious skeptics, as well as connoisseurs of the arts and sciences. As a result, Jews were welcomed and treated well. The renowned Jewish traveler of the twelfth century, Benjamin of Tudela, gives a vivid portrait of the prosperous Jewish communities flourishing in his time in such old Provençal cities as Narbonne, Marseilles, Lunel, Béziers, Posquières, and Montpellier.

We have already noted that fourteenth-century Provençal Jewry produced, in the person of Gersonides, the foremost Jewish philosopher and scientist of his age and the most original thinker after Maimonides in medieval Judaism. Spanish-Jewish philosophy and science were introduced among the Jews of Provence much earlier, in the first half of the twelfth century. It was then that the astronomer, mathematician, and religious philosopher, Abraham bar Ḥiyya (fl. early 12th cent.), came to Provence from Spain and began his educational work. Abraham bar Ḥiyya brought with him a wealth of scientific knowledge gleaned from sources written in Arabic, and made much of it available to his Provençal brethren, who did not read that language, in Hebrew. Bar Ḥiyya laid the foundations of scientific terminology in Hebrew, and was also a major figure in transmitting Greco-Arabic science to the Christian world. In his moral-religious treatise *Hegyon Ha-Nefesh* (*Meditation of the Soul*), a rather somber, heavy, and unoriginal work, he also introduced Provençal Jewry to philosophical ways of thinking about Judaism. His pioneering enlightening activity was continued by Abraham ibn Ezra (1089–1164), who spent some years in various Jewish communities of Provence and assumed the task of acquainting them, as well as the Jews of Italy (among whom he also sojourned for a time), with the riches of Spanish-Jewish literature. In the middle of the twelfth century many other Jewish scholars from Spain came to Provence, some of them seeking refuge from the persecutions of the fanatical Almohades. Two families, the Kimḥis and Tibbonids, proved to be of particular importance in transmitting Spanish-Jewish culture to the Jews of southeastern France.

Joseph ben Isaac Kimḥi (ca. 1105–ca. 1170), who arrived from Spain in 1150 and settled in Narbonne, was a gifted and prolific writer as well as a talented translator. His works include a translation from Arabic into Hebrew of Baḥya ibn Pakuda's *Ḥovot Ha-Levavot* (*Duties of the Heart*), grammatical and philological studies, a commentary on virtually the whole Hebrew Bible, religious hymns and poems, and a collection of maxims and proverbs in verse entitled *Shekel Ha-Kodesh* (*Holy Shekel*). Of special cultural-historical significance is his polemic tract *Sefer Ha-Berit* (*Book of the Covenant*), written, as he indicates, to aid "those who must carry on debates with apostates from our people, who spread lies and preach falsehood and presumptuously believe that with childish stories and foolish arguments they can overthrow the words of the living God." Apparently the Catholic Church was already employing Jewish converts as missionaries in its efforts to proselytize the Jews. The most remarkable aspect of Joseph Kimhi's *Sefer Ha-Berit*, which is composed in the form of a debate between a *maamin* or believing Jew and a *min* (literally a "heretic" or "sectarian") or Christian, is the bold freedom with which the author not only argues for the superiority of Judaism over Christianity, but permits himself to castigate Christian life and conduct. Thus, for instance, he calls attention to the sexual irregularities of priests and even of bishops and cardinals. Such freedom was not to be permitted later in the long history of written and oral disputation between Jews and Christians in medieval Europe.

Joseph Kimhi's sons, Moses and David, followed the footsteps of their father in pursuing Jewish scholarship. Moses Kimhi, the elder son, was the author of a Hebrew grammar, *Mahalach Shevilei Ha-Daat* (*Course of the Paths of Knowledge*), which in the era of the Protestant Reformation became the text from which most Christian scholars derived their first knowledge of Hebrew. It was translated into Latin by the Christian Hebraist Sebastian Muenster and published in Basel in 1531. In addition, Moses wrote commentaries on several books of the Bible. Far more renowned as a philologist and Bible exegete was his brother David (ca. 1160–1235), known in Hebrew literature as Radak (an acronym for Rabbi David Kimhi). In his two-volume *Michlol* (*Compendium*) David Kimhi so expertly summarized and systematized the vast grammatical and lexicographic discoveries made by the great Hebrew grammarians of the Spanish school that his work eventually completely displaced theirs. As a commentator on the Bible, he was widely read by Jews and also became enormously popular in the world of Christian scholarship, where several of his commentaries were translated into Latin and employed by the Christian translators of the Bible into European languages. David Kimhi's biblical exegesis clearly reflects the influence of Maimonides, for whose philosophy he had an inordinate admiration, as well as the rabbinic midrashic method and the *peshat* interpretations of Rashi. His rationalist explanations of the "work of creation" (*maaseh bereshit*) and "lore of the Chariot-Throne" (*maaseh merkavah*) infuriated the pietistic rabbis of northern France, but Kimḥi was not deterred. When the first major controversy between the followers and opponents of Maimonides was reaching its climax, the aged scholar played a prominent role as an ardent protagonist of the Maimonidean party. Like his father, David Kimḥi was also involved in disputations with Christian scholars and priests, and included polemical remarks on Christianity in his commentary to the Psalms.

While the Kimḥis were primarily grammarians, Bible exegetes, and polemicists, the Tibbonid family made its major contribution to Jewish history and thought in the realm of translation. It was chiefly because of them that non-Arabic speaking European Jewry gained access to the most important works of the great Spanish-Jewish philosophers and scholars.

The founder of the dynasty was Judah ben Saul ibn Tibbon (ca. 1120–after 1190), a native of Granada who settled in the Provençal city of Lunel at about the same time that Joseph Kimḥi took up residence in Narbonne. He began his translating activity from Arabic into Hebrew with Baḥya ibn Pakuda's *Ḥovot Ha-Levavot* (*Duties of the Heart*), being dissatisfied with Kimḥi's rendering of the work. Thereafter he proceeded to translate Judah Halevi's *Kuzari*, Solomon ibn Gabirol's *Mivḥar Ha-Peninim* (*Choice of Pearls*), Saadiah Gaon's *Sefer Ha-Emunot Veha-Deot* (*Book of Beliefs and Opinions*), and the grammatical works of Jonah ibn Jannaḥ. Judah ibn Tibbon was largely responsible for creating a philosophical-scientific vocabulary in Hebrew, and he fully deserves the encomium "chief of the translators" that was bestowed on him. Provençal Jewry gained its appetite for philosophical reflection on Judaism mainly as a result of his efforts.

Judah ibn Tibbon's work was continued by his son Samuel (ca. 1150–ca. 1230), who surpassed his father in the quality of both his intellectual and literary gifts. By the time he began his translating activity the name of Maimonides already resounded throughout the Jewish communities of Provence; the great Talmudist and philosopher who lived in Fostat as the *nagid* of Egyptian Jewry was regarded not only as the supreme authority in halachic matters but as the peerless thinker and most reliable guide in all spiritual questions. As soon as they heard of the appearance of Maimonides' *Guide of the Perplexed* in Arabic, a number of the cultured Jewish leaders of Lunel commissioned Samuel ibn Tibbon to prepare a Hebrew translation of the work. Samuel agreed, and completed the task in 1204, just two weeks before Maimonides' death. In the meantime, another, less precise translation of the *Guide* was made by the wandering Spanish-Jewish troubadour Judah Alḥarizi, who was then living in southern France. Some time later the intelligentsia of Narbonne and Béziers, whose thirst for philosophical literature was not entirely slaked by Maimonides' treatise, requested the Italian scholar Jacob ben Abba Mari Anatoli, Samuel ibn Tibbon's son-in-law, to render Averroes' works into Hebrew.

The spread of Aristotelian ideas in the first years of the thirteenth century through the widely read writings of the Jewish and Arabic philosophers stimulated in certain intellectual circles among the Jews of Provence, as well as those of Spain, a desire to reconcile the anthropomorphisms and miracle tales of the Bible with Aristotelian conceptions of God and nature through symbolic and allegorical interpretation of biblical texts. This had been the method employed to some extent by Maimonides himself, who followed a long tradition stretching back to Philo of Alexandria and beyond. Allegorical exegesis of Scripture had also become widespread in the Christian world and was assiduously cultivated by many of its foremost theologians in the Middle Ages. Samuel ibn Tibbon, who had lifelong relationships with Christian scholars and was an ardent admirer of Maimonides, advanced the popularity of symbolic-allegorical interpretation of the Bible in Provençal Jewry. In his *Maamar Yikkavu Ha-Mayyim* (*Essay on "Let the Waters Be Gathered"*), a philosophical commentary on *maaseh bereshit*, he explains his reason for advocating it:

> Only Maimonides with his luminous intellect saw how little understood among us [Jews] are the symbols in the sacred writings, and he uncovered very profound matters, but unfortunately few among us grasped his allusions. Therefore, I, one of the youngest of his disciples, when I saw that the true sciences are much more widespread among the Christian peoples in whose midst I live than in the Moslem lands, deemed it necessary to enlighten the eyes of those who are eager for knowledge and to acquaint them with the little with which God has blessed me.[4]

The eagerness of the followers of Maimonides to apply symbolic-allegorical interpretations not only to the anthropomorphic expressions and miracle stories of the Bible but to its commandments as well aroused the wrath of the orthodox and contributed not a little to the controversy which soon erupted over the philosopher's works.

Before turning to this controversy, we note that Samuel ibn Tibbon's translating was continued by his son Moses (d. ca. 1283), who lived in Marseilles, where he practiced medicine and rendered numerous philosophical and scientific books, including Joseph ibn Zaddik's *Olam Katan* (*Microcosm*) and works by Maimonides, from Arabic into Hebrew. A distinguished fourth-generation representative of the Tibbonids was Jacob ben Machir (Don Profiat) ibn Tibbon (ca. 1230–1312). Born in Marseilles, he lived mainly in Montpellier, where he served on the medical faculty of the university. Jacob was a renowned scholar and scientist; his astronomical tables were translated into Latin and employed by Dante in his *Divina Commedia*, and among his translations from Arabic into Hebrew were works by Euclid, Averroes, and al-Ghazali. In the second great battle involving the works of Maimonides at the beginning of the fourteenth century he was an ardent champion of the rationalist party, and fought determinedly against the attempt to suppress the study of science and philosophy.

The first controversy about Maimonides had begun during the philosopher's own lifetime, when Rabbi Abraham ben David of Posquières in Provence sharply attacked his legal code, the *Mishneh Torah*, as well as his ambiguous attitudes on the question of the resurrection and the world to come. He was joined in similar criticism in 1202 by the aristocratic young scholar Meir ben Todros Abulafia of Toledo in a letter addressed to Maimonides' ardent admirers, "the scholars of Lunel." After receiving their indignant and insulting response, Abulafia turned to seven prominent French rabbis, apprising them of his apprehensions about Maimonides and his controversy with the Provençal scholars. Although these rabbis had little direct knowledge of Maimonides' works, their spokesman, the Tosafist Rabbi Samson of Sens, replied to the effect that they were in general agreement with Abulafia. Nothing more came of the matter at this time. Abulafia's protest was ignored in Provence, and he himself was ridiculed as an obscurantist in verse by some Jewish poets in Spain. In the generation after Maimonides' death in 1204, however, the popularity of his philosophy, now made readily accessible through Samuel ibn Tibbon's and Judah Alḥarizi's Hebrew translations of his *Guide of the Perplexed*, increased markedly among the Jewish intellectuals of Provence. Some of them, under the influence of their rationalist outlook, became indifferent to the traditional religious commandments. At the same time, following the suppression of the Albigensian heresy, the Catholic Church became progressively more militant, employing the Inquisition and the Dominican monks to ferret out heresy. The Fourth Lateran Council proscribed a number of philosophic works as heretical, and the University of Paris was ordered by Pope Gregory IX to remove them from its curriculum. The intensified hostility of the clergy toward the Jews also became apparent in the harsh anti-Jewish decrees issued at the Church Council held in Narbonne in 1227. Under these conditions, a reactionary spirit emerged in the Jewish communities of Provence as well; the orthodox leaders also began to fear heresy and to perceive a serious threat to Judaism in the rationalists, influenced by Maimonidean philosophy, who indulged in allegorical interpretation of the Torah and even permitted themselves infractions of the *mitzvot*. The battle that soon erupted between the proponents and opponents of Maimonides was inevitable.

In 1232–1233 the battle reached its unfortunate climax. A Talmudic scholar of Montpellier, Solomon ben Abraham, and two of his disciples, David ben Saul and Jonah ben Abraham Gerondi, had become deeply distressed by what they regarded as the heretical and destructive tendencies of the symbolic-allegorical interpretation of the Bible prevalent among the Jewish illuminati of Provence. In their campaign against it they applied to the rabbis of northern France. The latter responded by dispatching a proclamation to the Provençal communities in which they harshly attacked Maimonides and threatened to excommunicate anyone who dared to read his *Guide of the Perplexed* and *Sefer Ha-Madda* (*Book of Knowledge*—the introductory, philosophical part of the *Mishneh Torah*). In retaliation, the aroused Maimonideans summoned the communities of Provence, Catalonia, and Castile to take up the philosopher's cause and excommunicate Solomon of Montpellier and his followers. An attempt by the great rabbinic scholar Naḥmanides to effect a compromise between the warring parties proved to be of no avail; passions had already become too violent. The adversaries continued to pelt each other with insults, denunciations, and mutual excommunications, and in some places came close to exchanging blows. Finally, according to a report of the Maimonideans, Solomon, who felt himself pushed to the wall, went to the Dominicans of the Inquisition in Montpellier and denounced the works of Maimonides as heretical. The accuracy of this report is questionable; what is certain is that in 1233 the Dominicans of Montpellier confiscated and publicly burned all the copies of *A Guide of the Perplexed* and *Sefer Ha-Madda* that they could locate through a house-to-house search. Many copies of Maimonides' philosophical works are also reported to have been burned some time later in a public square of Paris, on a pyre lit, according to popular legend, by a candle taken from the altar of the Cathedral of Notre Dame.

This sad denouement frightened and grieved both parties, and for a time the overt controversy between the Maimonideans and anti-Maimonideans was suspended. It soon resurfaced, however, and continued to be a prominent element in Jewish life and literature throughout much of the thirteenth century. Kabbalah gained ever larger numbers of adherents throughout European Jewry as the century wore on, and the mystics and the orthodox Talmudists were united in their opposition to the freethinking tendencies of the rationalists, whose idol was Maimonides. At the end of the century the controversy between the two sides again erupted with explosive force, though its focus was no longer specifically the works of Maimonides but philosophy and secular learning in general.

Among the followers of Maimonides were undoubtedly some very sincere and high-minded men who were attracted primarily by his courageous spirit and independent, critical thought, and who honestly believed that these could be employed to purify and strengthen Judaism. But many of the rationalists, particularly among the court Jews and financial aristocracy of Spain and Provence and their young, were drawn to philosophical ideas chiefly because they realized that these might be exploited as a means of liberating themselves from the disciplines and restraints of Jewish law and winning the freedom to indulge without hindrance the desires of their hearts. Symbolic interpretation of the Torah and justification of its commandments on utilitarian grounds could be instruments for nullifying their authority and destroying their obligatory character. In the name of rationalism, some of these persons launched public attacks on Jewish observance. "Young people," complains the Spanish rabbinic authority Solomon ben Adret, "raise questions: Why do the silly Jews make fringes on their garments, affix *mezuzot* to their doors, and place phylacteries on their heads? Has it not long ago been shown that all these customs have no sense whatever?" [5] Another writer of the time, Crescas Vidal of Marseilles, expresses the fear that gripped many of his pious contemporaries: "The danger is great that through the philosophizing young people the whole earth will be covered with heresy and the Torah become a mockery and scorn." That this fear was not without foundation is attested by the fact that at the end of the thirteenth and beginning of the fourteenth centuries not a few Jews in Spain and Provence, under the influence of rationalist ideas derived from a reading (or misreading) of Maimonides, concluded that it was "unreasonable" to suffer the disabilities involved in fidelity to Judaism, and promptly proceeded to shed them at the baptismal font. Believing that indifference to the commandments of Judaism and, ultimately, conversion to Christianity were the inevitable consequences of rationalism, some orthodox Jews of Provence quickly organized a movement to stamp out the pernicious tendency.

The most militant leader of the antirationalists and opponents of science and philosophy, Abba Mari ben Moses Ha-Yarḥi (his Provençal name was Don Astruc de Lunel), applied in 1303 to the illustrious rabbi of Barcelona, Solomon ben Adret, for aid in his campaign. After initial hesitation and some serious misgivings, Solomon was persuaded to send a letter to the community of Montpellier, requesting its leaders to proscribe the study of philosophy by anyone under the age of thirty, and volunteering to countersign any ḥerem or ban that they would issue. In the summer of 1304 the letter was read in the synagogue of Perpignan, precipitating a bitter quarrel between the party led by Abba Mari and those Provençal scholars who adamantly opposed this suppression of free inquiry. The latter group, led by Jacob ben Machir of Montpellier (Samuel ibn Tibbon's grandson), protested strongly to the Spanish rabbi against his interference in the affairs of a sister community, and defended the values of philosophical and scientific study. Solomon ben Adret replied that his letter was advisory only, and that the Provençal communities were free to follow it or not, as they pleased.

In 1305, however, the leading rabbinic authority of Germany, Asher ben Yeḥiel (also known as Rosh or Asheri), after spending some time in Provence, where he had expressed his sympathy with Abba Mari and the antirationalist movement, came to Spain. At the suggestion of Solomon ben Adret he was soon elected chief rabbi of the old and prominent community of Toledo. With this new accession of strength to the traditionalist party, Solomon was persuaded to take decisive action. On July 26, 1305, in the great synagogue of Barcelona a proclamation subscribed by thirty-six rabbis was read, forbidding for fifty years, under a ban and anathema, anyone who had not yet reached the age of twenty-five from studying any Greek work on the natural sciences (with the exception of medicine) or reading books on Greek philosophy in Hebrew translation or in any other language, "lest these sciences entice them and draw their hearts away from the Torah of Israel, which transcends the wisdom of the Greeks." The rabbis of Barcelona circulated their ban not only throughout Spain but in the communities of Provence as well, adding a lengthy explanation of the motives for their action and charging the rationalists with falsifying the Torah through allegorical interpretation, preaching godless and impious sermons in the synagogue, breaking the commandments, and denying the divinely revealed character of the Mosaic law.

The enraged rationalists of Provence immediately responded with a counterban, condemning all parents who prevent their sons of any age from studying science and philosophy, all persons who insult the honor of Maimonides and his works, and all who defame any author who expresses the philosophical opinions that he sincerely holds. In addition, they sought support from the political authorities, requesting the governor of Montpellier to deny the orthodox party of that city permission to publish the ban of Barcelona. To show their utter contempt for this ban and its authors, Jacob ben Machir and his followers arranged for readings in the synagogues from Jacob Anatoli's rationalist commentary on the Torah, *Malmad Ha-Talmidim* (*Goad of the Disciples*), which Solomon ben Adret had found particularly heretical and offensive. In their struggle against suppression of free inquiry, the rationalists were joined by a number of distinguished figures who had no sympathy whatever with their religious and philosophical views but who were deeply committed to the preservation of the principles of freedom of thought and unrestricted access to scientific knowledge. Preeminent among these were the Provençal Talmudist Menaḥem ben Solomon Meiri (ca. 1249–1306) and the foremost poet of the age in Provence, Jedaiah Ha-Penini (ca. 1270–ca. 1340). Both men staunchly defended the necessity of scientific inquiry and protested against the ban of the Spanish rabbis.

The *Kulturkampf* in Provence might have grown more bitter and continued indefinitely had not the French king Philip the Fair put an end to it by suddenly issuing, in July 1306, a decree banishing all Jews from the country. The community of Montpellier, which now—as seventy years earlier—had been the major seat of the controversy, was dispersed. Abba Mari went into exile and soon disappeared from view. Menaḥem Meiri died the same year and was followed to the grave some time later by the aged Rabbi Solomon ben Adret. But the conflict between rationalism, which places logic and science at the peak of its scale of values, and traditionalism, which regards orthodox belief and practice as the supreme demands of Judaism, did not disappear from the Jewish world. It reemerged time and again in the centuries that followed, up to the modern age. Even today it is by no means stilled.

We must now cast a brief glance backward at the Jewish communities of Germany. Here conditions deteriorated progressively throughout the thirteenth century, as the animosity of the Church toward the Jews grew and kings and nobles ever more sharply restricted their trade rights and increased their burden of taxation. The woes of this melancholy century were climaxed in 1298 by the Rindfleisch massacres, in which thousands of Jews perished and scores of Jewish communities were destroyed. In the life and death of its foremost religious leader, Rabbi Meir ben Baruch of Rothenburg (ca. 1215–1293), the experience of thirteenth-century German Jewry is tragically reflected.

Rabbi Meir was one of the last and greatest of the Tosafists; his halachic interpretations shaped Jewish life in Germany not only in his age but for centuries afterward. As a legal decisor, he was clear and logical but tended generally to a strict construction of traditional principles. Typical are his rulings that the biblical prohibition against kindling a fire on the Sabbath means that an oven may not be heated in a Jewish home during the Sabbath even by a non-Jew, no matter how cold it may be, and that, to preclude any possible violation of the Talmudic prohibition against carrying any object on the Sabbath, garments worn on that day are to have no pockets. The zeal of medieval German Jewry for punctilious observance of the Torah and for adding new restraints that would isolate it even more from the larger world, a zeal both typified and in considerable measure produced by Meir of Rothenburg, was no doubt largely a reaction to the bitter coldness and hostility of that world. Having to be prepared always to sacrifice his fortune and even his life for the Torah, the German Jew of the Middle Ages became even more devoted to it and wished to enlarge its compass, to create for himself new ordinances and commandments. The vast structure of discipline and law that resulted no doubt contributed significantly to maintaining the spiritual equilibrium of the Jew in the ages of darkness and oppression. Later, in the eighteenth and nineteenth centuries, when the external world became less hostile and began to open its doors to Jews, the sheer magnitude and weight of this structure came to appear oppressive to many who lived under it.

As a young man in 1240, Rabbi Meir was in France when his teachers, the Tosafists Samuel ben Solomon of Falaise and Yeḥiel of Paris, engaged in a famous disputation over the *Talmud* with the apostate Nicolas Donin. Two years later, after witnessing the public burning of the *Talmud* in Paris by Christian authorities, Meir wrote his celebrated elegy "She'ali Serufah" ("Ask, O thou burned by fire"), which is still recited on the Ninth of Av by Ashkenazic Jews. Shortly thereafter he returned to Germany and settled in Rothenburg, where he remained for more than four decades. When still quite young he was renowned as the foremost Talmudic scholar of his age. Although he was probably not the chief rabbi of Germany in an official sense, he was universally regarded as such and served as the supreme court of appeals for all Ashkenazic Jewry. Over one thousand of his responsa, dealing with the most varied questions of Jewish ritual and civil law submitted by rabbis, judges, and communities in Germany, Austria, Bohemia, Italy, France, and Spain, have been preserved. The *yeshivah* over which he presided in Rothenburg attracted students from all over Europe, and many of these, who later became eminent scholars in their own right, followed their master's decisions and teachings and helped make them standard in Ashkenazic law and practice.

Rabbi Meir's life ended very sadly. After his election as Emperor of Germany, Rudolph I of Hapsburg began to insist that the status of the Jews as *servi camerae* (serfs of the treasury), which had evolved in the thirteenth century, meant that they were the personal property of the emperor and that he had the right to tax them over and above the assessments laid upon them by the local rulers. Upon the imposition of an imperial tax by Rudolph in 1286, thousands of Jews under the leadership of Meir decided to leave Germany. Since the departure of the spiritual leader of all of German Jewry would have encouraged an even larger emigration of Jews, and a consequent loss of considerable magnitude to the imperial treasury, Meir was arrested and imprisoned in the fortress of Enzisheim. His devoted followers offered the emperor a ransom of twenty-three thousand pounds of silver, but the aged scholar refused to allow them to submit to the emperor's stipulation that this be regarded as a payment of taxes, lest similar stratagems be utilized in the future to extort even larger sums. As a result, Rabbi Meir remained in prison for seven years until his death in 1293. Even after his death the imperial authorities refused to surrender his body to the Jews; it was not until 1307 that his remains were ransomed for a large sum of money and brought to burial in Worms.

Rabbi Meir's successor as the acknowledged leader of German Jewry was his chief disciple Asher ben Yeḥiel (ca. 1250–1327). Fearing that he would ultimately suffer the same fate as his teacher, Asher left Germany in 1303. After spending some time in Provence where, as we have noted, he gave his support to Abba Mari of Lunel in the latter's campaign against philosophy and science, he arrived in Spain and was soon elected chief rabbi of Toledo. An austere and authoritarian person, Asher was not beyond threatening with capital punishment an insubordinate rabbi in Valencia who declined to recognize his authority and insisted on his own view. It was as a result of his efforts that the Tosafist methods of Talmudic study and the more stringent interpretations of the *halachah* prevalent in Germany were introduced in Spain. His influence on the codification of Jewish law in the Middle Ages was vast, but it was his son Jacob who actually wrote what emerged as the standard halachic code of his own and later eras.

Jacob ben Asher (ca. 1270–ca. 1343) was born in Germany and accompanied his father and brothers when they moved to Spain. A deeply pious man, he would not accept rabbinic office and lived in extreme poverty, devoting all his life to study of the law. Sensing that the *Mishneh Torah* of Maimonides, who believed that the code he had written would suffice for all ages, was no longer adequate and required revision in view of the massive development of the law, particularly in France and Germany, Jacob ben Asher composed a new code, *Arbaah Turim* (*Four Rows*), which was intended to bridge the gap between the Spanish and Franco-German traditions. Maimonides in his *Mishneh Torah* had omitted, to the dissatisfaction of many critics, the sources on which he based his opinions and decisions. Jacob was punctilious in citing all his sources, which included both the *Palestinian* and *Babylonian Talmuds*, Geonic responsa, and later Spanish, French, and German commentators and codifiers—most notably his father, whose views he generally follows. Also unlike Maimonides, he excluded from his code those segments of the *halachah* that had become obsolete with the destruction of the Temple and the loss of Jewish national independence. An excellent systematizer, Jacob organized the enormous material of his code into a four-part arrangement which subsequently became classic. These parts are:

1) *Orah Hayyim* (*Way of Life*), dealing with the daily regimen of life from rising in the morning until retiring at night, and including the laws of prayer, Sabbath, and festivals; 2) *Yoreh Deah* (*Teacher of Knowledge*), containing the laws of ritual slaughter, dietary regulations, rules governing vows, mourning, and so on; 3) *Even Ha-Ezer* (*Stone of Help*), on family matters, laws of women, marriage, and divorce; and 4) *Hoshen Mishpat* (*Breastplate of Judgment*), on the whole range of civil law. Because of its comprehensiveness, superb arrangement, and clear and comprehensible language, *Arbaah Turim* eventually displaced its predecessors. Thus, this work, created on Spanish soil by a German-born scholar, came to be the major code of Jewish law and later served as the foundation of Joseph Karo's *Shulhan Aruch*.

In France and especially in Germany, the fourteenth century, in which *Arbaah Turim* was written, brought havoc to the Jews. The massacres attendant on the Black Death (1348–1350) destroyed many of the Jewish communities of the Rhineland and their ancient seats of learning. New *yeshivot* were established in Austria, in Vienna, Krems, and Neustadt, and from these came the most eminent rabbis of central Europe in the fourteenth and fifteenth centuries—scholars such as Jacob ben Moses Mölln, Moses Minz, Jacob Weil, and Israel ben Petahiah Isserlein. Among the battles which these men were compelled to wage was one against unqualified and sometimes disreputable occupants of rabbinic positions. In the destruction and turmoil which followed the Black Death, the number of competent Talmudic scholars was greatly reduced, and men of limited knowledge and inferior moral stature came frequently to hold rabbinic office. The leading figures of the age took measures to correct the abuses wrought by "ignorant and corrupt judges" and to raise the level of the rabbinate and of Talmudic scholarship. In time they succeeded, and the Jewries of Germany, Austria, and Bohemia, despite the fact that they remained subject to constant social and economic oppression, and that Jewish communities were banished periodically from one locality or another, continued throughout the fifteenth and sixteenth centuries to maintain their communal life at a high level and to produce distinguished Talmudists and halachists. But the declining economic situation and virtually incessant persecution had long before stimulated the beginning of a mass migration eastward on the part of the Jews of central Europe. The *Drang nach Osten* continued for many generations, leading to a large-scale population movement and a shift in the European Jewish center of gravity

from Germany to the Polish lands. It was in Poland that a great revival of rabbinic scholarship took place in the sixteenth and seventeenth centuries.

As for the Jews of France, they had been allowed to return to their
native country after the expulsion of 1306 for two brief and unhappy
periods (1315–1321 and 1361–1394), but in 1395 they were decisively
banished. Only in Provence, where royal authority had not yet been
consolidated, were they permitted to remain until the beginning of
the sixteenth century. Even thereafter small numbers of Jews were
to be found under papal rule in the Comtat Venaissin, in the "Four
Communities" of Avignon, Carpentras, Cavaillon, and L'Isle, where
they kept alive their special traditions and distinctive *Comtadin* liturgy. It was not, however, until some Marranos who eventually
reverted to Judaism settled in Bordeaux and Bayonne in the seventeenth century, and the Ashkenazic Jews of Alsace and Lorraine
came under French rule in the seventeenth and eighteenth centuries,
that France again had a numerically significant Jewish populace.
Strangely enough, it was this country which treated its Jews with
such barbarity in the Middle Ages that was the first (except for the
United States, where the number of Jews in the eighteenth century
was numerically insignificant) in the modern world, as we shall see
later, to grant them full civic and political equality.

CHAPTER

&IV&

Italian Jewry and
the Renaissance Era

JEWS FIRST CAME to the Italian peninsula, where they have lived uninterruptedly until the present time, as early as the second century B.C.E., if not before. In that century several of the Maccabean rulers of Palestine sent embassies to Rome, and other Jews soon followed as permanent settlers. The prisoners brought to Rome by Pompey after his invasion of Palestine in 63–61 B.C.E., most of whom appear to have been released after a brief period, swelled its Jewish population. The number of Jews in Rome must already then have been considerable, for in 59 B.C.E. the orator Cicero, defending a former proconsul in Asia Minor who had confiscated funds gathered by Jews for the Temple, pretended that the court was being intimidated by the large gathering of Jews at the trial. Some years later Julius Caesar, who was favorably disposed toward the Jews scattered throughout the Roman Empire and regarded them as a useful element in the new political order which he projected, made Judaism a *religio licita* and granted its adherents certain privileges and exemptions that made it possible for them to fulfill their cultic obligations. In the first century of the empire there were probably fifty thousand Jews in Italy, more than half of them concentrated in and around Rome. Substantial numbers were brought to Italy as prisoners after the suppression of the Judean revolt in 70 C.E., and these also were soon given their freedom. Although there were sporadic persecutions, several of the Roman emperors of the second and third centuries treated their Jewish subjects fairly and generously; the emperor Caracalla included the Jews when he granted citizenship to all freemen of the empire in 212.

Life appears to have been generally peaceful and calm for the Jews who lived in Rome and elsewhere throughout Italy in the first three centuries of the Christian era. Although largely employed in menial occupations and not distinguished for their high culture, they built synagogues and schools and faithfully followed the traditions of their ancestors. There was even a Talmudic academy in Rome in the second century under the leadership of the Tanna Mattiah ben Ḥeresh, and Jewish proselytizing activity succeeded in winning converts among certain strata of the population. However, after Christianity became the official religion of the Roman Empire by edict of the emperor Constantine at the beginning of the fourth century, conversion to Judaism was proscribed and Jews were forbidden to own Christian slaves. Some years later pagan slaves were also included in the prohibition (the effect was to drive Jews out of certain economic realms), and marriages between Jews and Christian women were forbidden on pain of death. Instead of "a distinguished religion, certainly permissible," as it had been regarded in the days of Julius Caesar and his successors, Judaism was now declared "a sacrilegious gathering" or "a pernicious sect." These acts were only the beginning of a sustained campaign by priests and bishops to degrade the Jews and restrict their social and economic rights. The campaign culminated in the assignment by the legal codes of Theodosius and Justinian of an inferior status to the Jews, and their exclusion from public office as well as from many professions. The goal of the bishops was not to destroy Judaism completely, for they recognized it as the background out of which Christianity had emerged, but to denigrate it. As for Jews, they were to be preserved as historical witnesses of certain truths proclaimed in the New Testament, but in a wretched condition befitting those who had rejected and killed the Christ.

We know little about the history of the Jews of Italy in the turbulent period of the Gothic and Byzantine invasions, but it is on record that Pope Gregory I (590–604) protected them from local bishops in Naples, Palermo, Ravenna, and other cities, and protested against their forcible conversion. It is also known that the occupation of

Sicily by the Saracens (827–1061) resulted in an amelioration of the condition of the Jews who lived on that island. Beginning in the ninth century we have more information about Jewish life in Italy, particularly in some of the cities of the south, thanks to the *Sefer Yuḥasin* (*Book of Genealogies*), a remarkable chronicle compiled in 1054 by Aḥimaaz bar Paltiel of Oria and relating events of the two preceding centuries.

It appears that in the middle of the ninth century a scholar from Baghdad named Abu Aharon came to Italy and stimulated the development of Judaic culture and scholarship, especially in the old cities of Oria and Bari in the south. At the beginning of the tenth century Oria produced the first Jewish scientist and scholar in Christian Europe whose name has come down to us, Shabbetai ben Abraham Donnolo (913–ca. 982). Donnolo, who knew not only Hebrew but Greek, Latin, and colloquial Italian, achieved such competence in the healing art that he was appointed court physician to the viceroy of the Byzantine emperor in Italy. This first known member of a long line of distinguished Italian-Jewish physicians was also mystically minded and wrote a commentary to the *Sefer Yetzirah* (*Book of Creation*) in which the scientist-mystic attempts to provide experimental proof for some of the cosmological notions of the ancient work. Donnolo, like Saadiah Gaon (with whose writings he may have been familiar), attempted to deanthropomorphize the biblical conception of God. He wished to show that the idea that man is made in the image of God really means that the human physical form mirrors the created world. Employing his anatomical knowledge, Donnolo sought to demonstrate that the structure of man, the microcosm, corresponds to that of the world, the macrocosm; thus man's head is like the heavens, his skull like the celestial firmament, his hair like the grass and forests that cover the earth, and his eyes like the sun and moon. Hence, he echoes the *Mishnah* by concluding: "Whoever destroys a single person, it is as if he destroyed a whole world."

A century before Shabbetai Donnolo, the liturgical poet Shephatiah (d. 886), whose father Amittai was also a *paytan*, lived in Oria. The family traced its descent back to forebears who had been brought to Italy by Titus after the destruction of the Temple. According to Aḥimaaz's *Sefer Yuḥasin*, when Abu Aharon came to Italy he transmitted the mysteries of the practical Kabbalah to Shephatiah, enabling him to perform miraculous deeds. It is related that when the Saracens attacked Oria in about 856, Shephatiah was dispatched in an attempt to buy the invaders off. Later he traveled to Constantinople on a mission seeking the annulment of the anti-Jewish decrees that had been promulgated by the Byzantine emperor Basil I, the "vile murderer steeped in blood," as he is called by Aḥimaaz. The latter reports that the poet was able, through mystical incantations, "to save one of the princesses from the power of a demon," i.e., cure her of mental illness. As a reward, he obtained exemption from the emperor's conversion decrees for the Jews of Oria and of four other communities; these were given the privilege of continuing to observe the commandments of Judaism without interference. Of the many hymns that Shephatiah wrote, only "Yisrael Nosha Ba-Adonai" ("Israel is saved by the Lord"), which is still recited in the Ashkenazic synagogue at the Neilah service of Yom Kippur, has survived. The fate of the literary legacy of his son Amittai, who followed the family tradition of poetry writing, was happier; a good many of his religious poems, some incorporated into the Italian and Ashkenazic liturgies, have come down to us. Amittai ben Shephatiah refers in his poems to the conversions forced upon Jews by Basil I, and to other contemporary persecutions. He also alludes to religious disputations between Jews and Christians, a practice which thus appears to have been of ancient origin and which became ever more frequent and more troublesome to Jews in Christian Europe as the Middle Ages wore on.

An anonymous work which, in the judgment of several competent scholars, derives from ninth- or tenth-century Italy (though others date it earlier and conjecture that it was written in Palestine or Babylonia), reflects a remarkable tolerance toward non-Jews. This is the lovely *midrash* entitled *Tanna De-Ve Eliahu* (*Student of the School of Elijah*) or *Seder Eliahu* (*Order of Elijah*), distinguished by its didactic aim of promoting the moral and religious values of the Bible, particularly those exemplified in the lives and deeds of the patriarchs, and by the beauty and originality of its language. The unknown author deplores the fact that the Jews of his day imitate the customs of their non-Jewish neighbors, eat with them, and even occasionally intermarry with them; he is concerned that Jews preserve their unique identity, and realizes that a necessary condition for this is a certain isolation from the non-Jewish world. But he also declares: "I call heaven and earth to witness that, whether Jew or gentile, man or woman, manservant or maidservant—on each the holy spirit rests according to his deeds." [1] He further admonishes that those who adhere to a different faith must be treated as brothers. While the author of *Tanna De-Ve Eliahu* stresses the importance of study of Torah, he ascribes even greater relative value to love of Israel. Indeed, a humanitarian and social concern permeates the entire *midrash*, which frequently asserts that a man may not confine himself to promoting his own interests but must share the troubles of the community and seek its welfare. The author expresses his strong disapproval of asceticism and self-mortification, and there is little mysticism or messianism in his work.

Very different in this respect is another literary creation which probably comes from the same age and which some scholars have attributed to an Italian source, although others believe that it was written by a Palestinian considerably earlier, at the beginning of the seventh century, when the Byzantine Empire achieved its last triumphs over Persia. Known as the Book of Zerubbabel, this work purports to describe the revelations concerning the End of Days given by the angel Michael, or Metatron, to Zerubbabel, the last ruler of the Davidic dynasty. Repeatedly copied in manuscript and published in many different collections of *midrashim*, this immensely popular work provided Jewry from the tenth to the seventeenth centuries with its standard envisagement of the eschatological events that would precede and accompany the advent of the Messiah. The first great medieval Jewish philosopher, Saadiah Gaon, based a chapter of his *Sefer Ha-Emunot Veha-Deot* (*Book of Beliefs and Doctrines*) on it, and Nathan of Gaza, the prophet and right-hand man of the messianic pretender of Smyrna, adduced proofs from it that Shabbetai Tzevi was the Messiah.

Composed in the style of the visions of Ezekiel and Daniel in the Bible, the Book of Zerubbabel tells of Messiah son of Joseph, forerunner of Messiah son of David, who will be slain by the monster Armilus. This monster (his name may be a corruption of Romulus, the legendary founder of Rome) is portrayed as the son of Satan and a stone statue of a woman, and represents both the Roman Empire and the Christian Church, or Caesar and the Pope. For a time he will conquer the whole world and no one will be able to withstand his power. But then Hephzibah, the mother of Messiah son of David, will rise to do battle against him, aided by the stars and planets. Finally Messiah son of David will come forth in glory; at his command the prophet Elijah will appear and Messiah son of Joseph will rise from the dead, and the three of them will march triumphantly through the gates of Jerusalem. All the martyrs who died for the sanctification of God's name will be resurrected, and the children of Israel will gather in the Holy Land from all the ends of the earth. Messiah son of David will kill Armilus with the blast of his breath, the Temple will be rebuilt on Mount Zion, and Israel will inhabit its land in peace forever. This vivid tale of wars, disasters, and ultimate redemption, reflecting the bitter feelings of the Jewish people toward the Roman Empire and the Christian Church and their yearning for an end to the Exile, was accepted as a true forecast of the End of Days by almost all Jews in the Middle Ages, except for the followers of Maimonides and other rationalists.

The Book of Zerubbabel mirrors the hopes and dreams of the medieval Jew for the future. Another anonymous work called *Josippon*, probably written in the tenth century in southern Italy, which was widely read by the Jewish masses in the original Hebrew as well as in translations into Arabic, Ethiopic, Latin, English, Yiddish, Czech, Polish, and Russian, dwells on the past, particularly the period of the Second Temple. Based on a Latin version of Flavius Josephus' *Jewish Antiquities* and *The Jewish War*, as well as a Latin translation of the apocryphal Books of Maccabees, *Josippon* came to be erroneously attributed to the Jewish historian of the first century. Its author was an excellent stylist with superb narrative gifts and, for a man of the tenth century, possessed of remarkably keen historical insight. His glorification of Jewish heroes and vivid portrayal of dramatic incidents in Jewish history instilled pride in many generations of readers. *Josippon* is far superior to most of the chronicles and histories written by Jews in the Middle Ages, and rightfully earned the honored place it held in the affections of Jews for centuries.

By the beginning of the second millennium according to the Christian reckoning, Talmudic study had been firmly established in Italy; *yeshivot* were to be found not only in the southern cities of Bari, Otranto, Oria, and Venosa, but in Rome and Lucca as well. According to a legend first reported by Abraham ibn Daud in his *Sefer Ha-Kabbalah* (*Book of Tradition*), four rabbinic scholars, taken captive at sea after setting out on a voyage from Bari, were released and later founded Talmudic academies in various Mediterranean cities. Whatever kernel of truth there may be in the legend, it would seem to indicate that the then popular saying "For the Torah shall go forth from Bari and the word of the Lord from Otranto" was more than idle boasting. But the Torah of Italy was not, for a long time, characterized by any significant degree of creativity or originality. Only at the beginning of the twelfth century was a major work of Talmudic scholarship produced in Italy. This was the *Aruch*, a lexicon of the *Talmud* and *midrashim* completed in 1101 by Nathan bar Yeḥiel (1035–ca. 1110) of the famous Anaw family in Rome. Nathan, who with his brothers, headed the *yeshivah* in Rome and contributed a splendid synagogue and ritual bathhouse to the community, not only provides definitions and etymologies of many difficult words in the rabbinic literature, but also describes numerous customs, notes decisions and interpretations by the Geonim of Babylonia and other earlier scholars, and quotes from *midrashim* that were later lost. The historic importance of the *Aruch* consists not only in the fact that it provided the basis for all later lexicographical studies of the *Talmud* in Europe, but that its author preserved significant elements of the heritage of the Babylonian academies which might otherwise have completely disappeared.

A generation after Nathan bar Yeḥiel Italian Jewry was stimulated to further cultural creativity by the great itinerant Spanish-Jewish scholar Abraham ibn Ezra, who spent some time in Lucca, Mantua, Rome, and other cities. Ibn Ezra familiarized the Jews of Italy with the important discoveries in Hebrew grammar that had been made by the Jewish philologists of Moslem Spain, and attempted to arouse their interest in poetry and belles-lettres. He polemicized particularly against the archaic style and corrupted Hebrew of the old *paytan* Eleazar Kallir, then generally regarded as the master and classical exemplar in the realm of liturgical poetry. Ibn Ezra's fruitful activity among the Jews of Italy was continued by his pupil Samuel ben Abraham Parḥon, who was also a student of Judah ha-Levi and lived for a time in Salerno, where he completed his well-known lexicon, *Maḥberet He-Aruch*, in 1160. This work, which was widely studied, contributed much to popularizing Arabic-Jewish scholarship in Italy and other Christian lands.

In the period of the Crusades the seaports of Italy gained new importance and created a wave of prosperity. Through them hordes of Crusaders passed to and from their way to the Holy Land. They also became the entrepôts of the flourishing trade that developed with the Moslem East. The Jews, who performed a highly significant function as the bankers and moneylenders of the era, shared in the growing prosperity. The attitude of the Church toward them was highly ambiguous. On the one hand, there was the bull *Sicut Judaeis* issued in the early part of the twelfth century by Pope Callixtus II, which promised them freedom to practice their religion and protection from conversionist pressures, as well as security of person and property, and which was reconfirmed by subsequent popes. On the other hand were the repressive edicts of the Third and Fourth Lateran Councils (1179 and 1215), prohibiting Jews from employing Christian servants and instituting the hated Jew-badge. Later in the thirteenth century the Inquisition, led by zealous Dominican friars, began to concern itself with the Jews. At the same time as the Dominicans and Franciscans carried on their implacable war against heresy and free thought, however, new universities and scientific institutes were established in southern Italy, where the influence of Saracen civilization was strong. Jews played a notable role in these, contributing especially to the fame of the medical schools of Salerno and Naples.

The enlightened and liberal emperor Frederick II (1194–1250) was a special patron of the Jews, aiding them both materially and culturally. His court in Naples became a scientific and cultural center at which Christian, Moslem, and Jewish scholars were handsomely supported and encouraged to collaborate in learned enterprises. Frederick himself commissioned a number of Jews to translate Arabic philosophical and scientific works into Hebrew and Latin. Perhaps the most gifted of the Jewish scholars patronized by the emperor was Jacob ben Abba Mari Anatoli. This ardent rationalist and promoter of Aristotelian philosophy translated several works by Averroes into Hebrew (some of these were later translated from Hebrew into Latin). He was also chiefly responsible for the original dissemination of Maimonidean ideas among the Jews of Italy, both through his preaching in the synagogues and his book of collected sermons *Malmad Ha-Talmidim* (*Goad to Scholars*). Anatoli was a determined opponent of superstition and external piety; he insisted that genuine fulfillment of the *mitzvot* and true prayer must be based on a grasp of the rational and moral values implicit in them. As a champion of the allegorical interpretation of Scripture he also sought to disclose what he considered the abstract metaphysical truths concealed in it. His enthusiastic advocacy of Maimonides aroused intense opposition in orthodox circles both in Italy and France, where he spent his earlier years, but he remained unshaken in his convictions. Anatoli spoke eloquently of human brotherhood and the equality of all men; at the same time he betrayed contempt for the unlettered masses because of their incapacity to comprehend philosophical verities.

No less thoroughgoing a rationalist than Jacob Anatoli was Zerahiah ben Isaac ben Shealtiel Gracian (Ḥen), scion of a well-known family of Barcelona, who lived in Rome in the last part of the thirteenth century and gave lectures on philosophy, especially that of Maimonides, and biblical exegesis to a group of admiring disciples. Like Anatoli, he insisted that there are deeper philosophical truths behind the literal words of the Bible, and wrote commentaries on Job and Proverbs to expound these truths. Reason, for Gracian, was the ultimate authority in matters of religion; faith and tradition must prove that they are not inconsistent with reason if they are to be accepted. Consequently, he explained away the miracles of Scripture and derided Kabbalah and everything that smacked of mysticism. Gracian's allegorical interpretations of the Bible are frequently extreme, but he found, according to his own report, an enthusiastic audience in the "company of the delightful youths in the community of Rome."

It must not be thought, however, that Maimonidean rationalism completely dominated the religious outlook of the Jews of thirteenth-century Rome, or that all of them found its *jeunesse dorée*, who dabbled in philosophy and sought to enjoy all the pleasures of life that wealth could buy, quite as "delightful" as Zeraḥiah Gracian. Traditional Talmudic learning was cultivated by a number of Roman scholars, most notably Zedekiah ben Abraham of the distinguished Anaw family. Zedekiah wrote an important work called *Shibbolei Ha-Leket* (*The Ears of the Gleaning*), which represents the first major attempt made in Italy to codify rabbinic law. Also a halachist of distinction was Zedekiah's brother, Benjamin ben Abraham Anaw (ca. 1215–ca. 1295). Benjamin, however, achieved fame mainly as a liturgical poet and satirist of contemporary manners and mores. His poems include laments occasioned by the attacks on Judaism of the apostate Nicholas Donin, the burning of the *Talmud* in France, and the desecration of the Jewish cemetery in Rome; many of them were incorporated into the Italian Rite *Maḥzor*. As for his satire *Massa Ge Ḥizzayon* (*The Burden of the Valley of Vision*), it is one of the finest works of its genre in Hebrew literature. Benjamin mocks the arrogance of the wealthy Jewish parvenus of Rome—their shallowness, their love of luxury, and their conspicuous consumption. An intellectual aristocrat himself, he cannot forgive their contempt for learning and scholarship.

Within the satirist, of course, is a moralist whose sense of right and decency has been outraged. Benjamin's moralism is explicit. He summons his contemporaries to renounce their idols of gold and silver, to abandon their boasting and arrogance, and to return to the ancient paths of the Torah—humility, justice, and truth. After composing his satire Benjamin wrote a long poem entitled *Shaarei Etz Hayyim* (*The Gates Leading to the Tree of Life*), in which he denounced various vices and extolled such old-fashioned virtues as love, hospitality, faithfulness, gratitude, and charity. This Roman Talmudist and poet appears to have had no use for philosophy or rationalist exegesis of the Bible; he championed the old aggadic interpretations and even discussed with his brother Zedekiah the language spoken by the angels.

Benjamin's didactic preaching was continued by his relative Yehiel ben Yekutiel ben Benjamin Ha-Rofe Anaw, who wrote one of the most popular Hebrew books of *musar*, or moral instruction, in the Middle Ages, *Maalot Ha-Middot* (*Excellencies of Virtue*). Almost forty manuscript copies of this widely read moral treatise based on the *Talmud, midrashim*, and other sources have survived, and it was published in numerous editions after the invention of printing. In sincere and tender fashion the author seeks to inculcate the ancient virtues. "My children," he writes, "come hither. I would teach you to follow God's way. Not out of pride do I do this, nor because I wish to become renowned or parade my wisdom. I desire only to familiarize you with what our fathers taught us with their wise words, their heartfelt instruction." [2] It is interesting to note that this renowned moralist, who was also a highly regarded poet, devoted a great deal of time, as did many other notable scholars of his age, to the arduous task of copying religious manuscripts. [3] Indeed, the only complete extant manuscript of the Jerusalem *Talmud*, which is now located in the Leiden Library, was copied by Yehiel in 1289, and from it the Venice edition of 1523–1524 was printed.

If, as we have observed from the work of several members of the Anaw family (others of the clan distinguished themselves in various fields in Italy up to the twentieth century), the rationalist outlook and modernist teachings of Jacob Anatoli and Zerahiah Gracian did not completely captivate the minds of the thirteenth-century Roman-Jewish community, they found prominent expression in the work of the greatest Jewish poet of Italy, Immanuel of Rome (ca. 1261–after 1328), known in Italian as Manoello Giudeo, "Immanuel the Jew." This contemporary of the author of the *Divina Commedia* [4] conducted the official correspondence of the Jewish community of Rome and composed orations for festive occasions. His collection of poems and rhymed prose compositions, entitled *Maḥbarot*, comes close in literary splendor to the work of the great Spanish-Jewish masters Solomon ibn Gabirol, Judah ha-Levi, and Judah Alḥarizi, who were his models. Immanuel's poetry is distinguished by a consummate mastery of language, a punning wit, and a frank, unabashed eroticism that is virtually unparalleled in all of Hebrew literature. Some of the descriptions of feminine charms and amorous affairs in the *Maḥbarot* are analogous to those subsequently included by Giovanni Boccaccio in his *Decameron*. In later, more puritanical generations, Immanuel's frivolity and celebration of physical love came to be regarded as indecent and immoral. Moses Rieti, the Italian rabbi and poet of the fifteenth century, denounced his poems, and Joseph Karo, the great codifier of the sixteenth century, ruled in his *Shulḥan Aruch* (*Prepared Table*) that it is forbidden to read them either on Sabbath or weekday because of the prohibition against "sitting in the seat of scorners." [5]

Immanuel of Rome, however, was not merely a singer of the joys of love and passion. Fond as he was of the company of beautiful women, especially in his youth, he did not neglect the life of the mind, and in fact acquired a wide range of knowledge. Zeraḥiah Gracian was one of his teachers, and he had a profound reverence for Maimonides, describing him as "the light that illuminates everything deep and hidden." One of the poems in the *Maḥbarot* is on the philosopher's Thirteen Articles of Faith, and it is not the only one of a religious or philosophical character in the collection. Despite the fact that he deprecated his own religiosity, asserting in one of his Italian sonnets "I am not a good Jew, but also no Moslem, and I do not follow the doctrine of the Christians," there is no reason to doubt the authenticity of his loyalty to Judaism. As a Maimonidean, Immanuel insisted that the way to God is through knowledge and thought, and he repeatedly extolled the values of scientific inquiry. "The higher man ascends the ladder of knowledge," he wrote, "the closer he comes to God."

The last composition in Immanuel's anthology, which is called *Ha-Tofet Veha-Eden* (*Hell and Heaven*) and which he wrote late in life, is one of the most interesting. The poet who once confessed that he was capable of building idolatrous altars to feminine beauty, now transformed into a preacher and reprover, relates his visionary journey through the netherworld and paradise, following the schema of Dante's great poem. Immanuel locates in hell those who were concerned only with bodily pleasures when they were alive and therefore neglected the quest for wisdom, as well as those obscurantists who regarded the study of science as foolishness. In hell also are the hypocrites who assumed a mantle of piety while secretly doing the most corrupt deeds, as well as communal leaders who achieved their high estate through deception and exploitation and hated the poor "as Moslems hate swine and Nazirites despise beautiful women."

Immanuel assigns to heaven not only the patriarchs and prophets, the sages and God-fearing Israelites of all generations, but also the righteous gentiles who attained the supreme levels of wisdom and consequently became tolerant of faiths other than their own. These are the persons who, considering the question of God, concluded:

Every people calls Him by a different name, but we say, whatever name He may have, we believe in the primordial creative power which exists throughout all eternity and which brought the world into being and guides it in wisdom. Hidden and incomprehensible by reason of His greatness, He reveals Himself in His wisdom and grace which he pours out on all creatures and then summons them back to Himself and illuminates them with His glory.[6]

The liberal attitude of the Jewish poet stands in sharp contrast to that of his great Catholic contemporary, who resolutely barred from Paradise anyone who had not been saved by baptism and membership in the Church.

Despite his fervent admiration for Maimonides, Immanuel of Rome—in this, as in other respects, a mass of contradictions—was also a devotee of mysticism and studied Kabbalist works with great avidity. In his enthusiasm for Kabbalah, however, he was by no means singular. His contemporary in Rome, Kalonymos ben Kalonymos, a trenchant satirist and distinguished translator, testifies to the widespread popularity among Italian Jews of his day of such mystical texts as the *Sefer Yetzirah* and *Shiur Komah*. Apparently the interest in mysticism aroused in Italian Jewry by the Babylonian Abu Aharon in the ninth century was maintained continuously throughout the centuries. It was intensified after the appearance of the *Zohar* toward the end of the thirteenth century, and indeed this classical text of medieval Kabbalah found its first major expositor in an Italian Jew, Menaḥem Recanati, who was a contemporary of Immanuel. His *Perush Al Ha-Torah Al Derech Ha-Emet* (*Commentary on the Torah by Way of Truth*) and *Taamei Ha-Mitzvot* (*Reasons for the Commandments*) are permeated with the thinking of the *Zohar* and earlier Kabbalist writings, such as the works of Judah the Pious, Eleazar of Worms, and Naḥmanides. Recanati, claiming to have visions and revelations from heaven, stresses the interdependence of the upper and lower worlds and expounds the Zoharic doctrine that man is a reflection of the ten *sefirot*. He also emphasizes the great mysteries inherent in the commandments, all of which are connected with the heavenly "Chariot-Throne," and in the words of the traditional prayers. Italian Jewry's fondness for Kabbalah, expounded by Recanati and other scholars, grew as the Renaissance progressed, and in time, as we shall see, its major documents and ideas evoked intense interest on the part of many of the leading Christian humanists of Italy.

The renewed interest in, and fervent admiration for, the world of classical antiquity, the revival of humanistic learning and the substitution of Platonic modes of thought for the Aristotelianism that had dominated the mentality of Christian Europe, the remarkable efflorescence of literature, painting, sculpture, architecture, and music—all these central elements of the Renaissance era seem to have had relatively slight effects on the creativity of the Jews of Italy. To be sure, they welcomed the liberal and tolerant spirit that the Renaissance fostered and that was exemplified even by some of the popes and prelates of the Church, especially those belonging to the House of Medici. Many Jews also took advantage of their freedom to study medicine and the sciences at the Italian universities, and contacts between Jewish and Christian scholars were probably friendlier and more extensive in Renaissance Italy than at any previous time or place in history. But Jews were not themselves greatly stimulated to new creativity in the arts or literature. The art historian Giorgio Vasari, in his *Vite de' più eccellenti architetti, pittori, e scultori italiani* (1550), tells of the great admiration aroused by Michelangelo's colossal sculpture of Moses among the Jews of Rome, and how hosts of them pilgrimaged every Sabbath to marvel at the masterpiece. Throughout the entire Renaissance era, however, Italian Jewry did not produce a single painter or sculptor of eminence. In music there were a considerable number of celebrated instrumentalists but comparatively few illustrious composers. As for belletristic literature, Jewish achievements were not impressive. Immanuel of Rome, the most gifted of Hebrew poets in Italy, flourished when the Renaissance had barely begun, and none of his successors produced anything that can sustain comparison with his work.

The major Italian Jewish poetic work of the fifteenth century, Moses Rieti's *Mikdash Meat* (*Small Sanctuary*), must be judged pallid and tedious when set beside Immanuel's vivid and sparkling *Maḥbarot*. Rieti (1388–after 1460), known in Italian as Maestro Gaio, may be regarded, by reason of his versatility and mastery of several fields of learning, as approximating the Renaissance ideal of the *uomo universale*. He was not only a poet but a Talmudist, physician, student of philosophy and natural science, and connoisseur of Italian literature. For some years he served simultaneously as chief rabbi of Rome and body-physician to Pope Pius II. The immense acclaim given throughout Italy to Dante's *Divina Commedia* moved Rieti to attempt a similarly monumental work on Judaism in Hebrew. But the cantos of his *Mikdash Meat* can hardly be compared to their great Italian model. The poem is certainly comprehensive in subject matter. In the first part of his unfinished work Rieti deals with—among other items—Maimonides' Thirteen Articles of Faith, the Written and the Oral Torah, Kabbalah, physics, alchemy, mathematics, Aristotle's *Categories*, and Porphyry's *Isagoge ad Logicam;* in the second part he conducts the reader on a visionary journey through the celestial realms of the blessed spirits and discusses many of the sages of the *Talmud* (or the "ships of the soul," as he calls the *Mishnah* and the *Gemara*), the Geonim, and later Jewish scholars. But the poem, despite its elegant diction and Dantean terza-rima (which the author introduced into Hebrew poetry), has little aesthetic value and finally wears the reader out with its pedantic scholia. Nevertheless, in Jewish circles during the Renaissance era, Rieti's *Mikdash Meat* was lauded as a masterpiece and he himself was frequently referred to as "the Hebrew Dante."

An important exception must be noted to the absence of significant poets and original thinkers among the Jews of Renaissance Italy. One Jew did write a highly original work that reflects some of the most fundamental spiritual and intellectual currents of the Renaissance, and that enriched not only Judaism but the thought of the western world. This was Judah Abravanel (ca. 1460–after 1523), who was called in the Christian world Leone Ebreo or Leo Hebraeus. The eldest son of the aristocratic statesman Don Isaac Abravanel, revered leader of the Spanish Jews at the time of the expulsion, Judah was born in Lisbon, where he studied medicine. His father also gave him a thorough education in the classical sources of

Judaism and in Judeo-Arabic philosophy. After the expulsion from Spain, Abravanel went with his father to Naples, leaving behind a one-year-old son who had been secretly sent with his nurse to Portugal out of fear that he would be held as a hostage by the Spanish crown. The seizure of the infant by the king of Portugal in 1495, and his baptism, along with thousands of other Jewish children, grieved Abravanel intensely. Years later his sorrow over his child was still keen; it is expressed feelingly in his elegiac poem *Telunah Al Ha-Zeman* (*Complaint against the Time*), written in 1503. In Naples Abravanel became a renowned doctor and for a time taught medicine at its university and served as physician to the Spanish viceroy. He also immersed himself in the ideas and literature emanating from the famous Platonic academy in Florence and its foremost teachers, Count Pico della Mirandola and Marsilio Ficino. The illustrious Marrano physician Amatus Lusitanus, who flourished a generation after Abravanel's time, speaks of a philosophical treatise on the harmony of the spheres which his predecessor wrote for Pico, but this work was lost. According to the title pages of the second (1541) and third (1545) editions of the great work on which his fame rests, *Dialoghi di Amore*, first published in Rome in 1535, Judah Abravanel converted to Christianity in the last years of his life. The truth of this statement, however, is extremely dubious; in several passages of the *Dialoghi* Abravanel refers to himself as a Jew and speaks devotedly of Judaism. But the work is so broadly humanistic in conception, so nondogmatic and tolerant in spirit, and so replete with illustrations taken from the literature of classical antiquity as well as the Bible, that it would be difficult, apart from a few chance expressions, to determine the specific religious commitments of its author.

In the decade that this Spanish-Portuguese Jew spent in Italy before beginning to write his magnificent *Dialogues on Love*, he so thoroughly absorbed the mood and spirit of the Italian Renaissance and of the humanist movement that he became one of its chief exemplars and profoundest thinkers. The *Dialoghi* was one of the most widely read and influential philosophical works of the age. Between 1535 and 1607 more than a score of editions and printings appeared, and the book inspired innumerable essays, poems, and dialogues. Its influence is detectable in a great deal of the lyric poetry of sixteenth-century Italy, Spain, and France, including Michelangelo's sonnets and Torquato Tasso's *Minturno*, and in the philosophical outlook of Giordano Bruno and Baruch Spinoza.

The leitmotif of the three dialogues in Abravanel's work, which are carried on by two Platonic lovers named Philone and Sophia, is that love is both the origin and goal of the universe, and that its power permeates all things, from the celestial spheres to the stones and minerals of the terrestrial world. The divine love flows down incessantly from the Creator through all the gradations of being in nature, and conversely love flows up from the material to the spiritual world and from there to God Himself. The closest analogue to this current of love that pervades the cosmos is, according to Abravanel, the erotic love of man for woman. But whereas erotic love is ordinarily fulfilled in the possession of the beloved by the lover, and only in its higher stages achieves the bliss of true union, the cosmic love that energizes the universe has as its end not possession but the joy of the lover in union with the idea of the beautiful and the good that is incarnate in the beloved. The final goal of this love is the union of all of the created entities in the universe with the supreme Beauty that is in God—that Beauty which is simultaneously supreme Goodness and supreme Wisdom. Thereby the creature attains the *amore intelletuale di Dio* (intellectual love of God) which is also willed and enjoyed by God. In Abravanel's metaphysics the cosmos is a circle whose two halves yearn ceaselessly for reunion. The lower half strives toward God, and God strives to raise His creatures to Himself and to imbue them with His beauty and perfection. Through the mutual love of the Creator and the creature the mighty "circle of love," which sustains all things, is completed. At the center of this circle is man, whose soul is a "part of the infinite divine light." The human soul, with its capacity for knowledge and love of God, is the link which connects the divine Beauty with the physical world. The soul's love for God, Abravanel maintains, brings it to a superhuman wisdom and an ecstatic union with the divine. "This great love and desire of ours ravishes us into such contemplation as exalts our intellect till, illuminated by the special favor of God, it transcends the limits of human capacity and speculation and attains to such union and copulation with God most High as proves our intellect to be rather a part of the essence of God than an instrument of merely human form." [7]

The influence of Kabbalist modes of thought on Abravanel's philosophy is obvious. Like the Kabbalists, he perceives in the act of sexual union something divine and holy, a reflection of a heavenly, supernatural mystery. But while the Kabbalists had little conception of an ideal, romantic love which strives for far more than possession of its object, Abravanel expounded such a love in richly detailed imagery and proposed it as the key to the central mystery of reality.

Italian Jewry and the Renaissance Era

We noted earlier that the Jews of Italy were in general little affected by one of the fundamental currents of the Renaissance—its adulation of the ancient Greco-Roman civilization. No doubt one of the chief reasons for this was their rejection of the elaborate mythology of classical literature; the stories and legends about the pagan gods—their births, love affairs, intrigues, battles, deaths, and resurrections—offended their sober monotheistic convictions. This, however, was not the case with Abravanel, who shows no antipathy toward the myths of Greece and Rome. Indeed, in them he sees striking symbols of the thought, so dear to him, that all of nature participates in and reflects divinity, and that love is the most fundamental and pervasive power in the universe. Abravanel repeatedly endeavors to show the congruence between scriptural and rabbinic traditions and the inner meaning of the pagan myths. Thus the accounts of Jupiter's loves symbolize for him essentially the same meaning as the story of creation in the Book of Genesis. Nor did the author of the *Dialoghi* show any hesitancy in perceiving in figures of the Christian tradition illustrations of his favorite theses; St. John the Evangelist is included with Enoch, Moses, and Elijah among the four persons who attained both bodily and spiritual immortality.

Judah Abravanel's thoroughgoing humanism and universalism and his implicit deprecation of the theological distinctions separating Judaism, Christianity, and paganism were revolutionary and unprecedented phenomena in the Jewish world of his day. So also was his suggestion that all the rituals of the various historic religions are only symbols through which men adore the divine, and their diverse modes of worship are essentially similar instrumentalities for expressing their common love of God. A philosophy such as Abravanel's was certainly bound to raise the question why a Jew—or, for that matter, anyone else—should persist in fidelity to his own inherited religious tradition if other traditions were equally valid expressions of divine truth and love. There is no reason to suppose that Abravanel consciously posed this question to himself, or to assume that he abandoned the faith of his fathers. Nor does it appear that the rabbinic readers of the *Dialoghi* perceived any threat in it; no ideological attack was launched against Abravanel, and his work was eventually translated into Hebrew. Nevertheless, the question of reconciling universalist and particularist religious loyalties soon emerged into the forefront of Jewish life and became a deeply existential issue for many Jews in the era of enlightenment and civic emancipation. It is an issue that has still not been altogether satisfactorily resolved.

ᴇᴥᡠᏰᡣᴥ

We noted earlier that the popularity of Kabbalah increased among the Jews of Italy during the Renaissance. The literature of Jewish mysticism soon attracted the attention of a number of Christian scholars and humanists in Italy, some of whom perceived in it ideas confirming the truth of fundamental Christian dogmas and proceeded to develop a "Christian Kabbalah." Chief among these was the celebrated Count Giovanni Pico della Mirandola (1463–1494), who in his brief life of thirty-one years acquired magisterial learning in several branches of knowledge, including Semitic studies. This great contemporary and friend of Marsilio Ficino and Girolamo Savonarola sought out Jewish scholars who would teach him Hebrew and induct him into the mysteries of Kabbalah. Among his Jewish teachers were the theologian Elijah Delmedigo and the mystic Yoḥanan Alemanno. Pico was profoundly impressed by the philosophical wisdom of Kabbalah, especially its envisagement of the role of the human personality in the world. This envisagement is reflected in his *Oration on the Dignity of Man*, one of the noblest and most representative literary memorials of the Renaissance. But Pico's major concern was the reworking of Kabbalist conclusions "according to his own opinion" (*Conclusiones cabalisticae secundum opinionem propriam*) so as to give intellectual support to the truth claims of Christianity. One of his theses, condemned by the Church, was that "no science can make us more certain of the divinity of Christ than magic and Kabbalah." Other Kabbalist theses are contained in the nine hundred propositions derived from various scientific disciplines that Pico offered for public debate in Rome in 1486. That debate was never held, but Pico's sponsorship of Kabbalist ideas gave them notoriety and influenced other Christian scholars to reinterpret their faith Kabbalistically and to reformulate Kabbalah in a Christian fashion.

Pico himself first familiarized the famous German humanist Johannes von Reuchlin (1455–1522) with Jewish mysticism, and Reuchlin, in his *De arte cabalistica*, endeavored, like his teacher, to demonstrate the essential congruence of Kabbalah and Christianity. One of Reuchlin's most eminent pupils, the Austrian statesman, humanist, and Orientalist Johannes Albrecht Widmanstadt (1506–1557), who later became Rector of the University of Vienna and Chancellor of Lower Austria, was also deeply interested in Kabbalah. As a young man in Italy, this great Catholic scholar, along with his friend, the learned Christian Hebraist Egidio da Viterbo, received instruction in the literature of Kabbalah from the mystic Baruch of Benevento. Interest in Jewish mysticism was fostered by the highest authorities of the Church. Pope Sixtus IV (1414–1484) directed that a number of Kabbalist books be translated from Hebrew into Latin, out of the conviction that this might serve the purposes of the Church. Later, during the Counter Reformation, at the very time that the Dominicans were burning the *Talmud* and other Jewish books, numerous Kabbalist works were freely printed in Italy with the approval of the Catholic authorities. In 1559, when twelve thousand Jewish books were consigned to the flames in Cremona, the *Zohar* was published for the first time in two editions, in both Cremona and Mantua. This publication had the personal authorization of that bitter enemy of the Jews, Pope Paul IV, and of the agents of the Inquisition, and a significant role in the Cremona edition was played by the apostate Jew Vittorio Eliano (a grandson of the famous grammarian Elijah Levita), who had previously denounced the *Talmud* to the Dominican monks as an anti-Christian work and brought about its public burning.

The interest of many Christian humanists in the Hebrew language and in Jewish literature stimulated a renewal of philological and grammatical studies on the part of a number of Jewish scholars in Renaissance Italy. Several of these came to the aid of their Christian contemporaries in the latter's quest for Hebraic knowledge. Prominent among them was Jacob Mantino (1490–1549), court physician to Pope Paul III, professor of medicine at the University of Rome, and member of the rabbinic court of the Roman Jewish community. Mantino, who agitated against the messianic pretensions of Solomon Molcho and played a major part in bringing about the young Marrano's tragic downfall (for more on Molcho, see pp. 148–150), rendered several of Averroes' commentaries from Hebrew into Latin at the solicitation of his Christian friend Gianmateo Ghiberti, Bishop of Verona, and others. He also translated Maimonides' *Shemoneh Perakim* (*Eight Chapters*) and participated in the publication of the Latin version of the philosopher's *Guide of the Perplexed*. Another excellent scholar of the day who contributed significantly to the advancement of Semitic scholarship in Christian circles was Abraham ben Meir de Balmes (ca. 1440–1523). This eminent physician, philosopher, translator, and philologist obtained doctorates in both medicine and philosophy from the University of Naples by special authorization of

Pope Innocent VIII. Under the sponsorship of a prince of the Church, Cardinal Domenico Grimani, whom he served as personal physician, de Balmes translated a considerable number of medieval Arabic scientific and philosophical works from their Hebrew versions into Latin. He also wrote a logically oriented Hebrew grammar at the urging of Daniel Bomberg, the renowned Christian publisher of Hebraica in Venice. The work, *Mikneh Avraham* (*Cattle of Abraham*), was published with a Latin translation entitled *Peculium Abramae* shortly after the author's death, and for a long time was extensively utilized by Christian Hebraists.

Undoubtedly the most important figure in disseminating knowledge of the Hebrew language and grammar among both Jews and Christian humanists during the Renaissance was Elijah Levita (1468–1549), also known as Elijah Baḥur. Born in Germany, Levita spent most of his life in various cities of Italy, teaching Hebrew, working as editor and proofreader in the printing establishments of Christian publishers, and writing his numerous works. In his early years he composed epics and romances, based on medieval Italian and Provençal sources, in Yiddish verse; most of his work, however, was in the realm of sober philological scholarship. Levita's writings include a number of Hebrew grammars, Hebrew and Aramaic dictionaries, and an extremely valuable study of the technical terms and signs of the Masoretic text of the Bible; this last work, entitled *Massoret Ha-Massoret*, was published with an English translation and notes by Christian David Ginsburg in 1867, and recently (1968) reprinted. Among his Christian pupils were Sebastian Muenster and Cardinal Egidio da Viterbo. For some thirteen years Levita lived in the prelate's house in Rome and received financial support from him, so that he could devote all his time to research and writing. The Jewish scholar, who instructed Cardinal da Viterbo in Kabbalah and translated some Kabbalist works for him, was criticized by several rabbis of his day for teaching the Torah to gentiles; he defended himself by noting that many Christian Hebraists became friends and protectors of the Jews, and calling attention to the beneficial results of their sponsorship of Hebraic scholarship. The depth of Levita's own loyalty to Judaism is indicated by his refusal of an attractive offer to teach Hebrew at the Collège Royal in Paris because he did not wish to be the only member of his people allowed to live in France, and was not certain that he could properly fulfill his religious duties there. Two of his grandsons, however, converted to Christianity and became detractors of Judaism and Jewish literature.

Italian Jewry and the Renaissance Era

We have indicated that the Renaissance did not stimulate any great flowering of literature and thought among the Jews of Italy, nor did it produce, with the notable exception of Judah Abravanel, any highly creative Jewish thinkers. But it did contribute to the emergence, in substantial numbers, of a type of Jew only rarely known earlier in Christian Europe—a Jew thoroughly devoted to his own people and their traditions, but at the same time at home in and deeply influenced by all aspects of the larger cultural world of his time (not only its science and philosophy). Perhaps the best exemplar of the type is Judah ben Joseph Moscato (ca. 1530–ca. 1593), for many years rabbi in Mantua and probably the most brilliant preacher in the history of Italian Jewry. Moscato was a master of rabbinic learning and well acquainted with medieval Jewish philosophy, although his own mystical bent drew him strongly to Kabbalah. He also had an extensive knowledge of Greco-Arabic philosophy and was an ardent admirer of the "divine Plato," as he calls him. Beyond this, Moscato was profoundly interested in music, medicine, astronomy, and classical literature, as well as the works of contemporary Italian writers and thinkers. The cultural synthesis he achieved is evident in his published sermons; stories from the Bible are followed by tales from Greek mythology, and maxims from the *Talmud* are interwoven with quotations from Heraclitus, Aristotle, Plato, Cicero, Quintilian, Ovid, and Pico della Mirandola. These sermons are works of art, distinguished by their eloquent style and symmetrical construction. Didactic and moralistic elements are not absent from them, but aesthetic sensibility predominates. Never before had Jewish preaching attained such elegance and artistry, and only rarely did it again achieve this level. The fact that Moscato's sermons attracted appreciative listeners testifies that he had numerous coreligionists in Mantua who shared at least some of his wide-ranging culture. Many other such Jews were to be found throughout Italy in the sixteenth century.

Under the influence of the general Renaissance concern with history and antiquity, as well as the impact of the colossal tragedy that befell Spanish Jewry on its expulsion in 1492 (the aftereffects of which continued to be felt for many decades), the Jews of sixteenth-century Italy developed a keen interest in the past of their own people. A number of remarkable chroniclers and historians appeared to

[103]

satisfy that interest. One of the first and greatest was the Spaniard Solomon ibn Verga, who lived in the second half of the fifteenth and first half of the sixteenth centuries. After the exile from Spain Ibn Verga resided for some years as a Marrano in Portugal, and came in 1506 to Italy. There he later wrote his *Shevet Yehudah (Staff of Judah)*, an account of the many persecutions suffered by Jews from the time of the Palestinian revolt against Rome in the first century to his own day. In this work, characterized by a remarkably effective style, the author provides not only a historical survey of his subject but weaves into his moving narration imaginary disputations between Jewish and Christian protagonists, his personal reflections on the question of why the Jews have been the object of such intense hatred through the centuries, and his own highly critical animadversions against several popular Jewish philosophers, among them Judah ha-Levi and Maimonides. It is interesting to note that Ibn Verga regards hatred of the Jews as stemming mainly from religious fanaticism, ignorance, and jealousy, and suggests that perhaps the best remedy available (he is rather pessimistic about its efficacy) for counteracting these is for Jews to behave more modestly, be less conspicuous in their consumption and display of wealth, and practice greater mutual tolerance between themselves and adherents of other faiths. He has little use for the shopworn theological clichés about the suffering of the Jews being a mark of their superiority and of God's special love for them, and he scorns the notion, widespread among his contemporaries, that messianic redemption is imminent and will vindicate all their agonies. In his criticism of the subtleties and abstractions of the medieval Jewish schoolmen, the empirically and analytically minded Ibn Verga follows the attitude of many Christian humanists of the Renaissance era toward the Christian scholastics.

Of a different character than *Shevet Yehudah* is the work of another Jew of Sephardic descent whose family was exiled in 1492. This is Samuel Usque's *Consolaçam as tribulaçoens de Israel (Consolations for the Tribulations of Israel)*, published in Ferrara in 1553 and dedicated to Gracia Nasi, the famous patroness of Jewish culture in Constantinople. Unlike Solomon ibn Verga, Usque employs, in his survey of Jewish history from the beginning to his own day, standard apologetic themes, and endeavors to show that Israel, despite its age-long trials and sufferings, has not been forsaken by God and that its messianic redemption is at hand. Written in classical Portuguese prose, *Consolaçam* was intended to persuade Marranos who had fled from Spain and Portugal to revert to Judaism. Its intent apparently was understood by the Inquisition, whose agents burned most of the first edition soon after its publication. The work is distinguished by its frequently stirring portrayal of the whole panorama of Jewish history, and by the fact that it is written in the form of a typical pastoral dialogue of the Renaissance era. Two of the shepherds, Zicareo and Numeo, represent the prophets Zechariah and Nahum, and the third, Yacobo, represents the patriarch Jacob, symbol of the Jewish people as a whole.

Upon reading Usque's Portuguese book, another descendant of the Spanish exiles, Joseph Ha-Kohen (1496–1578), decided to write a similar work in Hebrew, and entitled it *Emek Ha-Bacha (The Valley of Tears)*. Joseph, who spent most of his life practicing medicine in various cities of Italy and composing historical works, was well equipped as a historiographer, for he had a comprehensive knowledge of European languages, history, literature, and science. His command of Latin and other languages made it possible for him to employ non-Jewish sources. This, added to his keen mind and remarkable critical-historical sense, led to the writing of works which so impressed the Christian Hebraist Jacques Basnage that he called Joseph the "second Josephus." Passages from *Emek Ha-Bacha*, which chronicles in detail the persecutions, expulsions, and forced conversions imposed on the Jews, came to be read annually on the Ninth of Av in a number of Italian communities. Joseph also slaked the thirst of his contemporaries for knowledge of world history. His *Divrei Ha-Yamim Le-Malchei Tzarefat Ule-Malchei Bet Ottoman Ha-Togar (History of the Kings of France and Turkey)*, published in Sabbioneta in 1554, deals only peripherally with the Jews and is concerned mainly with general European history from the end of the Roman Empire to his own generation, when the Ottoman Empire had become a world power threatening the nations of Europe. In Joseph's day the Jews of Italy had also developed a strong interest in geography, especially that of the recently conquered lands of South America and Mexico. The learned physician sought to satisfy this interest by translating Latin and Spanish works on the subject into Hebrew.

Perhaps the most widely read Jewish historian of the sixteenth century was Gedaliah ben Joseph ibn Yaḥya (1515–1578), a scion of the renowned Sephardic family Yaḥya, who was born in Italy and spent most of his life in the papal cities. Although he wrote voluminously, only his *Shalshelet Ha-Kabbalah (The Chain of Tradition)*, first published in Venice in 1587 and later many times reprinted, has survived. The popularity of the work was no doubt due to the inclusion of many midrashic legends and stories, along with historical information derived from *Josippon*, Abraham ibn Daud's *Sefer Ha-Kabbalah*, and other earlier Hebrew chronicles. The legendary and hagiographical elements of *Shalshelet Ha-Kabbalah* were extremely appealing to the masses. However, they led such a critical scholar as Joseph Solomon Delmedigo (Yashar of Candia) to characterize it as a "chain of lies." No doubt its major historical value lies in the information ibn Yaḥya provides about contemporary Jewish figures whom he knew personally or of whom he had accurate knowledge; this information makes the work one of the major sources for the history of Italian Jewry during the Renaissance. Gedaliah ibn Yaḥya appears to have been another of the type of *uomo universale* that Italian Jewry produced in the fifteenth and sixteenth centuries. The second part of his *Shalshelet Ha-Kabbalah* contains brief essays on a wide range of diverse subjects, including magic, ghosts, angelology, heaven and hell, astronomy, medicine, embryology, coins and measurements, and the manufacture of paper. Sober reportage of fact is generously mingled with fantasy and superstition.

Undoubtedly the greatest Italian-Jewish historian and finest Hebraic scholar of the Renaissance era, and a man of incomparably greater critical mentality than Gedaliah ibn Yaḥya and most of his contemporaries, was Azariah ben Moses dei Rossi (ca. 1511–ca. 1578). Born in Mantua into the renowned Min Ha-Adummim family, which traced its settlement in Rome to the time of the emperor Titus in the first century C.E., he studied medicine as a youth and earned a scant living from its practice in various Italian cities, including Ferrara, Ancona, Bologna, Sabbioneta, and his birthplace. His real interest, however, was literary scholarship, and he pursued it with passionate intensity throughout his life. No Jewish scholar before dei Rossi, and few after him, commanded a similar knowledge of the whole sweep of classical, medieval, and Renaissance Italian literature. The authors quoted in his work include—to mention but a few—Homer, Plato, Aristotle, Pythagoras, Herodotus, Xenophon, Aesop, Euclid, Virgil, Terence, Seneca, Cicero, Livy, Plutarch, Caesar, Dio Cassius, Pliny, Strabo, Eusebius, Jerome, Augustine, Justin Martyr, Clement of Alexandria, Thomas Aquinas, Isidore of Seville, Hugo of St. Victor, Dante, Petrarch, and Pico della Mirandola. No less magisterial was his knowledge of classical Jewish literature—the Bible, the *Talmud*, and Hellenistic-Jewish writings. The last of these, particularly the works of Philo of Alexandria, were of special interest to dei Rossi. Indeed, it was he who revived the philosophical commentaries of Philo, which had been preserved by the

Church Fathers but completely neglected by Jews for a millennium and a half, in Jewish scholarly circles. Dei Rossi revolutionized the study of the history of Judaism in the era of the Second Temple and the rabbinic age by employing not only Talmudic but Greco-Roman sources, both Jewish and non-Jewish, and by daring to give preference to the non-Talmudic literature in matters of history and chronology.

The great Italian-Jewish savant seems to have pursued scholarship throughout most of his life simply out of love, without any desire to publish the fruits of his researches, and his first and major work was printed when he was past sixty. The writing of this work, entitled *Meor Einayim* (*Enlightenment of the Eyes*), was occasioned by an extraordinary event. In 1571, when dei Rossi was living in Ferrara, the city was struck by an earthquake during which many of its residents were killed. Deeply moved by the catastrophe, in which he piously saw the hand of God, he wrote a vivid account of it called *Kol Elohim* (*The Voice of God*). Apparently reminded by the earthquake of the precariousness of human life, and apprehensive that his own learning would perish with him, he decided to write more. While residing as a refugee in a village outside Ferrara after the earthquake, dei Rossi had encountered a Christian scholar who asked him about the Hebrew original, which he assumed was extant, of the Greek pseudepigraphical work known as the Letter of Aristeas. Informing the Christian that there was no such original, and forced to admit further that Jews knew nothing of this important work dealing with the origin of the Septuagint, or Greek version of the Hebrew Bible, dei Rossi decided to translate the Letter into Hebrew under the title *Hadrat Zekenim* (*The Glory of the Elders*). The account of the earthquake in Ferrara and the translation of the Letter of Aristeas form the first two parts of *Meor Einayim*, which was published in 1573–1575. The third and largest part, *Imrei Binah* (*Words of Understanding*), consists of sixty chapters which summarize dei Rossi's findings in his studies of the development of the Bible and of Jewish history and literature, especially their chronology.

Employing the kind of critical analysis that did not become prevalent in Jewish scholarship until more than two centuries after his time, in the heyday of *die Wissenschaft des Judentums*, dei Rossi demonstrated that the Jewish calendar reckoning the years from the putative date of creation, which was universally accepted in his age and is still maintained in traditional Jewish circles, was of relatively recent vintage. Even in the early Middle Ages more ancient calendars, especially one that counted time from the conquest of Palestine by

Alexander the Great in 331 B.C.E., were in use among Jews. He further showed that adequate sources for reconstructing the chronology from the time of creation to the present are lacking, and that the claims of the traditional calendar can therefore not be admitted. Dei Rossi also argued that many of the stories in the *Talmud* and *midrashim* have no foundation in historical fact and must be regarded as legendary. Similar critical and independent judgment was brought to bear on a host of other topics having to do with Jewish history and literature.

Even before *Meor Einayim* came off the press in Mantua, rumors of its "heretical" content were abroad. The rabbis of Italy were scandalized by news of a Jewish scholar reported to have the temerity publicly to deny the validity of the calendar sanctified by tradition, and to question the authenticity of accounts set forth in the *Talmud* and midrashic literature. In 1574, when publication of the work was still not completed, the Venetian rabbinate, led by Samuel Judah Katzenellenbogen, issued a *herem* or ban against the reading, or even possession, of *Meor Einayim* by anyone who had not first obtained special permission from the rabbis of his locality. Dei Rossi was not himself attacked, since his personal conduct met the most rigorous standards of orthodoxy, but similar bans against his work were published in Rome, Ferrara, Padua, Verona, and Ancona. Even in distant Safed the *bet din* issued a *herem*, which went forth without the signature of the great halachist Joseph Karo only because he died before he could sign it, against *Meor Einayim*.

The aged scholar was deeply distressed by the attacks on his work and sought patiently to answer them. While *Meor Einayim* was still on the press he modified and softened some of the statements that had proved so offensive. All this, however, was of no avail. The assailants of his work were not mollified, and the ban remained. Around 1578 dei Rossi wrote a reply to his critics entitled *Matzref Le-Kesef (The Purification of Silver)*, dealing mainly with the question of the calendar and chronology, and shortly afterward went to his grave, no doubt regretting that he had ever published the results of the researches he had pursued so lovingly and assiduously throughout his days.

❦

The fact that dei Rossi's work was so vehemently attacked, and that the ban against *Meor Einayim* endured for over a century, during which it was rarely read and its author's name hardly ever mentioned, testifies that the great scholar lived before his time. It also bears witness to the intellectual regress and "failure of nerve" that were in full swing among the Jews of Italy toward the end of dei Rossi's lifetime. The springtime of the Renaissance was over, and Renaissance values and ideals were losing their power. The Catholic Counter Reformation, with its persecutions and forced ghettoization of Jews, as well as its burning and censorship of Jewish books, had already had its impact on Italian-Jewish life. (For a discussion of these events, see pp. 151–153.) Reactionary moods in the Jewish community were intensified, and the spirit of free thought and inquiry was dampened. The rabbis of Italy, who came increasingly from Germany, with its more rigid tradition of halachic observance, were not inclined to tolerate expressions of freedom and dissent which might weaken commitment to the *mitzvot*. While participation in the rich secular culture of Italy by the Jews residing there did not by any means cease, it became more limited and muted. The leaders of the beleaguered Jewish community sought to rally its strength by preaching unswerving fidelity to the ancestral traditions and removal from the corrupting "ways of the world."

That liberal and critical moods did not die out in Italian Jewry in the period after the Counter Reformation is perhaps best attested by the life and career of Leon da Modena (1571–1648), who lived two generations after Azariah dei Rossi and wrote most of his works in the first half of the seventeenth century. Since da Modena is one of the very few Jews of premodern times who wrote an autobiography, and since many of his letters have been preserved, more is known about him than virtually any other Jew of his or preceding ages.

Da Modena, born in Venice but brought up in Ferrara, was a *Wunderkind*. At the age of two and a half he read the prophetic lection in the synagogue, and at the age of three was able to translate passages from the Pentateuch into fluent Italian. As a five year old, he reports, he already dreamed of literary fame and was saddened by the thought that he might die before achieving it. In his youth da Modena studied with the foremost Hebrew grammarian of that age in Italy, Samuel Archivolti, who exercised a great influence on his style and all of his literary activity. The latter began at the age of twelve with his translation into Hebrew verse of the first canto of Ariosto's poem *Orlando Furioso*. A year later he wrote a tract against gambling entitled *Sur Me-Ra* (*Turn Away from Evil*). He himself, however, was a compulsive cardplayer throughout his life, and his losses at the gaming table kept him constantly in debt. This was by no means the only inconsistency in his character. An ardent rationalist and vehement assailant of Kabbalah and mysticism, he also dealt in amulets and nostrums and composed magical incantations.

The list of twenty-six occupations in which da Modena, according to his autobiography, engaged at various times in order to support his family (rarely above the poverty level) and pay his gambling debts is interesting. He: 1) tutored Jewish students; 2) tutored Christian students; 3) taught letter writing; 4) served as a preacher; 5) composed sermons for other preachers to deliver; 6) was a cantor in a synagogue; 7) acted as secretary of various societies; 8) served as a rabbi; 9) wrote rabbinic responsa; 10) acted as a *dayyan;* 11) taught in a *yeshivah;* 12) wrote official documents; 13) wrote letters; 14) taught music; 15) composed wedding poems and tombstone epitaphs; 16) wrote Italian sonnets; 17) wrote comedies; 18) rehearsed theatrical productions; 19) put together the form of legal contracts; 20) was a translator; 21) was a proofreader; 22) earned royalties from his own books; 23) taught the art of writing nostrums and amulets; 24) sold books of nostrums; 25) was a commercial broker; and 26) was a marriage broker.

Da Modena commanded considerable respect in the Jewish community of Venice because of his extensive Talmudic knowledge, but his reputation in its Christian society was even greater. Christians came in considerable numbers to listen to his eloquent preaching in various Venetian synagogues, and many Italian scholars regarded him as the most learned Jew of his day. But da Modena, the victim of his own compulsions and extremely unfortunate in his family life (of his three sons, the most promising died at the age of twenty-six as a result of lead poisoning contracted in experiments with alchemy, the second was killed in a brawl, and the third emigrated to Brazil and was never heard from again; one of his daughters and both his sons-in-law died young, and his wife became insane), was a bitter and resentful man. Considering his poverty and the wreckage of his family, he could not help but rail against the Jewish commandment to increase and multiply:

O how greatly they blinded our eyes and darkened our souls with this precept. They destroyed our body and our material existence, saddened and embittered our whole life with it. How many sins, how many wicked deeds does a man commit to support his wife and children. A heavy millstone have they hung about our necks so that we should not be able to lift our heads. . . . Large volumes would not suffice to describe how all our trouble and crimes, all our poverty and distress, derive from this commandment.[8]

This was not the only commandment that aroused da Modena's ire. Although a rabbi and rabbinic judge, he came in time to have the utmost contempt for rabbinic law. His *Kol Sachal* (*The Voice of a Fool*), which da Modena, who had no desire to play the martyr's role, put forth as a statement of the views of a "heretic" named Amittai ben Yedaiah which he supposedly wished to refute, contains the most caustic and thoroughgoing indictment of the Oral Law to be written in Hebrew until the era of Haskalah and Reform in the nineteenth century; proponents of both of these movements, in fact, repeated many of its arguments. Da Modena categorically rejects the claim that the Oral Law was divinely revealed at Sinai; this is a myth fabricated by the rabbis of the Talmudic age to bolster its authority and their own power. He castigates their multiplication of prohibitions and commandments and insists that their motivation was simply lust for power and self-aggrandizement.

Only after the destruction of the second Temple did our "sages" show what they could do. In reality, with the destruction of the Temple and the loss of its land by the Jewish people, many commandments and precepts became null and void. The teachers of the people ought to have adapted the Torah to the new circumstances prevailing in the exile. They should have lightened the yoke of the punctilious commandments for the miserable exiles, with their difficult situation in the land of their enemies and oppressors, so that it would not hinder them in their struggle to live nor arouse hatred for them among the surrounding populace. But our leaders did just the opposite. All the strict regulations which the Pharisees ordained particularly for the pietists who wished to separate themselves from the world, they enlarged even more fearfully and imposed upon all the people. They endlessly multiplied their prohibitions and commands, which press like a heavy burden on every individual, embitter and grieve his life, and make the whole people a mockery and a scorn. All this they did with a definite purpose: to rule over the people, so that the people might be completely dependent upon them, so that they might not be able to take a single step without them, the scholars and law-givers.[9]

Da Modena's *Kol Sachal* is undoubtedly idiosyncratic and does not reflect a mood widely shared by his contemporaries. Its author did not dare publish it; neither it nor *Shaagat Aryeh* (*The Roar of a Lion*), the brief and pallid response under da Modena's own name to the heterodox arguments of the imaginary Amittai ben Yedaiah, were printed until the middle of the nineteenth century. But that thoughts such as those in *Kol Sachal* could still be entertained shows that the spirit of free criticism and liberalism was still not completely stifled in seventeenth-century Italian Jewry. Further and perhaps more decisive evidence is provided by da Modena's sermons that have come down to us, rivaling those of Judah Moscato in artistry and classic style. It is also instructive that, as a halachic decisor, the Venetian rabbi saw no objection to going about bareheaded or playing ball games in the ghetto on the Sabbath.

In his old age, as a man of sixty-eight, Leon da Modena wrote his famous polemic against Kabbalah, which he had earlier defended on occasion. The work is entitled *Ari Nohem* (*The Roaring Lion*) and continues the tradition of anti-Kabbalist polemic inaugurated in Italy by Elijah Delmedigo in the fifteenth century. Da Modena not only demonstrates that the *Zohar* could not possibly have been written by the second-century Tanna Simeon bar Yoḥai, but also derides the irrationality of Kabbalah in general and of practical Kabbalah in particular. He has nothing but contempt for the Kabbalist ascription of miraculous powers to amulets, incantations, and combinations of letters. The "wisdom" of Kabbalah, da Modena concludes, is not only void of wisdom and its claim to great antiquity unfounded; it is also theologically pernicious, insofar as its *sefirot* doctrine undermines the central foundation of Jewish faith—the unity and incorporeality of God. Not without good reason, he urges, are Jewish apostates and Christian mystics so keenly interested in Kabbalah.

For Christian dogmatics da Modena had no use whatever. His *Magen Va-Ḥerev* (*Shield and Sword*) is one of the most incisive anti-Christian polemics ever written in Hebrew. With relentless logic the author exposes the offense to reason of the major articles of Christian faith and the perversity of Christian exegesis of the Hebrew Bible.

It is clear from his autobiography that Leon da Modena considered his life, both as a man and as a writer, a failure. He had no expectation that his work would be remembered. The epitaph he composed for his own tombstone reflects his hopelessness:

> Here on the field is a plot of four cubits
> That were determined by God Himself
> For Judah Aryeh, born in Modena.
> Here he lies buried, hidden and lost.

Da Modena's name and memory were, indeed, largely lost and forgotten for many generations. But the spirit he represented—the spirit of free thought and independent inquiry—continued to flicker fitfully and even, at times, to flare into incandescence in the Italian ghetto long after it had been totally snuffed out elsewhere in the Jewish world.

CHAPTER

❧ V ❧

East European Jewry

WHEN JEWS first settled in eastern Europe has not been definitely established. Archaeological evidence indicates that Greek-speaking Jews already lived in the region presently known as the Crimea in the first Christian century, and had their own communal organizations and synagogues. In the course of time the first settlers, who probably came from the Jewish colonies in Greece and the Aegean islands, seem to have been joined by others from Mesopotamia who trekked northward into the area. We have virtually no information about the early history of these Jews. We do know, however, that in the eighth century the major center of the Jewish settlement in the Crimea and the Caucasus was in Phanagoria (or Tamatarcha), which came to be virtually an all-Jewish town.

It is also known that in the eighth century Bulan, the ruler of an energetic people known as the Chazars who lived in the lower Volga region and had their capital at Itil, adopted Judaism as his religion, and that he was followed in this by some four thousand members of the nobility and upper classes of the state. The Chazar kingdom prospered for more than two centuries. Its power extended westward to Kiev; one of its princesses married the emperor of Byzantium, and her son ascended the Byzantine throne as Leo IV (775–780). In the tenth century Ḥasdai ibn Shaprut (ca. 915–ca. 970), the Jewish statesman and patron of learning who held high office at the courts of the caliphs Abd er-Raḥman III and Ḥakam II at

[113]

Cordova in Spain, is reported to have learned of the existence of the kingdom and sent an enthusiastic letter to its ruling Khakan, Joseph, through two Slavic Jews who had come to Cordova on a mission. Not long afterward, in 965–969, most of the land of the Chazars was conquered by Russian armies, and within a few decades the last vestiges of the once powerful and independent state disappeared. It may be, however, that descendants of the Chazars survived among the Karaites of the Crimea, the Krimchaks, and other Jews of east European origin.

The Christianization of the Slavic territories seems to have brought troubles to the Jews dwelling there; we hear of Byzantine bishops and abbots who despised Jews and of sporadic anti-Jewish riots. Nevertheless, Jewish merchants from western and central Europe continued to penetrate what they called the "land of Canaan." Jewish communities were established in such major trading centers as Novgorod and Kiev, and small settlements were also gradually formed in what is now Poland. Polish coins of the twelfth and thirteenth centuries struck by Jewish mintmasters and carrying Hebrew inscriptions have been discovered; these indicate the significant role played by Jews in the economic life of the country.

Poland did not fall under Tartar sovereignty as a result of the invasions of 1240–1241, as did Russia, but these incursions leveled its cities, leaving its industry ruined and its economy shattered. Commercial activity had virtually disappeared. To rebuild the economy and to establish a middle class between the *szlachta* or nobility and the peasants, the Polish kings, from the middle of the thirteenth century on, embarked on a systematic and highly successful effort to recruit merchants and artisans from Germany. With the German Christians, and following them, came many German Jews. They were impelled to leave their native country by the repressions and persecutions which became ever more frequent and severe in the Rhineland from the beginning of the era of the Crusades, and were attracted to Poland by the economic possibilities it offered. The German Jews were warmly welcomed by the Polish sovereigns. In 1264 King Boleslav the Pious granted the Jewish immigrants a model charter of protection, called the "Statute of Kalisz," guaranteeing them security of person and property as well as freedom of economic opportunity. These privileges were enlarged by Casimir the Great (1333–1370), who (according to some reports, persuaded by his Jewish mistress Esther) ratified the charter of Boleslav and accorded the Jews further rights, including travel and residence wherever they wished in the country, and the right to lease estates, or hold them in mortgage, even from the nobility and clergy. Since the city magistrates were generally prejudiced against Jews, Casimir also placed all litigation between Jews and Christians under the jurisdiction of the Crown. The theory underlying the charters granted by the Polish sovereigns was that the Jews were the *servi camerae regis*, the property of the Crown. Even more extensive rights than those given Jews in Poland were awarded in Lithuania (then an independent duchy but united with Poland in 1501) by the Grand Duke Vitovt (or Vitold) to the Jews of Brest-Litovsk in 1388 and to the Jews of Grodno in 1389. The royal policy of encouraging immigration of Jews and protecting their rights was, with few exceptions, maintained until the collapse of the Polish monarchy in the eighteenth century.

Given this encouragement and protection, Jews migrated to Poland in large numbers, mainly from Germany but from other European countries as well. They were not always greeted affectionately by the general populace, even in the early period of their settlement. The Christian merchants and artisans who had come from Germany in the *Drang nach Osten* tended to see them as competitors and despised them; the peasantry resented them as agents of the exploiting landowners; the Catholic clergy preached hatred of them as infidels and deicides, demanding that they be subjected to the restrictions and indignities decreed by the Lateran Councils. At the time of the Black Death in the middle of the fourteenth century, Jews in Poland, like their brethren throughout Europe, were massacred as a result of the accusation that they had poisoned the wells and rivers of the country. In 1399 the rabbi and thirteen elders of Posen were burned at the stake on charges of desecrating the Host; in 1407, at Easter time, the Jewish quarter of Cracow was sacked and many Jews were killed when a mob became incited by a rumor that the Jews had murdered a Christian child. Half a century later the zealous Franciscan monk John of Capistrano, the "scourge of the Jews" who instigated murderous riots with his rabid preaching in many places in Europe, carried his campaign against the Jews to Poland, with devastating results. Nevertheless, compared with most of Europe in the fifteenth and sixteenth centuries, Poland was a land of freedom and security for Jews, and they continued to migrate to it uninterruptedly not only from Germany but from Moravia, Bohemia, Italy, Spain, and the Crimea. In the sixteenth century Rabbi Moses ben Israel Isserles declared in his responsa that "it is preferable to live on dry bread and in peace in Poland" than to remain in other countries of Europe; he explained the Hebrew term for Poland, *Polin*, as deriving from *poh lin*, "here shall he rest." The Jewish population of Poland grew rapidly. It is estimated that at the beginning of the sixteenth century there were no more than fifty thousand Jews in Poland; within a century and a half their number had increased tenfold. The Jewish settlement in Poland and the neighboring territories eventually became the largest in Europe.

Unlike the Jews of other European lands who, in the late medieval period, were largely restricted to earning a living through moneylending and petty trade, the Polish Jews in that era were engaged in a wide variety of other occupations. A good many of them were craftsmen, merchants, and manufacturers. Considerable numbers were employed by the Polish nobles and landowners as managers of their estates, administering the farms, timber forests, and mines on their lands. More than a few, among them some who achieved great wealth, were tax-farmers and fiscal agents to the king. A significant percentage served in the dual role of village innkeeper and tax-collector. Among the Jews of Poland were also some who had studied medicine in Italy (particularly at the University of Padua) and who, despite the attacks frequently launched against them by jealous Christian physicians, were highly regarded by both the nobility and the general populace; a few even became court physicians to the Polish kings. Jews were not confined to the large cities, although places like Lemberg, Cracow, Posen, and Kalisz had large Jewish populations, but were scattered throughout the whole country, including the rural areas and small villages.

The Jews who began migrating to Poland from Germany in the thirteenth century soon outnumbered the older settlers, and before long their religious outlook, culture, mores, and language became dominant in Polish-Jewish life. German Talmudists, the spiritual heirs of Rabbi Meir of Rothenburg and Rabbi Asher ben Yeḥiel, brought with them their strict interpretation of the *halachah* and imposed it on the Polish settlement. The dress and manners of the German-Jewish communities became normative in Poland. The *Jüdisch-Deutsch* or Judeo-German dialect, essentially Middle High German with an admixture of Hebrew terms, spoken by the Jews of the Middle Rhine region from the eleventh century on, was imported into Poland. With the addition of many Slavic words and expressions, it evolved into Yiddish and quickly became, and remained for centuries, the vernacular of the masses of Ashkenazic Jewry. Before the Nazi Holocaust decimated the Jewish communities of Europe, Yiddish was the mother tongue of almost two-thirds of the Jews of the world.

Whereas elsewhere in Europe autonomous Jewish communities or *kehillot*, ruled by their own officials in accordance with Talmudic law, were usually recognized de facto by the various governments, in Poland the autonomy of the Jews was officially guaranteed by royal decree. Sigismund I (1506–1548) had appointed Michael Josefovicz as elder ("senior") of the Jews of Lithuania and Abraham of Bohemia as elder of the Jews of Poland, but the Jews resisted the authority of these royal appointees. They also opposed the designation in 1541 by the king of two chief rabbis, Moses Fischel of Cracow and Shalom Shachna of Lublin, over the province of Little Poland. In 1551 Sigismund Augustus (1548–1572), the last of the Jagellonian dynasty, officially authorized the Jews of his kingdom to elect their own chief rabbi and judges and granted their courts full jurisdiction to act according to Jewish law; the king's decree specified that any Jew who resists "the censures and bans imposed upon him by the rabbi, judge, or other Jewish elders . . . shall be beheaded." This system was intended to facilitate the collection of the taxes imposed on the Jewish community as a whole.

In time a national *Vaad* or council, which came to serve as the supreme legislative and judicial body of Polish Jewry, evolved. As early as the first half of the sixteenth century it became customary for Jewish merchants, gathered from all parts of Poland in Lublin at the great annual mercantile fair, to discuss issues of common concern, seek settlement of disputes between communities, and allocate the sum that each Kahal or local community organization was to contribute to the general tax imposed on the Jews of the country collectively. It also became customary for the rabbis gathered at the fair, many of whom were wealthy merchants or had business interests, to adjudicate civil cases submitted to them according to rabbinic law. Gradually these practices, sanctioned by the Polish sovereign, were institutionalized, and the *Vaad* became the officially recognized supreme authority for all of Polish Jewry.

Initially this body was known as the Council of Three Lands, comprising Great and Little Poland, Lithuania, and Polish Russia. Since the Grand Duchy of Lithuania had its own independent tax administration, the Lithuanian Jewish communities seceded and established their own organization in 1623. Later the *Vaad* was called the Council of Four Lands, with each of the four provinces of the Polish kingdom—Great Poland, Little Poland, Podolia-Galicia, and Volhynia—serving as constituents. Meetings of the Council were held twice every year, generally at the fair in Lublin in the spring and at the fair in the Galician town of Jaroslav in late summer before the High Holy Days, although emergency sessions were at times convened elsewhere. The membership of the Council consisted of thirty delegates, twenty-four layman and six rabbis, representing the major communities. While its central task was the apportionment of the collective government taxation among the various districts, the Council was also concerned with regulation of Jewish life as a whole and with the promotion of the general welfare of Polish Jewry. *Shtadlanim* or lobbyists, usually men of wealth with influential connections at court or among the higher nobility, were dispatched by the Council to sessions of the Polish Diet in Warsaw to protect Jewish interests, and money was provided for disbursement when it was felt that discreet gifts to strategically placed officials might prevent the passage of inimical legislation or promote favorable enactments. One of the major concerns of the Council was to maintain untroubled relations between the Jewish community (as well as its individual members) and the central government. To enforce its decisions the Council relied mainly on its power of excommunication, authorized, along with stricter penalties, by the decree of Sigismund Augustus in 1551.

Until its official dissolution by royal edict in 1764, the Council of Four Lands continued to regulate the life of Polish Jewry. It frequently issued sumptuary rules to control conspicuous consumption in dress, adornment, and entertainment, attempting thereby to prevent envy and hostility on the part of the Christian populace. It prescribed the structure and organization of the districts and communities and was particularly concerned with proper administration of the educational system, specifying duties of teachers, content of curriculum, and methods of examination. The Council also exercised strict supervision over Hebrew printing and sought to protect copyrights from violation. To prevent cutthroat competition, it laid down detailed laws regulating the conduct of business, as well as leases and rents. It prescribed rules for administration of justice in local rabbinic courts, and its own high tribunal served as a court of appeal and adjudicated disputes between communities. Thus, for a century and a half, the Council exercised control over virtually every aspect of Polish-Jewish life. In the precarious condition of Polish Jewry, particularly after the Chmielnitzki massacres in the middle of the seventeenth century, it was a remarkably effective instrument for en- suring discipline and solidarity in the face of a hostile world. Not a few Jews smarted under the authority of the *Vaad*, as well as that of the Kahals or local community councils. It was these institutions, however, that kept Jewish life in Poland from disintegration and chaos.

◈◈◈

The first significant figure in Polish-Jewish scholarship was Rabbi Jacob Pollak (ca. 1460–1541). As a young man Pollak studied in the *yeshivah* of Nuremberg and served in the rabbinate of Prague, then one of the major centers of Jewish learning and culture in central Europe. In 1503 he was appointed by King Alexander chief rabbi of Poland, but the Jews resisted a chief rabbi whom they had not them- selves elected, and Pollak was compelled to withdraw. He left his impress on Polish Jewry, however, by establishing, with the finan- cial aid of his widowed mother-in-law (who was rich and prominent enough to be received at the Polish court), a *yeshivah* in Cracow. Until that time Talmudic study had been little cultivated in Poland. The establishment of Pollak's academy changed this situation; from it came a number of young men who organized *yeshivot* in other cities and, within a few decades, there was hardly a country in the world where Talmudic learning was pursued as intensively as it was in Poland. Pollak himself, who was embroiled in bitter controversies over legal matters with other rabbis of his time, appears to have visited Palestine late in life and then returned to Lublin, where he died.

It was Jacob Pollak and one of his chief disciples, Shalom Shachna (1500–1559) of Lublin, who introduced into Polish Jewry, and firmly established in its *yeshivot*, the curious mode of Talmudic study called *pilpul*, which persisted for centuries and had a vast influence, largely negative in character, on Jewish intellectual and spiritual life.

In the Talmudic age the term *pilpul* (derived from *pilpel*, "to pep- per" or "to season") meant the method of resolving apparent contra- dictions and textual problems by acute logical analysis and reason- ing; its goal was the attainment of a clear understanding of the law. Even then the question was debated as to who contributes more to the promotion of Torah study—*sinai*, one who faithfully maintains the accepted texts and traditions, or *oker harim*, "the uprooter of mountains," the original scholar who employs reason and logic in interpreting the text and arriving at his conclusions. But the view was prevalent that *pilpul* is essential in connecting the Written Torah with the Oral, and that it is a valuable instrument for developing the reasoning capacity of students. According to a Talmudic tradition,[1] proficiency in *pilpul* was a prerequisite for membership in the Sanhedrin. While *pilpul* was not unknown to the scholars of the Geonic era and the Franco-German commentators before Rashi, it was not a major concern among them. A renewed appreciation of the method developed among the Tosafists of France and Germany and in the Talmudic academies of Spain in the twelfth and thirteenth centuries. In these circles its aim was no longer so much to clarify a single, apparently contradictory text, as cleverly to harmonize different passages and opinions in the *Talmud*. The Ḥasidei Ashkenaz, the "Pious of Germany," expressed their displeasure with the pilpulists of their time for stressing casuistry and mental ingenuity over the search for truth. The use of casuistry and sharp disputations, based on *ḥillukim*, or subtle divisions and differentiations, became even more widespread, however, in the German *yeshivot* of the fifteenth and sixteenth centuries. It was from these that the new *pilpul* was imported by Jacob Pollak into Poland, where it received intensive cultivation and grew riotously.

A typical procedure in the pilpulist method was to take two passages from the *Gemara* or two laws which seemingly have no relationship whatever with each other, or even blatantly contradict each other, and then, through tortuous distinctions and exceedingly subtle explanations, show that the passages or laws are really closely related and resolve all the apparent contradictions between them. Thereupon it is shown that the explanations just given are inconsistent with each other and, to reconcile *their* contradictions, new explanations and subtleties are devised. This procedure can be continued indefinitely, as long as the patience and resourcefulness of the "reasoner" last. Alternatively, the pilpulist might take a Talmudic passage or law whose meaning seems crystal clear and proceed to find in it the most baffling difficulties, bringing into the discussion endless quotations from elsewhere in the *Talmud*, comments of the Geonim, theories of the commentators, and decisions of the codifiers. Once the insolubility of the difficulties had been established through the most refined argumentation and the invocation of numerous citations and authorities, the dialectician would proceed to demonstrate, through equally subtle argumentation, that all the difficulties are only apparent and that the passage or law in question really means what it says.

Pilpulist exercises of this kind could obviously help develop the mental agility of their practitioners, but they also led to an infatuation with sterile sophistry. Men came to devote themselves zealously to *pilpul* not in order to obtain truth, knowledge, or accurate understanding, but purely as a means of displaying their skill in mental gymnastics, and regarded this as the whole substance of "studying Torah." In the sixteenth and seventeenth centuries excellence in *pilpul* became the major goal of most of the *yeshivah* students of Poland, for it was not only accorded universal admiration but was also rewarded tangibly by social status and preferment in rabbinic office; thorough and conscientious scholars who disdained its sophistry and casuistry were frequently passed over in official appointments and compared unfavorably with superficially clever pilpulists. A number of eminent rabbis, including Judah Loew ben Bezalel (the Maharal of Prague), Isaiah Horowitz, Ephraim of Luntschitz, and Yair Ḥayyim Bacharach, strongly deplored the tendency to make *pilpul* an end in itself, as well as the distortion of truth that resulted from its hairsplitting dialectics. They also criticized its practitioners' pursuit of personal glory and profit. Nevertheless, the popularity of *pilpul* in the *yeshivot* and in the larger religious life of east European Jewry did not wane significantly until the beginning of the nineteenth century. It was carried from the study hall of the *yeshivah* to the pulpit of the synagogue, and preachers vied with each other in applying its techniques in their homilies on the Bible and the *midrashim*. *Pilpul* did foster sharp-wittedness, but it also encouraged an arid scholasticism and a preoccupation with empty sophistries that had deleterious effects on east European Judaism. It also prepared the way for the warm reception that the Ḥasidic movement, with its liberating message of simple faith and piety, obtained when it burst on the scene in Poland in the middle of the eighteenth century.

Once Jacob Pollak, Shalom Shachna, and their successors, of whom we shall speak presently, established their *yeshivot*, Talmudic study became widespread in Poland. Perhaps in no other time or place in Jewish history did rabbinic learning engage so broad a segment of the population as in sixteenth- and seventeenth-century Poland. A contemporary chronicler, Nathan Hannover, writes of the period before the massacres of 1648:

In all the dispersions of Israel study was nowhere so widespread as in Poland. Every community had its Talmudic academies. The head of the *yeshivah* was paid generously so that he might be able to devote himself to it entirely, heart and soul, without extraneous concerns. The whole year through he would not cross the threshold of the academy except to go to the synagogue, but would sit and study Torah day and night. The students of the *yeshivah* were also maintained by the community, and each received a fixed stipend every week. Every student would be given at least two boys to teach so that he might accustom himself to transmit to others what he himself had learned and become competent in *pilpul*. Meals were provided for the students from the community charity fund or from the communal soup kitchen. A community of fifty householders would support no less than thirty Talmudic students. Each student, with his two boys whom he taught, would live with a householder. Even if the student obtained his requirements from the community, the householder would nevertheless feed him at his table like his own son. . . . In the whole land of Poland there was hardly a single home where Torah was not studied. Either the master of the house himself, or his son, or his son-in-law, or a student who took his meals in his home, was a scholar. Frequently all of them together were students and scholars.[2]

It would be naive to assume that Polish Jewry's fervid preoccupation with rabbinic learning was simply an expression of religiosity or disinterested love of intellectual pursuits. Though such motives were not absent, more practical considerations undoubtedly played a larger role. The Jewish community was, after all, self-governing, and its regulative legislation was the vast corpus of rabbinic law. Proficiency in this law was the prerequisite not only for successful conduct of one's daily affairs, but for status and recognition in society. As a great modern historian of Jewish literature has put it:

To study Torah day and night, to be well versed in the *Talmud* and codes, was not only a manifestation of piety, of great devotion to the commandments wherewith one purchases life in the world-to-come; it was also the most assured way which led to influence in communal life, gave one the possibility of attaining the highest degrees of power and honor in the community: to become a rabbi, a principal of a *yeshivah*, a president of a court, a *parnass*.[3]

◈

We have noted that Shalom Shachna was appointed chief rabbi of Little Poland by royal edict in 1541. The *yeshivah* that he established in Lublin attained great prominence and attracted students from all over Europe. Lublin became a major center of Talmudic scholarship and one of the two regular meeting places of the Council of Four Lands. Although Shachna strongly advocated the use of *pilpul*, his own responsa reveal a large measure of sober common sense and responsible concern for meeting contemporary needs.

More renowned than Shachna was his son-in-law and foremost pupil, Moses ben Israel Isserles (ca. 1525–1572), commonly known by the acronym Rema. Born into a family of great wealth in Cracow, Isserles was sent to Lublin to study in Shachna's *yeshivah* and married his teacher's daughter. The young woman died in 1552 when she was only twenty, and a year later her grieving husband built in her memory a synagogue in Cracow which is still standing; his own grave adjoins this synagogue, and until World War II thousands of Jews from everywhere in Poland, which is now virtually devoid of Jews, pilgrimaged to it annually on Lag Ba-Omer, the anniversary of his death. While still quite young Isserles founded a *yeshivah* in Cracow, presiding over it and supporting its students from his private fortune until his death. He quickly gained world fame as a halachist; almost all the great rabbinic scholars of his time consulted him on legal questions. His pupils included most of the leading figures in the religious and intellectual life of Polish Jewry in the generation after his.

In his own lifetime Moses Isserles came to be regarded as the Maimonides of Polish Jewry. Lacking the philosophical brilliance of the Sephardic scholar, Isserles did share his speculative outlook, his commitment to the secular sciences as well as the *Talmud*, and his concern with systematic methodology. His literary works embraced not only the fields of *halachah* and Kabbalah but metaphysics and science. Historically the most important of Isserles' legal works is his collection of glosses on Joseph Karo's *Shulḥan Aruch* (*Prepared Table*), known as *Haggahot* (*Corrections*, or *Marginal Comments*) or *Ha-Mappah* (*The Tablecloth*). This collection contains comments and supplements to Karo's work and includes the Ashkenazic customs and practices which the Sephardic codifier in Turkey had ignored. Thus, for instance, the custom of *Kapparot*, i.e., of swinging a fowl over one's head on the eve of the Day of Atonement while praying that the bird, when slaughtered, might serve as a vicarious atonement for the individual's sins—a custom which Karo had branded as "foolish" but which was very popular among the Ashkenazic Jews—is included. In *Ha-Mappah* Isserles also occasionally takes exception to some of Karo's halachic rulings and follows the decision of Asher ben Yeḥiel and his son Jacob rather than that of Alfasi and Maimonides. It was only by preparing his "tablecloth," noting Ashkenazic practice, to Karo's *Shulḥan Aruch* (*Prepared Table*) that Isserles made the latter work universally acceptable throughout the Jewish world, to Ashkenazim as well as Sephardim. The first edition combining the *Shulḥan Aruch* and *Ha-Mappah* was published in Cracow in 1569–1571, when both Isserles and Karo, with whom the Polish scholar corresponded on halachic matters, were still living.

Unlike many of his predecessors and successors, Isserles, as a legal decisor, tended to be lenient in interpreting the *halachah*, especially "in cases of emergency and where substantial financial loss is involved." He also attempted to give *minhag*, or traditional custom, the status of law, even when it had no foundation in the *Talmud* or conflicted with Talmudic *halachah*. He was not, however, blindly subservient to *minhag;* on occasion he declares emphatically, "This custom is wrong" or "Had I the power, I would nullify this custom, for it is based on error and there is no reason to follow it." Other Talmudists of his day, particularly Ḥayyim ben Bezalel, who had studied with Isserles under Shalom Shachna, attacked his attitude toward *minhag* and his lenient tendencies, as well as many of his specific rulings. Isserles' decisions and practices, however, became normative for Ashkenazic Jewry.

In his philosophical works, chiefly *Torat Ha-Olah* (*Law of the Burnt Offering*), Isserles attempted to establish the essential congruence of the basic principles of medieval Jewish philosophy, exemplified in Maimonides' *Guide of the Perplexed*, and the theosophy of Kabbalah, for both of which he had a profound admiration. The attempt was, of course, an abysmal failure. Isserles appears to have had no appreciation of the fact that Aristotelian rationalism and Kabbalah represent two fundamentally different worlds of ideas, and that *pilpul*, of which he was a master, is incapable of reconciling them. Convinced that "the wisdom of Kabbalah and the science of philosophy speak of one and the same thing but in different words," [4] Isserles ended with a weirdly eclectic mixture in which metaphysical theories about the role of the "active intellect" in the cosmos are followed by discussions of the miracles that may be wrought, and the compulsions that may be placed on the planets, by "combinations of letters." The Polish rabbi could not suppress his astonishment that so keen a thinker as Maimonides should have rejected belief in the power of combinations of letters when the Kabbalists have such incontrovertible knowledge of the marvelous force that inheres in the divine "names" and their mysterious letters. Yet he was enough of a rationalist to seek reasons for the commandments, give nonliteral explanations of some strange rabbinic *aggadot,* and mildly qualify biblical anthropomorphism by suggesting that the term "the hand of God" really means an angel.

Half-heartedly rationalist as it is, Isserles' *Torat Ha-Olah* was the only "philosophical" work produced in Polish rabbinic circles in the course of the sixteenth and seventeenth centuries. But even this much philosophy was utterly repugnant to Isserles' older relative, Solomon ben Yeḥiel Luria (ca. 1510–1574), known as Rashal or Maharshal. Luria, whose eminence in Talmudic scholarship approximated that of Isserles, was incensed that the latter should have manifested any interest in philosophy or science. Upon reading one of Isserles' responsa in which an Aristotelian argument had been cited, he indignantly wrote to him:

Like a knife cutting into living flesh have your words wounded me. You have surrounded me with whole packs of sciences, but mainly with secular sciences. . . . You always mention the gentile Aristotle, and the true wisdom, our Torah, is veiled in sackcloth. She laments that her children forsake her. . . . When I saw how you hold on to the wisdom of the gentile Aristotle, I cried out: Woe is me that my eyes see and my ears hear that the best and loveliest is hidden in the words of this unclean one and the sages of Israel endeavor—God forbid—to adorn our sacred Torah with these words! [5]

Although he had nothing but contempt for philosophy and science, Solomon Luria, who served as rabbi and rector of *yeshivot* in Ostrog, Brest-Litovsk, and Lublin, manifested remarkable independence of mind in his halachic rulings and in the critical methodology he brought to the study of the *Talmud.* He was hostile to *pilpul,* though it was used in his *yeshivah,* and insisted on methodical study of the Talmudic text. Unlike most of his contemporaries and successors, Luria refused to abdicate his own judgment before the opinions and decisions of the *Rishonim,* the Talmudic codifiers and commentators of previous generations. For his own rabbinic contemporaries, mesmerized by *pilpul,* he had, with few exceptions, scant respect. He complains:

Because of our numerous sins, there are among us many who have *semichah* [ordination] but very few competent scholars. The number of the ignorant increases. As soon as such a one obtains *semichah,* he makes himself

great and gathers around himself young students, like the nobles who surround themselves with a retinue of servants. . . . There are those who cannot understand any subject in the *Talmud* whatever or properly explain a
halachah . . . but these also rule over the community and over scholars,
prohibit and permit, and grant ordination to pupils who have not even studied with them but have given them payment and favors.[6]

Highly critical of others, Luria seems to have had little personal
vanity; it was his custom to spend an hour every day listening to the
moral exhortations of an ordinary preacher.

For Luria the only authoritative source for halachic decisions was
the *Talmud* itself, both its Babylonian and Palestinian recensions. He
undertook a systematic, critical study of its text, and his collection of
glosses and emendations, *Ḥochmat Shelomoh* (*The Wisdom of Solomon*), is
a remarkable example of rigorous and acute scholarship. The labor
expended on this work was only a preparation for his magnum opus,
Yam Shel Shelomoh (*The Sea of Solomon*), which was projected as a compendium of all the laws of the *Talmud*, systematically organized and
critically explicated on the basis of primary sources. In the introduction to each of the tractates Luria tells of the painstaking
thoroughness with which he carried through his work. Two whole
years were spent on the laws in the first half of the tractate *Yevamot*,
a full year on the first two chapters of the tractate *Ketuvot*, and six
months on a single chapter dealing with the laws of levirate marriage. It is hardly surprising that Luria managed to complete his
work on only a few of the tractates of the *Talmud*.

❧

After Isserles and Luria, Polish Jewry continued to produce large
numbers of eminent scholars, but few showed interest in anything
but rabbinic studies. An exception was Mordecai ben Abraham Jaffe
(ca. 1530–1612), a native of Prague who studied in both Poland and
Italy and later served as rabbi in Grodno, Lublin, Kremenetz,
Prague, and Posen. Jaffe wrote a commentary to Maimonides' *Guide
of the Perplexed* and gave his qualified approval to philosophy and
science, declaring that one may study books dealing with these subjects which are completely free of heretical ideas, and that only those
who have already attained a high degree of proficiency in Talmudic
learning may concern themselves with them. Despite his own admiration for Maimonides and his competence in mathematics, Jaffe,

who acquired fame with his halachic work *Levush Malchut* (*Royal Garment*), which for a time contended for supremacy with the *Shulḥan Aruch*, firmly believed in magic, demons, incantations, and transmigration of souls. Such beliefs were typical of the scholars of that age. Credulousness and superstition lived peaceably with the most acute mentality. The renowned Rabbi Meir ben Gedaliah of Lublin (1558–1616), known as the Maharam, who was a consummate master of *pilpul*, elaborated the most subtle *ḥiddushim* or novellae to the most difficult tractates of the *Talmud*, and wrote responsa that commanded the highest respect in the rabbinic world, deals at length in one of his responsa with the following question: What is the law with regard to a married woman who has had sexual intercourse with a demon who at first appeared to her in the form of her own husband and the second time in the guise of a Polish nobleman?

Although Rabbi Meir of Lublin and other scholars, notably Joel Sirkes (1561–1640), opposed the *Shulḥan Aruch* and sought to prevent it from becoming the definitive rabbinic code, their efforts were unsuccessful. The authority of Joseph Karo's work, combined with the supplement of Moses Isserles, continued to grow in Polish Jewry, and it soon became the standard code consulted by rabbis, judges, and communal leaders. The *Shulḥan Aruch* was studied no less assiduously than the *Talmud* itself, and some of the foremost rabbis of the first half of the seventeenth century made their reputations with their commentaries to it. Joshua Falk Ha-Kohen (1550–1614), who presided over the Council of Four Lands after Mordecai Jaffe, is famed in rabbinic literature as "the Sema," the first letters of his commentary to the *Shulḥan Aruch* (reprinted in almost all subsequent editions of that work) entitled *Sefer Meirat Einayim* (*The Book of the Enlightenment of the Eyes*). David ben Samuel Ha-Levi (ca. 1586–1667), Sirkes' pupil and son-in-law, is frequently referred to as "the Taz," from the initial letters of his commentary *Turei Zahav* (*Rows of Gold*). And Shabbetai ben Meir Ha-Kohen (1621–1662), the most brilliant of seventeenth-century Polish rabbinic scholars, is known as "the Shach," from the title *Siftei Kohen* (*The Lips of the Priest*) that he gave to his great commentary, completed when he was only twenty-four years old, to *Yoreh Deah*, the ritual part of the *Shulḥan Aruch*.

It must not be supposed, however, that *halachah* or law exhausted the spiritual concerns of the sixteenth- and seventeenth-century Polish rabbis or Polish Jewry at large. We have already referred to Moses Isserles' mystical bent and his intense interest in Kabbalah. In these he was followed by a great many of his rabbinic contemporaries and successors and by a large segment of the Jewish masses. The mystical tendencies so widespread at that time in Poland, and indeed throughout the Jewish world, find their finest and fullest expression in the work of Isaiah ben Abraham Ha-Levi Horowitz (ca. 1565–1630), known universally as Ha-Shelah Ha-Kadosh, "the holy Shelah," from the initials of his great work *Shenei Luḥot Ha-Berit* (*The Two Tablets of the Covenant*).

Isaiah Horowitz was born in Prague but moved as a youth to Poland, where Rabbi Meir of Lublin and Joshua Falk were among his teachers. Later he served as a rabbi in several Polish cities as well as in his birthplace and in the ancient community of Frankfurt-am-Main. In 1621 Horowitz settled in Jerusalem, becoming the rabbi of its Ashkenazic community. Here his lifelong mystical interests were intensified by study of the manuscript writings of the great Kabbalists who had lived and worked in Safed a generation or two earlier. Kabbalah, he was convinced, was the doctrine of "the sages of truth who entered the secret of the Lord received in unbroken oral tradition from Moses at Sinai." Unlike some other Kabbalists of his day, who restricted their teaching to small circles of initiates, Horowitz believed that the time had come to reveal publicly the mysteries of the *Zohar*, for his was the "final generation" that would see the "end," the messianic redemption eagerly awaited everywhere in the Jewish world.

In his *Shenei Luḥot Ha-Berit*, begun in Prague but completed in Palestine in 1623 and published in Amsterdam after his death, Horowitz, who was an outstanding halachist and pilpulist (he seems to have regretted the latter role, writing "I spent most of my life devising ingenious and marvelous *ḥillukim* [subtle distinctions]; I have sinned, I have committed iniquity, I have transgressed; I come therefore to admonish future generations, that thereby my deliberate sins may be changed into merits" [7]), combined Kabbalah with *halachah* and didactic preaching in order to teach his readers how to live a truly moral and God-fearing life. He summarizes the traditional six hundred and thirteen commandments of the Torah and gives Kabbalist reasons for them, declaring that each symbolizes a holy mystery that "no mortal can fathom, even if he were to live a thousand years." The Torah, for him, is a continuous revelation, "a flowing fountain that never ceases" and whose precepts prevent uncleanness. Observance of the commandments serves not only human but divine purposes. "For into man's hands are actually given . . . the inner

. . . and outer keys; and not merely to open a way for himself does he go forth but for the needs of the Most High, to profess the unity of the Great Name." Man's deeds, Horowitz follows the *Zohar* in teaching, influence the "supernal worlds," for he is stamped with the seal of God, and it is this seal that binds him to divinity "as with a hanging chain whose last links dragging on earth influence the links that are on high."

The author of *Shenei Luḥot Ha-Berit* deals with the problem of evil along the lines of the Lurianic Kabbalah. Primordially everything was good, and the universe was filled with divine light. Evil existed only as a potentiality, but Adam, through allowing himself to be tempted by the serpent, converted it into a reality; the divine light was obscured, spirit was transformed into *kelippah* or material shell, and good was mingled with evil. The primal harmony, however, may be restored. Through a life dedicated to hallowing all things, the Jew can help bring about the time when the reign of "all good and all light" will once again prevail. This is his mission: to sanctify everything around himself, to illuminate the earthly and material with the divine light. "My children," Isaiah Horowitz teaches, "think always, day and night, of increasing holiness and nearness to God." He regards the Jewish people—"this little lamb among wolves, exposed to the sword, hunger, enslavement, and shame"— as unique and as standing necessarily, by reason of its inner holiness, in opposition to the other peoples of the world.

Isaiah Horowitz's book was published just after Polish Jewry was stricken by the fury of the Cossack uprisings. To grieving souls mourning the tens of thousands of dead and mutilated, *Shenei Luḥot Ha-Berit*, which speaks movingly of suffering and martyrdom and of their redemptive consequences, brought a desperately needed message of consolation, and its somber and ascetic tone was well suited to the chastened mood that dominated Polish-Jewish life after the middle of the seventeenth century. Not only in the era that experienced the massacres but for many generations afterward the "holy Shelah" was deeply revered and his book widely read by Jews throughout eastern Europe.

❧⟡☙

The catastrophe of 1648 came upon the Jews of Poland unexpectedly, catching them totally unprepared. To be sure, for a long time they had been the objects of intense hatred by the Polish Catholic clergy, who regarded them as collaborators and instigators of the Protestant reformers and anti-Trinitarians. Numerous accusations of ritual murder and desecration of the Host were lodged against them in the sixteenth and first half of the seventeenth centuries, and scores of Jews were killed and tortured as a result of these charges, despite repeated papal pronouncements condemning them as utterly groundless. Anti-Jewish agitation by the Jesuits, who obtained dominance in Polish Catholicism during the Counter Reformation, led to frequent riots and massacres in Vilna, Posen, Cracow, Lublin, and elsewhere. But the terror of 1648 came from a different direction and was unanticipated. In the spring of that year the Cossacks of the Ukraine, who professed the Greek Orthodox faith, rose under the leadership of their new *hetman* Bogdan Chmielnitzki against their Polish rulers. This was a popular rebellion directed primarily against the gentry of Poland, who had ruthlessly oppressed the Cossack peasants politically, economically, and religiously. The Jews, in the view of the Cossacks, were deeply implicated in this oppression. They were the stewards and administrators of the Polish nobles' estates which the exploited peasants farmed, and the lessees of their mills, fisheries, mines, timber forests, and inns. They were the tax-collectors who exacted payment of the heavy tolls imposed by the Polish lords. Furthermore, their religion was even more hateful to the Cossacks than the Roman Catholicism of the Poles.

It was inevitable that the Cossacks should have detested the Jews as much as and even more than the Poles, and that they should have directed their bitterest rage against them. Immediately after the defeat of the main Polish army by Chmielnitzki near the Korsun River in May 1648, the serfs throughout the Ukraine rose in murderous fury against the Polish nobility and their Jewish agents. The atrocities that followed were virtually unprecedented in the annals of man's cruelty to his kind. The major Jewish chroniclers of that age— Nathan Hannover in his *Yeven Metzulah*, Shabbetai ben Meir Ha-Kohen in his *Megillat Efah*, Abraham ben Samuel Ashkenazi in his *Tzaar Bat Rabbim*—relate these in heart-rending descriptions. The throats of infants and children were slit before the eyes of their horrified mothers. The bellies of pregnant women were ripped open and then sewed up again after live cats had been inserted in them. Girls and women were brutally raped in the sight of their helpless fathers and husbands. Thousands of Jews were massacred in the region east of the Dnieper in towns like Pereiaslav, Piriatin, Lokhvitza, and Lubny; only a few who accepted the Greek Orthodox religion managed to save their lives. Many Jews who lived on estates in the open countryside fled to cities with fortified walls, such as Ostrog, Nemirov, and Tulchin, in the hope of finding safety there. The hope was illusory; most of them were slaughtered, in some cases betrayed to the Cossacks by the duplicity of the Polish residents. The "sanctification of the name," or martyrdom, of which Isaiah Horowitz had spoken so movingly in his *Shenei Luḥot Ha-Berit* became a daily occurrence.

Nathan Hannover describes the destruction of the Jews in Tulchin after that city was besieged by the Cossacks. The Polish *szlachta*, or nobility, there conspired to hand over their courageous Jewish fellow-battlers to the enemy in order to save themselves. The Jews, who learned of the conspiracy, wished to attack the Poles. "Then," Hannover relates, "the rector of the *yeshivah*, Rabbi Aaron ben Meir, arose and cried out, 'Hear me, my brethren! We are in exile among foreign peoples. If you fall upon the *szlachta*, other cities will quickly learn of it, and they will—God forbid—avenge themselves on our brethren there. If this be a decree of Heaven, we must accept it in love and trust in God's mercy. How are we better than our brethren?' " [8] After the Cossacks took away all the possessions of the Jews, they locked them up in a large garden. The three rabbis who were there admonished the people to prepare themselves to die as martyrs for their faith, and all responded "Hear, O Israel, the Lord our God, the Lord is One!" For three days the Jews were locked up; then a Cossack herald came with a banner in his hand, fixed its staff in the ground, and called out, "Whoever accepts the Christian faith will remain alive!" Not a single Jew responded. Three times the herald made his proclamation, and all were silent. The Cossacks then broke in and slaughtered all fifteen hundred of the Jews. Afterward, contemptuous of the treachery and cowardice of the Poles, they proceeded to murder them as well.

The massacres of 1648–1649 inaugurated a long era of travail for Polish Jewry. In 1654 the czar of Russia, to whom Chmielnitzki had transferred his allegiance, invaded the eastern regions of Poland. As the cities of White Russia and Lithuania surrendered to his armies, their Jews were either driven out or killed. Among the eminent scholars who fled into exile were Moses Rivkes, who settled in Amsterdam and there published his *Be'er Ha-Golah* (*The Well of Exile*) on the sources of Karo's *Shulḥan Aruch* and Isserles' *Ha-Mappah*; Shabbetai ben Meir Ha-Kohen, the author of *Siftei Kohen* and *Megillat Efah*, who became a rabbi in Moravia; and Samuel Aaron Koidanover, who later served as rabbi in Fürth, Nikolsburg, and Frankfurt-am-Main. At the same time the armies of Sweden under Charles X invaded Poland from the west and brought devastation and misery to the Jews, for the Poles suspected the Jews of pro-Swedish sympathies and massacred many of them after reconquering territory that had been taken by the Swedes. It is estimated that at least a hundred thousand Jews perished in Poland in the turmoils of the decade from 1648 to 1658. Thousands of others were taken captive by the Cossacks and their Tartar allies, and dazed and destitute Jewish refugees roamed the highways of Europe. Even when the wars ended, the sufferings of the Jews of Poland continued. Many had been reduced to penury and were never able to reestablish themselves. The burden of taxation increased progressively, and before long many communities found themselves on the verge of bankruptcy. Furthermore, blood libels and local disturbances became ever more frequent.

For four centuries—from the era of the First Crusade to the aftermath of the expulsion from Spain—the movement of Jewish migration had been eastward, from France, Germany, and Spain to Poland and Turkey. In the wake of the Chmielnitzki massacres and the terrors of 1648–1658, the direction was reversed. Jewish refugees from Poland and Lithuania, for whom these lands had become one huge cemetery or who could no longer hope to earn a living on their ravaged soil, began to stream into Hungary, Austria, Germany, the Netherlands, Italy, and even England. The new Jewish communities in the great mercantile centers of northwestern Europe which Marranos fleeing from Spain and Portugal had established at the end of the sixteenth and the beginning of the seventeenth centuries proved a godsend. The Sephardic pioneers were quickly followed by Jews from Germany, and these, in turn, by Polish Jews who, in a few generations, outnumbered the others. For almost three hundred years the westward migration was to continue—at times a trickle, at times a flood—until the Jewish population of Europe was completely redistributed both in that continent and in America.

Despite the drain of emigration, the high birth rate among Polish Jewry maintained and even increased its numerical strength in the century after the Chmielnitzki massacres. But much of the dynamism of its life and institutions had disappeared, replaced by a crippling rigidity and inertia. Furthermore, tensions within the Jewish communities which had remained largely underground in the expanding economy and optimistic climate of pre-Chmielnitzki Poland now erupted into the open, frequently bringing conflict and rebellion. The Kahals, faced with the necessity of paying the growing debts they incurred to buy off threatening attacks and blood libels, which multiplied greatly in this era, had to continue raising taxes. At the same time the oligarchic structure of the Kahals and the domineering posture of the larger communities toward the smaller irritated the masses of the Jewish populace and magnified their natural resentment of the rich and powerful. Even before the Cossack risings, the popular preacher Ephraim Solomon ben Aaron of Luntschitz (1550–1619) had, in his eloquent sermons before the Council of Four Lands, denounced the oppression of the poor by the wealthy and the learned, and castigated the latter's arrogance and hypocrisy.

Among the Torah students of our generation humility is nowhere to be found. On the contrary, nowhere in the world are there men so proud and arrogant as they. He who knows anything at all of the Torah thinks that there is no one like him, and let him only imagine that you have somehow impugned his puffed-up honor, he will thereupon consider nothing but avenge himself more than the primordial serpent. Each of these sages of the generation believes himself greater than the whole world and refuses to recognize another. Each insults the other, speaks every possible evil of him, endeavors to show that he is an ignoramus, a base man who understands and knows nothing.[9]

Ephraim repeatedly assailed the rich for their avarice and love of luxury, and for their failure to aid the needy and impoverished among their brethren. Wealth, he insisted, corrupts the characters of men who regard it only as an instrument of power and self-aggrandizement and do not understand its proper purpose.

Even more scathing is the denunciation of Tzevi Hirsch Koidanover (d. 1712), a Polish rabbi who, after achieving wealth and prominence in Vilna in the post-Chmielnitzki era, was imprisoned for four years on a false charge apparently brought by some leaders of the Kahal. Upon his release he moved to Frankfurt-am-Main, where in 1705 he published his *Kav Ha-Yashar*, a moralistic treatise in one hundred and two chapters which became extremely popular among the masses of east European Jewry. This work, besides reflecting the suffering and despair engendered by the Cossack massacres and later by the tragic denouement of the Shabbetai Tzevi movement, mirrors the economic struggle in the Polish Jewish communities and the frequent exploitation of the poor by the oligarchies that controlled the community councils. He writes:

Like the cloud which disperses and disappears, like the wind that is carried away and returns no more, so is the ruler and leader who does not conduct himself as befits a guide in Israel and does not take upon himself the burden of the children of Israel. He perishes and departs suddenly from the world, and no memory remains of his children. In this net many leaders are caught, on account of their arrogance and lordliness and the fact that they cast excessive fear upon the people—and this not for the sake of God's name. They enjoy all pleasures and delights and do not help the people with the taxes and imposts. They make the tax burden light for themselves and increase it as much as possible for others. When it comes to honor and glory, they take their share first. Their faces are always florid, fat, and healthy, for they indulge in all the pleasures their hearts desire. In other peoples' troubles they take no part; they are not moved by their sufferings. And God's assembly, the children of Abraham, Isaac, and Jacob are crushed and degraded. They go about naked and barefoot because of the taxes whereby the agents and servants of the community rob them. These agents and servants come into their homes cruelly, seize and plunder whatever they find and see to it that the owners are left naked and bare. They take away even their clothing, even their prayer-shawls, and sell these for paltry sums, so that nothing remains to them except the straw in their beds. In the season of cold and rain they shiver, and the householder and his wife and children each weep in a separate corner. But if the leaders helped pay the taxes, the burden would not be so great on the average householder and on the poor people. There is, however, an even greater sin: the leaders eat and drink from communal charity funds, and from these give dowries and wedding presents to their sons and daughters. And this money is always from the taxes that have been robbed and from the labor of the hands of Jews. Before each such *parnass* and leader a proclamation goes forth and exclaims: "This is he who eats the flesh and blood of the holy people of Israel! He robs poor people, orphans, and widows!" And the proclamation curses him with many curses, and his prayer is not heard. May God, blessed be He, preserve us from this punishment.[10]

The Chmielnitzki massacres and their melancholy aftermath not only brought into the open and intensified the latent conflict between the rich and the poor, the leaders and the masses, in the Jewish community; it also dealt a terrible blow to Jewish learning in Poland. Many of the *yeshivot* were wrecked, their students and teachers killed or scattered to the winds. Rabbi Moses ben Eliezer Ha-Kohen (Katz) of Narol, who managed to escape when the Cossack marauders de-

stroyed his community, reflects the despair that gripped Polish rabbinic circles in an elegy he composed at that time:

O delicate Poland, thou chosen in Torah and knowledge, there has been
none like thee since the people went into exile. Now thou art wasted and
homeless, forgotten and forsaken. There all the shepherds of the people
were accustomed to assemble, there the foundations of the faith were wont
to be established, there the laws and statutes for the entire people used to
be studied. To whom shall I now liken thee, O land of Poland? Where are
the *yeshivot* with their scholars? Who will now explain the laws, who will
reveal the mysteries of the Torah, who will conduct us over the depths of
the wisdom of the *Talmud?* The house of Jacob has become ashes, God's holy
ark had been taken away from us. . . .[11]

In time the *yeshivot* were rebuilt and rabbinic learning flourished
once more in Poland. Scholars again pored day and night over the
Talmud and halachic codes and wrote supercommentary upon commentary. But whatever breath of free inquiry and philosophical rationalism had been fitfully drawn in the intellectual life of the Jewish
community in pre-Chmielnitzki Poland was now extinguished. The
arid scholasticism and *pilpul* that reigned unrestrictedly in the Talmudic academies could not satisfy ardent souls longing for the vivifying experience of religious enthusiasm; so the people turned more
and more to Kabbalah for fulfillment of their religious needs. Isaiah
Horowitz's *Shenei Luḥot Ha-Berit* became one of the most popular
books of the generation. Jews throughout the land determined to
remove themselves from the sinful world, lead an ascetic life, and
mortify their flesh with fasting and flagellation, in order to triumph
over the power of the *kelippot* (shells) and hasten the "end," the messianic redemption.

The terrors of the Cossack rising had brought mystical-messianic
expectations to a hysterical pitch. Witnessing the atrocities committed by Chmielnitzki's hordes, many Jews could make sense of them,
and retain their sanity, only by interpreting them as the *ḥevlei ha-
mashiaḥ*, the agonies which, according to tradition, must accompany
the advent of the Messiah. Mystical calculations yielded the discovery that *ḥevlei ha-mashiaḥ* is equivalent in *gematria* to the Hebrew letters for 1648, and that the name of the Cossack leader, Chmil, is the
notrikon for *ḥevlei mashiaḥ yavou le-olam*, "the agonies of the Messiah
will come to the world." Hence it is not surprising that when the
proclamation of the Kabbalist of Smyrna, "I, your Messiah, Shabbe-

tai Tzevi!" resounded throughout the Diaspora, Polish Jewry responded with boundless faith and untrammeled excitement. The response came with the greatest speed and intensity in the provinces bordering on Turkey. According to Galatovski, the Ukrainian writer of that era:

> The Jews triumphed. Some abandoned their houses and property, refusing to do any work and claiming that the Messiah would soon arrive and carry them on a cloud to Jerusalem. Others fasted for days, denying food even to their little ones, and during that severe winter bathed in ice-holes, at the same time reciting a recently-composed prayer. Faint-hearted and destitute Christians, hearing the stories of the miracles performed by the false Messiah and beholding the boundless arrogance of the Jews, began to doubt Christ.[12]

From the south the messianic hysteria spread with lightning rapidity throughout the Polish kingdom, reaching even the distant cities of White Russia. A contemporary monastic chronicler reports that mysterious inscriptions proclaiming the Jewish Messiah "Sapsai" appeared on the walls of churches in Moghilev.

Shabbetai's conversion threw most of his followers into confusion, but it did not altogether destroy the movement he had inaugurated. Secret Shabbatian societies continued to exist in Poland and elsewhere. Numerous mystics appeared in the electric atmosphere of that age, summoning Jews to fasting and repentance and proclaiming that the redemption was at hand. Judah Ḥasid (1660?–1700) of Shedletz, a Shabbatian preacher who wandered from city to city and spoke of the coming redeemer in the synagogues and studyhouses with a Torah scroll in his hands, made a particularly powerful impression. Adherents to the order of Ḥasidim (the pious) which he established, who wished to hasten the "end" through fasting and mortification of the flesh, constantly increased. In the year 1700 a host of thirteen hundred Jews, dressed in white shrouds as a symbol of penitence, set out, under the leadership of Judah Ḥasid, for Palestine, convinced that there they would welcome the Messiah. After some five hundred of the travelers had died en route, Judah and his followers, recruited from Shabbatian circles in Poland, Austria, Germany, and Italy, arrived in Jerusalem on October 14, 1700. There Judah suddenly died a few days later. His dejected Ḥasidim split into factions. Some remained in Jerusalem, while others returned to Europe and joined Shabbatian societies in Poland and Germany.

Still others, in despair over the disappointment of their messianic hopes, converted to Islam or Christianity.

The debacle of the Shabbetai Tzevi movement and its unfortunate aftermath led, in western and central Europe, to a progressive decline in the attractiveness of Kabbalah and mysticism in general as the eighteenth century wore on. This development was furthered by the rationalist spirit of the Enlightenment, which began, in the second half of the century, to penetrate the Jewries of these sections of the continent. However, this was not so among the Jews of eastern Europe. There Enlightenment tendencies were strongly resisted, and Kabbalah retained its powerful hold, giving rise, as we shall see, to the mass movement of Ḥasidism. Both the continuing appeal of Kabbalah and the resistance to rationalism and modernism are exemplified in the life and work of the most brilliant and significant figure in eighteenth-century east European Jewry—Rabbi Elijah ben Solomon Zalman (1720–1797), known universally as Elijah Gaon or the Gaon of Vilna.

Born into a family with a rich scholarly tradition, Elijah became renowned as an *ilui*, or child prodigy. Although he studied briefly with some eminent rabbis of his day, he acquired most of his immense learning on his own and was thus saved from the fruitless *pilpul* that so entranced most of his contemporaries. As a youth Elijah studied not only the Bible and the *Talmud* but Kabbalist literature as well; indeed, even before he was *bar mitzvah* he experimented with *Kabbalah Maasit* (practical Kabbalah) and, by his own admission, once sought to create a *golem*. Such mystical interests, however, did not prevent him from acquiring a substantial knowledge of astronomy, mathematics, and geography from medieval Hebrew sources. Shortly after his marriage Elijah undertook a long journey through Poland and Germany, visiting some of the major communities, including Berlin. Later hagiographical accounts of his life were to recount how the young Polish Talmudist astonished learned professors in the Prussian capital with his profound knowledge of the sciences. Returning from his journey, Elijah settled with his wife in Vilna, where he remained for the rest of his life, rarely leaving his house and engrossed in ceaseless study. It is reported that, to avoid distraction, the shutters of his windows were never opened and he read always by candlelight. Only on the eve of the Sabbath and festivals would he interrupt his studies briefly to join his wife and children. According to his sons, Elijah never slept more than two hours a day. Not until he was forty did he modify this hermitlike regimen somewhat and begin to give lectures to a chosen group of distinguished scholars who gathered in his house and recorded his comments and explanations of difficult passages in the *Talmud*.

Elijah repeatedly refused to accept rabbinic office in Vilna; involvement in communal affairs, he felt, would keep him away from his studies. But the Kahal, throughout much of the period of his residence in the Lithuanian city, provided him with housing and a weekly stipend, so pleased were they at having in their midst the great scholar whose fame increased from year to year. The major exception to Elijah's general policy of noninvolvement in community matters was his participation in the battle against the Ḥasidim. He was convinced that the new sect was a menace and several times authorized excommunication of its members. When two of the outstanding leaders of Ḥasidism, Menaḥem Mendel of Vitebsk and Shneour Zalman of Liadi, sought an audience with the Gaon in an attempt to persuade him that the new movement was in no way a threat to traditional Judaism, he sternly refused to see them on the grounds that the Torah forbids holding converse with heretics. In 1796, a year before his death, when the Ḥasidim circulated a rumor that Elijah had come to regret his twenty-five years of implacable hostility to Ḥasidism, the aged Gaon dispatched a letter by special emissaries to the communities of Lithuania and White Russia in which he wrote: "I will continue to stand on guard, and it is the duty of every believing Jew to repudiate and pursue them [the Ḥasidim] with all manner of afflictions and overcome them, for they have sin in their hearts and are like a sore on the body of Israel."

The range of Elijah's interests was remarkably extensive. Naturally he was concerned with the Bible, the *Talmud*, the *midrashim*, and halachic literature, but he also had a lively interest in mathematics, astronomy, and medicine—insofar as these subjects impinged on Judaism and might contribute to a better understanding of the Torah. When the physician Baruch of Shklov translated Euclid's *Elements* into Hebrew, the Gaon wrote in approbation of the project, "To the degree that a man is deficient in knowledge and the secular sciences he will be deficient a hundredfold in the wisdom of the Torah," and strongly encouraged the translation of similar works. According to another statement, he deplored the total neglect of the secular sciences by most of the Talmudic scholars of his day as resulting in mockery of the Jews among the nations, "who, like the roaring of many waters, will raise their voices against us, saying, 'Where is your wisdom?' and the name of God will be profaned." But Elijah did not share the critical spirit or the secularizing and modernizing tendencies of the German Haskalah, which in his last years was beginning to attract a few adherents in east European Jewry. Indeed, it is recorded that he imposed a severe punishment on the luckless preacher and battler for enlightenment Abba of Glusk, made famous by the German writer Adelbert von Chamisso in a poem describing his tragic fate, when Abba permitted himself some mildly critical comments about Rashi's interpretation of Scripture.

The *maskilim*, or enlighteners, whom the Gaon knew were all firmly rooted in the soil of traditional Judaism, and he could therefore only commend their activities. There is no doubt, however, that he would have thoroughly condemned Haskalah if he had recognized its essential trends and the direction in which it was moving. For if there was a central element in the Gaon's world outlook, it was his conviction regarding the all-embracing scope, utter sanctity, and total eternity of the Torah. "Everything that was, is, and will be," he wrote, "is included in the Torah. And not only principles, but even the details of each species, the minutest details of each species, the minutest details of every human being, as well as of every creature, plant, and mineral—all are included in the Torah." For the Gaon the Torah and its commandments were the ultimate value, the goal and purpose of the world and of human existence. The ascetic scholar is reported to have said that dying was a matter of regret to him only because he would no longer be able to observe any of the commandments. When he lay on his deathbed during the festival of Sukkot he would not let the palm branch and citron out of his rigid hands, and breathed his last holding on to them.

Although he was relentlessly opposed to Ḥasidism, the Gaon of Vilna regarded the *Zohar* as well as other early Kabbalist works, such as the *Sefer Yetzirah* and *Sefer Ha-Bahir* (on all of which he wrote commentaries), as holy and an essential part of the Torah. To be sure, his interest in Kabbalah in the latter part of his life was chiefly intellectual and directed to establishing the correct reading of the texts. His central aim was so to expound the Kabbalist sources as to remove any contradiction between them and the rabbinic writings, since he sincerely believed that such inconsistencies could only be the result of misinterpretation of either or both. But while he explained the Kabbalist literature through the same methodology that he applied to the Talmudic, and in both cases sought to arrive at an understanding of the texts in their ordinary signification, his pupils reported that in his literal interpretations the deeper esoteric meanings were clearly implicit. It was also primarily his reverence for Kabbalah that led Elijah Gaon to regard philosophy as an "accursed" thing, and to condemn study of it. He criticized Moses Isserles for his philosophical interests and opinions, and launched an especially vehement attack on Maimonides because the latter had denied the efficacy of incantations containing divine "names" and of amulets and charms.

Elijah Gaon lived at the end of an old era and the beginning of a new one in the spiritual life of east European Jewry. In his interest in secular sciences he was the harbinger of the Haskalah movement that was soon to irrupt into eastern Europe from its birthplace in Germany. In his Talmudic scholarship and uncompromising commitment to the minutest punctilio of rabbinic *halachah* he was the heir of the centuries of intense learning and piety that preceded him. He died shortly before the end of the eighteenth century, but the typically "Litvak" or Lithuanian-Jewish union of rigorous scholarship, critical mentality, and religious orthodoxy to whose fashioning he contributed so importantly reached its consummate expression in the great *yeshivot* of Volozhin and Mir in the nineteenth century. Indeed, it continued to exert a powerful influence on Lithuanian-Jewish life well into the twentieth century, and still survives in the remnants of this life that have managed to reestablish themselves in America, Israel, and elsewhere.

CHAPTER

❦ VI ❧

Two Melancholy
Centuries

AT THE END of the fifteenth century western and central Europe stood on the threshold of a great new era. The world across the Atlantic had just been discovered, and tremendous social and economic energies were soon to be released in its colonization and settlement. The spiritual and intellectual thralldom in which the Catholic Church and its scholastic philosophy had held men for centuries was weakening perceptibly. Within a few years the Protestant Reformation would erupt, eventually bringing in its train a somewhat greater measure of religious freedom for the individual who wished it. New philosophies would appear and scientific discoveries be made that would help remove the blinders scholasticism had placed on men's eyes and direct them to a world far vaster than they had imagined before. The spirit of the Renaissance would spread from Italy to other parts of the continent, diminishing the ascetic, otherworldly mood of the Middle Ages and bringing a renewed sense of joy in life and of the value and dignity of the individual personality. With the development of nation-states in Europe great national poets and dramatists would arise to create masterpieces that would not only refine the language and literary taste of their countrymen, but enlarge their vision of the world and the possibilities of the human spirit. To be sure, religious and territorial wars were to plague Europe in the sixteenth and seventeenth centuries and inflict untold misery on its population, but, on the whole, these centuries were to be an era of great progress and high achievement.

Not so for the Jews. The fifteenth century ended with a massive tragedy—the expulsions from Spain and Portugal and destruction of some of the most cultured and creative Jewish communities in history. For the Jews of western and central Europe the next two centuries were to be largely a period not of achievement and progress but of stagnation and regress. With few exceptions, there was to be no advancement in Jewish religious or philosophic thought; in fact, the mental horizons of the Jew were to become more restricted. It is true that in Italy, as we have observed, Jews continued their long tradition of interaction with the larger world into the sixteenth century and beyond, and Italian Jewry, under the residual rays of the Renaissance, produced some of its finest literary and scholarly monuments; but in the second half of the sixteenth century the reactionary spirit of the Counter Reformation, with its persecutions and imposition of the ghetto throughout Italy, placed a damper on further creativity. It is also true that the Talmudic scholarship of Polish Jewry attained its peak in the sixteenth and first half of the seventeenth centuries, but that elevation was to be maintained only for a relatively short time; we have noted its rapid decline in the aftermath of the Chmielnitzki massacres of the mid-seventeenth century. Elsewhere in Europe Jews had either been driven out of the countries where their ancestors had lived for generations (such was the case not only in Spain and Portugal but in France and England as well) or else, as in the German states, were allowed only a precarious existence, largely cut off from the cultural influences of the larger world through ghettoization, reduced to the most degrading forms of earning a livelihood, and constantly threatened with expulsion or—worse—violence and slaughter at the hands of an incited mob.

The fact is that, in the sixteenth century, the center of gravity of Jewish life was once again in the East, in the Ottoman Empire. When the rulers of Spain and Portugal ruthlessly expelled their Jews, and the mobs and princelings of Germany hounded theirs, the sultans of Turkey welcomed Jews and provided a refuge for them.

As early as the close of the fourteenth century many Jews fleeing from massacres and persecutions in Spain had found new homes in the Moslem lands of North Africa. Some outstanding Spanish rabbis arrived and quickly established their religious authority. After the

expulsion of 1492, the numbers of refugees from the Iberian peninsula settling in the Levant increased greatly. All along the Mediterranean littoral there emerged Spanish-Jewish communities whose
members continued to cling tenaciously for centuries to their Ladino
tongue and the religious traditions and customs they had practiced in
their old home. Although subject to certain discriminatory restrictions by their Moslem rulers and often compelled to live in a special
quarter called the *mellah*, these Jews found life here much more toler-
able than in Christian Europe.

The largest number of Spanish exiles established themselves in the
central provinces of the Ottoman Empire, whose government
strongly encouraged their immigration. "Do you call this Ferdinand
wise—he who impoverishes his own lands to enrich mine?" Sultan
Bajazet is reported to have asked. The Spanish refugees were soon
joined by others from Portugal, as well as from Italy, Provence, and
Germany. Substantial Jewish communities developed within a few
decades in Constantinople, Salonika, Adrianople, Nicopolis, Brusa,
Smyrna, and elsewhere in the Ottoman Empire; indeed, in the sixteenth century the virtually all-Jewish city of Salonika and the capital of the empire, Constantinople, had the largest Jewish communities in all of Europe. The religious and cultural life of the ancient
Jewish settlements that had existed for centuries in the Byzantine
Empire was revitalized by the large influx of Jews from Europe arriving at the encouragement of the Ottomans, who built their powerful state on the ruins of Byzantium and realized that its economic development could be aided greatly by Jewish artisans and merchants.
The Karaites particularly, who had long since lapsed into intellectual
slumber, were awakened to new creativity by their contacts with
Jews of the rabbinic tradition. In fifteenth- and sixteenth-century
Constantinople and elsewhere in the Ottoman Empire, Karaite-
Rabbanite relationships were, with some exceptions, remarkably
amicable.

No Jew attained greater wealth and power in the Turkish Empire
than Joseph Nasi (ca. 1520–1579), a descendant of a Spanish family
that had fled to Portugal at the time of the expulsion and became
Marranos. Active in the immensely successful international banking
business built up by his uncle, Joseph came with his aunt, the celebrated Gracia Nasi (ca. 1510–1569), and their families to Constantinople, where they publicly reverted to Judaism. While Gracia Nasi
devoted herself to countless philanthropic and rescue enterprises in
support of her coreligionists and became the most admired Jewish

woman of the age, Joseph aided them through the vast influence which he commanded at the court of the sultan. For a time one of the most powerful figures at the Sublime Porte, which created him Duke of Naxos and the Cyclades in recognition of his services to the state, he frequently exercised his position to protect Jews and Jewish interests both in Turkey and abroad. Joseph Nasi, it appears, also envisioned the possibility of creating a semiautonomous Jewish territory in Palestine. After being granted by the sultan seignioral rights over the ancient but long-ruined city of Tiberias and a sizable area in its vicinity, he proceeded to rebuild and fortify the city, provide an economic basis for its future by developing a textile and silk industry, and arrange for its colonization by Italian-Jewish immigrants. Unfortunately the experiment did not succeed, but it did serve as an inspiration for later and more successful efforts in the nineteenth and twentieth centuries.

Despite the failure of Joseph Nasi's attempt to develop Tiberias on a sound economic footing, a great upsurge of Jewish life took place in Palestine in the sixteenth century. The groundwork for this upsurge was laid in the closing decade of the preceding century with the arrival in Palestine, then a Mameluke province, of the Italian Talmudist Obadiah di Bertinoro (ca. 1450–ca. 1510), author of a classic commentary on the *Mishnah*. Having come in 1488 to Jerusalem, like thousands of pious Jews before and after him, to spend his last years there, Obadiah found a disorganized and demoralized Jewish community. The Mameluke officials and tax-collectors were rapacious and dishonest, and their Jewish agents no less so. In a long letter to his father in Italy which has survived, he describes how the "wicked elders" of Jerusalem oppressed the Jewish refugees from Germany, placing intolerable tax burdens on them, and sold the hospitals, the synagogue furnishings, the crowns and ornaments of the Torah scrolls, and the scrolls themselves to please their overlords and fulfill their avaricious demands. Obadiah's moral authority, fine scholarship, and eloquent oratory quickly brought him recognition as the spiritual leader of the Jews of Jerusalem; he employed his position to reorganize the community, create new charitable and philanthropic agencies, improve relations with the Moslems, and raise the religious and educational level by establishing a *yeshivah*. The Italian rabbi was highly regarded by both Jews and Moslems, and his writ ran not only in Jerusalem but throughout the land.

Large-scale immigration to Palestine began after its conquest from the Mamelukes in 1517 by the sultan Selim I, who also annexed Syria and Egypt and was acclaimed by many Jews of the Turkish Empire and Europe as the "scion of Cyrus." Under his tolerant rule considerable numbers of the exiles from Spain and Portugal, as well as refugees from other countries of Europe, decided to settle in the ancient land sanctified by memory and hope. Within a relatively brief period large communities of Jews were to be found in Jerusalem and Safed, and smaller ones in Tiberias and Hebron—the four "holy cities" of Palestine. Of the immigrants, many of whom were ardent pietists and mystics, some earned a living through artisanry and trade, but most wished to devote all their time to study of Torah and prayer. They depended for material support on the generosity of Jews in the Diaspora who could not themselves fulfill their desire to live and die in the Holy Land, but felt they might share vicariously in the privileges attendant thereon by contributing to the maintenance of its students and scholars and their *yeshivot*. For generations emissaries of the Palestinian communities, some of them deeply learned in the law, traversed the highways and sealanes of the world, going as far as India, the Caribbean islands, and North America, to collect offerings that were gladly given. Concerning these, a modern historian justly notes that "they constituted over many centuries an important element in the life of the Jewish people, bringing the latest currents of thought and scholarship into the most remote communities, keeping alive the memory of the Holy Land, and maintaining personal contact between the far-flung offshoots of the Jewish world." [1]

Throughout the sixteenth century the Jewish population of Palestine continued to increase. At the end of that century Safed alone, according to the report of a contemporary traveler, boasted more than three hundred rabbis, twenty-one synagogues, and eighteen *yeshivot*. Stimulated by this remarkable growth in numbers and the presence of such large numbers of Talmudic scholars in his immediate vicinity, one of the leading rabbis of Safed, Jacob Berav (1474–1546), who was born in Spain and later served as rabbi in Fez in Morocco, undertook in 1538 what proved to be an abortive effort to revive rabbinic ordination (*semichah*). Official ordination to the rabbinate had lapsed with the abolition of the Palestinian patriarchate in the fifth century. While scholars in the Middle Ages assumed the title of rabbi, and the conferring of the diploma attesting their competence in Talmudic law was still called *semichah*, this was a restricted form of ordination and bestowed only the power to teach and apply the inherited *halachah*, not to mold it as the Tannaim and Amoraim had done. It was understood, however, that, on the unanimous consent of all scholars living in Palestine, the earlier type of full ordination could be reinstituted. Jacob Berav apparently believed that such consent might be obtained, and that restoration of *semichah* would make it possible to reestablish the Sanhedrin, thereby uniting Jews everywhere in the world under a single religious authority that could legislate for its needs and would also hasten the advent of messianic redemption. He was mistaken, however, in believing that he could obtain unanimous agreement for his proposal. The chief rabbi of Jerusalem, Levi ibn Ḥaviv, and other scholars were adamantly opposed; after a bitter controversy, the proposal was abandoned. One can only speculate on how differently the subsequent course of Jewish law and religious life would have developed if Berav's plans had succeeded.

⋰⋱

It was in Safed, as we observed in Chapter II on the Kabbalah, that a great revival of Jewish mysticism took place in the sixteenth century. Near the city, at Meron, lay the grave of the saintly Tanna, Rabbi Simeon ben Yoḥai, reputed author of the *Zohar*, and to it were drawn mystics and ecstatics from all over the Jewish world. Messianic expectancy filled the air of Safed, and many of its residents fasted and mortified their flesh with penances to hasten the coming of the redeemer. Religious life was at a high peak of intensity in Safed, which quickly became the major center of mystical Judaism. There Moses Cordovero developed his great synthesis and philosophical interpretation of Kabbalist doctrine, and Isaac Luria initiated the new school of mystical-messianic theosophy which was to have such a melancholy result in the Shabbetai Tzevi movement of the seventeenth century.

One of the most fervent mystics of Safed was Joseph Karo (1488–1575), the great legist and author of what is still today the most widely consulted code of Jewish law and the authoritative guide of orthodox practice, the *Shulḥan Aruch* (*Prepared Table*). A small child at the time of the expulsion from Spain, he was taken by his father and first teacher, Ephraim, to Turkey. After living at Nicopolis, Salonika, and Adrianople, where he acquired renown as a foremost Talmudist and Kabbalist, Karo went to Palestine in 1536 and settled in Safed. He was soon recognized as a leading member of the local circle of scholars and mystics and assiduously pursued his researches into the *halachah*, at the same time serving as the principal of a large *yeshivah* and head of the community's *bet din*. Shortly after his arrival in Safed Karo became one of the four scholars ordained by Jacob Berav, and he joined the latter in his unsuccessful attempt to revive *semichah*. Equipped with a keen and brilliantly analytic legal mind, Karo was nevertheless convinced throughout his adult life that he was regularly visited and guided in his actions by a kind of heavenly mentor, whom he called his *maggid* and whom he conceived as the personified *Mishnah*, or the soul of the *Mishnah*. It appears that on occasion he would also fall into an ecstatic state during which the voice of his beloved *maggid* would issue from his lips, "singing of itself." The mystic and ecstatic in Karo, however, did not significantly influence the sober halachic authority pronouncing judgment on questions of Jewish law. Only a very small number of legal allusions are to be found in his *Maggid Mesharim* (*Messenger of Uprightness*), the mystical "diary" in which he recorded the visits and words of his mentor-angel. The latter spoke to him mainly of the supreme importance of living an ascetic life and of not desisting for a moment from his study of Torah. He also promised that Karo's fondest hopes would be fulfilled. These were that his legal works would be unspoiled by any error and become authoritative among all the Jews of the Diaspora; that he might be found worthy of settling in the Holy Land (apparently this ardent desire obsessed him for many years before he finally came to Safed); and that he might die a martyr's death at the stake, thereby sanctifying the name of God.

The last hope was not realized. But Karo did spend the last forty years of his life in the Holy Land, and his expectation that his books would ultimately obtain universal acceptance in the Jewish world was not disappointed. While still living in Adrianople as head of the local *yeshivah* he began a monumental work which was to occupy him for two decades. This was *Bet Yosef* (*House of Joseph*), the first edition of which appeared in four large folio volumes in 1555–1559. In form *Bet Yosef* is a commentary on Jacob ben Asher's *Arbaah Turim*, tracing each law back to its original sources in the *Talmud*, indicating how it was treated by various commentators and codifiers, presenting the arguments in support of conflicting interpretations, and bringing its development down to Karo's own day. This immense work, magnificently organized and systematized, won its author recognition in his own lifetime as the foremost halachist of the age. On the basis of *Bet Yosef*, Karo later wrote a shorter, practical code which he finished in 1555 and entitled *Shulḥan Aruch*. Intended, according to its author, for "young students" (*talmidim ketanim*), the *Shulḥan*

Aruch, which was first published in Venice in 1564–1565, was disseminated with amazing rapidity throughout the Diaspora and was soon universally acknowledged as the standard code of rabbinic law and practice, particularly after Moses Isserles in Poland, as we have noted (pp. 123–124), added to the "prepared table" his "tablecloth" (*Ha-Mappah*) containing the different legal decisions and religious customs of the Ashkenazic tradition.

Acceptance of the *Shulḥan Aruch* as the final halachic authority proved, in many respects, regrettable. It meant that the *halachah*, which had already lost much of its original plasticity, now became quite congealed. Every one of its decisions—trivial or weighty, illiberal or enlightened—became sacred and unalterable in the minds of the orthodox. Only one stereotyped pattern of Jewish religious life came to be regarded as legitimate; all divergences were branded by its defenders as rebellion not only against tradition but against God Himself. Furthermore, use of the *Shulḥan Aruch* as the authoritative code contributed significantly to the rapid decline of rabbinic scholarship in the late sixteenth and seventeenth centuries. Particularly in southern Europe and the Near East (much less so in Poland), study of the *Talmud* and *midrash*, as well as of the works of the great medieval commentators and codifiers, fell increasingly into desuetude. The perils of a mechanical conformity to a rigid pattern, unenlivened by the breath of moral fervor and intellectual questing, were realized in more than a few lives, even though the majority of Jews may have found faithful adherence to the precepts of the *Shulḥan Aruch* deeply satisfying. Sooner or later a reaction on the part of the disaffected was bound to come. It manifested itself in the Ḥasidic movement of the eighteenth century and the antitraditionalist movements of the nineteenth.

We have noted that one of Joseph Karo's strongest wishes was to die at the stake as a martyr. This wish was undoubtedly inspired in significant measure by his association with Solomon Molcho (ca. 1500–1532). The life of this Kabbalist, messianic dreamer, and enthusiast is emblematic of the mystical-messianic moods that played so large a role in sixteenth-century Judaism, and were to erupt with such explosive force in the seventeenth century. Born Diogo Pires of a Marrano family in Portugal, Molcho had begun a promising career as secretary in one of the high courts of justice in Lisbon when he was moved to return to Judaism, apparently by the appearance of David Reuveni. This colorful adventurer, on arriving in Rome in 1524, identified himself as the ambassador of his brother Joseph, king of the tribe of Reuben, on a mission to solicit the aid of the crowned heads of Europe in his war against the Moslems. Reuveni was received at the Vatican, where his story was accepted, and the Medici Pope Clement VII gave him letters of introduction to a number of princes and potentates. Coming to Portugal, the Jewish "ambassador" was again highly successful and aroused enormous excitement among the Marranos.

In this highly charged atmosphere the young Diogo Pires had himself circumcised and assumed the Jewish name Solomon Molcho. Embarking on a regimen of ascetic exercises, he began to have visions of a heavenly messenger who soon ordered him to leave Portugal for Turkey. He went to Salonika where he studied with, and made a profound impression on, the Kabbalist circle of Rabbi Joseph Taytazak, among whose members were Joseph Karo and the renowned mystic Solomon Alkabetz. At the end of 1529 Molcho appeared in the Italian city of Ancona, where his sermons on the advent of the Messiah created a sensation. Some time later he came to Rome and spent thirty days praying and fasting among the beggars who congregated before the papal palace, thus fulfilling some of the rabbinic legends about the conduct of the Messiah. Received by Clement VII, Molcho accurately predicted a flood that soon thereafter ravaged Rome (on October 8, 1530). The pope, deeply impressed by the young mystic who appears to have believed himself the forerunner of the Messiah, or Messiah ben Joseph, provided sanctuary for him in his palace and protected him from the Inquisition when its authorities decided to burn him as a heretic and renegade from Christianity.

Many Jews of Rome accepted Molcho's messianic pretensions, but the Jewish physician and communal leader Jacob Mantino denounced him vitriolically. Only when Molcho left the safety of the Vatican and decided to go with David Reuveni to Ratisbon in an attempt to persuade Emperor Charles V of the truth of their fantastic claims did he fall into the clutches of the Inquisition. He was burned as a renegade at Mantua in March 1532. It is reported that, when approaching the stake, he was offered pardon if he would recant, but replied that his highest wish was to become "a burnt-offering of sweet savour unto the Lord," and that his only regret was that he had been a Christian in his youth. Joseph Karo never forgot his early association with Molcho and throughout his life cherished the memory of his "chosen Solomon." Many other Jews followed him in veneration of the mystical dreamer who remained faithful to his visions and did not desecrate through apostasy the hopes of those who believed in him, as did Shabbetai Tzevi a century and a half later.

At the end of the sixteenth century the great age of Judaism in Turkey was virtually over. The Ottoman Empire, now frequently headed by incompetent and fanatical rulers, manifested clear symptoms of decline, and with it the position of the Jews began to deteriorate as well, although there were no intense or widespread persecutions. Jewish cultural life also declined, but not before producing the most gifted Hebrew poet since the golden era of Hebrew poetry in Moslem Spain. This was Israel Najara (1555?–1625?), a native of Damascus who served as rabbi in Gaza. Najara wrote hundreds of religious hymns whose melodious language and rich imagery gained them immense popularity in the Oriental countries. One of them, *Yah Ribbon Olam Ve-Alemaya* (*God of the World, Eternity's Sole Lord*), which is written in Aramaic, also became a favorite of the Ashkenazic Jews and is still widely sung in their synagogues and homes.

❧§❧

The sixteenth century, during which the Jews of the Ottoman Empire enjoyed peace and relative freedom, was a bitter period for Jews and Judaism in Christian Europe. At first it appeared that the Protestant Reformation might bring some improvement in their condition. Martin Luther, in the early years of his war against the papacy, had vigorously condemned persecution of the Jews and urged that they be treated with greater tolerance and Christian charity. In his 1523 tract *Dass Jesus Christus ein geborener Jude sei* (*That Jesus Christ Was Born a Jew*), the German reformer defended the Jews' refusal to accept the "papal paganism" that the Catholic Church had misrepresented to them as authentic Christianity, and declared: "Had I been a Jew and seen such fools and blockheads teaching the Christian faith, I should rather have become a pig than a Christian." Luther hoped that his "purified" brand of Christianity would soon win over the Jews, who had failed to respond to the proselytizing efforts of Catholicism not so much because of their own "obstinacy and wickedness" as because of the "absurd and asinine ignorance and wicked and shameless life of the popes, priests, monks, and scholars." Many Jews in Europe eagerly welcomed the disturbances in the Christian world and expected that the Reformation would not only break the power of the Catholic Church but also usher in an era of tolerance for all religions, including their own. Some even hailed

Luther as a "secret Jew" who was attempting to steer errant Christianity back to Judaism.

When it became clear that the Jews were no more prepared to embrace Lutheranism than Catholicism, Luther's tolerant attitude was exchanged for one of increasing hostility. His *Table Talks* of the 1530s frequently complain of "the stiffnecked Jews, ironhearted and stubborn as the devil," and in tracts written in the early 1540s, including one entitled *On the Jews and Their Lies*, he describes them as "thieves and robbers," "poisonous and virulent," and "disgusting vermin." Shortly before his death in 1546 the quondam defender of the Jews preached a sermon in which he admonished Christian princes to tolerate them no more but expel them from their domains—something a number of Protestant rulers had already done, and others, following Luther's advice, were soon to do. Centuries after Luther's death, Protestant Europe was no more strongly disposed to treat Jews with elementary decency than was Catholic Europe. Moreover, the reformer's vitriolic defamations remained a permanent legacy not only of the Lutheran Church but of German culture in general; it was always there to be exploited by enemies of the Jewish people, and it resurfaced, close to four hundred years after his death, in the murderous onslaughts of the Nazi propaganda machine.

While the Reformation brought no healing balm to Jews living in the lands where Protestantism prevailed, the Counter Reformation in Italy and other Catholic territories magnified their misfortunes. The Catholic Church, casting about for scapegoats on whom to place the blame for its troubles, had no difficulty in discovering the Jews among the chief malefactors. The people whom Luther had maligned so outrageously were charged with contributing significantly to the Reformation. Perhaps the only shred of truth in the accusation was that Luther had urged his followers to return to the Bible and to personal study of its text, and some reforming theologians, wishing to understand the text more accurately, had taken lessons in Hebrew from Jewish scholars. This was sufficient to convince the authorities of the Church that good Catholics must be protected from infectious contact with the Jews even more than they had been previously. The old restrictions and quarantines decreed by the Lateran Councils of 1179 and 1215, which had frequently been winked at (and especially so in the Papal States), now had to be rigorously enforced.

The prime executioner of the policy of systematic degradation and repression of the Jews (a policy which was to be maintained for two and a half centuries until Napoleon's armies overthrew the old order) was the fanatical Cardinal Gian Pietro Carafa, founder of the Theatines and—along with the founder of the Jesuits, Ignatius of Loyola—chief architect of the Counter Reformation. At Carafa's instigation, the *Talmud* was summarily put on trial by a papal commission and condemned as containing scurrilous attacks on Christianity. On the second day of Rosh Hashanah, 1553, all copies of the *Talmud* that could be located in a house-to-house search in Rome by agents of the Inquisition were publicly burned in the Campo dei Fiori. The scene was soon reenacted in Bologna, Ferrara, Mantua, Venice, and elsewhere in Italy. Thus the great Jewish work which a generation earlier had been printed for the first time by the Christian publisher Daniel Bomberg under the sponsorship of the cultured Pope Leo X was now consigned to the flames as blasphemous and pernicious. Still greater misfortunes were in store for the Jews when Carafa ascended the throne of St. Peter as Paul IV in 1555. For several decades the city of Ancona had served, with the approval of the popes, as a place of refuge for Marranos from Portugal. This was intolerable to the new pope. Without notice he canceled the Marranos' letters of protection and ordered them handed over to the Inquisition. Many escaped from Ancona, and others who were Turkish subjects were released by the Inquisition when Sultan Suleiman the Magnificent addressed an imperious letter to the pope demanding that they be set free, but twenty-four men and one woman were burned at an auto-da-fé on May 24, 1556.

Paul IV was not content with killing and torturing Marranos. Shortly after assuming the position of vicar of Christ, the new pope issued on July 12, 1555, his infamous bull *Cum nimis absurdum*, according to which Jews were henceforth to be restricted to their own special quarter in each city (later known as the ghetto, from the name of the quarter of Venice, the *Getto Nuovo* or New Foundry, where officials of the Venetian Republic had segregated its Jews earlier in the century), around which a high wall was to be built, with gates that were to be locked each night. The papal bull further decreed that Jews could no longer own real estate, practice medicine among Christians (in an earlier era more than one pope had a Jew as his personal physician), employ Christian servants or workmen, and bear honorary titles. In addition, the special badge decreed by the Fourth Lateran Council, now to assume the form of a yellow hat, was made mandatory. With a few brief intermissions, these oppressions and indignities were strictly carried through in Catholic Europe until the beginning of the nineteenth century. The policy of the Papal States toward the Jews became the pattern emulated by much of the rest of the continent.

Of all the restrictions placed upon the Jews in the era of the Counter Reformation, compulsory ghettoization probably had the most far-reaching and negative consequences. The institution of the ghetto spread under different names from Italy to other countries (in southern France it came to be known as the *carrière des juifs*, in the Germanic lands as the *Judengasse* or *Judenstadt*), and everywhere led to a narrowing of horizons and intellectual decline. To be sure, the ghetto was not simply a "prison"; it was also a "fortress," both in a physical and spiritual sense, inasmuch as its walls frequently provided protection from the attacks of the mob as well as a sheltered environment in which loyalty to Judaism was not threatened by the corrosive influences of the larger, non-Jewish world. But the intellectual inbreeding that it fostered, the movement within a closed circle of ideas and attitudes without stimulation and fresh impulses from without, took its inevitable toll. More than a few brilliant minds that might have achieved insights and discoveries of immense importance to mankind at large, had they been applied to larger concerns and with a wider field for their exercise, went to waste in fruitless mystical speculation about the nature and interrelationships of the *sefirot* or in endless weaving of pilpulistic subtleties on minute points of rabbinic law. As for Judaism itself, it probably became more stagnant and uncreative in the period of ghettoization than in almost any previous era of its long history. By and large, the Jewish religious leaders and thinkers who lived in the age and milieu of compulsory segregation from the larger world were inferior in intellectual power, poorer in imagination, narrower in sympathy, and less innovative in response to emergent conditions than those who came before and after them. However, it must also be said that, despite the obscurantism and narrowness that dominated the intellectual life of the ghetto, its residents vigorously maintained the centuries-old Jewish traditions of family solidarity, philanthrophy, and communal responsibility. Furthermore, their eagerness to fulfill the commandment of Torah study kept alive almost universal literacy and a high degree of mental alacrity.

⋦§⋧

While the shadows of the Counter Reformation darkened Jewish life in southern and central Europe in the second half of the sixteenth century, places of refuge that were to prove more tolerant to Jews and Judaism were emerging in cities along the northern seas of the continent. With the discovery of America and the westward movement of European imperialism, the Mediterranean cities had begun to yield their place as the centers of world trade to the seaports of the North Atlantic. Groups of enterprising Marranos began to turn their steps to these burgeoning emporiums of international commerce, and by the end of the sixteenth century small colonies were established in Antwerp, Amsterdam, Hamburg, and London. Before long many of their members found it possible and desirable to throw off their Christian disguise and become publicly professing Jews. Within a short time descendants of the Jewish exiles from Portugal and Spain who had been scattered all over the Mediterranean world followed them, and these were followed in turn by Ashkenazic Jews from central and eastern Europe. By the end of the seventeenth century most of the great mercantile centers of northern Europe had substantial settlements of both Sephardic and Ashkenazic Jews who organized their separate communities and synagogues and generally sought to have as little to do with each other as possible. It was through the energy and courage of the pioneering Marrano merchants that these European settlements, as well as the centers of Jewish life that were to emerge in the western hemisphere, were made possible.

Undoubtedly the most important of the new Jewish communities in the north of Europe established by Marranos was that of Amsterdam. After the northern provinces of the Netherlands declared their independence of Catholic Spain in 1571, Marranos from Spain and Portugal began to settle in the city, soon to become a major entrepôt of international trade, in which few questions were asked about men's religious beliefs. They were followed by an influx of Sephardic Jews, and in the 1620s Ashkenazic settlers began to arrive. Within a short time synagogues and schools were established, and a flourishing Jewish community life developed. The school called *Talmud Torah*, founded in 1616, became famed throughout the Jewish world for the breadth of its curriculum and the excellence of its instruction; not only rabbinic literature but Hebrew grammar and poetry were taught in its classes. From among its graduates came rabbis of many Sephardic communities throughout Europe and the Levant, as well as a number of Hebrew poets. With the establishment of presses by Jews for printing Hebrew, Spanish, and Portuguese books beginning in 1627, Amsterdam became a leading publishing and cultural center. Its presses distributed their products throughout the Diaspora in the seventeenth and eighteenth centuries. The glories of Amsterdam

Jewry were everywhere rehearsed, and the architecture of its magnificent Sephardic synagogue, dedicated in 1675, was copied in many communities.

Quite early in its history the Jewish community of Amsterdam was riven by religious dissension. Among the Marranos who reverted to Judaism were men of broad learning and critical mentality. Exposed to the freedom of the relatively liberal Dutch society in which they lived, some of these resented the harsh authoritarianism and unyielding dogmatism of the rabbis and the majority of lay leaders. The congregation Beth Jaäcob split in 1619 and remained divided for two decades, with an orthodox and a liberal faction. Ultimately the authority of the community's rabbis, led by Saul Levi Morteira (ca. 1596–1660), prevailed, and freethinking tendencies were rigorously suppressed. It was the rabbis who played a major role in the excommunication of seventeenth-century Amsterdam's two most celebrated heretics, Uriel da Costa (1585–1640) and Baruch Spinoza (1632–1677).

The first of these is a tragic figure. Born in Portugal into a Marrano family virtually all of whose members had turned into devout Catholics, da Costa became a minor official of the Church in Oporto in 1615 after studying at Coimbra. Then, according to his own report, a close reading of the Bible brought about his reversion to Judaism. He thereupon converted his family, including his four brothers, and moved with them to Amsterdam, where he hoped to practice his religion openly and without fear. But da Costa soon discovered that the version of Judaism which he had derived from his study of the Bible, the religion of Moses and Isaiah as he conceived it, was very different from that practiced in his new home. He could not conceal his disappointment and criticized the "Pharisees of Amsterdam" for what he regarded as their excessive ritualism and formalism. He also raised questions about the truth of the idea of the immortality of the soul, maintaining, in Sadducean fashion, that the doctrine was not biblical. When da Costa expressed his views in writing in 1624, his tract was burned and he himself was arrested, indicted before the magistracy for uttering views subversive of both Jewish and Christian faith, fined three hundred gulden, and excommunicated by the rabbis.

Returning to Amsterdam after a sojourn in Hamburg, the former Marrano in 1633 requested readmission to the Jewish community, even though he had not changed his views. Isolated from both Jewish and Christian society, he had come to feel an urgent need for fellowship and decided, as he put it, "to become an ape among apes." But once restored to membership in the synagogue, da Costa quickly began to entertain doubts about the divinely revealed character of the Torah and to ask whether all institutional religions were not simply human artifacts. His thinking moved toward a kind of philosophical deism or natural religion, without any ecclesiastical dogmas or cultic forms. God, he argued, is the ruler of nature but has no concern with either religious doctrines or forms of worship, all of which are nothing but vanity. The only religion da Costa could accept consisted of the moral principles contained in the seven Noahide commandments. Putting his convictions into practice, he ceased to observe Jewish rituals and also sought to dissuade some Christians from converting to Judaism. Again he was excommunicated but this time remained in Amsterdam, where as the years passed he found his isolation (even his closest relatives shunned him) increasingly unbearable. Once more da Costa applied, in 1640, for readmission to the Jewish community. His petition was granted after he submitted to the stipulation of the *bet din* that he publicly renounce his heretical opinions, be flogged thirty-nine times with a lash, and lie on the threshold of the synagogue so that all the congregation could trample over him. Crazed with despair over the indignities to which he had been 'subjected, the proud da Costa went home, dashed off a few pages of a moving autobiography which he called *Exemplar Humanae Vitae (Specimen of a Human Life)*,[2] and blew out his brains.

It may be said in extenuation of the harsh treatment accorded Uriel da Costa by the rabbis and community leaders of Amsterdam that they could hardly have been expected to stand calmly by and see the faith for which some of them had suffered so deeply attacked by a brash and semiinformed newcomer. Furthermore, they were undoubtedly apprehensive that harboring in their midst, without severe punishment, a man whose views were as subversive of Christian doctrine as of Jewish might compromise them in the eyes of their gentile neighbors. The fact remains that da Costa's life exemplifies the tragedy of the independent thinker who refuses to be silent in an atmosphere of religious intolerance, as well as the brutalities of which sincerely religious men are capable when they feel threatened by radical criticism. In the rationalist climate of the nineteenth century a number of dramas, novels, and operas portraying the heretic of Amsterdam as a martyr in the cause of freedom of thought were written, and the twentieth-century novelist Israel

Zangwill included an idealized portrait of him in his *Dreamers of the Ghetto*.

◆§◈§◆

It is possible, as some scholars have suggested, that da Costa served as an inspiration for the other great heretic expelled from its midst by the Jewish community of Amsterdam in the middle of the seventeenth century, Baruch Spinoza. But Spinoza was a far more original and strong-minded thinker than da Costa, and never wavered in clinging to the rationalist principles which he employed to construct one of the most celebrated metaphysical systems in the history of western philosophy. As consistent in his actions as in his thought, when he found that he could no longer accept the dogmas and disciplines of Judaism he left the synagogue even before he was officially excommunicated, and in the last twenty years of his brief life had virtually no contact with the Jewish community.

Born into a prominent Sephardic merchant family of Amsterdam, Spinoza studied Hebrew, Bible, and *Talmud,* as well as the works of the medieval Jewish philosophers and the commentaries of Abraham ibn Ezra, at the communal school. It is likely that among his teachers were Saul Morteira and Menasseh ben Israel. He also learned Latin and a good deal about mathematics and the natural sciences from Franz van den Ende, a freethinking ex-priest then living in Amsterdam. As a young man he also became familiar with the work of René Descartes, who inaugurated a new era in European philosophy. Shortly after Spinoza left the *yeshivah*, rumors that he was becoming infected with heretical views began circulating in the Jewish community. It appears that he was formally questioned and expressed heterodox opinions about angels, the immortality of the soul, and the bodily nature of God. It is also claimed that Saul Morteira offered him an annual stipend if he would not give public utterance to his beliefs, and that the young Spinoza firmly declined the offer. In any case, on July 27, 1656, he was formally excommunicated and anathematized by the *bet din*, with the action duly reported to the Amsterdam magistracy.

Even before his official expulsion, however, Spinoza had severed his contacts with the Jewish community and formed a circle of friends and disciples most of whom belonged to the Mennonite sect known as the Collegiants. After his excommunication he resided in several different places in the Netherlands, earning a modest living

by grinding lenses and in his leisure hours writing his great philosophical works. In his own lifetime he achieved vast fame and was in
correspondence and personal contact with such eminent figures in
the scientific and philosophical worlds as Count von Tschirnhausen,
Henry Oldenburg, Christian Huygens, and Gottfried Wilhelm Leibniz. He was also a close friend of the Dutch statesman Jan de Witt.
A few years before his death from tuberculosis at the age of forty-
five Spinoza was offered a professorship of philosophy at the University of Heidelberg by the Elector Palatine, on condition that he
would teach nothing that might disturb the established religion, but
he politely declined the preferred appointment. He ended his days
neither a Jew nor a Christian, steadfastly maintaining his unique
religious and philosophical convictions.

When Spinoza's *Tractatus Theologico-Politicus* was published, without the author's name, in 1670, it at once aroused a storm of vehement opposition. This work, in which the mild lens grinder of the
Hague presented his critique of supernatural religion and his arguments for a liberal, secular state in which freedom of thought and
religion would be major cornerstones, was formally proscribed by
the Synod of Dort and by the States General of Holland, Zealand,
and West Friesland. To avoid censureship, the *Tractatus* had to be
sold under false title pages. Spinoza himself was charged with
blatant atheism and irreligion and felt compelled to defend
himself against the accusation, which he believed was thoroughly
unmerited.

In point of fact the *Tractatus Theologico-Politicus* is a devastating assault on the foundations of revealed religion, both Christian and
Jewish—but more pointedly directed at the latter than the former.
Spinoza here appears as one of the chief originators of modern biblical criticism, although it is clear that he is indebted for many of his
judgments to the veiled statements of the medieval Jewish exegete
Abraham ibn Ezra. He rejects the Mosaic authorship of the Pentateuch, notes its composite character and its numerous repetitions and
inconsistencies, ascribes late dates to the Psalms and Proverbs, questions the authenticity of much of the Book of Daniel, and discloses
many contradictions in the prophets' conceptions of natural and religious phenomena. Most importantly, however, Spinoza, despite
the fact that he overtly speaks of the divine origin of Scripture, denies that the words of the prophets are literally divine revelation and
that the teachings of the Bible are factually true. The Bible does not
provide truths but only useful moral lessons. Its stories are not to be

taken literally, he insists, for they were adapted to the limited mentality of the multitude, which is incapable of comprehending abstract concepts and definitions. Furthermore, he argues, the miracles recounted in Scripture are utterly impossible; nothing can happen that violates the eternal and unalterable laws of nature.

A good deal in Spinoza's view of the Bible is reminiscent of the rationalism of Maimonides and his followers, but his criticisms go much further. It is clear that he is actually intent on destroying the truth-claims of the Bible and reducing it to a textbook of popular morality. Thus, unlike Maimonides, who maintained that the inspiration of the prophets derived from the perfection both of their reason and imagination, Spinoza regards it as dependent on imagination only, and reduces the prophets to the status of soothsayers. Moreover, while Maimonides insisted that all the legislation of the Torah is of divine provenance, Spinoza categorically rejects this idea. God is not the giver of laws, even of moral laws, which a man may obey or disobey, but the source of eternal and necessary truths. The only sense in which He may be considered the source of moral principles or rules to guide human action is that the eternal order which derives from Him contains certain actions that have beneficial results, and others which are destructive and which the prudent man will therefore avoid. Furthermore, the cultic and ceremonial laws of the Torah are, according to Spinoza, not only nondivine in origin but have now become superfluous. Their significance was merely political, insofar as they contributed to preservation of the Jewish state; with the cessation of autonomous Jewish national existence, they have lost all value.

It may also be noted that Spinoza polemicizes against the traditional doctrine of the election of Israel. The Jews were not singled out for any special divine vocation by God, nor are they distinguished from other peoples either in intellect or virtue. Other nations, he emphasizes, also had their prophets, and the apostles of Christianity were superior to the Hebrew prophets. Indeed, the philosopher who laid such great stress on equanimity, and insisted that the wise man will never surrender to the passion of anger, had some rather harsh things to say about his biblical ancestors.

How divergent Spinoza's philosophy is from the mainstream of Biblical-Rabbinic Judaism becomes even more apparent when we consider the views of God, man, and the world, and their interrelationships, that he developed in his greatest philosophical work, the *Ethics*. This masterpiece of rationalist metaphysics is constructed in

Euclidean logical-mathematical form, i.e., as a series of propositions following from definitions and axioms and demonstrated by rational argument. It is written in the most arid and precise Latin, with barely any trace of emotion, following the rule its author had set for himself in his philosophizing: *non ridere, non lugere, neque detestari, sed intelligere* (not to laugh, not to weep, not to hate, but to understand). Spinoza was convinced that the system so constructed was eternally and irrefutably true. As he put it in one of his letters: "I do not presume that I have found the best philosophy; I know that I understand the true philosophy. And if you ask me how I know it, I answer: In the same way as you know that the three angles of a triangle are equal to two right angles." [3]

In the first book of the *Ethics* the philosopher develops his view that God or Nature (*Deus sive Natura*) is the only possible substance, for the definition of substance is "that which is itself, and is conceived through itself," and nothing finite is self-subsistent. Individual souls and material objects are not independent entities but simply modes or aspects of the one, infinite divine being. This pantheistic conclusion, according to Professor Harry Wolfson, [4] appears to have been derived by Spinoza from his reflection on the theorizing of medieval philosophers, especially Jewish thinkers, on the question of whether there can be two Gods, and whether God is different from the world. From the principle that God or Nature is the only substance, Spinoza proceeds to show that everything in the universe follows through logical necessity from the essence of God and those two of His attributes which alone are comprehensible to man— thought and extension. God is in no sense unpredictable. We may regard Him as free, but His freedom consists simply in following the order that is the expression of His being. *"Deus ex solis suae naturae legibus et a nemine coactus agit*—God acts only in accordance with the laws of His own nature and is coerced by no one." [5] What this means further, Spinoza asserts, is that God has no purposes and does not strive to achieve any goals. Men may ascribe a purposeful character to events and objects in nature and conceive them as good or bad, but this is simply a result of their human egotism, ignorance, prejudice, and fear. All things are as they are necessarily and could not be otherwise.

The determinism which, for Spinoza, governs nature also embraces man. He, too, is simply another mode of the infinite divine substance and subject to the iron laws of necessity. But he can be liberated from that further bondage in which he is placed by his own unclarified emotions, or passions, through rising above them to a true comprehension of the world and through acting according to reason. The wise or enlightened man, having gained an understanding of the order of events in nature and why they cannot be otherwise than they are, will not be governed by the external powers of ignorance and passion but by the laws of his own nature. He will live beyond either hope or fear and will eschew sorrow and regret, "for he who repents of an action is doubly wretched or infirm." [6] When the wise man achieves such a level of universal understanding that he sees all things, as does God, "under the aspect of eternity or necessity," then he will attain that "intellectual love of God" which, according to Spinoza, is "part of the infinite love with which God loves Himself." [7] In such wisdom, and not in any illusory immortality or afterlife, consist man's blessedness and salvation.

Spinoza's philosophy, here sketched in briefest outline, is obviously an impressive intellectual achievement, but it is far removed from the world view of classical Judaism. There is little doubt that certain aspects of his thought were influenced by Maimonides, Ḥasdai Crescas, and other medieval Jewish philosophers, as well as by the Kabbalist tradition, but in its totality it represents a complete negation of some of the central affirmations of mainstream Judaism— God as personal spirit who loves man and makes ethical demands of him, the world as created and guided by God but not identical with Him, man as a free and morally responsible personality who transcends the order of nature, hope for a messianic fulfillment ushering in a new world in which the evils and negativities of present existence will finally be overcome. Many a nineteenth-century *maskil* idolized Spinoza as a victim of the reactionary synagogue and a courageous battler for freedom of thought against fanatical orthodoxy, and more than a few uncritical admirers have sought to show the authentically Jewish character of his thought. These attempts, however, must be pronounced a failure. Spinoza was undoubtedly a great thinker who contributed significantly to the treasury of western philosophy, but he was not an essentially Jewish thinker, and he did not enrich the life and thought of the people from whose midst he came and whom he abandoned before they abandoned him.

❧⚜❧

An older contemporary of Spinoza's and perhaps one of his teachers, Menasseh ben Israel (1604–1657), accomplished a good deal in winning a sympathetic hearing for Judaism in the Christian world of his day. Born a Marrano in Madeira, he grew up in Amsterdam, where he gained renown as a child prodigy and while still in his teens succeeded Rabbi Isaac Uzziel as preacher in one of the city's important congregations. A few years later he founded Amsterdam's first Hebrew press, which he continued to operate throughout his life and from which a series of Hebrew, Spanish, and Portuguese works flowed. Thoroughly proficient in Latin and with an extensive knowledge of both Jewish and Christian philosophical-theological literature, Menasseh acquired his initial reputation in the Christian milieu with the first part of his *Conciliador,* a work written in Spanish and soon translated into Latin and English,[8] in which he attempted to harmonize seemingly discordant passages in the Bible. Thereafter he wrote a series of theological tracts in Latin directed primarily toward a non-Jewish audience. These writings, as well as his preaching in the synagogue, which attracted some of the most prominent figures in Amsterdam's Christian society, led to Menasseh's recognition in that society as the foremost living exemplar of Hebraic scholarship. He became a friend of Hugo Grotius and Rembrandt van Rijn, who painted his portrait. He also corresponded with the great contemporary patroness of science and scholarship, Queen Christina of Sweden. A restless, ambitious man whose manifold activities never seem to have brought him a satisfactory livelihood, he once planned to leave Holland and seek his fortune in Brazil, as some of his Jewish townsmen in Amsterdam had done, but he did not carry out his plans.

Of historical significance was Menasseh's involvement in the developments which led to resettlement of the Jews in England after the Puritan revolution. This involvement stemmed from his fervent Kabbalist convictions. Like many Kabbalists as well as contemporary Christian mystics, Menasseh awaited with intense excitement the "apocalyptic" year 1666, which he believed would bring the advent of the Messiah and the redemption of Israel. But he also believed that the exile of the Jews could not end and their triumphant return to the Holy Land could not take place before they had been dispersed to the "ends of the earth" and the Ten Lost Tribes of Israel had been recovered. Impressed by the reports of a Marrano traveler that he had discovered remnants of the tribes among the Indians of Ecuador, Menasseh wrote a work entitled *Esperança de Israel* (*The Hope of Israel*), describing the reported discovery and proclaiming that the biblical prophecies concerning the coming of the Messiah would soon be fulfilled. In 1650 he dedicated the Latin edition of this work to the Parliament of England, hoping to gain its approval for the return of the Jews to that country; this, he was persuaded, would complete their dispersion to *Ketzeh Ha-Aretz* (the end of the earth), the term in medieval Hebrew for Angle-Terre, and fulfill the necessary condition for the arrival of the Messiah.

A few years later, in 1655, Menasseh went to London to negotiate personally with Oliver Cromwell the official readmission of the Jews to England (a small colony of Marranos had already been living there for some time). At the end of that year a sizable assemblage of government officials, lawyers, and theologians was convoked at Whitehall to deliberate the matter. Cromwell, who appreciated the commercial value of the Marrano merchants, was known to be sympathetic to the readmission of Jews to the country, but the conference could reach no agreement. The lawyers noted that there was no statutory bar to Jewish settlement in England, but the theologians, urged on by Christian merchants, were either opposed or would give their approval only on seriously restrictive conditions. Cromwell thereupon dissolved the conference before it could reach any definite decisions. Although no formal authorization for Jews to settle was issued by Cromwell, a petition submitted some time later by the small Marrano colony in London to open a synagogue and establish a cemetery was granted. Thus the resettlement of Jews in England, from which they had been banished more than three and a half centuries earlier, came about de facto rather than de jure. Within a relatively short time there were thriving communities in London and other major commercial centers. As for Menasseh ben Israel, though disappointed that no official action was taken by Cromwell, he was pleased by the Lord Protector's gesture of personal sympathy in awarding him a pension of one hundred pounds per year. While in England, Menasseh wrote his famous *Vindiciae Judaeorum* (1656), eloquently defending the Jews against various attacks then being launched against them.

Even before Marrano merchants established new Jewish communities in the northern European centers of Amsterdam, Hamburg, and London, other Marranos had settled in some of the seaports of southern France, chiefly Bordeaux and Bayonne. Since France was Catholic, these immigrants could not cast off their Christian guise and publicly profess Judaism, but little attention was paid to their activities as long as they called themselves Christians and conformed outwardly to the practices of the Church. Hence, styling themselves "New Christians," attending church, and receiving the sacraments, they proceeded to develop a parallel Jewish life, complete with synagogues, rabbis, and Talmudic academies, in which they could express their true faith. It was plain to everyone that they were really Jews, but the pretense that they were loyal Christians was studiously maintained. It was only in the first half of the eighteenth century that this elaborate charade was abandoned and the New Christians of southern France were more or less formally acknowledged to be Jews. Toward the end of the century they were the first Jews to be granted French citizenship by the National Assembly.

We observed that Menasseh ben Israel was a devoted adherent of Kabbalah. The Kabbalists, he believed, had fathomed the deepest secrets of existence, and he regarded the teachings of Lurianic mysticism, despite his European education and substantial familiarity with the Jewish rationalist philosophic tradition, with the greatest reverence. "I know very well," he writes, "that the wisdom of Rabbi Isaac Luria rises above the highest mountains," and he fervently exclaims, "Blessed is the generation that was privileged to have him in its midst!" [9] Menasseh's enthusiasm for Lurianic Kabbalah was shared by many of his fellow Jews in Amsterdam, and it is therefore not surprising that its shattering consequence, the Shabbetai Tzevi messianic movement, found some of its most ardent followers in the Dutch capital.

Menasseh ben Israel was already dead when Shabbetai Tzevi put forth his claim to be "the Messiah of the God of Jacob," but among those who gathered to dance jubilantly around the platform of the synagogue in Amsterdam at the news were such cultured and prominent men as Abraham Pereira, Benjamin Mussafia, Benedict de Castro, and Manuel Teixeira. The epidemic of messianic frenzy spread like wildfire to communities all over Europe, Asia, and Africa. Everywhere in that amazing year 1665–1666 Jews prophesied ecstatically and spoke in tongues, flagellated themselves and performed ascetic exercises, married off their young children so that they might give birth to others into which the few unborn souls still remaining in the celestial storehouse might enter and the final bar to redemption thereby be removed, and shipped their belongings to the nearest harbor so that they might follow the Messiah to Palestine as soon as he should give the signal.

An interesting contemporary account of the pathological moods that prevailed at the time is given in the Yiddish memoirs of that doughty lady, Glückel of Hameln (1645–1724), who was then living in Hamburg:

[164]

Two Melancholy Centuries

When I remember the penance done by young and old, it is indescribable, though it is well enough known in the whole world. O Lord of the Universe, at that time we hoped that You, merciful God, would have compassion on Your people Israel and redeem us from our exile. We were like a woman in travail, a woman on the labor-stool who, after great labor and grievous pains, expects to rejoice in the birth of a child, but finds it is nothing but wind. This, my great God and King, happened to us. All Your servants and children did much penance, recited many prayers, gave away large amounts in charity, throughout the world. For two or three years Your people Israel sat on the labor-stool, but nothing came except wind. We did not merit to see the longed-for child, but because of our sins we were left neither here nor there but in the middle. Your people still hope every day that You, in Your infinite mercy, will redeem them and that the Messiah will come—if it be Your divine will to save Your people Israel. The joy, when letters arrived, is not to be described. Most of the letters were received by the Portuguese. They took them to their synagogue and read them aloud there. The Germans, young and old, went into the Portuguese synagogue to hear them. The young Portuguese on these occasions all wore their finest clothing and each tied a broad green silk ribbon round his waist. This was Shabbetai Tzevi's livery. So all, "with kettledrums and round dance" went with joy like the joy of the Festival of the *Bet Ha-Shoevah* to hear the letters read. Many people sold home, hearth and everything they had, hoping for redemption. My father-in-law, peace unto him, who lived in Hameln, moved from there, leaving things standing in the house just as they were, and went to Hildesheim. He sent us here, to Hamburg, two big barrels of linenware. In them were all kinds of food—peas, smoked meat, all sorts of dried fruits—that would keep without spoiling. The good man thought they would leave from Hamburg for the Holy Land. These barrels were in my house for more than a year. At last, afraid that the meat and other things would be spoiled, he wrote that we should open the barrels and take out all the food, so that the linen underneath should not spoil. They remained here for three more years, my father-in-law always expecting to need them at a moment's notice for his journey. But this did not suit the Almighty.[10]

Virtually the only significant voices raised in protest against the mass intoxication of the Shabbetai Tzevi movement were those of Rabbi Jacob ben Aaron Sasportas (ca. 1610–1698) and the Frances brothers, Jacob (1615–1667) and Immanuel (1618–ca. 1710). Sasportas, who had accompanied Menasseh ben Israel on his journey to England in 1655 and himself served for a brief period as rabbi in London, leaving because of the Great Plague of 1665, fiercely denounced the movement, its chief prophet Nathan of Gaza, and its followers.

Maintaining the traditional conception of the messianic age, he pointed out how different it was from what was happening at present. An ardent Kabbalist and follower of Isaac Luria, Sasportas perceived strong antinomian tendencies in the Shabbetai Tzevi movement and feared that it would turn into a revolution against the rabbinic tradition. In it he saw close analogies to Christianity and warned that its adherents might become a heretical sect and break away from Judaism altogether. The Italian Frances brothers, thoroughgoing rationalists who had no use for mysticism and Kabbalah, attacked Shabbetai Tzevi in satirical poems and lampoons as a "wolf who disguises himself as a lamb," and predicted that the movement he had inaugurated would end in destruction and untold misery for the Jewish people. But theirs, as well as Sasportas', were voices crying in the wilderness. The Shabbetai Tzevi madness gained increasing momentum and ran its course to its catastrophic conclusion.

We noted earlier that the virus of messianic fervor did not die out with the conversion of the would-be messiah of Smyrna to Islam. Some of his ardent followers tenaciously maintained their belief in his messiahship and followed their master's example by becoming Moslems, at the same time continuing to practice a kind of messianic Judaism. These half-Moslems and half-Jews, known as Dönmeh from the beginning of the eighteenth century, abrogated the practical commandments of what they called the "material Torah" and based their religious existence on eighteen precepts which they attributed to Shabbetai Tzevi. Included among these is a parallel version of the Ten Commandments, similar to the biblical except that the commandment concerning adultery appears more as a positive recommendation than a prohibition. Among this strange sect, which still has a small number of members in Turkey today, belief in the divinity of Shabbetai Tzevi became a central principle. The Dönmeh also practiced exchange of wives and conducted orgiastic rites in connection with their annual *Ḥag Ha-Keves*, or Festival of the Lamb, celebrated at the beginning of spring.

Others who clung to their belief in Shabbetai Tzevi's messiahship did not leave the Jewish fold but formed secret conventicles dedicated to venerating him and following his teachings. For generations after his death not a few rabbis renowned for scholarship and piety were suspected of covert Shabbatian sympathies, and more than one community was torn apart by accusations of Shabbatian heresy hurled against its teachers and leaders. In the middle of the eighteenth century virtually all the leading rabbis of Europe were caught up in an acrimonious and protracted dispute between Rabbi Jacob Emden (d. 1776) and Rabbi Jonathan Eybeschütz (d. 1764), which erupted when the former accused the latter of having written some amulets containing hidden references to Shabbetai Tzevi. In the heat of the controversy tempers flared and excommunications and counterexcommunications were freely issued against each other by the contending parties and their adherents. When the dust had settled, the net result became apparent: many Jews could no longer greatly respect a rabbinate that could devote itself with such intense zeal for so many years to a debate over such a matter.

The seventeenth century, despite certain peaks of achievement, was truly melancholy. In their longing for redemption from present woes, thousands of Jews had rushed headlong into a frantic messianic movement that bitterly disappointed their hopes. For many, mystical fantasies had replaced rational thought and sober expectations; the realm of dreams in which the world would be miraculously saved and Israel emerge in triumphant splendor was obviously far more attractive than the reality in which an unredeemed world continued to despise and oppress Jews. Nevertheless, the seeds of a new order of Jewish existence in which messianism and mysticism would no longer have the same powerful attraction were already planted. But before these flowered toward the end of the eighteenth century, the age-old mystical-messianic drive in Judaism gave birth to one more creation of immense vitality and religious importance—the Ḥasidism of Israel Baal Shem Tov and his disciples.

CHAPTER

❦ VII ❧

Ḥasidism

A T THE BEGINNING of the eighteenth century Jewish religious
life on the European continent, where the majority of the world Jewish population was then concentrated, had lapsed, by and large, into
a state of rigidity and of unquestioning conformity to traditions of
the past. The great achievements in philosophy and poetry of the
Spanish-Jewish community in its "golden age" were now no more
than faded memories, and even the halachic innovations of Franco-
German Jewry in its heyday were not duplicated anywhere in
Europe after the sixteenth century. Isolated spiritually and also
frequently physically through enforced ghettoization, victimized by
economic and social discrimination, threatened relentlessly by expulsion and persecution, Jews found stability and sustaining purpose in
clinging to their inherited faith which assured them of the special
and unbreakable relationship between God and their people. They
kept alive, despite the recent debacle of the Shabbetai Tzevi movement, hope for ultimate messianic redemption. Further meaning to
Jewish existence accrued from obedience to every punctilio of the
sacred law which Jews believed had once been revealed at Sinai to
their fathers and which was now codified in the paragraphs of the
Shulḥan Aruch, and from participation in the activities of the highly
organized and largely autonomous community life that had developed over the ages.

The intellectual revolution that occurred in Europe in the seven-

[168]

teenth century, the period which Alfred North Whitehead once called "the century of genius," seems to have had only the slightest effect on the inner life of European Jewry, with the exception, perhaps, of the Jews living in Italy, where there had long been a tradition of participation in science and scholarship and in the broader cultural life of the country. Elsewhere, however, probably not so much as the names of the authors of this revolution—among them men like Galileo, Harvey, Newton, Descartes, Huyghens, and Pascal—were known to any but the rarest resident of the ghetto. It is true that European Jewry in the seventeenth century produced, in the person of Baruch Spinoza, one commanding figure destined to have a profound effect on European thought and life and to be accorded an honored place in the history of western philosophy. But this son of the Jewish community of Amsterdam, as we have seen, was early separated from the life of his people, and had, at least in his lifetime, little, if any, influence over them. Nor did the first half of the eighteenth century, in which the age of the Enlightenment with its promotion of a rational and scientific approach to religious, social, political, and economic questions had its birth, appreciably affect the Jews of Europe. It was not until the middle of that century that the barriers separating Judaism from the intellectual and spiritual life of Christian Europe began to break down for a small number of Jews in the western and central parts of the continent, and not until toward its end, with the downfall of the *ancien régime*, that large masses of Jews in these areas were brought into full contact with that life. These events naturally wrought havoc with the stable structure of Jewish existence that had evolved in the Middle Ages and remained generally unchanged as long as Jews lived in virtually complete isolation from the major currents of European thought.

While civic emancipation and emergence from the confines of the ghetto in the wake of the French Revolution were to produce vast changes in Judaism and in the character of Jewish life in western and central Europe, it was in eastern Europe, where the separation of Judaism from the outside world continued largely unbroken until relatively recent times, that the most important movement in Jewish religious life of the eighteenth century emerged. This movement, which came to be known as Ḥasidism and which quickly engaged the loyalty of great masses of Jews in the East, may in a sense be regarded, despite the seeming paradox, as the last major manifestation of medievalism and the first important manifestation of modernism in the Jewish world. It is an expression of medievalism because it is a direct outgrowth of the mysticism that was, as we have observed, perhaps the most significant and powerful factor in Jewish religious thought throughout the late Middle Ages. It may be viewed as an expression of modernism, among other reasons, because of its emphasis on the inner psychic experience of the individual, an emphasis which became the hallmark of a major trend in post-Enlightenment interpretations of both Jewish and Christian religion.

Hasidism arose in Poland and is historically connected with the Shabbatian movement, remnants of which, as we have noted, survived the great disillusionment which followed Shabbetai Tzevi's conversion to Islam. Although the Polish rabbis sought vigorously to root out the Shabbatian heresy from their midst, it persisted for many decades, leading finally to the emergence of the Frankists in the middle of the eighteenth century. The founder of this messianic, antinomian sect, Jacob Frank (1726–1791), was a Polish Jew who had been brought up in a Shabbatian society and ultimately put forth the claim of being Shabbetai's successor. After organizing a group among whose members sexual license was exalted to the level of religious duty, Frank engaged in a number of disputations with the Polish rabbis in the course of which he repudiated the *Talmud*, proclaimed a fantastic trinitarian interpretation of Judaism with himself occupying the position of the second person, and even revived the old ritual murder charge. Finally, in 1759, after numerous copies of the *Talmud* had been publicly burned as a result of his accusations, Frank and his followers, numbering some fifteen thousand, had themselves baptized in the Catholic Church. After Frank's death his sect gradually disappeared as a separate entity and was absorbed into Polish society. Frankism itself was the last excrescence in the painful, century-long history of Shabbatian messianism, fueled by the popular longing for redemption. With Frankism this messianism died out, but the widespread demoralization he and his movement wrought in the life of Polish Jewry remained and provided fertile ground for the spread of Hasidism, which also proclaimed a message of redemption, but of a very different character.

The gloom which settled upon the Jews of Poland as a result of their bitter disillusionment with messianic movements was aggravated by a continuing decline in their social and economic position, and by the hostility of the surrounding world. The Chmielnitzki massacres of the middle of the seventeenth century had not only decimated Polish Jewry's population but also wrecked the foundations of its economic life. In the decades that followed, other massa-

cres and persecutions left many more Jews homeless and ruined.
With the passing years the Jewish communities of Poland came constantly closer to total bankruptcy, and individual Jews sank ever
lower into poverty and degradation. Trapped in the misery of the
disintegrating Polish kingdom, regarded with contempt by the gentile world, and eking out a bare livelihood in their squalid villages
and towns, the Jewish masses had little in the way of either material
or spiritual consolation. Hope of messianic redemption had become
somewhat weakened and, in any case, removed to the far distant future. Nor could the average Jew, who was not always able to observe
all the minutiae of the Law, any longer be confident that he had fulfilled the requirements for entrance after death into the bliss of "the
world to come." As for the present world, its darkness was aggravated by the rampant superstitious belief that it was peopled on all
sides by malevolent demons. The great longing of the masses, a
longing which Shabbatian-Frankist messianism had promised to fulfill but finally betrayed, was for redemption from the misery of their
daily existence.

The religious leaders of the period were unable to meet the needs
of the people. Rabbinic scholarship had declined sharply from the
peaks reached in Poland in the sixteenth and seventeenth centuries,
and Jewish learning was no longer widespread among the populace
at large. Most of the rabbis concentrated their efforts on hair-split-
ting Talmudic dialectic, endlessly elaborating subtle distinctions in
the Law but offering little that could speak directly to the mind or
heart of the simple Jew who had neither the leisure nor the ability to
follow them in their learned disquisitions. A growing gulf yawned
between the pious but unlettered masses and the intellectual aristocracy consisting of the rabbis and the relatively few Jews who were
proficient in Talmudic study.

The times cried out for a different kind of spiritual leader and for
a religious outlook other than that offered by the rabbis. Such a
leader arose in the person of Israel Baal Shem Tov, and such a different and liberating outlook was to be found in the teaching he imparted to his followers, who soon came to call themselves by the ancient name *Ḥasidim* (the pious).

The story of Israel's life, as it has come down to us in the literature of the Ḥasidim, is a strange blend of fact and fiction, reality and

fantasy. All sorts of legendary and miraculous incidents were woven into the biographies written after his death by devoted followers. Setting aside these hagiographical embellishments, we find that Israel was born in 1700 in the small town of Okup in the province of Podolia in Poland. Having lost both parents in infancy, he grew up as a ward of the community. Although introduced, as was customary at the time, to a regimen of Torah study at an early age, the young Israel did not display any great enthusiasm for learning. His biographers tell us that he would frequently slip away from the dismal *ḥeder* to spend entire days wandering in the wood that skirted his native village. There, he often later told his followers, amidst the beauties of nature, he felt more in the presence of God than in the schoolroom.

As a young man Israel served first as an assistant to a private teacher, then as a servant in a school, and then as a teacher himself. For some time after his marriage, he and his wife lived in isolation in a small village at the foot of the Carpathian mountains where they earned their living through lime digging. Here Israel also gave himself up to further study of the Kabbalah, in which he had been interested from his early youth, and to solitary contemplation. Wandering about on the mountains and in the woods, he was frequently carried away, according to the testimony of his disciples, by ecstatic religious experiences. When he was thirty-six years old, Israel concluded that the time had arrived for him to begin his real work. He became a *baal shem*, that is, a practitioner of the healing and miracle-working art, and began to travel around the countryside prescribing herbal remedies, exorcising demons, and writing out charms and amulets to cure and ward off disease. The practitioners of this profession, much of whose lore was derived from the "practical" Kabbalah, received the title *baal shem*, "master of the name," because they were presumed to possess knowledge of the secret names of God, which they would invoke in their incantations. Israel, however, did not employ any of the holy names of God in the charms he distributed, but only his own and his mother's, "Israel son of Sarah." As a *baal shem* Israel was highly successful, gaining, in addition to his fame as a "wonder worker," a wide reputation throughout Galicia, Podolia, and the Ukraine for his religious enthusiasm, generosity, keen personal interest in those he served, and inspiring instruction. Around the year 1745 Israel gave up traveling as a *baal shem* and settled in the town of Medzhibozh in Podolia. Here he established a *bet midrash*, a house of study, to which many admirers, among them some prominent rabbis and scholars, were attracted by his teaching as well as by the power of his personality. Israel remained at Medzh-ibozh, living in joyful communion with a growing company of devoted followers, until his death in 1760.

Israel himself wrote nothing, but his disciples incorporated fragments of his teaching in their writings. From these it is clear that much of his doctrine was founded on the Lurianic Kabbalah in which he had steeped himself from youth. However, it must be emphasized that he also deviated from it in significant respects. His chief concern was redemption, the "liberation of the 'sparks of holi-ness,' " bringing the individual closer to God—just as Luria's had been. But in place of messianic visions of future deliverance, Israel (who did not reject the traditional belief in the ultimate coming of the Messiah) stressed the possibilities of redemption in the here and now. God, he insisted, was active at all times and everywhere in the universe, and men could come into communion with Him and participate in His redemptive activity. Through this communion and participation they would know the joy of present fulfillment. It was a doctrine peculiarly adapted to the needs of the time.

Central in the teaching of the founder of Ḥasidism was the idea of the omnipresence of God. While accepting the Lurianic doctrine of *tzimtzum*, or concentration, he understood it to mean not that God at creation had withdrawn from Himself to Himself, but that He had radiated His infinite light everywhere, only modifying its intensity according to the capacity of the creatures to bear it. Thus, there is no place and no thing that is not in some measure infused with the divine. Israel is reported to have said: "God, blessed be He, fills the entire world with His glory, and every movement, even every thought, comes from Him." Another of his statements, transmitted by his disciple, Rabbi Jacob Joseph of Polonnoye (d. ca. 1775), was: "The *Shechinah* permeates all four orders in nature, the inanimate things, the plants, the living beings, and man; it is inherent in all creatures of the universe, whether they are good or bad." That Israel's teaching was actually pantheistic, as some of its later opponents charged, is doubtful. He does not appear to have wished to identify God and nature, something that would have been totally at variance with the whole weight of Jewish tradition and, furthermore, inconsistent with the rest of his own teaching. His intention was rather to emphasize the consoling idea that God is not merely a transcendent First Cause but present and active everywhere in the universe, so that men can come into communion with Him by many and diverse routes.

Observance of the law prescribed in the *Talmud* and traditional codes as a way of entering into relationship with God was never rejected by Israel Baal Shem Tov. A faithful upholder of the rabbinic tradition, he insisted on the indispensability of its precepts. Nevertheless, he was not generally as rigorous in his demands as the traditional rabbis. For him, assiduous study of the Torah and exact obedience to its commandments carried no greater promise of acceptance than the sincere faith and intention of the humble Jew who, though he cannot study much or always pray at the designated time and place, yet surrenders himself and his life to God in simple trust and confidence. One of his biographers relates that when in his travels Israel would sometimes see groups of Jews with bowed heads, bent backs, and sorrowful faces, he would stop and ask them: "Why are you so sad, why are your faces so miserable?" They would answer: "We have not prayed properly. We have not studied in the right way. We have not yet accomplished even a fraction of our duties to our Creator, praised be His Name." Israel would then say:

Stop! Sorrow is an evil. If you have not studied enough—study is not the principal thing. If you have not prayed rightly, believe! A Jew works all day long in the marketplace; towards evening, at dusk, he trembles and says to himself "Woe unto me! I almost forgot to say the evening prayer." And he rushes into a house and says his prayer, without knowing what his lips are saying, and yet—I tell you—all the angels tremble at his prayer. No, the chief thing is the intention, the purity of heart and thought. Now, therefore, leave sorrow and sadness; man must live in joy and contentment, always rejoicing in his lot.[1]

From the teaching of its founder that God and "sparks of holiness" are present in all things, Ḥasidism drew the conclusion that He can be worshiped not only through prayer and observance of the commandments of the Torah but even in the humblest acts of daily life. This idea—the "hallowing of the everyday" [2]—became one of its chief emphases and finds repeated expression in its literature.

Only ordinary people think that they can serve God solely by prayers and Torah. In reality it is not so, for His dominion rules over all, and even gross matter can serve as a vehicle of divine worship. Just as there is a significance in spiritual matters—in the Torah, prayers and the performance of precepts—in that they serve to elevate the fallen sparks, so there is the same significance in earthly things—eating, drinking, and all kinds of work.

Believing so intensely that God was in all things and in all men, Israel Baal Shem Tov could not accept the idea that anything was irremediably evil or that any man was totally depraved. Evil for him was not, as for the Lurianic Kabbalah, a positive demonic power, deriving from the realm of darkness, but only an inferior manifestation of good in which some measure of the divine light still inhered. "The *Shechinah*," he declared, "permeates all stages of life, from the highest to the lowest. Even when a man commits a sin the *Shechinah* is in him, because otherwise he could not have carried out the act or moved any organ, for it is God who endows man with vitality and power." [3] Since sin and evil have their source in God, the sinner, on abandoning his ways, could be confident of God's ready forgiveness. Even in a sinful act there are some "sparks of holiness," namely, the possibility of repentance.

In keeping with these views, Ḥasidism rejected the obsession with sin and retribution in hellfire that was characteristic of many traditional Jewish preachers of the period in which it arose. It taught instead that brooding over sin and evil, and the gloom which ensued upon such brooding, were themselves evil and to be avoided at all costs. One of the later masters, Rabbi Isaac Meir of Ger, stated the predominant Ḥasidic view when he said:

Whoever talks about and reflects upon an evil thing he has done is thinking the vileness he has perpetrated. And what one thinks, therein is one caught. With one's whole soul one is caught utterly in what one thinks, and so he is still caught in vileness. And he will surely not be able to turn, for his spirit will coarsen and his heart rot, and besides this, a sad mood may come upon him. What would you? Stir filth this way or that, it is still filth. To have sinned or not to have sinned—what does it profit us in heaven? In the time I am brooding on this, I could be stringing pearls for the joy of heaven. That is why it is written: "Depart from evil, and do good"—turn wholly from evil, do not brood in its wake, and do good. You have done wrong? Then balance it by doing right. [4]

In the triad of cardinal virtues that Israel Baal Shem Tov and Ḥasidism proclaimed, joyfulness (*simḥah*) occupied the first place. This, they felt, was absolutely essential. God could not be properly worshiped in sadness or through self-laceration and mortification of the flesh. In contrast with the Lurianic Kabbalah, Ḥasidism generally opposed asceticism and self-denial. When Israel learned that one of his former disciples was imposing an ascetic regimen on himself, he wrote to him:

I hear that you think yourself compelled from religious motives to enter upon a course of fasts and penances. My soul is outraged at your determination. By the counsel of God I order you to abandon such dangerous practices, which are but the outcome of a disordered brain. Is it not written, "Thou shalt not hide thyself from thine own flesh"? Fast then no more than is prescribed. Follow my command and God shall be with you.[5]

The Ḥasidim, as we have noted, did not regard eating, drinking, sleeping, and other ordinary functions of the body as essentially indifferent and nonreligious acts. When carried out in the proper spirit of joyfulness and directed toward God, these activities, they believed, were also sacramental, as truly forms of divine service as the more conventional religious disciplines of prayer and study. Indeed, the service of God through enjoyment of the pleasures of life was considered by some Ḥasidic teachers as perhaps of even greater value than that expressed in spiritual activities, for, through the former, the sparks of holiness imprisoned in the material are raised to their spiritual source. Thus cheerfulness and love of life, frequently expressed in the fondness of the Ḥasidim for song and dance, became one of the hallmarks of their communities.

The second cardinal virtue of Ḥasidism was humility or modesty (shiflut). The Baal Shem Tov himself never wearied of extolling these qualities and contrasting them with their opposites—pride, vanity, smugness. He is reported to have said:

It should be indifferent to a man whether he be praised or blamed, loved or hated, reputed to be the wisest of mankind or the greatest of fools. The test of the real service of God is that it leaves behind it the feeling of humility. If a man after prayer be conscious of the least pride or self-satisfaction, if he thinks, for instance, that he has earned a reward by the ardor of his spiritual exercises, then let him know that he has prayed not to God but to himself. And what is this but disguised idolatry? Before you can find God you must lose yourself.[6]

The Ḥasidim believed that for an individual to achieve what they regarded as the supreme goal of the religious life, the state of "adhesion" or "cleaving" to God (devekut), it was essential that he overcome his natural egotism and self-assertion and remove from himself all vanity and conceit. These, they were convinced, constituted a barrier to the sense of the omnipresence of God and the experience of communion with Him. But it should not be thought that the emphasis of Ḥasidism on humility led to any derogation of man or a low view of his status in the world. Morbid self-flagellation and obsessive contrasting of the nothingness of man with the majesty of God were quite alien to its ethos. One of the later Ḥasidic masters aptly summed up the need for a proper balance between humility and self-regard in the human spirit. "Everyone," he said, "must have two pockets, so that he can reach into the one or the other, according to his needs. In his right pocket are to be the words: 'For my sake was the world created,' and in his left: 'I am but dust and ashes.' " [7]

In addition to joyfulness and humility, Ḥasidism stressed a third major virtue, enthusiasm or fervor. In the literature of the movement this quality is called *hitlahavut*, which means a "kindling" or "setting on fire." The Ḥasidim believed that the perfunctory, rote performance of any *mitzvah*, unaccompanied by burning enthusiasm and an intense surging of love for God, was of little consequence. Prayer especially was regarded as pointless if offered mechanically and without fervor. "Man," Israel Baal Shem Tov is quoted as having said, "must concentrate his entire heart and mind on his prayers, and he must immerse the very life of his soul in each word he pronounces." [8] To attain this kind of ecstatic fervor in prayer the Ḥasidim were advised by some of their teachers to make use of all available stimuli, including swaying bodily movements, gesticulations, loud singing, dancing, and even somersaulting. These came to be viewed by many not only as methods of reaching the state of *hitlahavut* but as manifestations of it. However, wordless prayer, in which the soul is entirely absorbed in ecstatic communion with God, was declared by some Ḥasidic masters to be the superlative form.

❧⚬❧

Although Talmudic Judaism valued prayer highly, it nevertheless tended at times to place it lower in the scale of religious duties than intensive study of Torah. Ḥasidism dissented from this view and made prayer the center of its religious life. While it held, as we have already observed, that man could worship God in a great variety of ways, it nevertheless generally insisted that prayer is the supreme instrument of communion with Him. "In prayer," said the Baal Shem Tov, "man rises to the stage where there is no veil between himself and God, where even his profane thoughts become sanctified, for even in such thoughts there are sparks of holiness which mingled with them when the breaking of the vessels occurred." [9] Prayer was regarded not only as the most effective means of liberating the holy sparks and thus advancing the repair and ultimate redemption of the flawed world—what both Kabbalah and Ḥasidism called *tikkun ha-*

olam—but also as the chief instrumentality for bringing practical benefits from God to the individual. Through prayer, the founder of Ḥasidism taught, disease may be cured, wealth obtained, misfortune averted, and all kinds of blessings secured. He himself believed that every individual had the capacity to offer prayer of such efficacy, but his immediate successors taught that this capacity was beyond the average person and inhered only in the saint, or perfectly righteous man. It was largely from their teaching that both the concept and the institution of the *tzaddik*, which were to play an extremely important role in the history of Ḥasidism, developed.

While the Baal Shem Tov glorified the saintly man, or *tzaddik*, as "the messenger of the *Shechinah*" and urged men to follow his directions, the idea of the *tzaddik* as an actual mediator between the people and God was introduced by his chief disciple and immediate successor, Dov Ber of Meseritz (1710–1772). Dov Ber, also known as the Great Maggid (Preacher) because of his extraordinary preaching ability, was the organizer of Ḥasidism as a mass movement, sending throughout the Ukraine and elsewhere emissaries who won adherents to its teachings by the thousands. Believing as he did that the ordinary Ḥasid could not attain the level of constant communion with God at which prayer becomes fully efficacious, Dov Ber urged each individual to attach himself to a *tzaddik* who had attained this level. Through such attachment and following of the holy man's example, the Ḥasid himself would not only rise to a higher degree of holiness but also obtain the benefits of his master's intercessory powers. "The will of the *tzaddik*," Dov Ber taught, "agrees with the will of God." [10]

Rabbi Jacob Joseph of Polonnoye continued the tendency to exalt the person and power of the *tzaddik*. "The *tzaddik*," he wrote, "is the soul and vital force of the world; the rest of the generation is like the body, which is the garment of the soul. He is the channel through which the divine influence flows to the common people who make up the body of Israel." [11] But what of the fact that a *tzaddik* may be seen at times descending in his conduct to the weakness and sinfulness of ordinary mortals? For such "descents" Jacob Joseph had a simple explanation: "The *tzaddik* must himself possess a particle of uncleanness [*tumah*], so as to be able to join with the common or gross man in order to raise him to a higher state." [12] Every appearance of deviation from holiness on the part of a *tzaddik* thus came to be regarded by his followers as mere illusion; when the master seemed to be indulging in the pleasures of the world or pursuing fame and fortune, he was in fact attempting to liberate the holy sparks imprisoned in matter and to elevate them to their divine source. The corrupting possibilities of such a theory are obvious, and it is hardly surprising that they were occasionally actualized in the later history of Ḥasidism by some unscrupulous *tzaddikim* who managed to behave in thoroughly unsaintly ways without incurring a word of criticism from their adoring followers.

In the period after the death of Dov Ber, Ḥasidism achieved enormous success, winning to its standard within fifty years nearly half the Jewish population of eastern Europe. The movement consisted of numerous local and independent communities, or groups of families, each centering around its own *tzaddik*, who was also known as "the *rebbe*." The latter title was used to distinguish the Ḥasidic leader from the *rav*, or rabbi, of the traditional Talmudic type. Unlike the *rav*, the *rebbe* did not owe his position to his scholarship (though he might be extremely learned) and was not primarily an interpreter of the Law. He derived his authority from his obvious charismatic endowments, the power of his personality, and the firm belief of his followers in his special access to God. (Later on, being born to or descended from a *tzaddik* sufficed.) As for his function, it was not so much to impart to his followers the traditional teachings of the Torah—indeed, some Ḥasidim looked upon their *rebbe* as himself a "living Torah" and believed that his slightest words and acts were manifestations of divine wisdom—as to help bring them closer to God and to mediate God's gifts to them.

Many of the early Ḥasidic leaders—among them men like Mendel of Vitebsk (d. 1788), Pinḥas of Koritz (d. 1791), Mosheh Leib of Sassov (d. 1807), Levi Yitzḥak of Berdichev (d. 1809), and Naḥman of Bratzlav (d. 1811)—were saintly personalities possessed of rare spiritual powers. Each of these great *tzaddikim* developed a unique pattern of worship and piety, as did many of the *tzaddikim* of later generations whose saintliness was no less genuine and original than their predecessors'. In time, however, it came to be believed that the merit of a *tzaddik* was automatically transmitted to his offspring, and the leadership of many Ḥasidic communities became dynastic. That the system of hereditary "tzaddikism" often led to a sad decline in the quality of Ḥasidic leadership need hardly be stated.

The Ḥasidic community itself was a unique kind of society and represents one of the most original contributions of the movement to the history of Judaism. Martin Buber, the foremost modern exponent of Ḥasidic thought, called Ḥasidism "the one great attempt in the history of the Diaspora to make a reality of the original choice and to found a true and just community based on religious principles." [13] The bond that united the members of the Ḥasidic community was their common reverence for their *tzaddik*, a reverence which often approached worship. Not only did he serve them as a living pattern of holiness, but he was their friend and adviser, taking upon himself the burden of their troubles and guiding them in their problems, small and great. His followers would come to his house for counsel and for *segullot* (formulas for good health, success in business ventures, and so on), in return for which they would make a contribution according to their means either to some charity or toward the expenses of his own household.

The home of the *tzaddik* was also the gathering-place of his disciples for worship on Sabbaths and festivals, and especially for the "third meal" of the Sabbath, when they would sit at their beloved master's table, listen to his teaching, and join him in the singing of mystical hymns and melodies. At the High Holy Days no disciple of the *rebbe* would think of worshipping anywhere but in his house, and even the Ḥasid who had moved far away would make every effort to return for the season. United in their devotion to the *rebbe* and basking in the glory reflected from him, his followers formed a closely knit fellowship. Differences of age, learning, and position became irrelevant among the members of the Ḥasidic community. All considered themselves members of a single family and were eager to share each other's joys and sorrows, as well as material goods. The Baal Shem Tov and his successors had stressed in their ethical teaching the imperative of love for all men, even for evildoers and enemies. The true Ḥasid made strenuous efforts to live according to this rule of love, following it especially in his relationships with his fellow Ḥasidim. Thus, the Ḥasidic community was, in a sense, a "welfare" society whose members offered each other mutual support and affection on a continuing basis.

The ability of the Ḥasidic community to give its members a powerful sense of joyous fulfillment, as well as security and self-esteem, was no doubt the chief factor in the extraordinary success of Ḥasidism as a movement in the first half-century of its existence. To be sure, the religious ideas proclaimed by Israel Baal Shem Tov and his successors answered the deeply felt needs of the masses for a message of redemption and appealed more strongly to them than either the legalism and intellectualism of traditional Talmudism or the fantasies of Shabbatian-Frankist messianism. But it is doubtful that merely the ideas of Ḥasidism, without their institutionalization and concretization in the life of real communities, would have had any significant impact. For the community of the Ḥasidic type to come into being and maintain itself, the *tzaddik* appears to have been essential; without him it would have lacked an organizing center and been deprived of its cohesive power. Thus, the institution of "tzaddikism," while responsible in considerable measure, as we shall point out, for the later decline of Ḥasidism, was also necessary for its early flowering and growth.

⋘⧂⧉⧃⋙

The teaching of the Baal Shem Tov and most of the subsequent *tzaddikim* was of a simple, unsystematic, and nonphilosophical character, despite the fact that it employed the ideology and vocabulary of Kabbalist theosophy. Its major vehicles of expression were the parable and the anecdote, and it was intended that it be readily comprehensible to both the unlearned man and the scholar. Ḥasidism, however, also had its theoretical exponent, Rabbi Shneour Zalman (1748–1813) of Liadi, who developed a more intellectual version of it which, while remaining deeply mystical, came closer to the rational and legal spirit of traditional rabbinism.

Born in the northern province of Lithuania, where Jewish scholarship was still intensively cultivated, Shneour Zalman, after receiving a thorough Talmudic education, came to Meseritz to hear the teaching of Dov Ber, the Great Maggid, from his own lips. He became a zealous convert to Ḥasidism and decided to introduce it to the Jews of his native region. But the simple, emotional form of Ḥasidic teaching that had appealed so strongly to the relatively unlearned Jews of southern Poland would not, he realized, have the same attraction for the better-educated Jews of Lithuania. He therefore began the task of formulating a more theoretical system of Ḥasidism which came to be known as *Ḥabad*. The title is an acronym, deriving from the initial Hebrew letters of the names of the three highest *sefirot* of the Kabbalist tradition, *Ḥochmah* (Wisdom), *Binah* (Understanding), and *Daat* (Knowledge).

In his *Likkutei Amarim* (popularly known as the *Tanya*) Shneour Zalman set forth the basic ideas of *Ḥabad* Ḥasidism concerning God and man. The omnipresence of God, the cardinal point in Israel Baal Shem Tov's doctrine, is again stressed and given a complex and systematic exposition. Briefly, according to Shneour Zalman, God's

[181]

creative word, i.e., His power, permeates everything in the universe and brings it from nonbeing into being; were this power to be withdrawn from any entity even for a moment, that thing would immediately return to nothingness. Indeed, apart from God, neither the world nor anything in it has real existence. These are regarded by men as existing independently only because the light of God, or the divine power that sustains them, is covered by their outward form. This view of Shneour Zalman's led to the charge of heresy, and he was accused by his opponents of being a pantheist. It is clear, however, that his view is very far from the classical pantheism of Spinoza. God, for him, is not identical with nature or the universe; in fact, from the point of view of God, according to Shneour Zalman, there is no universe. Yet it can hardly be supposed that his metaphysics is really as acosmistic as it appears. Shneour Zalman must have granted at least relative existence to the created world. Otherwise, man's religious life and God's providential activity in the world, to both of which he ascribed the utmost importance, would be meaningless.

The founder of Ḥabad Ḥasidism also expounded a distinctive view of man. In the *Tanya* man is described as a creature of two souls, the *nefesh ha-behemit* (animal soul) and the *nefesh elohit* (divine soul). The first, according to Shneour Zalman, is located in the left side of the heart and is derived from the "shell" (*kelippah*), or material power in the world, while the second is located in the brain and emanates from the *sefirot*, or divine power. The animal soul is the source of man's passions and vices; the divine soul is the source of his reason (described as consisting of the stages of wisdom, understanding, and knowledge) and his ethical qualities. The normal or average person (*benoni*) experiences an ongoing struggle between these two souls. While, unlike the *tzaddik*, the average person cannot altogether overcome the impulses of the lower soul which lure him to the pleasures of the world, he can subordinate it to the divine soul and make the mind rule the heart.

The means to this goal, Shneour Zalman taught, is study and observance of Torah. The activity of the divine soul is expressed in the powers of thought, speech, and action. All these are to be directed by the average man to study of the Torah and fulfillment of its *mitzvot*. Thereby he can succeed, as it were, in embracing God, for the Torah is the earthly "garment" of God's will and wisdom. In this way also the average man contributes to the process of cosmic redemption. Although he cannot himself "break the shells" and "raise the sparks," he can, through his performance of the *mitzvot*, cause the divine presence to enter the world and add power to the *tzaddikim* in their carrying through of the task of redemption. By proclaiming this teaching, *Ḥabad* Ḥasidism restored Torah study and observance to their former position of centrality in the life of the Jew, retaining at the same time the mystical outlook characteristic of Ḥasidism in general.

While Shneour Zalman reaffirmed the common Ḥasidic exaltation of the *tzaddik* as the instrument of redemption and the channel of divine grace and blessing, he appears to have been disturbed by the spread of the cult of "tzaddikism." He begged his followers to offer their own prayers for their material needs, and not come to him for aid in obtaining them. Furthermore, he refused, as did his successors in *Ḥabad* Ḥasidism, the title *tzaddik*, and chose instead the more traditional title of rabbi, thereby indicating that, in his conception of Ḥasidic leadership, Talmudic learning was more important than the possession of charismatic gifts. In keeping with his more restrained and rationalistic pattern of piety, he also forbade his followers to engage in the vehement bodily movements in prayer which most of the *tzaddikim* encouraged.

❧⟨§⟩❧

In the first years of its expansion throughout the Ukraine, Podolia, and Galicia, the Ḥasidic movement encountered little hostility from the traditional rabbinic authorities. Only when Ḥasidism penetrated into Lithuania, the citadel of rabbinism, did effective opposition arise. The first attack occurred in Vilna in 1772, when the leaders of the community discovered that a small Ḥasidic congregation had arisen in their midst. The community council ordered the congregation to disband. With the consent of Rabbi Elijah ben Solomon Zalman, the Gaon of Vilna, who, as we have observed, was the foremost rabbinic scholar of the age and the acknowledged spiritual guide of Lithuanian Jewry, it issued a ban or *ḥerem* against Ḥasidism, excluding its followers from participation in the activities of the Jewish communities. Thus began a period of strife, lasting for many years and producing bitter dissension throughout much of Russian-Polish Jewry, between the Ḥasidim and their opponents, who came to be called Mitnaggedim. At the center of the struggle stood the revered figure of Elijah, the Gaon of Vilna.

Elijah and the Mitnaggedim attacked Ḥasidism on a number of

grounds, perhaps the most important of which was the *tzaddik* worship of the Ḥasidim. In this their opponents saw a departure from the fundamental Jewish principle that no man requires a mediator between himself and God. They were also apprehensive that the exaltation in Ḥasidism of the *tzaddik* as "a living Torah" would lead to a diminution of the authority of the traditional Torah; indeed, an incipient tendency toward antinomianism is discernible in some early writings of the movement. Minor innovations in traditional practice made by some of the Ḥasidic leaders, such as their adoption of the *Nusaḥ Ari*, or Lurianic version of the prayerbook, and their introduction of a slight change in the method of ritual slaughter, were perceived by the Mitnaggedim as indications of antiauthoritarian and possible schismatic tendencies. Above all, the veneration of the Ḥasidim for the *tzaddik* as the vessel whereby God's grace and blessing is transmitted to men aroused apprehension among the Mitnaggedim that a new and dangerous pseudomessianism might arise out of Ḥasidism. The Mitnaggedim could not overlook the fact that the movement arose in precisely those regions of Poland where Shabbatianism and Frankism had flourished, and they may well have suspected the existence of some affinities between these heresies and Ḥasidism.

The priority given by the Ḥasidim to religious enthusiasm and pietistic emotion over intensive study of Torah and strict observance of its precepts also aroused the wrath of the Mitnaggedim. In this they saw not only a reversal of the classic rabbinic hierarchy of values but also the possibility of a movement toward growing laxity in observance. When Ḥasidism began openly to disparage Talmudic learning and scholarship and even to impugn the character of the traditional rabbis, as in *Toledot Yaakov Yosef* (published in 1780) of Jacob Joseph of Polonnoye, animosity toward the Ḥasidim was intensified, and a new ban against them was endorsed by the Gaon of Vilna.

The Mitnaggedim were also deeply disturbed by the extreme immanentism of the Ḥasidic teaching about God. In the doctrines both of the Baal Shem Tov and of Shneour Zalman they detected pantheistic tendencies and a failure to draw a sufficiently precise distinction between God and the world. To regard God as present in all things and events, including acts of sin, seemed to them to endanger the distinction drawn so sharply by the classic rabbinic tradition between good and evil, the holy and the profane. In this tradition the immanence and transcendence of God had been maintained with equal emphasis, and the tension between these two apparently contradictory envisagements of deity had remained unbroken. In the mystical teaching of Ḥasidism the Mitnaggedim were inclined to see a serious peril that the idea of God's transcendence to the universe might be lost.

Eventually the struggle between the Ḥasidim and their opponents lost much of its bitterness and intensity. This, however, did not happen before some shameful acts, including the denunciation of the Ḥasidim by the Mitnaggedim as subversives and the consequent imprisonment of Shneour Zalman in a czarist dungeon in St. Petersburg, had been perpetrated in the heat of controversy. As the years passed, Ḥasidism, especially in its *Ḥabad* version, abandoned some of its extravagances in the practice of worship that so annoyed the more sober Mitnaggedim, became less radical in its mysticism, and demonstrated that it really posed no substantive threat to preservation of the fundamental norms of the rabbinic tradition. As for the Mitnaggedim, many of them, while remaining generally unfriendly to Ḥasidism, could not fail to be impressed by the emotional zeal and fervent piety of the Ḥasidim and in time came, albeit grudgingly and partially, to acknowledge their religious authenticity. Although the hostility between the groups did not die out completely, it was further abated by their eventual recognition that the real threat to the continued existence of each was not the other but rather an ideology inimical to both—Haskalah, the secularist and humanist movement of enlightenment that succeeded in attracting a growing number of adherents from among east European Jewry as the nineteenth century wore on.

Within fifty years of its beginning as a movement Ḥasidism had already passed the peak of its success, both in terms of intrinsic spiritual power and ability to gain followers, and entered upon its decline. The chief cause of this decline was undoubtedly its *tzaddik* worship, which not only Elijah Gaon and the Mitnaggedim but Shneour Zalman as well had sought in vain to check. Unfortunately, Shneour Zalman's relatively sober and rational brand of Ḥasidism found a significant number of followers only in Lithuania. In Poland, Hungary, and Rumania, where the great masses of the Ḥasidim were concentrated, a far less restrained and less sophisticated version of Ḥasidism, in which the cult of the *tzaddik* was central, prevailed. Here the Ḥasidim came increasingly to look upon their *tzaddikim* as wonder workers. In their credulity, intensified by their lack of even the rudiments of scientific knowledge and education, they ascribed the most extraordinary powers to the *tzaddik* and clamored for miracles from him. While some of the *tzaddikim* strongly repudiated the role of wonder worker, others succumbed to the temptations of power and prestige inherent in their followers' view of them and implicitly or explicitly encouraged their fantastic expectations. This, of course, necessitated opposition on their part to every effort to spread enlightenment and knowledge. With the passing years Ḥasidism became increasingly fanatical, obscurantist, and reactionary, firmly setting its face against all progress and change.

Many of the later *tzaddikim* were deeply religious men who sought only to build with their followers the same kind of holy fellowship at which the early Ḥasidic masters had aimed. But there were also not lacking opportunistic *tzaddikim*, especially among those communities in which the leadership had become hereditary, who did not hesitate to exploit their followers' devotion in the interests of self-aggrandizement and increasing the power of their own dynasty. These men often lived luxuriously within an establishment organized like a royal court. They also engaged in unseemly competition for adherents with other Ḥasidic courts and dynasties. The rivalry among the *tzaddikim* and the consequent fragmentation of the Ḥasidic movement contributed significantly to the attenuation of its religious vitality.

❦

Despite the abuses of "tzaddikism" and the steadfast hostility of the Ḥasidic leaders to all the forces of modernism and progress seeking to penetrate their environment, and notwithstanding its own progressive decline in attractive power, Ḥasidism continued to be a major force in the life of a considerable segment of east European Jewry until that Jewry itself was largely destroyed in the Nazi Holocaust. Today remnants of the movement still survive in Israel and the United States, numbering their strength no longer in the millions but in tens of thousands. Perhaps the most influential of the present-day Ḥasidic groups is the *Ḥabad* school known as Lubavich. With headquarters in New York since 1940 and under the leadership of descendants of Shneour Zalman, the Lubavich Ḥasidim have managed to establish a sizable network of schools and publishing houses to propagate their teachings. They also send throughout the world hundreds of dedicated young missionaries who seek to bring secularly minded and nonobservant Jews back to the practice of Judaism. Devoted followers of the Lubavicher *rebbe* are to be found not only in New York but throughout the world, and form a closely knit brotherhood.

It is difficult to assess the overall impact of Ḥasidism on the millions of Jews who were caught up in it. There is no doubt that it not only brought fresh hope and a new buoyancy to many of its adherents, but also provided them with an authentic religious experience, a strong sense of the presence of God not otherwise easily obtainable, and a profound experience of genuine fellowship and community. It also revived in its followers an appreciation of the glories and beauties of the world of nature—an appreciation to which the official rabbinic tradition makes a perfunctory bow but does not seriously foster. Perhaps these values more than compensate for the obscurantism and dogmatism, the superstition, and the fanatical resistance to scientific knowledge, social progress, and all nonreligious culture that so frequently characterized its later stages.

One of the most valuable legacies of Ḥasidism to contemporary Judaism is its rich treasure of folklore, legend, parable, and gnomic wisdom. The mode of teaching most favored by many of the Ḥasidic masters, beginning with the Baal Shem Tov, was the brief parable or short, pregnant saying expressive of deep religious and moral truth. As the Ḥasidic tradition developed, legends and tales about the earlier masters, their deeds and their words, were elaborated in riotous profusion. Few of the Ḥasidic preachers and storytellers, with the notable exception of Naḥman of Bratzlav, had any sense of aesthetic form or literary style; the original versions of their parables, maxims, and tales—located in arid and crabbed Yiddish and Hebrew texts—are frequently formless and crude. But under the masterful polishing of such gifted writers and stylists as I. L. Peretz and Martin Buber, who have retold and translated them, the dross has fallen away and the pristine splendor is clearly revealed. Buber's version of the Ḥasidic legends and sayings has had a particularly marked impact not only on the contemporary religious consciousness of Judaism but on that of the larger world as well. The recovered lore of Ḥasidism—and, indeed, some of its general mood and spirit—have also inspired a considerable number of modern Jewish musicians, painters, dramatists, and choreographers in their creativity.

In recent years in the United States a mild flirtation with what might be called "pop" Ḥasidism has developed among some American Jews not raised in a traditional Ḥasidic environment, particularly among adolescents and college students. It is appropriate to term the object of their interest and devotion "pop" Ḥasidism, because few of these enthusiasts appear to have any substantive knowledge of Ha-sidic-Kabbalist modes of thought, and fewer still seem to be pre-pared to accept the theology of Hasidim or to commit themselves to following the Hasidic way of life, including the discipline of full ob-servance of the *halachah*. Frequently it is some of the superficial and immediately accessible aspects of Hasidism—its fondness for singing and dancing, its emotionalism, its reverence for charismatic leaders—that elicit their admiration. Insofar as their interest is an expression of longing for authentic faith and for religious spontaneity and immediacy, it is an encouraging phenomenon. Whether this in-terest will deepen and lead to a substantive accretion in the ranks of genuine Hasidism within American Jewry would be hazardous to predict.

CHAPTER

❧ VIII ❧

Into the Modern World

WHILE east European Jewry in the last decades of the eighteenth century was caught up in the ferment created by the rise and spread of Ḥasidism, it did not then, or for a long time thereafter, emerge out of the general social and intellectual isolation from its larger environment that characterized the medieval European Jewish community as a whole. At that very time, however, the Jews of central and western Europe were witnessing social changes and the emergence of new ideological currents that were soon to result in the breakdown of their long separation from non-Jewish society, and to catapult them into the mainstream of the life of the modern world.

Many factors converged to bring about the entrance of Jews into western society. Not the least significant was the mercantilist capitalism which the European nation-states of the seventeenth and eighteenth centuries had come to espouse as their economic philosophy. Mercantilism was not conducive to the maintenance of religious prejudice and persecution. These were soon recognized as likely to entail definite disadvantages in the effort of a nation to attain for itself the mercantilist goal of a favorable balance of trade. Jews, with their long experience in the intricacies of finance and commerce, came increasingly to be regarded as an economic resource of which constructive use had to be made; they could not simply be left to wither in ghetto isolation. Thus, small numbers of Jews, whose commercial talents might be expected to help increase the nation's prosperity, were given "toleration" and the right to live and carry on business activities in their realms by the rulers of the Netherlands, England, Denmark, France, and Prussia. In the German states of the seventeenth and eighteenth centuries a number of Jews rose out of the ghetto to attain the privileged status and title of *Hofjuden*, or Court Jews. Some of these Court Jews, who amassed great wealth as bankers and business agents of the rulers and as purveyors to their armies, did not hesitate to act as *shtadlanim*, or intercessors, for their fellow Jews, exercising their influence at court to obtain rights and privileges which foreshadowed the emancipation of later times.[1] In general, however, it was not the sporadic influence of the relatively few *Hofjuden* and Jewish financiers but the increasingly prominent and indispensable role played by ever larger numbers of Jewish merchants and traders throughout the economies of practically all the nation-states of western and central Europe that served as a significant factor in the eventual grant of civic and political rights to all Jews in these states.

Another contributory factor was the rapid progress of science and the prestige of scientific method in this era. The advance of scientific knowledge was accompanied by a corresponding decline in the authority and credibility of the traditional ecclesiastical structures and dogmas which had for centuries dominated the mentality of the European populace, and which, along with other factors, had conspired to reduce the Jew of the Middle Ages to the status of a pariah, outside the boundaries of Christian society. The revolutionary discoveries of Copernicus, Galileo, Kepler, and Newton succeeded finally not only in undermining the cosmological doctrines taught by the Church but in leading many to a denial of supernatural revelation and to an affirmation of the capacity of the unaided human mind to attain a full understanding of the universe. Reflecting the new scientific approach, the great British empiricist, who may also be regarded as one of the chief progenitors of the philosophy of the Enlightenment, John Locke (1632–1704), in his *Essay Concerning Human Understanding*, rejected "innate ideas" as the source of knowledge and insisted that all knowledge is ultimately derived from sensation. Revelation, in his view, could not disclose any truths not discoverable through experience and reflection.

As the scientific and rationalist spirit of the Enlightenment gained ascendancy, the Church and its dogmas came under increasingly trenchant criticism. Included in this criticism was its intolerant attitude toward non-Christians and their consequent exclusion from civil rights in the Christian state. Locke himself, in his "Letter Concerning Toleration," published in 1689, had maintained that "neither Pagan, nor Jew, ought to be excluded from the civil rights of the commonwealth because of his religion." This view, as well as the more general proposition that the state ought to be organized entirely as a secular institution, free of all ecclesiastical control, and that religion should be a matter solely of individual conscience with religious freedom guaranteed to every man, was to be defended by a number of other influential figures in the century that followed, not only in England but also in France and the German states.

The broad humanitarianism that generally pervaded the thought of European intellectuals in the Age of Reason, and the liberal, non-dogmatic spirit of the deistic religious outlook which, for many who had been imbued with the ideas of the Enlightenment, came to replace supernaturalist Christian faith, also contributed significantly to the eventual emancipation of the Jews. The idea of the natural equality of all men had been powerfully advocated by some important European thinkers in the sixteenth and seventeenth centuries. Now the concept of a universal human nature and a universal rationality in which all men share became increasingly popular, leading to widespread condemnation of such institutions as slavery, the slave trade, and the European prison system. But if the essential humanity of the Negro slave or of the victim of a cruel and irrational penal system could no longer be overlooked, neither could that of the Jew. Liberal spirits such as Charles Louis Montesquieu arose to question the morality as well as the rationality of continuing the persecutions and ghetto restrictions so long inflicted upon the Jews.

As the eighteenth century progressed and the humanitarian ideals of the Enlightenment gained strength, demands for ameliorating the conditions under which the Jews lived came occasionally to be voiced. Not all of the leading figures of the Enlightenment championed the cause of the Jew. No less a person than Voltaire, who so scathingly denounced the irrational prejudices and outmoded social institutions of the *ancien régime*, continued to harbor such intense hostility to the Jews that he was moved to write in his article "Juifs" in the *Dictionnaire philosophique:* "We find in them only an ignorant and barbarous people who have long united the most sordid avarice with the most detestable superstition and the most invincible hatred for all peoples who have tolerated and enriched them." (To which, however, he added, "Still we ought not to burn them.") Nor did some of the other French *philosophes*, including men like Baron d'Holbach and Denis Diderot, cherish a much friendlier attitude toward the Jews. But others, under the sway of the humanitarian spirit of the Age of Reason, felt keenly the injustice of the prejudices and restrictions visited upon the Jews and were impelled to call for their removal. One such was the famous German dramatist and critic Gotthold Ephraim Lessing. Another was the noted Prussian historian and councilor of state Christian Wilhelm von Dohm, who in 1781 wrote an important and influential pro-Jewish tract entitled *Über die bürgerliche Verbesserung der Juden* (*On the Civic Amelioration of the Jews*) in which he sought to demonstrate that noble and magnanimous persons were to be found even among that people which had for so long been despised by the Christian world as the enemies of Christ.

Long before the spirit of the Enlightenment converged with the other factors mentioned above to bring civic emancipation to the Jews of central and western Europe, these Jews were to experience an Enlightenment movement within their own midst and to enjoy the beginnings of a cultural emancipation which prepared them, at least in some measure, for the political emancipation to come. At the center of the movement for Jewish enlightenment and cultural emancipation was Moses Mendelssohn (1729–1786). Mendelssohn occupies an important place in the history of modern Judaism not only because of his major contributions in facilitating the transition of the Jew from ghetto isolation into the mainstream of European civilization, but also because he was the first thinker to recognize and wrestle with the basic problem that inevitably confronted the Jew once he had made the transition. This problem, reduced to its essentials, was how to maintain loyalty to the ancient religious tradition of Judaism and affirm its continuing validity in the face of the challenges hurled at it by the philosophies and ideologies of the larger world.

Mendelssohn's own life represents a remarkable metamorphosis that was unique among Jews of his age—from a humble youth spent in the Jewish ghetto of a provincial German town to a maturity in which he was admired, indeed lionized, by the leading intellectual lights in the Berlin of the *Aufklärung* era.

Born the son of an impoverished Torah scribe in 1729 in Des-

sau, the young Mendelssohn received the traditional Jewish education of his time. He early demonstrated such mental agility and
thirst for learning that he was taken under the wing of the rabbi of
Dessau, David Frankel, who personally guided his studies in the
Bible and rabbinic literature and even introduced him to the subtleties of Maimonides' *Guide of the Perplexed*. When Frankel left Dessau
in 1743 to become chief rabbi of Berlin, the fourteen-year-old Mendelssohn followed his teacher to the Prussian capital. Enrolling in
Frankel's academy, he continued his Talmudic studies, but also,
after quickly achieving command of the German language, began
an intensive exploration of secular fields of learning. In Berlin at
the time there were already a number of Jews well versed in science,
classical languages, and philosophy. Mendelssohn attracted the notice of several of these, who gave him instruction in mathematics and
Latin and led him to the writings of some highly admired German
philosophers, especially Leibniz and Christian von Wolff.

In his twenties Mendelssohn was introduced to Gotthold Lessing,
who became his lifelong friend and encouraged him to begin writing
on philosophical and literary subjects. In 1763 the young Jew
achieved the distinction of winning first prize in an essay contest
sponsored by the Prussian Academy on the subject of *die Evidenz in
metaphysischen Wissenschaften* for an entry in which he sought to demonstrate that metaphysical (i.e., religious) principles are as susceptible of logical demonstration as are the principles of science. The reputation Mendelssohn thereby achieved in the intellectual circles of
Berlin was immensely heightened when a few years later, in 1767,
he published his book *Phaedon*, a defense of the idea of the immortality of the soul modeled after Plato's *Phaedo*. Marked by no great
originality of thought, the book apparently answered a widespread
contemporary need, for it attained instantaneous success. Translated
from German into several languages, *Phaedon* found large numbers of
admiring readers all over Europe. Because of it Mendelssohn came to
be widely known as the "Jewish Plato" and the "German Socrates,"
and achieved general recognition as one of the outstanding representatives of the German Enlightenment. Many travelers to Berlin, including members of the French and German nobility, regarded their
visit to the Prussian capital as incomplete if they could not call on
the remarkable Jew who wrote so eloquently and with such brilliant
literary style on profound philosophical questions.

Although Mendelssohn was in his youth and remained to the end
of his days a traditional and observant Jew, his chief interest in his

twenties and thirties was the world of German literature and philosophy. Already in this period his religious thinking was influenced by the "natural theology" then being expounded by a number of Protestant theologians in Germany. These theologians, whose thought was nourished by the rationalist spirit of the Enlightenment, held that the truth of certain fundamental religious principles—the existence of God, the reality of divine providence, and the immortality of the soul—could be apprehended by any man of reason and common sense, and did not require supernatural revelation for their validation. They further maintained that these principles constituted the common foundation of all higher religions. Mendelssohn espoused their concept of "the religion of humanity" and perceived in it nothing inconsistent with his Judaism. He apparently hoped that in its light Jews and Christians would eventually come to recognize each other as sharing, despite their differences, the fundamental principles of a common faith, and would learn to live with each other in amity and mutual tolerance. But this hope was shattered when, two years after the publication of his *Phaedon*, he was publicly challenged by a Swiss theologian, Johann Caspar Lavater, in the latter's preface to a book by the Geneva naturalist and philosopher Charles Bonnet which he had translated and published under the title *An Examination of the Proofs for Christianity*, either to refute the book's arguments or to do "what truth and honesty demand and what Socrates would have done had he read the book and found it irrefutable"—i.e., abandon his former faith and become a Christian. Mendelssohn had always shunned religious polemic, but Lavater's public challenge forced him to justify his personal loyalty to his ancestral religion. It also impelled him to a deeper and more intensive concern with Judaism and Jewish life than he had previously manifested.

In his *Open Letter* replying to Lavater, Mendelssohn defended his adherence to Judaism in strong terms:

> My study of the foundations of my religious faith does not date from yesterday. Very early in my life I had already become aware of the need to examine my views and actions. . . . If my decision, after all these years of study, had not been entirely in favor of my religion, I would certainly have found it necessary to make my convictions known publicly. . . . However, inasmuch as my investigations strengthened me in the faith of my fathers, I was able to continue in it quietly, without feeling that I had to render an account of my convictions to the world.[2]

Reproaching Lavater for his proselytizing zeal, Mendelssohn called his attention to the fact that Judaism, unlike Christianity, does not seek to convert men of other faiths, but concedes that every man can be "saved" by his own righteous conduct. "All who live in accordance with the religion of nature and of reason," he wrote in a formulation that owes as much to the Enlightenment conception of a universal natural religion as to Talmudic teaching, "are called 'the righteous among other nations'; they too are entitled to eternal bliss." [3]

Mendelssohn declined to polemicize against Christianity in his *Open Letter* to Lavater, but it is evident from other letters of his written in 1770 and 1771 that he believed that Judaism was superior to Christianity inasmuch as it did not, in his view, demand belief in any supernatural dogmas that are contradicted by human reason. These letters also make clear that the conception of Judaism which he was to formulate more than a decade later in his *Jerusalem*—that it consists of the principles proclaimed by the universal "religion of reason" together with a particular "revealed legislation" intended for and binding upon the Jewish people alone—was already in his mind at the time of the Lavater affair.

The controversy with Lavater and its unpleasant aftermath were personally disillusioning experiences for Mendelssohn, but they had the effect of intensifying his Jewish self-consciousness and deepening his concern with the problems of his own people. He realized that he could not serve the cause of improving the situation of his fellow Jews merely by setting an example of high personal virtue and achieving renown as a philosopher and writer. Henceforth, much of Mendelssohn's work was to be directed toward two goals: First, changing those aspects of contemporary Jewish life which, he believed, prevented the individual Jew from gaining general acceptance as a Jew within the larger society, and, second, advocating such a reconstruction of the political foundations of that society that the Jew might participate fully in its life and yet remain a Jew.

Within the Jewish community itself the chief barrier which kept Jews apart from the larger German world, Mendelssohn felt, was their cultural isolation. To be sure, in the Berlin of his day there were already a few Jews who had acquired a considerable degree of secular learning, but for the vast majority of Jews in Germany the thought and culture of the outside world were *terra incognita*. Their intellectual horizons were completely bounded by the Talmudic studies of the traditional Jewish school. The fact that even their language was not German but the Judeo-German (Yiddish) dialect effectively barred them from the knowledge and thought of the larger world and enclosed them in a world of their own that had scarcely changed from the time of the Middle Ages. This isolation, Mendelssohn was convinced, had to be broken down and the spirit of the Enlightenment allowed to penetrate the Jewish community.

In furtherance of this goal he and some of his disciples advocated a different kind of education for Jewish children, and worked for the establishment of a new type of school that would combine Jewish and secular studies, along with vocational training. Young Jews, they urged, must not only have a knowledge of Hebrew and of the Bible and *Talmud* but must also learn German thoroughly and acquire some familiarity with science, mathematics, geography, and history. The curriculum of the Jewish Free School (*Jüdische Freischule*) of Berlin, the establishment of which in 1778 was encouraged by Mendelssohn, attempted to meet these requirements. Both religious and secular subjects were included, and all were taught in German.

It also appears to have been at least partly with the deliberate intent of weaning his fellow Jews away from the use of Yiddish and spreading among them knowledge of the German language, thereby providing the indispensable key for access to the realm of European thought and culture, that Mendelssohn undertook his celebrated translation of the Pentateuch into German. The translation, in Mendelssohn's elegant German, was printed in Hebrew characters, the only alphabet which most Jewish readers knew, and accompanied by a commentary in Hebrew, known as the *Biur*, in the writing of which Mendelssohn enlisted the aid of several collaborators. Completed in 1783, the translation aroused a storm of controversy among orthodox leaders in Europe. While a few rabbis, among them the Gaon of Vilna and the chief rabbi of Berlin, Herschel Levin, welcomed and approved Mendelssohn's work, many others attacked it vociferously out of their apprehension that a knowledge of German would inevitably weaken the attachment of Jews to their traditional religious studies and lead them instead to concentration on secular learning.

Despite this opposition, Mendelssohn's Bible translation was widely read and intensively studied both when it first appeared and in later years. It undoubtedly served as the means whereby many Jews, not only in Germany but in eastern Europe, gained their knowledge of German and were thus enabled to pass from the intellectual isolation of the ghetto to their first acquaintance with European culture. The nineteenth-century Jewish historian Heinrich Graetz was probably guilty of some overstatement when he wrote of

Mendelssohn's translation, "thousands of *Talmud* students from the great houses of study in Hamburg, Prague, Nikolsburg, Frankfort-on-the-Main, Fuerth, and even from Poland, became little Mendelssohns. . . . The inner freedom of the Jews . . . dates from this translation"; [4] but that it had a considerable effect in furthering the cultural emancipation of European Jewry in the late eighteenth and early nineteenth centuries can hardly be denied.

◦⟨⟩◦

Concerned as Mendelssohn was to effect the broadening of the intellectual horizons of his fellow Jews and their cultural emancipation, he also understood that the civic and political emancipation he desired for them depended ultimately on the overthrow of the idea and institution of the "Christian state," in which citizenship was considered the right only of those who belonged to the state religion, and on the emergence, in its stead, of a secular, pluralistic society all of whose members would enjoy religious freedom along with political equality. To the advocacy of such a society he devoted a major part of his little book entitled *Jerusalem: Or on Religious Power and Judaism*. Published in 1783, *Jerusalem* sets forth not only Mendelssohn's vision of the kind of society in which Jews would obtain complete freedom and the right to live as Jews but also presents his mature philosophy of Judaism. From the perspective of the history of Judaism, it is unquestionably the most significant of his writings.

In the first part of *Jerusalem* Mendelssohn defined what he regarded as the separate and distinct spheres of authority of the state and of religion respectively. While both are concerned with man's actions as well as his beliefs, only those actions and beliefs arising out of his relationship with his fellows are the legitimate province of the state, while those deriving from his relationship to God belong to the sphere of religion. "Insofar as man's actions and convictions, which serve the common good, spring from the relations between man and man, they are the domain of the civil law; where the source of man's actions and convictions is his relationship to God, they are the domain of church, synagogue, and mosque." [5] Whereas the state, Mendelssohn further urged, may rightfully employ the sanctions of the law and its powers of coercion to regulate the behavior of its citizens in such a way as to secure the common welfare of society, religion may have recourse to no methods other than teaching and persuasion to gain adherence to its precepts and practices. Moreover, the individual's freedom of thought and conscience in religious matters must in no way be infringed by either civil or religious authority: "Neither church nor state has the right to impose any restraint upon a man's principles and convictions or to make his status, rights, or claims contingent upon these principles and convictions." [6] Although at this point he explicitly demanded total religious freedom for the individual and maintained that a person's citizenship rights in the state should not be dependent upon his religious beliefs and affiliations, Mendelssohn's position was not sufficiently free of inconsistency to prevent him from writing in another place in *Jerusalem* that "the state must be vigilant, so that no doctrines will be spread which are detrimental to public welfare or which, like atheism or Epicureanism, might undermine the foundations of society." [7]

Mendelssohn's concern in the first part of *Jerusalem* was not only to defend—without, as we have observed, complete absence of contradiction—the individual's religious freedom from interference by the state, but also to safeguard it against the coercive power of ecclesiastical authority, including that of the rabbis. Religious sentiment and loyalty, he believed, cannot be forced. Thus he condemned the use of the ban or excommunication, to which the Jewish religious authorities of his day seem to have resorted rather frequently as a means of enforcing discipline within the community. To expel a dissenter from the religious community, instead of seeking to change his views by means of rational persuasion, is, he declared in *Jerusalem*, "like denying a sick person admission to a pharmacy." [8]

The general thrust of Mendelssohn's argument in the first half of *Jerusalem* was that in a properly organized society a man's religious beliefs ought to be regarded as his personal affair, and that neither civil nor religious authority should be granted the power to compel religious conformity by expelling from the community, or otherwise punishing, the dissident. Opposition to the use of coercion by rabbinical authorities had already been expressed earlier by Mendelssohn in the preface he had written in 1782 to Marcus Herz's German translation of *Vindiciae Judaeorum*, the apologetic treatise composed by the famous seventeenth-century rabbi of Amsterdam, Menasseh ben Israel. But was such a view really compatible with Judaism, which, in its authoritative literature, set forth a complex system of rewards and punishments to enforce compliance with its precepts? Was Mendelssohn not destroying the authority of the Torah by rejecting the propriety of punishment for its violators? Could he, in the light of his views, still be regarded as an authentic

Jew? These were among the questions and challenges that had been put to him by unfriendly critics in reaction to the plea he had made for the abandonment of religious coercion in his preface to *Vindiciae Judaeorum*. In an attempt to answer them, he devoted the second half of *Jerusalem* to an exposition of his own conception of the essential nature of Judaism as a religion.

The fundamental theological tenets of Judaism—which Mendelssohn understood as consisting of its belief in the existence and unity of God, divine providence, and the immortality of the soul—are not, he maintained, peculiar to Judaism; they are the elements of the "common religion of humanity." Nor are they the products of a particular supernatural revelation communicated at a specific time and place; instead they must be recognized as eternal and universal principles—*vérités de raison*, to use Leibniz's term—whose validity is self-evident to every rational understanding. If the term "revelation" is at all appropriate in connection with these tenets, it is only in the sense that "the supreme Being has revealed them to all rational creatures through concepts and events inscribed on their souls with a script that is legible and intelligible at all times and in all places." [9] Since the eternal truths of religion are indispensable to man's happiness, Mendelssohn argued, they must be available equally to all men. To suppose that God revealed them to only a part of mankind and abandoned the rest of the human race to darkness would be, in effect, to deny His essential goodness.

Beyond the fundamental tenets whose truth is universally acknowledged by all rational creatures, Judaism, Mendelssohn urged in *Jerusalem*, has no authoritative dogmas, no articles of belief which its adherents must accept on faith. Mendelssohn was aware that Maimonides in the twelfth century had formulated thirteen theological principles which the overwhelming majority of Jews accepted as the substance of their faith, but he insisted that this was an "accidental effort," and that neither the attempt of Maimonides to formulate a creed for Judaism nor similar attempts by later Jewish thinkers of the Middle Ages had forged any "shackles for our beliefs." In support of his contention that Judaism is nondogmatic and noncreedal and allows its adherents complete freedom of religious thought, Mendelssohn pointed out that "among the precepts and ordinances of the Mosaic law, there is none saying, 'You shall believe' or 'You shall not believe.' All say, 'You shall do' or 'You shall not do.' " And he added: "You are not commanded to believe, for faith accepts no commands; it accepts only what comes to it by reasoned conviction." [10]

Judaism commands not faith but deeds. According to Mendelssohn, it is then essentially not a creed or a religion in the ordinary sense, but rather a system of laws and commandments, or, in his own terminology, a "revealed legislation." While in his view the fundamental theological principles of Judaism are identical with the eternal, universal, rational, nonrevealed truths of the common "religion of humanity," its laws and commandments must be acknowledged as the product of a particular supernatural revelation. These, Mendelssohn declared, following classic Talmudic teaching, were given exclusively to the Jews and were to be binding on them alone as the expression of God's special will for the Jewish people. "The lawgiver," he wrote, "was God—God not as Creator and Sustainer of the universe, but God as Protector and covenanted Friend of their ancestors; God as Redeemer, Founder and Leader, as King and Sovereign of this nation. He solemnly sanctioned His laws, enjoining them upon the people and their descendants as unalterable obligations." [11] It is these revealed laws, not the rational theological principles which Judaism shares with the universal "religion of humanity," that constitute its unique substance.

In the biblical era the laws revealed by God to Israel, Mendelssohn pointed out in response to those critics who had challenged his view that coercion and punishment have no place in Judaism, served as the constitution of a Jewish state. Since they were simultaneously religious and civic legislation, and since they constituted the foundation of the social-political order, it was necessary and proper that those who violated them be subject to punishment. But the biblical state, with the Torah as its constitution, was a special and temporary phenomenon. "This constitution existed only once. . . . It has disappeared, and only the Almighty knows among what people and in which century something similar may appear once again." [12] With the end of the Mosaic state, Mendelssohn explained, those laws of the Torah which governed its social-political life or which had to do with the cult of the Temple no longer apply. However, all the rest of the Torah, its legislation regulating the life of the individual Jew, remains fully in force, since it was openly and publicly revealed by God and has never been revoked by Him. On this point Mendelssohn was emphatic: "Personal commandments, duties imposed upon every son of Israel, which are unrelated to Temple service and land ownership in Palestine, must, as far as I can see, be strictly observed according to the words of the law until it will please the Most High to set our conscience at rest and to proclaim their abrogation clearly and publicly." [13] But the duty of observing these commandments, he held, is a matter between the individual Jew and God and ought not to be the subject of any communal or ecclesiastical coercion.

Thus Mendelssohn, the rationalist philosopher of the Enlightenment who could admit no belief that contradicted reason, proclaimed, paradoxically enough, that Judaism consisted not of any unique theological doctrines but of a set of special laws that had been given to the Jewish people through a supernatural revelation. He remained enough of a rationalist to urge that all the laws of the Torah "refer to, or are based upon, eternal verities, or remind us of them, or induce us to ponder them." [14] But he was not willing to conclude from this that these laws are to be observed by the Jew only if he happens to discover in them some rational or moral significance, and otherwise they may be ignored. As the revealed will of God, they are all obligatory upon every Jew, and he must not presume to set himself up as their judge and decide for himself which he will fulfill and which neglect.

Mendelssohn apparently sensed no contradictions in his theory of Judaism. In his own personal life a commitment to reason and freedom of thought in matters of religious belief lived in peaceful coexistence with a profound conviction that the Torah is a God-given discipline that no Jew may cast off. That he had not demonstrated how the latter conviction could be logically reconciled with the former commitment seems not to have troubled him. Nor does he appear to have been aware of any difficulty in assuming, as he did, that the God apprehended by all men of reason as "the Creator and Sustainer of the universe" is identical with the God who, in His giving of the Torah to Israel, reveals Himself as the "Protector and covenanted Friend," the "Founder and Leader," the "King and Sovereign" of the Jewish people.

Identifying the unique content of Judaism with the supernaturally revealed ceremonial legislation of the Torah, Mendelssohn urged his fellow Jews to remain uncompromisingly loyal to it. But his conception of Judaism as essentially revealed law found little acceptance among his contemporaries and successors, nor, as events proved, did it succeed in keeping Jews from leaving the fold of Judaism. Neither the rationalistic spirit dominating the Enlightenment era, which was already drawing to a close, nor the sentimental, pietistic mood of the Romantic era, which was soon to dawn, could find much attractive power in a religion that had been reduced to a set of ritual and cultic observances. If Judaism, as Mendelssohn had taught, has no theological uniqueness as a faith but simply shares the tenets of the universal religion of reason, if what is peculiar to it is only a series of legal prescriptions whose claim to being of divine origin cannot be justified on any rational ground, and if, furthermore, observance of these prescriptions comes to be felt (as happened in the case of some of Mendelssohn's own followers and admirers who did not share his reverence for Jewish law) as burdensome, anachronistic, and lacking any profound religious significance, why—a considerable number of Jews apparently began to ask themselves—persevere in adherence to Judaism, especially when conversion to the dominant faith could mean release from the prejudices and disabilities visited upon the loyal Jew?

Mendelssohn himself can hardly be charged with significant responsibility in the matter, but the fact remains that the last decades of the eighteenth century and the first decades of the nineteenth century were a period of large-scale defection of Jews from Judaism in Germany. The philosopher's own children, with the single exception of his son Joseph, all became converts either to Protestantism or Catholicism shortly after his death, and their example was followed by thousands of other Jews of the time. Obviously Mendelssohn's practical formula for living as a Jew in a non-Jewish world—"adopt the mores and constitution of the country in which you find yourself, but be steadfast in upholding the religion of your fathers, too" [15]— proved an overly simplistic solution incapable of coping with the complexities of the situation faced by Jews on their entry into the mainstream of European life. He had been made keenly aware of the problems involved in being a Jew faithful to his traditional religious heritage and at the same time a full participant in the intellectual and cultural life of the larger world, and he had struggled with them long and hard. But the solution that had proved efficacious for him personally did not prove so for Jews generally, and the philosophy of Judaism that he elaborated in *Jerusalem* yielded little guidance for those who came after him.

⋰§§⋱

Mendelssohn had been confident that the civic emancipation of his coreligionists would not be long delayed. And indeed, the process of officially abrogating the restrictions and disabilities which the Jews of Europe had borne for centuries and of extending citizenship rights to them by the various nations in which they lived began not long after his death. Political emancipation, however, was not obtained by the European Jew overnight, nor, once obtained, was it always a permanently secured possession. Frequently citizenship rights were given to a nation's Jews to be enjoyed for a few years, then suddenly revoked or sharply curtailed. Complete political equality was not finally achieved by the Jews of such countries as Germany and Italy until the 1870s, and most of the Jews of eastern Europe had to wait until the twentieth century for any significant degree of civic emancipation.

The first European nation to grant its Jews citizenship rights was France. The revolutionary National Assembly which convened in Paris in 1789 proceeded in August of that year to issue its celebrated "Declaration of the Rights of Man," and proclaimed the principle that no one must be "disturbed" on account of his religious beliefs. The specific question of the political status of the Jews soon engaged the attention of the Assembly. This body showed little hesitation in granting civic rights to one of the two French Jewries, the Sephardim, who were concentrated in Bordeaux and Bayonne. These Jews of Spanish and Portuguese extraction, arriving in France in the second half of the seventeenth century as Marranos and reverting to Judaism, had accumulated both wealth and culture through their international trading activity. In point of fact they had already achieved many of the rights and privileges they desired, and the granting of political rights by the National Assembly on January 27, 1790, was largely a *pro forma* gesture.

But the Ashkenazic Jews living in Alsace-Lorraine, most of them poor and engaged in petty trade and moneylending, presented the Assembly with a more difficult problem. They had not, generally speaking, adapted their way of life to French culture and were cordially despised by most of their Christian neighbors. On behalf of the Ashkenazic Jews Lippmann Cerf-Berr, a prominent member of the Strasbourg community, and other Jewish leaders presented to Count de Mirabeau and Abbé Henri Gregoire, two of the most influential figures in the Assembly, both of whom had already proclaimed their strong support for the cause of emancipating the French Jews, a petition for the enfranchisement of all their people. In the sharp and extensive debate that followed in the Assembly, the eloquence of Mirabeau and Gregoire finally carried the day against those deputies who sought to withhold political equality from the hated Jews of Alsace-Lorraine. On September 29, 1791, the rights that had been granted earlier to the Sephardim were extended to all French Jews.

These emancipatory acts of the National Assembly signalized the beginning of a new epoch in the history of Judaism and the Jewish people. At long last Jews were no longer aliens everywhere in Europe; in revolutionary France they had achieved the status of free and equal citizens. But this status carried a price tag. It would have to be paid for by Jews through a progressive abandonment of what had been their mode of existence throughout the medieval period as members of a relatively strong, independent, self-governing, and cohesive ethnic-religious group. Henceforth French Jews would be expected to live as Frenchmen whose personal faith happened to be Judaism, rather than as members of an autonomous, self-enclosed Jewish community with a powerful sense of kinship to one another and to the Jewish people as a whole. The price to be exacted for emancipation had been made quite clear in the declaration of the liberal deputy Count Clermont-Tonnerre to the National Assembly: "To the Jew as an individual—everything; to the Jews as a nation—nothing." It became even clearer, as we shall presently see, when Napoleon convoked his Assembly of Jewish Notables and his so-called "Sanhedrin" some years later.

In the first flush of excitement over their attainment of citizenship, many French Jews responded with exuberant expressions of gratitude to the land that had suddenly become for them, too, *La Patrie*. In a Parisian journal Samuel Levy rhapsodized: "France, which has been first to remove from us the shame of Judea, is our Land of Israel; its hills, our Zion; its waters, our Jordan. Let us drink its living waters, the waters of freedom. . . . The people that was enslaved more than any other will pray for the people that broke its fetters . . . for France, the haven of the oppressed." The previously mentioned Lippmann Cerf-Berr wrote ecstatically to his fellow Jews in Alsace:

At length the day has arrived on which the veil is torn asunder which covered us with humiliation. We have at last again obtained the rights of which we have been deprived for eighteen centuries. How deeply at this moment should we recognize the wonderful grace of the God of our forefathers! On the 28th of September we were the only inhabitants of this great realm who seemed doomed to eternal humiliation and slavery, and on the very next day, a memorable day which we shall always commemorate, didst Thou inspire these immortal legislators of France to speak one word which caused sixty thousand unhappy beings, who had hitherto lamented their hard lot, to be plunged suddenly into the intoxicating joys of purest delight. God chose the noble French nation to reinstate us in our due privileges and to bring us to a new birth, just as in former days He selected Antiochus and Pompey to degrade and oppress us.[16]

In the war of the Republic against Prussia and Austria (1792–1793), Jews sought to prove their loyalty and gratitude to France by eagerly joining the National Guard in large numbers and serving with notable bravery in the French army. Some congregations even contributed their synagogue plate and ornaments to the war effort. During the Robespierre Terror of 1793–1794, when both churches and synagogues were temporarily closed, there were even a few Jews who voluntarily joined the new "Cult of Reason" and gladly came to worship in its major temple, formerly known as the Cathedral of Notre Dame. The great majority, however, continued loyally to practice their ancestral religion.

In the two decades that followed the political emancipation of the French Jews the armies of France, sweeping across Europe, brought with them temporary civic equality in greater or lesser degree to the Jews of almost every state and territory they occupied—the Netherlands, Belgium, the Italian cities of Venice, Rome, and Leghorn, and a number of the German states. Not everywhere, however, was the gift of civic equality accepted with unalloyed enthusiasm by its recipients. In the Netherlands the more conservative leaders of the Jewish community resisted it, fearing that the price to be paid—loss of Jewish communal autonomy, increased susceptibility to the blandishments of assimilation, and general weakening of the traditional Jewish mode of life—was far too high.

The justification of the apprehensions of these and other Jews who viewed political emancipation as, at best, a mixed blessing became more evident after Napoleon Bonaparte assumed the title of emperor. Responding to complaints that Jewish moneylenders were extorting usurious rates of interest and foreclosing mortgages among the peasants in Alsace, as well as to reports that Jews generally were evading military conscription, Napoleon, whose personal attitude toward the Jews was always rather ambivalent, in 1806 issued a rescript declaring a one-year moratorium on all debts held by Jewish creditors against farmers in the eastern departments of France. At the same time he ordered the convening of a "Jewish States-General" that would prepare articles abolishing usury and take measures toward reviving among Jews "the sentiments of civic morality that have unfortunately been moribund among too large a number of them by reason of the state of degradation in which they have long languished."

The Assembly of Notables, a carefully selected group of one hundred and twelve prominent businessmen, financiers, and rabbis who assembled at Napoleon's command at the Hôtel de Ville in Paris on July 29, 1806, were immediately informed by the emperor's representative, Count Louis Mathieu Molé, that their task was to prove themselves deserving of the rights of French citizens by providing satisfactory answers to a series of twelve questions. The first three of these dealt with Jewish attitudes toward polygamy, divorce, and intermarriage of Jews and Christians; underlying them was the basic question whether Jews were willing to be governed by the civil legislation of France rather than their own religious law in these matters. The next three focused on Jewish attitudes toward non-Jews and the degree of Jewish loyalty to France: Were Jews willing to consider Frenchmen their brothers and to grant them the status of monotheists under Jewish law? Did Jews regard France as their homeland? Were they willing to fight in its defense and to accept its civil code? The remaining questions dealt with the nature and scope of religious authority within the Jewish community, and the permissibility of lending money on usurious terms. What Napoleon clearly desired from the Notables, it is apparent from these questions, was an assurance that the jurisdiction of rabbinic *halachah* in civil and judicial matters would give way before the supremacy of French law, and, more importantly, a complete renunciation by Jews of all claims to Jewish nationhood and separate corporate status within France.

The Assembly of Notables and the so-called "Sanhedrin" which Napoleon convoked the following year to ratify its answers gave the emperor what he wished. They were able to give satisfactory replies to virtually all the questions posed to them (of course Jews were opposed to polygamy; of course they considered Frenchmen their brothers and would fight in defense of France—*jusqu'a la mort;* of course the authority of the rabbis is only spiritual; of course only fair rates of interest are permitted) with full sincerity, while remaining in complete accord with the principles of Jewish law. Only on the subject of intermarriage did they feel compelled to give an evasive answer. But the effect of their pronouncements, though they themselves probably had no clear grasp of it at the time, was to reinterpret Judaism in individualistic, religious terms and to prepare the way for its dissociation among significant segments of western Jewry in the nineteenth and twentieth centuries from the distinctive, organic Jewish communal structure which for ages had been its foundation and the chief source of its vitality. Portalis fils, one of Napoleon's commissioners, did not greatly exaggerate the revolutionary significance of the "Sanhedrin" when he later wrote that through it "the Jews ceased to be a people and remained only a religion."

The resolutions of the Assembly of Notables and the "Sanhedrin," gratifying as they were to the emperor, did not lead to any expansion of Jewish rights in France. Quite the contrary. While French Jewry as well as Jews all over Europe were still basking in the afterglow of the "Sanhedrin," Napoleon in March 1808 issued a series of regulations (Jews quickly titled them the "Infamous Decree") arbitrarily restricting the economic activities and rights of residence of French Jews. At the same time he promulgated an "Organic Regulation on the Mosaic Religion" which, pronouncing Judaism one of the "official" religions of France, established a state-supervised consistorial system to regulate Jewish religious life. Among the major obligations of the officials of the consistories under the terms of the "Organic Regulation" were the promotion of patriotism and respect for French law among their coreligionists, and the insuring of an adequate supply of young men for conscription into the French army.

۞

If Napoleon's decree of 1808 represented something of a retreat from the emancipation Jews had won in France in 1791, this retreat was quite minor in comparison with the wholesale cancellation and restriction of Jewish rights elsewhere in Europe following Napoleon's downfall in 1814. Most of the statesmen assembled at the Congress of Vienna (1814–1815) were determined to restore "legitimacy" and "normalcy" to Europe, to wipe out all traces of the liberal and cosmopolitan ideas that had been fostered for a generation by the French Revolution. As far as the Jews were concerned, this meant that they must be put back in their former places.

Especially in Germany, where a wave of "Christian Teutomania" swept the country in the second decade of the nineteenth century, the old repressions were once more imposed upon the Jews almost everywhere. In Frankfurt the ghetto was reestablished; in Lübeck and Bremen movements were launched to expel the Jews entirely. Anti-Jewish feeling was fanned not only by the ignorant but by high-placed representatives of the *Gelehrte*. For example, Professor Friederich Rühs of the newly established University of Berlin urged the restoration of the medieval Jew-badge "so that a German, even if he be deceived by looks, behavior and speech, can recognize his Hebrew enemy," [17] and Professor J. F. Friess of the University of Heidelberg in 1816 published a book, *On the Menace of the Jews to the Welfare and Character of the Germans*, which advocated their total expulsion from Germany. In Italy and Spain as well, the rights gained by Jews in the generation of Napoleon were drastically reduced and in certain cases rescinded outright.

To be sure, the movement of political liberalism and, with it, the cause of civic rights for the Jews ultimately triumphed in the second half of the nineteenth century in most of western and central Europe. But the triumph came only after long agitation and intensive struggle. In the vanguard of the liberal movement were such noted Jews or born-Jews as Heinrich Heine, Ludwig Börne, and Gabriel Riesser. The revolution of 1848 inaugurated an era in which substantive civic equality was once again granted to many of the Jews of Germany, although even thereafter rights in various parts of the country were often curtailed and complete formal emancipation was not achieved until 1871. The Jews of Austria had to wait until 1867 to be declared legal equals of Christians, those of Hungary until 1895. In Italy Jews were granted full political and civic rights only in 1870, and in Switzerland in 1873. Even in England a Jew was not admitted to a seat in the House of Commons until 1858, and to academic degrees at Oxford and Cambridge until 1871. Much of the history of the western and central European Jew in the nineteenth century is a history of the struggle to secure the emancipation first promised in the last decade of the eighteenth century and rudely snatched away a generation later.

In the early nineteenth century the first withdrawal of the promise, and the threat of an enforced return to the disabilities and restrictions of the ghetto, produced among a considerable number of Jews the desire to escape their predicament through abandonment of their Judaism and conversion to Christianity. These followed the path of many Jews who, as we have noted, had succumbed as early as the time of Mendelssohn to the blandishments of the rationalist ideology of the Enlightenment, and later to the influence of the Romantic era, and left their people and faith. But philosophical and religious reasons figured rather slightly in the conversion of most Jews in the first decades of the nineteenth century; their motives were, in the main, frankly opportunistic. Heinrich Heine, who was himself baptized in 1825, summed up the spirit in which a large number of his contemporaries made their trip to the baptismal font. "The baptismal certificate," he declared cynically, "is the ticket of admission into European civilization." Many young Jews, fretting under the burden of a freedom only half-attained and still extremely precarious, longing for acceptance in the larger society, and realizing that only as Christians could they hope for such things as a professional or academic career, had little compunction about paying the price of the ticket.

Given the challenge to the Jewish faith and way of life posed by the rationalism of Enlightenment and the sentimentalism of Romanticism, given the corrosive effects of the new secularist political orders emerging in Europe on the traditionally autonomous and self-contained Jewish community, and given the immense losses sustained by Jewry through conversion or simple abandonment of all commitment to their ancestral heritage by many of its ablest sons and daughters, the future of Judaism in western and central Europe in the first decades after the emergence of its Jews from their ghettos seemed highly problematic. Many a concerned and thoughtful Jew of the time must have experienced grave apprehensions in assessing the prospects for the survival of Judaism in the face of its exposure to the shattering stresses and challenges of the new era. Judaism and the Jewish people, however, not only survived the shock of their entry into the modern world, but manifested their continuing vitality and resilience by producing, under the impact of that entry, a number of significant movements—the movement of humanism and enlightenment called Haskalah, the new and rich scholarship known as *die Wissenschaft des Judentums*, the Reform, Conservative, and Neo-Orthodox reinterpretations of Judaism, and Zionism. These movements, among the most important phenomena in the history of modern Judaism, will engage our attention in the chapters that follow.

CHAPTER

ᨣᢱ IX ᢱᨣ

Haskalah

THE TERM *Haskalah* denotes the complex movement of life and literature which emerged in the middle of the eighteenth century as the specific response of the European Jewish community to the general movement of enlightenment and secularization fostered by the rationalist spirit that dominated the social and intellectual life of the century. From its birthplace in Germany it moved to eastern Europe, where it achieved its full flowering in the nineteenth century. Although Haskalah proved to be merely a transitory phenomenon and ended in frustration and disillusionment, and though it had, as we shall see, its negative sides, it must be regarded on the whole as a movement of considerable positive value. Its major significance in the history of Judaism lies in the fact that it laid the foundations for the modern revival of Hebrew literature and played a large role in preparing the way for Zionism by creating, particularly in eastern Europe, a substantial body of Jews who, while molded by the values and ideals of classical Hebraic culture and loyal to the traditions of their people, were also highly responsive to the secularist-rationalist social and political ideologies of the modern world.

The central theme of Haskalah, persisting throughout its life as a movement, was the supremacy of reason (the word itself derives from the Hebrew word *sechel*, "reason" or "intelligence"). Its essential aim was to enlighten Jews, to familiarize them with the world of European civilization, to rationalize and modernize Jewish life. This aim was particularly compelling among Jews reaching out, as many did at different times in the various lands of Europe in the eighteenth and nineteenth centuries, for political rights and social emancipation. Many believed that the chief obstacle to attainment of these desiderata was the Jews' cultural distinctiveness (or "backwardness," as some would have it). They were persuaded that once Jews exchanged their own peculiar language for the vernacular of the country in which they lived, modernized and rationalized their educational system through the introduction of secular subjects, absorbed the culture of the larger European world, and cultivated its manners and mores, they would be regarded as worthy of having civic rights and social equality accorded to them. But Haskalah was also nurtured by more universal, humanistic ideals. Many of the *maskilim*, as the protagonists of Haskalah are called, were inspired by a fervent faith in the central ideas of the Enlightenment era as a whole—reason, humanity, progress. They were convinced that the individual Jew would inevitably attain a larger, freer, happier, more humane life, and that the Jewish people would share in the ongoing march of human progress, by energetic devotion to the cultivation of reason and the pursuit of practical knowledge.

The origin of Haskalah as a dynamic, militant movement is to be located in the Berlin of Moses Mendelssohn's time. To be sure, long before Mendelssohn a considerable number of well-to-do Jews could be found not only in Berlin but in Königsberg, Breslau, and elsewhere in Germany. These Jews—at least some of them—had moved both physically and spiritually from the Jewish ghetto into the larger German society and had become enthusiastic admirers of its language, literature, philosophy, and science. Several hundred Jews had managed to attend German secondary schools and universities. Even within the rabbinate such staunch traditionalists as Jonathan Eybeschütz and Jacob Emden, whose celebrated controversy in the middle of the eighteenth century over amulets and accusations of Shabbatian heresy bears all the hallmarks of medieval obscurantism, both manifested considerable interest in the natural sciences. But it was Mendelssohn, acting on his conviction that Jews must overcome their long intellectual isolation, who took the first important steps specifically intended to provide access to the world of European culture to the generality of his fellow Jews, and who may therefore be regarded as the prime initiator of Haskalah and its most distinguished figure in its early period.

Around Mendelssohn gathered a group of disciples who were inspired by the enlightening ideals he represented, and who shared his desire to make them operative in the Jewish community. Among these were men whose extreme rationalism and assimilationist bent ultimately led them to a general indifference, if not contempt, for traditional Judaism and Jewish life. Such, for instance, was David Friedländer, who once seriously offered in a letter to William Abraham Teller, provost of the consistory in Berlin, to have his family and several other Berlin Jewish households baptized into the Lutheran Church, provided they would not have to subscribe to such "irrational" Christian dogmas as the Trinity or the divinity of Jesus. Such also was the brilliant vagabond thinker and interpreter of Kantian philosophy, Solomon Maimon, who repeatedly castigated Judaism for what he regarded as its obscurantism and backwardness. But most of Mendelssohn's disciples were men who were genuinely devoted, as he himself was, to Judaism and the preservation of Jewish life.

We have already noted the importance of Mendelssohn's advocacy of secular education and of his German translation of the Pentateuch in breaking down the intellectual and cultural isolation of his fellow Jews. But Mendelssohn also made other contributions to incipient Haskalah, most notably in encouraging a revival of interest in the Hebrew language. It was Hebrew, and more specifically biblical Hebrew, that most of his disciples and successors in the Jewish movement for enlightenment in both Germany and eastern Europe chose as the vehicle of expression for their ideas, considering it a far nobler language than the Yiddish spoken by the Jewish masses. Yiddish, despite its antiquity (it dated from the eleventh century), widespread use, and the fact that it had already produced some remarkable literary works (although the great flowering of secular Yiddish literature did not occur until the end of the nineteenth and the beginning of the twentieth centuries in eastern Europe), was regarded by the majority of the *maskilim* as a "despicable jargon." As early as 1750, when Mendelssohn was only twenty-one, he began issuing in collaboration with a friend a Hebrew pamphlet, in imitation of the *Tatler* and *Spectator*, entitled *Kohelet Musar* (*Collection of Ethical Essays*) in which he sought to arouse the interest of young Jews in the fundamental ethical principles of their religion as well as in contemporary thought, and to cultivate and refine their aesthetic sensibilities. Although *Kohelet Musar* appeared only three times, Mendelssohn did not lose his youthful interest in stimulating a renaissance of Hebrew. The Hebrew style of his own contribution to the *Biur*, the commentary accompanying his translation of the Pentateuch, served as a model for many of the *maskilim* both of his time and of later generations.

It was under the direct influence of Mendelssohn that a group of his disciples, led by Isaac Euchel, Menaḥem Mendel Breslau, and the brothers Simon and Zenvil Friedländer, established in Königsberg in 1783 a Hebrew monthly entitled *Ha-Meassef* (*The Gatherer*). This journal, which appeared, with numerous and sometimes long interruptions, until well into the nineteenth century, was perhaps the chief instrument of German Haskalah. The *Meassefim*, as its contributors came to be called, published poetry and essays, compendiums of knowledge in various scientific fields, historical studies, explanations of biblical passages, book reviews, and discussions of current events. Mainly, however, the pages of *Ha-Meassef* were filled with Hebrew translations from European literature, especially German, French, and English, in an attempt to popularize among Jews the moral and aesthetic standards prevalent in the larger world, to make them appreciate the "beauty of Japheth" and the "wisdom of the Gentiles."

The underlying theme of the *Meassefim* was the necessity for Jews to cultivate *ḥochmah* (wisdom). This meant a rationalist approach to the Jewish tradition (the *Meassefim* wished, as did the Haskalah movement as a whole, to repudiate the whole mystical tradition of Judaism) and the acquisition of secular knowledge in general and scientific and practical knowledge in particular. In such knowledge they were disposed to see nothing less than an instrument of salvation. Typical of the quasi-religious reverence with which the *Meassefim* regarded *ḥochmah* is the following panegyric by one of them, Isaac Satanov:

Because God loved Wisdom, He adopted her as His daughter. He Himself lovingly brought her up. Before He made heaven and earth, she was His delight; before the mountains were born, ere the hills were formed. Because He willed to span heaven and earth, to do good to His creatures, to whom He would thus reveal the beatific splendor of His kingdom, He called upon Wisdom to present herself before Him, and to her He said, "My daughter, it is my intent to rear a dwelling place that will be inhabited by a multitude of beings. It is my will to establish my throne, and have my footstool upon the earth—therefore, be thou with me to give me sweet counsel. For I shall do nothing without thee. . . ." And she was henceforth with the King at His work. He took counsel with her; how to spread the sky with skill, and give the stars their measurements and rhythms . . . then, because God loved man, He sent Wisdom to walk upon the earth, that her delightful employ be with man, who would choose her in order to survive unto great salvation.[1]

The most representative spokesman of German Haskalah after Mendelssohn was Naphtali Herz Wessely, who contributed frequently to the early issues of *Ha-Meassef*. A faithful disciple of Mendelssohn and a participant in his *Biur*, Wessely energetically propagated his master's views on the need for reforming the traditional Jewish educational system. Given the pressure to adapt to the new intellectual, social, and economic environment which the Jew was then entering, and under the impact of novel Enlightenment schemes of education such as that propounded by Jean Jacques Rousseau in his *Émile*, the reform of Jewish education had come to be regarded as one of the major problems of the time. In a series of open letters to the Jews of the Austrian Empire, *Divrei Shalom Ve-Emet* (*Words of Peace and Truth*), written in response to the *Toleranzpatent* (edict of toleration) issued in 1782 by Emperor Joseph II and promising his Jewish subjects greater occupational, residential, and educational rights, Wessely applauded the emperor's promises and strenuously advocated modernization of the Jewish school to include secular and vocational subjects. Anticipating the objections of the orthodox, he attempted to show that a knowledge of such sciences as geography and mathematics, besides having intrinsic utility, would lead to an improved understanding of the Bible and *Talmud*. But his progressive educational views aroused strong opposition among such leaders of orthodoxy as Rabbi Ezekiel Landau of Prague and Rabbi David Tevele of Lissa, and led to extensive and acrimonious controversy. This, indeed, was the typical experience of the protagonists of Haskalah in that era as well as in later times: to the ultra-pious, determined to maintain the traditional pattern unchanged, the *maskilim* seemed heretics bent on "throwing off the yoke of the Torah" and threatening to undermine the very foundations of Jewish life.

In point of fact, most (not all) of the Hebrew writers of the first Haskalah period centered in Germany treated Jewish tradition with considerable respect. Generally they attacked only superstitions, foolish customs, and narrow-minded resistance to enlightenment and secular culture. The majority of them had a genuine reverence for Judaism, the Hebrew language, and Jewish history. Representative of this spirit is Wessely's own lengthy epic poem dealing with the exodus from Egypt, *Shirei Tiferet* (*Songs of Glory*). Despite its excessive didacticism and numerous literary defects, this work must be regarded as one of the most significant creations of German Haskalah, and one that exercised a considerable influence on the further development of neo-Hebrew poetry.

The Hebrew Haskalah of Germany is important mainly because it was a pioneering effort. Its literary productions are not distinguished by any special beauty or genuine profundity. Furthermore, its career was short-lived. By the end of the second decade of the nineteenth century many Jews in Germany no longer required any admonitions to acquire secular culture. Knowledge of German had become widespread at the same time that familiarity with Hebrew was declining, and the young were matriculating eagerly and in growing numbers at the universities. The positive program of Haskalah seemed an unnecessary belaboring of the obvious, and its rationalist spirit an anachronism in a world that no longer glorified Enlightenment and in which rationalism had been superseded by Romanticism. Moreover, within the Jewish community the central problem was no longer to supplement Jewish life and learning with secular knowledge, but to maintain Jewish loyalty among the young in the face of the disintegrative effects of the general European civilization which they were determined to absorb wholly and in comparison with which their own culture and religious tradition appeared to many of them relatively unattractive. It was to this problem, as we shall see, that the *Verein für Cultur und Wissenschaft der Juden*, founded by Leopold Zunz and his associates, as well as the German Reform movement, addressed themselves.

While Haskalah had run its course and become obsolete in Germany, it found a fertile field in eastern Europe, where it came to be a powerful influence and inspired new and important expressions in Jewish life throughout the nineteenth century.

It was in the Galician cities of Lemberg, Brody, and Tarnopol, the major crossroads of the growing commerce between Germany and the East, that the influence of the German Haskalah first penetrated and struck roots. Mendelssohn, in his later years, had been a magnet attracting to himself a considerable number of young Polish, Austrian, and Russian Jews eager to expand their intellectual horizons and become familiar with European philosophy, literature, and science. Some of these, after their sojourn in Berlin, settled in the

Galician commercial centers, where they found, particularly among the well-to-do Jewish merchants and tax-farmers, a congenial atmosphere for the dissemination of the Enlightenment ideals of which they had become zealous partisans.

The most prominent of the early east European *maskilim* directly influenced by Mendelssohn, and one who played a major role in connecting the Berlin Haskalah with the Jews of the East, was Mendel Lefin, also known as Levin (1749–1826). While in his twenties Lefin spent three years in Berlin as a member of the Mendelssohnian circle, and managed during that time to master several European languages and to acquire a considerable knowledge of mathematics, natural sciences, and philosophy. In 1791, encouraged by his friend and patron, the liberal Polish statesman Prince Adam Casimir Czartoryski, he published a brochure in French entitled *Essai d'un plan de réforme, ayant pour objet d'éclairer la nation juive en Pologne et la redresser par ses moeurs.*[2] Lefin lauded the rationalist tendencies in Judaism represented by Maimonides and Mendelssohn, deplored the spread of Ḥasidism, and urged the incorporation of secular studies in the curriculum of the Jewish school as a prerequisite for political emancipation. The pamphlet, however, had no effect; the short-lived Polish Constitution of 1791 granted no rights to the Jews. Later Lefin settled in Brody, where he continued his energetic enlightening activity until the end of his life. Among his Hebrew works, written in a clear and a lucid prose style emulated by many later *maskilim*, are essays expounding the elementary principles of various sciences, a translation of a popular medical work by the French physician Tissot, and a translation and elaboration of Benjamin Franklin's *Poor Richard's Almanac* entitled *Heshbon Ha-Nefesh* (*Examination of the Soul*). The last of these works was widely read and went through numerous editions. Curiously, it was republished by the very orthodox exponent of *musar*, Rabbi Israel Salanter, and even inspired the organization of a number of societies of young men in Podolia and Galicia which aimed at helping their members order their lives by its rules.

The great age of Galician Haskalah, however, began with the teaching activity and scholarly research in the modern fashion of Solomon Judah Rapoport and Naḥman Krochmal in the 1820s and 1830s. We shall deal with their important contributions in Chapter XI while discussing the rise of *die Wissenschaft des Judentums* and Jewish philosophy in the nineteenth century. Here it must suffice to note that Rapoport and Krochmal, by virtue of their brilliant use of critical and scientific methods in the study of Jewish history and personalities of the Talmudic and especially post-Talmudic eras, as well as the immense reputation both achieved in the realm of Jewish scholarship, made Galicia renowned throughout the Jewish world as a center of learning and enlightenment.

But if Galicia was noted as a seat of culture because it harbored the great scholarly *maskilim* Rapoport and Krochmal and a few others of lesser stature, it was also a major center of Ḥasidism, which by this time had largely degenerated into tzaddikism, as well as of a rigid rabbinic orthodoxy which set its face sternly against all humanistic and enlightening tendencies. The lengths to which the zealotry of some of the orthodox leaders could be carried is indicated by the fact that in 1816 Jacob Orenstein, the chief rabbi of Lemberg and a renowned Talmudic scholar, did not hesitate to place under the *ḥerem* (ban or excommunication) Rapoport and several of his friends suspected of harboring Enlightenment views. In their struggle against such fanaticism and their attempt to overcome the ignorance and superstition prevalent in the Ḥasidic communities, a few of the leading Haskalah writers of Galicia in the early decades of the nineteenth century had resort to the weapons of satire and caricature.

The first of the Hebrew satirists was Joseph Perl (1773–1839), a native of Tarnopol. By reason of his wealth and influence in government circles he was the leader of the Haskalah movement in Galicia in its infancy, and served as the maecenas and protector of other *maskilim*. Inspired by the ideals of the German Haskalah, Perl founded a modern school at Tarnopol in 1813 and was also instrumental in establishing a synagogue in which certain reforms in worship, including regular preaching in German, were introduced. Eager for the spread of Enlightenment among his people, Perl saw the chief obstacle to his projects in the hold of Ḥasidism on the Jewish masses. Like virtually all his colleagues in the Galician Haskalah, including even the great Krochmal, Perl was totally oblivious to the residue of authentic spirituality and religious depth that still survived in Ḥasidism. Annoyed by its crude exterior, repelled by its vehement emotionalism, and disgusted by the adulation with which its adherents regarded the *tzaddikim* and ascribed miraculous powers to them, he found it impossible to penetrate beneath the unattractive surface phenomena of Ḥasidism, and came to view the entire movement in an extremely one-sided way as a mass of superstition and quackery.

In 1819 Perl published his *Megalleh Temirin* (*Revealer of Secrets*), which quickly became popular in the enlightened circles of Galicia. Modeled after the famous *Epistolae Obscurorum Virorum*, written three hundred years earlier by a friend and defender of Johannes von Reuchlin at the beginning of the humanist movement in Germany, *Megalleh Temirin* purports to relate the adventures of a pious Ḥasid named Obadiah ben Petaḥiah. The hero, having come into possession of the sacred writings of Rabbi Adam, the teacher of Israel Baal Shem Tov (the founder of Ḥasidism), is thereby enabled to render himself invisible and observe the secret proceedings at the courts of the *tzaddikim*, and to read their private correspondence. The letters which he publishes, ostensibly for the sake of "glorifying" Ḥasidism, present an appalling picture of corruption and duplicity at the Ḥasidic courts. The *tzaddikim* and their henchmen are portrayed as unprincipled and greedy men who do not recoil before the most shameless acts in their effort to gain power for themselves and to win advantages over their opponents through working on the credulity and naivete of the masses of the Ḥasidim. The portrait, of course, is a caricature, grossly exaggerating the defects undoubtedly to be found in the Ḥasidic movement and altogether overlooking its genuine spirituality and religious values. It was this portrait that helped, in considerable measure, to shape the extremely negative and hostile view of Ḥasidism taken by such German-Jewish historians of the nineteenth century as Isaac Marcus Jost and Heinrich Graetz.

Perl's satirization of Ḥasidism was continued and carried to even greater lengths by his far more gifted younger contemporary and colleague, the physician Isaac Erter (1795–1851). A man of deep moral earnestness, Erter was dismayed by the backwardness and obsession with absurdities which, he felt, were suffocating the life of the Jewish masses in Galicia and eastern Europe generally. He devoted his considerable literary talents to writing a series of satires in which he mercilessly castigated this life and, in the spirit of Enlightenment, pleaded for reforms. Erter's essays, originally printed in various periodicals, were collected and published posthumously in 1856 under the title *Ha-Tzofeh Le-Bet Yisrael* (*The Watchman of the House of Israel*), and represent some of the choicest examples of Hebrew prose in the entire Haskalah period.

Erter did not confine himself to chastising the Ḥasidim only for their attachment to what he regarded as blatant superstition and obscurantism. He also directed his satires against the rabbis of the Mitnaggedim, reproving them for their hypocrisy and fanaticism, their casuistic learning and proclivity to plagiarism, and their fanatical opposition to all projects for enlightenment. Even the enlighteners, his fellow *maskilim*, were not spared; Erter criticized them severely for their egotism and materialism, their aloofness and alienation from the people, and their slavish imitation of German models in composing their Hebrew poems. But the satirist reserved his sharpest barbs for the Ḥasidim, deriding especially their infatuation with angelology and the notion of transmigration of souls, both of which greatly offended his rationalist temperament. Ridiculing the idea of metempsychosis in his longest and best-known satire, *Gilgul Nefesh* (*The Transmigration of a Soul*), Erter has the soul of a frog, which he represents as having previously been lodged in the body of a Ḥasid, sarcastically describe the Ḥasidic way of life:

I became a Ḥasid—a man who drinks brandy like water, who abandons his father and mother, his wife and children, to go to his rabbi and imbibe his obscure teachings, to seize the crumbs from his plate with lightning agility. As I prayed I would leap and run, clap my hands and behave like a madman. When I sang the Sabbath and festival hymns all who heard me vowed that both the cormorant and the bittern dwelt in my throat. My cry rose to the heavens; I skipped like a ram on the tables and benches. And when my throat became dry and my tongue failed for thirst, brandy poured into me like water, into my entrails like a rushing stream . . . until, inflamed by the liquor, I myself was consumed by fire, rising as an unsavory burnt offering unto the Lord.[3]

The extreme anti-Ḥasidism of such typical representatives of the Galician Haskalah as Perl and Erter did not, however, go unchallenged, even among the ranks of the "enlightened." Disgusted by what he considered the barrenness of Haskalah ideology and dismayed by its vehement and unfair attacks on the Ḥasidim, Jacob Samuel Byk (ca. 1770–1831), who had been a lifelong champion of Enlightenment, finally decided to sell publicly his copy of Maimonides' *Guide of the Perplexed* (the most honored emblem of Jewish rationalism among the *maskilim*) and to declare his sympathy with Ḥasidism. To his friend Solomon Judah Rapoport, who shared the general Haskalah antipathy to the Ḥasidim, Byk chidingly explained: "Why have you, who loves Schiller so deeply and has translated his poems into Hebrew, not taken to heart for yourself his cosmopolitan verse '*Diesen Kuss der ganzen Welt!*' You do not fulfill this verse toward the people of Israel. Embrace and kiss all our Jewish brothers with a whole heart and an undivided soul, even if one must pay with both reason and soul." [4]

Having given rise to such seminal figures in Jewish scholarship as Rapoport and Krochmal, such keen satirists and proponents of rationalism and enlightenment as Perl and Erter, and a small band of lesser scholars, essayists, and poets, the Galician Haskalah quickly exhausted itself. After the resumption of Polish control over Galicia, a general assimilation to Polish culture, going far beyond the aim of modernizing and rationalizing Jewish life espoused by the Haskalah, became dominant in the circles of the Jewish intelligentsia. The mass of Galician Jewry, however, rejected both Polonization and the ideology of Haskalah and remained committed to preservation of the traditional patterns of Jewish life, until it was itself largely destroyed in the Nazi Holocaust.

❧❦❧

Haskalah in Russia enjoyed a longer and more variegated career than it did in Galicia. The Jews of the czarist empire, particularly in the province of Lithuania, were generally far more learned in Jewish lore than their Galician brethren, and also far more receptive to the pursuit of secular knowledge. As early as the second half of the eighteenth century, and even earlier, young Russian Talmudists traveled to the universities of Padua, Göttingen, Halle, Königsberg, and Cambridge to study medicine, mathematics, and other sciences. A few found their way into Moses Mendelssohn's circle and became contributors to his *Biur* and to *Ha-Meassef*. No less a rabbinic authority than Elijah, the Gaon of Vilna, strongly advocated study of the natural sciences. "Every lack of knowledge in secular subjects," he declared, "causes a hundredfold lack in the study of the Torah, for Torah and knowledge are intertwined." [5] The Gaon also urged reforms in the traditional Jewish educational system, and himself composed treatises on Hebrew grammar, trigonometry, geometry, algebra, and astronomy. One of his ardent admirers, Baruch Schick of Shklov (1740–1812), who studied medicine in England and translated Euclid and other mathematical works into Hebrew, wrote: "The Vilna Gaon advised me to translate as many scientific books as possible into our sacred tongue to disseminate learning in Israel, lest the Gentiles ridicule us for our ignorance and in their pride ask, 'Where is your wisdom?' " [6]

Toward the end of the eighteenth century the enlightened Joshua Zeitlin, who had amassed a fortune as a purveyor to the czar's armies during the Turkish war, established a research institute for

Haskalah

maskilim as well as traditionalist scholars on his estate at Ustye near Shklov. There, Baruch Schick organized a laboratory for chemical experiments, and the ascetic Benjamin Zalman Riviles, a disciple of the Gaon of Vilna, established a botanical collection from which he extracted medical remedies. There also Mendel Lefin wrote his *Heshbon Ha-Nefesh* and Rabbi Menaḥem Naḥum composed his commentary to the Tosefta, *Tosafot Bikkurim*.

Positive attitudes toward secular learning became somewhat more widespread among the Jews of Russia during the first part of the reign of Alexander I (1801–1825). The czar's proclaimed liberalism inspired flickering hopes of emancipation, at least among the wealthy Jewish merchants and military contractors. When the Russian universities were opened to them for the first time in 1811, a number of young Jews matriculated to study for the professions. The *maskilim* rejoiced and proceeded to organize modern Jewish schools in various cities. Societies for the promotion of Enlightenment were also organized, among them the *Shoharei Or Ve-Haskalah* (Seekers of Light and Culture) in Berdichev, the Maskilim Society in Raseiniai, and the Maskilim Group led by Mordecai Aaron Günzburg in Vilna. A small group of *maskilim* had also organized themselves in the new Jewish community that came into existence in St. Petersburg at the end of the eighteenth century. Some of their leaders, however, became apostates, thus arousing the hostility of the masses of Jews toward the entire Haskalah movement. In addition, Alexander's abandonment of liberalism after the Congress of Vienna and his attempts in the last years of his reign to convert his Jewish subjects to Christianity brought the incipient Haskalah movement into even greater disrepute among the masses.

Their distrust was greatly intensified during the regime of Nicholas I (1825–1856). His brutal conscription ukase of 1827, his subsidy of the proselytizing "Jewish Committee," and his edict establishing government or "crown" schools for Jewish children made it clear that his intent was not to educate the Jews and ameliorate their condition but to win them away from Judaism. When the Enlightenment-minded German rabbi Max Lilienthal (1815–1882) toured the major Jewish cities of Russia in 1840 to urge Jews to accept the proposed government schools, he encountered tremendous opposition everywhere and was denounced by the orthodox as a covert missionary. Haskalah now became a term of odium, and its advocacy of secular study was regarded as the first step to apostasy. The leaders of the Ḥasidim and Mitnaggedim, despite their own sharp differences, considered Haskalah their common enemy and joined forces in a bitter and protracted struggle against it.

Despite all opposition, Haskalah succeeded in establishing itself in Russia in the first half of the nineteenth century, and eventually grew into a significant force. This was due in considerable measure to the persistent efforts of Isaac Ber Levinsohn (1788–1860), whose enlightening activity won him the title "the Russian Mendelssohn." Born in the Volhynian town of Kremenetz, where he received a good secular as well as Jewish education, Levinsohn as a young man spent some years in Galicia, teaching for a time in the modern Jewish school of Brody. There he became acquainted with some of the leading Galician *maskilim*, including Rapoport, Krochmal, and Erter, and was influenced by their modernizing and rationalist attitudes toward Jewish life. Returning to his native city in 1820, Levinsohn began his career as a propagandist of Enlightenment. Like his Galician friends, he felt that the chief enemy of progress was the Ḥasidic movement, and his first work was an anonymously published satire directed against the Ḥasidim and entitled *Divrei Tzaddikim* (*The Words of the Tzaddikim*). This was followed in 1828 by the publication of an apology in behalf of Haskalah and the modernization of Jewish life, *Te'udah Be-Yisrael* (*A Testimony in Israel*). This work so impressed Russian officialdom, then bent, as we have observed, for its own anti-Jewish purposes on promoting secular education among the Jews of the empire, that Nicholas I awarded Levinsohn a subsidy of a thousand rubles for it.

Levinsohn's *Te'udah Be-Yisrael* is hardly a profound or original work, but it was widely read and managed to convince a good many Jews of the essential compatibility of Haskalah ideals and Jewish religion. In it he raised for discussion five "major problems" regarding enlightenment: Is a pious Jew obliged to know the Hebrew language in correct, grammatical fashion? Is he permitted to learn foreign languages? May he study secular sciences? What benefits will he obtain from studying languages and sciences? Will the benefits outweigh the possible injuries to religious faith? These were hardly new problems; they had been discussed ad nauseam by protagonists of both the German and the Galician Haskalah. But Levinsohn brought them to the forefront in Russia, where they were intensively debated for many years. Quoting voluminously from Talmudic literature and rabbinic authorities, Levinsohn demonstrated that the first three questions must clearly be answered in the affirmative. Similarly, he argued that the study of languages and sciences would not only brighten the image of the Jew among the Gentiles and advance his economic and political prospects but also help him better to understand and practice Judaism. Such study, he urged, would strengthen faith rather than injure it. By thus making the enhancement of Judaism the primary concern, by speaking always in the most respectful way of Jewish tradition, by producing sanctions for his educational suggestions from the *Talmud* and other accepted sources, and by conducting his own life in a thoroughly traditional and pious manner, Levinsohn seemed to provide living proof that Haskalah and Judaism were not fundamentally irreconcilable.

Levinsohn concluded his *Te'udah Be-Yisrael* with a strong plea that Jews recognize the duty of manual labor, particularly of cultivating the soil. To strengthen his appeal and demonstrate that the dignity of labor is an ancient Jewish ideal, he proceeded to supply numerous examples of important Jewish figures of the past who engaged in agriculture. Even Pliny and Aristotle were invoked to provide general philosophical support for his thesis. The ancient Egyptians were also cited as having valued agriculture so highly that they deified farm animals. This emphasis of Levinsohn's on the dignity and value of agricultural labor was to be repeated by many of the later Russian *maskilim* (though generally not in his effusive and grandiloquent terms) and was ultimately appropriated by some of the pioneers of Zionism as an essential part of their ideological program.

Levinsohn's advocacy of Haskalah found particularly fertile soil in Lithuania, where the influence of the Gaon of Vilna, with his positive attitude toward secular studies, persisted. Vilna itself became a major center of enlightenment and produced some of the foremost scholars and poets of the Russian Haskalah. Among the latter were Abraham Dov Lebensohn (1794–1878) and his son Micah Joseph Lebensohn (1828–1852). The former, whose pure biblical style profoundly influenced later Hebrew writers in Russia, polemicized in his allegorical drama *Emet Ve-Emunah* (*Truth and Faith*) against ignorance and superstition, and argued that authentic Jewish faith must be based on truth and guided by reason. As a poet he was far surpassed by his son, who, in a tragically brief life, wrote a number of epics in which his personal search for truth and beauty, his melancholia, and his passion for life in the face of approaching death are projected onto great personalities of the Bible. The romantic glorification of the biblical past, expressed with genuine artistry in these epics, became a major theme in the poems and novels of other Haskalah writers of the period.

The high point of this romantic tendency to focus attention on the age of the Bible is to be found in the novels of Abraham Mapu (1808–1867), a native of Lithuania and a *maskil* who earned his living as a teacher in the Russian government school for Jews at Kovno.[7] His two major historical novels, *Ahavat Tziyyon* (*The Love of Zion*, 1853) and *Ashemat Shomron* (*The Guilt of Samaria*, 1865), proved immensely popular. Despite their wildly contrived and implausible plots, these stories of love, war, and intrigue in the days of the biblical kings and prophets, with their vivid descriptions of the Palestinian countryside, opened to countless Jews living amidst the squalor and sordidness of the Pale of Settlement in czarist Russia a new world of heroism, romance, and natural beauty hitherto undreamed of. To *yeshivah* students, poring over their dry and intellectualist texts, Mapu's colorful novels provided a means of emotional release and an outlet for the expression, even if only in imagination, of their longings for a larger world of heroic action and feeling. These romances stimulated pride in the Jewish past among several generations of young Hebrew readers in eastern Europe, and directed their attention to an era when the Jews had been a free people living on their own soil through the labor of their own hands. It is probably no exaggeration to say that Mapu's books made a not insignificant contribution to the awakening of the national sentiment which culminated in the Zionist movement.

The reforms in the Russian social order introduced in the early years of Alexander II's reign (1855–1881) inaugurated a new phase in the Russian Haskalah, which now began to direct its attention away from a sentimental idealization of the past to a practical concern with the problems of the present. The "Czar Liberator" who emancipated the Russian serfs also appeared genuinely disposed to improve the condition of the Jews. The special regulations governing the military conscription of the Jews were repealed, the entire empire was opened for settlement to certain classes of Jews, and Jewish lawyers were admitted to the bar and even to the magistracy. Under the warming rays of the new era which seemed to be dawning, Haskalah gained greater support than it had ever enjoyed before. A group of financiers in St. Petersburg, led by Baron Joseph Günzburg and the wealthy Polyakov and Rosenthal families, in 1863 organized the *Hevrat Mefitzei Ha-Haskalah* (Society for the Promotion of Enlightenment). Its projects, intended to educate Jewry into "readiness for citizenship," included dissemination of knowledge of Russian within the Jewish community, establishment of night schools and libraries, provision of financial aid to needy students, and publication of educationally useful pamphlets and books.

Also in the 1860s, *maskilim* who had been educated in Russian-Jewish schools began to hold rabbinic office with the introduction of the institution, repugnant to traditionalist Jews, of *kazyonny ravvin* (government-appointed rabbi). In addition, a series of new periodicals aggressively devoted to propagating the cause of Haskalah were founded, including the Russian-language *Razsvet* (*Dawn*), the Hebrew *Ha-Melitz* (*The Interpreter*), and the Yiddish *Kol Mevasser* (*The Proclaiming Voice*). Through these journals tens of thousands of Russian Jews were introduced to secular ideas and values; thousands of others were similarly influenced by their attendance at Russian gymnasia and universities. Under the far-reaching influence of the contemporary Russian "positivist" essayists Tchernishevski, Dobroliubov, and Pissarev, who attacked all forms of romanticism, aestheticism, and intellectualism, and crusaded vigorously for practical reforms in Russian society, many of the Haskalah writers who now came to the fore abandoned the romanticism of their predecessors, turned a critical eye on their own Jewish society, and became ardent champions of its reformation. The spirit of this "positivist" and "realist" phase of Haskalah is best represented in its foremost spokesmen, Judah Leib Gordon (1830–1892) and Moses Lilienblum (1843–1910).

Gordon, generally regarded as the poet laureate of the Russian Haskalah, was born in the intellectual center of Lithuanian Jewry, Vilna, where he obtained a standard Talmudic education. While still in his teens, however, he was drawn into the circles of the enlightened and thereafter devoted himself to secular studies for a period of time, mastering Polish, French, and German. For a number of years he served as a teacher and principal in various Jewish government, or "crown," schools. In 1872 Gordon was called to St. Petersburg to become secretary of both the Jewish community and the Society for the Promotion of Enlightenment. Seven years later he was exiled for a few months as a result of a false accusation that he belonged to a revolutionary party. Though soon cleared, he was not reinstated in his official post and spent the last years of his life in St. Petersburg in journalistic work as a contributing editor of *Ha-Melitz*.

Gordon's early Hebrew poetic works, such as "The Love of David and Michal" and "David and Barzillai," are biblical idylls redolent with the mood and spirit of Romanticism. But a new note appears in his poems "The Way of the Daughter of My People" and "Awake, My People," the latter written in 1863 after Alexander II's emancipation of the serfs. Gordon was convinced that a new era was dawning for Jews as well, and exulted:

> This paradisical land will be opened to you,
> Its sons will now call you "our brother,"
> . . . .
> And they will remove the burden from your shoulder,
> And lift the yoke from your neck;
> They will remove from their hearts causeless hatred and vanity,
> They will give you their hand, greet you with peace.[8]

How should Jews react to these happy phenomena? Gordon's answer became the watchword of the enlighteners: "Be a man when you go out and a Jew in your tent, a brother to your countrymen and a servant to your king." [9] The Russians, he believed, would abandon their enmity toward the Jews and greet them as brothers once the Jews themselves fulfilled the standard precepts of Haskalah:

> All understanding men will study science,
> Workers and artisans will learn arts and crafts,
> The stout-hearted will serve in the army,
> Farmers will buy fields and plows.[10]

Beginning in this period, criticism of ghetto existence with its fanaticism and superstition, and diatribes against the excessive religiosity and overspiritualization of Jewish life, its constriction to "the four ells of the *halachah*," become increasingly prominent motifs in Gordon's work. His historical ballad "In the Lion's Teeth," which describes the sad fate of a Jewish soldier who had fought against the Romans in Jerusalem and meets his death in a Roman circus, contains a denunciation of the ancient Jewish teachers who, like their contemporary counterparts in the Pale of Settlement, "taught you, alas, to go against life, to keep yourself behind fences and walls, to be dead on earth and alive in heaven, to dream while awake, and to be sunk in fancies." [11] Particularly angered by what he regarded as the abuses of rabbinic Judaism, Gordon wrote a series of bitterly satirical poems in which he castigated the "cruelty" of the rabbis who, in their insistence on strict adherence to the letter of the law, did not flinch from inflicting immense suffering on innocent persons. In the best known of these, "The Point of a Yod" (1876), he laments the fate of a beautiful young Jewess who is prevented from marrying her beloved and condemned to a life of loneliness as an *agunah* (deserted woman) because a stubborn rabbi nullifies her divorce document from her first husband on the grounds that it contains a single minor spelling error.

Talmudic Judaism, Gordon insisted, cannot serve the needs of the Jew entering the full-bodied life of the modern world, and he strongly urged religious reform. He wrote:

Can we really continue the same way of life by the waters of Europe and other countries that we led by the waters of Babylon? Are the philosophies and teachings of ancient times appropriate for the times we live in, and are they adapted to the present status of knowledge? The *Talmud* is dear to us as an ancient book, a precious chronicle of historical events, a source for enriching our language (of course, purifying it and sifting it with thirteen sieves). It is as important and valuable as the poultice on a wound. But if the *Talmud*, with its pedantry, with its overlapping additions and rabbinic commentaries, becomes a guide for our people, then we will be like those who follow the pillar of clouds in the night and we will wander bewildered in the world. We shall be sealed forever in the desert without hope of ever returning to the world around us, to a life of bodily vigor.[12]

In the last years of his life Gordon came to realize that the bright hopes he had entertained when he wrote "Awake, My People" were not to be realized. Alexander II's abandonment of liberalism after 1870, the progressive curtailment of the rights of Jews, and finally the pogroms of 1881 made it clear that the promise of full emancipation through Haskalah was no more than an empty dream. Considering how little fruit Haskalah had borne, realizing that religious reforms would hardly succeed in maintaining the integrity of Jewish life, and seeing the growing assimilationism of many of the enlightened Jews of the day, who were forsaking not only the Hebrew language but the Judaism which, despite all his criticism of it, remained precious to him, Gordon despaired of the future. In one of his late poems, "For Whom Do I Labor," he wondered sadly whether he might not be the "last of the singers of Zion."

❧⟨§⟩❧

The critical attitude toward Jewish life and the demands for reform expressed in the mature work of Judah Leib Gordon are paralleled in the early writings of Moses Lilienblum. Born in the small

Lithuanian town of Keidany, Lilienblum received a traditional Jewish education and, following the prevalent custom, was married at
the age of fourteen. He then moved to Vilkomir where, in 1865, he
established a *yeshivah* as a means of earning a livelihood. Having
become interested in the new Hebrew literature of the Haskalah, he
also managed a small library in town for the young people. The
rigidly orthodox townspeople suspected him of "atheistic" Enlightenment tendencies and began to persecute him severely. When in 1868
Lilienblum published his *Oreḥot Ha-Talmud* (*Paths of the Talmud*) in
Ha-Melitz, urging some reforms of Talmudic law and pleading sincerely with the rabbis for relaxation of its severities and abandonment of its anachronisms, the persecutions were intensified.

Forced to flee, Lilienblum moved to Odessa, where he hoped to
find a cultured community devoted to Hebrew literature and an
enlightened form of Judaism and Jewish life. Instead he discovered
among the *maskilim* of that city a general indifference to Judaism
and a cynical careerism. Losing faith in Haskalah and disillusioned
about the prospects of religious reform, he wrote a despairing biographical document, *Hattot Ne'urim* (*The Sins of Youth*, 1876), which
became perhaps the most widely read Hebrew book of the time
because it portrayed with such searing honesty the conflict between
orthodoxy and rationalism that not only he but young Jews throughout eastern Europe were then experiencing so sharply. At this time,
when the futility of his existence and efforts weighed heavily upon
him, Lilienblum encountered the works of the Russian positivist
writers. Pissarev's essays and Tchernishevski's *Chto Delat* (*What Is To
Be Done?*) made a profound impression on him. Turning away from
the old Haskalah, and rejecting as useless and wasteful its concern
with Hebrew poetry, scholarship, and religious reform, he now advocated practical, utilitarian education, the teaching of productive
occupations to the youth, as the means necessary for curing the ills
of ghetto life, and preached socialism and cosmopolitanism.

Lilienblum might have followed the logic of this position to its assimilationist conclusion had it not been for the emergence of a strong
anti-Jewish movement in Russia led by such eminent intellectuals as
Aksakov and Dostoevsky, and the shattering effect produced on him
by the pogroms of 1881. The latter, as he indicated in his *Derech
Teshuvah* (*The Way of Repentance*), which he wrote many years later
as an autobiographical supplement to his youthful *Ḥattot Ne'urim*,
brought home to him the emptiness of the hope for emancipation
and convinced him that the only salvation for the Jews as a people
lay in their return to Zion.

We dream that we will become children of the European nations, children with equal rights. What can be more fatuous? For we are aliens and will remain aliens. Our future is fearful, without a spark of hope or a ray of light—slaves, aliens, strangers forever. Yet why should we be aliens in alien countries if the land of our fathers has not yet been forgotten and remains vacant? It can absorb our people! We must cease to be aliens and return to our fatherland. We must buy land there, little by little, becoming rooted there, like other people who live in the land of their fathers. We are being uprooted from the land of our residence; the gates are open for us to leave. We are, in fact, fleeing. Why, then, flee to America and be alien there too, instead of to the land of our fathers? [13]

A far more eloquent spokesman of the nationalist ideology which the movement for Enlightenment adopted in the last stages of its career in eastern Europe, and the chief standard-bearer of Zionist Haskalah, was Lilienblum's contemporary Peretz Smolenskin (1842–1885). After receiving a traditional Talmudic education and spending some years at Ḥasidic courts in Lubavich and Vitebsk, Smolenskin came to Odessa, where he studied music and modern European languages while earning his living as a singer in a synagogue, a preacher, and a Hebrew teacher. Intent on publishing a Hebrew journal, he settled in Vienna in 1868, and a year later his monthly *Ha-Shahar* (*The Dawn*) began to appear. The journal continued for almost seventeen years, with Smolenskin serving not only as editor and major contributor, but also as manager, proofreader, and distributor until shortly before his death of tuberculosis at the age of forty-three.

Ha-Shahar was devoted to the cause of disseminating culture and enlightenment among the Jews, and like other organs of Haskalah in eastern Europe, it polemicized against the fanaticism and obscurantism sometimes displayed by orthodox Judaism and Ḥasidism. But, under the influence of Smolenskin, who saw with utmost clarity the destructive effects of the assimilationist currents in the Mendelssohnian Haskalah which the *maskilim* of Germany and their Russian successors promoted, it advocated loyalty to the Torah and the traditional values of Judaism. Above all, it strongly championed the cause of Hebrew and the strengthening of the newly awakened nationalist sentiments among the Jewish masses.

Smolenskin himself made major contributions to the development of modern Hebrew literature through such rambling philosophical novels as *Ha-To'eh Be-Darchei Ha-Hayyim* (*The Wanderer on Life's Paths*), *Simhat Ḥanef* (*The Joy of the Godless*), *Kevurat Ḥamor* (*The Burial of an Ass*), and *Ha-Yerushah* (*The Legacy*), all published originally in the pages of *Ha-Shaḥar*. These works won him recognition as the fore-most Hebrew novelist of his time. But it is in his exposition of the philosophy of Jewish nationalism that Smolenskin's chief historical significance lies.

Long before the pogroms of 1881 Smolenskin developed his theory of spiritual Jewish nationalism. In the major studies *Am Olam* (*The Eternal People*) and *Et Laasot* (*A Time To Act*), published in *Ha-Shaḥar* in 1872 and 1873, he elaborated his thesis that the triple cord bind-ing Israel together through all the centuries of homelessness and dispersion consisted of Torah, the Hebrew language, and the mes-sianic hope. The Jewish people is not merely a religious group, as the Reformers and many of the German and Russian *maskilim* held, but a nation. If it is to reverse the process of disintegration which is consuming its substance, it must resolutely affirm its nationhood. This is the only way, Smolenskin urged, through which it can main-tain and increase its self-respect as well as respond meaningfully to anti-Semitism, whose origin he then tended to perceive primarily in the contempt of the nations for the Jews' deficient national status.

The pogroms of 1881 strengthened Smolenskin's conviction that political emancipation, on which several generations of *maskilim* had pinned their hopes, would prove illusory. They also persuaded him that spiritual nationalism would not suffice to heal the ravaged body of the Jewish people. Jews, Smolenskin eloquently urged in more than a score of articles in the last three volumes of *Ha-Shaḥar*, must return to their ancient homeland in Palestine and undertake all the political, economic, cultural, and religious activities necessary for the eventual establishment of a Jewish state. The pogroms in Russia and the recrudescence of anti-Semitism in Germany, he argued prophet-ically, were not lamentable but essentially ephemeral manifestations of social regress. They were harbingers of far greater atrocities yet to come for the Jewish people, which would be in mortal peril if it did not rebuild its national life in Palestine and create a place of refuge for those caught in the storms that would break over Europe.

Mainly through Smolenskin and many of his followers, who en-thusiastically joined the *Ḥovevei Tziyyon* (Lovers of Zion) movement, Haskalah in large measure passed over into Zionism, having pro-vided for the latter movement much of its fundamental ideology as well as the basis for the renaissance of Hebrew as a living language. Thus the assimilatory direction in which Haskalah had been moving in certain Jewish circles was generally reversed. A considerable number of young Russian Jews, to be sure, joined underground revolutionary movements in the last decades of the Romanov dynasty, convinced that with the overthrow of the czarist regime Jews would be fully emancipated and totally absorbed in Russian society. And a few *maskilim* continued to uphold the traditional Haskalah program and to maintain their faith in the amelioration of the condition of the Jews and, ultimately, the award to them of full social and political equality. This group of irrepressible "hopefuls" in Russia centered their activities around the newspaper *Voskhod* (St. Petersburg, 1881–1906). The majority of Jews who had been touched by Haskalah, however, found in Zionism the commitment that gave substance and purpose to their Jewish existence.

CHAPTER

⤙ X ⤚

New Interpretations
of Judaism

In the case of a considerable number of Jews in western and central Europe, civic emancipation and entry into the life of the larger European society at the beginning of the nineteenth century destroyed all loyalty to their people and their ancestral faith. Many simply abandoned all religious identification; many more, not infrequently motivated chiefly by desire for the obvious social and financial benefits accruing therefrom, converted to the dominant religion of their countries. The majority remained loyal to the synagogue and the Jewish people, but even among the faithful there were not a few in whom exposure to the religious life and institutions of their Christian countrymen and to the general culture of the Enlightenment era produced rankling dissatisfaction with various aspects of Jewish life and practice.

The source of perhaps the most widespread discontent initially was the relative unattractiveness of the synagogue service—its general lack of decorum and orderliness, the rote mumbling of little understood Hebrew prayers by many worshipers, and the virtually complete absence of European aesthetic standards. Deficiencies such as these, rendered all the more obvious and irritating by comparison with the Christian churches and cathedrals with their hushed solemnity, colorful pageantry, great choirs, and Bach chorales, were the focus of concern of the first Jews who undertook to "reform" their religion in Germany in the opening decades of the nineteenth century. These persons, mainly laymen with a limited understanding of Jewish tradition and little rabbinic guidance or support, believed that the remedy for disaffection with the synagogue consisted essentially in abbreviating the prayers, having sermons preached in German, introducing unison singing by congregation and choir to the accompaniment of the organ, and adding some prayers and hymns in the vernacular to the traditional Hebrew liturgy.

Such were the reforms inaugurated in 1810 by Israel Jacobson (1768–1828), a wealthy Jew of the Duchy of Brunswick and generally regarded as the initiator of the Reform movement in Germany, in the chapel connected with the modern boarding school which he established in the town of Seesen. These innovations proved attractive to many Jews and were continued in the worship services Jacobson began to hold in his home in Berlin, where he settled a few years later. Indeed, the crowds drawn to these services, attracted especially by several young Jewish intellectuals of Berlin who presented sermons at them, soon necessitated their removal to the larger mansion of Jacob Beer. However, the orthodox "defenders of the faith," to whom the innovations were anathema, employed their influence with the Prussian government to have these services proscribed in 1817 under a law of 1750 which forbade Jewish worship outside the confines of the official synagogue. Although the holders of the Reform services of Berlin were soon given permission to resume them, they were again banned by royal decree at the end of 1823, thus stifling for many years the progress of the Reform movement in the Prussian capital.

Meanwhile, in the free city of Hamburg a Reform temple was established in 1818 under the leadership of Eduard Kley, a disciple of Israel Jacobson and one of the young men who had served as preacher in the services conducted at the home of Jacob Beer in Berlin. Kley collaborated with Rabbi Gotthold Salomon (1784–1862), a vigorous champion of Reform and a widely admired preacher, in sermonizing at the services. The innovations of the Hamburg Temple were vehemently opposed by the learned orthodox rabbi of the community, Isaac Bernays (1792–1849), although he himself favored the modernization of Jewish education, made German the language of instruction in the Hamburg *Talmud Torah*, and was the first traditionalist rabbi to preach in German.

[233]

The hostility of the orthodox was intensified when, in 1819, the Hamburg Temple issued a prayer book in which some of the classical petitions for the advent of the Messiah, the reinstitution of the Temple and the sacrificial cult, and the restoration of Jewish national life in Palestine were removed and, in their place, a more universalist prayer calling for establishment of a worldwide kingdom of human brotherhood and righteousness was inserted. While the reformers argued that these changes were necessitated by the demands of intellectual integrity (after all, they considered themselves citizens of the *Vaterland* and had no desire for the reestablishment of a Jewish state in Zion, and certainly none for the restoration of sacrifices), the orthodox contended that it was heresy and blasphemy to abandon prayers that had been central in the Jewish liturgy for so many centuries. In this the traditionalists rightly perceived a threat to the authority of the entire Oral Torah and proceeded to place the prayer book of the Hamburg Temple under the *herem*, or ban.

The conflict between the reformers of Berlin and Hamburg and the upholders of tradition evoked a literature of intensive polemic. In 1818 the Talmudist Eliezer Liebermann published a brief volume entitled *Nogah Ha-Tzedek* (*The Light of Righteousness*) containing responsa by four rabbis—Shem Tov of Leghorn, Jacob Recanati of the rabbinical college of Verona, Moses Kunitzer of Budapest, and Aaron Chorin of Arad in Hungary—sanctioning, on the basis of Talmudic sources, such innovations of the reformers as the use of instrumental music in the synagogue on the Sabbath, prayer in the vernacular, and employment of the Sephardi pronunciation of Hebrew. To these responsa Liebermann added his own fervent plea for the reform of Jewish practice, maintaining, oddly enough, that the "outlandish" religious practices of the Jews, their disdain for science and secular culture, and their deficient patriotism were the fundamental causes of the hostility and persecution that had been directed against them through the centuries.

Liebermann's *Nogah Ha-Tzedek* naturally enraged the traditionalists. The orthodox rabbinate of Hamburg responded in 1819 with a collection of responsa entitled *Eleh Divrei Ha-Berit* (*These Are the Words of the Covenant*). In their responsa some of the foremost traditional rabbinic scholars of Europe, including Akiba Eger of Posen (1761–1837) and Moses Sofer of Pressburg (1763–1839), vehemently condemned the reforms approved in *Nogah Ha-Tzedek*. However, their narrow Talmudic casuistry, failure to take serious account of the intellectual problems raised by the reformers, and highly intemperate language did not impress many Jews seeking light rather than heat in the struggle.

As the conflict continued into the third and fourth decades of the century, both parties on occasion appealed to German government authorities for intervention and protection of their respective positions, although in fairness it must be said that the orthodox resorted to this measure somewhat more frequently than the reformers. Not a few Jews on the sidelines of the acrimonious struggle responded with the attitude of "a plague on both your houses"; more, however, took sides and vigorously defended their views.

Until the middle of the 1830s the movement of Reform was promoted primarily by laymen, few of whom had any profound knowledge of Judaism. Their concerns were largely practical and their efforts motivated by the belief that the "beautification" of the synagogue service along lines approved by the canons of western aesthetic taste would revivify flagging loyalties to Judaism and check the flood of conversions to Christianity. To be sure, the theological problem of the continuing validity of Jewish messianic expectations and hopes for national restoration asserted itself, but it was rarely dealt with systematically or consistently by the early reformers. The importance of the pioneering efforts of these laymen in Germany should not, however, be minimized. Their attempts at making Jewish worship more attractive were emulated by Jews elsewhere on the continent—in major cities in England, Denmark, Austria, and Hungary—and even in distant America; by the mid-1830s Reform was a significant factor in Jewish religious life.

❦

It was at this juncture that a number of rabbis appeared in Germany who energetically espoused the cause of Reform. Several of these were men of extraordinary ability, with a profound knowledge of both Judaism and European culture. Almost all of them were greatly influenced by the new Jewish scholarship that was beginning to emerge in Germany and elsewhere in Europe—the so-called *Wissenschaft des Judentums*, which we shall discuss in Chapter XI. Under the impact of this scholarship, which examined Jewish history and literature critically, these rabbis could no longer subscribe to the traditionalist view that Judaism was a monolithic and stable structure, enduring essentially unchanged from Sinai to the present day. Their historical studies made it obvious to them that Judaism had evolved over the centuries and assumed sharply differing forms in re-action to various challenges and environments. If changes had taken place in the past, albeit unconsciously, then—these men con-cluded—it is perfectly legitimate to make them now, and to do so in consciously directed response to the needs of the contemporary situation.

Preeminent among the German rabbis who assumed leadership in the growing Reform movement and proceeded to give it some theo-logical substance and direction was Abraham Geiger (1810–1874). Born into a prominent orthodox family in Frankfurt, Geiger received an intensive Talmudic education as a child and adolescent. At the age of nineteen he matriculated at the University of Heidelberg, where he studied classical philology and Oriental languages. Later he continued his studies at the University of Bonn. Here one of his closest friends was his future theological adversary and the guiding spirit of the Neo-Orthodox movement, Samson Raphael Hirsch, with whom he collaborated in organizing a group of young men interested in developing their homiletic skills. At Heidelberg and Bonn, Geiger thoroughly absorbed the scientific-critical approach to the study of history, and his doctoral dissertation at Bonn, *Was hat Mohammed aus dem Judenthume aufgenommen?*, dealing with the influence of Judaism on the Koran, was the first of his many significant contributions to *die Wissenschaft des Judentums*. In 1832 Geiger became rabbi in Wies-baden, where he began to work for several moderate reforms in worship and greater decorum in the synagogue. Strong opposition to his innovating proposals from some laymen led to his resignation after five years of service. In Wiesbaden Geiger began to issue a learned journal, *Wissenschaftliche Zeitschrift für jüdische Theologie* (6 vols., 1835–1847), which included among its contributors some of the foremost Jewish scholars of the time. It was in Wiesbaden also that he organized, in 1837, the first meeting of German rabbis with Reform sympathies. The meeting, however, produced little in the way of practical consequences.

Known for his proclivities toward Reform and his critical-scien-tific approach to the Bible, the *Talmud*, and other sources of Ju-daism, Geiger was elected, in 1838, by the community of Breslau, many of whose members desired modernization of the synagogue rit-ual and other aspects of Jewish life, as *dayyan* and assistant to its se-nior rabbi, Solomon A. Tiktin, an unyielding defender of ortho-doxy. The unseemly controversy thus precipitated between the two men made it impossible for Geiger to occupy his position until 1840.

After he assumed office, the Breslau congregation issued a two-volume work, *Rabbinische Gutachten über die Verträglichkeit der freien Forschung mit dem Rabbineramte* (*Rabbinic Opinions on the Compatibility of Free Investigation with the Rabbinic Office*), containing strong statements by some leading proponents of Reform. Even following Tiktin's death in 1843 and the election of Geiger to the office of senior rabbi, the controversy in Breslau was not stilled, since the orthodox party managed to have Tiktin's son elected assistant rabbi. Some years later the orthodox minority seceded from the official community and established its own congregation. The breach between the two factions was not to be healed until 1856.

During his tenure in Breslau Geiger played a prominent role in the deliberations of the conferences of liberal rabbis held in 1844, 1845, and 1846 in Brunswick, Frankfurt, and Breslau respectively. Since the participating rabbis were united only by a general sentiment in favor of reforming Jewish practice, theoretical and theological issues were avoided as much as possible; the conferences focused on such concerns as liturgical change (prayer in the vernacular and organ music in the synagogue), mitigating some of the rigors of the traditional rules for observance of the Sabbath, and reforming marriage and divorce laws so as to give the Jewish woman increased rights. The participants constantly appealed to traditional (mainly Talmudic) sources in justification of the changes they proposed, and insisted that they did not consider Reform a sect departing from the mainstream of historical Judaism; their attitude toward the authority of the *Talmud* was, however, obviously ambiguous. It is interesting to note that the rabbis were quite hostile toward the group of laymen in Frankfurt styling themselves the "Society of the Friends of Reform" who, in 1843, had issued a manifesto which, among other things, rejected circumcision, completely denied the authority of the *Talmud*, repudiated belief in the Messiah, and, on the positive side, stated only their conviction that "the Mosaic faith is capable of limitless development." Most of the conferees were also negatively disposed to the radical *Reformgemeinde* founded in Berlin in 1845.

Besides being the guiding spirit of the rabbinical conferences, Geiger was instrumental in establishing in 1854 the Jüdisch-Theologisches Seminar of Breslau, which became one of the major centers of *die Wissenschaft des Judentums* in the second half of the nineteenth century. To his keen disappointment, however, the principalship of the school was denied him because of opposition from the conservatives and given instead to Zacharias Frankel. In 1862

Geiger established another journal, *Jüdische Zeitschrift für Wissenschaft und Leben*, which continued for over a decade and in which he published numerous scholarly and topical papers. In 1863 he was appointed to the rabbinate of the Reform congregation in Frankfurt. From 1870 until his death in 1874 he served as rabbi of the Berlin congregation. Only in 1872 did he achieve his lifelong ambition of holding an academic post. In that year he joined three other scholars, David Cassel, Israel Lewy, and Hermann Heymann Steinthal, on the faculty of the Hochschule für die Wissenschaft des Judentums, the institute for critical Jewish scholarship and the training of liberal rabbis that had just been established in Berlin, and was also appointed its director.

While still in his thirties Abraham Geiger emerged as the major theoretician and spokesman of the Reform movement in Germany. His reputation as a brilliant scholar whose intellectual interests embraced virtually the whole of Jewish history and literature, as well as his active involvement in all the significant concerns and causes of German Jewry of his day, combined to lend authority to his reforming ideas and proposals.

As a result of his historical studies, Geiger was persuaded that Judaism is an ongoing, evolutionary process. Its pristine origin lay in the divine revelation granted the Hebrew prophets—their insight that God is essentially Moral Will and that He alone created and rules all things. On this foundation the Jewish religious tradition was established and began to develop. The teachers of the Talmudic age, in Geiger's view, both criticized and expanded their religious legacy. They did not regard biblical law as eternally valid; they interpreted it creatively and energetically adapted it to the demands of their own time. Only with the close of the *Talmud* in the sixth century C.E. did Judaism begin to lapse into orthodoxy, into a lifeless and petrified nomism from which, Geiger urged, it was now the central task of Reform to deliver it.

Geiger affirmed the reality of divine revelation but refused to regard it as an isolated event that occurred at Mount Sinai and then ceased forever. Instead, he developed the concept of "progressive revelation," the idea that God continuously reveals His truth through the discoveries of scientists and the insights of poets and philosophers. New truth is constantly being made available in every generation; hence no document of the Jewish tradition—neither the Bible, *Talmud*, nor any other—divinely inspired though it may be, can lay claim to being the full and definitive disclosure of God's wisdom and will. Furthermore, since revelation is always mediated through fallible human beings, no document recording it is simply and unqualifiedly divine; on the contrary, it is an amalgam of the divine and human, of God's truth and man's limited and frequently distorted grasp of it. Thus Judaism must be regarded as a living process, developing from primitive origins to its full moral, spiritual, and intellectual stature.

That stature, according to Geiger, must be made manifest by approaching the Jewish tradition critically and removing those excrescences that have attached themselves to Judaism over the centuries, obscuring its nobility and truth. Its rituals, customs, and ceremonies especially require fearless critical evaluation. Geiger was not intrinsically opposed to ritual, but he insisted that, in keeping with the teaching of the Hebrew prophets, it must be regarded as secondary and subordinate to what is the essence of Judaism—its morality. Ritual has instrumental value in dramatizing and vivifying the moral and intellectual truths of Judaism and inspiring the Jew who performs it, but it is not itself sacred and unalterable. Its forms have changed in the past, and if they are now no longer successful in inspiring the contemporary Jew, or are repugnant to his sensibilities, there ought to be no hesitation in again changing them or even abandoning them altogether. New forms may also be constructed. However, since Judaism ought not and cannot break with its past, this should be done out of the halachic materials of the historical tradition.

In practice, Geiger was quite moderate when it came to reforming Jewish ritual, and became even more so as he grew older. At the Frankfurt rabbinical conference in 1845 he opposed retention of Hebrew in the synagogue service, arguing that the language was unknown or insufficiently known by the majority of worshipers, and that authentic spirituality demanded prayer in a familiar tongue. Despite his contention, the prayer book that he issued for his congregation in Breslau in 1854 retained the Hebrew, along with prayers in German. References to the restoration of the Jewish people to Palestine, however, were deleted, and such a phrase in the traditional liturgy as *meḥayyeh metim* (who quickens the dead) was translated in German as *Quell ewigen Lebens* (Source of eternal life). Geiger was also opposed to the abrogation of the rite of circumcision, although he admitted in a letter to Leopold Zunz that he personally considered it a "barbaric, bloody act." In addition, Geiger was hostile to the substitution of Sunday services for the traditional Sabbath (a practice adopted by the radical Reform congregation in

Berlin under the leadership of Samuel Holdheim), but he gave his assent to instrumental music in the synagogue on the Sabbath. Indeed, as time went on his sympathy for tradition increased to the point that during his rabbinate in Berlin in the last years of his life he even reinstituted observance of the second day of the festivals, a practice he had eliminated in Breslau. The major reasons for his growing conservatism were his desire that Reform Judaism not become a schismatic sect alienated from the main body of Judaism, and his aversion to all customs smacking of usage by the Christian Church, to which he was intensely antipathetic.

Despite his personal antagonism to Christianity, however, Geiger insisted on envisioning the Jewish people in terms of the model of the Christian Church. Israel or the Jewish people is, in his view, not a nation with a distinctive faith, but a religious community pure and simple. Its raison d'être is to serve, as Deutero-Isaiah put it, as "a light to the nations." The mission of the Jewish people is to bear witness in the world to God and His moral law by living its corporate life, and having its individual members conduct their lives, in accordance with that law. According to Geiger, the loss by ancient Israel of its national independence and territory was not, as the mainstream of rabbinic tradition contended, divine punishment visited upon it for its sins. On the contrary, the dispersion of the Jews was a crucial element of God's beneficent plan for mankind, and was intended essentially to enable Israel to fulfill its appointed task of teaching, by example as well as precept, the truth of ethical monotheism to all the peoples of the world. In consonance with this view, Geiger believed that the Jews must abandon, now and for the future, all claims to national existence or even ethnic distinctiveness and come to regard themselves as a faith community commissioned by God to play a central role in the drama of world redemption.

That world redemption—what Jewish tradition included in its concept of "the days of the Messiah"—was not far off was one of Geiger's cherished convictions. Despite all the evidence of the recrudescence in Europe of discrimination against and active persecution of the Jews, and despite the failures of some of the liberal revolutions that he witnessed in his own lifetime, he remained persuaded of the validity of the Enlightenment's favorite watchword—Progress. The movement of history, Geiger devoutly believed, was essentially forward, and the ideals proclaimed by the revolutionaries of France— liberty, equality, fraternity—would soon be generally realized. The essence of biblical Judaism, its moral code and its prophetic view of

The interior of the synagogue at Livorno,
a painting by Solomon A. Hart (1806–1881).

Synagogue in Toledo, Spain, built around the beginning
of the thirteenth century. Now the
Church of St. Maria La Blanca.

The medieval synagogue of Rabbi Isaac Abouhab in
the old quarter of Safed, Palestine.

Tempio Israelitico Spagnola, Venice, 1584.

Dedication of the Spanish-Portuguese Synagogue, Amsterdam, 1675.

Interior of the wooden synagogue, formerly in Kirchheim,
Bavaria, Germany, eighteenth century.

The wooden synagogue in Wolpa, Poland, built in 1781.

Touro Synagogue in Newport, Rhode Island, built in 1763. It is the
oldest synagogue still standing in the United States.

Prayer for the Emperor at the installation of the Chief Rabbi of Paris
in the synagogue on the rue Notre-Dame de Nazareth.

A Jew in prayer shawl
and phylacteries awaiting
execution by the Nazis.

Round-up of Jews by Nazis
in the Warsaw Ghetto.

ABOVE LEFT: A. D. Gordon (1856–1922),
apostle of the "religion of labor"
and ideologist of Labor Zionism.

ABOVE RIGHT: Abraham Isaac Kook (1865–1935),
Chief Rabbi of Palestine
and mystical thinker.

LEFT: Solomon Schechter (1847–1915),
leader of Conservative Judaism
and major builder of the
Jewish Theological Seminary of America.

Isaac Mayer Wise (1819–1900),
builder of Reform Judaism in America
and founder of the Hebrew Union College.

Kaufmann Kohler (1843–1926),
theologian of Reform Judaism in America
and president of the Hebrew Union College.

Abba Hillel Silver (1893–1963),
rabbi, scholar, and foremost Zionist
leader in America.

Mordecai Kaplan (b. 1881),
founder of the Reconstructionist
movement in American Judaism.

the consummation toward which history tended (which, in Geiger's view, were also the ultimate source of the ideals and values of nineteenth-century European liberalism), would become the core of a world faith uniting all men in universal brotherhood.

Despite its facile optimism, romanticism, and blindness to facts which did not escape the notice of more realistic and perspicacious observers of historical and intellectual tendencies, Geiger's was a noble faith that inspired not only himself but numerous followers. There is no evidence that he and his disciples were fundamentally motivated, as some have charged, by a desire to curry favor with their Teutonic neighbors and win greater political and social acceptance for Jews in German society. Nor were they impelled by any desire for a rapprochement with Christianity; Geiger himself, as we have noted, had a strong disdain for the Christian faith and its tenets and practices. To be sure, the effect of his reforming efforts and those of his successors was to make Judaism appear, at least externally, more like Christianity, but this was not their intent. They were motivated basically by a desire to refashion the Judaism they had inherited into a religious faith that would speak compellingly both to their hearts and minds, the former open and generous and the latter questioning and critical.

❦

Geiger, we have observed, was rather moderate in his reforms of Jewish practice. Far more cavalier in his attitude toward traditional customs and values was the chief spokesman of radical Reform in mid-nineteenth-century Germany, Samuel Holdheim (1806–1860).

Born in Kempno in the province of Posen, Holdheim attended a *yeshivah* and received an intensive Talmudic education of the old-fashioned type. Later, after his divorce from the educated woman who had introduced him to the world of secular German culture, he studied at the universities of Prague and Berlin and received a doctorate from the University of Leipzig. Following some years of service in Frankfurt-am-Oder and as *Landesrabbiner* (chief rabbi) of Mecklenburg-Schwerin, he assumed, in 1847, the rabbinate of the Reform congregation of Berlin, the so-called *Reformgenossenschaft*, which, in its radicalism, had already seceded from the official Jewish community in the Prussian capital and incurred the intense disapproval of most of the liberal rabbis of Germany. Under Holdheim's leadership the Berlin congregation became even more radical; indeed, it was the most extreme exemplar of Reform in all of Europe. The hostility directed against him was so great that, on his early death at the age of fifty-four, his opponents refused to pay him the funerary honors customary for a distinguished rabbi; one of them even attempted to prevent his interment in the section of the Berlin cemetery reserved for rabbis. The attempt was unsuccessful, and Abraham Geiger, who sharply disagreed with many of Holdheim's views while respecting his integrity and scholarship, preached the funeral oration.

Holdheim's views are expressed in his collection of sermons preached at Frankfurt-am-Oder, *Gottesdienstliche Vorträge* (*Worship Addresses*, 1839), *Über die Autonomie der Rabbinen und das Prinzip der jüdischen Ehe* (*On the Autonomy of the Rabbis and the Principles of Jewish Marriage Law*, 1843), his Hebrew work *Maamar Ha-Ishut* (*An Essay on Marriage*, 1861), his three published volumes of sermons given in Berlin, and numerous essays. On the basis of tortuous and frequently rather specious reasoning from Talmudic statements, reflecting his early training in *pilpul* in a traditional *yeshivah*, Holdheim sought to justify abandonment of all nationalist and ethnic elements in Judaism and complete adaptation of Jewish law and custom to the legal systems of the nation-states of which Jews were becoming citizens. In so doing he carried to their logical (and destructive) conclusion the program and attitudes of the Assembly of Jewish Notables and the "Sanhedrin" convened in Paris by Napoleon several decades before his time.

Taking as his proof-texts the principle of the third-century Babylonian Amora, Mar Samuel, that in civil matters *dina de-malchuta dina* (the law of the state is the law [for its Jews]),[1] as well as the dictum of the *Mishnah* to the effect that "any religious duty that does not depend on the Land [of Israel] may be observed whether in the Land or outside of it; and any religious duty that depends on the Land may be observed in the Land [alone]," [2] Holdheim concluded that all the laws of the Bible and *Talmud* that were in effect when the Jews lived as a sovereign nation with their own territory and government had lost their legitimacy. Judaism now requires a new system of legislation that will be in accord with both the letter and spirit of the laws of the nations in whose midst the Jews live as free and equal citizens.

Even laws whose source is God Himself, Holdheim urged, must be regarded as valid only for a particular time and place. As he put it:

The present requires a principle that shall enunciate clearly that a law, even though divine, is potent only so long as the conditions and circumstances of life, to meet which it was enacted, continue; when these change, however, the law also must be abrogated, even though it have God for its author. For God Himself has shown indubitably that, with the change of the circumstances and conditions of life for which He once gave those laws, the laws themselves cease to be operative, that they *shall* be observed no longer because they *can* be observed no longer.[3]

Thus, Holdheim urged that the Talmudic and biblical laws governing marriage, divorce, and personal status are now nugatory, and that in these areas Jews should be ruled completely by the civil legislation of the state. Apparently he believed that these laws could no longer be observed, but why is not at all clear. In any case, taking this position, Holdheim could find no religious objection to intermarriage; the halachic prohibition of marriages between Jews and non-Jews and the refusal of Jewish law to recognize the validity of such marriages were proper only when the Jews lived in their own territory as members of a sovereign nation. Holdheim appears to have been little troubled by the idea that the sanctioning of exogamy would inevitably weaken the fabric of Judaism, and might ultimately lead to the extinction of the Jewish people. He was quite prepared to officiate at intermarriages and did virtually nothing to discourage them. Holdheim also did not refrain from declaring openly in 1844 that circumcision is not the essential rite that makes a Jewish male a member of the household of Israel, and that its observance must therefore be considered a matter of choice for the infant's parents; Jewish status is conferred simply by being born of a Jewish mother. From the formal halachic point of view, there was no doubt a good deal that could be said in justification of this position. That tremendous emotional power was impacted in the symbol of induction into the Covenant of Abraham through circumcision, that it had been one of the most deeply rooted and cherished observances among Jews for centuries, made little difference to Holdheim's prosaic and rationalist mind; circumcision was formally and legally dispensable, although he personally preferred its retention. In reforming the worship of the Berlin Temple, Holdheim was again quite indifferent to Jewish law and tradition. Sunday eventually became the sole weekly day of worship there, although at first services were conducted on both Saturdays and Sundays, and the second day of the festivals (except for Rosh Hashanah) was abolished. The liturgy was greatly abbreviated and almost entirely in German.

Holdheim's influence on the course of the development of Reform Judaism in Europe was not highly significant. He found no imitators of his radical tendencies on the continent, but his antinomian spirit was exemplified to some degree by many leaders of the Reform movement. In Europe Abraham Geiger's more restrained and conservative version of Reform, with its fundamental respect for history and tradition, was regnant. Only in America in the second half of the nineteenth century did Holdheim's radicalism win a few disciples and emulators, but even here Geiger's moderate Reform was the dominant influence.

By the middle of the nineteenth century Reform Judaism had achieved an established place in the life of German Jewry, but its original impetus appears to have been largely spent. Some of its foremost rabbinical leaders migrated to America, especially in the wake of the reaction that followed the revolutions of 1848, and so did many liberal-minded Jewish laymen. These contributed to the building of a vital Reform movement in the United States, but their departure diminished the strength of the liberal cause in Germany. The religious excitement which generated and accompanied the rabbinical conferences of the 1840s could not be mustered again in Germany. Indeed, no liberal rabbinical conference was convoked for more than twenty years. It was not until 1869 that a Reform synod, consisting of both rabbis and laymen, was held in Leipzig. It was reconvened in Augsburg in 1871. The effect of these synods, however, was negligible, since each of the Reform congregations in Germany insisted on complete autonomy; even the acceptance of a common prayer book had to wait more than another fifty years. But though Reform Judaism in its native land came to lose much of its pristine vitality, its historical importance should not be minimized. German Reform pioneered in adapting Judaism to the needs and demands of a new age, and while its specific programs and proposals were challenged by other movements of religious adaptation, the latter were clearly influenced by the original movement. Furthermore, German Reform gave rise to Reform movements of greater or lesser strength elsewhere in Europe—in Austria, Hungary, France, England, and other countries—and, most significantly, in America.

❧❧❧

Reform Judaism fulfilled the religious needs of considerable numbers of Jews who were no longer at home in the world of traditional Jewish piety. It responded to the *Zeitgeist*, the "spirit of the times," to employ a favorite expression of more than a few of its champions. Reform met the requirements of those Jews who desired a less restrictive and disciplined regimen of ritual observance, who longed for worship more in keeping with western tastes and sensibilities, who were searching for a faith that would require less of a *sacrificium intellectus* than did classical Judaism as formulated by Maimonides in his Thirteen Articles of Faith, and who wanted a religion that would give them a sense of mission and purpose in their Jewish existence and in their relationship as Jews to the larger world. Many, however, even among those Jews who shared these requirements, came to feel that Reform Judaism as it developed in Germany in the first half of the nineteenth century was moving too rapidly and recklessly, that it threatened to cut itself off from its roots in the soil of historic Jewish tradition, and that a more moderate reconstruction of Judaism was the real desideratum of the age. Sooner or later a conservative reaction against Reform was bound to arise. It came in the 1840s in the form of a new movement which presently began to call itself the Positive-Historical School and whose outstanding leader was Zacharias Frankel (1801–1875).

It has become customary among historians of Judaism to signalize the genesis of this school with the dramatic walkout of Frankel from the conference of liberal rabbis at Frankfurt in 1845 in protest against the stand taken by the conference on the use of Hebrew in synagogue worship. This incident may well be regarded symbolically as the beginning of the Conservative movement in Judaism in Germany, although sharp criticism of the program of the reformers by rabbis and scholars with liberal tendencies, and by Frankel himself, actually antedated the Frankfurt conference by years.

One of the early critics of the reformers was the great scholar Leopold Zunz, who in the initial years of the Reform movement had himself preached at the Reform services conducted in the home of Jacob Beer in Berlin, and later (1835–1836) served briefly as rabbi of a private Reform association in Prague. Zunz's first major work, *Die gottesdienstlichen Vorträge der Juden* (*The Devotional Addresses of the Jews*) (1832), was motivated in large measure by his desire to demonstrate that preaching in the synagogue in the vernacular was an ancient and honored custom in Judaism, and that the synagogal liturgy had changed substantially over the centuries—from which it followed that the introduction of the German sermon and the liturgical modifications proposed by the reformers were no radical departure from tradition. As time went on, however, Zunz became more skeptical about the value and utility of many of the changes advocated by the

Reform party, particularly by its radical wing. In 1843 he came to the defense of the practice of wearing *tefillin* in worship, a practice which had been discarded by many of the reformers, arguing that this and other symbolic rituals served the indispensable purpose of concretizing and dramatizing the religious and moral values of the Jewish tradition, and that without them Judaism would be seriously impoverished. A year later, responding to the manifesto of the Frankfurt "Society of the Friends of Reform," which denounced the rite of circumcision as a primitive, barbaric, and outmoded relic, Zunz again admonished that Judaism could not survive merely as a set of abstract doctrines without tangible practices symbolizing them and making them come alive. And in a letter written in 1845 to Abraham Geiger, who had deplored his growing conservatism, Zunz protested against the Reform attitude toward the Jewish dietary regulations, urging that "we must reform ourselves, not our religion."

Zunz's early ardor for Reform cooled, in addition, because of his historical sense, which made him ascribe much greater value and importance to the *Talmud* than did many of the Reform rabbis. Furthermore, he had little use for modern rabbis as a group, regarding their professional functions as a "waste of time" and once even classifying them with soothsayers and quacks. He suspected the rabbinical leaders of Reform of harboring ecclesiastical ambitions of which he strongly disapproved, and was apprehensive that they might become religious autocrats. Zunz, however, was too engrossed in his scholarly work to become the polemicist and champion of the reaction against Reform. This role was assumed to a degree by Zacharias Frankel, who, like Zunz, was also an outstanding protagonist of *die Wissenschaft des Judentums* and made some notable contributions to it.

Born in Prague in 1801 into a wealthy and prominent family, Frankel obtained a standard Talmudic upbringing in the city's *yeshivah* as well as a comprehensive general education. At the age of thirty he received, simultaneously with rabbinic ordination, a doctorate in classics from the University of Budapest for a dissertation on the Septuagint. Becoming rabbi of the congregation of Teplitz and appointed *Kreisrabbiner* (district rabbi) of Leitmeritz by the Austrian government, Frankel proceeded to institute several slight innovations in the synagogue service, including the introduction of a choir of boys, elimination of the medieval liturgical poems that had been added to the statutory prayers, and preaching in the vernacular. However, in response to the president of his congregation, who ventured the hope that the new rabbi would rectify the "abuses" (*Miss-bräuche*) of synagogal life, Frankel declared that he knew of no such abuses and that, in any case, it was not within the competence of laymen to interfere in such matters. In 1836 he was called to the chief rabbinate of the community of Dresden, where he gained increasing fame for his scholarship and advocacy of the cause of conservatism. When the Jüdisch-Theologisches Seminar was established in Breslau in 1854, Frankel, as we have noted, was elected to its directorship. For the next twenty years, until his death, he remained at the seminary, pursuing his scholarly investigations and training numerous rabbis and teachers in the Science of Judaism.

Although Judaic learning in the spirit of *die Wissenschaft des Judentums* was Frankel's central interest throughout his adult life, he was not without a practical concern for the welfare of his fellow Jews. One of the important services he rendered them was contributing to the abolition of the degrading oath *more Judaico*, the special formal oath imposed by the government of Saxony on Jews participating in judicial processes, justified by the argument that Jews supposedly repudiated all their vows and promises annually through the recitation of the *Kol Nidrei* prayer. In a learned study entitled *Die Eidesleistung bei den Juden in theologischer und historischer Beziehung* (*The Jewish Oath in Theological and Historical Context*, Dresden, 1840), Frankel showed the absurdity of this supposition, and the oath *more Judaico* was soon withdrawn by Saxony and later by other states of Germany as well. Another work of Frankel's on legal procedure, *Der gerichtliche Beweis nach Mosaisch-Talmudischen Rechte* (*Judicial Evidence in Mosaic-Talmudic Law*, Berlin, 1846), also aided Jews involved in court proceedings. Prussian law stipulated that the testimony of a Jew against a Christian was admissible only in civil cases, and in these only when a sum of less than fifty thalers was involved. As a result of Frankel's study, which was quoted as an authority in the Prussian Diet, this discriminatory legislation was revoked in 1847. Frankel's other scholarly works, dealing largely with rabbinic literature and the history of the *halachah*, were more theoretically oriented. Even these, however, were of considerable practical significance in shaping his views, as well as those of his colleagues and disciples, on the kind of response to the contemporary world they believed was required of Judaism—a response quite different from that of the reformers.

The key element in Frankel's conception of Judaism is his assumption that the Jewish legal tradition, which is the heart of Judaism, is fundamentally the product of the Jewish people and the people's creative spirit. Frankel could not accept the orthodox dogma that Talmudic law, or the Oral Torah, is the content of a supernatural divine revelation given to Israel at Mount Sinai. Its source, for him, was the Jewish *Volksgeist*, the living spirit of the people, which, in response to historical circumstances, the environment, and its own creative impulses, always produced new institutions and forms when these were required, and sloughed off old ones when these had lost their value or become dysfunctional in the life of the people. To be sure, the Pentateuch, or Written Torah, was, according to Frankel, the product of divine revelation supernaturally communicated to Israel. But he held that the law of the Written Torah, though theoretically eternal and unalterable, had, in practice, undergone continuous interpretation and modification at the hands of the teachers of the people, at certain times resulting in a strengthening of its severity, at other times in a relaxation of its rigor, and at still others in virtually complete alteration of its substance. This process of interpretation and modification, Frankel believed, was perfectly legitimate and in accord with the divine will, for the Torah had been given by God *to Israel*, and Israel (i.e., the Jewish people as a whole, although not necessarily its individual members) may be trusted to understand God's will rightly and to preserve the essence of the Torah. From this it follows that the substance of Judaism consists of the beliefs, values, institutions, practices, and forms created and maintained in the historical experience of the Jewish people, and that this historical experience is not to be overruled or ignored by any individual Jew or small group of Jews.

Holding such a view of the nature of Judaism, Frankel had necessarily to react critically to the innovations and proposals of the advocates of Reform. His first major published statement on Reform appeared in 1842 and was a response to the controversy evoked by the publication in 1841 of a revised version of the Hamburg Temple Prayer Book and the consequent warning by the orthodox *hacham* of Hamburg, Isaac Bernays, that the *herem* issued against the first edition some two decades earlier was still in effect. Frankel strongly deplored the use of the *herem*, defended the leaders of the Hamburg Temple against the accusation of atheism and heresy made by Bernays and other traditionalist "defenders of the faith," and declared changes in the liturgy permissible in principle. At the same time he assailed the reformers for their lack of historical perspective and for relying too heavily on their personal, idiosyncratic reasoning and sentiment, and ignoring the historical experience of the Jewish people as a whole that is embedded in tradition.

The *Siddur* and *Maḥzor*, Frankel maintained, represent the beliefs, values, and aspirations of Israel in its entirety; they are the distillation of centuries of spiritual travail and searching. No individual Jew or group of Jews is entitled to adopt a cavalier attitude toward them and arrogantly substitute his or its own convictions and feelings for those of the Jewish people as a whole. To do so is destructive of the unity of Israel and of the historical continuity of Jewish tradition. If any particular idea, prayer, or liturgical formulation is dead or obsolete, Israel in its corporate character may be depended on eventually to eliminate or modify it. This is what has occurred in the past, and it is sure to occur in the present and future. Activist and individualist reforms are not only unnecessary; they are pernicious and must be rejected.

In the prospectus for the journal he founded in Dresden in 1844, *Zeitschrift für die religiösen Interessen des Judenthums*, Frankel wrote:

In these pages we shall emphasize the progress of Judaism. We shall conceive it to be our task to avoid the kind of negative reform which leads to complete dissolution, but instead, to show how the teachings of Judaism itself contain the possibility of progress. . . . Many people display nothing but a dull indifference instead of the deep religiosity of former days, and we notice that there are many who, misunderstanding the depths of Judaism, wish to dissolve it in the general mood of the modern age. The synagogue faces a crisis, but this must not dishearten us nor must we give way to doubts that it can be victorious, for the innermost content of Judaism is guaranteed both in its continued existence as well as in its latent possibilities of self-development. How such development shall take place must be determined by scientific research based on positive historical foundations.[4]

One of the major theological bugbears of the reformers, as we have noted, was traditional Jewish messianism, with its proclamation of a personal Messiah and its hope for national restoration of the Jewish people in Palestine and reconstruction of the Temple on Mount Zion. Not only extreme reformers like Samuel Holdheim but also moderate spokesmen of Reform such as Abraham Geiger rejected the whole doctrinal complex of orthodox messianism as wildly irrational and, furthermore, inconsistent with the new political status of Jews as citizens of the nations in whose midst they lived. They substituted the expectation of the ultimate advent of a "messianic age," a universal society of brotherhood, justice, and peace, toward which it was Israel's mission to help lead all the nations of the world. To Frankel the attitude of the reformers was deeply repugnant. Writing in 1842 in *Literaturblatt des Orients* of the elimination in the

Hamburg Temple Prayer Book of the petitions for the restoration of Zion, he declared: "There is nothing wrong with the yearning to re-establish our nationality in a corner of the world linked with our holiest memories, where it might again march forward in freedom and win the respect of the nations which, we are taught by melancholy experience, is given only to those who have worldly power." [5] Frankel vigorously denied that the Jewish messianic expectation implied the slightest deficiency in patriotism or devotion to the *Vaterland* on the part of Jews. What it proved rather was that "despite thousands of years of suffering and persecution, we have still not lost hope and can still grasp the idea of independence and renewal." [6]

While Frankel may properly be considered a "proto-Zionist," he was not a Zionist in the full sense of the term. To be sure, in his day no organized movement had yet arisen setting as its goal the establishment of a Jewish homeland in Palestine that might ultimately gather within its borders all the dispersed members of the household of Israel and become a great center of a revitalized Judaism and Hebraic culture. But Frankel did not himself advocate establishment of such a movement, and his vision of a rebuilt Zion was restricted to a place of refuge for the oppressed Jews of the world. Nevertheless, even his limited Zionism served as a protest against what many regarded as the empty and utterly visionary universalism and cosmopolitanism of the majority of the German champions of Reform. An encouraging attitude toward the nationalist aspirations of the Jewish people eventually became one of the hallmarks of the Positive-Historical School and of its followers in Germany, as it did of the later Conservative movement in America. To this result Frankel contributed significantly.

Although, as we have observed, Frankel had himself moved far away from dogmatic orthodoxy, he regarded with growing alarm the manifestations of radical Reform in the 1840s, such as the Berlin *Tempel-Verein* and *Reformgenossenschaft* and the Frankfurt "Society of the Friends of Reform." The manifestos of these groups and the pronouncements of other left-wing Reform leaders aroused in him the apprehension that Reform was pursuing a schismatic course and threatened to become a sectarian movement in German Jewry. While he had not attended the first conference of liberal rabbis in Brunswick in 1844, and indeed had reacted negatively to its proceedings and conclusions, he decided to come to the second conference in Frankfurt a year later. The basic motivation behind this decision apparently was his belief that he might persuade his rabbinical colleagues to move far more slowly and moderately with their reforming proposals. If that was Frankel's hope, he was grievously disappointed.

Much of the discussion at the Frankfurt conference revolved around the use of Hebrew in the synagogue service. Geiger, Holdheim, and several other Reform leaders argued that Hebrew was by no means essential to Jewish worship, and proved, through copious citations from the *Talmud* and the rabbinic codes, that tradition clearly sanctioned prayer in the vernacular. To insist upon Hebrew, they urged, was to defend the letter against the spirit, for many Jews no longer understand the sacred tongue and it is far better that they pray with sincerity and conviction in a language familiar to them than mumble words in incomprehensible Hebrew. Frankel took a completely contrary position. Hebrew, he maintained, is sacred to Jews, hallowed by history and tradition. Not only is the Hebrew language one of the major, unique, and irreplaceable expressions of the Jewish spirit, but worship in Hebrew has served as a common bond among Jews, uniting the generations of the past with the present. If, in any given generation, Jews have neglected their religious duty to study Hebrew and have lost their familiarity with it, that is no reason for destroying what is a "vital historic element in our religion."

When the arguments of Geiger and the reformers prevailed and the Frankfurt rabbinical conference adopted a resolution to the effect that Hebrew was not at all indispensable in Jewish worship but that for the present it was "advisable" to retain it, Frankel and one of his colleagues left the meeting in protest. In a letter dated July 18, 1845, and published in a Frankfurt journal, he announced his withdrawal from the conference then meeting in the city and his inability, as a matter of conscience, to cooperate further with a group of rabbis so disdainful of Jewish tradition. As for himself, he declared, he would be faithful to the principle of "positive historical Judaism."

To the regret of those who place a high value on ideological clarity, Frankel did not give a precise theoretical definition of this principle, which became the watchword of the Conservative movement in Germany and, later, in America. But it is fairly clear what he meant in practice. Tradition, which the "positive historical" experience of the Jewish people enshrines, must be normative in Judaism if it is to survive in the present and retain its identity, or at least its essential historical continuity, with the forms it has manifested in the past. Judaism cannot endure if it is constantly to be reformulated in accordance with the capricious "spirit of the times." Certain beliefs, values, institutions, and usages have been so fundamental and so deeply impacted into the structure of Judaism that its endurance without them is inconceivable. That is not to say that Judaism has been or must now be a monolithic, unalterable structure of belief and practice. Historical inquiry clearly shows that Judaism has changed in the past, and it will undoubtedly change in the future. Many of its beliefs and practices have proven themselves ephemeral and dispensable; history has rendered them obsolete and nugatory. It will do the same with others, and will no doubt create new forms in the future, as it has so richly in the past. No planned, reasoned intervention in the historical process on the part of individual Jews or small groups of Jews is either necessary or desirable.

Historical research in the spirit of *die Wissenschaft des Judentums*, Frankel urged, is required to discover what is enduring and permanently valuable in Judaism. "Jewish science," he wrote, "is not a mere autopsy on the corpse of Judaism. By means of it we must inquire into the principal foundations of Judaism from ancient times, for the preservation of which we must wage a determined struggle. We may not tamper with these fundamentals. They are memorials that have been acquired at the cost of blood and great sacrifice." [7] Free and critical historical inquiry by the individual is permissible and indeed laudable, but it does not entail any prescriptive right to make alterations in the structure of Judaism. "Any Jew is at liberty to pursue independent thought or investigation, but only the Jewish community as a whole has the authority to bring about reforms in Judaism. What has been fully accepted by the people and sealed in its history is sacred." [8]

The people, then, the Jewish community in its entirety, both vertically and horizontally, Jewry of the past and the present—what Solomon Schechter, one of Frankel's chief later disciples, was to call "catholic Israel"—is the ultimate authority in Judaism. In Judaism's great "trinity"—God, Torah, and Israel—the last became primary in the German Positive-Historical and the later American Conservative schools. It is not much of an exaggeration to say that the three great movements of modern Judaism, Reform, Neo-Orthodoxy, and Conservatism, came to be essentially distinguished by which of these three elements received their central stress. Reform, with its theological orientation, emphasized God and His moral will and tended to see Judaism as a "confession," a religious faith and an ethical doctrine; Neo-Orthodoxy, concentrating on Torah understood primarily as *halachah*, conceived Judaism as a divinely ordained system of legislation whose punctilious observance is obligatory on every Jew; and Conservatism, with its historical and sociological focus, apotheosized Israel and came eventually to express with utmost clarity in its last major American version—Mordecai Kaplan's Reconstructionism (see pp. 415–419)—the logical conclusion of its position by defining Judaism as the historical civilization of the Jewish people.

In reaction to Reform, and largely under the leadership of Frankel and the faculty of the Jüdisch-Theologisches Seminar in Breslau, a substantial group of rabbis emerged in Germany and elsewhere in Europe in the second half of the nineteenth century who led congregations in which ritual modifications were made slowly, and only when it became clear that they were demanded by the majority of the people. The members of this Positive-Historical School, as they styled themselves, also contributed leadership to the Conservative movement in America when some of them emigrated to the New World in the last decades of the century.

❧

We have noted that Frankel did not give a clear-cut definition of what he meant by "positive historical" Judaism when he withdrew from the Frankfurt rabbinical conference. Neither did he respond some eight years later to the demand addressed to him by Samson Raphael Hirsch (1808–1888) on his assumption of the directorship of the Jüdisch-Theologisches Seminar that he present a statement of the religious principles which would govern instruction at the seminary. Soon after the publication by Frankel of his *Darchei Ha-Mishnah* (*Ways of the Mishnah*) (Leipzig, 1859), Hirsch wrote a series of articles in which he attacked the vagueness of the author's definition of rabbinic tradition and his understanding of the history of rabbinic controversies. Frankel again avoided a direct response to Hirsch's challenge, restricting himself to arguing that not everything termed a "law" and reported as having been given to Moses on Mount Sinai is really of Mosaic origin.

When the director of the Breslau seminary was attacked by Hirsch, the latter had already achieved recognition as the major champion of the "new traditionalism," or Neo-Orthodoxy, as the third great religious movement that emerged in nineteenth-century German Jewry came to be called.

Born in 1808 in Hamburg into a leading orthodox family, Samson

Raphael Hirsch grew up in the atmosphere of intense controversy generated by the establishment of a Reform temple in that city and the struggle waged against it for many years by the *hacham* Isaac Bernays. Studying Judaica under the tutelage of Bernays and later in the *yeshivah* at Mannheim of Rabbi Jacob Ettlinger (1792–1871), he came to combine the complete loyalty to Jewish religious tradition and the devotion to German secular learning so happily exemplified by his teachers. Although he had only one year at the University of Bonn (where Abraham Geiger was among his closest friends), and the critical-scientific approach of the university toward the study of history and literature never affected his vision of Judaism, Hirsch maintained a lifelong love affair with German *Kultur* and was one of its most ardent promoters among his coreligionists.

It was while serving in his first rabbinical post, as *Landesrabbiner* of the Principate of Oldenburg (1830–1841), that Hirsch wrote two of his major works on Judaism. These were *Neunzen Briefe über Judenthum, von Ben Uziel* (*Nineteen Letters on Judaism by Ben Uziel*, 1836) and *Horeb: Versuche über Jissroel's Pflichten in der Zerstreuung* (*Horeb: Essays on Israel's Duties in the Diaspora*, 1838). Both works achieved considerable renown in their time and are still widely read by Hirsch's Neo-Orthodox followers today.

After serving for several years as chief rabbi of Moravia and Austrian Silesia, with headquarters in the large Jewish community of Nikolsburg, and becoming a member of the Austrian parliament, Hirsch in 1851 accepted an invitation to become the leader of a small and struggling orthodox congregation in Frankfurt. In that city, where he remained until his death thirty-seven years later, he managed to restore and enlarge the prestige of Orthodoxy which had long been overshadowed by Reform, to establish excellent schools committed to his philosophies of Judaism and education, to found and edit his monthly magazine *Jeschurun*, and to write numerous learned works, including a large commentary on the Pentateuch, which made his name famous throughout European Jewry. It was also in Frankfurt that Hirsch in 1876 arranged the secession of his orthodox *Religionsgesellschaft* from the central *kehillah*, on the grounds that Jews faithful to the Torah could not in good conscience cooperate in any way with a community dominated by Reform Judaism or in which Reform institutions and principles were accepted. This splitting of the community, on which Hirsch insisted despite considerable concessions to the traditionalists by the Reform leadership of Frankfurt, evoked strong disapproval even among some of the ultraorthodox rabbis of Germany.

New Interpretations of Judaism

What essentially distinguishes Hirsch's Neo-Orthodoxy from the *Altgläubigen*, or orthodox "old believers," was his insistence on the legitimacy, and indeed necessity, of secular culture along with fidelity to the precepts of the Torah. As the motto of the schools and congregation he led in Frankfurt, Hirsch selected the dictum of the *Mishnah*, "An excellent thing is study of Torah combined with worldly occupation [*Torah im derech eretz*]." [9] But by *derech eretz* he understood not worldly occupation but the culture of the age. *Torah im derech eretz*, "Both Torah and secular culture"—this became the central plank in Hirsch's Neo-Orthodox platform. Against the older orthodox rabbis who regarded Torah as fully sufficient for the Jew's intellectual as well as moral and religious life, and who deplored secular learning as likely to lead to heresy, or—at best—as being a waste of time, Hirsch adopted the position of Moses Mendelssohn that scientific knowledge and secular culture were not only compatible with unqualified loyalty to Judaism but essential to its practice. Familiarity with them, he therefore urged, is a religious obligation.

We maintain that an acquaintance with all those elements which lie at the root of present-day civilization and a study of all the subjects required for such an acquaintance are of the highest necessity for the Jewish youth of our day (as it was in fact in all times), and should be looked upon as a religious duty. This will be denied by no Jew who recognizes what Judaism demands. We are ourselves fortunate enough to live in a time which we can regard as the dawn of a new era of justice in human affairs, in which the members of the Jewish people also will be invited to take an active part in all humane, social and political activities among the nations. Our contact with general culture no longer bears the passive character which it had in the times of our fathers. But even if this were not so, how religiously important it would be to provide our youth with the knowledge which would enable them to form a true and just appreciation of the personal, social, political and religious conditions and relations in which they would have to live as men and Jews. How religiously important it would be to give them the knowledge for properly appraising the European culture by which they are surrounded and for absorbing with zest all that is good and noble in it! [10]

Mendelssohnian also is Hirsch's insistence that Judaism is a non-dogmatic religion, a religion of practice rather than of creed. One dogma, however, is central in his version of Judaism, as it is in Mendelssohn's, and distinguishes Neo-Orthodoxy from both Reform and Positive-Historical Judaism. This is the divinely revealed character of the whole Torah. In *Horeb* as well as in *Nineteen Letters* Hirsch envisions Judaism's teaching and praxis as consisting of six categories: *Torot* (doctrines), *Edot* (testimonies), *Mishpatim* (judgments), *Ḥukkim* (positive ordinances), *Mitzvot* (commandments), and *Avodah* (worship). All of these—whether *Edot* such as the Sabbath and festivals which serve to further Israel's moral education, or the *Mishpatim* which are intended to promote social justice and fair dealing between men, or such arbitrary *Ḥukkim* as the dietary laws—are of divine origin, revealed by God to Israel at Sinai or Horeb in the presence of more than two million souls, and therefore eternally incumbent upon the Jewish people and the Jew.

The task of the present-day Jew, Hirsch maintained, is not to eliminate or modify any of the principles or practices revealed to him by God, but to understand the profound meaning inherent in them. Hirsch himself undertook to provide in his *Horeb* and other writings an explication of the deeper significance of many of the teachings and laws of Judaism through a symbolic and metaphorical interpretation which is, at times, strongly reminiscent of the method of Philo of Alexandria. Like Philo, he frequently resorts to far-fetched etymological explanations of Hebrew terms for homiletical purposes. The etymology in many instances is, from a scientific point of view, extremely dubious, but the explanations breathe a genuine and intense religious fervor. It may be added that, on Hirsch's own view of the laws of Judaism as divinely revealed, any human defense of them is supererogatory, since their status as expressions of God's will provides more than adequate sanction for their observance; nevertheless, Hirsch obviously felt that the Jews of his day required an apologetic rationale such as his own as a stimulus for fulfillment of the *mitzvot*.

In the Reform movement Hirsch saw a distortion of authentic Judaism. The reformers were presuming to decide, on the basis of their own reason and sentiment, how God is to be served. But God Himself has clearly and unambiguously prescribed the service He demands of the Jew, as well as his duties to the world and his fellowmen. The Torah is the Jew's eternal and unfailing guide, and service of God through observance of its precepts is his prime task and unique destiny. To adapt Judaism to the ephemeral values of the contemporary world or to the tastes and standards of one particular, time-bound civilization, as Hirsch believed the reformers were attempting to do, was—in his judgment—to destroy it. The divine and eternal Torah must be the judge of current values and ideas, not vice versa. Hirsch therefore assailed the way of Reform, which, he declared, was to adopt "a standpoint outside of Judaism, to accept a conception derived from strangers of the purposes of human life and the object of liberty, and then, in correspondence with this borrowed notion, to cut, curtail and obliterate the tenets and ordinances of Judaism." [11]

To serve God through a life of obedience to the commandments of the Torah is the divinely appointed purpose of the Jew, Hirsch maintained, and thereby the Jewish people also fulfills its mission to the world. In *The Nineteen Letters of Ben Uziel* he wrote:

> Because men had eliminated God from life, nay, even from nature, and found the basis of life in possessions and its aim in enjoyment, deeming life the product of the multitude of human desires, just as they looked upon nature as the product of a multitude of gods, therefore it became necessary that a people be introduced into the ranks of the nations which, through its history and life, should declare God the only creative cause of existence, fulfillment of His will the only aim of life; and which should bear the revelation of His will, rejuvenated and renewed for its sake, unto all parts of the world as the motive and incentive of its coherence. [12]

It is clear that Hirsch's conception of the mission of Israel is not radically different from that of Abraham Geiger and other proponents of Reform. Where he differed from most of the reformers was in his insistence that the Jewish people, in order to fulfill its moral task among the peoples of the world, must maintain its apartness from the world and preserve its unique way of life through observance of the ritual and ceremonial commandments that God has laid upon it alone, and that it may not repudiate.

Such isolation, Hirsch maintained, is spiritual and religious only; it does not imply withdrawal from secular concerns or nonparticipation in the affairs of the world. Jews must collaborate with their fellow citizens of non-Jewish faith in all matters having to do with promoting the general welfare and social progress of the community. To do so is one of the great privileges made available to them by their political emancipation. While Hirsch perceived in emancipation the possibility of "a new trial, much severer than the trial of oppression," [13] and recognized that it might draw the Jew away from fidelity to religious observance, his dominant attitude toward it was highly positive and optimistic. If the Jew now, under the benevolent rays of emancipation, remains loyal to the Torah and conducts himself toward the non-Jew as it ordains, he will not only further his God-given mission to the larger world, but also win that world's admiration and affection. Thus Hirsch preached enthusiastically:

Practice righteousness and love as the Holy Law bids you; be just in deed, truthful in words, bear love in your heart for your non-Jewish brethren, as your Law teaches you; feed his hungry, clothe his naked, console his mourners; heal his sick, counsel his inexperienced, assist him with counsel and deed in need and sorrow, unfold the whole noble breadth of your Israeldom, and can you think that he will not respect and love you, or that there will not result as great a degree of social intimacy as your life can concede? [14]

Hirsch would probably have been just as astounded as many of his disciples were at the strange response, fifty years after his death, of the "German Christians" and Nazis to several generations of ardent wooing by the Jews of Germany of their non-Jewish fellow citizens.

As a corollary of his view of the promise of emancipation, Hirsch categorically repudiated the Jewish nationalism and Zionism that were being proclaimed in the last years of his life by voices such as those of Moses Hess, Tzevi Hirsch Kalischer, Peretz Smolenskin, and Leo Pinsker. He would not, as many of the reformers had done, remove the ancient petitions for the restoration of Jewish nationhood in Palestine from the *Siddur*, but he insisted that these prayers must not lead to any practical activity by Jews for their realization. Hirsch wrote in *Horeb*:

Not in order to shine as a nation among nations do we raise our prayers and hope for a reunion in our land, but in order to find a soil for the better fulfillment of our spiritual vocation in that reunion and in the land which was promised and given, and again promised for our observance of the Torah. But this very vocation obliges us, until God shall call us back to the Holy Land, to live and to work as patriots wherever He has placed us, to collect all the physical, material and spiritual forces and all that is noble in Israel to further the weal of the nations which have given us shelter. It obliges us, further, to allow our longing for the far-off land to express itself only in mourning, in wishing and hoping; and only through the honest fulfillment of all Jewish duties to await the realization of this hope. But it forbids us to strive for the reunion or the possession of the land by any but spiritual means. [15]

Hirsch's views are in effect identical with those of the later orthodox Agudas Yisroel and of the Satmarer "rebbe" and the Neturei Karta today, still tenaciously maintained long after the establishment of the State of Israel.

New Interpretations of Judaism

❧⳩⳩❧

Next to Samson Raphael Hirsch, the outstanding champion of Neo-Orthodoxy in nineteenth-century Europe was the Italian Samuel David Luzzatto (1800–1865), commonly known by the acronym Shadal. Born into an extremely poor family distinguished for its scholarly traditions, Luzzatto was appointed professor at the newly established Collegio Rabbinico Italiano in Padua in 1829. His entire career, devoted to teaching and writing voluminously on the Bible, Hebrew grammar, poetry, philosophy, and Jewish history, was spent at the Collegio. The encyclopedic range of his scholarship is manifest in his published correspondence on learned matters with most of the outstanding representatives of *die Wissenschaft des Judentums* of the mid-nineteenth century, including Leopold Zunz, Abraham Geiger, Solomon Judah Rapoport, Isaac Samuel Reggio, and Moritz Steinschneider.

Luzzatto was a modern scholar and by no means a fundamentalist, but he adamantly rejected biblical criticism and, indeed, the critical spirit itself when applied to the foundations of Judaism. Amidst the jubilant chorus of admiration raised by nineteenth-century Jewish scholarship in general for Maimonides and Abraham ibn Ezra, his was a dissenting voice. Luzzatto argued that Greek philosophy, which Maimonides especially had embraced so wholeheartedly, is essentially antagonistic to the ethos of Judaism. So also is Kabbalah, but its theosophy, in his view, was the inevitable reaction to rationalist philosophy.

Luzzatto set himself sternly against the *Zeitgeist* of the nineteenth century and repudiated its espousal of Hellenism (or as he called it, Atticism), with its apotheosis of reason and its pretension to the capacity for attaining a total intellectual understanding of the universe. In his theological essays, as well as his letters, he sought to develop a Jewish theology based on faith in divine revelation and the election of Israel, and on the authority of tradition. Judaism—that is, the Torah and its commandments—must not be rationalized or relativized, as was being done by the school of historical criticism. Judaism is based not on reason or on history but on revelation, and its ethic flows from the fundamental quality of *ḥemlah*, human compassion or empathy.

The great watchword of the enlighteners of the eighteenth and nineteenth centuries was Progress. For Luzzatto, progress was an idol and its claims outrageously false. The rational principles and methods exemplified in Atticism may have achieved extraordinary results in science, philosophy, literature, and art, but they had not produced a more humane or morally mature society. The European civilization of his day was, in Luzzatto's view, rotten to the core. The advancement of science had only magnified the horrors of poverty, and the Industrial Revolution had raised the destructiveness of war to a new dimension. These disasters were the judgment of God on a presumptuous intellectualism, and the road to salvation lay in a return to obedience to the moral imperatives of the divine Torah, and to a renewal of compassion for all men.

Unlike Hirsch, whose writings were mainly homiletic and apologetic, Luzzatto made many notable contributions to Jewish scholarship. Having access to the great collections of Judaica in various libraries in Italy, he could study rare Hebrew books and manuscripts and inform his colleagues elsewhere in Europe of them. Among his major works is an edition of the poems of Judah ha-Levi which contributed significantly to a revival of interest in medieval Hebrew poetry. The Collegio Rabbinico in Padua, of which he was the leading light for more than thirty years, did not long outlast him, but another rabbinical seminary which carried on in his spirit was established in Florence after the unification of Italy.

In central Europe the seminary that would provide the leadership for the development and maintenance of Neo-Orthodoxy was the work not of Samson Raphael Hirsch but of his colleague and friend Azriel Hildesheimer (1820–1899). After obtaining a thorough Talmudic education, Hildesheimer studied Semitics, philosophy, and history at the universities of Berlin and Halle, and eventually obtained a doctorate from the latter for a study on the Septuagint. Elected to the rabbinate of the Austro-Hungarian community of Eisenstadt in 1851, Hildesheimer proceeded to establish there a *yeshivah* which included secular studies in its curriculum and attracted students from all over Europe. The innovations in his *yeshivah*, however, were strenuously opposed by the orthodox rabbis. Frustrated by the opposition of both the ultraorthodox and Reform elements in Hungarian Jewry, Hildesheimer decided in 1869 to accept a call to the rabbinate of the newly founded orthodox congregation Adass Jisroel in Berlin. Soon afterward he established in the Prussian capital a modern rabbinical seminary which became the major institution for the training of Neo-Orthodox rabbis in Europe. In it scientific study of Jewish sources, while certainly not carried to the same critical extreme as in the Hochschule für die Wissenschaft des Judentums, was permitted, with no apparent diminution of orthodoxy or commitment to the halachic tradition.

Although closely associated with Samson Raphael Hirsch, Hildesheimer could not endorse Hirsch's separatist philosophy for orthodoxy and advocated cooperation among all Jewish groups for the sake of unity. He saw a particular need for consolidating the Jewish community's strength in its battle against German anti-Semitism. Hildesheimer also differed from Hirsch in his intense devotion to the pro-Zionist tendencies and activities becoming prominent in the last decades of the nineteenth century. He urged that as many of the Jews fleeing from the pogroms in Russia as possible be resettled in Palestine instead of America. While still living in Eisenstadt, he had been instrumental in collecting large sums of money to improve the condition of the Jews living in Jerusalem, and he remained an ardent supporter of the Palestinian *yishuv* to the end of his life. Hildesheimer's contacts with the German Foreign Office in Berlin were instrumental in securing government support for institutions dedicated to raising the educational, cultural, and vocational standards of the Jews living in Palestine. His activities in this connection, however, drew upon him the bitter wrath and violent hostility of the ultraorthodox, old *yishuv* in Jerusalem, whose leaders placed him under the *ḥerem* or ban.

Azriel Hildesheimer's work was continued by his distinguished pupil, David Hoffmann (1843–1921). A product of various Hungarian *yeshivot*, Hoffmann also studied at Hildesheimer's seminary in Eisenstadt, as well as at the universities of Vienna, Berlin, and Tübingen, and became a teacher of *Talmud*, rabbinic codes, and the Bible in the new seminary which his master founded in Berlin. After Hildesheimer's death in 1899, Hoffmann became rector of the seminary and in the last decades of his life was considered the supreme halachic authority of German Orthodox Jewry. On his seventy-fifth birthday in 1918 he was awarded the honorary title of Professor by the German government.

Despite the fact that he was thoroughly orthodox in halachic matters and strenuously opposed Reform, David Hoffmann applied historical-critical methods to a degree in his valuable studies, written in German, on the *Talmud* and rabbinic literature. He was unshakeably opposed, however, to the higher criticism of the Bible and regarded his polemic writings against it as "a holy undertaking . . . an obligatory battle to answer decisively these new critics who come as oppressors to violate the sacred Torah." The methods and conclusions of Julius Wellhausen and his Protestant colleagues in the "scientific" study of the Bible, which were beginning to find a considerable response in Reform Jewish circles and among secularist Jews, were denounced by Hoffmann as utterly destructive of Judaism.

By virtue of his personal humility and modesty, as well as his massive scholarship in many branches of Jewish study, Hoffmann was revered not only by the orthodox but also by the liberal Jews of Germany, and gained respect and support for the movement he represented.

The new interpretations of Judaism that emerged in the nineteenth century all had their rise, as we have observed, in Germany, the land where the challenges to the traditional Jewish faith and practice of the premodern era posed by the civic and political emancipation of the Jews appeared most sharply. It was these religious movements that gave German Jewry much of the ferment and élan that characterized it in the century before its tragic end. From Germany they were transplanted to Jewish communities all over the world. While they struck roots virtually everywhere, it was probably in America, to which they were carried by large numbers of European émigrés, that they enjoyed their fullest flowering and most notable success. Even at present these German-born movements, modified and adapted to the conditions of the American scene, continue to play a prominent role in determining the character and quality of American-Jewish religious life.

CHAPTER

ᥱ XI ᥲ

The Science of Judaism and Nineteenth-Century Jewish Philosophy

AT THE BEGINNING of the nineteenth century precise knowledge of the complex course of historical evolution through which the Jewish people and Judaism had passed was virtually nonexistent among the Jews of Europe. Since the time of Josephus, some seventeen hundred years earlier, no truly first-rank historian of comparable stature had emerged within Jewry. Throughout the Rabbinic period, the Geonic era, and the entire Middle Ages, systematic investigation of the past had attracted scant attention among Jewish scholars. The chronicles and historical writings that were produced—with a few notable exceptions, such as the studies of the Italian-Jewish scholars of the Renaissance era, Solomon ibn Verga, Joseph Ha-Kohen, and Azariah dei Rossi—were hardly noted either for accuracy or for any significant measure of critical objectivity. The general indifference to precise history persisted into the eighteenth century, even in the circles of the "enlightened," among whom infatuation with logical abstractions and "eternal verities" precluded

[263]

any real concern with the "merely historical." Moses Mendelssohn himself admitted: "What do I know of history? All that bears the name history . . . has never gotten into my head, and I yawn all the time when I am bound to read anything historical." [1]

By the end of the nineteenth century, however, the whole of the Jewish past—its outstanding personalities, institutions, and ideas, as well as its vast literature—had undergone careful and exhaustive investigation at the hands of a small army of Jewish scholars utilizing the modern techniques of critical historical, philological, and literary investigation. In addition, these men brought to light hundreds of important Jewish religious, legal, moral, philosophical, and poetic works—some published in the first decades after the invention of printing, but many in manuscript and gathering dust in libraries throughout Europe and the Near East—which had hitherto been ignored, their very existence often unknown to the generality of Jewish students. These works, a good many of which were now issued in fine critical editions, demonstrated the continuous creativity that had characterized Jewish life throughout the centuries. The total achievement of these scholars has come to be known as "the Science of Judaism" (die Wissenschaft des Judentums, as those of its protagonists who wrote in German referred to it, or Ḥochmat Yisrael, as those who wrote in Hebrew called it). Their work had more than the purely intellectual aim of making possible a genuine understanding of how the Jewish people and Judaism had developed in the course of their history. In certain cases, as we shall see, it was also intended to aid the Jew's struggle to obtain an accepted and honored place in the larger European society, and it contributed, as we have noted, to the shaping of the new interpretations of Judaism that emerged in the nineteenth century.

There is little doubt that the Science of Judaism, in Germany at least, was stimulated by the historicism and romanticism which came to dominate German intellectual life in the first half of the nineteenth century, as Haskalah in its early period had been stimulated by the regnant rationalism and universalism of the Enlightenment era. The thinkers of the post-Kantian period in Germany turned their attention away from the "eternal truths" of metaphysics to the empirical facts of history, and exchanged for the rationalist ideal of universal humanity the romantic ideal of the nation with its particular qualities created by its unique historical experience and constituting what Herder had called its Volksgeist. As a result, a new and powerful enthusiasm for the study of the past emerged, and historical research was eagerly cultivated in the German universities. At the University of Berlin, for instance, where Leopold Zunz, the foremost German representative of the Science of Judaism, studied, the professors who influenced him most deeply—Friedrich August Wolf, August Boeckh, and Friedrich Carl von Savigny—were all great historians in various fields. These men insisted that genuine understanding of the literary monuments of the past could only be attained through rigorous and comprehensive philological scholarship. From his studies, under their tutelage, of ancient history, Greek philosophy, and Roman law, Zunz learned the critical techniques and methods which he was later to apply in his own work in Jewish history and literature.

We shall return to a discussion of Zunz's seminal and pioneering contributions to the Science of Judaism. First, however, we must note that, at the very time he was undertaking his work in Germany, important studies in Jewish literature and history of the modern, critical type were already being produced in Galicia. Their authors, who wrote in Hebrew, were the great Galician scholars Naḥman Krochmal (1785–1840) and Solomon Judah Rapoport (1790–1867).

Krochmal's renown rests on his *Moreh Nevuchei Ha-Zeman* (*Guide for the Perplexed of the Time*), which was published in 1851, eleven years after his death, by his friend Zunz, and which represents almost all of his literary legacy. Zunz gave fame to the otherwise obscure Galician town in which the work was written by placing on the title page the words *Scripsit Nachman Krochmal Incola Zolkiewiensis*. In Krochmal's lifetime—a lifetime plagued by bad health, family misfortunes, and the necessity for earning his livelihood through distasteful work as a liquor-tax farmer, but also spent in unremitting study and reflection—he achieved a measure of renown primarily as a teacher who shared his vast learning and profound thought with a group of admiring disciples whom he stimulated to think critically and historically about Judaism. *Der ewige Student*, as Krochmal called himself, he was extremely reluctant to publish the results of his own researches, and finally agreed to do so only under pressure from his disciples and friends. He also had no desire for the prestige that might accrue to him from occupying a prominent rabbinic position. Even when he was offered the chief rabbinate of Berlin, he declined, writing: "It has never entered my mind to fill the post of a keeper of conscience, or to occupy myself with the conduct of the religious affairs of a community; such a purpose would have been in harmony neither with my theological researches nor with my whole personality." [2]

While still a youth Krochmal had come under the rationalist influence of Maimonides' *Guide of the Perplexed*. Later in life he steeped himself in the works of the great German philosophers—Kant, Fichte, Schelling, and Hegel. Unlike other Jews of his day raised in the orthodox Talmudic tradition who, after being exposed to the science and philosophy of the contemporary world, came to doubt the value of Judaism, Krochmal was persuaded that Judaism contained eternal rational values and that the "spirit" of the Jewish people represented the most comprehensive and complete devotion to the "absolute Spirit," or God. But the essence of the Jewish spirit had been obscured, in Krochmal's view, by excrescences of fanaticism, superstition, and neglect of the moral and rational meaning of Judaism's precepts in favor of mechanical obedience to the letter of the law. To recover the genuine and eternal qualities of the Jewish spirit, to distinguish between the accidental and the essential, between the transitory and the permanent, Krochmal urged, it was imperative to go back to its sources and trace their development in their various manifestations. This enterprise—"to search out, to reveal, and to establish all the phenomena of Judaism in and through the actual period of their origin," as it is formulated in the preface of his book—required rigorous critical-historical study.

A considerable part of *Moreh Nevuchei Ha-Zeman* is devoted to a presentation of Krochmal's philosophy of Jewish history. Only the barest outline can be given here.

Borrowing from the theory of historical development propounded by the great eighteenth-century Italian philosopher Giovanni Battista Vico (1668–1744), Krochmal maintained that every nation or people passes through three stages in its development—efflorescence and growth, maturity, and then progressive decline and disappearance from the stage of history. God (or to use the Hegelian term, the Absolute Spirit) is partially realized in every nation or people through the particular idea or spirit which it represents. Thus, the ancient Greeks, for example, represented the spirit of beauty and philosophic speculation, and the Romans the spirit of law and political administration. Once these ideas or spiritual forms of a people are realized, their original bearers vanish from the historical arena, but the ideas themselves, adopted by other peoples, continue to be operative in history. The Jewish people, however, has been unique, according to Krochmal, because the idea for whose sake it came into being and for which it has lived is not partial or limited but the Absolute Spirit itself, i.e., the everlasting God. Since its idea is eternal and universal, it, too, is eternal and universal. All the spiritual powers in the universe, by and for which the various nations have lived, are included in the "universal soul" of Israel.

According to Krochmal's reading of Jewish history, the Jewish people passed three times through the cycle of birth, maturity, and decline characteristic of all peoples. The first cycle lasted from the era of the patriarch Abraham to the Babylonian Exile (586 B.C.E.); the second from the Return under the Persian emperor Cyrus (536 B.C.E.) to the suppression by the Romans of the revolt led by Bar Kochba (132 C.E.); and the third from the time of the redaction of the *Mishnah* by Rabbi Judah Ha-Nasi (ca. 200 C.E.) to the expulsion of the Jews from Spain in 1492. At the end of each cycle the Jewish people might have been expected to follow the course of other nations and die; but each time it sprang, phoenixlike, to new life from its own ashes. This was so because its goal always was to attain the Absolute Spirit, which is the fountainhead of all ideals and, as pure spirituality, by nature imperishable. Krochmal did not explicitly assert it, but it seems to have been his conviction that in his day the Jewish people was in the stage of efflorescence in the fourth great cycle of its eternal historical pilgrimage.

Although Naḥman Krochmal had scant sympathy for contemporary German reformers of Judaism, they had no hesitation in helping themselves liberally to those of his ideas that suited their general ideology. Thus it was primarily from him that they took their favorite notion that Israel was invested by God with the mission of serving as teacher of the nations of the world. However, they ignored Krochmal's suggestion that the exile and dispersion of the Jewish people were not to be regarded as permanently beneficial, but rather as temporary evils to be endured and to be employed for the strengthening of those elements of national consciousness and cohesiveness which would eventually lead to the restoration of Israel to Zion. Nor did they give heed to his warning against the perils of a de-Hebraization of Jewish life and culture when he spoke of the assimilated, Greek-speaking Jews of ancient Alexandria who disappeared virtually without a trace from history and from the memory of the Jewish people because, as he suggested, "they forsook the holy tongue of their inheritance." [3]

Besides its unique philosophy of Jewish history, Krochmal's *Moreh Nevuchei Ha-Zeman* also contains a series of brilliant chapters exemplifying the author's application of the critical-historical method which he developed all alone in his long years of quiet reflection in his obscure Galician town, without the benefit, enjoyed by Leopold Zunz and many of the later contributors to the Science of Judaism, of a university education and the intellectual stimulus of living in a major cultural center. These chapters include discussions of such topics as Alexandrian Judaism, the development of the *halachah* in its different stages, the character of the *Aggadah*, and the relation between ancient Gnosticism and medieval Kabbalah. The essay on the evolution of Jewish law proved particularly important, inspiring practically all the later scholarly efforts in the field.

Reviewing Krochmal's pioneering studies, Solomon Schechter, one of his intellectual heirs in the Science of Judaism, rightly underscored their historic importance:

He it was who taught Jewish scholars how to submit the ancient rabbinic records to the test of criticism and the way in which they might be utilized for the purpose of historical studies; he it was who enabled them to trace the genesis of the tradition, and to watch the inner germination of that vast organism. . . . I may assert with the utmost confidence that there is scarcely a single page in Krochmal's book that did not afterwards give birth to some essay or monograph or even elaborate treatise, though their authors were not always very careful about mentioning the source of their inspiration. Thus Krochmal justly deserves the honorable title assigned to him by one of our greatest historians, who terms him the Father of Jewish Science.[4]

It was to Krochmal that the second major east European pioneer in the Science of Judaism, Solomon Judah Rapoport, was largely indebted for his critical approach to research into the Jewish past. In his youth in Lemberg Rapoport had come under the influence of the Haskalah movement, which was then penetrating into Galicia from Germany, and, like other early *maskilim*, occupied himself with translating European poetry into Hebrew. His encounter with Krochmal, with whom he maintained constant and close personal relationships for the next thirty years, turned his interest toward the investigation of Jewish history. Lacking his friend's speculative capacities, Rapoport made no attempt to develop any broad, philosophic interpretation of Jewish history, but focused on examination of restricted topics. His belief that the spirit of the Jewish people is best reflected in the life and work of its great figures led him to concentrate his early efforts on the field of biography.

In 1829 Rapoport published in *Bikkurei Ha-Ittim*, a Hebrew annual printed in Vienna, his first biographical monograph, on Saadiah Gaon. This essay, with its mastery of detail and remarkable acumen, aroused the admiration of other scholars, including Zunz, who hailed it as the first significant modern work of Jewish biography. It was followed by several other studies of notable figures of the early Middle Ages—the author of the first Talmudic lexicon, Nathan ben Yehiel of Rome, the liturgical poet Eleazar Kallir, and the Geonim Hai, Hananel, and Nissim. Through these biographies, provided with detailed notes and addenda displaying his amazingly wide erudition, Rapoport managed to present for the first time an accurate portrait of medieval Judaism at several important junctures in its evolution. As exemplars of superb critical methodology in historical research, these essays served many other investigators as a model for emulation.

To complement his early biographies, Rapoport planned a comprehensive work under the title *Anshei Ha-Shem* (*Men of Note*), which was to include all the great figures in the history of Judaism from the prophets to his own time. This work was never written; the author's duties as rabbi in Prague, where he spent the last twenty-eight years of his life, left him comparatively little leisure for scholarly pursuits. Nor was his projected Talmudic encyclopedia, *Erech Millin*, completed. Only one volume, embracing the letter *alef*, appeared in 1852. Even this one volume, however, throws brilliant illumination on many questions concerning the history, literature, and institutions of the Talmudic era. Its articles, some of them almost full-scale monographs, stimulated a vast amount of research on the part of later practitioners of the Science of Judaism. So also did Rapoport's essays in various periodicals and his published volume of learned correspondence carried on with other scholars, mainly with his friend Samuel David Luzzatto in Italy, over many years.

Luzzatto's fervent orthodoxy on all questions regarding religious faith and practice occasionally brought him into sharp conflict with Rapoport, for the latter did not hesitate at times to express scholarly views that to a traditionalist seemed heretical. Fundamentally, however, Rapoport's attitudes toward Judaism, especially on matters of halachic observance, were quite conservative. He was distressed by the activities of the German Reformers in the 1840s and sharply rebuked them for what he regarded as their destructive radicalism.

In letters addressed to the rabbinical conference at Frankfurt in 1845 Rapoport warned the Reformers that their removal of references to the messianic redemption and the return to Zion from their prayer books was an act of faithlessness toward the Jewish past as well as the future, and would hardly achieve its apparent aim of making Jews more acceptable to the peoples among whom they lived. Furthermore, he declared that the cavalier attitude of the Reformers toward the *halachah*, if continued, would surely isolate them from the Jewish people as a whole and lead them to the same fate as the Samaritans or the Karaites. Time itself, he urged, would sweep away from Judaism those practices and customs that had become obsolete; there was no need for the reckless surgery advocated by the extremist proponents of Reform. Considering his general views on Jewish nationalism, tradition, and halachic observance, it seems appropriate to regard Rapoport as an early protagonist of what later came to be called the Positive-Historical School of Judaism (or Conservative Judaism).

Krochmal and Rapoport may be considered the founders of the east European branch of the Science of Judaism. Inspired by their work and following their methods, a considerable number of other scholars in eastern Europe in the second half of the nineteenth century devoted themselves to critical and objective study of Jewish history and literature. It was in Germany, however, that the Science of Judaism attained its fullest flowering and produced its most prominent results. The initiator and the towering figure of the movement there throughout much of the century was Leopold Zunz (1794–1886).

In his childhood years at a dreary orphan asylum and old-fashioned school in Wolfenbüttel known as the Samson Free School, Zunz laid the foundations of his extensive knowledge of Talmudic literature. With the arrival in 1807 of a new director at the school, the cultured *maskil* Samuel Meyer Ehrenberg, the curriculum was broadened to include German literature, French, history, and geography, and entirely new intellectual horizons were opened before Zunz and his classmates. Encouraged by Ehrenberg, Zunz entered the advanced department of the Wolfenbüttel gymnasium, from which he was the first Jewish student to graduate. In 1815 he left Wolfenbüttel for the University of Berlin where, during four years of intensive study of classical philosophy, Semitics, law, history, and philosophy under the masters of the *wissenschaftlich* approach to learning to whom we alluded earlier, he acquired their methodology and spirit as well as a vast body of humanistic knowledge.

In 1818, while still a student in Berlin, Zunz published his first work, a fifty-page pamphlet entitled *Etwas über die rabbinische Literatur* (*Notes on Rabbinic Literature*), in which he sketched a program of Jewish research inspired by the ideal of *Wissenschaft* which he had absorbed from his teachers at the university. The corpus of post-biblical Jewish literature, he pointed out, had been left almost entirely untouched by critical investigation. But the social and cultural factors that had produced this literature were now disappearing, and the literature itself was about to come to an end. This very fact demanded an accounting of it. The chief value of a critical study of Jewish literature, Zunz suggested, would be universal; it would constitute a contribution to the knowledge of mankind, "which is the most worthy goal of all research." [5]

Apparently Zunz was here adopting the stand of the detached observer, viewing the Jewish tradition and its creativity from the outside rather than from within. But the detachment was not total; a practical concern with Jewish life and a mildly apologetic motivation are apparent even in this rather extreme essay of Zunz's youth. Scientific research into Jewish literature, he suggested, would aid the cause of reforming Jewish life, by making it possible "to know and distinguish the old which is still of use, the antiquated which has become pernicious, and the new which is desirable. . . ." [6] It would further help remove some of the prejudices with which the rabbinic literature is regarded in certain circles. The fact is that, while constantly upholding the highest standards of exact scholarship and rigorous objectivity, Zunz was also throughout his life a devoted Jew, and his scholarly labors were significantly inspired by a deep concern for the welfare of his people.

This concern is manifested in his leading role in the establishment of the *Verein für Cultur und Wissenschaft der Juden* (*Society for the Culture and Science of the Jews*). The *Verein* consisted of a group of young Jewish intellectuals who came together in 1819, at a time when indifference to, and ignorance about, Judaism was rampant in the Berlin Jewish community and many Jews were abandoning it for Christianity, out of a desire to intensify their own Jewish identity and strengthen the wavering loyalties of others. The group, whose membership besides Zunz included such figures as Eduard Gans, Joel

List, Moses Moser, Isaac Marcus Jost, and later Heinrich Heine, wrestled with the problem of what could cement their commitment to Judaism in the face of the overwhelming pressures to assimilate completely to the dominant German culture. The young men decided that the most promising approach was to attempt to overcome the image of the Jew as a spiritually and intellectually defective creature, and to disclose the universal values inherent in Jewish culture by exploring Judaism and the history of the Jewish people through the new critical-scientific methods. During the five years of its existence (1819–1824) the *Verein* organized programs on Jewish culture as well as a school at which Heine gave lectures on Jewish history. Perhaps its most significant undertaking was the publication in 1822–1823 of a journal edited by Zunz, entitled *Zeitschrift für die Wissenschaft des Judentums*, in which the scholarly young editor published several articles, including his memorable biography of Rashi.

The *Verein* met with general disapproval from orthodox Jews, large-scale indifference among the enlightened and wealthy members of the Berlin Jewish community with Reform sympathies, and an almost complete lack of attention in non-Jewish society. Discouraged, most of its members drifted away, and the *Verein* itself was soon dissolved. Eduard Gans, its founder, became a Christian and was followed to the baptismal font not long afterward by Heine. Zunz, however, persevered in his devotion to Jewish scholarship, inspired and encouraged by Solomon Judah Rapoport, with whom he carried on a learned correspondence.

In his younger years Zunz was in sympathy with the emerging Reform movement; indeed, in the early 1820s he served for a time as preacher in the Reform congregation in Berlin and later led a Reform association in Prague. Congregational work, however, proved uncongenial, and Zunz subsequently earned his living by working for a daily newspaper in Berlin and directing the Jewish community's primary school. Still later, from 1840 to 1850, he was the head of a Jewish teacher-training seminary in the Prussian capital. His hope of many years that the University of Berlin or one of the other great universities of Germany would include Judaica in its curriculum and appoint him to a professorship proved illusory; the German academic establishment was not yet prepared to recognize Jewish studies as a respectable and valuable discipline. The idea of an independent seminary or institute for Jewish studies, unaffiliated with a university, did not greatly appeal to Zunz, who was apprehensive that such an organization might make the Science of Judaism parochial and isolate it from the larger cultural and intellectual life of Germany. Hence, his scholarly work was carried on in splendid loneliness, as well as frequently in dire poverty.

In 1832, when Zunz was thirty-eight, his epoch-making *Die gottesdienstlichen Vorträge der Juden* (*The Devotional Addresses of the Jews*) appeared. In this great work, one of the pioneering monuments of the Science of Judaism in the nineteenth century, Zunz traced the evolution of preaching among the Jews from the time of the biblical prophets through the Tannaim, Amoraim, Geonim, and later teachers. It is a work of immense scholarship, displaying a magisterial control of hundreds of literary sources. Zunz intended to write a rigorously scientific and critical work, and his book is largely that. Nevertheless, motives of an apologetic character are quite prominent in *Die gottesdienstlichen Vorträge*. In the introduction the author deplores the political and civic disabilities of his coreligionists in Germany and expresses the hope that a fuller appreciation of Jewish literature and of the rich cultural heritage of Jewry will induce the nation's leaders to grant full emancipation to the Jews. Zunz also urged that Jews who obtained a better acquaintance with their own history and literature would thereby understand how to reform and revitalize obsolete religious rituals and practices. At the end of his book Zunz heartily endorsed many of the changes and innovations that had been instituted in the synagogue service by the Reformers of his day. Later on he apparently changed his mind about the value of religious reforms and, as we have observed, disparaged the efforts and motivations of the Reform rabbinical conferences of the 1840s.

Most of Zunz's research in the last decades of his scholarly career focused on synagogal liturgy and poetry. His three major works on this subject—*Die synagogale Poesie des Mittelalters* (*The Synagogal Poetry of the Middle Ages*) (1855), *Der Ritus des synagogalen Gottesdienstes* (*The Rite of the Synagogue Service*) (1859), and *Die Literaturgeschichte der synagogalen Poesie* (*The Literary History of Synagogal Poetry*) (1865)—are contributions of great and enduring significance. For his research Zunz visited many of the foremost libraries of Europe, including the Bibliothèque Nationale of Paris, the British Museum, the Bodleian library of Oxford University, and the de Rossi library of Parma (as a Jew he could not enter the Vatican library in Rome to examine its priceless collection of Hebrew books and manuscripts).

While Zunz was a master of virtually all Jewish literature, he shared the progressivist and rationalist bias of many lesser protagonists of the Science of Judaism as well as of Haskalah in the nineteenth century and tended to deprecate the *Talmud*, and especially the literature of the Kabbalah. Although he had no direct disciples, his methodology and its published results inspired numerous contemporaries and successors who found in his work an enormously helpful model for their own researches.

~§§~

The Science of Judaism made immense strides in various European countries in the first half of the nineteenth century. In Germany Isaac Marcus Jost (1793–1860), Zunz's colleague and fellow worker in the ill-fated *Verein für Cultur und Wissenschaft der Juden*, wrote a massive, nine-volume historical survey of the Jewish people from the Maccabean age to his own time, *Die Geschichte der Israeliten (The History of the Israelites)* (1820–1829), which did not lose its value or importance even after the appearance of Heinrich Graetz's greater work. In Italy Samuel David Luzzatto (1800–1865), the staunchly traditionalist scholar who opposed all proposals for the reform of Jewish belief and practice and deplored the corrosive effects of enlightenment and emancipation, pioneered in the study of Hebrew linguistics and modern biblical exegesis. He also discovered and published scores of significant Hebrew manuscripts, among them Judah ha Levi's *Diwan* (1844). In Galicia, Solomon Judah Rapoport and Naḥman Krochmal, as we have already observed, pursued their invaluable investigations of Jewish history and literature. In France, Salomon Munk (1803–1867) was one of the first among the founders of the Science of Judaism to delve into Arabic sources for the study of medieval Jewish literature and philosophy. In his *Mélanges de philosophie juive et arabe (Mixtures of Jewish and Arabic Philosophy)* (1859), a work of seminal importance, Munk identified Solomon ibn Gabirol as the author of *Fons Vitae (Fountain of Life)*, which had until then been universally ascribed to a Christian or Moslem thinker. His critical edition of the Arabic original of Maimonides' *Guide of the Perplexed* (1856–1866), and translation of it into French, provided the indispensable basis for the modern study of medieval Jewish philosophy.

While the Science of Judaism found ardent practitioners throughout Europe, it was in Germany that it achieved its greatest triumphs in the nineteenth century. The major rabbinic figures in both of the new interpretations of Judaism that arose in the first half of the century, Reform and Positive-Historical (Conservative) Judaism, were scholars thoroughly committed to the *wissenschaftlich* method so brilliantly exemplified in the work of Leopold Zunz. Zacharias Frankel (1801–1875), who may properly be regarded as the chief protagonist of the Positive-Historical School of Judaism, laid the foundations for a critical exploration of the history of Jewish biblical exegesis, the *Talmud*, and *halachah* in general in his important works *Vorstudien zu der Septuaginta* (*Preliminary Studies on the Septuagint*) (1841), *Über den Einfluss der palästinischen Exegese auf die alexandrinische Hermeneutik* (*On the Influence of Palestinian Exegesis on Alexandrian Hermeneutics*) (1851), *Darchei Ha-Mishnah* (*Ways of the Mishnah*) (1859), *Entwurf einer Geschichte der Literatur der nachtalmudischen Responsen* (*Sketch of a History of the Literature of Post-Talmudic Responsa*) (1856), and *Mevo Ha-Yerushalmi* (*Introduction to the Jerusalem Talmud*) (1870). His *Darchei Ha-Mishnah* especially irritated many traditionalist rabbis, including Samson Raphael Hirsch, who sensed that Frankel had departed considerably from the orthodox view of rabbinic tradition and the revelation of the law at Mount Sinai, and therefore sharply attacked him.

Abraham Geiger, the leading German theoretician of the Reform movement, also undertook studies of the development of the *halachah*, as well as of ancient versions of the Bible and of sectarian groups in Judaism. Geiger's reforming tendencies both derived from and in turn influenced his scholarly studies, occasionally to the detriment of the cause of scientific objectivity. Nevertheless, he made major contributions to the Science of Judaism, opening the possibility of a critical history of Jewish religious thought and practice. Although Geiger used the conclusions of his research into the history of Judaism as polemic material to serve what he regarded as the demands of religious reform and of the political emancipation of the Jew, his chief works—*Urschrift und Übersetzungen der Bibel* (*The Original Text and Translations of the Bible*) (1857), *Sadducäer und Pharisäer* (*Sadducees and Pharisees*) (1863), and *Das Judentum und seine Geschichte* (*Judaism and Its History*) (3 vols., 1865–1871)—are of enduring scholarly value.

Perhaps the foremost German protagonist, besides Zunz, of *die Wissenschaft des Judentums* was Moritz Steinschneider (1816–1907), generally regarded as the greatest bibliographer of Judaica in the nineteenth century. His catalogues of the Hebrew books and manuscripts in the libraries of Leyden, Berlin, Hamburg, Munich, and—most important of all—the Bodleian of Oxford University, revealed numerous literary treasures whose very existence had previously been unknown even to the most learned of Jewish scholars. Steinschneider's works on the Hebrew translations made during the Middle

Ages and on Judeo-Arabic literature are landmarks in the history of the Science of Judaism, and his survey of Jewish literature written for a German encyclopedia and translated into English under the title *Jewish Literature from the Eighth to the Eighteenth Century* (1857) was the first comprehensive overview of virtually all works written by Jewish authors in any language during the thousand-year period with which it deals.

In the first decades of its existence the Science of Judaism was largely in the hands of individuals working alone and without institutional support. The establishment in Breslau in 1854 of the Jüdisch-Theologisches Seminar, which was headed for the next twenty years by Zacharias Frankel, placed research in Judaica on an organized basis and made it possible for a group of distinguished scholars, including the eminent historian Heinrich Graetz, to devote themselves entirely to it. The Science of Judaism was greatly furthered by the establishment of still other modern seminaries and research societies in the years that followed—Jews' College in London (1856), the École Rabbinique in Paris (1859), the Bet Ha-Midrash Lilmod U-Lelamed in Vienna (1863), the Hochschule (Lehranstalt) für die Wissenschaft des Judentums in Berlin (1870), the Hebrew Union College in Cincinnati (1875), the Landesrabbinerschule in Budapest (1877), and the Société des Études Juives in Paris (1880), to name the most important. In this period the two foremost learned journals, in which many of the scholars of the Science of Judaism published their studies, were the *Monatsschrift für Geschichte und Wissenschaft des Judentums*, established by Frankel in 1851 and continuing publication until it was destroyed by the Nazis in 1939, and the *Revue des Études Juives*, founded in 1880 through the efforts of Zadoc Kahn and Isidore Loeb, and with a history of continuous publication, except for a hiatus during World War II, until the present day. In 1889 the *Jewish Quarterly Review* began publication in London under the editorship of Israel Abrahams and Claude G. Montefiore, and at once became the major English-language journal of the Science of Judaism. In 1910 it was moved to Philadelphia, where it is still published today.

Before concluding our discussion of nineteenth-century Science of Judaism, we must note that a large part of its effort in the second half of the century was devoted to exploration of the history of the Jewish communities of various countries and their major cities. This was, in significant measure, a response to the struggle for political rights and against anti-Semitism. Many Jewish scholars believed that by demonstrating the antiquity of Jewish settlement in Europe and the valuable contributions made by Jews to general European civilization they would strengthen Jewish claims to emancipation and allay anti-Jewish sentiment. That this belief proved largely illusory does not detract from the fact that the historical investigations of the Science of Judaism managed to instill a higher degree of self-respect in many Jews and to diminish the tendency to self-hatred among Jews provoked by the hostility of the external world.

❦

The same result was no doubt furthered by the foremost works in the field of Jewish philosophical thought that appeared in nineteenth-century Europe. Naḥman Krochmal's insistence, in his *Moreh Nevu-chei Ha-Zeman*, on Judaism as the bearer of eternal rational values, and his contention that the Jewish people represents the fullest and most comprehensive devotion to the Absolute Spirit, have been noted above. We have also suggested that he was influenced by the Italian Vico and the great German philosophers—Kant, Fichte, Schelling, and Hegel—whom he avidly read. The same intellectual influences, especially the philosophical idealism of Schelling and Hegel, and to some degree a similar view of Judaism and the Jewish people, are encountered in the philosophy of Solomon Formstecher (1808–1889), widely recognized as one of the major thinkers of the German Reform movement.

Born in Offenbach, Formstecher studied at the University of Giessen and later served as rabbi in his native city from 1842 until his death. In 1841 he published his *Die Religion des Geistes* (*The Religion of the Spirit*), in which the Jewish religion is portrayed as essentially a great idea whose scope and value is disclosed in the progressive development of humanity. Judaism, according to Formstecher, is the religion of absolute, final, and true revelation, proclaimed by the prophets of Israel, who were not speculative metaphysicians but men of profound intuition and sentiment in touch with the objective source of ultimate values—God. The God of Judaism, in Formstecher's view, is not, like the God of the philosophers, an idea obtained through speculation and reason, but the absolute and purely moral being who transcends both terrestrial and spiritual nature.

Judaism, Formstecher maintained, is unique among the religions and philosophies of the world. The other religions—with the qualified exception of Judaism's two daughter faiths, Christianity and

Islam—are essentially pagan; they are religions of nature. Like his Christian mentor Schelling, the Jewish philosopher conceived paganism or the religion of nature as the expression of man's longing for universal life, in which the spirit appears as the "soul of the world." It is in this pagan aspiration that Formstecher also saw the origin of the philosophy of pantheism and of speculative metaphysics in general. Even in the early Schelling's philosophy the "world soul" was bound to nature. Judaism, on the other hand, Formstecher declared, is the religion of the spirit; it is the expression of the longing for the realization and embodiment in the world of the absolute moral ideal, which derives from God and divine revelation. Its goal, unlike that of the pagan religions, is not to unite men with a God conceived as immanent in nature, but to make them similar to the God who transcends the universe by having them fulfill His moral imperatives. Through all its changing historical forms Judaism has held fast to this goal, and Jews have thereby been distinguished and isolated among the nations of the world, who are dominated by pagan modes of life and thought which are by nature antithetical to Judaism.

Unlike many of his rabbinic colleagues in the German Reform movement, Formstecher did not envision the conversion of the nations to ethical monotheism as the divinely appointed mission of Judaism. The Jewish people and Judaism fulfill their divine task by preserving their own devotion to the ideal of the spirit. It is through the historical religions to which Judaism helped give rise, Christianity and Islam, in which natural and spiritual strands are interwoven, that paganism has been progressively vanquished and replaced by yearning for the realization of the absolute moral ideal of the spirit. The history of Christianity is essentially the history of the struggle between its pagan and Jewish elements. The spirit, Formstecher believed when he wrote his *Die Religion des Geistes* in his thirties, would eventually triumph completely and unite all men and nations in a universal faith whose substance would be dedication to the absolute moral ideal. But as long as Christianity has not fully liberated itself from its pagan elements, there is a place for Judaism as a separate religion. Ultimately it will become superfluous, Formstecher held, and it can even now make itself ready for the triumph of the universal religion of the spirit by abandoning the particularist elements in its belief and practice, and especially by progressively surrendering its unique rituals and ceremonies.

Similar in many respects to Formstecher's philosophy of Judaism is that of his contemporary, Samuel Hirsch (1815–1889). Like Formstecher, Hirsch was one of the pioneers of the Reform movement in Germany. Born in Prussia, he served for more than twenty years (1843–1866) as chief rabbi of the Duchy of Luxembourg, and then emigrated to America to become rabbi of the Reform Congregation Keneseth Israel in Philadelphia, where his tenure again lasted over two decades (1866–1888). Hirsch was the leading spirit at the important conference of Reform rabbis held in Philadelphia in 1869 and, together with his son Emil G. Hirsch (see pp. 299–300), rabbi of Chicago's Sinai Temple, figured prominently at the meeting of rabbis in Pittsburgh in 1885 which formulated the so-called Pittsburgh Platform, the programmatic guide of American Reform Judaism for the next half century. His reputation as a scholar and thinker came very early in his career when in 1842, at the age of twenty-seven, he published what was to be his major work, *Die Religionsphilosophie der Juden (The Religious Philosophy of the Jews)*.

Deeply influenced by Hegel, Hirsch understood the function of philosophy of religion in precisely the terms defined by the great German Idealist: its task is to convert the content given in immediate religious consciousness into the consciously known content of spirit or mind by conceiving it as rational necessity and intelligible truth. Unlike Hegel, however, the Jewish philosopher denied that religion contains the truth of spirit only in the inadequate form of representation, and that when philosophy understands this truth conceptually it fundamentally alters its content. For him religious and philosophic truth are identical; the truth given in immediate religious feeling or awareness—expressed, according to Hirsch, fully and absolutely in the Hebrew Bible—is essentially the same as that which philosophy obtains through thought. As far as historical criticism of the Bible is concerned, Hirsch simply rejected it in his *Religionsphilosophie* and, in his later works, argued that historical questions about the origin of the various books of Scripture have no bearing on its absolute truth. Biblical stories, such as that of Adam and Eve in the Garden of Eden, may be mythical, but myth is not poetic fantasy; it is the presentation of an inner event in the vestment of an external occurrence.

The Bible, Hirsch notes, understands man essentially as a being endowed with freedom. In his capacity to say "I" to himself and to contrast himself with the world of nature, man becomes aware of his freedom. But the primordial freedom of man is abstract and requires that it be given specific content. One possible content is "natural" freedom, the ability to do whatever one wishes. This kind of freedom, according to Hegel, is necessarily in contradiction with abstract freedom, and the consciousness of the inevitable inner conflict in man, who understands himself as simultaneously a creature with a natural will and a creature destined for reason, is the consciousness of "sin." Hirsch, however, maintained that sin is not inevitable, that man may but need not sacrifice his freedom to nature; it is possible for him to use his freedom so as to subordinate nature by subjecting his sensual impulses to reason. To each of these alternatives corresponds a different consciousness of God. Men who sacrifice their freedom to nature justify their behavior by holding that the force of sensuality is indomitable, and they attribute absolute power to nature and raise it to the status of divinity; this, for Hirsch, is the origin and foundation of paganism in its various forms. Those, however, who subordinate nature to their freedom envision God as Moral Will transcending nature; such an envisagement is the heart of Judaism.

Hirsch proceeds to an analysis of the history of religions that is quite similar to Formstecher's. But while Formstecher considered paganism a partial apprehension of a valid ideal immanent in spirit, Hirsch regards it as totally empty and the result of a complete perversion of man's moral consciousness. Employing Hegelian dialectic, he shows that pagan religions could develop only in such a way as finally to disclose their nothingness and vanity. But Judaism, once it discovered (in the time of Abraham) the ultimate truth that religion is moral freedom, had no essential further development; one can speak of development in Judaism only in the sense of the ongoing moral education of man by God and his growing appropriation of the content of genuine faith.

According to Hirsch, original Christianity, as exemplified in the life and work of Jesus, was thoroughly Jewish. Jesus had no desire to transcend Judaism but sought to make every Jew, like himself, a "son of God," prepared to triumph over sin and to assume the burden of being the suffering servant of the Lord. In so doing Jesus was fulfilling the mission of Israel, and remained entirely within the orbit of Judaism. Christianity's rupture with Judaism came only when the apostle Paul became convinced that mankind was laboring hopelessly under the total dominion of sin, and could be saved from it only through faith in the risen Christ. Not until the teaching of Paul, his doctrine of original sin and salvation through Christ, is utterly repudiated by the Church, Hirsch argued, can the gap between Judaism and Christianity again be bridged. Then Christianity may fulfill its task of being an "extensive" religion, a religion for the whole world, while Israel continues to cultivate its "intensive" religiosity, fulfilling its mission to the world by preserving itself as a holy community and demonstrating the power of its faith by realizing it in its life. In the eschatological era of absolute truth, in the days of the Messiah, extensive and intensive religiosity will be unified, and Judaism and Christianity will be identical. However, even when Israel becomes one with all mankind, it will, according to Hirsch, retain its distinct identity and continue to maintain its special cult, the eternal symbol of its historic mission.

While Samuel Hirsch, Solomon Formstecher, Naḥman Krochmal, and most of the lesser lights of nineteenth-century Jewish philosophy sought to reconcile Judaism with philosophical idealism, one major thinker set Judaism in categorical opposition to all forms of rational philosophy. This was the poet and religious philosopher Salomon Ludwig Steinheim (1789–1866). Unlike most of the Jewish philosophers of the century, Steinheim was not a rabbi or professional scholar. He studied medicine and practiced it in Germany for many years. The last twenty years of his life were spent mainly in Rome. In addition to collections of verse and works on medicine and natural science, he published a book on Moses Mendelssohn and his school, and a study of what he regarded as the permanent and transitory elements in Judaism. His magnum opus, *Die Offenbarung nach dem Lehrbegriffe der Synagoge* (*Revelation According to the Doctrine of the Synagogue*), was published in four volumes between 1835 and 1865.

Steinheim did not participate in the controversies raging in his day between the traditionalists and the reformers of Judaism, but managed to irritate both—the traditionalists by drawing a sharp distinction between revelation and biblical-Talmudic literature, and the reformers by his supranaturalism and antirationalism. Religious truth, he held, is given only through revelation, which is not a function of human consciousness or thought but comes to man from without, from God, and all attempts to identify the content of religion and reason are futile and false. Rational speculation leads invariably to a dualistic vision of the universe, to seeing it as split between elements of good and evil, spirit and matter; but the revelation contained in the Hebrew Bible teaches creation out of nothing and the absolute unity of God. Furthermore, rational philosophy considers reality a system of mechanical necessity, while biblical revelation regards freedom as the fundamental fact in the universe. Corresponding to these different visions are two kinds of religion—natural religion, which understands God as necessarily subject to the laws of His own being and identical with an eternal material universe, or at least dependent on it, as in the various forms of paganism or in Spinoza's pantheistic system, and the religion of revelation, which knows God as the absolutely free and omnipotent Creator who brings the universe into being *ex nihilo* and without any compulsion outside Himself. Creation, according to Steinheim, is the central pillar of revealed religion; its other basic principles are the unity of God, the unity and freedom of man, and the immortality of the soul. While these principles are not the product of human reason and are given to man "from outside," reason is "compelled" to confirm their truth. Steinheim is explicitly antirationalist, and yet the fundamental elements of the faith that he considers revelation alone capable of yielding—God, freedom, and immortality—are identical with the religious postulates that Immanuel Kant had maintained are necessarily implied by moral reason.

Formstecher and Hirsch were nineteenth-century philosophical idealists, and Steinheim may properly be regarded as a forerunner of modern religious existentialism. But while differing radically in their philosophical presuppositions, all three arrive finally at the same understanding of the substantive content of Judaism. For all of them Judaism is essentially a moral and personalist religion, standing in full theoretical and practical opposition to paganism. They perceive it as revolving around belief in a personal creative God who transcends the universe of which He is the source, in the ethical freedom and dignity of the human personality, and in the moral communion of God and man which is eternal and endures beyond the individual's death. Though far less deeply rooted in the tradition of Jewish life than were the great medieval Jewish neo-Platonists and Aristotelians, such as Solomon ibn Gabirol and Maimonides, and far more radical in their attitude toward the *halachah*, the nineteenth-century thinkers did not allow the speculative systems from which they borrowed to influence their theological understanding of Judaism as massively as did those of medieval times, and were much more faithful to the fundamental categories of biblical-rabbinic faith. Nevertheless, it is probably fair to say that the philosophers of the Middle Ages, for whom at least the divinely revealed character of the law was an unquestioned axiom, contributed more to the cause of keeping Jews loyal to Judaism than did their latter-day successors.

The Science of Judaism

❦

In view of the prevalence among nineteenth-century Jewish philosophers of the conviction that the heart of Judaism is its morality, it is surprising how little effort was devoted to systematic, theoretical exposition of Jewish ethics. The major, and one of the very few, attempts in this area is Moritz Lazarus' *Die Ethik des Judentums* (*The Ethics of Judaism*), the first volume of which was published in 1898 and the second posthumously in 1911. Lazarus (1824–1903) obtained a thorough traditional Jewish education, exchanging Talmudic study for philosophy and psychology only in his twenties. His was one of the most brilliant academic careers of any professing Jew in nineteenth-century Europe. After serving as professor of philosophy at the University of Berne and becoming rector of the university, he moved to Berlin, where he was soon appointed to a professorship at its university and also later taught at the Hochschule für die Wissenschaft des Judentums. Together with his brother-in-law, Hermann Heymann Steinthal, he developed a discipline known as *Völkerpsychologie*, "the psychology of nations," and for many years edited a journal devoted to the subject. His most famous psychological work is the three-volume *Das Leben der Seele* (*The Life of the Soul*), which went through several editions. Throughout his life Lazarus maintained a strong interest in Judaism and was deeply devoted to his people. For a quarter of a century he was a member of the Jewish community council of Berlin and also served as head of the Leopold Zunz Institute. His second wife, Nahida Ruth Remy, who was a zealous convert to Judaism, also wrote extensively on Jewish subjects.

In *Die Ethik des Judentums* Lazarus purports to follow an "objective-immanent" rather than the "constructive-speculative" method followed by Formstecher and Hirsch—i.e., deriving Jewish teaching empirically from an analysis of the classical Jewish sources rather than bringing a ready-made philosophical framework and perspective to the sources. Philosophy, he urges, can only serve as a methodological instrument for discovering the "objective unity" of the "ethical cosmos" as it appears in the major documents of Jewish literature. However, it is clear that Lazarus actually employs (rather loosely and uncritically) philosophy, particularly Immanuel Kant's moral philosophy, to interpret the content of Jewish ethics. Furthermore, he is temperamentally more attracted to the sane, balanced, and moderate ethical judgments of the Talmudic rabbis than to the intense and uncompromising sense of justice and injustice and unconditional moral demands manifested by the biblical prophets. The spirit of a sober, kindly, bourgeois nineteenth-century gentleman scholar hovers over the work.

Kant had insisted on the autonomous nature of moral demands. The categorical imperative—"Act only according to a maxim which you can at the same time will that it shall become a general law"—is not derived from any source (divine or other) outside man, nor is it based on utilitarian grounds or any purpose beyond itself. Kant wished, as he himself put it, to construct "a pure moral philosophy which is completely freed from everything which may be only empirical and thus belong to anthropology." [7] Lazarus applies the Kantian notion of autonomy to Jewish ethics, but he means by it that ethical judgments, from a Jewish perspective, are accompanied by an immediate inner certainty of their validity, and that the motive for the fulfillment of moral obligations should be nothing but love of God and aspiration to imitate Him. For Lazarus, the ethics of Judaism is religious, and religious ethics differs from philosophical in recognizing God as the source of moral imperatives. In Kantian terms, religious ethics is not autonomous but heteronomous. Lazarus, however, is unwilling to accept this conclusion and seeks to evade it by asserting that God Himself is subject to moral norms: what He commands is right and good not because He commands it, but He commands it because it is independently right and good. The Jewish scholar apparently wished to have his Kantian "autonomous" cake and eat it too, and many later critics of his system charged him with inconsistency and with not doing justice to the clearly heteronomous, or, more accurately, theonomous, character of Jewish ethics.

Lazarus attempted to show that, formally, Jewish ethics is deontological, i.e., an ethics of duty, but that materially it posits love and the inner harmony of man as the supreme ideal. He was also concerned with demonstrating that in Judaism religious ethics does not overthrow man's natural moral impulses and aspirations, but simply points to their transcendent source. Against the argument of many nineteenth-century Christian theologians who wished to establish a radical disjunction betweeen "Old Testament" and rabbinic ethics, Lazarus contended for their essential continuity and endeavored to show how prophetic ethics is developed and concretized in the *Talmud*. Also, no doubt with some apologetic motives, he maintained correctly that Jewish ethics is all-embracing, suited to the needs of both the individual and society, and that its thrust is clearly universal. Not content with expounding general principles, he also wished to make clear how abstract moral ideals find specific expression in the actual life of the Jewish people, permeating its institutions and its ritual practice. Here his lifelong interest in social psychology interpenetrated his concern with ethical theory. To be sure, the mass of concrete details and insights do not contribute to the logical unity of his study, but Lazarus was not primarily a logician. Moreover, it is not at all clear that the materials of Jewish ethics are susceptible of conceptual unification. It is, in fact, in its multiplicity of detail and diffuseness that much of the value of *Die Ethik des Judentums* lies.

We have alluded to apologetic and polemical motives in the writings of Moritz Lazarus. Similar motivations are apparent in the work of his predecessors. Krochmal, Formstecher, and Hirsch were all concerned, in greater or lesser degree and more or less consciously, with challenging Hegel's contention that Christianity is the "absolute religion." The Galician thinker maintained that the Jewish people manifested the most all-embracing and total devotion to the Absolute Spirit, and the two German Reform theologians vigorously argued Judaism's superiority over Christianity and were willing to attribute only relative validity to the latter, inasmuch as its Jewish "essence" had been corrupted by an admixture of pagan and anti-Jewish elements. In an age when Hegel was the regnant deity in the philosophical pantheon, and when many Jews were succumbing to the lure of conversion to Christianity, it seemed necessary not only to reaffirm the traditional doctrine of Israel's chosenness but to defend it through philosophical and moral arguments.

Nineteenth-century Jewish philosophy was apologetic in another sense as well. With the notable exception of Salomon Ludwig Steinheim (and somewhat less unambiguously so of Naḥman Krochmal), its major representatives endeavored to justify Jewish theology and ethics rationally and to interpret them in such a way as to demonstrate their complete consistency with the temporarily dominant philosophical outlook, whether Hegelian or Kantian. Orthodox teachers and scholars did not follow this way (indeed, they were not inclined to provide any philosophical or theological exposition), but it was not until the twentieth century that liberal expositors began to recognize its futility and to apply themselves to the task of presenting Judaism in its own right—in the intellectual idiom of the age, to be sure, but without assuming that its philosophical presuppositions were self-evidently valid and that it was the truth-claims of Judaism that required demonstration.

CHAPTER

❦ XII ❧

American Judaism from Its Beginnings to the End of the Nineteenth Century

IN 1654 twenty-three penniless Jews landed in the harbor of the Dutch trading colony of New Amsterdam to establish the first Jewish settlement in North America and the nucleus from which its great Jewish community was to develop. They were refugees fleeing from Portuguese persecution in Brazil. Originally a colony of Portugal, Brazil had attracted a considerable number of former Marranos and other Jewish immigrants from Holland after its conquest by the Dutch in 1631. In 1654 the Portuguese recaptured Brazil, and its Jews were compelled to flee. Many of them found refuge and re-established themselves in various islands of the Caribbean. Some, like the first twenty-three who came to New Amsterdam, settled on the American mainland, where they were soon joined by other Jewish immigrants, largely of Marrano extraction, from Holland and England. By 1658 there was a Jewish community in Newport, Rhode Island, where Roger Williams had decreed that neither "Papists nor Protestants, Jews nor Turks be turned away," as well as in New Amsterdam (which in 1664 passed into British hands and became New York).

Before the end of the eighteenth century Jewish communities of sufficient size to establish a synagogue were also to be found in Philadelphia, Richmond, Charleston, and Savannah. However, after nearly a century and a half of Jewish settlement, the number of Jews residing in the United States in 1800 was probably no more than three thousand. The largest Jewish community in America, that of Charleston, boasted about five hundred members.

The Jews who migrated to America in the colonial era and in the first decades of the republic were mainly Sephardim, i.e., of Spanish and Portuguese descent. But among them were also a substantial number of Ashkenazim, Jews of central and east European origin. The members of the two groups did not always welcome each other with the most fraternal of embraces. Generally, the Sephardim, who believed themselves superior in refinement and culture, regarded their Ashkenazic coreligionists somewhat condescendingly. Nevertheless, the two groups did come together (at least in the first one hundred and fifty years) in the synagogues on American soil, thus breaking the pattern prevalent in the seventeenth and eighteenth centuries in European Jewish communities such as those of Amsterdam and London, where Sephardim and Ashkenazim not only kept aloof from each other socially but maintained separate places of worship.

The synagogues of North America were not led by ordained rabbis until well into the nineteenth century. On the eve of the American Revolution not a single rabbi lived permanently in the colonies, although the Jewish communities of Jamaica, Curaçao, and Surinam each had one. In the congregations of New York, Philadelphia, and other cities on the mainland the chief functionary was the *ḥazzan*, the traditional precentor or leader of the prayer service. As time went on, the *ḥazzanim* in America came increasingly to adopt the role of the Protestant pastor and to serve the same functions. As far as their Jewish learning was concerned, most of them were undistinguished. A few, however, such as Gershom Mendes Seixas (1745–1816), who led the communities of New York and Philadelphia around the time of the Revolution, participated in George Washington's inauguration, and was for many years a trustee of King's College (later Columbia University), were men of high ability and left a permanent impress on the life of their communities and congregations. Another such notable figure was Isaac Leeser (1806–1868), who served several synagogues in Philadelphia from 1829 to 1868, pioneered in introducing the sermon in English as a regular part of the Sabbath service in America, and translated into English not only the Hebrew Bible but the Ashkenazic and Sephardic Prayer Books as well.

As we have noted, in Europe in the Middle Ages, and indeed up to modern times, the Jews were organized into largely autonomous communities or *kehillot*, officially recognized by the government and vested with the right of taxing all Jews within their vicinity for the maintenance of communal institutions—bathhouses, hospitals, ritual slaughtering facilities, matzah bakeries, cemeteries, funds for relief of the indigent and ransom of captives, schools, prayerhouses, and a host of others. The official leaders of the community managed its affairs, including the appointment of the rabbis, who were not functionaries of individual synagogues but served the entire *kehillah*. In the New World, however, the Jewish communities rarely obtained governmental recognition or legal powers of taxation and coercion over their members. To be sure, the early American synagogues performed many of the functions of the autonomous and officially recognized Jewish communities of Europe, but affiliation with them was a matter of personal and voluntary decision for the individual Jew. While the *parnassim*, or officers, of the congregation Shearith Israel of New York (still in existence today and popularly known as the "Spanish and Portuguese Synagogue," although its present membership is almost entirely of Ashkenazic descent) during the colonial and revolutionary periods did attempt imperiously to dictate the conduct of their membership and high-handedly imposed fines and other penalties for nonconforming behavior, any member could escape their constraints simply by withdrawing. However, social pressure and the lack of a viable alternative, except for conversion to another faith (which appealed to relatively few even of the most malcontent of Jews), generally dissuaded him from doing so.

Until 1836 Jewish immigration to America was a mere trickle, consisting of random individuals and families who, for various reasons, chose to leave their homelands and settle in the New World. But in that year began a relatively large-scale migration of Jews from Germany to America, largely as a result of continuing and increasingly oppressive social and economic restrictions in the *Vaterland*, combined with the slump in trade that then depressed the German economy. German, Austrian, and Bavarian Jews continued to come to the United States in significant numbers until almost the end of the century. It was chiefly they who raised the Jewish population of the country to approximately fifteen thousand by 1840, fifty thousand by 1850, one hundred and fifty thousand by 1860, and a quarter of a million by 1880. The immigrants from central Europe, unlike the Sephardim who concentrated their settlements on the Atlantic seaboard, penetrated into the West and South, following the expansion of the frontier. In the 1840s they settled and established congregations in Pittsburgh, Cleveland, Louisville, Chicago, Saint Louis, and—in 1849, the year of the Gold Rush—San Francisco. It was the arrival of these Jews and the numerical predominance they quickly attained that produced radical changes in the religious life of American Jewry.

⚜

The earlier Sephardic and Askenazic immigrants, though rarely well versed in the tradition, were generally orthodox in religious belief and practice. So also were most of the German-speaking Jews who began arriving in the 1830s. Among the latter, however, were some who had already broken with traditionalism and whose religious ideology had been influenced by the burgeoning Reform movement in Germany and elsewhere on the continent.

Indeed, the first stirrings of Reform in America manifested themselves even earlier, and their authors were largely Jews of German ancestry who had already lived in America for some time but were apparently inspired by the example of the Hamburg Temple and reports they had heard of other attempts at Reform in Germany. In 1824 forty-seven members of the old orthodox and largely Sephardic congregation Beth Elohim of Charleston, South Carolina (founded in 1750), petitioned its trustees to adopt a number of moderate changes in the synagogue ritual: an abridgement of the long service, repetition of some of the more important Hebrew prayers in English, removal of references to the resurrection of the dead, and a regular discourse in English on the scriptural reading prescribed for the week. When their petition was denied, twelve of the signatories, led by Isaac Harby, a noted journalist and playwright, seceded from the congregation and established what they called a Reformed Society of Israelites. Within a comparatively short time the membership of the dissident group had multiplied fourfold. Its prayer services were not only abbreviated and conducted to a considerable extent in English, but also included instrumental music and worship with bared heads on the part of the male members of the congregation. The statement of principles published by the Reformed Society of Israelites in 1831 indicates how far they had moved away from tradition and how pathetically eager they were to conform their religious practices to what they regarded as the demands of the American environment. An important part of the statement declares: "They subscribe to nothing of rabbinical interpretation, or rabbinical doctrines. They are their own teachers, drawing their knowledge from the Bible, and following only the laws of Moses, and those only as far as they can be adapted to the institutions of the Society in which they live and enjoy the blessings of liberty." [1] By 1840 the reformers were numerically strong enough to take control of the old Congregation Beth Elohim, aided by its sympathetic "minister," the Reverend (as he styled himself) Gustav Poznanski, who was born in Poland but had been educated in Germany before assuming the Charleston pulpit in 1836.

Pozanski was the first Jewish clergyman with marked Reform tendencies in America. Many others were to come in the next few decades as the immigration of German Jews grew larger, particularly after the failure of the liberal revolutions of 1848, which led many educated and intellectual Jews in central Europe to despair of any amelioration of its social order and to resolve to settle in the "land of liberty and justice." In the 1840s and 1850s groups of German Jews, impressed by the development of the Reform movement in the *Vaterland* and repelled by the obscurantism, ignorance, and superstition they frequently encountered in the synagogues of America, began to organize so-called Reform Vereine. Out of these soon emerged full-fledged Reform congregations, some of which in time managed to acquire distinguished European rabbis, eager to abandon the stifling atmosphere of the Old World and to live and work in the New. Thus, in 1842 Congregation Har Sinai of Baltimore, which a dozen years later obtained the services of an outstanding German rabbi, David Einhorn, was established. So also in 1845 Congregation Emanu-El of New York, which grew out of a "cultus society" advocating reforms in Jewish worship in order (among other things) "to occupy a position of greater respect among our fellow citizens," was formed and drew to its pulpit Rabbi Leo Merzbacher; 1860 saw the founding of Temple Sinai of Chicago which, for the next half century, was led by a series of prominent German rabbis—

American Judaism–Its Beginnings

Bernhard Felsenthal, Kaufmann Kohler, and Emil Gustav Hirsch.

Surpassing all these and other noted rabbinic figures in the effectiveness of his work on behalf of the Reform movement in America, though hardly the equal of some of them in intellect and scholarship, was Isaac Mayer Wise (1819–1900), who has been called, with no little justification, "the master builder of American Reform Judaism."

Born in the Bohemian village of Steingrub, Wise apparently received rabbinic ordination in Prague in 1842. He also studied for a time at the universities of Prague and Vienna. For two years he served the congregation in the small town of Radnitz, where he found himself frequently in conflict with his laity. In addition, he deliberately violated the regulations of the government authorizing only a limited number of Jewish marriages in any year. In 1845 Wise was present as an observer at the second conference of Reform leaders at Frankfurt. Feeling increasingly frustrated in his rabbinic career in Europe, he decided to emigrate to America with his wife and little daughter. He arrived in New York City in the summer of 1846 after a sea voyage of sixty-three days, and a few months later was appointed rabbi of the traditionalist Congregation Beth El of Albany, New York. Here he began urging reforms in the synagogue service, such as the introduction of family pews, preaching in the vernacular, a mixed choir, and the ceremony of confirmation—all of which he managed eventually to obtain. He also sought to give women more rights, including eligibility to be counted in the *minyan* (quorum of at least ten persons required for public worship).

Wise's reform proposals did not go unopposed by some of the more articulate and irascible laymen committed to orthodoxy. In 1850 a sharp controversy erupted in Congregation Beth El, resulting in Wise's resignation from the pulpit and the formation of a new congregation, Anshe Emeth, by his friends and adherents. Wise served the new group until 1854, when he was invited to become rabbi of the important congregation Bene Yeshurun of Cincinnati. Here he remained until his death forty-six years later. Cincinnati and Bene Yeshurun provided him with an effective base for pursuing his tireless labors, which were directed chiefly toward the unification of the scattered local synagogues on a national level and promoting the cause of Reform Judaism.

Soon after his arrival in America Wise became convinced that if Judaism were to flourish in the New World, the religious anarchy resulting from the fact that each congregation was completely autonomous and followed its own way according to the whims of its lay or rabbinic leadership must come to an end. The local congregations must organize themselves into a national federation that would make possible standardization of worship (virtually every prominent rabbi of the time was issuing his own prayer book) and consultation and cooperation on common problems of religious faith and practice. They must also collaborate in the establishment and maintenance of a seminary for the training of indigenous rabbis, so that the American congregations would no longer be dependent on European-born and European-educated spiritual leaders who were not always sufficiently attuned to their new environment. Isaac Leeser, the highly respected ḥazzan-minister of Philadelphia and editor of the influential monthly journal *The Occident* (founded in 1843), which was circulated throughout the country, had already called for a national union of congregations as early as 1841, but without success. Two years after his arrival in America, in 1848, Isaac Mayer Wise summoned the "ministers and other Israelites" of the United States to form a union in order to overcome the anarchy which he believed threatened the survival of Judaism in the land. His summons was published in *The Occident* and heartily endorsed by Isaac Leeser, but again the rabbis and congregations were not yet ready to cooperate. Wise did not despair. Almost immediately after settling in Cincinnati he began to publish two weeklies, *The Israelite* (later *The American Israelite*) in English and *Die Deborah* in German, to serve as vehicles for the dissemination of his views, particularly those regarding the need for a union of congregations and a rabbinical seminary. His position as leader of one of the most prominent congregations in the country, his editorship of *The Israelite* and *Die Deborah*, and his numerous books ranging in subject matter from Jewish history to philosophy and theology to romantic fiction (Wise wrote voluminously, though not always brilliantly or even sensibly) quickly made him a national figure in Jewish circles. Invitations poured in to speak to Jewish gatherings all over the country. Wise rarely declined, glad of the opportunity to employ the speaker's platform to propagandize his favorite projects.

It was not until 1855 that Wise managed to convene a national conference of rabbis, both Orthodox and Reform, in Cleveland. The traditionalists and the liberals, of course, found themselves in sharp conflict on many fundamental issues. But Wise, who presided over the conference, was prepared to compromise his own position for the sake of unity. The majority of the conference adopted the following resolution, each party satisfied that it had triumphed over the other: "The Bible, as delivered to us by our fathers and as now in our possession, is of immediate divine origin and the standard of our religion. The Talmud contains the traditional, legal and logical exposition of the biblical laws, which must be expounded and practiced according to the comments of the Talmud." [2] That Wise actually believed this, even at the moment of affixing his signature to the resolution, is almost inconceivable.

The result of the Cleveland conference was a sharp attack on Wise from both extremes of the rabbinic spectrum—the Orthodox and the radical Reform. The latter group, led by David Einhorn of Baltimore, assailed Wise for his religious and intellectual pusillanimity in not maintaining a consistent Reform position and in subscribing to a document which, *inter alia*, acknowledged the binding authority of the *Talmud*. Wise also became the object of acrimonious criticism by traditionalists, whose leader was Isaac Leeser, because of the prayer book which he brought forward as a result of the conference. Wise had long urged that the proliferation of prayer books by individual rabbis was destructive of the unity of American Jewry, and that a standard prayer book was a prime desideratum. At the conference he was appointed to a committee charged with the responsibility of editing such a book. The result, entitled *Minhag America* (*American Rite*), on drafts of which he had been working for several years, was almost entirely the product of Wise's own labors. While far less radical in its excisions and departures from the traditional *Siddur* than prayer books such as David Einhorn's *Olat Tamid* (*Regular Offering*) (published in 1858), it was deeply offensive to the Orthodox, since it excluded the traditional petitions for the reestablishment of Zion, the Temple, and the sacrificial cult. Most of the Reform congregations of the South and the West eventually adopted it; those of the Northeast, however, preferred Einhorn's more consistently Reform work. To Wise's credit, it must be said that he was motivated by a genuine concern for promoting greater unity in American Judaism. When the Central Conference of American Rabbis, which he himself founded and presided over until his death, in 1894 published its *Union Prayer Book*, based to a considerable extent on Einhorn's *Olat Tamid*, Wise voluntarily withdrew his *Minhag America* and adopted the new prayer book for worship in his own congregation.

That Wise's religious positions were often blatantly inconsistent with each other, that he was the most obvious of intellectual fence-straddlers, can hardly be disputed. Unlike most of his Reform contemporaries in both Germany and America, he took the quintessentially orthodox position that the divine revelation at Mount Sinai reported by the Bible was a real historical event, confirmed by the unanimous testimony of six hundred thousand eyewitnesses. In contradistinction to orthodoxy, however, and with no apparent rational foundation for his view, Wise held that only the Decalogue was directly revealed by God to Israel from heaven (*min ha-shamayim*). He frequently rhapsodized about the moral grandeur of the Ten Commandments, describing them as both the essence of Judaism (ignoring the fact that the rabbis of the Talmudic age proscribed their regular recitation in the synagogue service precisely because Christianity maintained that they alone constituted Judaism's essential character) and universal ethical principles, valid for all peoples, places, and times. The Torah as a whole, however, Wise followed Moses Mendelssohn in asserting, was meant only for Israel; contrary to Mendelssohn, he insisted that it was obligatory on Israel only for a definite term and cannot be regarded as still, in its entirety, God's prescriptive will for the present-day Jewish people.

Wise stressed the historic importance of *halachah* in Judaism and his own personal commitment to it: "To be sure, I am a reformer, as much as our age requires; because I am convinced that none can stop the stream of time, none can check the swift wheels of the age; but I have always the *halachah* for my basis; I never sanction a reform against the *din*." [3] This, however, did not prevent him (although his Reform innovations were far more moderate than those of many of his contemporaries, e.g., Samuel Holdheim in Germany and David Einhorn and Emil G. Hirsch in America) from actively sanctioning clear-cut departures from Talmudic law and from frequently inveighing against "legalism" as a distortion of Judaism (he did not spare Pauline antinomianism either).

Wise could champion the cause of the *Talmud* against attacks launched by Christian theologians as well as by his more radical colleagues in the Reform movement; yet he could also write, in the introduction to his *Judaism—Its Doctrines and Duties*, "the author of this little volume ignores the three Talmuds (Jewish, New Testament, Koran), reads the Bible from its own standpoint, and proves that it contains the complete and rational system of religion for all generations and countries." [4]

Wise's favorite adjectives for characterizing Judaism—rational, humane, universal, liberal, progressive—clearly demonstrate that he read the history of Judaism through the highly distorting lenses of the eighteenth- and nineteenth-century liberalism and rationalism that were already being abandoned by many of the more romantic and venturesome spirits of his day. He could also be sufficiently opaque to the actual social, intellectual, and religious currents of his age to predict a number of times—in utmost seriousness—that not too long after the beginning of the twentieth century the majority of Christians in America would abandon their "superstitions" and embrace the rationally pure and enlightened Jewish faith; ethical monotheism—and its originator and historic bearer, Judaism—would become the dominant religion of the land.

If Judaism was to realize its divinely ordained destiny and become the universal religion, Wise urged, it had to be "denationalized." All the accretions of rite and ceremony that had come into the Jewish religion over the centuries in consequence of the effort to make it distinctive and to differentiate the Jew from the non-Jew had to be stripped away, in order "to launch the universal religion based exclusively on the Ten Commandments." Such was Wise's theory and such his rhetoric. In practice, however, he declined to abrogate the *halachah* as such and insisted on its indispensability as the central means of hallowing Jewish life. The strength of his residual loyalty to historic tradition is discernible in numerous instances, but especially in his loyalty to the traditional Sabbath and his opposition to Sunday services (introduced by a number of his contemporaries) either in place of or in addition to Sabbath services.

It is clear that Isaac Mayer Wise did not favor a reform of Judaism so extreme that it would sever its connections with historic Jewish faith and practice, although he frequently employed language that might suggest otherwise. His was an essentially moderate Reform position. What he envisaged and worked for was a liberalization of Judaism that he believed would be acceptable to, and eventually engage the loyalty of, all American Jews, if not America and the world at large. His penchant for compromise and his lack of consistency, while repugnant to the logical purist, may well be regarded as virtues rather than defects. It was apparently these qualities that kept him from strictly following the logic of his position to the point of virtually de-Judaizing the synagogue. This was done by some of his colleagues, such as Emil G. Hirsch of Chicago's Sinai Temple, who went so far as to substitute Sunday services entirely for Sabbath and to eliminate regular reading of the Torah from his worship exercises.

Some Reform rabbis of Wise's time went even further and followed the logic of their ideological position to its complete conclusion. For them Reform *Judaism* seemed overly particularistic and tribal; it had to be transcended by a universal religion of ethical humanism. Thus, Felix Adler (1851–1933), son of Rabbi Samuel Adler of Temple Emanu-El in New York and expected to succeed his father as spiritual leader of the congregation after completing his general and rabbinic education in Germany, discovered upon his return to America that even Reform Judaism was too constricting, supernaturalist, and nationalistic for his tastes. He also found at least some of its beliefs intellectually embarrassing. He later wrote:

Was I to act a lie in order to teach the truth? There was especially one passage in the Sabbath Service which brought me to the point of resolution: I mean the words spoken by the officiating minister as he holds up the Pentateuch scroll, "And this is the law which Moses set before the people of Israel." I had lately returned from abroad, where I had had a fairly thorough course in Biblical exegesis, and had become convinced that the Mosaic religion is, so to speak, a religious mosaic, and there is hardly a single stone in it which can with certainty be traced to the authorship of Moses. Was I to repeat these words? It was impossible. It was certain that they would stick in my throat. On these grounds, the separation was decided on by me.[5]

Alder proceeded, in 1876, to establish the Ethical Culture Society, and drew into its membership many erstwhile Reform Jews. Similarly, two rabbis of Temple Israel in Boston felt constrained to abandon Reform Judaism for more "universalist" work and vistas; in 1893 Rabbi Solomon Schindler resigned its pulpit to become a promoter of Edward Bellamy's socialism, and in 1911 his successor, Rabbi Charles Fleischer, left the congregation to found a community church in Boston.

The indefatigable efforts of Isaac Mayer Wise over a period of more than two decades to establish a national federation of congregations finally bore fruit in 1873. In July of that year representatives of thirty-four synagogues met in Cincinnati to establish the Union of American Hebrew Congregations. Wise had hoped that all the Jewish congregations in America would join his federation, but that hope was not to be fulfilled; only the more liberal and modernized synagogues agreed to cooperate in his Union. Some which joined the Union eventually left it in protest against what they considered a reckless and precipitate pace of reform by its leadership. But the instrumentality had been created for an organized Reform movement that was to prove highly successful, if not to be the dominant force in American-Jewish religious life. A century after its birth, the Union of American Hebrew Congregations could boast a membership of over six hundred congregations. Throughout its history the Union has exercised a considerable influence on American Judaism, although in the last half century its Conservative and Orthodox counterparts, the United Synagogue and the Union of Orthodox Jewish Congregations, have shared its influence. It was only appropriate that Isaac Mayer Wise, who almost single-handedly founded the Union, should have been elected its first president in 1873.

With the Union firmly established, Wise could proceed to concentrate his efforts on what he regarded as its first major task—formation of a seminary for the training of rabbis and teachers in the liberal environment of America. As early as 1855, a year after his arrival in Cincinnati, he had made an abortive attempt to establish such a school in an institution which he called Zion College. In the 1860s Isaac Leeser and several other traditionalist rabbis had organized Maimonides College in Philadelphia as a rabbinic training school, but it had been compelled to close its doors after only a few years. Now, with the financial support of the Union of American Hebrew Congregations, Wise succeeded in opening the Hebrew Union College in the vestry rooms of the Plum Street Temple of Cincinnati in 1875; he ordained its first graduating class of four rabbis in 1883. The founder of the College was, of course, also its first president, and served in that capacity, as well as carrying an extensive teaching load, until his death in 1900.

❧

As we have observed, Wise's forte was in organizing ability, not in theology. Probably the most influential theologian of American Reform Judaism in its first era was David Einhorn, who, after his arrival in the United States in 1855, ministered successively to congregations in Baltimore, Philadelphia, and New York until his death in 1879. Einhorn had participated in the historic Reform conferences at Frankfurt in 1845 and Breslau in 1846. Deeply devoted to German culture and the German language, Einhorn, unlike Wise, declined to preach in English, which he considered deficient and crude in comparison with his native tongue. In his journal *Sinai* (published from 1856 to 1862) he wrote: "It takes little familiarity with the condition of American Jewish religious life to recognize that the English ele-

[297]

ment under present circumstances is a brake to Reform strivings. German research and science are the heart of the Jewish Reform idea, and German Jewry has the mission to bring life and recognition to this thought on American soil." [6] Einhorn also differed from Wise in his attitude toward the slavery question; he was an eloquent abolitionist and spoke out so strongly on the issue that he was forced to leave the pulpit of Har Zion Temple of Baltimore in 1861, whereas his colleague remained in Cincinnati and vacillated on the matter.

While still living in Europe and serving as rabbi of the Reform synagogue in Pest, Einhorn had adopted the typical Reform position that, since Judaism is a religion of progressive divine revelation, Talmudic *halachah* is not binding on the contemporary Jew. Only the Decalogue could be considered the permanent and unalterable law of Judaism; all other ordinances were temporal and changeable. He also vehemently denied the national character of Judaism and insisted that Jews did not constitute a people but only a religious community, charged by God with the "mission" of bringing knowledge of Him and His moral law to those that knew them not. When this mission was completed, the Jews could regard their obligation to maintain a distinct identity as discharged and merge with all of a humanity now possessed of both ethical and rational enlightenment. Only provisionally, until the fulfillment of their responsibility (and Einhorn and his colleagues in the more radical Reform wing of American Judaism apparently believed that that fulfillment was not far off), was it necessary that Jews remain a separate and identifiable group.

Einhorn, as we have noted, had little sympathy or tolerance for Isaac Mayer Wise's compromises at the Cleveland rabbinic conference of 1855, and Wise's further inconsistencies and vacillations on both practical and theological issues displeased him even more. In 1869 Einhorn joined eleven other Reform rabbis, most of them serving congregations in the East, at a rabbinic conference in Philadelphia chaired by Samuel Hirsch (1815–1889), who, as we have noted, had gained renown in Europe for his important work *Die Religionsphilosophie der Juden* (on Samuel Hirsch as a philosopher, see pp. 278–281) and served as rabbi of the Grand Duchy of Luxembourg before coming to Philadelphia in 1866 to assume the pulpit of Reform Congregation Keneseth Israel. This conference issued a statement, in German, that expressed clearly the views of the left wing of the contemporary American Reform rabbinate. Among other things, it utterly rejected the national character of Judaism, declaring that the destruction of the Jewish state was to be understood "not as a punishment for the sin of Israel, but as a result of the divine intention," which was to scatter the Jews "to all parts of the world, so that their high priestly mission—leading the nations to the true knowledge and worship of God—might be realized." The conference ringingly proclaimed (in defiance of centuries-old tradition) that "Israel's messianic aim is not the restoration of the ancient Jewish state . . . but the unification of all God's children." [7] It also declared that the idea of the immortality of the soul should be substituted in the prayers for that of physical resurrection.

As far as Jewish practice is concerned, the Philadelphia conference of 1869, among its other actions, abrogated the rite of *ḥalitzah*, authorized the *agunah* to remarry if civil law permitted it, generally accepted civil divorce and dispensed with the traditional *get* or divorce, and permitted the bride and groom to exchange rings and vows in the marriage ceremony.

Succeeding David Einhorn as probably the outstanding spokesman of radical Reform in the last decades of the nineteenth century and the first decades of the twentieth was Emil G. Hirsch (1851–1923), Einhorn's son-in-law and the son of Samuel Hirsch. During his long ministry (1882–1923) at Chicago's Sinai Temple, to which he came after graduating from the University of Pennsylvania and four subsequent years at the universities of Berlin and Leipzig and at the Hochschule für die Wissenschaft des Judentums (where he studied with such great German Jewish savants as Abraham Geiger, Israel Levy, Hermann Steinthal, and Moritz Lazarus), he may well have commanded a larger audience and exercised greater influence than his brother-in-law Kaufmann Kohler, who served as president of the Hebrew Union College from 1903 to 1922. Besides performing his rabbinical duties, Hirsch taught Jewish literature and philosophy for many years at the University of Chicago; he was invited to join its faculty by the University's first president, William Rainey Harper, himself an outstanding Hebraist. He was also one of the chief editors of the *Jewish Encyclopedia* and contributed an impressive number of major articles to it. But it was as a preacher that Hirsch won his greatest fame, achieving an international reputation for his oratory. His sermons, many of them published in the *Reform Advocate* of Chicago, are models of lucidity, scholarship, and style. They present his radical philosophy of Judaism with extraordinary clarity and eloquence. For the student of Jewish thought this philosophy holds considerable interest as a remarkable attempt to harmonize Judaism with the general intellectual climate of the age. Hirsch may well be the most original figure in late nineteenth- and early twentieth-century American Jewry, and his philosophy of Judaism is more clearly thought out and better articulated than that of any other Reform thinker of his age.[8]

We have noted that for many years a controversy was sustained between the moderate Reform rabbis, led by Isaac Mayer Wise, and the more radical reformers, whose leaders included David Einhorn and Emil G. Hirsch. In 1885, under the impetus of sharp attacks on Reform Judaism launched by such Conservative spokesmen as Rabbi Alexander Kohut (1842–1894) of New York, the two factions assembled in Pittsburgh and largely compromised their differences. Nineteen rabbis, including a number of nonordained "ministers," convened at the call of Kaufmann Kohler, then serving as rabbi of Temple Beth El in New York, at a conference presided over by Wise. The conference adopted a statement of principles that came to be known as the Pittsburgh Platform and served for more than half a century as the quasi-official theological program of the American Reform rabbinate.

The Pittsburgh Platform, which was largely formulated by Kohler, took certain positions that were more extreme than any adopted by the Reform conferences and synods in Germany. Its eight principles are worth quoting in full:

First—We recognize in every religion an attempt to grasp the Infinite One, and in every mode, source or book of revelation held sacred in any religious system the consciousness of the indwelling of God in man. We hold that Judaism presents the highest conception of the God-idea as taught in our holy Scriptures and developed and spiritualized by the Jewish teachers in accordance with the moral and philosophical progress of their respective ages. We maintain that Judaism preserved and defended amid continual struggles and trials and under enforced isolation this God-idea as the central religious truth for the human race.

Second—We recognize in the Bible the record of the consecration of the Jewish people to its mission as the priest of the One God, and value it as the most potent instrument of religious and moral instruction. We hold that the modern discoveries of scientific researches in the domains of nature and history are not antagonistic to the doctrines of Judaism, the Bible reflecting the primitive ideas of its own age and at times clothing its conception of divine providence and justice dealing with man in miraculous narratives.

Third—We recognize in the Mosaic legislation a system of training the Jewish people for its mission during its national life in Palestine, and today we accept as binding only its moral laws and maintain only such ceremonials as elevate and sanctify our lives, but reject all such as are not adapted to the views and habits of modern civilization.

Fourth—We hold that all such Mosaic and Rabbinical laws as regulate diet, priestly purity and dress originated in ages and under the influence of ideas altogether foreign to our present mental and spiritual state. They fail to impress the modern Jew with a spirit of priestly holiness; their observance in our day is apt rather to obstruct than to further modern spiritual elevation.

Fifth—We recognize in the modern era of universal culture of heart and intellect the approach of the realization of Israel's great Messianic hope for the establishment of the Kingdom of truth, justice and peace among all men. We consider ourselves no longer a nation but a religious community, and therefore expect neither a return to Palestine, nor a sacrificial worship under the administration of the sons of Aaron, nor the restoration of any of the laws concerning the Jewish state.

Sixth—We recognize in Judaism a progressive religion, ever striving to be in accord with the postulates of reason. We are convinced of the utmost necessity of preserving the historical identity with our great past. Christianity and Islam being daughter religions of Judaism, we appreciate their mission to aid in the spreading of monotheistic and moral truth. We acknowledge that the spirit of broad humanity of our age is our ally in the fulfillment of our mission, and therefore we extend the hand of fellowship to all who co-operate with us in the establishment of the reign of truth and righteousness among men.

Seventh—We reassert the doctrine of Judaism, that the soul of man is immortal, grounding this belief on the divine nature of the human spirit, which forever finds bliss in righteousness and misery in wickedness. We reject as ideas not rooted in Judaism the belief both in bodily resurrection and in Gehenna and Eden [hell and paradise], as abodes for everlasting punishment or reward.

Eighth—In full accordance with the spirit of Mosaic legislation which strives to regulate the relation between rich and poor, we deem it our duty to participate in the great task of modern times, to solve on the basis of justice and righteousness the problems presented by the contrasts and evils of the present organization of society.[9]

While most of the text of the Pittsburgh Platform was Kaufmann Kohler's work, it should be noted that the eighth principle was proposed by, and adopted at the insistence of, Emil G. Hirsch. This principle was to serve as the justification of many of the "social justice" pronouncements and activities of Reform rabbis in the first decades of the twentieth century.

❦

Adoption of the Pittsburgh Platform in 1885 was the major direct stimulus for the organization of a movement of counteraction against Reform on the part of a number of distinguished Conservative rabbis shocked by its radical repudiation of classical Jewish positions. The religious sensitivities of these men, who generally styled themselves proponents of Historical Judaism rather than Conservative Judaism, had already been outraged by an incident that had taken place two and a half years earlier in connection with the ordination of the first graduating class of the Hebrew Union College in Cincinnati in 1883. A member of that class, Rabbi David Philipson, who was to become one of the major modern historians of Reform Judaism, describes it vividly in his autobiography:

The convention of the Union of American Hebrew Congregations, whereof this rabbinical ordination was the peak, closed with a great dinner at a famed hilltop resort, the Highland House. Knowing that there would be delegates from various parts of the country who laid stress upon the observance of the dietary laws, the Cincinnati committee engaged a Jewish caterer to serve the dinner. The great banqueting hall was brilliantly lighted, the hundreds of guests were seated at the beautifully arranged tables, the invocation had been spoken by one of the visiting rabbis, when the waiters served the first course. Terrific excitement ensued when two rabbis rose from their seats and rushed from the room. Shrimp had been placed before them as the opening course of the elaborate menu. . . . The Highland House dinner came to be known as the "*terefa* banquet." The Orthodox Eastern press rang the changes on the *terefa* banquet week in and week out. The incident furnished the opening to the movement that culminated in the establishment of a rabbinical seminary of a conservative bent.[10]

Until the Highland House incident virtually all the major synagogues in the United States were affiliated with the Union of American Hebrew Congregations. Besides this, a number of prominent Conservative and more or less traditional rabbis supported, and even participated in the work of, the Hebrew Union College, regarding it as a school that would be likely to provide rabbis and teachers for all segments of American Jewry. The ordination banquet of 1883 disabused them of their belief, and the extremist principles of the Pittsburgh Platform of 1885 confirmed their conviction that they would have to organize a countermovement. The first task of this movement would be the establishment of another rabbinical seminary, if the cause of a more traditional version of Judaism in America was not to be weakened and eventually disappear.

The reins of Conservative leadership were taken by the Italian-born Sabato Morais (1823–1897), rabbi for many years of the Sephardic congregation Mikveh Israel of Philadelphia, in whose pulpit he had succeeded Isaac Leeser in 1851. Morais was a disciple of the great Italian-Jewish scholar Samuel David Luzzatto and had served for a number of years as a teacher in one of the schools of the Spanish and Portuguese synagogue in London before coming to America. For a long time he had collaborated with Isaac Mayer Wise, cooperating with him first in establishing the Hebrew Union College and then serving as one of its examiners until 1885. With the adoption of the Pittsburgh Platform in that year by a group of rabbis among whom Wise was included, Morais felt—despite Wise's vociferous insistence that the platform was not obligatory on, and did not necessarily represent the mind of, either the Union of American Hebrew Congregations or the Hebrew Union College—that he could no longer work with the Reformers.

In his project of creating a new seminary in New York City, Sabato Morais enlisted the aid of several eminent colleagues who shared his conservative views. Among these rabbis, all of whom had been more or less influenced by the Positive-Historical position of Zacharias Frankel in Germany, were the already mentioned Alexander Kohut, who achieved scholarly fame for his edition of the Talmudic lexicon *Aruch Completum;* Marcus Jastrow (1829–1903), who also compiled a valuable work entitled *A Dictionary of the Targumim, the Talmud Babli and Yerushalmi, and the Midrashic Literature;* Benjamin Szold (1829–1902), for more than four decades rabbi of Congregation Oheb Shalom of Baltimore, author of *A Hebrew Commentary to the Book of Job,* and editor of a popular prayer book; and Henry Pereira Mendes (1852–1937), the young minister of the old congregation Shearith Israel of New York. These and several other rabbis collaborated with Morais in the formation of the Jewish Theological Seminary Association in 1885.

The charter of the Association made it perfectly clear that the Seminary was intended to counteract what the Conservative leaders regarded as the reckless extremism and assimilationism of the Reformers:

The necessity has been made manifest for associated and organized effort on the part of the Jews of America faithful to Mosaic Law and ancestral traditions, for the purpose of keeping alive the true Judaic spirit; in particular by the establishment of a seminary where the Bible shall be impartially taught and rabbinical literature faithfully expounded, and more especially where youths, desirous of entering the ministry, may be thoroughly grounded in Jewish knowledge and inspired by the precept and example of their instructors with the love of the Hebrew language and a spirit of devotion and fidelity to the Jewish Law.[11]

Sabato Morais had proposed naming the new rabbinical school the Orthodox Seminary, but was persuaded by Alexander Kohut to call it the Jewish Theological Seminary, to indicate, apparently, that it would follow the program of Historical Judaism practiced and taught at the Jüdisch-Theologisches Seminar in Breslau which had been presided over by Zacharias Frankel. After long months of planning, the dedication exercises of the Seminary were conducted on January 2, 1887, at Lyric Hall, and classes inaugurated at the Shearith Israel synagogue. Among the eight students in the first class was Joseph Herman Hertz (1872–1946), later to become chief rabbi of the British Empire.

There were, to be sure, some significant theological differences between the Reformers and the members of the Historical school who united to establish the Jewish Theological Seminary, but the major issues between them were in the realm of religious practice. Most of the rabbis who claimed adherence to the Historical school desired some moderate reforms in the synagogue (some even went so far as to favor introduction of family pews and organ music), but they were adamant in their refusal to abandon the traditional Sabbath, worship conducted largely in Hebrew, and the dietary laws. It was primarily these practices that they hoped to preserve through the Seminary.

Perhaps the major ideological issue between the two camps was the question of Zionism. Already in the 1880s a proto-Zionist movement had sprung up in eastern Europe as a result of the Russian pogroms, and small bands of young Jews were proceeding to Palestine to establish colonies and settlements. These activities were generally decried by the Reform rabbis. A few notable dissenting spirits, including such figures as Bernhard Felsenthal, Maximilian Heller, and Gustav Gottheil, were warmly disposed and later responded eagerly to Theodor Herzl's program of political Zionism directed toward the establishment of a Jewish state in Palestine, and aided in the founding of the American Federation of Zionists. The dominant mood within both the rabbinate and laity of Reform, however, was vehement opposition to Herzlian Zionism. They considered it a repudiation of the universalist spirit of Judaism and of the idea that the Jews were a religious community only, not a nation. Even such a moderate Reformer as Isaac Mayer Wise spoke deridingly of "Ziomania." The Conservative rabbis, on the other hand, by and large greeted the idea of building a Jewish state with fervent enthusiasm. In 1894 Benjamin Szold helped establish the first American Zionist society in Baltimore, and other Conservative leaders, notably Marcus Jastrow and Henry Pereira Mendes, gave strong support to the movement for national restoration.

In the 1890s the Jewish Theological Seminary did not appear to have a very promising future; indeed, when its founder Sabato Morais died in 1897, it seemed that it might soon have to close its doors. Not only was there a momentary lack of leadership, but a number of the important congregations that supported the Seminary financially at its inception had turned to Reform a dozen years later. Undoubtedly the major factor that rescued the Seminary, as well as the cause of Conservative Judaism, was the massive influx to America of east European Jews beginning in the early 1880s. By the end of the century some of these immigrants, and even more of their sons and daughters, were ready for the modified version of traditional Judaism represented by Conservatism.

❦

In 1880 the majority of the quarter of a million Jews resident in the United States who were affiliated with any synagogue probably belonged to Reform congregations. Jews of German and central European extraction dominated the congregations of the land, of which there were almost three hundred at the time, as well as the Jewish fraternal orders and philanthropic societies. Two decades later, three quarters of a million Jews from eastern Europe had settled in America, radically altering the religious and social complexion of the Jewish community.

To be sure, Jews from eastern Europe had come to America long before the pogroms which began in Russia in 1881 inaugurated a wholesale Jewish exodus from the czarist empire. Thirty years earlier, in 1852, New York already had a synagogue, the Beth Ha-Midrash, whose membership consisted largely of Russian and Polish Jews, and ten years earlier, in 1872, there existed in that city close to thirty congregations following east European orthodox practice. In

1874 there were already enough Yiddish-speaking Jews in New York for an orthodox weekly in Yiddish, *Die Yiddishe Gazette*, to commence publication. Nevertheless, 1881 signalized the beginning of a tidal wave of Jewish immigration to America from eastern Europe that was to continue unabated until after World War I.

The new immigrants, who fled from the squalid, poverty-stricken *shtetl* of the Pale of Settlement and from czarist persecution, were a different breed of Jews from the Sephardim and Ashkenazim who preceded them in America. Coming from areas of dense Jewish population in which a largely autonomous and self-contained Jewish culture had long been maintained, most of them huddled together in the New World and sought to recreate on its soil as much as possible of the life and culture they had known in the Old. The expansion of the American frontier westward had virtually ceased by the time they arrived, and so they concentrated their settlement chiefly in the great cities of the eastern seaboard (as had the Sephardic immigrants of the colonial era)—largely in New York, but in Boston and Philadelphia as well. Here jobs were available, particularly in the needle trades. Lacking entrepreneurial skills and ambitions, most of the immigrants, in the years immediately after their arrival in the country, earned a meager livelihood in the factories and sweatshops of the growing American commercial and industrial centers.

It is likely that the majority of the east European Jewish immigrants who came to the United States in the 1880s and 1890s were quite orthodox in religious belief and practice. Many of the men had studied in famous *yeshivot* in their youth and commanded a considerable knowledge of Judaism, especially of its vast and complex legal tradition. These Jews proceeded to establish congregations of their own, frequently on a *Landesmannschaft* basis, i.e., men coming from the same European city or town would band together to form a synagogue in which they could cultivate and maintain memories of the "old home." These congregations felt no need for rabbis or "spiritual leaders." While they might be happy to find a musically talented *ḥazzan* or chanter of prayers, in most cases practically all the adult males in any congregation could and did function quite competently as *shaliaḥ tzibbur*, the leader of the congregation in worship. Their synagogues, although located amidst the crowded tenements of New York's Lower East Side or similar areas of dense Jewish settlement in other cities, were frequently virtual replicas of the synagogues of the *shtetl*.

By no means did all the immigrants maintain a pristine and unalloyed attachment to religious orthodoxy. Many of them had been exposed to the ideological influences of the Haskalah movement while still in Europe and had become thoroughly secularized in their attitudes and beliefs. Some had become ardent Zionists and interpreted Judaism and Jewishness solely in nationalist terms. Some, through membership in the *Bund* and other influences, had been attracted to socialism and envisaged salvation as the emergence of an international socialist order. Virtually every ideology that had penetrated east European Jewish life was represented among them, but only one attracted few adherents, and that was total assimilationism. Among even the most secularized and radical, a strong sense of Jewish identity and a desire to maintain it—be it only by the preservation of Yiddish—prevailed.

Some of the bourgeois, semiassimilated German Jews who had long lived in America regarded the influx of these masses of unwashed coreligionists from eastern Europe with unmitigated horror. The foreign dress, cacophonous speech, and tenacious clinging to "old country" ways of the Russian and Polish "greenhorns" appeared to threaten their own hard-won status as Americanized "adherents of the Mosaic faith." Would not their gentile neighbors identify them with these uncouth persons who were "fellow Jews"? Even more frightening to not a few of the prosperous, middle-class German Jews was the social and economic radicalism of some of the new immigrants. Were there not among them individuals who professed socialism and even anarchism?

To the credit of the German Jews it must be said that most of them soon overcame their personal repugnance to the *Ostjuden* and proceeded to aid them in a variety of ways—by organizing relief societies to support the indigent, by establishing manual training schools and courses for the teaching of English, and by instructing them in American manners and mores. To be sure, underlying many of these efforts was the desire to Americanize the Russo-Polish Jews and rid them of their embarrassing foreign habits and ways as quickly as possible. But whatever may have been the motivations, the efforts themselves were frequently of substantial benefit to the immigrants and eased their adjustment to the new environment.

One thing most of the German Jews of the 1880s and 1890s were not quite prepared to do was to extend an invitation to the east European Jews to join their Reform congregations. Nor would such an invitation have been welcomed or accepted by any significant number. As far as the more orthodox immigrants were concerned, the Reform synagogue, with its bare-headed worshippers, mixed choir, prayers and sermons in English, and mingling of men and women, was not much different from a Christian church and hardly deserved the name synagogue. As for the radicals, while some might have appreciated the denunciations of social and economic injustice and the glowing pronouncements about human equality and the brotherhood of man that issued from the lips of rabbis preaching "prophetic" Judaism, they would also have suspected some hypocrisy on noting that these denunciations and pronouncements came from well-fed and well-tailored gentlemen who seemed generally quite content with eloquent words and only rarely attempted to realize their "ideals" through action.

If the Reform synagogues could hardly have succeeded in winning the interest and allegiance of the east European immigrants, even had their rabbis and lay leaders genuinely wished it, this was not the case with the more traditional congregations and rabbis who had banded together to establish the Jewish Theological Seminary. Recognizing that the Seminary was in a moribund condition in the late 1890s, a small group of Jews in New York and Philadelphia, led by the ubiquitous Cyrus Adler (1863–1940), then on the Semitics faculty of Johns Hopkins University and assistant secretary of the Smithsonian Institution in Washington, and including Rabbi Henry Pereira Mendes of New York's Shearith Israel and Rabbi Bernard Drachman who served on the Seminary faculty, conceived the idea of reorganizing the Seminary and making it an instrument for reaching the masses of new immigrants. Their intent was simultaneously to Americanize the east European Jews and confirm their loyalty to traditional Judaism by attracting some of their brighter young men and making of them modern, English-speaking, university-educated rabbis with a solid knowledge not only of the *Talmud* and *halachah*, but of the whole range of Jewish religious literature and experience.

Cyrus Adler and his colleagues hoped to gain a mass constituency, as well as to further their stated intentions, through the establishment of a federation of Orthodox congregations that would look to the Seminary as the source of its rabbinic leadership. Orthodox congregational life, particularly in New York City, was utterly chaotic in the 1880s and 1890s. New congregations, worshiping in storefronts or tenement basements, were constantly springing up, only to be torn apart by factionalism within a short time. As early as 1879 an attempt had been made to organize the Orthodox congregations of New York and to import a chief rabbi from Europe as their leader, but that attempt proved abortive; apparently no suitable candidate could be located. In 1888, however, a number of the larger east European congregations of the city banded together to bring Jacob Joseph (1848–1902), a distinguished rabbinic scholar and the official preacher of the great Jewish community of Vilna, to America as chief rabbi. The consequences were personally disastrous for Rabbi Joseph and scandalous for the association of Orthodox congregations. The latter insisted, despite warnings that the plan was not only undignified but unworkable, on financing the chief rabbi's office through a tax on kosher food products. The total failure of this plan, in addition to the hostility of the many Orthodox synagogues which refused to join the congregational association, doomed the chief rabbinate from its inception. The association of synagogues was dissolved in an atmosphere of intense acrimony and Rabbi Joseph died a broken and disillusioned man at the age of fifty-four. Even his funeral on July 30, 1902, when more than fifty thousand mourning Jews thronged the streets of New York to follow his bier, was marked by a public disturbance in which several persons were severely injured.

An Orthodox enterprise with a happier outcome was the establishment of a *yeshivah* in New York in 1896, named Yeshivat Rabbenu Yitzhak Elhanan in memory of Rabbi Isaac Elhanan Spektor (1817–1896), the great Lithuanian rabbinic authority and exponent of *Musar* who had died a few months earlier. The *yeshivah*, in its beginning, was devoted strictly to the study of *Talmud* and rabbinic codes in the east European fashion, and did not conceive its mission as the training of rabbis. Out of it, however, eventually developed a distinguished Orthodox rabbinical seminary as well as the great institution known today as Yeshivah University.

To Rabbi Henry Pereira Mendes, Cyrus Adler, and their associates, the *yeshivah* at that time did not seem likely to grow into a school that would furnish the kind of rabbinical leadership that was required; this, they believed, could only be done by the Jewish Theological Seminary, restructured and revivified. In 1898 a call for an Orthodox Jewish Congregational Union was published in English and Hebrew. Of the thirteen signatories, eleven were faculty members and trustees of the Seminary; only two were acknowledged leaders of orthodoxy. On June 18, 1898, the convention that officially established the Union of Orthodox Jewish Congregations was held with one hundred delegates in attendance, and Mendes was elected president of the new organization.

At first, out of respect for Mendes, the Union adopted a resolution supporting both the Seminary and the *yeshivah*, but it soon became apparent that the majority of the Orthodox congregations and rabbis were not prepared to recognize the Seminary as an authentic rabbinical school. For them, study of the *Talmud* and rabbinic codes in Yiddish in the traditional east European mode was the essence of rabbinic education, while the general style of the Seminary was clearly that of *die Wissenschaft des Judentums* and most of its classes were conducted in English. At a later convention, with Mendes himself presiding, a resolution was adopted rejecting the rabbinical authority of the Seminary's graduates.

This, however, was only a temporary setback for the Seminary and the Conservative movement as a whole. Even in the 1890s the Seminary was attracting a few students from among the east European orthodox immigrants, and before too many years had passed congregations led by its graduates were drawing large numbers of the immigrants, and particularly their children, into membership. Orthodoxy continued to be powerful, its ranks constantly replenished by the masses of Russian, Polish, Rumanian, and Hungarian Jews who continued to stream into the United States each year until the early 1920s. But great numbers of second and even first generation American Jews lost their attachment to the *shtetl*-like Orthodox synagogues and flowed into the modernized and Americanized Conservative congregations. In 1901, at the urging of Cyrus Adler, a group of wealthy Reform Jews of German extraction—led by Jacob Schiff and including, among others, Mayer Sulzberger, Louis Marshall, Leonard Lewissohn, and Daniel and Simon Guggenheim—collected a fund of half a million dollars to expand the program of the Jewish Theological Seminary and enable it to bring the great rabbinic scholar, Solomon Schechter, from Cambridge University to New York to serve as its president. Under Schechter's brilliant leadership from 1902 to 1915 the Seminary and Conservative Judaism blossomed. But the account of their achievements must await a later chapter in which we shall discuss American Judaism in the twentieth century.

Here it need only be said that the major factor which undoubtedly impelled many of the sons and daughters of the east European immigrants ultimately to abandon the congregations of their parents and move to Conservatism was their growing estrangement from, and dissatisfaction with, synagogues which obdurately refused to make any concessions to the demands of the American environment, and insisted on modeling themselves after the *bet midrash* and *shtibl* of the Russian Pale of Settlement. Perhaps most irritating to many second as well as first generation Jews was the system of religious education fostered, or at least tolerated, by east European orthodoxy in America. The most common type of venture in this system was the *ḥeder* or one-room school in which a *melamed*—generally a *Luftmensch* who, only after a series of dismal failures in everything else, discovered that he had a vocation for teaching—attempted to instruct a group of bored youngsters in the elements of Hebrew and in mechanical reading of the *Siddur*. To be sure, here and there even in the 1880s and 1890s there was a *Talmud Torah* or *yeshivah ketanah* with several different classes and a more or less graded curriculum. In these schools, sometimes financed by the larger congregations but more frequently by the Jewish community in general, an attempt was made to present the substance of the traditional east European Jewish education in a more rational way. But such schools were relatively rare before the turn of the century. Most of the children of east European immigrants who received any Jewish "education" at all did so in the *ḥeder* under the tutelage of a knuckle-rapping *melamed* who attempted, usually in vain, to enforce discipline with a heavy ruler or worse. The effect on the student was, in not a few cases, a lifelong antipathy to all things Jewish.

This unfortunate system was made even worse by the fact that the substance of the Jewish instruction imparted in the *ḥeder* (and this was true to a considerable extent in the *Talmud Torah* and *yeshivah ketanah* as well, though the methods of these institutions were somewhat more enlightened) was generally restricted to rote reading of Hebrew, the *Siddur*, a bit of *Ḥumash* with Rashi's commentary, and traditional religious practices and customs. Little, if any, attempt was made to teach the history of the Jewish people (certainly not beyond the biblical or, at best, the Talmudic age), the ethics of Judaism, or Jewish religious ideas and values. The results were frequently destructive, as far as loyalty to Judaism was concerned. Nathan Glazer has well summarized the situation:

One was brought up to observe the commandments, and, for this reason, as soon as one came in touch with a kind of thought which questioned fundamentals, one was at a loss. In other words, it may be said Jews lost their faith so easily because they had no faith to lose: that is, they had no doctrine, no collection of dogmas to which they could cling and with which they could resist argument. All they had, surrounding them like an armor, was a complete set of practices, each presumably as holy as the next. Once this armor was pierced by the simple question, Why? it fell away, and all that was left was a collection of habits.[12]

For many, the habits themselves sufficed to keep them in the Orthodox synagogue. For others the habit structure was too weak to prevent them from drifting into thoroughgoing secularism and, ultimately, assimilation. Still others, however, found in the Conservative and, later, in the Reform synagogue a version of Judaism that could command their loyalties.

❧

Before concluding this survey of American Judaism to the end of the nineteenth century, we must again cast a glance at Reform Judaism in the final decade of the century. Having graduated several classes of rabbis from his Hebrew Union College, Isaac Mayer Wise in 1889 organized his alumni and most of the Reform rabbis in the country into the Central Conference of American Rabbis. Wise, of course, was elected president of the organization, holding the office until his death in 1900. The Conference, which from an initial membership of less than fifty grew in 1974 to more than a thousand, promptly passed resolutions asserting its historical continuity and ideological identification with the previous Reform rabbinical conferences and synods that had taken place in both Germany and the United States. One of the first major items on its agenda, at Wise's urging, was appointment of a committee to prepare a uniform prayer book for the Reform congregations of America. Wise still felt, as he had forty years earlier, that the proliferation of prayer books written by individual rabbis was productive of a calamitous diversity and disharmony in the ranks of Reform Judaism. When the Conference in 1894 ratified the text of the *Union Prayer Book*, which was based more on David Einhorn's *Olat Tamid* than on his own *Minhag America*, Wise, as we have noted, withdrew his prayer book from use in his own congregation in Cincinnati in favor of the new ritual. Most, but not all, of the Reform congregations of the United States soon adopted the *Union Prayer Book*. Over the past eighty years this prayer book, several times revised, has probably been the major unifying factor in the American Reform movement.

In the 1890s the growth rate of Reform Judaism, which until then had been quite rapid, began to slacken somewhat. It had, as we have observed, little appeal for the masses of east European immigrants, though the overwhelming majority of German and central European Jews who identified themselves in religious terms were in its membership. In time it was to be profoundly influenced by the Jews of Russian and Polish extraction who ultimately flowed into its congregations, but that was not to happen until well into the twentieth century. Reform had evolved as a version of Judaism adapted to the tastes of prosperous, middle-class, rationalistically minded Jewish citizens who kept whatever fervent religious emotions they may have had under strict control, and whose major goal apparently was to achieve financial success and social acceptance by their non-Jewish fellow citizens. Distinctively "Jewish" customs and rituals, which might have called attention to the Jew's "difference" from the white, Anglo-Saxon Protestant, were generally regarded with disfavor. Furthermore, the millennial hope of the Jewish people for a return to Zion was, as we have observed, widely rejected, mainly no doubt out of the sincere conviction that it was no longer required in view of the progressively larger measure of political and civic rights granted to Jews in the more democratic nations of the world. The rejection also arose, to a considerable extent, out of apprehension that the maintenance and fostering of Jewish nationalist ambitions might lay Jews open to the charge of "dual loyalties" and lead to some retrenchment of their hard-won rights and privileges. Also, the rationalist disdain of tradition, folklore, and mythology, characteristic of much of American religion in general in the last decades of the nineteenth century, was clearly reflected in American Reform Judaism.

Despite all its concessions and accommodations to the American social and intellectual environment, late nineteenth-century Reform Judaism maintained a visceral loyalty to the Jewish people and the cause of keeping it alive. This is manifested perhaps most clearly in the vehement opposition to intermarriage proclaimed by virtually all the Reform rabbis and the largest segment of the laity. Marriages of Reform Jews with non-Jews were not infrequent, but they were the object of the intense disapproval of even most of those leaders of Reform who spoke with greatest fervor of the eventual emergence of a universal religion based solely on the fatherhood of God and the brotherhood of man—a religion which, in their view, would ultimately replace Judaism and render it superfluous. The same emotional attachment to the maintenance of Jewish identity is reflected in the preservation, among practically all Reform families, even the most assimilated, of the covenant of Abraham. The requirement of circumcision for adult male converts was declared nugatory by the Central Conference of American Rabbis in 1893; all that was required was a declaration by the prospective convert, orally and in writing, in the presence of a rabbi and at least two associates, that he accepted Judaism as his personal faith and intended to live by it. But the circumcision of newborn boys, even if performed by a physician rather than by the traditional *mohel* and frequently without any religious ceremony, continued to be practiced almost universally in Reform circles. Furthermore, abandonment of the seventh day as the Sabbath and transference of the major synagogue worship service to Sunday, while fairly widespread in the 1880s and 1890s among American Reform congregations, had come to be severely criticized by Reform leaders toward the end of the century. Even Kaufmann Kohler, who inaugurated the Sunday service while serving as rabbi of Sinai Temple in Chicago, eventually regretted it and ardently championed a return to the traditional Sabbath. Clearly, American Reform had not completely severed its associations with traditional Judaism and *Kelal Yisrael*. But it had to wait until almost the mid-twentieth century for the appearance of a powerful internal movement advocating renewal of, and return to, the historical roots of Judaism.

Something must be said, before concluding this chapter, about the state of Jewish culture and scholarship in America at the end of the nineteenth century. As early as the 1840s a fairly lively Jewish press, consisting of journals in English and German edited and largely written by one energetic person, e.g., Isaac Leeser or Isaac Mayer Wise, had become part of the American-Jewish cultural scene. Later, with the influx of the east European immigrants, journals in Yiddish and Hebrew as well, some with relatively advanced literary and intellectual standards, emerged. The first Jewish Publication Society was founded, largely under the leadership of Isaac Leeser, in Philadelphia as early as 1845; unfortunately it came to an end only half a dozen years later when fire destroyed the building housing its plant and stock. In 1888 the still extant Jewish Publication Society was established and by the end of the century had published a number of significant books. In 1892 the American Jewish Historical Society was founded and began its sponsorship of a program of research and publication which has continued to the present day. "In 1900," notes Herbert Friedenwald, then Recording Secretary of the American Jewish Historical Society, in his article on Jews in the United States in the *Jewish Encyclopedia*, "there were in the United States 415 Jewish educational organizations, 291 of which were religious schools attached to congregations with 1127 teachers and an attendance of about 25,000 pupils. There were also 27 Jewish free schools, chiefly in large cities, with about 11,000 pupils and 142 teachers." [13] The largest collection of Judaica at that time was in neither the Hebrew Union College nor the Jewish Theological Seminary but in the New York Public Library. Of Jewish poets, novelists, editors, and writers on Jewish themes who had gained eminence in nineteenth-century America, Friedenwald mentions Emma Lazarus, Michael Heilprin, Abraham Cahan, Annie Nathan Mayer, Mary Moss, Emma Wolf, Martha Wolfenstein, and Morris Rosenfeld.

Of Jewish scholarship in the strict sense there was virtually none in America until after the middle of the century. Most of the early Reform rabbis, including Isaac Mayer Wise, had neither the training, leisure, or capacity for serious scholarship; a few, like David Einhorn and Samuel Hirsch, had the requisite background and ability, but wrote and published comparatively little. Among the leaders of the Conservative or Historical school the outstanding scholars were Marcus Jastrow, who compiled a fine Talmudic dictionary, and Alexander Kohut, whose eight-volume, four thousand-page *Aruch Completum* (published in Vienna, 1878–1892), begun while he was still in Hungary and representing twenty-five years of unremitting labor, is undoubtedly one of the chief monuments of nineteenth-century Jewish scholarship. No truly outstanding Orthodox scholars who published their work appeared in America until the twentieth century.

The establishment of the Hebrew Union College and the Jewish Theological Seminary gave a major stimulus to the cause of Jewish learning. Among early faculty members of the College who made notable contributions were the Talmudist Moses Mielziner (1828–1903); the historian Gotthard Deutsch (1859–1921), a disciple of Heinrich Graetz; the philologists and biblical scholars Max L. Margolis (1866–1932) and Moses Buttenwieser (1862–1939); and the student of medieval Jewish philosophy and Judaeo-Arabic literature, Henry Malter (ca. 1864–1925). Associated with the Seminary were, besides Jastrow and Kohut, such figures as the rabbinic scholar Bernard Drachman (1861–1945) and later the great polymath author of

The Legends of the Jews, Louis Ginzberg (1873–1953), and the eminent Solomon Schechter (1850–1915).

In the late nineteenth century a number of distinguished Jewish scholars of Judaica were also appointed to professorships in American universities. It was no longer absolutely necessary that one be a Christian in order to serve as a professor of Hebrew, as had generally been the case earlier in the United States. In 1886 Richard James Horatio Gottheil (1862–1936), the son of Rabbi Gustav Gottheil of New York's Temple Emanu-El, was appointed to a chair in Semitics at Columbia University, and a year later Cyrus Adler, (born in Van Buren, Arkansas!) was invited to membership in the Semitics faculty of Johns Hopkins University, where he was joined in 1902 by William Rosenau (1865–1943). We have already noted that Emil G. Hirsch was appointed to the faculty of the University of Chicago by its first president, William Rainey Harper. In 1892, the year that Hirsch began teaching rabbinic literature and Jewish philosophy at Chicago, Morris Jastrow, Jr., was called to teach Semitic languages at the University of Pennsylvania. Only in the most sophisticated and research-oriented American universities could Jewish professors of Judaica be found in the late nineteenth century, but the groundwork had been laid for what was to become a far more substantial program of university-sponsored research and teaching in Jewish Studies in the twentieth century.

As the nineteenth century was drawing to its close, a group of American-Jewish scholars came together to plan the production and publication of a great Jewish encyclopedia in English that would give "in systematized, comprehensive, and yet succinct form, a full and accurate account of the history and literature, the social and intellectual life, of the Jewish people—of their ethical and religious views, their customs, rites and traditions in all ages and in all lands," and that would "cast light upon the successive phases of Judaism, furnish precise information concerning the activities of the Jews in all branches of human endeavor, register their influence upon the manifold development of human intelligence, and describe their mutual relations to surrounding creeds and peoples." [14]

The idea of such an encyclopedia was not new. Moritz Steinschneider, the "Nestor of Jewish bibliography," had proposed such a work in Germany as early as 1844 in the pages of the *Literaturblatt des Orients*, but nothing came of it, aside from the prospectus and a preliminary listing of subjects to be included. The German scholars Ludwig Phillipson in 1869 and Heinrich Graetz in 1887 had also suggested the need for such an encyclopedia, but their suggestions bore no fruit. Only after Isidore Singer (1859–1939) had devoted ten years of unflagging labor in promoting the enterprise and, following arduous efforts at enlisting the interest and cooperation of European Jewish scholars, had arrived at the conclusion that only in America could it succeed, was the *Jewish Encyclopedia* born.

The preliminary work was done in the winter of 1898–1899 in New York by a triumvirate consisting of Singer, Richard Gottheil, and Kaufmann Kohler. These were soon joined by Cyrus Adler, Gotthard Deutsch, Marcus Jastrow, Morris Jastrow, Louis Ginzberg, Frederick de Sola Mendes, the great Christian Hebraist and rabbinic scholar George Foote Moore, the Christian scholar of Hellenistic literature Crawford H. Toy, and the Anglo-Jewish historian Joseph Jacobs of London. All these men, with the exception of Professor Moore, who was compelled to withdraw after assuming the responsibility of serving as president of Andover Theological Seminary, served as members of the editorial board and editors of the major departments of the *Encyclopedia* under the managing editorship of Isidore Singer.

The American board of consulting editors included Bernard Drachman, Bernhard Felsenthal, Gustav Gottheil, Emil G. Hirsch, Henry Pereira Mendes, Moses Mielziner, George Foote Moore, and David Philipson. Among the members of the foreign board of consulting editors were Israel Abrahams, Senior Tutor at Jews' College in London; Wilhelm Bacher, Professor at the Jewish Theological Seminary of Budapest; Hartwig Derenbourg, Professor of Literary Arabic at the Special School of Oriental Languages in Paris; S. M. Dubnow of Odessa; Ignaz Goldziher, Professor of Biblical Philology at the University of Budapest; Moritz Güdemann, Chief Rabbi of Vienna; Baron David Günzburg of St. Petersburg; Abraham Elijah Harkavy, Chief of the Hebrew Department of the Imperial Public Library in St. Petersburg; Zadoc Kahn, Chief Rabbi of France; Moritz Lazarus, Professor Emeritus of Psychology at the University of Berlin; Anatole Leroy-Beaulieu, Professor at the Free School of Political Science in Paris; S. H. Margulies, Chief Rabbi of Florence and Principal of its Jewish Theological Seminary; Abbé Pietro Perreau, formerly Librarian of the Reale Biblioteca Palatina in Parma; Solomon Schechter, Professor of Hebrew at University College in London and Reader in Rabbinics at the University of Cambridge; Ludwig Stein, Professor of Philosophy at the University of Bern; Hermann L. Strack, Professor of Old Testament Exegesis and Semitic Languages at the University of Berlin; and Charles Taylor, Master of St. John's College in Cambridge.

In 1901 the first of the twelve volumes of the *Jewish Encyclopedia*, a monumental work of scholarship which was not rendered altogether obsolete even by the publication of the new *Encyclopedia Judaica* in Jerusalem in 1972, appeared in New York.

At the turn of the century American Jewry stood at the threshold of great promise, both religiously and culturally. Would the promise be fulfilled? Time would tell.

CHAPTER

ৼXIIIৡ

The Recrudescence of Anti-Semitism and the Rise of Zionism

A LARGE PART of the history of the western and central European Jew in the nineteenth century, we have noted, revolves around his struggle to secure the political emancipation and civic equality first promised him in the wake of the French Revolution. By the 1870s victory in this struggle had apparently been achieved; for the Jews of England, France, Italy, Switzerland, Germany, and Austria full rights of citizenship had been confirmed by governmental action. A mood of buoyant optimism, reflected perhaps most clearly in the pronouncements of the leading theologians and philosophers of Reform Judaism, dominated the Jewries of these countries. Many were deeply persuaded that the time would not be long in coming when all the ancient prejudices from which Jews had suffered so long and grievously would be dissipated by the rays of growing enlightenment and knowledge. Even the czarist empire, it was believed by more than a few Jews both inside and outside of Russia, would eventually be compelled, under the influence of the example set by the rest of

[319]

Europe, to terminate its persecution and repression of its Jewish inhabitants. In the very midst of their euphoria, however, the Jews of both the progressive, constitutional states of western and central Europe and of the autocracy of the East were struck by a new wave of intense anti-Jewish sentiment and activity. Although the truth could hardly have been recognized at the time, this was only a prelude to the Holocaust that was to end with the virtual destruction of the largest centers of European Jewry some seventy years later.

Many factors were involved in this recrudescence of anti-Semitism. Obviously major was the fact that the ghost of the standard medieval caricature of the Jew as tormentor and killer of Christ, malevolent enemy of mankind, blood-sucking moneylender, and cunning exploiter of guileless Christians, had never really been laid to rest. It survived subliminally in the consciousness of many Europeans, not only among the unlettered masses but in the circles of the cultured and privileged. Religious myths apparently die hard; it is noteworthy that as late as the 1960s the Second Vatican Council of the Roman Catholic Church found it necessary solemnly (and, unfortunately, rather half-heartedly) to issue an admonition to the faithful against portraying the Jews as deicides. Perhaps a more significant factor in the renewal of anti-Semitism in the 1870s was the wave of intense nationalism that washed over Europe in this era. To the ardent nationalist the Jew—no matter how assimilated linguistically, culturally, and even religiously—was an "outsider," a foreign element in the state whose acculturation could only be superficial and who would forever remain troublesomely "different" and a threat to the cause of national unity. In addition, economic factors, such as the stock market collapse and financial panic of 1873 in Germany and the long depression that followed, created an environment in which the Jew became a convenient scapegoat on whose head the blame for all the ills of the nation could be placed.

In 1879, the last year of the depression in Germany, Wilhelm Marr, a petty journalist who had converted from Judaism to Christianity, published a pamphlet entitled *Der Sieg des Judentums über das Germantum* (*The Triumph of Judaism over Germanism*). His thesis was that the Jews, materialists by their very nature, had organized a complex system of industry and finance in order to gain control over the peoples of Europe and eventually obtain world hegemony; Semitism was now on the verge of achieving total victory over idealistic Germanism and would succeed in its nefarious plot unless Germans awoke to their mortal peril and concentrated all their energies in struggling against it. The same year Marr organized a society called The Anti-Semitic League whose avowed purpose was to "save" the fatherland from Judaization. A year before, Adolf Stöcker, son of a jail warden who eventually became Protestant chaplain at the imperial court and was elected to the Reichstag a number of times in the 1880s, founded the Christian Socialist Workers Party, which, in addition to proposing a program of social reform (including trade corporations, a government insurance system, and other welfare measures), made the curbing of Jewish "domination" in German economic, political, and social life a central plank in its platform. The demagogical Stöcker was the first to raise the slogan *Deutschland, erwache!* (Germany, awake!), which was to be resurrected, together with his spurious socialism, half a century later by Hitler's Nazis. According to Stöcker, the two chief enemies of the middle class and workers—big business and Marxist socialism—are both Jewish conspiracies. "The Jews," he thundered, "are at one and the same time the pace-setters of capitalism and of revolutionary socialism, thus working from two sides to destroy the present political and social order." [1]

The agitation against the Jews of Germany carried on by Wilhelm Marr, Adolf Stöcker, and others of their ilk intensified the anti-Semitic attitudes already widespread among all classes in Germany. In 1881 a petition signed by two hundred and fifty-five thousand persons, denouncing Jewish influence in Germany and calling for the disenfranchisement of its Jews and prohibition of further Jewish immigration into the country, was submitted to the German chancellor Bismarck. "The blending of the Semitic with the German element of our population," the petition declared, "has proved a failure. We are now faced with a loss of our national superiority through the ascendency of Judaism, the steadily increasing influence of which springs from racial characteristics which the German nation cannot and must not tolerate unless it wishes to destroy itself." "The Jewish race," the document concluded, "is a menace not only to the economic well-being of the German people but to their culture and religion." [2]

Noteworthy in this petition are the clear references to the Jewish race and racial characteristics. It was the allegedly scientifically proved doctrine of racial differences, particularly the notion that the Jews represent a stock that is physically and morally inferior and threatens to corrupt the superior Aryan race, whose noblest representatives are the Germans, that was one of the most powerful elements in the new anti-Semitism that emerged in Europe in the second half of the nineteenth century, and that culminated in Hitler's death camps and gas chambers.

Perhaps the major source of the new racial anti-Semitism was a book published in 1853–1855 by the French writer and diplomat Comte Joseph Arthur de Gobineau, entitled *Essai sur l'inégalité des races humaines* (*An Essay on the Inequality of the Human Races;* English trans., 1915). The author contrasted the blond, tall, idealistic, creative, and civilizing Aryan with the dark, short, materialistic, selfish, and parasitical Semite, who is himself incapable of creating anything novel or worthwhile and has merely exploited the high civilization forged by the Aryans. Gobineau's racist ideas were introduced to Germany by his friend and admirer, the composer Richard Wagner, in the 1870s. Wagner himself frequently indulged in anti-Semitic slurs and admonished his "noble" Teutonic countrymen that they were in danger of being corrupted and degraded by the mean-spirited and parasitical Jews. Both Gobineau's and Wagner's racism was carried further by the composer's son-in-law and the son of a British admiral, Houston Stewart Chamberlain, whose *Die Grundlagen des Neunzenjahrhunderts* (*The Foundations of the Nineteenth Century;* English trans., 1910), which appeared in Germany in 1899 and quickly obtained enormous acclaim and circulation, is probably the most blatantly racist work produced before the era of the Nazis. The Jews, Chamberlain charged in his work, which was so admired by Kaiser Wilhelm II that he read it aloud to his children, are "the product of an incestuous crime against nature," and have never been anything more than middlemen and imitators, sponging on the glories of the civilization created by the Aryans. The great figures of the Old and New Testaments—King David, Isaiah, Jeremiah, Jesus, the apostle Paul—whose creative genius was universally acknowledged, presented something of a problem to Chamberlain; he disposed of it simply by asserting that these men were not Semites at all but what he termed "Aryan Amorites."

It must be noted that the anti-Semitism of late nineteenth-century Germany was not fostered merely by yellow journalists, self-seeking clerical politicians, megalomaniacal composers, and pseudoscientific anthropologists such as Wilhelm Marr, Adolf Stöcker, Richard Wagner, and Houston Chamberlain, but by some very eminent figures in German scholarship and intellectual life. Heinrich von Treitschke (1834–1896), who taught at the University of Berlin after 1874 and was undoubtedly one of the foremost German historians of the century, was a notorious Jew-baiter. When signatures were being collected for the anti-Semitic petition of 1881, Treitschke published his *Ein Wort über unser Judentum* (*A Word on Our Jewry*), three essays in which he "proved" that anti-Semitism was "a natural reaction of the German national feeling [*des germanischen Volksgefühles*] against a foreign element which has usurped too large a place in our life." [3] With smug hypocrisy and self-righteousness he wrote: "In the circles of highly educated Germans, who would indignantly protest against any thought of religious or nationalist intolerance, a single cry is heard, 'The Jews are our misfortune.' " [4]

Treitschke was joined by many lesser lights in the German academic world in his espousal of anti-Semitism. But Jews also had a few defenders in the universities. The famous historian Theodor Mommsen (1817–1903), author of the classical *History of Rome*, who was Treitschke's colleague on the faculty of the University of Berlin, courageously denounced anti-Semitism and called his fellow historian to account for what he regarded as his intellectual and moral irresponsibility. But observing the rising fury of the mob against the Jews, Mommsen later became deeply pessimistic about the effectiveness of any rational antidote. "Whatever I or anybody else could say," he wrote, "are in the last analysis reasons, logical and ethical arguments, to which no anti-Semite will listen. They listen only to their own hatred and to the meanest instincts. There is no protection against the mob, be it the mob of the streets or of the parlors. . . . One must patiently wait until the poison has consumed itself and lost its virulence." [5] The virulence did subside for a time in Germany in the first decades of the twentieth century, but it remained latent and erupted with murderous force in the Third Reich.

The resurgence of anti-Semitism in late nineteenth-century Europe was by no means restricted to Germany. France, the first European nation to emancipate its Jews, was also strongly infected with anti-Jewish sentiment. In 1886 a journalist named Eduoard Drumont published a bitterly anti-Semitic tract entitled *La France Juive* (*Jewish France*), accusing the Jews of a conspiracy to gain control of the country. Drumont's book enjoyed immense popularity. The hatred of Jews which it fostered was intensified shortly afterward by the bankruptcy of the French Panama Canal Company, during the formation of which a number of its promoters, including some Jews, had been involved in bribing members of the government, and the collapse of which ruined thousands of its stockholders. The anti-Semitism thereby engendered was diligently cultivated by the Royalist party and press, which sought the overthrow of the Third Republic and restoration of the monarchy and found its adherents and sympathizers chiefly among the nobility, the officer corps, and the

Catholic clergy. Republicanism, the Royalists argued endlessly and raucously, was controlled by corrupt Jewish financiers who manipulated it for their own nefarious purposes.

Anti-Semitism in France reached a new peak in 1894 when Captain Alfred Dreyfus, a nominally Jewish officer attached to the French General Staff, was accused of selling military secrets to the German government. The whole matter was from the beginning part of a campaign against the Republic instigated by the army. For months the *affaire Dreyfus* was the chief topic of discussion in the press, in the streets, and in the Chamber of Deputies, arousing violent anti-Jewish feeling. On January 5, 1895, quietly proclaiming his innocence, Alfred Dreyfus, having been convicted by a military court, was publicly degraded on a parade ground in Paris and sentenced to life imprisonment on Devils Island. Even when it was discovered that the document upon which his conviction hinged was a forgery committed by another French officer, nothing was done to rectify the gross injustice. After the famous novelist Emile Zola took up the captain's cause in his eloquent *J'accuse* (*I Accuse*), and was joined in his demand for a new trial by such eminent figures as Anatole France and Georges Clemenceau, France was divided into pro- and anti-Dreyfus factions. Colonel Henri, an officer of the General Staff, perpetrated further forgeries to maintain Dreyfus' guilt and committed suicide when his treachery was disclosed. Only in 1899 was Dreyfus returned to France for retrial. Even then the Council of War sitting at Rennes reaffirmed his conviction, but the verdict was so manifestly unjust that the president of the Republic pardoned him and Dreyfus was later restored to his rank in the French army.

The anti-Semitism of Germany and France, while real and virulent enough, did not lead to widespread rioting against the Jews or any serious attempt on the part of the government to curb their civil rights. This, however, was not the case with the anti-Semitism that flared up with unprecedented violence in czarist Russia in 1881. On March 13 of that year Emperor Alexander II, who had been about to grant a limited constitution to his disaffected subjects, was assassinated by a revolutionary terrorist. In this charged atmosphere the advocates of reaction and autocracy gained complete control and within a matter of weeks the Jews of Russia felt the full brunt of their fury. On April 27 a riot directed against the Jews broke out in Elisavetgrad on the hoary pretext of the blood libel. For two days the mob raged without the slightest intervention on the part of the Russian officials or the soldiery in the garrison. Many persons were killed; dozens of women were raped; five hundred houses, a hundred shops, and several synagogues were destroyed. By the autumn of 1881 the outrages perpetrated in Elisavetgrad had been repeated in scores of other cities and towns in southern Russia, with especially large-scale rapine in Kiev and Odessa. In December another series of riots began in Warsaw, continuing until the following summer.

Although it was not definitely established that the pogroms, as they came to be called, had actually been instigated and organized by the government, it was obvious that the government did nothing to prevent them, or to bring them under control, or to punish the perpetrators of atrocities. The attitude of the czarist regime toward its Jewish subjects was made clear by Konstantin Pobiedonostzev, Chief Procurator of the Holy Synod of the Russian Orthodox Church from 1880 to 1905, principal adviser to Czar Alexander III, and for a time the most powerful man in Russia, who is reported to have said that the solution to the Jewish problem of the empire lay simply in converting one-third of its Jews, bringing about the emigration of another third, and killing the rest. The pogroms of 1881–1882 evoked no government measures against the rioters who had killed, raped, burned, and looted, but instead a new policy of repression against their victims. In May 1882 the notorious "May Laws," whereby Jews were barred from residence in all villages and rural areas even in the Pale of Settlement, outside of Poland, were decreed. The pretext for the decrees was that Jewish liquor dealers, tavern-keepers, and moneylenders were demoralizing the Russian peasantry. Mass meetings of protest against the pogroms and the May Laws, which deprived untold numbers of Jews of their living and reduced them to destitution, were held in London, Paris, and New York, and a number of Western governments protested through their embassies in St. Petersburg. The czarist government, however, remained unmoved, with minor exceptions, from its anti-Jewish policy until the downfall of the Romanovs in 1917. Contemplating the catastrophes of 1881 and 1882, hundreds of thousands of Jews in Russia concluded that their only salvation lay in flight, and the great westward migration, particularly to America, began. Within a few decades the world Jewish population was to be massively redistributed.

❦

It was the reemergence and maintenance of a barbaric policy toward the Jews in the czarist empire and the resurfacing of anti-Semitism in the lands of central and western Europe at the end of the nineteenth century that provided the immediate impetus for the launching of an organized Zionist movement, dedicated to the establishment of a Jewish homeland in Palestine. This movement, which was to be of the profoundest historical significance in the life of the Jewish people, had, of course, much more ancient and deeper roots.

Zionism was rooted, first of all, in an intense religious bond to the land of Palestine which had been fostered for centuries, ever since the destruction of the Second Jewish Commonwealth in 70 C.E. The hope for eventual restoration of Jewish national life in the land of the patriarchs was never abandoned. It was kept alive in the liturgy; every morning and evening, in his daily prayers, the faithful Jew repeated the ancient formula: "And to Jerusalem, Thy holy city, return in mercy . . . rebuild it speedily in our days." It was also maintained through numerous Jewish customs and ceremonies. Soon after the destruction of the Temple in Jerusalem it became customary for preachers in the synagogue to end their addresses with a petition for the coming of the redeemer and redemption, understood as restoration to Palestine. Other practices, such as the shattering of a glass by the groom at the marriage ceremony and leaving a corner of a new home unplastered and unpainted, were interpreted as symbols commemorating the destruction of the Temple and the Jewish state. The Passover *seder* was concluded with a special formula: "Next year in Jerusalem." To die and be buried in the sacred soil of Palestine was the fervent hope of many a pious Jew, and more than a few over the ages undertook the arduous journey to the Holy Land to spend their last years there and mingle its dust with their own. For centuries Jews from every corner of the Diaspora who could not themselves go to the Holy Land sent their contributions for the maintenance of Torah scholars and schools there. As we have noted, there were also a number of explosive messianic or pseudomessianic movements, most importantly the Shabbetai Tzevi movement of the seventeenth century, whose goal was restoration of a Jewish state in Palestine. When modern political Zionism arose at the end of the nineteenth century, it could draw on a deep reservoir of authentic sentiment and ardent attachment to Palestine that had been inculcated for centuries among Jews by religious belief and practice.

Even though hope for an ultimate ingathering of the exiles was one of the most deeply cherished elements in Judaism throughout the centuries of dispersion, nonmessianic proposals to the effect that Jews themselves actually return as a nation to Palestine and begin colonizing it were not seriously put forth, with minor exceptions (such as Joseph Nasi's project for Tiberias in the sixteenth century), until the middle of the nineteenth century. Undoubtedly the major factor in the development of a secular nationalist movement revolving around Palestine among the Jews at that time was the prevalent and intensive nationalist spirit of Europe. Everywhere on the continent ethnic groups with a distinctive cultural and linguistic identity were demanding recognition as sovereign nations and the right to self-determination. Among the groups which struggled for national independence in this era were the Greeks, the Serbians, the Rumanians, and the Bulgars. Furthermore, lands such as Germany and Italy, which had a common language and culture but for centuries had been divided into dozens of rival principalities and states, were now achieving national unity. The resurgence of nationalist feeling throughout Europe between the Congress of Vienna and the Congress of Berlin, and the example of successful struggle on the part of formerly subject and disunited ethnic groups to obtain national independence, unquestionably encouraged the emergent nationalist sentiment in certain segments of European Jewry.

One of the earliest and intellectually most significant advocates of Jewish national restoration was Moses Hess (1812–1875), the German-Jewish thinker who may properly be regarded as the father of Zionist socialism. Born in Bonn, Hess was given a standard religious education by his orthodox grandfather. Later, however, he abandoned most of his Jewish associations, married a Christian woman (feeling personally responsible for the corrupt social system that forced women into prostitution, Hess chose for his wife a "lady of the night"; the marriage was highly successful), and became one of the leading spirits of the nascent German Socialist movement. Hess exerted a certain influence on the youthful Karl Marx and Friedrich Engels, though both later attacked him for his romantic "ethical" version of socialism and his rejection of the philosophy of dialectical materialism. In his youth Hess believed that the Jews had already fulfilled their historic mission and that they should now assimilate and invest all their energies in building an international socialist order in which all specifically Jewish problems would automatically disappear. As far as his personal life was concerned, he regarded himself as fully German in every sense.

Hess's own experiences of anti-Semitism and his historical and anthropological studies eventually led him to the conviction that the national independence of oppressed peoples is an essential precondition for social progress. His sense of identity as a Jew was reawakened, and in 1862 he published his classic *Rom und Jerusalem* (*Rome and Jerusalem*). In the very first letter of this work he wrote:

> After an estrangement of twenty years, I am back with my people. I have come to be one of them again, to participate in the celebration of the holy days, to share the memories and hopes of the nation, to take part in the spiritual and intellectual warfare going on within the House of Israel, on the one hand, and between our people and the surrounding civilized nations, on the other. For though the Jews have lived among the nations for almost two thousand years, they cannot, after all, become a mere part of the organic whole. A thought which I believed to be forever buried in my heart has been revived in me anew. It is the thought of my nationality, which is inseparably connected with the ancestral heritage and the memories of the Holy Land, the Eternal City, the birthplace of the belief in the divine unity of life, as well as the hope in the future brotherhood of men.[6]

Moved by the success of the Italian Risorgimento under the leadership of Mazzini, Garibaldi, and Cavour, Hess believed that the Jewish people might experience a similar national renaissance and liberation. The coming world order would be a concert of various national cultures, each devoted to promotion of its unique ethical ideals. The Jewish religion, Hess maintained, is the best instrument for preserving Jewish nationality and must therefore not be disturbed (he criticized the reformers of his day severely) until a Jewish state is reestablished in Palestine and a new Sanhedrin can revise Jewish law and adapt it to the requirements of the times.

Moses Hess's *Rome and Jerusalem* was received with indifference by almost all of the few Jews of his day who read it. It was especially ridiculed by the reformers, to whom the whole idea of Jewish nationalism appeared regressive and unnecessary. Abraham Geiger disposed of Hess as "an alienated Jew gone bankrupt on socialism and similar swindles." Only with the birth of political Zionism was his work resurrected and appreciated. In his diary entry of May 2, 1901, Theodor Herzl wrote: "The nineteen hours of this round trip were whiled away for me by Hess with his *Rome and Jerusalem*, which I had first started to read in 1898 in Jerusalem but had never been able to finish properly in the pressure and rush of these years. Now I was enraptured and uplifted by him. What an exalted, noble spirit! Everything that we have tried is already in his book. The only bothersome thing is his Hegelian terminology. . . . Since Spinoza, Jewry has brought forth no greater spirit than this forgotten Moses

Hess." [7] Modern Israel has recognized its indebtedness to this pioneering theoretician of Zionism; in 1961 Hess's remains were transferred to Israel from the Jewish cemetery near Cologne where he had been buried in 1875.

Interestingly enough, in the very year that Hess's *Rome and Jerusalem* appeared, another work was published in Hebrew calling for the rebuilding of Palestine. This was Tzevi Hirsch Kalischer's *Derishat Tziyyon (Seeking Zion)*. Kalischer (1795–1874) was an orthodox rabbi who served the community of Thorn for forty years. Observing the sufferings of the Jews of eastern Europe, as well as the struggle of the Poles against Russia for reestablishment of Polish independence, Kalischer advocated the colonization of Palestine as a solution to the problem of Jewish misery. Although unalterably opposed to the reformers and staunchly committed to traditional Jewish faith and practice, including belief in the coming of the Messiah, he urged his fellow Jews to hasten the messianic consummation through their own efforts. He wrote:

> The redemption of Israel for which we long is not to be imagined as a sudden miracle. The Almighty, blessed be His Name, will not suddenly descend from on high and command His people to go forth. He will not send the Messiah from heaven in a twinkling of an eye, to sound the great trumpet for the scattered of Israel and gather them into Jerusalem. He will not surround the Holy City with a wall of fire or cause the Holy Temple to descend from the heavens. The bliss and the miracles that were promised by His servants, the prophets, will certainly come to pass—everything will be fulfilled—but we will not run in terror and flight, for the redemption of Israel will come by slow degrees and rays of deliverance will shine forth gradually. . . . The redemption will begin by awakening support among the philanthropists and by gaining the consent of the nations to the gathering of some of the scattered of Israel into the Holy Land. [8]

Kalischer rebuked the Jews of his day for their indolence and contrasted their passivity with the heroic activism of other peoples:

> Why do the people of Italy and of other countries sacrifice their lives for the land of their fathers, while we, like men bereft of strength and courage, do nothing? Are we inferior to all other peoples, who have no regard for life and fortune as compared with love of their land and nation? Let us take to heart the example of the Italians, Poles, and Hungarians, who laid down their lives and possessions in the struggle for national independence, while we, the children of Israel, who have the most glorious and holiest of lands

as our inheritance, are spiritless and silent. We should be ashamed of ourselves! All the other peoples have striven only for the sake of their own national honor; how much more should we exert ourselves, for our duty is to
labor not only for the glory of our ancestors but for the glory of God who
chose Zion! [9]

Rabbi Kalischer was not merely a theoretical but a highly practical
Zionist. He proposed the establishment of farming settlements in
Palestine and the purchase of land for colonization. It was chiefly as
a result of his tireless badgering that the Alliance Israelite Universelle, the organization established by French Jewry in 1860 for the
protection of Jewish rights throughout the world, founded the first
Palestinian agricultural colony, Mikveh Yisrael, and an agricultural
school near Jaffa in 1870. Independently wealthy, Kalischer after
1860 traveled throughout Europe to organize Palestinian colonization
societies, providing the foundations for the movement that later
came to be known as *Hovevei Tziyyon* (*Lovers of Zion*).

When Moses Hess and Tzevi Hirsch Kalischer wrote their works
in the early 1860s the time was not yet ripe for widespread acceptance of their ideas. The resurgence of anti-Semitism in France and
Germany in the 1870s and 1880s and the pogroms of Russia in
1881–1882, however, radically changed the climate of opinion. Many
Jews, especially in eastern Europe, came to regard Zionism as the
only practical answer to the problem of Jew-hatred. We have observed that the foremost representatives of Haskalah were moving
toward a Zionist position, that Moses Lilienblum, under the impact
of the pogroms, became a fervent preacher of Zionism, and that both
before and after the pogroms Peretz Smolenskin eloquently advocated Jewish nationalism. In the few years of his life that remained
following the pogroms and the May Laws, Smolenskin abandoned
his abstract theorizing about the Jews as a "spiritual nation" and called
for wholesale removal of east European Jewry to Palestine.

Perhaps historically more important than either Lilienblum or
Smolenskin as an advocate of Zionism in the wake of the Russian
atrocities was Leo Pinsker (1821–1891). Educated as a physician at
the University of Moscow, Pinsker practiced medicine in Odessa for
many years, becoming one of the leading doctors in the city and
receiving a decoration from Czar Nicholas I for his services during
the Crimean War. Throughout his life Pinsker had been an ardent

proponent of Russification and took a prominent part in the activities of the Society for the Dissemination of Culture Among the Jews of Russia after its establishment in 1863. The pogroms of 1881 were a shattering blow to his assimilationist stance. The fact that it was not only the ignorant peasantry who attacked the Jews, but respected journalists, academicians, and government officials as well, persuaded him that the hopes of the Jews of Russia for emancipation through enlightenment and Russification were completely illusory. "New remedies, new ways" were now essential. Shocked by the brutalities of the pogroms, Pinsker traveled to the capitals of central and western Europe to discuss with Jewish leaders his new conviction that the majority of the Jewish people must be resettled in a national home of their own. He found few who shared his views. Adolph Jellinek, the distinguished scholar and chief rabbi of Vienna, who had been a friend of his father's, suggested to him when they met in the spring of 1882 that he was emotionally disturbed and should seek medical attention. The heads of the Alliance Israelite in Paris spurned his proposals. One of the few persons who responded positively was Arthur Cohen, a member of the English parliament and chairman of the Board of Deputies of British Jews in London.

Returning to Russia, Pinsker in 1882 published anonymously in German a pamphlet entitled *Autoemanzipation: Mahnruf an seine Stammesgenossen von einem russischen Juden (Self-Emancipation: An Admonition to His Kin by a Russian Jew)*, calling upon the Jews to abandon hope for emancipation by the governments of the nations among whom they lived and to summon up their own forces and liberate themselves. The heart of the Jewish problem, he maintained, is that in every nation the Jews are a distinct ethnic group which cannot be assimilated. They have become a ghostlike people and it is psychologically understandable that they inspire the same dread and revulsion that ghosts normally evoke. The fear of the Jews, Pinsker urged, will not be dissipated, either in the near or distant future, for Judeophobia is a hereditary psychic disease which has been transmitted for two millennia and is essentially incurable.

In his passionately written tract, which reflects his anguish over the events that had recently destroyed his lifelong convictions and his intense concern for the welfare of his people, Pinsker also notes the corrupting effects of anti-Semitism on the Jews themselves:

When we are ill-used, robbed, plundered and dishonored, we dare not defend ourselves, and, worse still, we take it almost as a matter of course. When our face is slapped, we soothe our burning cheek with cold water;

and when a bloody wound is inflicted, we apply a bandage. When we are turned out of the house which we ourselves built, we beg humbly for mercy, and when we fail to reach the heart of our oppressor, we move on in search of another exile. . . . If no notice is taken of our descent and we are treated like others born in the country, we express our gratitude by actually turning renegades. For the sake of the comfortable position we are granted, for the fleshpots which we may enjoy in peace, we persuade ourselves and others that we are no longer Jews, but full blooded citizens. Idle delusion! [10]

Pinsker was not solicitous over wounding the tender feelings of his fellow Jews, but frankly called attention to the absurdity of the Jewish position in the world.

Indeed, what a pitiful figure we cut! We are not counted among the nations, neither have we a voice in their councils, even when the affairs concern us. Our fatherland—the other man's country; our unity—dispersion; our solidarity—the battle against us; our weapon—humility; our defense —flight; our individuality—adaptability; our future—the next day. What a miserable role for a nation which descends from the Maccabees! [11]

With sober realism Pinsker noted the economic as well as the psychological foundations of anti-Semitism. He also ridiculed the pronouncements of the German reformers who regarded dispersion of the Jews throughout the world as a precondition for the fulfillment of their religious "mission." At the same time he scored the quietism of the orthodox who counseled passive acceptance of suffering and patient waiting for the Messiah, whom God will send in his own good time. The only meaningful solution is to transform the Jewish people into an independent nation living a normal life, like other peoples, on its own soil. It is wishful thinking to believe that the spread of enlightenment and the general advance of mankind will bring salvation to the Jews:

We must learn to recognize that as long as we lack a home of our own, such as the other nations have, we must resign forever the noble hope of becoming the equals of our fellowmen. We must recognize that before the great idea of human brotherhood will unite all the peoples of the earth, millenniums must elapse; and that meanwhile the people which is at home everywhere and nowhere must everywhere be regarded as alien. The time has come for a sober and dispassionate realization of our true position.[12]

When he wrote his *Self-Emancipation* Pinsker was still undecided as to whether Palestine or some territory in America should be the locale of the Jewish homeland. But he was soon persuaded by Moses Lilienblum and others to give his support to the movement for a return to Palestine that was already in existence. In fact, it was only among the recently organized Ḥovevei Tziyyon or Ḥibbat Tziyyon groups, whose aim was the establishment of agricultural colonies in Palestine, that Pinsker's analysis of the situation of the Jewish people found warm acceptance. Most of the leaders of western and central European Jewry rejected his views as overly pessimistic; anti-Semitism, they insisted, was not a permanent but a temporary condition, an aberration that would soon disappear. As for the orthodox Jews of eastern Europe, they could not follow anyone so clearly estranged from traditional Jewish faith as Pinsker was.

The Ḥovevei Tziyyon societies, whose members were electrified by Pinsker's pamphlet, had begun to emerge shortly after the pogroms of 1881 in Russia, where they had to meet in secret since the czarist regime had declared Zionist activity illegal. From Russia they spread to Rumania as well as to Austria, Germany, and Switzerland, where a considerable number of Russian-Jewish students who could not attend universities in their own country because of the strict Jewish quota had gone to seek higher education. Members of the societies, recruited mainly from university students and intellectuals, undertook fund-raising activities, organized courses for the study of Hebrew, and prepared a few hardy souls for emigration to Palestine. On November 6, 1884, an international convention of Ḥovevei Tziyyon societies, attended by members from Russia and abroad, was held in Kattowitz in Upper Silesia. It was the first significant proto-Zionist assemblage in modern Jewish history. The convention, which wished to attract the support of western Jews, did not proclaim as its goal the establishment of an independent Jewish state in Palestine but only the promotion of agriculture among Jews and the encouragement of Jewish farming settlements in Palestine. Pinsker consented to serve as chairman of the executive committee and continued, despite grave doubts about the effectiveness of the Ḥovevei Tziyyon movement, to work for it until his death.

Between the Russian pogroms of 1881–1882 and the first Zionist Congress convened by Theodor Herzl in 1897, over twenty thousand Jews, mainly from eastern Europe, actually migrated to Palestine. The vast majority of these members of the First Aliyah, as they came to be called, did not, however, settle on the soil but joined the approximately thirty thousand Jews already living in the country, many of them supported by *ḥalukah*, or charity, and residing mainly in the cities of Jerusalem, Jaffa, Haifa, and Hebron. Only small numbers, notably a group of students from the University of Kharkov, who formed a society known as Bilu (from the initial letters of their Hebrew motto "O House of Jacob, come, let us go"), actually made a heroic attempt to establish a cooperative agricultural colony in Palestine.

Most of the immigrants of the First Aliyah opened shops or became artisans in the cities. A few hundred settled on the land and established farming colonies such as those at Petah Tikvah, Rishon Le-Tziyyon, Zichron Yaakov, and Rosh Pinnah. These colonies, founded mainly by young idealists and theoreticians who had no practical agricultural experience, encountered virtually insuperable hardships in their first years and were saved from ruin only through the financial assistance of Baron Edmond de Rothschild of Paris, who granted them generous subsidies. While the pioneers of Bilu and the Hovevei Tziyyon societies fulfilled the historic and essential task of obtaining a foothold on the soil of Palestine, it was obvious that tiny settlements of the kind which they established would never create the Jewish state that Hess and Pinsker had envisioned. A new program and a powerful leader of great vision and imagination were demanded if the Zionist goal was to be achieved. That program and leadership appeared in the person of Theodor Herzl (1860–1904), the mesmeric figure who is properly regarded as the father of the Jewish state.

⚜

In the 1880s and 1890s, when the Hibbat Tziyyon colonies were being established in Palestine, Theodor Herzl still had only the slightest sense of identification with his people and was completely devoid of any conception of Jewish nationhood. He had been born in Budapest into a rather assimilated Jewish family, moved to Vienna with his parents at the age of eighteen, graduated with a doctorate in law from the university of that city, become renowned while still in his twenties as the author of clever feuilletons, philosophical stories, and dramas, and been appointed as the Paris correspondent of the Viennese *Neue Freie Presse*, the most influential newspaper in the Hapsburg Empire. Herzl served in the French capital from October 1891 to July 1895. The growing anti-Semitism that he observed in France disturbed him profoundly, and he at first entertained the idea that the plague might be removed by mass conversion of the Jewish youth and their joining the socialist movement. He soon realized, however, that this was an impossible solution. His attendance at the court-martial and subsequent public degradation of Captain Alfred Dreyfus, when the Parisian mob shouted "Death to the Jews!", persuaded him that the only answer to the Jewish problem was removal of the Jews from the countries in which they now lived and resettlement in a territory of their own. The Jews, he became convinced, were a people who must reestablish themselves as a nation on their own soil.

When Herzl reached this conclusion in 1895, he knew nothing of the writings of the great proponents of Jewish nationalism who had preceded him—Hess, Kalischer, Smolenskin, Lilienblum, and Pinsker; the idea of Jewish nationhood was something he discovered entirely on his own. The idea obsessed him and in a matter of weeks, writing with furious speed, he completed the first draft of his little book *Der Judenstaat (The Jewish State)*, published in February 1896 and translated that same year into Hebrew, English, French, Russian, and Rumanian.

The central theme of the book, which aroused considerable excitement and at once catapulted Herzl into a position of prominence in the Jewish world, is that the Jewish problem cannot be solved by assimilation, for two fundamental reasons: the inevitable anti-Semitism of the nations, and the Jews' own will to survive. Anti-Semitism is bound to become more malignant in view of the abnormal social and economic conditions of the Jews in their host countries. But these nations can solve their embarrassing Jewish problem by providing Jews with a territory either in Palestine or in Argentina where they could establish an independent state of their own. Herzl himself preferred Palestine. Mass migration and settlement would have to be preceded by an international political agreement securing the foundations of the state. The state would be established on a modern scientific and technological basis with a commitment to progressive social principles. To realize his plan Herzl proposed immediate organization of two bodies, a Society of Jews, which would be the official representative of the worldwide Jewish people, and a Jewish Company, which would raise from the great and smaller Jewish banking firms of Europe and America the large sums required for the settlement of hundreds of thousands of Jews in the national home and would supervise the actual work of settlement and construction.

Only after his plan was peremptorily rejected in personal interviews by Baron Maurice de Hirsch, the greatest Jewish philanthropist of the day, and Baron Edmond de Rothschild, whose approval might also have gained for it the general support of the Jewish leadership in the western world, did Herzl decide to organize the Jewish masses. With the encouragement of a few friends—notably Israel Zangwill, the Anglo-Jewish novelist, Max Nordau, the eminent Viennese physician, social psychologist, and writer, and David Wolffsohn, a businessman from Cologne—and cheered on by the wildly enthusiastic response of the crowds of Polish and Russian Jews who met him at railroad stations on a journey that he made through eastern Europe, he decided to issue a call for an international Zionist congress at which steps would be taken to implement his plans for establishment of the Jewish state.

Despite widespread and vehement opposition from the central and western European Jewish leaders, and even from within the ranks of the Hovevei Tziyyon societies, some two hundred delegates from almost every nation in which there was a significant Jewish community were called to order by Herzl in the Swiss city of Basel on August 29, 1897. In his address to the Congress, while acknowledging the value of the small-scale colonization efforts of the Hovevei Tziyyon, he insisted that what was now required was massive settlement, and the prerequisite for this was realization of the basic aim which he defined for the Zionist movement: "To create a publicly recognized, legally secured home for the Jewish people in Palestine." This became the central plank of the so-called Basel Platform adopted by the First Zionist Congress.

Herzl was enthusiastically elected president of the World Zionist Organization, established by the Basel Congress in its three-day meeting. Shortly afterward he began negotiations to organize the Zionist bank, the Jewish Colonial Trust, in London. At the close of the Congress Herzl wrote in his diary: "At Basel I founded the Jewish State. If I said this out loud today, I would be answered by universal laughter. Perhaps in five years, and certainly in fifty, everyone will know it." [13]

It is clear in retrospect that Herzl's great achievement was transforming Zionism from a relatively unorganized, small-scale colonization effort, with rather ill-defined goals, into an effective mass political movement, specifically directed toward obtaining for the Jewish people an internationally recognized homeland in Palestine and establishing the structures and institutions required to realize the goal. Within a short time after the Basel Congress, Zionist societies and federations were springing into existence in almost every nation of the world where there was a substantial Jewish community, and Jews by the thousands were formally joining the movement through an annual purchase of a shekel. The imagination of the masses, particularly in eastern Europe, was fired by the great vision Herzl had conceived and defined in the Basel Platform.

In the special undertaking to which Herzl directed most of his own massive energies in the few remaining years of his life after the First Zionist Congress—acquisition of a legal charter for the Jewish state from Sultan Abdul Hamid of Turkey—he had no success. Driven by the notion that the best means to this goal was personal diplomacy, Herzl obtained interviews with the leading figures of Europe—the sultan himself, the Pope, Kaiser Wilhelm II of Germany, high government officials such as German Chancellor Bernhard von Bülow and Russian Minister of the Interior Wenzel von Plehve, international bankers, and so on—but all to no avail. He was convinced at one point that if only he could have obtained several million pounds from the Rothschild family to help the financially troubled Turkish government pay off its insistent European creditors he would have received the charter from the sultan; his belief was probably naive and mistaken.

Realizing that his negotiations with the Turkish government were unproductive, Herzl turned to the British Foreign Office, which from the beginning had shown a lively interest in his proposals. The Colonial Secretary, Joseph Chamberlain, raised the possibility of establishing a Jewish commonwealth either on the island of Cyprus or in the Sinai Peninsula. When difficulties with these suggestions arose, Chamberlain in the summer of 1903 offered a territory in Uganda in British East Africa. Herzl, who had just toured the Russian Pale of Settlement where he had been greeted with a tumultuous reception by the Jewish masses and had seen at first hand the misery of the Jewish populace now streaming out of the country in larger numbers than ever before in the wake of the massacre at Kishinev, decided, in consultation with his friend and collaborator Max Nordau, to propose the Uganda project to the Sixth Zionist Congress which was scheduled to meet in Basel on August 23, 1903. Nordau, who submitted the plan at the opening session of the Congress, made it clear that Uganda was not a substitute for Palestine as the ultimate goal of the Zionist movement; it was merely a *Nachtasyl*, an asylum for the night, a temporary refuge until Palestine could be obtained. Herzl was astonished at the bitterness of the debate that ensued and the vehemence of the objections raised to the Uganda plan. When the vote on the resolution to explore the plan was taken, it was passed by a small margin because of Herzl's personal prestige and authority, but almost all the east European delegates left the hall in protest and gathered in another room, where many of them wept and sat on the floor as if in mourning for the death of Zionism. Herzl was compelled to swallow his pride and plead with the dissident delegates to return to the sessions. They finally agreed to do so, but their opposition to the Uganda scheme was implacable.

The aftermath of the Sixth or Uganda Congress, as it came to be known—meetings of rebellious Zionist leaders in Russia and Austria, intrigues, protests, demonstrations, an attempt on Max Nordau's life by a Russian Jew in Paris, and finally withdrawal of the Uganda offer by the British government—placed an unbearable strain on Herzl's already weakened heart. On July 3, 1904, Jews all over the world, particularly those who had joined his movement, were stunned by the news that their leader was dead at the age of forty-four. His coffin, draped in the Zionist flag, was carried back to Vienna and was followed by ten thousand mourners through the streets of the city to be buried next to the grave of his father, where Herzl had specified in his will that he wished his body "to stay until the Jewish people will carry my remains to Palestine." Forty-five years later, in August 1949, the remains were flown to the State of Israel and buried in an immense tomb on a ridge facing Jerusalem and renamed Mount Herzl. Herzl himself had written his own best epitaph when he noted in his diary entry of January 24, 1902: "Zionism was the Sabbath of my life. I believe my effectiveness as a leader may be attributed to the fact that I, who as a man and as a writer have had so many faults, made so many mistakes, and done so many foolish things, have been pure of heart and utterly selfless in the Zionist cause." [14]

Herzl's work and the institutions he created made Zionism the central topic of discussion in Jewish life everywhere in the world. Both the proponents and opponents of nationalism marshaled their arguments and sought to win adherents to their respective positions, and in the Zionist movement itself a number of factions, representing differing goals and emphases, emerged. The debates were conducted with great passion and energy for many years.

The most strenuous opposition to Zionism in its early period came from the extremes of the Jewish religious spectrum, i.e., the radical reformers and the unswervingly orthodox. The reformers, with some notable exceptions both in Europe and America, categorically rejected the idea of Jewish nationhood and insisted that the bond uniting Jews was religious only and that the ancient hopes for restoring the Jewish people to its own soil were no longer either valid or necessary. The Pittsburgh Platform of 1885, which summarized the majority position of the German-trained Reform leaders of America, asserted flatly: "We consider ourselves no longer a nation but a religious community and expect no return to Palestine." Despite the fact that a number of Reform rabbis in America, such as Stephen S. Wise, Gustave Gottheil, Bernhard Felsenthal, and Maximilian Heller supported Herzlian Zionism from its inception, both the rabbinic leadership and laity of the American Reform movement generally opposed Zionism until the 1930s, when the rise of Nazism and the sword hanging over European Jewry brought about a widespread change of attitude.

The ultraorthodox, on the other hand, opposed political Zionism because they regarded it as an impious and arrogant "forcing of the end." The return to Palestine and the ingathering of the exiles, they maintained, must be left to the pleasure of God, who will send His Messiah when He chooses. Furthermore, there was widespread distress among the orthodox that the foremost leaders of the Zionist movement—Herzl, Nordau, Zangwill, and others—were secularist Jews without any commitment to traditional religious belief or practice. A considerable number of orthodox Jews in eastern Europe and elsewhere, however, adopted the views that had been proclaimed by Tzevi Hirsch Kalischer forty years earlier and fervently espoused the cause of establishing a Jewish state. Their special concern was that the state be organized on a religious foundation and governed by the traditional *halachah*. These orthodox proponents of Zionism, under the leadership of the great Lithuanian Rabbi Isaac Jacob Reines (1839–1915), established their own organization, called Mizraḥi, in 1902 and enlisted the support of a growing number of adherents.

Against both Mizraḥi and the general political Zionism advocated by Herzl and his followers, some Jews insisted that the Jewish state must be built on socialist lines and with a determination to create a welfare society in which class distinctions would be erased. The chief theoreticians of socialist or Labor Zionism, as it came to be called, were Naḥman Syrkin (1867–1924) and Ber Borochov (1881–1917). Unlike most of the more orthodox and dogmatic Jewish

Marxists of eastern Europe, who opposed all nationalist activity on the part of the Jews and urged them to work for establishment of an international socialist order, Syrkin and Borochov maintained that socialism and Zionism are by no means inconsistent and that, indeed, there is a specifically Jewish problem which only the inextricable combination of the two ideologies could solve. Neither of these two exponents of Labor Zionism settled in Palestine, but their views greatly influenced many members of the so-called Second Aliyah, i.e., those who migrated to Palestine between the time of Herzl's death and the beginning of World War I, and of the Third and Fourth Aliyot, comprising the immigrants of the periods 1919 to 1923 and 1924 to 1928, respectively. A considerable number of these men and women came with the intention of founding cooperative agricultural communities in which they would themselves work the soil, without exploiting hired labor, whether Arab or Jewish.

Syrkin and Borochov provided economic theory and socialist ideology. The foremost spiritual guide of many of the *halutzim,* or pioneers, who actually settled on the land in the first three decades of the century, however, was Aaron David Gordon (1856–1922). This mystical dreamer and romantic, who laid the foundations of what came to be known as "the religion of labor" (though he himself did not use the term), spent the largest part of his life in his native Russia, employed for more than two decades in the financial management of Baron Joseph Günzburg's estate. Only at the age of forty-eight did he leave Russia to settle in Palestine alone, bringing his wife and daughter over a few years later.

Gordon was deeply influenced by Count Leo Tolstoy, the great Russian novelist who in his last years gave up his previous mode of life as an aristocratic nobleman, dressed in peasant garb, worked on the soil of his estate at Yasnaya Polanya, and wrote fervent tracts extolling the redemptive power of physical labor. On coming to Palestine, Gordon also insisted on earning his living by working as a manual laborer in the vineyards and orange groves of Petah Tikvah and Rishon Le-Tziyyon and in various villages of Galilee. Sharing the lot of many of the other migrant Jewish workers of his day—poverty, unemployment, malaria—he spent his leisure hours writing articles on the theme of self-renewal through contact with nature and tilling the soil. Within a few years Gordon became a well-known figure throughout Palestine and was recognized as the spiritual father of the *halutzim,* many of whom came from all parts of the land to visit him in his humble lodgings, talk with him about their hopes and frustrations, and confirm their faith in the value of the enterprise upon which they had embarked.

The last years of Gordon's life were spent at the *kevutzah*, or cooperative colony, of Degania near the Jordan River. Although he was both a Zionist and a socialist, he had no great faith in social ideologies or organizations as such, not even the *kevutzah*. Gordon opposed orthodox Marxism because he believed that its attempt to reorganize society without first effecting a fundamental change in man was misguided and would inevitably prove unsuccessful. The primary task, he insisted, is the spiritual regeneration of the individual. In Gordon's world-view, expressed in his numerous rhapsodic essays and articles, man and nature, or the cosmos as a whole, are an essential unity. Man feels intuitively—and this is the heart of the religious sentiment—that he is an organic part of creation and that his soul is purposefully related to a "hidden" part of the cosmos; the experience of the unity of the self and nature is the experience of holiness and of the "hidden mystery" of God. But modern man, with his exaltation of reason and scientific knowledge at the expense of intuition, and with his alienation from the life of nature, has lost his sense of cosmic unity and holiness. The relationship of technological and urbanized man to nature and other persons has become abstract, contractual, and utilitarian, and when such a relationship predominates the religious sentiment cannot survive. It is possible, however, to recover fullness of life, an awareness of the meaning and purpose of human existence. The best road to such a recovery, Gordon fervently maintained, is again to subordinate intellect to intuition and to return to nature "through the medium of physical labor."

Although Gordon's "religion of labor" concentrated on the self-renewal of the individual, it did not ignore the social matrix within which personal fulfillment must occur. Individual and social regeneration, Gordon held, are interdependent. But genuine social renewal is not possible for an accidentally constituted aggregate of persons but only for an organically interrelated community, i.e., a nation or people. "The nation," Gordon wrote, "may be likened to a funnel: at its wide receiving end endless existence is poured in, while through its concentrated, restricted end the funnel empties its contents into the soul of man. The nation, therefore, is the force which creates the spirit of man. It is the link which unites the life of the individual to the life of mankind and to the world at large." [15] A nation or people is, for Gordon, a natural community exemplifying a living cosmic relationship. The endeavor to transcend or by-pass the specific historic people into which one is born and to achieve directly the cosmopolitan status of "citizen of mankind" is an illusory undertaking and must end in reducing one's existence to an abstraction. In place of such cosmopolitanism Gordon proclaimed the ideal of *am-adam*, "people-humanity" or "people embodying humanity." This is the purpose and task he assigned to the Zionist movement; the Jews returning to Palestine are to create a nation "in the image of God," one which strives to exemplify the highest ideals of morality in all its social, political, and economic structures. "We must direct it [the nation] toward the development of the human spirit, toward the search for truth and righteousness in its relations with other peoples and with all mankind." [16] Jews whose life has been renewed by a return to nature and by work on the soil would, Gordon hoped, obtain the moral courage and strength to build a nation that would serve as a shining example to the world.

Gordon's preaching on the regenerative effect of toiling on the land, his ethical and universalist vision of the goal of Jewish nationhood, and his personal idealism were significant factors in inspiring the rapid growth of cooperative farming settlements on nationally owned land in Palestine in the period after World War I. The first such collective, or *kevutzah*, was Degania, established in 1909. In it, as in the *kevutzot* that were later formed and based on its model, all property, except for small personal items, was to be jointly owned by the members of the group, who came together voluntarily in the hope of establishing a completely communitarian and democratic society. Hired labor was to be strictly avoided, the members themselves performing all the work and sharing the various tasks. Meals were to be served in a community dining room and children raised in a common nursery, spending only a few hours a day with their parents. A similar type of collective village, the *kibbutz*, which was distinguished at first from the *kevutzah* by incorporating industry as well as agriculture into its economy, permitting wage labor, and removing restrictions on the size of the community, originated during the Third Aliyah. In recent years the distinction between the *kevutzah* and the *kibbutz* has become progressively less significant. Both types of community, though attracting only a small percentage of the country's population into their membership, have contributed importantly to shaping its ideology and social structure.

While Aaron David Gordon's mystical "religion of labor" and idealized nationalism made a profound impression on many *ḥalutzim*, another more rationalist and intellectualist vision of the Zionist task came to be highly influential in the thought and activity of both the Diaspora and the *Yishuv*, or Jewish community of Palestine. This was the Cultural Zionism of Asher Hirsch Ginsberg (1856–1927), better known by his pseudonym Aḥad Ha-Am (One of the People). In 1889, considerably before the appearance of Theodor Herzl and political Zionism, this Ukrainian Jew, who after receiving a traditional Jewish education went on to obtain a broad knowledge of western culture entirely through self-study and became one of the foremost Hebrew essayists of modern times, strongly criticized the Ḥovevei Tziyyon societies and their program in his first major article, entitled *Lo Zeh Ha-Derech (This Is Not the Way)*. Aḥad Ha-Am opposed the policy of fostering immediate settlement in Palestine and insisted that cultural and educational work must be given primary place on the Zionist agenda. He himself became the intellectual guide of the secret (because of the czarist police censorship) Zionist order Benei Mosheh, which dedicated itself to fulfilling the ideas expressed in *Lo Zeh Ha-Derech*.

After the rise of Herzl's political Zionism, Aḥad Ha-Am, who had visited Palestine twice in the early 1890s and surveyed the condition of the Jewish settlements, continued his polemic against a program which, as he believed, mistakenly assumed that the Jewish problem was essentially economic and political. The heart of the problem, he contended, is the weakness of national consciousness and sentiment among Jews. The assimilation that had proceeded apace among the Jews of Europe for a century and more in the wake of their political emancipation had produced this result, as well as a pathological condition which he defined as "living in slavery in the midst of freedom." Instead of finding fulfillment and meaning in the rich moral and spiritual heritage of their people, Jews, corrupted by assimilationist tendencies, had lost their self-respect and dignity and become obsessively concerned with their standing vis-à-vis the gentile world, and with winning its approval.

The "national will to existence," Aḥad Ha-Am urged, needed to be revitalized. The commitment of Jews to the specific values of Judaism—monotheism, the messianic vision, the ideal of absolute justice or "the quest for truth in action"—must be strengthened. A great revival of the Jewish spirit is an essential precondition for a genuine national renaissance.

As a Zionist, Aḥad Ha-Am did not envision the goal of the Zionist movement as an ultimate ingathering of all Jews to Palestine. The majority of the Jewish people, he believed, would continue to live in the lands of the Diaspora. The small Jewish state in Palestine, however, would serve as a "spiritual center" for world Jewry. Living in an independent and completely Jewish society, the Jews of Palestine would no longer suffer from the constraints of being a minority in a non-Jewish world, but would be able to build a model social order exemplifying moral and cultural values that would provide inspiration to all Jews of the world and guarantee their continued survival and unity as a people. It is interesting to note that after the issuance in 1917 of the Balfour Declaration, which he played a role in obtaining, Aḥad Ha-Am argued for a small Jewish state in Palestine, distinguished for moral and intellectual excellence rather than numerical strength, out of a concern for the national aspirations of the Palestinian Arabs as well as because of his "elitist" conception of the nature of the Zionist enterprise.

While by no means an orthodox believer, Aḥad Ha-Am rejected Reform Judaism as misguided and essentially assimilationist. The essence of Judaism, as far as he was concerned, was Hebrew culture and the unique Jewish morality which regards justice as an ethical principle superior to love. The traditional *halachah* or religious law of Judaism, he believed, certainly required modification, but the changes would come naturally under the influence of the renewed Jewish life in Palestine.

The Cultural Zionism typified by Aḥad Ha-Am, who spent only the last five years of his life in Palestine after living for a long time in London, served as a powerful influence on the settlers of the Second Aliyah. Hebrew, they were convinced, must be revived as the language of the *Yishuv*. Yiddish, which many of them regarded as a degraded jargon, would not do. A protracted and intensive effort had been made by the dedicated philologist Eliezer ben Yehudah (1858–1922) and a group of colleagues to modernize Hebrew and expand its vocabulary so that it might again be a living language, adapted to the requirements of the contemporary world. Through the work of ben Yehudah, as well as the inspiration of Aḥad Ha-Am's Cultural Zionism, Hebrew soon became the vernacular of the Jewish community in Palestine. Gifted poets and novelists began to write in the language and quickly developed a remarkable literature. An excellent school system was also established, capped by the Hebrew University, whose cornerstone was laid in Jerusalem in 1918. The university, which opened its doors in 1925 under the presidency of Dr. Judah Leon Magnes, once rabbi of New York's Reform Temple Emanu-El, became within a few years a major seat of learning and gained added strength when a significant number of Jewish scholars and scientists fleeing from Nazi Germany in the 1930s joined its faculty.

⚜

A milestone in the development of the Zionist movement was the issuance on November 2, 1917, of a statement by British Foreign Secretary Arthur James Balfour, declaring that the British government favors "the establishment in Palestine of a national home for the Jewish people, and will use their best endeavors to facilitate the achievement of this object, it being clearly understood that nothing shall be done which may prejudice the civil and religious rights of existing non-Jewish communities in Palestine, or the rights and political status enjoyed by Jews in any other country." This statement came after long and intricate negotiations on the part of Chaim Weizmann, Nahum Sokolow, and other Zionist leaders with the British Foreign Office beginning shortly after the outbreak of World War I. In part the Balfour Declaration was a gesture of gratitude to Weizmann, whose chemical researches had aided the British war effort, but in greater measure it was calculated to win the support of the Jews of Russia against the Bolsheviks, who wished to withdraw from Russian participation in the war, as well as the sympathy of Jews in the areas of central and eastern Europe under the control of the Central Powers. It was also encouraged by Lord Balfour's visit to the United States in the spring of 1917 and his meeting with President Woodrow Wilson, who had come to sympathize with the Zionist cause through the advocacy of Justice Louis D. Brandeis and other American Zionist leaders.

Although it was not unopposed in Jewish circles—the presidents of both the Board of Deputies of British Jews and the Anglo-Jewish Association argued that it would endanger the position of Jews everywhere—the Balfour Declaration evoked great jubilation throughout the Jewish world. Many Jews regarded it as a guarantee of the fulfillment of the Zionist goal. Their hopes were strengthened with the ratification of the Balfour Declaration by the Allied Powers, including the United States, and the grant, in the postwar settlement, of the mandate for Palestine to Great Britain, with the charge that it proceed toward the realization of the objective stated in it. Within a few years many leading western Jews who had opposed a Jewish state in Palestine on the basis of ideological principles came to see it, particularly in the light of the rapidly deteriorating conditions of Jewish life in Poland and eastern Europe generally, as essential and justifiable on humanitarian grounds; only Palestine seemed to offer a place of refuge for any significant number of Jews seeking to emigrate from countries in which their lives had become an endless succession of miseries and indignities. The change in attitude was signalized by the accession in 1929 to membership on the executive of the enlarged Jewish Agency for Palestine, which was concerned with the practical task of financing and administering the settlement of Jews in the country, of such outstanding non-Zionist leaders as Louis Marshall of the United States, Léon Blum of France, and Lord Melchett of Great Britain.

With the end of World War I immigration of Jews to Palestine had resumed. The Third Aliyah (1919–1923) brought in some thirty-five thousand persons, many of them young and idealistic *ḥalutzim*, or pioneers, who, together with the veterans of the Second Aliyah, built roads, forested eroded hills, changed malarial swamps into fertile farmlands, irrigated desert areas, expanded the network of *kevutzot* and *kibbutzim*, and established the Histadrut Ha-Ovedim with its manifold economic, social service, and educational activities. In the Fourth Aliyah (1924–1928) there were also a number of such pioneers, but most of the sixty-seven thousand immigrants of this period were middle-class Jews fleeing from Poland and other countries of eastern Europe where life was becoming increasingly intolerable; the majority of these settled in the cities and built workshops and small factories. During the decade of the Fifth Aliyah (1929–1939), the number of immigrants rose to more than two hundred fifty thousand and the character of the *Yishuv* was radically altered. Over seventy thousand of these immigrants were refugees from Nazi Germany; included in their number were more than a few world famous academicians and scientists, as well as many professionals and businessmen who brought capital and entrepreneurial skills with them. In this period also thousands of children and young people were brought to Palestine from Germany and elsewhere in Europe by the Youth Aliyah, a movement initiated by Recha Freyer in the early 1930s and headed from 1933 to 1945 by Henrietta Szold.

In May 1939, as thousands of Jews in Nazi Germany and elsewhere in Europe were still seeking frantically to leave their countries and escape the fate, far worse than they could then imagine, that awaited them and millions of their fellow Jews, the British government, headed by Neville Chamberlain, issued a White Paper officially declaring that a maximum total of seventy-five thousand Jewish immigrants would be allowed to enter Palestine in the next five years, and that thereafter immigration of Jews would cease entirely and the building of the Jewish homeland under the terms of the Balfour Declaration and the mandate would be regarded as complete.

This callous decision, which even in Britain was denounced by the Labour Party as an "act of moral betrayal," came as the conclusion of a series of reports by government commissions dispatched from London to investigate the growing deterioration of relations between the Jewish and Arab segments of the Palestinian population. The rising tide of Arab nationalism, the intensity of which was frequently underestimated by the Zionist leadership, had manifested itself in increasing resentment and bitterness on the part of many Arabs in Palestine; these regarded the Jewish immigrants as an alien people from the West infiltrating a land which did not belong to them and determined to transform it into a Jewish state. Spurred on by the rabid Haj Amin al-Husseini, who had been made Grand Mufti of Jerusalem with British support, Arab bands had attacked Jewish homes and settlements and massacred hundreds of Jews in Hebron and elsewhere in 1929. In 1936, again incited by the Grand Mufti and aided by the German Nazi and especially the Italian Fascist governments, both intent on embarrassing Great Britain in the Middle East, armed Arab raiders from Palestine and "volunteer" guerrillas from neighboring Arab countries had once again launched a nationwide attack on Jewish settlements. The *Yishuv*'s defense forces, organized in the Haganah, followed a policy of self-restraint which precluded terrorism and reprisals against Arab communities during the three years of violence that followed. But British officialdom, long inclined toward a policy of placating the Arabs at the expense of the Jews and of whittling down the commitments of the Balfour Declaration and the mandate, responded with its White Paper of 1939. The stunned Jews of Palestine did not waver in their determination to rescue as many as possible of the Jews fleeing from Europe, and proceeded in the war years to smuggle into the country all the refugees that they could. In the meantime the members of the *Yishuv* waited impatiently for the day when, as a free and independent people and masters of their own destiny, they would be in a better position to save Jews from nations either bent on destroying them or utterly indifferent to their fate.

Zionism, whose origin, early growth, and various forms we have outlined, may have been a retreat from the universalist dreams that so enchanted many Jews of western and central Europe in the nine-teenth century. But it was the product of a sobering encounter with reality. Under the impact of that reality Jews developed a renewed sense of their peoplehood and gained dignity, self-assurance, and a sense of the meaningfulness of Jewish existence. Not only those who returned to Palestine, but hundreds of thousands who could not or would not return, were transformed by the resurgent nationalist spirit. In Poland and elsewhere in eastern Europe between the two world wars the *Tarbut*, or Hebrew culture, schools that were orga-nized by the Zionist movement, and the hopes that the movement proclaimed, infused vigor and vitality into a community whose spiri-tual as well as physical resources were being rapidly deplenished. That community was to be largely swallowed up a few years later in the fires of the Holocaust, but the renewal of the Jewish spirit gen-erated by Zionism, and its later culmination in the establishment of the State of Israel, spread throughout the Jewish world. It is still far from exhausted today.

CHAPTER

❦ XIV ❧

European Jewry in the Twentieth Century

I T IS NOT LIKELY that in the year 1900 even the most keen-sighted and prescient observer could have foreseen that before the new century had run half its course Jewish life in the central and eastern parts of the continent, where the largest and most creative Jewry in the world had been concentrated for ages, would be almost completely annihilated. Nor could he have predicted that almost six million Jews—a third of the total world Jewish population—would be swept away in a cataclysmic tragedy whose magnitude and horror beggar description and before which all previous misfortunes in the millennial history of Jewish suffering pale into relative insignificance. Historical hindsight may lend the tragedy the semblance of inevitability, but the supposition that it could have been anticipated in anything approximating its actual form, or that it might have been prepared for, seems altogether gratuitous.

We cannot, in the compass of a chapter, hope to provide even the barest sketch of the complex and tortuous course of events that led to this crushing tragedy and its aftermath, but must content ourselves with a discussion of the historical developments, personalities, and ideas in European Jewry of the twentieth century that are of major significance for the history of Judaism, Jewish culture, and the inner life of the Jewish people.

᠂ᢒᢢᢀ

In the opening years of the century the largest Jewry in Europe, that of the Russian empire, continued to suffer from the brutal policies of the czarist regime. Indeed, under the impact of increasing social unrest among the Russian masses and intensified terrorist activity by revolutionaries bent on overthrowing the government through violence, Nicholas II and his advisers became even more determined fomenters of anti-Semitism, hoping to make the Jews the scapegoats on to whose heads the resentment of the peasants and workers might be deflected. Once again violence erupted. In April 1903 forty-five Jews were massacred, scores of others wounded and maimed, and hundreds of Jewish homes and shops burned down by an incited mob at Kishinev. Within the next four years pogroms and riots, many of them under the direct auspices of the so-called "Black Hundreds," reactionary terrorists determined to defend czarist autocracy against liberalism and constitutionalism, occurred in almost three hundred other Russian towns, and the estimated total of Jewish casualties reached fifty thousand. Under these circumstances, wholesale emigration of Russian Jews to the West—mainly to the United States, but also to Austria, Germany, France, and England, as well as to Argentina and other South American countries— proceeded without abatement and assumed even greater proportions.

Among the masses of Jews who remained in eastern Europe religious and cultural life continued to be intense and variegated. The majority in the towns of the Pale of Settlement as well as in the larger cities of Russia, Poland, and the Ukraine remained staunchly loyal to traditional Judaism, following its precepts to the letter, sending their children to the ubiquitous *ḥeder*, and thronging the synagogues and study-houses. Thousands of young men attended the great *yeshivot* of Lithuania and other parts of the empire, spending years in intensive study of the *Talmud*, while Hasidic conventicles, each centered around a revered *tzaddik* or *rebbe*, flourished everywhere. Especially in the larger urban centers, such as St. Petersburg, Odessa, Kiev, Warsaw, and Vilna, there were, however, more than a few Jews who, under the influence of the Haskalah movement and assimilationist tendencies, had abandoned traditional Jewish faith and practice and become completely secularized. A rigorously enforced *numerus clausus* made it impossible for more than a few Jews to attend Russian universities, but hundreds managed to go abroad to study at universities and technical institutes in Germany, Switzerland, and Austria and returned home imbued with western ideas and attitudes.

Russian Jewry at the turn of the century boasted a large number of outstanding scholars, both traditional Talmudists who studied the classical rabbinic writings in the time-honored fashion and modern investigators who critically explored every facet of Jewish history and literature. The books written by these men were widely read, as was the extensive periodical literature in Hebrew, Yiddish, and Russian devoted to discussion of scholarly matters as well as contemporary questions. Perhaps the most hotly debated issue was Zionism, pushed to the forefront of Jewish life by the appearance of Theodor Herzl and the establishment of the World Zionist Organization. The leading Hebrew periodical of the age was the monthly *Ha-Shiloah* (1896–1927), published until 1920 in Odessa, the center of the Hebrew literary revival in Russia, and edited originally by Ahad Ha-Am, who utilized its pages for his polemics against Herzl's political Zionism. Also an editor of *Ha-Shiloah* for some years was Hayyim Nahman Bialik (1873–1934), the "singer of the Jewish national renaissance" and perhaps the most brilliant Hebrew poet since Judah ha-Levi. After studying at the famous *yeshivah* of Volozhin, Bialik moved to Odessa in 1891 and published his first poem there in the same year. While teaching at Sosnowice from 1897 to 1900 he completed his great poems *Ha-Matmid* (*The Perpetual Student*) and *Achen Hatzir Ha-Am* (*Surely the People Is Grass*), expressing his rebellion against the traditional environment and his bitter criticism of east European Jewish society, with its melancholy synagogues and houses of study from which the glory of the Shechinah had departed.

In Odessa in 1902 he wrote his *Metei Midbar* (*The Dead of the Wilderness*) in revolt against the Diaspora, and in 1903 *Be-Ir Ha-Haregah* (*In the City of Slaughter*), fiercely castigating the passivity and nonresistance of the Jews of Kishinev at the time of their massacre. The latter poem stirred the organization of Jewish self-defense groups throughout Russia in anticipation of the pogroms still to come. In the years that followed Bialik visited Palestine and wrote numerous Zionist poems, folk songs, and verses for children—all marked by an incomparable lyricism. Several years after the Bolshevik revolution the poet, who had also become a noted publisher, left Russia for Berlin, where he established the Devir publishing house, which was later removed to Tel Aviv. A legend in his own time, Bialik himself settled in Tel Aviv in 1924 and spent the last decade of his life there, becoming the focus of the Hebrew cultural activity of the Palestinian *Yishuv*. In Tel Aviv he collaborated with his friend Y. H. Ravnitzki in producing superb editions of the poems of Solomon ibn Gabirol and Moses ibn Ezra, and wrote stories and poems for children. Here Bialik also inaugurated the *Oneg Shabbat*, a modernized version of the traditional Sabbath *seudah shelishit*, or "third meal." In the poet's re-creation it was transformed into a gathering on late Saturday afternoons for lectures and Jewish cultural programs, and became a popular institution in both Palestine and the Diaspora.[1]

Among the welter of diverse Zionist ideologies and organizations that emerged in eastern Europe at the end of the nineteenth and the beginning of the twentieth century, one that proved particularly attractive was socialist Zionism. Socialist ideas had already become widespread, especially among the workers in the industrial centers of Poland and Russia, and they were now welded in the minds of many Jews to the nationalist aspirations that had been awakened. In the first decade of the new century isolated groups calling themselves Poalei Zion (Workers of Zion) were organized in a number of Russian cities, followed by the establishment of similar societies in other European countries, as well as in the United States and Palestine. In 1907 a number of these groups combined in an international conference held at the Hague to form the World Confederation of Poalei Zion. The ideology of socialist Zionism was formulated chiefly, as we have noted, by two Russian Jews, Nahman Syrkin and Ber Borochov. While Syrkin, whose socialism was predominantly of a humanitarian and utopian character, set forth a program of "Socialist Constructivism" in which the orthodox Marxist doctrine of the role of the class struggle was minimized and cooperative effort emphasized, Borochov, who worked for a time in the revolutionary Social Democratic Party in Russia, applied the categories of Marxist economic determinism to an analysis of the Jewish situation in the world. Establishment of a Jewish state, Borochov argued, is a historical inevitability because of the pressures deriving from the fact that every economic class within the Jewry of any given country is in competition with a parallel non-Jewish class; this will necessarily lead to displacement and emigration. The working class in the Jewish state that will be formed must organize to protect and advance its own interests and to fight for a socialist society.

The Poalei Zion groups of eastern Europe contributed a high proportion of the immigrants of the Second and Third Aliyot. It was largely their members who pioneered in the creation of the collective settlements and the cooperative sector of the economy in Palestine. From their ideologies also emerged the Labor parties that presently dominate the political life of the State of Israel.

Not all the Jewish socialists of eastern Europe by any means wedded their socialism to Zionism. Tens of thousands joined the Marxist-socialist Allgemeiner Yiddisher Arbeiterbund in Lite, Poilen un Russland (General Jewish Workers' Union in Lithuania, Poland, and Russia, commonly known as the "Bund"), which was adamantly opposed to Zionism, regarding it as a reactionary nationalist movement of the bourgeoisie. The Bund, formally established in Vilna in 1897, emerged out of a Jewish workers' movement that had been developing for many years and functioned originally both as a labor union and a revolutionary political party. Most of the first branches of the Bund were in Poland and Lithuania, but it soon spread to many places in Russia, where it was declared illegal by the czarist regime and its members frequently subjected to arrest and severe punishment. Members of the Bund played a major role in the founding in 1898 of the Social Democratic Party, in which the left-wing Bolsheviks became predominant a few years later under the leadership of Lenin, and they also played a prominent role in the unsuccessful Russian revolution of 1905. In 1903 Lenin opposed the continuance of the Bund in the Social Democratic Party on a national-federal basis because he believed that the Jews, lacking a territory of their own within Russia, were not a nation, and that they ought, in any case, to become totally assimilated. The Bund thereupon seceded and became an independent party, but it rejoined the all-Russian party as a distinct entity in 1906. After the Bolshevik revolution of 1917, the Russian and Ukrainian Bund organizations were absorbed into the Communist Party. Only the Polish Bund remained independent and continued to be a significant factor in Polish-Jewish life until the Nazi invasion in 1939. Briefly reactivated after the war, it was forced to amalgamate with the Polish Communist Party in 1947.

In general, the program of the Bund, which was constantly torn by internal ideological strife in its attempt to reconcile its Jewish identity with socialist internationalism, approximated that of late nineteenth-century German socialism. It steadfastly refused to consider the Jews a worldwide national entity (as Zionism maintained) and insisted that they were irrevocably bound to the countries in which they lived (*dokeit*, "hereness," in Bund terminology) and obliged to struggle alongside their fellow citizens for a classless society.

[353]

After a good deal of initial vacillation, the Bund, in the years before World War I began to claim the right of Jewish cultural autonomy in every country, and to advocate such measures as the guaranteeing to Jews of freedom of rest on the Sabbath and the establishment of state Yiddish schools. Throughout its history it was strongly committed to the Yiddish language and opposed Zionist attempts to deprecate Yiddish in favor of Hebrew. While promoting the interests and class-consciousness of Jewish workers in eastern Europe, it also contributed to the development of moderate socialism and trade unionism in the United States. Among the prominent leaders of the American labor movement who spent their formative years in the atmosphere of the Bund were Sidney Hillman and David Dubinsky.

At the same time that the Bund was moving toward advocacy of Jewish cultural autonomy, a theory of "Diaspora Nationalism" or "National Autonomism" was set forth by Simon Dubnow (1860–1941). This eminent Russian-Jewish historian, who wrote an eleven-volume universal history of the Jewish people (in which, in opposition to Heinrich Graetz, he emphasized social and economic as against religious and intellectual factors), as well as important histories of the Jews of Russia and Poland and of the Hasidic movement, began his career as an advocate of Russification and assimilation but soon reversed his direction and developed an ardent appreciation of Jewish spiritual and cultural values. Dubnow came under the influence of the then popular idea of "a state consisting of various nationalities" which might preserve the unity of such multiethnic empires as the Russian and Austro-Hungarian while fulfilling the demands for self-determination of the various peoples out of which these empires were constituted. He thereupon developed the view that the Jews, who already had a long experience throughout their history in the Diaspora of living in a state of spiritual independence and judicial autonomy, should be formally recognized as a "nation" within the framework of the state and guaranteed the rights to preserve their own language and culture and to live as a respected minority, sharing fully the privileges and responsibilities of citizenship and free of all discriminatory restrictions. Dubnow opposed both the Zionists, because they tended to write off the Diaspora, whose necessity and positive value he himself affirmed until the end of his life, and the Bundists, whose Marxist ideology he could not wholly accept and many of whom he suspected of being assimilationists. To promote his own solution of the Jewish problem, Dubnow in 1906 formed his Jewish People's Party, but it never gained a large number of adherents or exercised widespread influence and it was dissolved in 1918. After the Bolshevik revolution, the great historian, denied a university professorship in Lithuania, settled in Berlin. He fled to Riga on Hitler's accession to power in 1933. When that city was captured by the Germans in 1941 and its Jewish community dispatched to a death camp, the aged scholar was murdered by a Gestapo officer who had once been his pupil.

Both Simon Dubnow in his mature period and the Bundists were strong partisans of Yiddish language and literature. Yiddish had, of course, been the vernacular of the east European Jewish masses for hundreds of years, and in the sixteenth century some notable works had been written in it, although Hebrew was regarded both then and later as the appropriate vehicle for serious literature. Perhaps the most popular early Yiddish work was the *Bovo-Buch*, an epic in verse on the adventures of Prince Bovo of Antona (also known as Bevis of Hampton), written by the great Hebrew grammarian Elijah Levita in 1507–1508. Also widely read was the *Maaseh-Buch* (*Book of Tales*), a collection of Talmudic legends and of folktales derived from many different peoples and centuries. Jewish women especially favored the *Tze'enah U-Re'enah*, containing stories and homilies based on the Bible, and *techines*, devotional prayers in Yiddish. Literary creativity in Yiddish continued in the seventeenth and eighteenth centuries, but at a somewhat inferior level. When the Haskalah movement arose at the end of the eighteenth century, most of its protagonists spurned Yiddish as a corrupt "jargon" and determined to write only in Hebrew. However, some Haskalah writers of the first half of the nineteenth century—e.g., Mendel Lefin (ca. 1749–1826), Solomon Ettinger (ca. 1801–1856), Abraham Ber Gottlober (1810–1899), and Isaac Meir Dick (ca. 1807–1893)—also employed Yiddish for their tracts, stories, satires, and translations. These men contributed—as did the developing Jewish labor movement in eastern Europe, with its warm espousal and affirmation of the dignity of Yiddish—to a new appreciation of the language, and prepared the way for the three foremost masters of modern Yiddish literature: Mendele Mocher Seforim, Isaac Leib Peretz, and Sholem Aleichem. All three reached the apogee of their popularity at the end of the nineteenth and the beginning of the twentieth centuries and are still widely read today by Jews both in the original and in the numerous translations that have been made of their works.

Mendele Mocher Seforim ("Mendele the Bookseller," a pseudonym; his real name was Shalom Jacob Abramovitch; ca. 1836–1917), who spent many years as principal of the *Talmud Torah* in Odessa, began his literary career by writing in Hebrew but turned to Yiddish in the 1860s. In his early Yiddish stories—*Dos Kleine Menshele* (*The Little Man*), *Fishke der Krummer* (*Fishke the Lame*), *Die Takse* (*The Kosher Meat Tax*), and *Die Klyatshe* (*The Mare*)—he was the trenchant satirist, ridiculing the ignorance, superstition, and pettiness of Jewish life in the Pale of Settlement. Even here, however, his love and compassion for his poor brethren rotting in the squalor and backwardness of the *shtetl* is manifest. Mendele also translated the Psalms into Yiddish and collaborated with Bialik and Ravnitzki in a Yiddish translation of the Pentateuch. In his hands Yiddish prose achieved an unprecedented plasticity and expressiveness, and he has rightly been called the "grandfather of modern Yiddish literature."

Possessed of far greater sophistication, psychological insight, and literary artistry than Mendele was Isaac Leib Peretz (1852–1915). Although brought up in a traditional religious environment in Zamosc, he early acquired an extensive knowledge of German and Polish literature and studied Russian law, practicing as an advocate for ten years before his disbarment on an accusation of participating in the revolutionary movement. Later, in 1891, he obtained employment as a minor official in the cemetery department of the Jewish community organization of Warsaw, remaining in this position until his death, despite the fact that his poems, short stories, and dramas brought him renown throughout the Jewish world of eastern Europe. Peretz's first collection of Yiddish tales, *Bilder fun a Provintz-Reize* (*Sketches from a Provincial Journey*), portrayed the poverty and degradation of Jewish life in the Pale of Settlement. It was based on impressions collected during a tour he made in 1890 of many small towns and villages in the province of Tomaszow as a member of an expedition to gather statistical data financed by the Warsaw philanthropist Jan Bloch, a Jew who had converted to Christianity.

In the mid-1890s Peretz was powerfully attracted to the new currents and styles prevalent in western European literature, neoromanticism and symbolism. Their influence is discernible in his *Folkstimliche Geshichten* (*Folktales*, 1909) and his collection of Ḥasidic stories, begun in 1904. Although hardly a Ḥasid himself, Peretz recognized the kernel of moral grandeur and mystical profundity within the obscurantism and ignorance-ridden existence of the Ḥasidim. His lyrical, symbolistic tales in Yiddish about the life and faith of these simple pietists anticipated the later re-creation of the legends of Ḥasidism by Martin Buber in German, and contributed significantly to a renewed appreciation of the great mystical movement whose pristine fire had long since died down but in which sparks of authentic spirituality still flickered. In his stories, poems, and dramas, as well as his life (an ardent socialist, he was arrested in 1899 for attending an illegal meeting and subsequently imprisoned for several months), Peretz was always a champion of the poor and the oppressed. But, above all, he was a masterful writer who greatly enriched both Yiddish and Hebrew literature.

If Isaac Leib Peretz was the great psychologist of Yiddish literature, Sholem Aleichem (a nom de plume; he was born Sholem Rabinovich; 1859–1916) was its great humorist. At an early age this immensely prolific writer (an incomplete edition of his collected works runs to twenty-eight volumes) began to write novels, poems, and plays in three languages—Russian, Hebrew, and Yiddish—and found the last of these his most congenial medium. In his twenties he married the daughter of a rich landowner of the Kiev region and for a time lived in luxury; he soon lost his wealth, however, through speculation on the Russian stock exchange. Throughout his life he continued to write unremittingly (much of his work appeared in the Yiddish newspapers of St. Petersburg, Warsaw, and New York) and also embarked on extensive lecture tours in order to support himself and his "republic," as he called his large family, in proper style. Utilizing his extraordinary gift for seeing the comical elements in the pervasive sadness and pathos of east European Jewish life, he created a whole series of unforgettable characters who made Jews throughout the world alternately laugh and sigh—Hapke, the pock-marked maid, Menachem Mendel, the incurably optimistic *Luftmensch* and promoter of harebrained schemes, and Tevye, a philosopher in the guise of a milkman who drives a rickety wagon to eke out a bare livelihood but whose thoughts range through all realms, physical and metaphysical, and reach up to God. (The portrait of Tevye served as the inspiration for the enormously successful American musical play and movie in the 1960s and 1970s, *Fiddler on the Roof.*) Sholem Aleichem's immense popularity, which began in Russia in the 1880s and soon became international, did not wane after his death in New York in 1916. His Yiddish works were translated not only into Hebrew but into English, Russian, and other European languages and avidly read by hosts of Jews and non-Jews as well. In the last half century dramatic versions of his stories, as well as several of the plays that he wrote, have been performed repeatedly by outstanding companies in America, England, Argentina, Israel, the Soviet Union, Poland, and many other countries. Critical opinion, which once tended to regard him merely as a popular and entertaining writer for the masses, has come to acknowledge his genius.

The three classical masters of Yiddish literature were joined by a host of lesser contemporaries who contributed significantly to its development. In fiction there were Jacob Dinesohn (1856–1919), author of the widely successful *Der Shwartzer Yungermanchik* (*The Dark Young Man*); Mordecai Spector (1858–1925), whose *Der Yiddisher Muzhik* (*The Jewish Peasant*) promoted the ideas of the Hovevei Tziyyon societies; S. An-Ski (pseudonym of Solomon S. Rapoport; 1863–1920), composer of *Die Shvueh*, the hymn of the Bund, and of the celebrated drama *The Dybbuk*, still widely performed on the stage today; Nahum Meir Shaikevitch (1849–1905), author, under the pen name Shomer, of scores of extremely banal and undistinguished best sellers in Yiddish; and Sholem Asch (1880–1957), undoubtedly the best-known Yiddish novelist and playwright of the twentieth century, whose works were translated into many languages and helped bring Yiddish to the attention of the larger world.

The founder of the Yiddish theater was Abraham Goldfaden (1840–1906), who in 1876 organized in Rumania the first modern Yiddish dramatic company, which he served in the multiple capacities of producer, director, playwright, and actor. Goldfaden composed many plays and traveled with his troupe throughout Europe and the United States, where he died. His work was continued by Jacob Gordin (1853–1909), who came to America from Russia in 1891 and wrote more than eighty plays, many of them obtaining wide popular acclaim, for the Yiddish stage in New York. Other Russian-born Yiddish dramatists whose major works were composed in America were Leon Kobrin (1873–1946) and David Pinski (1872–1959). Kobrin migrated to the United States in 1892 and, after working for a time in a sweatshop, wrote a series of highly successful plays. Pinski's popular comedy *The Treasure* was performed in Germany as well as America, and his *The Eternal Jew* was produced by the noted Ha-Bimah company in Moscow in 1919. He was also the author of a major novel, *The House of Noah Eden*, which portrayed the decline of Jewish loyalty through three generations in America and argued eloquently against assimilation.

In the early years of the twentieth century in eastern Europe Yiddish was also adopted for a considerable number of scholarly works, although most learned writers continued to prefer Hebrew or Russian. Scholarship in Yiddish was given a powerful impetus by the organization in 1925 in Vilna of YIVO (*Yiddisher Visenshaftlicher Institut*, Institute for Jewish Research), which devoted itself to the scientific study of Jewish life and culture throughout the world, but gave particular stress to east European Jewry and its Yiddish-speaking off-shoots. At the beginning of World War II, when the major center of YIVO was transferred from Vilna to New York, the organization had branches in thirty different countries. After the war, part of the archives and library in Vilna that had been saved from the ravages of the Nazis was brought to New York. Among the distinguished scholars who participated in the research and publications of YIVO in its Vilna period were Simon Dubnow, Elias Tcherikower, Saul Ginsburg, Abraham Menes, Jacob Shatzky, Max Weinreich, Alexander Harkavy, S. Niger, Zalman Rejzen, Jacob Letschinsky, and A. A. Roback. Several of these men who found refuge in the United States continued their work at YIVO in New York.

One of the most important scholarly works written in Yiddish in Russia in the twentieth century is Israel Zinberg's *Geschichte fun der Literatur bei Yidn* (*History of Jewish Literature*), now beginning to appear in English translation.[2] Zinberg (1873–1939), a chemical engineer by profession, was a major contributor to the *Yevreyskaya Entziklopediya*, the Russian-Jewish encyclopedia which appeared in St. Petersburg (later Leningrad) in sixteen volumes between 1906 and 1913. He also participated in the work of the Jewish Academy, officially named Higher Courses in Oriental Studies, that was established in that city in 1908 by the scholarly philanthropist Baron David Günzburg (the Academy, whose lecturers included Simon Dubnow and J. L. B. Katzenelson, was attended by Zalman Shazar, Joshua Guttman, Yehezkel Kaufmann, and Solomon Zeitlin, as well as many others who later attained fame as scholars and writers). Zinberg devoted years of intensive study to the Jewish books and manuscripts in the great libraries and Judaica collections of St. Petersburg, including Baron Günzburg's. He began his massive eight-volume history of European Jewish literature from the Spanish period to the end of the Russian Haskalah in 1915, and continued to work on it indefatigably until his arrest by the Soviet police and deportation, in 1938, to Vladivostok, where he died shortly afterward. Zinberg's *Geschichte*, written in the spirit of *die Wissenschaft des Judentums*, but in a vivid and enthusiastic style, is one of the last and greatest individual monuments of European Jewish scholarship.

[359]

Despite the repressions and brutalities of the czarist government, Russian Jewry continued to maintain its religious and cultural life at a high and creative level. World War I, however, was a shattering blow. Large masses of Jewish civilians were caught between the German and Russian armies (in both of which many thousands of Jews served as soldiers) as the battle lines on the eastern front ebbed and flowed. Several hundred thousand Jews perished of hunger, exposure, and disease during the war years, and the end of the war brought little remission in the suffering of many who survived. In the turbulent aftermath of the Bolshevik Revolution in Russia, Jews in the Ukraine particularly suffered large-scale pogroms and massacres during the period from 1919 to 1921 as the Red Army fought and eventually defeated the Ukrainian nationalist forces led by Simon Petlura and the White Russian armies under the command of General Denikin.

The largest segment of the Jewry that had formerly lived in the czarist empire found itself, after the war, living in the reestablished and once again independent nations of Poland and Lithuania. More than two and a half million, however, remained in what in 1922 came to be called the Union of Soviet Socialist Republics, under the dictatorship of the Bolsheviks. The fact that a significant number of leading Bolsheviks and Lenin's closest associates—men such as Leon Trotsky, Jacob Sverdlov, Grigori Zinoviev, Maxim Litvinov, Karl Radek, and Lazar Kaganovich—were of Jewish birth proved of no practical help to the Jewish populace. To be sure, the Soviet government under Lenin declared anti-Semitism counterrevolutionary and illegal, but the enforced collectivization of the economy undertaken by the communist regime inflicted special hardships on the Jews. Many of them had been engaged as middlemen in petty trade, and they now discovered themselves, along with the relatively few of their brethren who had formerly been successful businessmen, without an economic function and branded as "ex-capitalists" and "exploiters of labor." Eventually they were absorbed into the new economy, but a significant number of those who could fled the Soviet Union, as did also many Jewish intellectuals who found the thought control and repression of the new totalitarian order intolerable.

Among the émigrés was Lev Shestov (born Lev Isaakovich Schwarzmann; 1866–1938), one of the profoundest Jewish philosophers of the twentieth century. Born into a wealthy Jewish family in Kiev, Shestov studied at the universities of Moscow and Kiev and obtained a law degree, but soon turned to his first loves, literature and philosophy. His brilliant books and essays on Shakespeare, Brandes, Chekhov, Nietzsche, Tolstoy, and Dostoevsky, written before World War I, earned him a European reputation. A few years after the Bolshevik Revolution, Shestov settled with his family in Paris and spent the rest of his life there. During the war years and their aftermath he had become obsessed with what he called "the nightmare of godlessness and unbelief that has taken hold of humanity," and his interests turned decisively in a religious direction. Most of his later writing, culminating in his *Athens and Jerusalem* (1938), is a sustained philosophical polemic, written in the most elegant Russian prose and reflecting enormous erudition in the whole range of European literature and philosophy, against the claims of rationalism and scientism. The ungrounded pretensions to truth of "Athens," representing rationalist philosophy and science, with their tendencies toward a mechanist and determinist view of the world must be exposed, Shestov argued, in order to make room for "Jerusalem," with its proclamation of human freedom and a creator God "for whom nothing is impossible." In recent years the contributions of the great Russian-Jewish philosopher to the revolutionary movement of modern existentialist religious thought have gained growing recognition.[3]

Upon seizing power in Russia, the Bolshevik regime that Shestov and many others felt compelled to flee embarked on a militant campaign to stamp out religious belief, which it regarded as essentially bourgeois and hopelessly reactionary. Judaism, along with other faiths, was subjected to an intensive assault by the government. Public religious instruction was legally proscribed and atheism was taught in the Russian schools as an indispensable part of Soviet ideology. No one identified as "religious" was eligible to join the Communist Party. The rabidly antireligious members of the Jewish section of the party which existed for some years, the so-called Yevsektsia, as well as of the Commissariat for Jewish National Affairs established under the direction of S. M. Dimanshtein, considered it one of their major functions to root out Jewish religious observance and de-Judaize Jewish communal institutions. Although Yiddish was recognized as an official language in those parts of the Soviet Union where there was a large concentration of Jews, and secular Yiddish schools, libraries, newspapers, and theatrical companies were maintained under government auspices, the study of Hebrew was prohibited. In part this was an element of the campaign against religion, but Hebrew was also disapproved because of its association with Zionism, which was officially anathematized by the Bolsheviks on the grounds that it was associated with British "capitalist imperialism" and because Zionist sympathies were considered inconsistent with full loyalty to the Soviet state. Many Zionists were imprisoned, sent to labor camps, or exiled to Siberia. Further to counteract Zionism, the Soviet government collaborated in an effort, financed largely by American Jews, to establish Jewish agricultural settlements in the Ukraine and Crimea and, in 1928, on the initiative of President Kalinin, allocated a large tract of land called Birobidjan in eastern Siberia for the establishment of a republic in which Jews would enjoy cultural autonomy. The Jewish response in Russia, however, was meager, and Jews never constituted more than a quarter of Birobidjan's population. At present only a few thousand Jews live there.

By the outbreak of World War II, two decades of communist dictatorship had radically transformed Russian-Jewish life. Isolated from fellow Jews elsewhere in the world, its demographic and occupational pattern completely altered, many of its religious and intellectual leaders liquidated or exiled, and subjected to a relentless barrage of antireligious and anti-Zionist propaganda, Russian Jewry had become largely secularized and denationalized. It had also been greatly weakened by a high intermarriage rate. But it had by no means, as some of the "Jewish" commissars hoped would happen, become totally assimilated into the larger Soviet society and disappeared as a separate and self-conscious people.

Elsewhere in eastern Europe Jewish life in the period between the two world wars was characterized by progressive deterioration as much of the continent rushed headlong into political and economic fascism. The rights of Jews (and all other ethnic and religious minorities) to civic equality, economic opportunity, and cultural and linguistic self-expression in the new republic of Poland, whose population included some three million Jews, were supposedly secured by the "minority" clauses written into the peace treaties of Versailles which formally ended World War I. This was also ostensibly the case with the Jewries of Lithuania, Latvia, Estonia, Czechoslovakia, and Rumania, the last of which had tripled its Jewish population to eight hundred thousand with the annexation of large areas of the old Romanov and Hapsburg empires. But except for Czechoslovakia which, under the benevolent governments of Jan Masaryk and

Eduard Beneš, honored its word and granted Jews full equality, the states of eastern Europe began flagrantly to violate the "minority" clauses before the ink on the treaties they had signed had hardly dried.

Accompanied by an intensive campaign of anti-Semitic propaganda, which represented the Jews as the ringleaders of both international communism and international capitalism, unscrupulous politicians in virtually every east European country outside the Soviet Union allied themselves to the business interests that supported them and undertook a systematic program of economic, political, and educational discrimination against their Jewish citizens. The situation of the Jews declined rapidly with each passing year of the decade of the 1920s and became even worse in the 1930s when, after Adolf Hitler's accession to power in Germany, political leaders in Poland, Rumania, Hungary, and elsewhere began to emulate both Nazi ideology and tactics in their own countries. Large-scale immigration to America had become impossible after the imposition of highly restrictive quotas by the United States government in 1924, but tens of thousands of east European Jews in the 1920s and early 1930s still managed to find their way to the United States, England, France, Palestine, Mexico, and Argentina (where a sizable community quickly developed). For the masses, however, migration was out of the question, and they remained sunk in their growing misery. Thus, even before Hitler plunged Europe into World War II and made ready to implement his "final solution" to the Jewish problem, the majority of east European Jewry had been pauperized and reduced to desperation. Religious life in both Ḥasidic and Mitnaggedic circles, scholarship in every aspect of Judaica, socialist and Zionist activity, the writing of novels, plays, poetry, and learned works in Yiddish and Hebrew—all these continued in eastern Europe during the years before the Nazi Holocaust, but they were hampered by ever worsening social and economic conditions.

Nor did the Jewries of western Europe escape the intense anti-Semitism which flared up and quickly spread over the globe (including the United States) in the wake of the great economic depression that engulfed the world beginning in 1929. In England, France, and Italy, traditional centers of liberalism where Jews had long enjoyed not only civic but social equality and had contributed to the political, cultural, and scientific life of the nation in far greater measure than might have been expected from their numbers in proportion to the total population, anti-Jewish sentiment and activity assumed menacing dimensions in the 1930s and was institutionalized in anti-Semitic parties and organizations. These, to be sure, were repudiated by the masses of the people, but they nevertheless managed to attract a considerable number of sympathizers.

≈§§≈

English Jewry in the nineteenth century had prospered and, with the aid of such influential advocates as Robert Grant, Thomas Babington Macaulay, and the Duke of Sussex (son of George III and a keen Hebraist), eventually attained full political emancipation. Jews promptly began to play a prominent role in British public life. In 1837 Sir Moses Montefiore (1784–1885), the first English Jew to obtain a knighthood in modern times, became Sheriff of the City of London. Deeply religious and orthodox in practice, Montefiore acquired renown everywhere in the Diaspora through his mission with Isaac-Adolphe Crémieux to the Middle East in connection with the Damascus Affair in 1840, when he secured the release of a number of Syrian Jews who had been imprisoned and tortured on a ritual murder charge. His later journeys of intercession on behalf of the Jews of Russia in 1846 and again in 1872, of Edgardo Mortara (a Jewish child kidnaped from his parents' home in Bologna by papal agents to be brought up as a Christian on the pretext that his nurse had informally baptized him as a one-year-old) in 1858, of the Jews of Morocco in 1863, and of the Jews of Rumania in 1867, were regarded as quasi-official missions of the British government.

In 1858 Montefiore's friend Lionel de Rothschild was permitted to occupy the seat in the House of Commons to which he had been repeatedly elected, and in 1885 Lionel's son Nathaniel was elevated to the House of Lords. The great statesman and prime minister Benjamin Disraeli (1804–1881), although baptized a Christian at the age of thirteen, boasted of his Jewish origins and sympathies and contributed significantly to advancing the social and political position of British Jewry. In 1871 Sir George Jessel (1824–1883), one of the greatest of nineteenth-century English legal scholars, was appointed solicitor general. He was followed in public office in England in the twentieth century by a large number of eminent Jewish figures, most notably Herbert (later Viscount) Samuel (1870–1963), a philosopher who became a cabinet minister in 1909 and served as England's high commissioner for Palestine from 1920 to 1925; Edwin Samuel Montagu (1879–1924), who was minister of munitions in 1916 and later secretary of state for India; and Rufus Daniel Isaacs (later Marquess of Reading; 1860–1935), a nonobservant but concerned and loyal Jew who served successively as Britain's solicitor general, attorney general, lord chief justice, ambassador to the United States, viceroy of India, and foreign secretary. The prominence of Jews in Liberal Party politics in the Edwardian era as well as later, and their friendships in high circles, including even the royal family, fueled the anti-Jewish attitudes of such writers as Hilaire Belloc, G. K. Chesterton, and Rudyard Kipling. This literary anti-Semitism, however, was relatively innocuous compared to the physical attacks on Jews and Jewish property launched in the 1930s by the "Blackshirts" under the English fascist leader Sir Oswald Mosley.

It was not only in politics that British Jewry distinguished itself, but in literature, the arts, and scholarship as well. Sir Arthur Wing Pinero (1855–1934), Israel Zangwill (1864–1926), Alfred Sutro (1863–1933), and Louis Golding (1895–1958) are only a few of the famous Anglo-Jewish writers of the twentieth century. In art eminence was achieved by the painters Solomon J. Solomon (1860–1921) and Sir William Rothenstein (1872–1945), the latter for a time principal of the Royal College of Art, and by the sculptor Sir Jacob Epstein (1880–1959). Among the important Jewish figures in English scholarship and academic life have been Sir Sidney Lee (originally Lazarus; 1859–1926), the foremost Shakespearian scholar of his day and editor of the *Dictionary of National Biography;* Sir Israel Gollancz (1864–1930), professor of English at King's College in London for twenty-five years and organizer of the British Academy and its secretary from its establishment in 1902 until his death; Samuel Alexander (1859–1938), a profound metaphysician and professor of philosophy at the University of Manchester beginning in 1893; Harold Laski (1893–1950), foremost theoretician of the British Labor Party and one of the chief builders of the London School of Economics; Cecil Roth (1899–1970), reader in Jewish studies at Oxford from 1939 to 1964, when he settled in Israel and subsequently became editor of the newly published (1971) *Encyclopedia Judaica;* David Daube (b. 1909), Regius professor of civil law at Oxford and biblical scholar; and Sir Isaiah Berlin (b. 1909), professor of social and political theory at the same university and author of important works on philosophy, Russian history and literature, and political thought.

The pattern of Jewish religious life in England was largely set in the middle of the nineteenth century. Half a century earlier the Sephardic community had been forced to yield its preeminent position to the Ashkenazim. For a period of almost seventy years, from 1845 to 1911, Nathan Marcus Adler and later his son Hermann occupied the office of chief rabbi of the Ashkenazic community. Nathan Adler (1803–1890), a proponent of dignified orthodoxy, introduced modern standards into the English rabbinate and sought to extend his authority throughout the empire, as evidenced by his issuance, in 1847, of a document entitled *Laws and Regulations for All the Synagogues in the British Empire*. However, German Reform tendencies of a rather moderate character had already been introduced in 1840 with the establishment of the West London Synagogue of British Jews. (Because of the strenuous opposition of the traditionalists, led by Sir Moses Montefiore, it managed to organize branch congregations only in Manchester and Bradford before the end of the nineteenth century.) In 1855 Adler founded Jews' College, a seminary for training traditional ministers and rabbis which is still functioning in London and whose principals have included such scholars as Michael Friedlander, Adolph Büchler, and Isadore Epstein. In 1870, with the authorization of an Act of Parliament, he organized the United Synagogue, originally a federation of the Ashkenazic synagogues of the capital city that has since extended its activity into the provinces. Nathan Adler was also an early leader of the Ḥovevei Tziyyon and helped gain sympathy for Zionist ideas in England. His son and successor, Hermann Adler (1839–1911), served as president of Jews' College for thirty years before becoming chief rabbi in 1891. He continued his father's advocacy of the Ḥovevei Tziyyon movement and visited Palestine in its behalf.

During the last years of Nathan Adler's incumbency as chief rabbi and throughout Hermann Adler's, large-scale immigration from eastern Europe greatly enlarged and transformed the Jewish population of England; the community grew from sixty-five thousand in 1880 to three hundred thousand in 1914. Most of the proletarian, Yiddish-speaking, and predominantly orthodox immigrants settled in the East End of London, but large contingents also went to Manchester, Birmingham, Leeds, Liverpool, and Glasgow. At first maintaining their own prayer houses and schools, many of them, and especially their children, eventually joined the congregations of the United Synagogue, whose rite was broadly traditional. Among the immigrants was the distinguished Rumanian-born scholar Solomon Schechter (1850–1915), who came to England in 1882. A few years later he encouraged his friend and pupil Claude G. Montefiore to establish the learned journal *The Jewish Quarterly Review*, which has now been published for more than eighty years (in the United States since 1910). In 1890 Schechter was appointed reader in Rabbinics at the University of Cambridge, to which he brought back a large part of the Hebrew manuscripts in the ancient *genizah* of Cairo, and remained at Cambridge until he went to New York to assume the presidency of the Jewish Theological Seminary of America in 1902.

It was in that year that the Jewish Religious Union, which later led to the establishment of the Liberal Jewish Synagogue in London and a few other Liberal congregations elsewhere in Great Britain, was founded. These congregations were more left wing and closer to American Reform than the West London Synagogue, which, though it called itself Reform, approximated the pattern of the more moderate Liberal synagogues in Germany. The leading spirit of the new movement was Claude G. Montefiore (1858–1938). Blessed with inherited wealth, Montefiore, who studied at Balliol College, Oxford, under its famous master Benjamin Jowett, devoted his life to Jewish scholarship. His chief interest was the New Testament period and his major work is *The Synoptic Gospels* (2 vols., 1909 and 1927), but he was also deeply concerned with biblical and rabbinic literature, which he studied under the guidance of Solomon Schechter (whom he was instrumental in bringing to England). Sympathetic to the ethical teachings of Jesus in the Gospels and convinced that the time had come for the New Testament to be read and studied by Jews and given an honored place in present-day Judaism, Montefiore was nevertheless opposed to placing the New Testament on a level with the Hebrew Scriptures or reading from it in Jewish worship. His universalist vision of Judaism led him to adamant opposition to Zionism at a time when most of the leaders of British Jewry (including the new chief rabbi Joseph Herman Hertz, the Sephardic *ḥacham* Moses Gaster, the second Lord Rothschild, and Sir Herbert Samuel) warmly espoused it, and as president of the Anglo-Jewish Association he sought to prevent issuance of the Balfour Declaration.

Montefiore's close collaborator in the development of the Liberal Jewish movement in England (and also his coeditor of the first twenty volumes of *The Jewish Quarterly Review*) was the noted Hebraist and scholar Israel Abrahams (1858–1925). The son of an orthodox rabbi, Abrahams was a member of the faculty of Jews' College from 1891 until 1902, when he succeeded Schechter as reader in Rabbinics at Cambridge. Among his important scholarly works are *Studies in Pharisaism and the Gospels, Jewish Life in the Middle Ages*, and an edition of *Hebrew Ethical Wills*. Both Montefiore and Abrahams were inspired in their work for liberal Judaism by another doughty champion of the cause, Lilian Helen Montagu (1873–1963). Lilian Montagu, who was the daughter of the strictly observant and orthodox banker and philanthropist Samuel Montagu (later Lord Swaythling; 1832–1911) and sister of the Liberal Party politician Edwin Samuel Montagu, founded a girls' club in London in 1893 and devoted much of her long life to social work. In defiance of her authoritarian father, who broke with her on the issue, she joined her greatly admired friend Montefiore and Israel Abrahams in organizing the Liberal movement, and frequently preached from the pulpit of the Liberal synagogue in London. In 1926 Miss Montagu inspired the organization of the World Union for Progressive Judaism, a federation of the nonorthodox synagogues of England, Germany, France, and other European countries with the Union of American Hebrew Congregations and the Central Conference of American Rabbis, and remained its guiding spirit until her death.

The 1930s brought an immigration of some ninety thousand Jewish refugees, mainly from Germany, Austria, and Czechoslovakia, into England. This influx strengthened both the traditionalist and progressive religious movements of the country. Liberal congregations were revitalized by distinguished German Reform rabbis and scholars, and proponents of Samson Raphael Hirsch's brand of Neo-Orthodoxy gave an additional impetus to the separatist orthodox movement, contributing also to a marked shift to the right within the United Synagogue.

❧⳾❧

In France the opening of the twentieth century saw a Jewish community which, although somewhat smaller in size than England's, had become equally well established socially, economically, and politically. As early as 1834 a Jew, Benoît Fould, manager of the great Fould-Oppenheim banking firm, had been elected to the Chamber of Deputies. In 1842 his brother Achille Fould had also won a seat in the Chamber and later served as minister of finance, minister of state, and senator in the government of Louis Napoleon. Among the many Jews who achieved a high place in French society in the nineteenth century perhaps the most distinguished was Isaac-Adolphe Crémieux (1796–1880). Trained in the law, Crémieux served as a deputy from 1842 and became minister of justice when the French Republic was proclaimed in 1848. During the Second

Empire he was a foremost leader of the opposition movement of the Freemasons. In the Republican government of 1870 he was again appointed minister of justice and, while holding this office, signed the decree conferring French nationality on the Jews of Algeria. Crémieux, as we have noted, traveled to the Middle East with Sir Moses Montefiore in connection with the Damascus Affair, and also interceded with the French government to protect Jewish rights and interests on a number of other occasions. He was instrumental in the founding, in 1860, of the still actively functioning Alliance Israélite Universelle, which came into being as a result of the notorious Edgardo Mortara case and dedicated itself to working on a world-wide scale, with the financial support of wealthy French-, British-, and American-Jewish philanthropists, for the defense of Jewish civil and religious liberties, provision of educational and vocational opportunities to backward Jewish communities, and relief of Jewish victims of disaster. Crémieux served as president of the Alliance from 1863 to 1880, during which time it undertook the establishment of a network of schools, marked by a strong French cultural orientation, in various countries of the Balkans, Asia, and North Africa, as well as in Palestine.

We have observed that a wave of anti-Semitism, culminating in the Dreyfus trial and its turbulent aftermath, washed over France in the last decades of the nineteenth century. But with the failure of the anti-Semitic Royalists and clericalists to topple the Republic, French Jewry emerged unscathed and, indeed, strengthened. Although it had declined numerically with the loss to Germany, in 1870, of Alsace and Lorraine, it again grew substantially from 1881 to 1939 through a large immigration from Russia, Poland, and Rumania, as well as from Turkey and Greece. It is estimated that on the eve of World War II there were one hundred eighty thousand Jews (out of a total of some two hundred seventy thousand Jews in all of France) living in Paris, and that only a third of them belonged to the old French-Jewish community.

The contributions of Jews to the cultural life of France, which had already been of a high order in the nineteenth century, continued unabated in the twentieth. In the period before and after World War I a number of brilliant Jewish artists—among them Camille Pissarro, Chaim Soutine, Jules Pascin, Amadeo Modigliani, and Marc Chagall—contributed to the fame of Paris in the world of art. In literature and philosophy there were such outstanding figures as Marcel Proust, Henri Bergson, Émile Durkheim, Lucien Levy-Bruhl, and André Maurois. French-Jewish scholarship, which in the nineteenth century had boasted such eminent representatives as Salomon Munk, Adolphe Franck, Isadore Loeb, Joseph Derenbourg, and James Darmesteter, continued in the twentieth century with the work of men like Theodore Reinach and Georges Vajda. Much of the Jewish research has been carried on under the auspices of the Société des Études Juives (founded in 1880), which has by now published well over a hundred volumes of its learned journal *Revue des Études Juives*, containing articles not only by French-Jewish scholars but by others from all over the world.

The year 1905 marked the end of an era in French-Jewish religious life. In that year, as a result of the victory of the Dreyfusards, church and state were legally separated. The "consistorial" system, with its councils of *grand rabbins* and lay leaders for each department of France and its central council in Paris, under which French Jewry had lived since its imposition by Napoleon Bonaparte in 1808, was officially abolished, and state financial support for religious institutions withdrawn. However, the general structure of the consistorial system, sanctioned by a hundred years of tradition, continued on a voluntary basis and has been maintained to the present day. The central consistory in Paris was renamed the Union des Associations Cultuelles de France et d'Algérie, and the French Jewish community became in fact a voluntary federation of local communities with some joint central services, including a rabbinical seminary (originally established in Metz in 1829, it was moved in 1859 to Paris, where it still functions) and the chief rabbinate.

In 1905 Zadoc Kahn (1839–1905), a strong personality who had dominated the Jewish life of the country since his appointment as chief rabbi of Paris in 1868 (in 1889 he became chief rabbi of France), died. An eloquent preacher, Kahn had been largely responsible for reviving Jewish life in France after the loss of Alsatian Jewry, and played a leading role in gaining support for the Ḥovevei Tziyyon movement; it was he who interested Baron Edmond de Rothschild in supporting colonization efforts in Palestine. Some years before his accession to the chief rabbinate of Paris, the *grand rabbins* of France had gathered to formulate a common policy in response to both the assimilatory drift away from Judaism and the growing demands of many laymen, influenced by the development of the Reform movement in Germany, for modifications in worship and religious practice generally. Out of this assemblage came the decision to institute a number of moderate reforms directed mainly toward making the synagogue service more decorous (including the instruction that officiating rabbis were to wear garb similar to that of the Catholic clergy) and to improving the quality of religious education. These concessions, and the general grant of considerable latitude to local congregations and rabbis, warded off the development of an organized Reform movement like that in Germany, and it was not until later that a few Reform congregations appeared in France. Zadoc Kahn continued to foster the dignified traditionalism that had become the hallmark of French-Jewish religious life. After his death, with the influx—especially following World War I—of large numbers of refugees from the former Ottoman Empire and even larger groups from eastern Europe, a considerable number of more unqualifiedly orthodox congregations and schools were established by the newcomers. The Yiddish-speaking immigrants, who settled chiefly in Paris and tended to organize themselves in *Landesmannschaften*, contributed to the progressive "Ashkenazation" of the community and the revitalization of its religious life.

Even in France, which had known relatively little anti-Semitism for years, the general European movement toward fascism brought a renewal of Jew-hatred in the 1930s. The Cagoulards, or "Hooded Men," a secret society which aimed to overthrow the Republic and establish a dictatorship, were intensely anti-Semitic. They and other right wing and anti-Jewish groups were driven to special fury by the premiership of the Jewish socialist leader Léon Blum (1872–1950), who led the French government in 1936–1937 and again in 1938. Having survived imprisonment by Marshall Petain's Vichy regime and incarceration in the Buchenwald concentration camp by the Germans, Blum returned to head a brief interim government of France in 1946–1947.

It was in Germany, of course, that twentieth-century anti-Semitism reached its apogee, attaining a demonic frenzy and virulence that, in little more than a decade, brought death and destruction to the largest part of European Jewry. But anyone observing Germany and German-Jewish life at the opening of the century could hardly have foreseen the catastrophe that impended.

In 1900 there were six hundred thousand Jews in Germany, 1 percent of the total population. In the three decades since the establishment of the Reich Jews had come to occupy a prominent place in

German social, cultural, and economic life. Although, as we have seen, the anti-Semitism fostered by demagogues like Wilhelm Marr and Adolf Stöcker was widespread, and Jews were rarely appointed to official positions in the government or full professorships in the universities and could not become officers in the army, their participation in academic life, the liberal professions, science and technology, literature, the theater, the arts, and journalism was far out of proportion to their numbers. Jews were also among the founders and leaders of the Liberal and Social-Democratic parties, which usually had a number of Jewish representatives in the Reichstag. The prominence of Jews in many fields, and especially in science and medicine, grew in the first decades of the twentieth century; eleven of the thirty-eight Germans and three of the six Austrians awarded the Nobel prize before 1933 were Jews or of Jewish origin. Intermarriage and conversion kept on increasing in these decades (by the period 1921–1927 the mixed marriage rate had grown to almost 45 percent and five hundred conversions were taking place annually), but the steady influx of *Ostjuden* was an important factor in preventing total assimilation and maintaining the numerical strength of German Jewry.

With the fall of the monarchy and the establishment of a democratic republic after World War I, during which more than a hundred thousand Jews served in the imperial army, Jews came to the forefront of Germany in even greater degree. All existing barriers to full participation in public life were removed, and Jews quickly gained unprecedented power and influence in German politics. Two Jews, Hugo Haase and Otto Landsberg, were among the six "People's Commissars" who constituted the first postrevolutionary German government. The premier of the revolutionary republic in Bavaria was a Jew, Kurt Eisner, and the majority of the members of the government after his assassination in 1919 were Jewish intellectuals, including Gustav Landauer, Eugen Leviné, and Ernst Toller, of whom the first two were also killed in 1919 and the last later left Germany and came to the United States, where he committed suicide in 1939. The draft of the Weimar Constitution was prepared by a Jew, Hugo Preuss; another Jew, Walter Rathenau, a noted engineer and industrialist, served as minister of reconstruction and foreign minister in the German republican government and worked for Franco-German reconciliation before his assassination by young anti-Semitic extremists in 1922.

Anti-Semitism was rampant throughout the decade of the 1920s, fueled by the severe inflation that gripped the German economy in the postwar period and the humiliation inflicted upon Germany by the Treaty of Versailles; Jews provided a convenient scapegoat for both disasters. Nevertheless, despite anti-Semitism and the growing assimilationism to which we previously alluded, this decade was a highly creative period in the religious and cultural life of German Jewry. The communities were superbly organized, their right to collect dues from their members officially recognized by public law, and their synagogues (both traditionalist and liberal ones were to be found in many communities), schools, and philanthropic activities functioned at a high level. Zionism, which was gaining a growing number of adherents, had become an influential force and succeeded in winning a hearing for national Jewish interests in the face of the assimilationist, thoroughly Germanized tendencies of the older members of the communities. A number of distinguished cultural and learned societies flourished, continuing the scholarly tradition of *die Wissenschaft des Judentums* which had blossomed so magnificently in the nineteenth century. An ambitious *Encyclopedia Judaica* was begun under the editorship of Jacob Klatzkin (only ten volumes were published before the rise of Nazism forced suspension of tne project, and the work was, in a sense, completed after a hiatus of almost forty years with the publication of the new *Encyclopedia Judaica* in Jerusalem in 1971). In this decade, also, many refugee Hebrew publishers, writers, and poets from Russia, including Ḥayyim Naḥman Bialik and Saul Tschernichowski, found a home in Germany, and new Hebrew publishing houses were founded in addition to the established firms which had long been issuing valuable works of Judaica.

❦

The decade of the twenties also saw at the height of their powers a number of seminal German-Jewish figures whose work has been epochal for the development of Jewish religious thought in the twentieth century. Only the contributions of three of the most important of them—Franz Rosenzweig, Martin Buber, and Leo Baeck—can be briefly indicated here. First, however, something must be said about another major thinker, Hermann Cohen, who died shortly before the opening of the decade.

Hermann Cohen (1842–1918) was born the son of a cantor in the small town of Coswig and studied for a time at the Jewish Theological Seminary in Breslau. He gave up his original intention of entering the rabbinate and went on to a brilliant career as an academic philosopher. For nearly forty years, from 1873 to 1912, he taught at the University of Marburg, where he developed a new interpretation of Immanuel Kant's philosophy that came to be called the Marburg School of Neo-Kantianism and brought him worldwide renown. While writing highly abstract treatises on logic, ethics, and aesthetics, Cohen also became an ardent socialist, urging that a nation's treatment of its workers is an index of its moral maturity. Although he referred to Karl Marx as "God's historical messenger," his own socialism was of a humanistic and idealistic kind, devoid both of Marxist dialectical materialism and of atheism.

Cohen's first appearance in the arena of German-Jewish life came in 1880, shortly after the historian Heinrich von Treitschke had launched an attack on Judaism and declared that the Jews were Germany's misfortune. The philosopher of Marburg replied to the historian of Berlin in that year with his *Ein Bekenntnis zur Judenfrage* (*An Avowal on the Jewish Question*), in which he argued that German Jews had no "dual loyalties" but were becoming totally integrated into German society, and at the same time urged Jews to be more serious about their religion. In 1888 Cohen responded to a charge that Talmudic law permits Jews to rob and defraud non-Jews in a pamphlet entitled *Die Nächstenliebe im Talmud* (*Love for Fellow Man in the Talmud*). Here he went beyond the refutation of the false charge to an attempt at reconciling two seemingly incompatible notions, both fundamental to Judaism, i.e., that the Jews are the chosen people and that the unity of mankind is the goal of the messianic age. He developed the Jewish idea of God as the One in whose image all men are created, and as the father and protector of the stranger who wills the establishment of a society of perfect brotherhood on earth.

Even before retiring from his chair at Marburg in 1912, Cohen had lectured at the Hochschule für die Wissenschaft des Judentums. In that year he moved to Berlin, where he spent the last years of his life teaching at the liberal rabbinical seminary and writing two important books, one on religion in general, *Der Begriff der Religion im System der Philosophie* (*The Concept of Religion in the System of Philosophy*, 1915), and the other on Judaism, *Die Religion der Vernunft aus den Quellen des Judentums* (*The Religion of Reason out of the Sources of Judaism*, published posthumously in 1919).[4] In these works Cohen moved away from the views he had held in his Marburg period, when he regarded religion only as a primitive and deficient form of ethics and considered God merely a concept guaranteeing the eternity of nature and thereby providing the possibility for the fulfillment of man's never-ending ethical task. Now religion was recognized as an independent domain, dealing with the personal concerns of the individual and his quest for salvation, and not, as does ethics, with humanity, or moral man as a type. God also was transformed for Cohen in his late period from an idea into a real being. In his new theocentric system God, indeed, is the only being, and the changing and finite world is becoming. But being and becoming, God and the world, are "correlated" through the processes which religion has called creation, revelation, and redemption. The world is dependent for its existence on God (creation), as is the human mind (revelation), and man is appointed to be a "coworker with God in the work of creation" by imitating the divine holiness and laboring for the establishment of a united mankind in the messianic era (redemption). In his final work, on Judaism, *Die Religion der Vernunft*, Cohen applied his concept of "correlation" and his theological categories to a systematic interpretation of the specific beliefs and practices of Judaism in which he emphasized the primacy of its moral, prophetic, and universal values, but also insisted on the supreme importance of Jewish tradition and *halachah*. This work, as well as the author's personal teaching, decisively influenced several generations of Jewish thinkers and scholars, most notably his pupil Franz Rosenzweig, perhaps the most original Jewish theologian of the twentieth century.

The son of a rather assimilated family which gave him only a minimal Jewish education, Rosenzweig (1886–1929) studied philosophy and law at a number of German universities and received a doctorate for a dissertation entitled *Hegel und der Staat* (*Hegel and the State*). Even in his student days, however, he had become discontented with Hegelian rationalism and was searching for the kind of personal meaning in existence that could be provided by religious faith. Knowing little of Judaism, he was on the point of converting to Christianity when apparently the experience of a Yom Kippur service in an orthodox synagogue in Berlin in 1913 brought him back to Judaism. Rosenzweig thereupon undertook an intensive study of Jewish sources which he continued for the rest of his life; his favorite early mentor was Hermann Cohen. While serving in the German army during World War I he wrote a draft of his major philosophical-theological work *Der Stern der Erlösung* (*The Star of Redemption*, 1921).[5] In 1920 he established the Freies Jüdisches Lehrhaus in Frankfurt-am-Main, a unique academy for informal adult Jewish education in which some of the foremost Jewish scholars of Germany served as teachers. Shortly after the founding of the Lehrhaus Rosenzwieg was smitten with a paralysis that progressively robbed him of all power of communication, but his last years of illness were highly creative and he continued to work until the end. Besides writing numerous essays and translating the poems of Judah ha-Levi in this period, he also collaborated with Martin Buber on a great translation of the Hebrew Bible into German.

Rosenzweig's philosophy of religion is existentialist in mood and spirit, protesting against the rationalism that attained its consummate form in Hegel, and which exalted abstract thought over concrete reality and mankind in general over the individual person, with his fears, hopes, and agonies. Profoundly existentialist also is his insistence that ultimate human truths, such as those postulated by religious faith, are not, like mathematical truths, logically demonstrable, objective, and universal. A religious truth is "personal" truth; it is not what "is" eternally and universally true, but rather what is "made true," verified (*bewährt*) through decision, commitment, and risk-taking daring in the actual life of the individual who professes it. Rosenzweig further rejects what he regards as the sustained effort of the great representatives of the western philosophical tradition "from Ionia to Jena," from the pre-Socratics to Hegel, to demonstrate that the three fundamental entities which "sound common sense" directly perceives in experience—God, the world, and man—are one in essence. The various monisms that have attempted to derive God and man from the world, or the world and man from God, or God and the world from man, are all mistaken. None of the fundamental elements are reducible to one of the others, but biblical religion—in contrast to paganism—rightly perceives them as interrelated. God is related to the world through creation, which Rosenzweig understands as a continuous process in which divinity moves from hiddenness to self-disclosure. God is related to man through revelation, in which He shows His love for man—a love which makes possible, in turn, the human response of love for fellow man. And man's love for his fellow leads to the redemption of the world, an event that Rosenzweig conceives as supervening in its fullness only at the end of time, but glimpses of which may be experienced in the here and now.

For the Jew, according to Rosenzweig, the proper response to the divine love disclosed in revelation is not only love of fellow man but fulfillment, in the highest degree possible for him as an individual, of the *mitzvot* of the *halachah*, the historic structure of religious practice elaborated by the teachers of Judaism in response to their revelatory encounters with God. Rosenzweig did not accept the orthodox position that the *halachah* itself is divinely revealed, but urged his fellow Jews seeking to return to a fuller experience of Judaism to treat it with reverence and to discover for themselves, through serious attempts at observance, what elements of it could become transformed for them from *Gesetz*, or legal prescription, into *Gebot*, or religiously vital commandment, experienced as directly addressed to the self. On this issue he exchanged correspondence with his friend Martin Buber, who tended to deprecate the halachic aspects of Judaism.[6]

Having once been so strongly attracted to Christianity that he was on the verge of adopting it as his own faith, Rosenzweig was driven to defining its relationship to Judaism. The two biblical religions, he concluded, represent two different but equally valid covenants with God. Judaism is the "eternal life" and Christianity is the "eternal way." The divinely appointed task of the Church is to bring the pagan world to God, while the mission of the Synagogue is to preserve the Jewish people, already with God, as a holy community untainted by the moral ambiguities that involvement in the world necessarily entails and with its gaze fixed steadfastly on the ultimate redemption. Although Rosenzweig's conception of Judaism and Christianity has found a fair number of admirers in Christian theological circles, it has gained little support among Jewish thinkers. On the other hand, his philosophical explication of the categories of biblical faith and his view of *halachah* have had a profound impact on subsequent Jewish religious thought; echoes of them are strongly discernible in much Jewish theological discussion in America and elsewhere to the present day.[7]

While Rosenzweig's intellectual influence has been felt mainly in Jewish religious circles, that of Martin Buber (1878–1965) has probably been even greater in the Christian and general philosophical worlds than in the Jewish. His re-creation of the tales of the Ḥasidim [8] have perhaps found as many non-Jewish as Jewish readers, and his philosophy of dialogue has had an enormous effect not only on twentieth-century Christian theology but in many other areas as well, including contemporary ethical theory, psychotherapy, social work, and education.

Born in Vienna, Buber spent much of his childhood at the home of his grandfather, the distinguished scholar of the *Midrash* Solomon Buber, in Lemberg, acquiring a good Jewish education and exposed on occasion to the life of the Ḥasidim in the vicinity. After studying art history, comparative religion, and philosophy at several German universities, he became editor of the Zionist journal *Die Welt* at the age of twenty-three. Throughout his life he continued to work for the Zionist cause, frequently irritating those of its leaders who were guided only by considerations of *Realpolitik* with his insistence on the moral goals that a Jewish state must serve. In his twenties Buber undertook an intensive study of the literature of the Ḥasidim and began to write the stream of books and essays that made him the foremost interpreter of Ḥasidism to the western world. Having published his classic little volume *Ich und Du* (*I and Thou*),[9] presenting his philosophy of dialogue, in 1923, he was appointed professor of the philosophy of Jewish religion and ethics at Frankfort-am-Main a year later and held this post until his dismissal by the Nazis in 1933. In 1938 the world-renowned scholar left Germany and settled in Jerusalem, where he served as professor of social philosophy at the Hebrew University, and spent the remainder of his life there.

In *I and Thou*, upon which his fame as a philosopher rests, Buber distinguished between the "I-Thou" relation of a person to other persons and things in the world, a relation characterized by reciprocity, openness, presentness, and immediacy, and the "I-It" relation, characterized by the absence of these qualities. The tendency of the modern, technological world to make the manipulative and objective "I-It" relation massively dominant, he suggested, must lead to a further deterioration of authentic interpersonal relationships, which are dependent on a dialogue wherein the partners truly speak and respond to one another. This tendency also militates against a genuine experience of God, for God—or the Eternal Thou, as Buber calls Him—is known not through logical demonstration or metaphysical speculation but only through a person's particular I-Thou encounters with other persons, animals, nature, and works of art. In every finite Thou the Eternal Thou is present and speaks through the dialogical situation to the person sensitive to His voice. That God is not found in rare, supernatural events but in the human relationships of ordinary life, in the "hallowing of the everyday," is, Buber urged, one of the great insights of Ḥasidism.

Judaism, according to Buber, has stressed the reality of the dialogical encounter between man and God more than any other religion. The Hebrew Bible, in his view, is the record of a thousand-year-long dialogue between the I of the speaking God and the Thou of the hearing Israel. The dialogue finds its consummate expression in the covenant, which forever set Israel its historic task: the Jews were to become a holy nation and build a community in which the kingship of God would be realized in every aspect of its life—social, economic, and political. The first and second Jewish commonwealths failed the task, and the conditions of Diaspora life afterward made its fulfillment impossible, but the new Jewish state of our time, Buber repeatedly declared, provides another opportunity that must not be missed.

Buber the philosopher of dialogue and prophet of social justice has been highly revered among contemporary Jews. But many, particularly in the more Orthodox and conservative wings of Judaism, have questioned his competence to serve as a Jewish religious guide. The major reason for this is the fact that he was not personally observant of most traditional rituals and declined to attribute any special religious authority to the *halachah*. Existentialist both in ethics and religion, Buber insisted that authentic response must always arise out of the immediacy of the unique situation confronting the individual at a given moment, and cannot be dictated by a supposedly timeless and universally valid code of moral or ritual law. Although his attitude toward the *halachah* has made him suspect in certain quarters, Buber is likely to be a continuing source of inspiration to all future attempts to strengthen a biblically oriented understanding and appropriation of Judaism among Jews.

When Hitler came to power in 1933 Buber was appointed director of the new Central Office for Jewish Adult Education, established to provide educational opportunities for Jews now expelled from German schools. German Jewry in those dark years closed ranks and reaffirmed its heritage with a new vigor that produced a veritable cultural and religious renaissance in the brief time remaining before its extinction. It was responding to the spirit of the challenge placed before it by Robert Weltsch, editor of the influential Zionist journal *Jüdische Rundschau* in Berlin, who in April 1933, shortly after the Nazis organized their boycott of Jewish stores and plastered their windows with yellow six-pointed stars, wrote: "This was supposed to be a disgrace. Jews, pick up the Shield of David and wear it with pride!" Buber played a major role in organizing the spiritual resistance of the Jews in the first years after Hitler's rise to power. The leading figure and chief spokesman of German Jewry at that time, however, was Rabbi Leo Baeck (1873–1956), president of the Reichsvertretung der Juden in Deutschland. This was the official representative organization of the Jewish community that was established in

1933 and carried on social services, established schools, organized cultural programs, and facilitated the emigration of more than half of Germany's Jews before the doors clanged finally shut in 1941.

Baeck, who had served as a Liberal rabbi and professor at the Hochschule für die Wissenschaft des Judentums in Berlin since 1912, provided a superb example of dignity and tenacity, refusing invitations to rabbinic and academic posts abroad and affirming that he would remain with the last *minyan* of Jews in Germany. In 1935, after the Nuremberg laws reduced Jews to the status of pariahs in the Third Reich, Baeck composed a prayer which he sent to all rabbis in Germany to be recited at the Kol Nidrei service of Yom Kippur. It was not read at that time because it was discovered and suppressed by the Nazi police, but the text was inserted into the record of Adolf Eichmann's trial in Jerusalem in 1961. In this prayer Baeck had the courage to declare:

> We stand before our God. With the same fervor with which we confess our sins, the sins of the individual and the sins of the community, do we, in indignation and abhorrence, express our contempt for the lies concerning us and the defamation of our religion and its testimonies. . . . In our prayers, in our hope, in our confession, we are one with all Jews on earth. We look upon each other and know who we are; we look up to our God and know what shall abide.[10]

As a theologian Leo Baeck made his mark with his *Das Wesen des Judentums* (*The Essence of Judaism*),[11] published in 1905 as an apologetic response to Adolf von Harnack's *Das Wesen des Christentums* (*The Essence of Christianity*), written several years earlier. The book, which has gone through eleven German editions and has been translated into English, Hebrew, and Japanese, is the representative work of twentieth-century German Liberal Judaism. Under the influence of Kantian and neo-Kantian philosophy, and maintaining the classical position of the German-Jewish reformers, Baeck assigns the moral commandment the primary place in Judaism. In his view Judaism consists essentially of a dialectical polarity between "commandment" (*Gebot*) and "mystery" (*Geheimnis*). Its commandments do not necessarily form a legal system like the traditional *halachah*, but appear in the form of "instructions for action" that tear through the veil of the divine mystery like flashes of lightning. In the religious structure of Judaism there is a vital tension between order and freedom, between God's nearness, experienced in the commandment, and His distance and otherness, felt in the mystery out of which the commandment originates. Baeck criticized Christianity, which he characterized as a "romantic" religion of the abstract spirit yearning for transworldly salvation, and contrasted it with Judaism, the "classical" religion of the concrete spirit engaged in activity directed toward redeeming this world. Though not an active Zionist, he had a strong sense of Jewish peoplehood that finds its profoundest expression in his last work, *Dieses Volk (This People Israel*, 1955–1957).[12]

Leo Baeck survived Nazism. Deported to the concentration camp at Theresienstadt in 1943, he ministered indefatigably to its miserable inmates and encouraged them to endure their sufferings with a measure of faith and hope. When the American army liberated Theresienstadt in 1945, he was—miraculously—still alive. But almost six million of his fellow Jews had died in the Holocaust. Hitler had not succeeded in his professed aim of making Europe *judenrein*, but he and his minions had killed more than half of its Jewish population and virtually destroyed Jewish life in the central, eastern, and southern parts of the continent.

❦

We shall not attempt to give an account of the bestiality of the Nazi leaders as they engineered the extermination of their victims after conquering most of Europe, or of the valor of those Jews who in the uprising of the ghettos of Warsaw, Bialystok, and elsewhere decided to stage a last-ditch fight against their murderers. Nor shall we attempt to portray the courage—and the despair—of the millions of others who went without resistance and in bewildered incomprehension to their deaths. The details of the soul-sickening and mind-numbing tragedy are readily available in any recent history of the Jewish people, and some sense of its incredible horror is conveyed in the many diaries and memoirs, written both by victims who perished and others who survived, that have been published since 1945. We present here merely a table of comparative population figures for the nations of Europe with major Jewish settlements in 1933, when Hitler came to power, and in 1946, when the smoke of World War II and the Holocaust had cleared away. These figures indicate how effectively the Nazi executioners and their accomplices had done their work before their defeat by the American, British, and Russian armies, and how, with the exception of the Jewries of Great Britain, France, and the Soviet Union, those of practically all the other European countries had been rendered numerically insignificant and deprived of the strength that might give them promise of creative survival.

The Jewish Population of Europe

Country	1933	1946
U.S.S.R.	3,021,000	1,800,000
Poland	3,113,000	200,000
Rumania	728,000	360,000
Germany	503,000	85,000 *
Hungary	444,000	150,000
Czechoslovakia	356,000	50,000
Great Britain	280,000	400,000
France	260,000	180,000
Holland	102,000	30,000
Greece	73,000	10,500
Yugoslavia	68,000	10,000
European Turkey	51,000	50,000
Belgium	50,000	25,000
Italy	48,000	35,000

* Including displaced persons.

Events since the end of the war have further altered the demographic situation. Poland suffered the greatest losses in the Holocaust. Thousands of its Jews who had escaped to Russia returned shortly after the war and tried to rebuild their lives, settling mainly in Silesia and in the cities of Warsaw, Lodz, and Cracow. But pogroms by Poles against Jews, the worst at Kielce in 1946, and the general spread of anti-Semitism under the new communist regime, impelled many to flee, and by 1958 approximately one hundred forty thoussand Jews had emigrated to Israel. Another outbreak of intense anti-Semitism in 1968–1969 motivated the departure of most of the remainder, and Jewish life in Poland is now almost completely snuffed out.

In Rumania the postwar communist regime set about liquidating Jewish organizational life,, and between 1948 and 1952 over one hundred twenty-five thousand Jews left for Israel. In recent years the government of Rumania has left Jews undisturbed and even maintained diplomatic relations with Israel when all the other communist governments of eastern Europe broke off with her in the wake of the Six Day War of 1967. At present there are approximately one hundred thousand Jews left in the country, the majority concentrated in Bucharest and Jassy, with synagogues and schools functioning under the leadership of an energetic chief rabbi, Moses Rosen. But Rumanian Jewry today is no more than a pale shadow of what it was in the prewar period. The same is true of Hungarian Jewry. The accession to power of a communist government in 1948 led to the nationalization of Jewish institutions and the centralization of religious organizations under one authority. Many Jews fled the country in the wake of the unsuccessful revolution of 1956. Today there are fewer than one hundred thousand Jews in Hungary, most of them living in Budapest. Hungarian Jewry, however, can boast a unique phenomenon, the only rabbinical seminary in the communist world. The school, located in Budapest, has only a handful of students but is presently led by a distinguished scholar, Rabbi Alexander Scheiber (b. 1913), who has devoted himself to exploring the records of the once great Jewish community of his country and edited several volumes of *Monumenta Hungariae Judaica*. In Czechoslovakia half of the fifty thousand Jews who remained at the end of the war left for Israel in the period from 1945 to 1953. High positions were held in the postwar government by Jews, among them Rudolf Slansky, who was vice-premier and general secretary of the Czech Communist Party. But with the trial of Slansky and several of his associates in 1952 on charges of "Trotskyite-Titoist-Zionist activities in the service of American imperialism" and their subsequent execution, the number of Jews prominent in government and public life decreased markedly. The crushing by Russian troops in 1968 of a later liberal regime further dispirited the remaining Jewish community. At present Czechoslovakia has no more than twelve thousand Jews, and Jewish religious life is virtually nonexistent.

The end of the war found a few thousand Jews still alive in Germany, some of them survivors of concentration camps that had been liberated and some baptized or partners in mixed marriages who had somehow been saved by their "Aryan" relatives. Many other thousands spent a brief time in Germany as "displaced persons" before going to Israel or elsewhere. Of those who remained, a number felt that the presence of a Jewish community in Germany was necessary to prove that Hitler had not fully succeeded in his demonic plan of making Germany *judenrein*, and to serve as a living reminder to the German people of their guilt and obligation to atone. The government of West Germany under Konrad Adenauer, who entered into a reparations agreement with the State of Israel, and his successors, has contributed to the construction of new synagogues and the rebuilding of historical structures such as the Rashi Synagogue in Worms. German Jewry, numbering less than thirty-five thousand today (including several thousand in the communist German Democratic Republic), has well-organized communities, but religious and cultural life is at a low ebb. Its membership consists of an unusually large proportion of older people, and the intermarriage rate is very high. The future of Jewish life in Germany must be judged precarious.

☙ ❦ ❧

In the Soviet Union hundreds of thousands of Jews were ruthlessly murdered when the Nazis, in 1941, invaded and quickly occupied most of the areas with dense Jewish populations that had recently been annexed by Joseph Stalin—Belorussia, east Galicia, Bessarabia, Lithuania, and Latvia—and then penetrated into the Ukraine and Russia itself. Half a million Jews fought with great distinction in the Red Army during the war, knowing that the Nazis were especially intent upon exterminating their people; their patriotism and valor are attested by the large number who were decorated with the highest award, Hero of the Soviet Union. In 1941 the Soviet government created a Jewish Anti-Fascist Committee to solicit political and financial support among the Jews of the world for the Russian struggle against Germany. The Committee continued to function for a few years after the war as the unofficial representative body of Soviet Jewry and as a liaison with Jews in other countries, and it was instrumental in reviving the publication of Yiddish books and the activities of the Yiddish theater that had been largely suspended during the war years. This revival, as well as the unexpected support and endorsement by the Soviet government of the establishment of the State of Israel in 1948, encouraged hopes of happier days for Jewish life in Russia.

These hopes were rudely shattered shortly afterward. The sudden dissolution of the Jewish Anti-Fascist Committee and the arrest of most of its members in 1948 inaugurated a period of five "black years," as Russian Jews have come to call them. Soviet newspapers embarked on a venomous campaign against "cosmopolitanism," directed mainly at Jewish intellectuals. Synagogues and Jewish schools were denounced as hotbeds of subversion and summarily

[384]

closed. A wave of anti-Semitism broke across the country, and many Jews in government and academic life were dismissed from their positions. In 1952 twenty-five leading Jewish writers and intellectuals were executed on charges of treason, among them such outstanding figures as David Bergelson, Peretz Markish, Leib Kvitko, and David Hofstein. Shortly afterward, in January 1953, the arrest and impending trial of a group of prominent doctors, most of them Jewish, on a charge of conspiring to kill government leaders was announced. Only the death two months later of Stalin, whose paranoid fear of Jews in the last years of his life seems to have inspired these acts, ended the terror of Russian Jewry.

The "thaw" that followed Stalin's death under the regime of Nikita Khrushchev brought relief from the excesses of the preceding period, but the Jewish institutions destroyed in the "black years" were not restored. Synagogues continued to be closed down; according to Soviet sources, the number decreased from four hundred fifty to ninety-six in the period between 1956 and 1963. The printing of Jewish religious books was generally banned and the baking of *matzot* proscribed. Judaism was subjected to a special barrage of slander in newspapers and books, as was the State of Israel, against which the Soviet Union had allied itself with the Arab nations. The increasingly loud protests of both Jews and distinguished non-Jewish political figures in the western world beginning in the late 1950s and continuing into the 1960s brought some alleviation of the hardships suffered by Jews. A few concessions, such as the printing of a *siddur* and the restoration of permission to bake *matzot*, were granted by the government in response to the pressure of worldwide public opinion, but the Jews of Russia continued to be largely deprived of the freedom to express themselves either culturally or religiously without fear and hindrance.

But despite—or perhaps because of—the apparently determined effort of the government to annihilate all vestiges of significant Jewish identity among the two and a half million Jews living in the Soviet Union, many of them in recent years have begun to experience a heightened and defiant sense of Jewishness. Evidence of this was provided by the gathering of large crowds of young Jews, most of them nonreligious and Jewishly illiterate, in the street outside the Great Synagogue in Moscow on Simḥat Torah each year during the 1960s. Thousands of Russian Jews, it appears, have also begun to study Hebrew and Jewish history, often clandestinely. Tens of thousands have demanded the right, since they cannot fulfill themselves culturally or religiously and are apprehensive about their future as Jews in Russia, to leave the country and emigrate to Israel. And the Soviet regime, while permitting only a few hundred of its Jewish citizens to leave each year during the 1960s and banning emigration to Israel altogether after the Six Day War, suddenly reversed itself, apparently in response to the clamor of both Jewish and non-Jewish voices throughout the world, and permitted some twenty thousand Jews to depart for Israel in 1971. In 1972, although imposing an extortionate exit fee on Jews with a higher education who wished to leave, the Soviet authorities allowed over thirty thousand to go to Israel. In 1973 an even larger number was permitted to depart.

How long Russian Jews will be permitted to emigrate, and how many will choose to do so, are unpredictable. It seems probable, however, that a majority of the Jewish population of the Soviet Union will remain in its native land. Are the Jews who stay doomed to total loss of their cultural and religious substance within a few decades, and will Russian Jewry eventually disappear altogether? To assume this and to write off completely the possibility of a viable indigent Jewish community in Russia seems unjustified. It appears unlikely that all Jews in whom a strong sense of Jewish identity has been created or reawakened will leave. The spark that has already been fanned in some may spread to many others. It is certainly not beyond the realm of possibility that the Soviet government may develop a more significant degree of tolerance for religious belief and cultural diversity among its citizens, and that, under these circumstances, a religiously and culturally vital Jewish community may once again appear in Russia.

⋙⟡⋘

In western Europe only the Jewries of Great Britain and France appear to have sufficient numerical strength to maintain a meaningful level of Jewish life in the long run, although small Jewish communities, progressively eroded by assimilation and intermarriage, are likely to continue in Italy, Switzerland, the Netherlands, Belgium, Denmark, and Sweden.

British Jewry, as we have noted, obtained new strength from the thousands of refugees fleeing central Europe who came to England in the years before World War II. Other refugees arrived during and after the war, but not in great numbers. While hardly noted for its high degree of religious fervor, the staid traditionalist wing of the

Jewish community went through a traumatic experience in the 1960s when the chief rabbi vetoed the appointment of Rabbi Louis Jacobs to the principalship of Jews' College and his reappointment to his synagogue pulpit on the grounds that Jacobs did not believe that the entire Torah is of divine origin. The "Jacobs Affair" did not contribute to any marked revival of orthodoxy, and the new chief rabbi, Immanuel Jakobovits, declared after taking office in 1967 that the primary challenge confronting British Jewry, in view of "staggering losses by defections, assimilation, and intermarriage," was the survival of Judaism. Assimilation and a high rate of intermarriage continue apace, but there are still some four hundred synagogues functioning in Great Britain, and a strong sense of Jewish peoplehood, focused especially on concern for the State of Israel, permeates most of its Jewish population. The last Yiddish weekly in England suspended publication in 1967, but the *Jewish Chronicle* of London continues to be the finest Jewish newspaper in English anywhere in the world. In recent years nontraditionalist Judaism in Great Britain has grown somewhat stronger as many Jews, dissatisfied with the dogmatism of the United Synagogue, have joined both Liberal synagogues and the Reform congregations associated with the West London Synagogue. These two groups, subordinating their long rivalry, have moved toward a rapprochement and now collaborate in maintaining the Leo Baeck College, a training school for liberal rabbis.

France is the only European nation to which Jews migrated in large numbers after World War II. Indeed, its Jewish population has tripled since 1945 and now stands at five hundred fifty thousand, about 1 percent of the total population of the country. Some "displaced persons" and survivors of the concentration camps who passed through France after the war decided to settle there. Between 1954 and 1961 about one hundred thousand Jews from Egypt, Morocco, Tunisia, and Algeria, most of them French-speaking, moved to France. After the establishment of Algerian independence in 1962 immigration increased dramatically; by the end of 1963 virtually the whole Jewish community of Algeria, consisting of over one hundred thousand persons, had come to the mother country in which they held citizenship. In the late 1960s Algerian Jewry was followed by substantial contingents of Jews fleeing again from Tunisia and Morocco. The result of the massive influx from North Africa is that the majority of the French-Jewish community presently consists of Sephardim. Over 60 percent of the community is concentrated in Paris and its vicinity, but there are sizable settlements in

Marseilles, Lyon, Toulouse, Nice, and Strasbourg, as well as smaller ones throughout the country.

While religious life is rather weak in the contemporary Jewish community of France, it is effectively organized. The orthodox synagogues are united in the Consistoire Central Israélite and maintain two rabbinical seminaries, the École Rabbinique and the Séminaire Israélite de France. The few nontraditionalist congregations are organized into the Union Libérale Israélite, which is affiliated with the World Union for Progressive Judaism and trains rabbis at its Institut International d'Études Hébraïques. Cultural activities are in a more flourishing condition than religious life. There are several daily, weekly, and monthly journals in Yiddish, and many books on Jewish subjects and Israel are published each year. The universities of Paris and Strasbourg offer courses in Jewish history, literature, and sociology; eight other French universities, as well as many *lycées*, provide instruction in Hebrew. Although French Jewry was shocked by the vehement anti-Israel position taken by General Charles de Gaulle and his government after the Six Day War, it did not waver in its own support of Israel. And when de Gaulle in 1967 permitted himself to refer insultingly to the Jews as *"un peuple d'élite, sûr de lui-même et dominateur,"* he was publicly taken to task by the chief rabbi, Jacob Kaplan. While the Jewish community of postwar France has not yet attained full maturity, it has the potentiality of becoming an important and creative center of Jewish life. The high rates of intermarriage and assimilation, however, continue to pose serious problems.

Despite the fact that there has been a mass exodus of Jews from North Africa to France (many have also gone to Israel), there are still substantial numbers of Jews in Morocco and Tunisia. There are also a good many Jews left in several Asian countries—Turkey (more in European than in Asian Turkey), Iran, and Iraq. But the future of the Jewries of all these lands, as well as the small number of Jews remaining in Syria and Lebanon, is highly precarious. It is doubtful how long these remnants of the chain of once great and cultured communities of Sephardic Jews that stretched for centuries across North Africa and western Asia can survive.

❧❦❧

Before bringing this chapter to a close, we must say something about the offshoots of European Jewry living in what were formerly colonies of the British Empire and in Latin America, and about the character of their religious and cultural life.

A small number of Jews settled in Montreal after the British conquest of Canada, and in 1768 they organized the Sephardic congregation Shearith Israel. Ashkenazic Jews began to migrate to Canada from England, as well as Germany and eastern Europe, in the first decades of the nineteenth century, but it was only in 1858 that the Ashkenazic congregation Shaar Hashomayim was formed. In the meantime another Ashkenazic congregation had been established in Toronto. Jews moved westward and began to establish themselves in British Columbia during the gold rush of 1858. While several thousand Jews were settled as farmers in Saskatchewan by Baron Maurice de Hirsch's Jewish Colonization Association, large-scale migration to Canada began only after the pogroms of 1881 in Russia. In the single decade 1900–1910 the Canadian-Jewish population rose from sixteen thousand to seventy-five thousand. Many thousands more came from Europe in the years following World War I and continuing into the period after World War II, when Canada was one of the few places in the world with generally unrestrictive immigration policies. Today Canada has a Jewish community of more than three hundred thousand, boasting an excellent educational system including several *yeshivot* and teachers' seminaries, many large synagogues and Jewish libraries, a flourishing press, and an effective national representative organization in the Canadian Jewish Congress. The vast majority of Canadian Jewry is concentrated in the three cities of Montreal, Toronto, and Winnipeg.

When the British *raj* began in India in 1757 there were two small colonies of Jews living on the vast subcontinent. The first were the Cochin Jews on the Malabar coast, who may have established themselves in Cranganore as early as the sixth century C.E. but moved to Malabar after the capture of Cranganore by the Portuguese in 1523. These native Cochin Jews (or "Black Jews") were later joined by immigrants from Turkey, Syria, and Europe ("White Jews"), and a rigid caste system separating the two groups was maintained. Despite their isolation from the mainstreams of Jewry, the Cochin Jews maintained a strong religious and cultural life. Almost all of them have now moved to Israel, less than one hundred being left in India when they celebrated the four hundredth anniversary of their synagogue in 1968. The second colony were the Bene Israel, whose origins are lost in antiquity. Deprived for ages of all contact with the larger centers of Jewish life in Europe, Africa, and Asia, they had lapsed by the eighteenth century into a pattern of religious observance quite different from that generally followed in the Jewish world. Teachers from Cochin and Iraq later brought them back to more traditional norms of practice. Most of the Bene Israel, who had concentrated their settlement in Bombay under British rule, have now moved to Israel, where they maintain their own communities. In the early nineteenth century Iraqi Jews began to migrate to India and formed Arabic-speaking communities in Bombay, Calcutta, and elsewhere. In the later period of British rule several thousand European Jews also settled in the large cities. At present there are only about fourteen thousand Jews in India, and their religious and cultural activities are very limited.

In South Africa Jewish life appears to be flourishing. Jews began to arrive there early in the nineteenth century, establishing a synagogue in Capetown in 1841. After the discovery of gold toward the end of the century a considerable number of European Jews were drawn to South Africa, settling mainly in Johannesburg. In the period following World War I thousands of Jews, chiefly from Lithuania and Poland, came to the country, as did also a good number of refugees from Nazi Germany. South African Jewry, presently numbering over one hundred thousand, is concentrated largely in Johannesburg and Capetown, where traditional synagogues predominate, although a Reform movement inaugurated in 1933 has gained a growing number of adherents. The community is generally well-to-do and has strong Zionist sympathies. Its future, however, is clouded by the reactionary policies of the South African government, whose racist insistence on apartheid and suppression of the black masses of the population creates a potentiality for violence and revolution. Elsewhere in Africa some five thousand Jews live in Rhodesia, about equally divided between the cities of Bulawayo and Salisbury.

Australia has had a Jewish community since the early nineteenth century, when Jews from England began to settle there. A congregation was established in Sydney in 1831 and others were soon founded in Melbourne, Adelaide, and Brisbane. Substantial immigration began after the Russian pogroms of 1881, and many new settlers have arrived in the last few decades as a result of Australia's liberal immigration policies. Among the Jews achieving high position in the country have been Sir Isaac Isaacs, the first Australian-born governor-general, and Sir John Monash, commander of the Australian Expeditionary Force in World War I. Most of the congregations of Australian Jewry, numbering over seventy thousand, are orthodox and recognize the authority of the chief rabbi in London, but large liberal synagogues have also been established in Melbourne and Sydney. There is also a small Jewish community of some four thousand in New Zealand, mainly in the cities of Wellington and Auckland.

In general, the Jewries that came from Europe to the dominions and former colonies of the British Empire have prospered under the conditions of freedom and security they have enjoyed, and continue to maintain a fairly vigorous religious and cultural life.

As for Latin America, Jewish settlement there preceded the arrival of the Jews in North America. In the sixteenth century Marranos from Portugal came to the colony of Brazil, where they were sometimes harassed by the Inquisition. After conquest of Recife by the Dutch in 1631, some of the Marranos of Brazil reverted publicly to Judaism and many immigrants came from Holland to join them in establishing a flourishing Jewish community. With the reconquest of Recife by the Portuguese in 1654, the Jews had to leave. Some returned to Holland, others formed settlements throughout the West Indies, and a few, as we have noted, came to New Amsterdam. When Brazil became an independent nation in 1822, it became possible for Marranos to return to Judaism, and some did so. Later in the century Jewish immigrants began arriving from Europe and settling in the larger cities. Some Jews also came to Brazil from Russia and Rumania in the first decades of the twentieth century under the auspices of the Jewish Colonization Association, although the Association concentrated its efforts on bringing Jews to Argentina. A good many refugees from Nazi Germany arrived in the 1930s. Today the Jewish population of Brazil, settled mainly in Rio de Janeiro, São Paulo, and Porto Alegre, numbers some one hundred fifty thousand. While its religious life is not strong, Brazilian Jewry manifests considerable interest in Jewish culture.

Like Brazil, Argentina also attracted Marrano settlers in the sixteenth century, but these eventually disappeared into the Christian populace. Its present Jewry dates from the second half of the nineteenth century and was initiated with the organization of the Jewish community of Buenos Aires in 1862 by immigrants from France, England, and Germany. Large numbers of Jews from eastern Europe began arriving in the 1880s following the Russian pogroms, and especially after World War I a great many Spanish-speaking Sephardic Jews from lands along the Mediterranean littoral moved to Argentina. The attempts of the Jewish Colonization Association over a period of many years beginning in 1891 to settle east European Jews as farmers on Argentine soil, while supported by vast sums of money, did not prove spectacularly successful. In 1940 there were twenty-five Jewish agricultural colonies in Argentina with some twenty-eight thousand settlers, but the number of colonies and their inhabitants has greatly diminished through the move of families to the cities. At present the Argentine Jewish population is close to five hundred thousand, including eighty thousand Sephardim; and Buenos Aires with its three hundred sixty thousand Jews has one of the largest Jewish communities in the world. The capital city is particularly noted as a stronghold of Yiddish culture and has become in recent years a major center for the publication of Yiddish books. Buenos Aires boasts a Yiddish theater as well as two daily and four weekly Yiddish newspapers, in addition to periodicals in Hebrew, Spanish, German, and Hungarian. Religious life, as is generally the case throughout Latin American Jewry, is rather pallid.

The Jewish settlement in Uruguay, consisting chiefly of immigrants from eastern and central Europe, was established only in the twentieth century. Virtually all of Uruguay's fifty-four thousand Jews live in the capital city of Montevideo, where factionalism is a problem, as it is almost everywhere in Latin American Jewry; Montevideo's Jews are divided into three Ashkenazic (east European, German, and Hungarian) communities and a Sephardic community. Like Buenos Aires, Montevideo supports two daily Yiddish newspapers. It also has weeklies in Yiddish, Spanish, and German.

Chile attracted Marrano settlers while under Spanish rule beginning in the sixteenth century, but the Inquisition made public practice of Judaism impossible and the Marranos became totally assimilated. A few Jews came to the country after its independence was established early in the nineteenth century. The present community, however, dates largely from the period after World War I and includes a good many German refugees. Out of Chile's thirty-five thousand Jews, thirty thousand live in Santiago.

As in Chile, Marranos came to Mexico with the Spanish conquistadores in the sixteenth century, and two of them were burned in an auto-da-fé in 1528. While a few European Jews settled in Mexico in the nineteenth century, the present community of thirty thousand (twenty-eight thousand living in Mexico City) is largely of post-World War I origin. Half of Mexico's Jews are Ashkenazim who migrated from Poland, Russia, Lithuania, and Germany, and the remainder are Sephardim from Syria, Turkey, and Greece. Mexico City has flourishing religious, cultural, and educational institutions. Among the notable cultural achievements of the community is the ten-volume *Encyclopedia Judaica Castellana*, published between 1948 and 1951 and especially useful for its articles on Spanish and contemporary South American Jewry.

Elsewhere in South America there is a community of ten thousand Jews in Colombia, with half of them concentrated in Bogotá; twelve thousand in Venezuela, most of them in Caracas; and four thousand in Peru, with all but a few in Lima. Marranos lived in Peru from the early part of the sixteenth century, and during the period of the Peruvian Inquisition from 1570 to 1806 over one hundred were condemned on charges of Judaizing, and twenty-four were burned at the stake. The present Jewish community of Peru, like that of Colombia and Venezuela, is of twentieth-century origin.

While Jewish cultural activity in such major centers of population as Buenos Aires, São Paulo, Rio de Janeiro, Montevideo, and Mexico City is intense and varied, religious life almost everywhere is feeble. This is no doubt due in large measure to the general lack of effective religious leadership and modern rabbis and teachers, but it may also be a result of the larger religious environment and the fact that the dominant faith of Latin America, Roman Catholicism, engages the formal loyalty of the masses of the people much more than their genuine sentiment. Although many of its members have prospered in recent years, the future of Latin American Jewry in several countries where military dictatorships face revolutionary challenges from the disaffected classes, and where Jews are especially vulnerable economically because of their position as middlemen, remains doubtful.

At the beginning of the twentieth century nearly nine million Jews, more than 80 percent of the total world Jewish population, lived on the European continent, and Europe had for ages been the chief locus of Jewish culture and creativity. Only somewhat over one million, less than 10 percent of the total, lived in America, and somewhat fewer than fifty thousand were settled in Palestine. The tragic and turbulent events of the century brought not only the destruction of close to six million of Europe's Jews, but a massive redistribution of the world Jewish population and a radical change in its center of gravity. At the beginning of the 1970s all of Europe had only about four million Jews, and Europe had long ceased to be the principal center of Judaism. Well over six million Jews, more than 40 percent of the world's total, now lived in the United States, and over two and a half million, almost 20 percent of the total, were residents of the State of Israel.

America and Israel have obviously become the two major foci of Jewish life and of Judaism. To them we must now turn.

CHAPTER

XV

Jewish Life
and Religious Thought
in America in the
Twentieth Century

A<small>T THE THRESHOLD</small> of the twentieth century the number of
Jews in the United States was approximately one million, out of a
total population of seventy-six million. In the less than two decades
since large-scale Jewish immigration from eastern Europe had begun
in the wake of the Russian pogroms, the Jewish population of
America had increased fourfold and its character had been radically
transformed. The prosperous, homogenized, German-speaking but
increasingly Americanized and generally assimilationist constituency
of the Reform synagogue now represented only a minority of American Jewry; the majority consisted of immigrants from Russia, Poland, Rumania, and Austria-Hungary whose passage through Ellis
Island had occurred only a few years earlier.

In religious as well as cultural and intellectual respects, the new

[394]

immigrants exemplified an enormous diversity. Most of them remained orthodox both in practice and belief, but more than a few, under the indoctrination of the more radical tendencies of Haskalah or of Marxist ideology, had become skeptical and even militantly anti-religious while still in Europe, and they saw no reason to change their attitudes in the New World. Among the immigrants were Ḥasidim and Mitnaggedim, Zionists and anti-Zionists, socialists and anti-socialists, Hebraists and Yiddishists. The need to earn a livelihood was their most pressing and immediate concern, and for most of them the hours of labor were long and back-breaking, but the members of each group ardently promoted their respective positions and sought to win converts. The ideological diversity of the various factions in the areas of dense Jewish settlement in New York's Lower East Side and in other large cities, and the passion with which the controversies among them were conducted, gave greater color and intensity to American-Jewish life than it had known before. These became even more marked as the flow of immigrants from eastern Europe in the first years of the new century was transformed into a veritable flood (in the peak five-year period from 1904 to 1908 more than six hundred thousand arrived) and the Jewish population of America reached almost three million by the outbreak of World War I.

Some of the immigrants became peddlers and small shopkeepers, but most joined the urban proletariat, gravitating particularly toward the ready-made clothing industry in New York, Chicago, Philadelphia, Boston, Cleveland, Baltimore, and Rochester. It was in this industry that the Jewish labor movement, which began in the 1880s but gained significant strength only after 1900, developed. A landmark in the struggle of the Jewish trade unions for recognition and power was the successful three-month strike of sixty thousand cloakmakers directed by the International Ladies' Garment Workers Union following the catastrophic Triangle Shirtwaist Company fire of 1911, in which one hundred forty-six Italian and Jewish employees, almost all of them young girls, died in a New York factory where the most elementary measures to protect the safety of the workers were ignored. Distinguished native-born Jews such as Jacob Schiff, Louis Marshall, and Rabbi Judah Leon Magnes intervened in the bitter strike, which was finally settled chiefly through the efforts of Louis D. Brandeis, destined for appointment to the United States Supreme Court a few years later. By 1920 some two hundred fifty thousand Jews belonged to predominantly Jewish labor unions.

Associated with the Jewish labor movement was a secularist Yiddish culture which retained its vitality until well into the 1930s. Yid-dish daily newspapers, magazines, and books found avid readers, and the Yiddish theater was extremely popular. Some of the Yid-dishist ideologues were militantly antireligious, anti-Zionist, and so-cialist, but the masses of Yiddish-speaking Jews maintained at least a vestigial loyalty to Jewish religious practice, and many were sympa-thetic to the colonization efforts being made in Palestine. Extremely important to the Yiddish-speaking immigrants were their *chevras*, or societies, mainly established on a *Landesmannschaft*, or European home-town, basis. These societies provided not only fellowship and the possibility of maintaining longstanding friendships and associations but, in many cases, sick benefits and funeral arrangements. Around 1915 more than twelve hundred of these societies flourished in New York City alone. Some of them maintained orthodox and Yiddish-speaking synagogues, frequently housed in storefronts and lofts. Yiddish culture in America reached its peak in the early 1920s and declined steadily thereafter. With the cessation of large-scale Jewish immigration from eastern Europe after the enactment of restrictive congressional legislation, the Yiddish press, literature, and theater began to lose their clientele as the increasingly Americanized im-migrant generation was not replenished by new arrivals from over-seas, and the native-born generation largely lost touch with the loyal-ties of its fathers. Today only relics of the once vibrant Yiddish culture remain in America.

While Reform Judaism at the dawn of the twentieth century had long since lost its numerical supremacy in American Jewish life, as well as much of its original impetus, it continued to be an important movement—particularly in the Midwest and South, to which the east European immigrants at first came only in small numbers—and to retain the loyalty of the long-settled and more Americanized Jews throughout the country. In 1900 Isaac Mayer Wise, the pioneering builder of the institutions of American Reform Judaism whose per-sonality had dominated the movement for several decades, died. After a brief hiatus his office as president of the Hebrew Union College was assumed in 1903 by Kaufmann Kohler (1843–1926), who continued to occupy it until 1921. In the first two decades of the century Kohler was the generally recognized leader of the Re-form movement, although his actual influence may not have been as substantial as that of more eloquent spokesmen such as Emil G. Hirsch of Chicago.

Born in Fürth, Bavaria, into a rabbinic family, Kaufmann Kohler was given a traditional *yeshivah* education and studied for a time in Frankfurt-am-Main under Samson Raphael Hirsch, the leader of German Neo-Orthodoxy, whose religious point of view he later rejected but whose continuing influence he always gratefully acknowledged. Study at the universities of Berlin and Erlangen undermined his orthodox convictions and led him to a period of skepticism and spiritual confusion. His doctoral dissertation, *Der Segen Jacobs* (*The Blessing of Jacob*, 1867), reflected such a radically critical view of the Bible that it was difficult for him to obtain a rabbinic position in Germany. On the recommendation of Abraham Geiger, Kohler emigrated to America in 1869 and became rabbi of Congregation Beth El in Detroit. After marrying David Einhorn's daughter and serving for some years as rabbi of Sinai Congregation in Chicago, he succeeded his father-in-law in the pulpit of New York's Temple Beth El in 1879.

Kohler, as we have noted, was the chief architect of the Pittsburgh Platform of Reform Judaism, adopted in 1885. He was also one of the leading spirits in the preparation and publication of the *Jewish Encyclopedia*, serving as editor of its department of philosophy and theology and contributing some three hundred articles to it. On being called to the presidency of the Hebrew Union College at the age of sixty, he proceeded to revise its curriculum and to add several distinguished figures to its faculty, including the Talmudist Jacob Z. Lauterbach, historian of Jewish philosophy David Neumark, and biblical scholar Julian Morgenstern. He also engaged as librarian of the college Adolph S. Oko, who in the more than thirty years of his tenure contributed greatly to the building of its valuable collection of books and manuscripts. Kohler became embroiled in conflict with several of his faculty members on the issue of Zionism, to which he was adamantly opposed, but his presidency on the whole proved to be a period of growth both in size and quality for the Reform seminary and enhanced its reputation as a major seat of Jewish learning.

At the urging of Gustav Karpeles, president of the Society for the Promotion of the Science of Judaism in Berlin, Kohler wrote and published in German, in 1910, a ground-breaking work on the theology of Judaism. The book was later expanded and published in an English translation, in 1918, under the title *Jewish Theology Systematically and Historically Considered*. In this work Kohler set himself the task of "presenting Jewish doctrine and belief in relation to the most advanced scientific and philosophical ideas of the age, so as to offer a comprehensive view of life and the world [Lebens- und Weltanschauung]." [1] Drawing on the whole of Jewish religious literature from the biblical period to his own day, the author devoted the three parts of the book to the themes of "God," "Man," and "Israel and the Kingdom of God." Although insisting that his work was not apologetic, he vigorously defended the superiority of Jewish teaching over Christian and Mohammedan doctrine. Distinguished by a thorough knowledge of the sources and permeated with the standard nineteenth- and early twentieth-century liberal apotheosis of Reason and Progress, Kohler's *Jewish Theology*, which for several decades was regarded as a classic treatment of the subject, reflects a unique blending of pious faith, critical rationalism, and polemic argumentation.

Typical is Kohler's account of the Jewish conception of God in its most highly developed stage.

Judaism . . . teaches us to recognize God, above all, as revealing Himself in self-conscious activity, as determining all that happens by His absolutely free will, and thus as showing man how to walk as a free moral agent. In relation to the world, His work or workshop, He is the self-conscious Master, saying "I am that which I am"; in relation to man, who is akin to Him as a self-conscious rational and moral being, He is the living Fountain of all that knowledge and spirituality for which men long and in which alone they may find contentment and bliss. Thus the God of Judaism, the world's great *I Am*, forms a complete contrast not only to the lifeless powers of nature and destiny which were worshipped by the ancient pagans, but also to the God of modern paganism, a God divested of all personality and self-consciousness, such as He is conceived of by the new school of Christian theology, with its pantheistic tendency. I refer to the school of Ritschl, which strives to render the myth of the man-God philosophically intelligible by teaching that God reaches self-consciousness only in the perfect type of man, that is, Christ, while otherwise He is entirely immanent, one with the world. [2]

In defending the idea of the mission of Israel to the world, which had been so strongly asserted by Abraham Geiger and most of the major nineteenth-century protagonists of Reform in Germany and America as a central aspect of Judaism, Kohler found occasion to castigate the Zionists for their substitution of what he regarded as a narrow and ignoble nationalist vision of the destiny of the Jewish people. The Jew in the centuries after the rise of Christianity, he declared,

. . . proved to be the "Servant of the Lord who gave his back to the smiters," the "man of sorrows, despised and forsaken of men." . . . A two thousand years' history of martyrdom, a tragedy without parallel in the world, and yet sustained by a faith which never faltered and with words of praise and sanctification of the Most High which resounded throughout the centuries—this was the wondrous realization of the Deutero-Isaianic prophecy, for the grandeur of which our Nationalists have as little appreciation as have our anti-Semitic enemies. Well may the words of the English poet be applied here: "They also serve who only stand and wait." And for what did the Jew wait all these centuries? Not for his mere national resurrection or for the rebuilding of a state like any other, but for the new and grander revelation of God's glory, for the establishment of God's kingdom on earth.[3]

While Kohler in his early rabbinate had been a radical reformer, as evidenced by his transfer of the major worship service of the week to Sunday at Chicago's Sinai Temple in 1874, he tended in his later years toward a greater degree of conservatism. In opposition to Emil G. Hirsch and other rabbis who wished to extend Reform's revolutionary thrust, he advocated maintenance of worship on the traditional Sabbath, revitalization of such neglected festivals as Shavuot and Simḥat Torah, and more ceremonial observance in the Jewish home. Not all American Reform Jews by any means heeded his summons to a more traditional religious life, but his position as head of the Reform seminary lent a certain authority to his views and helped at least to retard the progressive de-Judaization of the Reform Synagogue.

We have noted that Kaufmann Kohler clashed with some of his faculty on the issue of Zionism. Pro-Zionist attitudes within the Reform movement, which remained generally negative to Jewish nationalist aspirations until the 1930s, were promoted in the opening decades of the century not only by several professors of the Hebrew Union College but also by a number of courageous rabbis who achieved nationwide recognition. The most eminent of these were undoubtedly Stephen S. Wise and Judah Leon Magnes, both of whom contributed importantly to the development of Jewish life in America.

Stephen S. Wise (1874–1949) in 1906 rejected the invitation of New York's prestigious Temple Emanu-El to become its rabbi because its trustees would not guarantee him complete freedom of the pulpit; a year later he established the Free Synagogue of New York, in which the pulpit was to be under no constraints whatever on the part of the lay leadership, the program of the congregation was to be

[399]

financed by voluntary contributions, and the pew ownership or rental system and all the class distinctions prevalent in most Reform congregations of the day were to be abolished. Wise was among the founders of the Federation of American Zionists, which later became the Zionist Organization of America. From 1916 to 1919 he was chairman of the Provisional Committee for Zionist Affairs and, as a friend of President Woodrow Wilson, played a part in the issuance of the Balfour Declaration and its prompt endorsement by the American government. In 1922, disturbed by the anti-Zionism that dominated the Hebrew Union College, he founded the Jewish Institute of Religion in New York as a school for training rabbis for all three denominations of American Jewry in the spirit of the progressive Judaism, Zionism, and political liberalism that constituted his own central commitments. Wise was also a founder of the still flourishing American Jewish Congress and served as its president for many years. While more than a few of his contemporaries in the Reform rabbinate preached eloquent sermons on social justice, Wise was particularly devoted to the cause of the worker and fought tirelessly for the strengthening of labor unions and social welfare legislation and against corrupt political machines. His vast energy and extraordinary oratorical power contributed to making him one of the foremost Jewish leaders in America during most of the first half of the twentieth century.

No less devoted to the Zionist cause was Judah Leon Magnes (1877–1948). Ordained at the Hebrew Union College in 1900, the California-born Magnes subsequently spent several years studying in Berlin and Heidelberg and during this period visited eastern Europe. He was deeply moved by the intense Jewish life he discovered there, and his Zionist sympathies were strengthened. Returning to America, Magnes served as rabbi of a Reform congregation in Brooklyn and subsequently became one of the rabbis of Temple Emanu-El. Convinced that Reform Judaism had taken a wrong direction and must return to the sources of Jewish tradition, and seeing no prospect of such a return, he resigned from the Reform ministry in 1910. In the ensuing years Magnes devoted himself with immense energy to the work of the Kehillah of New York City, serving as its president and guiding spirit. The Kehillah, founded in 1908 as the representative body of New York Jewry to advance and coordinate the chaotic activities of what had become the largest Jewish community in the world, sought to bring a measure of order into its religious life and to raise the standards of Jewish education. One of its enduring achievements was the organization, in 1910, of the first Bureau of Jewish Education in America, led for many years by the gifted educator Samson Benderley (1876–1944) and destined to serve as the prototype of similar professional agencies in most of the major centers of Jewish population in the United States. The Kehillah, under Magnes' leadership, was also involved in labor arbitration in the needle trades and other industries in which Jews were heavily represented, and it cooperated with New York's police department in helping to reduce criminal activity in the Jewish immigrant settlements. The very size and diversity of New York's Jewish populace made the efficient functioning of the Kehillah a virtual impossibility, and by 1922 it disintegrated. In the years that followed, however, many other sizable Jewish communities in the United States were more successful in establishing enduring and effective community councils.

As a result of his deep pacifist convictions, Magnes opposed the entry of the United States into World War I, though the Jewish community as a whole after 1917 vigorously supported it. His involvement in the peace movement weakened his authority both in the Kehillah and in the American Zionist movement, and by 1917 his brilliant career as a communal leader in the United States had reached an impasse. In 1921 Magnes emigrated with his family to Palestine, where he devoted himself to the organization of the Hebrew University. When the university was opened in 1925 he became its chancellor, and from 1935 until his death in 1948 he served as its president. It was largely as a result of his efforts that the university was established on a sound academic and fiscal basis. With the beginning of World War II, Magnes, despite the general pacifism which he continued to profess, called for war against Nazi Germany. He collaborated with his lifelong friend Henrietta Szold in the work of the Youth Aliyah and during the war directed relief activity among Jews throughout the Orient. Though an ardent Zionist of the Aḥad Ha-Am school, Magnes could not, with his pacifist and humanitarian ideals, remain unmoved by the growing animosity and violence in the relationships between Jews and Arabs in Palestine. In 1926 he collaborated with Arthur Ruppin in founding the *Berit Shalom* society to promote amicable relations between the two groups and to work for eventual establishment of an Arab-Jewish binational state in which each community would enjoy internal autonomy and cooperate with the other in the government on the basis of parity of rights. Later he worked with Rabbi Binyamin (Yehoshua Ha-Talmi),

[401]

Ernst Simon, Martin Buber, and others in the *Iḥud* organization, devoted to the same goals. Unfortunately, the binational ideal evoked little response from either the Arab or Jewish leadership, and violence continued, leading eventually to the partition of Palestine into separate Arab and Jewish states.

⋅⋅⋅⧼§⧽⋅⋅⋅

While still serving as a Reform rabbi in New York in the early years of the century, Magnes had been inspired to a return to religious traditionalism through his personal association with Solomon Schechter (1847–1915), who had recently arrived in America to assume the presidency of the Jewish Theological Seminary and into whose inner circle he was admitted. It was Schechter who, in the thirteen years of his presidency, raised the Seminary to a position of scholarly eminence and made it the fountainhead of a vital Conservative movement, ready to challenge Reform in a contest for the religious loyalties of the growing sector of Jews in the process of becoming Americanized.

Born in a small Rumanian town and brought up in an atmosphere of intense mystical piety (his father was a Ḥabad Ḥasid), Schechter later studied in Lemberg and at the Bet Ha-Midrash in Vienna. For several years he was also a student at the Hochschule für die Wissenschaft des Judentums and the University of Berlin, acquiring a critical methodology in the study of Jewish literature which he managed to combine successfully with an unqualified love of the Jewish tradition as a whole. In 1882 he was persuaded by his fellow student at the Hochschule, Claude G. Montefiore, to return with him to London and serve as his tutor in rabbinics. During his twenty years in England Schechter taught at Cambridge University, as well as University College in London, and acquired world fame as a rabbinic scholar. This fame was based largely on his recovery of the treasures of the Cairo *genizah*. With Charles Taylor, the noted Christian Hebraist and master of St. John's College, Schechter brought from Egypt to England and presented to Cambridge University over one hundred thousand old manuscripts and manuscript fragments. Seventy years later the history of the Jewries of the Mediterranean world is still being rewritten in the light of these documents.

In 1901 Schechter was induced by a number of outstanding American Jews, led by Judge Mayer Sulzberger of Philadelphia, to leave his comfortable position at Cambridge and come to New York to head the reorganized Jewish Theological Seminary, which some of them hoped would become a major instrument for the religious adjustment and Americanization of the masses of immigrants streaming into the country from eastern Europe. With funds provided by wealthy benefactors of the Seminary, most of whom were Reform Jews, Schechter attracted to its faculty several great scholars, including Louis Ginzberg, Israel Davidson, Alexander Marx, and Israel Friedlander. He also appointed as principal of the Seminary's new Teacher's Institute the young Mordecai Kaplan, destined to have an important influence on American-Jewish life and thought. Under Schechter's guidance, and with its remarkable faculty, the Seminary took its place as one of the major world centers of Jewish scholarship, and its graduates went forth to lead congregations that no longer sought to replicate the pattern of the east European *shul*, as did those of the unswervingly orthodox first generation immigrants, but to adapt tradition to the American environment without the major reformulation of worship and theology undertaken by the Reform movement.

After graduating several classes of rabbis from the Seminary, Schechter and his associates proceeded in 1913 to establish the United Synagogue of America, a national union of the Conservative congregations which now looked to the Seminary and its faculty for leadership and guidance. The goals of the United Synagogue were defined in thoroughly traditionalist and implicitly anti-Reform terms:

> The advancement of the cause of Judaism in America and the maintenance of Jewish tradition in its historical continuity; to assert and establish loyalty to the Torah and its historical exposition; to further the observance of the Sabbath and the Dietary Laws; to preserve in the service the reference to Israel's past and the hopes for Israel's restoration; to maintain the traditional character of the liturgy, with Hebrew as the language of prayer; to foster Jewish religious life in the home as expressed in traditional observances; to encourage the establishment of Jewish religious schools, in the curricula of which the study of the Hebrew language and literature shall be given a prominent place, both as the key to the true understanding of Judaism and as a bond holding together the scattered communities of Israel throughout the world. It shall be the aim of the United Synagogue of America, while not endorsing the innovations introduced by any of its constituent bodies, to embrace all elements essentially loyal to traditional Judaism and in sympathy with the purposes outlined above.[4]

Schechter's own understanding of Judaism had been molded by the Positive-Historical school of Germany and its leading protagonists—Zacharias Frankel, Solomon Judah Rapoport, Heinrich Graetz, and the later Leopold Zunz. Like them, he advocated the maintenance of all the customs and practices which still found general acceptance among the Jewish people as a whole—what he was pleased to call "Catholic Israel"—along with a critical, scholarly investigation of the Jewish past. Schechter also warmly espoused Zionism as "the great bulwark against assimilation" and, to the publicly expressed dismay of some of the Seminary's anti-Zionist, Reform trustees, opened its halls to Zionist activity. Although he wrote an important historical work entitled *Some Aspects of Rabbinic Theology* (1909), he was not a systematic theologian in the fashion of Kaufmann Kohler, and he did not share Kohler's penchant for theological platforms and manifestos. Perhaps his clearest statement on the crucial question of the revelatory character of the Torah and its authority in Judaism is one he wrote while still living in England, obviously reflecting the position of Frankel and the Positive-Historical school generally:

It is not the mere revealed Bible that is of first importance to the Jew, but the Bible as it repeats itself in history, in other words, as it is interpreted by Tradition. . . . Since, then, the interpretation of Scripture or the Secondary Meaning is mainly a product of changing historical influences, it follows that the center of authority is actually removed from the Bible and placed in some *living body*, which, by reason of its being in touch with the ideal aspirations and the religious needs of the age, is best able to determine the nature of the Secondary Meaning. This living body, however, is not represented by any section of the nation, or any corporate priesthood, or Rabbihood, but by the collective conscience of Catholic Israel, as embodied in the Universal Synagogue. . . . The norm as well as the sanction of Judaism is the practice actually in vogue. Its consecration is the consecration of general use—or, in other words, of Catholic Israel.[5]

Graduates of the Jewish Theological Seminary—or "Schechter's Seminary," as it was called even years after its famous president's death—managed to draw into their congregations many of the first and second generation immigrants who had become disaffected with the Judaism of their parents. In the Conservative synagogue they found rabbis who spoke fluent English and preached intelligible sermons, as well as a service which, while quite traditional, was conducted with dignity and decorum. Many Conservative rabbis and lay leaders joined the Orthodox in railing against the excesses of Reform, but in time some of the major innovations of Reform in worship—family pews, the late Friday evening service, recitation of some of the prayers in the vernacular, the confirmation ceremony, even mixed choirs and organ music—found their way into the Conservative synagogue. To be sure, significant differences remained. The Conservative synagogues were virtually all pro-Zionist, sought to provide as much Hebrew education in their schools as possible, and advocated observance of the dietary laws; if the latter were not universally followed by congregants in their homes, at least in the synagogue only kosher food was served. In addition, Conservative congregations generally maintained a liturgy that was largely traditional, retained observance of the second day of the festivals, and continued the custom of worship in *tallit* and headcover on the part of men. Nevertheless, as the years progressed and many Conservative congregations became more liberal at the same time as many Reform congregations were turning toward a greater traditionalism, the differences between the two movements were narrowed.

In its competition with Reform Judaism, the Conservative synagogue proved eminently successful. Perhaps it is not unfair to say that a major factor in this success was precisely the fact that the Conservative movement did not define its theological platform with any precision. While its practice made it plain that it did not acknowledge the revelatory character of the Torah or accept its unqualified authority, Conservatism continued to profess its general loyalty to tradition. Thus, many a sentimental Jew who recoiled at the idea of moving too far away from the faith of his ancestors, yet was unwilling to accept the disciplines of orthodoxy, could join a Conservative congregation without suffering the qualms of conscience that might be involved in affiliating with Reform Judaism, which forthrightly proclaimed its rejection of the plenary authority of the *halachah*.

While Conservatism proved highly congenial to a large segment of American Jewry, it did not by any means displace Orthodoxy. We noted earlier the difficulties encountered by the Orthodox synagogues of the country in the late nineteenth century in moving away from their jealously guarded independence and isolationism and banding together in a national organization for the achievement of greater strength. A milestone in this movement was the establishment of the Union of Orthodox Jewish Congregations in 1898. Equally significant was the formation, in 1902, of the Union of Orthodox Rabbis of the United States and Canada (Agudath Ha-Rab-banim), which came into being mainly through the efforts of several rabbis in cities of the Midwest who were more keenly aware of the lure of Reform than their colleagues in the teeming immigrant settlements of New York. With these two organizations Orthodox Jewish life in America found instrumentalities for the promotion of its central values and gained greater cohesion and effectiveness.

The Union of Orthodox Jewish Congregations and the Agudath Ha-Rabbanim turned their attention primarily to the promotion of Sabbath observance and *kashrut*, both made difficult for observant Jews by the conditions of American life. In 1905 they were instrumental in establishing the Jewish Sabbath Alliance of America, which sought in many ways—through teaching and exhortation, political activity directed toward gaining exemption for observant Jewish merchants and artisans from Sunday closing laws, lobbying for the right of public employees not to work on the Sabbath, bringing together Sabbath-observing employers and workers by means of special employment bureaus—to promote fulfillment of the traditional commandments regarding Sabbath rest and worship. Aided in their endeavors by a number of influential Conservative and Reform Jews, the Orthodox leaders of the Jewish Sabbath Alliance managed to stem at least to some extent the tide of abandonment of Sabbath observance. The traditional rabbis also attempted to bring some semblance of order into the area of kosher slaughtering and to correct the abuses and frauds frequently associated with the sale of kosher meats and other food products. Here their efforts were more often than not in vain, and many Jews who might otherwise have continued to observe the dietary laws abandoned them in disgust over the commercialism, profiteering, and other improprieties associated in more than a few cases with *kashrut*.

Somewhat more successful were the attempts of Orthodox rabbis and lay leaders in the first decades of the century to improve the quality of Jewish education within the constituency of their congregations. Under their prodding and with their support, a number of excellent communal Talmud Torahs, as well as a handful of Jewish day schools, were established, to replace the old-fashioned and all too frequently inadequate *ḥeder*. The cause of higher Jewish learning in America was also advanced when the Agudath Ha-Rabbanim undertook to support the Yeshivat Rabbenu Yitzchak Elchanan, which had been established in New York in 1896. The rabbis in 1908 sided against the faculty of the *yeshivah* in sanctioning the desire of many of its students to pursue secular studies at local colleges and universities in addition to their Talmudic studies. This was a major step in the emergence of an Orthodox rabbinate that could cope with the exigencies of the American environment and compete successfully with its university-trained Reform and Conservative counterparts.

Chiefly responsible for the development of the Yeshivat Rabbenu Yitzchak Elchanan as a significant force in American-Jewish life was Bernard Revel (1885–1940). Born in Kovno, Lithuania, Revel studied at the famous *yeshivah* of Telshe, one of the leading centers of Talmudic study in Russia (destroyed in 1940, the *yeshivah* was reestablished a year later in Cleveland, Ohio, by a few of its teachers and students and continues to flourish there with a present student body of over four hundred). At the age of twenty-one, already a master of rabbinic learning, he came to America and studied at New York University and later at the postgraduate Dropsie College for Hebrew and Cognate Learning in Philadelphia, where he received a doctorate for a dissertation on *Karaite Halachah and Its Relation to Sadducean, Samaritan and Philonian Halachah* which showed the groundlessness of Abraham Geiger's contention that Karaism represented a subterranean continuation of Sadduceeism.

A word may be said parenthetically about Dropsie College, which emerged as an important center of Judaic scholarship in America. Established through a bequest from the estate of Moses Aaron Dropsie (1821–1905), a Philadelphia lawyer, the college opened its doors in 1909 with two departments, Bible and Rabbinics, to which were soon added departments of Hebrew and Cognate Languages and of History. Its president for the first thirty years of its existence was Cyrus Adler. Adler, who served simultaneously as president of the Jewish Theological Seminary, was succeeded, in 1941, by historian Abraham A. Neuman, who was followed in turn, in 1967, by Abraham Katsh. Considerably expanded after World War II, Dropsie College, which has no denominational ties or orientation, has over the years trained a substantial number of students, including non-Jews, in all branches of Jewish learning through its doctoral programs. Its faculty has included some distinguished figures who have made notable contributions to scholarship.

Appointed in 1915 at the age of thirty as principal of the Yeshivat Rabbenu Yitzchak Elchanan, with which the Yeshivah Etz Chaim (founded in 1886) had just merged, Dr. Revel began to reorganize the amalgamated school along more modern lines and to expand its student body. Unlike the Reform and Conservative seminaries, the *yeshivah* did not restrict its students to those desiring to prepare for the rabbinate, but welcomed young men who might later follow other professions or engage in business to study in its halls. In 1916 Revel founded the Talmudical Academy, the first combined academic high school and *yeshivah* in America. Twelve years later he established Yeshiva College, the first liberal arts college organized under Jewish auspices and committed to the program summarized by Samson Raphael Hirsch as *Torah im Derech Eretz* (Torah along with secular culture).

Despite opposition from the more traditionalist Orthodox leaders, Yeshiva College flourished and by 1945 had become Yeshiva University. Today the university is a sizable institution, enrolling over seven thousand students at several locations in New York City. Its schools include the Rabbi Isaac Elchanan Theological Seminary, Yeshiva College for Men, Stern College for Women, the Bernard Revel Graduate School for Jewish and Semitic Studies, the Ferkauf Graduate School of Humanities and Social Sciences, the Belfer Graduate School of Science, the Wurzweiler School of Social Work, and, perhaps best known, the Albert Einstein College of Medicine and its affiliated Albert Einstein College Hospital. Although the greatest growth of Yeshiva University has taken place under the leadership of Dr. Samuel Belkin, who in 1943 succeeded to the presidency left vacant by Revel's death in 1940, it was Revel who laid the foundations for its development. Through the years the university has become the chief bastion of modern orthodoxy in America. Not only has its *yeshivah* ordained over eleven hundred rabbis since its foundation, but it has also trained a large segment of the Orthodox lay leadership. At present the university continues its important educational and scholarly enterprises and also serves the Jewish community through its Community Service Division, which arranges for the placement of rabbis and teachers, aids Talmud Torahs, day schools, and youth groups through providing pedagogic materials and services, and sponsors seminars for teen-agers and young adults.

❧❀❧

In the first years of the twentieth century religious institutions—synagogues, seminaries, congregational unions, rabbinical organizations—still played the dominant role in American-Jewish life, and their range of activities extended beyond the narrowly religious.

By the end of World War I, however, communal, philanthropic, social welfare, and cultural concerns had become incorporated into the program of a number of powerful secular organizations which challenged the religious institutions for leadership and influence in the Jewish community. The struggle, often muted and subterranean but sometimes overt and raucous, between the religious and secular institutions, and the growing ascendancy of the latter over the former, have continued throughout the century.

The pogroms of 1903 to 1905 in Kishinev and throughout Russia awoke American Jews to a renewed sense of responsibility for their fellow Jews elsewhere in the world and stimulated the organization of large-scale international relief activity. In 1905 the hastily assembled National Committee for the Relief of Sufferers by Russian Massacres quickly collected $1,250,000 to send to Russia. A year later the American Jewish Committee was established to "prevent the infraction of the civil and religious rights of Jews in any part of the world," to "secure for Jews equality of economic, social, and educational opportunity," and to "alleviate the consequences of persecution and to afford relief from calamities affecting Jews wherever they may occur." The Committee, which at first recruited its members (by invitation) from among the wealthy and prominent Jews of every city, but chiefly of New York, quickly became the most influential Jewish organization in America. In 1911 it undertook a movement to effect the abrogation of a longstanding treaty between the United States and Russia when the latter discriminated against Jewish holders of American passports. At the outbreak of World War I the Committee, which throughout its history has consistently taken a generally non-Zionist position, joined the Zionist Organization of America in dispatching emergency help to the *Yishuv* in Palestine and collaborated in the establishment of the American Jewish Joint Distribution Committee to carry on relief and rehabilitation work among Jews overseas.

During the war the American Jewish Committee, whose membership then consisted largely of well-to-do and somewhat assimilated Reform Jews of German descent who tended to be elitist, oligarchic, and rather distrustful of mass movements and democratic procedures, opposed the idea of establishing a permanent American Jewish Congress to consist of delegates democratically elected by Jewish communities and organizations, which was being vigorously promoted by various Zionist groups. However, it agreed to participate in a temporary congress that would limit itself to efforts toward

securing the rights of Jews in all countries at the Paris Peace Conference. At the conclusion of the Peace Conference the American Jewish Congress, in the election of whose delegates some three hundred
thousand Jews had participated and in which the national Jewish organizations had been represented directly, was dissolved. Its delega-
tion in Paris, led by Julian W. Mack and Louis Marshall, had succeeded in winning inclusion in the peace treaties of provisions
guaranteeing the civil, religious, and economic rights of the minority
groups in the various countries of eastern Europe—guarantees
which, as we have noted, ultimately proved meaningless. In 1922,
under the leadership of Rabbi Stephen S. Wise and Nathan Straus,
the American Jewish Congress was reestablished as a permanent organization. Unlike the American Jewish Committee, which, while
maintaining a favorable attitude toward Palestine and Israel, has
remained officially neutral on the question of Zionism, the Congress,
with a membership drawn chiefly from Jews of east European origin,
was and continues to be actively pro-Zionist. Both organizations,
however, fought determinedly against Nazism during the Hitler era,
and they have shared a common interest in combating not only anti-
Semitism but prejudice and discrimination against other minorities
in American society, as well as in defending the civil rights of threatened groups and individuals in the United States.

Concern over anti-Semitism, certainly not absent earlier, was to
become deeper and more widespread among American Jews in the
1920s and 1930s. Indeed, for many, especially among the dereligion-
ized and denationalized, the fear of anti-Semitism became their central passion as Jews. While the reaction of some Jews to it may have
been excessive, anti-Semitism itself was an undeniable reality, manifested in such phenomena as the imposition of quotas for Jewish
students in numerous private colleges and universities and the general refusal of these schools to appoint Jews to their faculties, discrimination against Jews in many other areas of employment, and
the spread of the racist anti-Catholic and anti-Jewish Ku Klux Klan,
as well as in the production and circulation of vehemently anti-
Jewish literature by other organizations and individuals. The most
notorious offender in the later realm was the automobile manufac-
turer Henry Ford, who published his *Dearborn Independent* and circulated the scurrilous *International Jew* in millions of copies until forced
by a 1927 lawsuit to desist from his anti-Semitic activity.

Both the American Jewish Committee and the American Jewish
Congress devoted much of their energies in the 1930s to exposing

and denouncing anti-Jewish propaganda and activity in Germany and elsewhere in Europe, and to fighting against indigenous movements that fomented hatred of Jews in the United States. They were joined in these efforts by the Anti-Defamation League, organized in 1913 specifically for the purpose of defending Jews against bigotry and discrimination by the Order of B'nai B'rith, the fraternal society which had been founded by German Jews in the middle of the nineteenth century and eventually became the largest middle-class men's organization in the Jewish community, counting its membership in the hundreds of thousands. Unfortunately, the three "defense agencies," as they came to be called, while performing useful and important work, squandered a considerable amount of their energy in duplicative efforts or in unseemly competition among themselves for prestige, and generally resisted proposals for amalgamating or effectively coordinating their activities.

We noted that the American Jewish Committee participated in the establishment of the American Jewish Joint Distribution Committee at the beginning of World War I. This organization, popularly known as the "Joint" or JDC, became, and has remained to the present day, American Jewry's chief international relief and reconstruction agency, and may well be regarded as one of its great glories. Its formation marked the assumption by the American Jewish community, which by the 1920s had become not only the wealthiest but the most populous of any country in the world, of major responsibility for aiding distressed Jewries everywhere. In its sixty years of existence the Joint, originally established under the leadership of such wealthy German-American Jews as Jacob Schiff, Felix Warburg, Nathan Straus, and Herbert Lehman, as well as prominent figures from the more recent east European immigrant community, has expended close to one billion dollars in its superbly organized and staffed network of enterprises designed to relieve the miseries of Jewish victims of war, persecution, disease, and economic disaster throughout the world.

During World War I the Joint Distribution Committee provided subsistence and medical care for tens of thousands of impoverished and homeless Jewish families in the ravaged countries of eastern and central Europe. In the period immediately after the war it saved many others suffering from famine and disease as a result of the pogroms and persecutions in the Ukraine. Later, the Joint contributed importantly to the reconstruction of Jewish life in Poland and elsewhere in eastern Europe through the provision of vocational training facilities, loan funds, and credit cooperatives, as well as financial support to religious and educational institutions. When the economic situation of the Jewries of Poland and other countries declined precipitously, it supplied emergency relief to destitute families and individuals. During the period of the rise of Nazism in Germany, as the Jews of that country were subjected to increasingly harsher persecution, it provided economic assistance and facilitated emigration. While the Nazi Moloch devoured its six million victims in the period 1939–1945, agents of the Joint continued to operate in Europe and carried on rescue and relief activity wherever possible. In the postwar period the Joint brought its skills and resources to the massive tasks of aiding the displaced persons and survivors of the concentration camps, reconstructing Jewish life in Europe, providing relief in Moslem countries, helping the emigration of hundreds of thousands of European and Oriental Jews to Israel, and caring for the aged and the sick once they had arrived there. Most recently the Joint has performed an invaluable service in facilitating the emigration of Russian Jews to Israel by maintaining a transit camp in Austria.

❧

The passage of a series of severely restrictive immigration acts by the United States Congress in 1921, 1924, and 1929 initiated a process that fundamentally changed the complexion of the American-Jewish community. While some immigration from Europe continued and American Jewry maintained a steady growth as a result of it, as well as of its own natural increase, massive infusions from abroad ceased. Within less than a generation the membership of the American-Jewish community became predominately native-born. The children and grandchildren of the immigrants who had toiled as ill-paid workers in the needle trades and other industries became, in many cases, prosperous business or professional men. The rise of American Jews on the economic ladder was seriously impeded but not halted by the Great Depression that began in 1929 and soon engulfed America in wholesale misery. A certain number of Jews, particularly among the intellectuals and academicians, turned to radical political thought and action as a solution to America's social and economic problems—after all, there had been a significant socialist tendency within American Jewry from the time of the early east European immigration in the late nineteenth century—but most Jews persevered, with eventual success, in their efforts to achieve economic security within the framework of America's capitalist system.

The Depression years struck hard at the religious and philanthropic institutions of American Jewry. As the economic crisis was intensified and unemployment grew, the income of synagogues, schools, and charitable agencies declined sharply. Drives to collect money for relief of Jews overseas, where needs were desperate, were almost abandoned for some years in the 1930s, and many synagogues, schools, and social agencies were compelled to default on their mortgage payments for the lavish buildings that had been constructed in the boom era of the 1920s and to cut back the salaries of their employees. But the religious, educational, and philanthropic organizations of the American-Jewish community continued to function, even if at a drastically reduced level.

The era after World War I had been marked by an upsurge in the development of social welfare institutions in the Jewish community—hospitals, old people's homes, child care agencies, family service bureaus, vocational service offices, recreational centers. Increasingly the fund raising for these enterprises, as well as for the large national welfare and philanthropic organizations, was centralized and coordinated by the local communities. Beginning in 1895 in Boston, federations of charities were organized for combined fund-raising campaigns and allocation of resources. The federation system continued to develop, establishing itself in virtually every city of any size and tending to assume leadership in the Jewish community. Amidst the welter of diverse organizations, of different religious or nonreligious identifications, and of the competing ideological and cultural loyalties maintained by Jews, the federation leadership could claim with considerable justification that philanthropy was the one bond uniting all Jews and that the federation was the "central address" of the Jewish community. The scope and influence of federations (or united welfare funds, as they are also sometimes called) grew as the twentieth century wore on, and they have now become probably the most powerful institutions in the American-Jewish community.

One peculiarly American-Jewish institution that enjoyed marked growth in the era between the two world wars was the Jewish community center. The center owes its origin to the Jewish young men's literary societies that sprang into existence in a number of larger cities in the middle of the nineteenth century and that imitated to a certain degree, but without the corresponding religious motivation, the program of the Young Men's Christian Associations. The first Young Men's Hebrew Association was formed in Baltimore in 1854 as a center for recreational and cultural activities. Similar associations were soon established elsewhere and became, with the influx of large numbers of Jews from eastern Europe beginning in the 1880s, primarily centers for providing recreational facilities and opportunities for progress in Americanization to the children of the immigrants under the patronage of long-settled Jewish philanthropists. In the period before World War I they were not much different from the settlement houses that were also established in the immigrant neighborhoods for the purpose of teaching the English language and American customs to the newcomers and supplying them with wholesome recreation. By the 1920s and especially the 1930s, however, these centers, now found in practically every city with a sizable Jewish population, no longer served young people or the children of poor immigrants alone. They had also drawn into their membership large numbers of adults from the middle-class segment of the community, and the change in name to Jewish community center followed.

By this time the center provided a secular, nondenominational, and nonideological meeting place for Jews of various persuasions, or no persuasion at all, who wished simply to associate with each other and express their sense of common ethnic identity through participation in a variety of shared activities. The center generally offered programs of athletics and physical education, dramatics, arts and crafts, summer camps for children, dances, lectures, concerts, forums, discussion groups, and a variety of clubs; with some notable exceptions, its Jewish cultural program tended to be minimal. For large numbers of Jews the center proved highly attractive and came to serve, in a sense, as a substitute for the synagogue and Jewish school. Not a few rabbis and synagogue leaders were alarmed by this phenomenon, which they correctly perceived as a manifestation of the growing secularization of the Jewish community; a great many second generation American Jews were, either through active rebellion or passive indifference, abandoning the ways of their immigrant parents, especially their religious loyalties. The apprehension of the religious leaders was not abated by the fact that a considerable number of the social workers who staffed the centers, while professing as one of their chief goals preservation of Jewish culture and Judaism, were quite ignorant of the culture and either indifferent or hostile to Jewish religious values.

In an attempt to compete with the Jewish community centers, and to win those Jews who were rapidly becoming alienated from the synagogue but still maintained a strong sense of ethnic consciousness back to Judaism as well as to "Jewishness" a number of congregations proceeded to establish "synagogue-centers" in which the standard athletic, recreational, social, and cultural activities of the center were to be carried on alongside the traditional synagogal program of worship and study. The pioneer in this movement was Dr. Mordecai Kaplan, professor of homiletics at the Jewish Theological Seminary and dean of its Teacher's Institute, who founded the Jewish Center in New York in 1918 as a synagogue-center and served as its rabbi for some years. Kaplan's model was followed by other congregations, mainly Conservative but Reform and Orthodox as well, which built elaborate recreational facilities that included gymnasiums, theaters, swimming pools, and so on. But the synagogue-center (or "*shul* with a pool," as some of its detractors called it) enjoyed only moderate success in achieving its major goal; of the many who came to swim, relatively few stayed to pray. Although, as we shall see, decline in the attractive power of the synagogue was temporarily reversed in the period after World War II, the secular Jewish community center continued to offer strong competition to the synagogue. Despite the fact that attempts have been made in recent years to expand the Jewish cultural and educational program of the center, it is still regarded by some rabbis more as a rival than a collaborator in the enterprise of insuring the loyalty of Jews to Judaism. The fact that Jewish community centers generally regard themselves as agencies obliged to serve the entire community, and that many of them have a substantial proportion of non-Jewish members, adds to the suspicion with which some of their harsher critics view their claim to being an effective instrument of meaningful Jewish survival.

While almost all Jewish religious leaders were distressed by the increasing drift of the American-Jewish community in the period between the wars toward secularization, and by the tendency of many Jews to replace loyalty to the traditional beliefs and practices of Judaism with an ethnically centered "Jewishness" in which a sense of common peoplehood and culture was stronger than faith-commitment, one outstanding figure accepted these phenomena and, in a sense, "validated" them in a new sociological interpretation of Judaism. This was Mordecai Kaplan who, in a series of books which he began issuing in 1934—*Judaism as a Civilization, The Meaning of God in Modern Jewish Religion, The Future of the American Jew,* and several others—developed the philosophy of Judaism that has come to be known as Reconstructionism.

Kaplan, who was born in Lithuania in 1881 but came to America with his family at the age of nine, was ordained at the Jewish Theological Seminary and served as the rabbi of an Orthodox congregation in New York before joining the Seminary's faculty, on which he remained for almost half a century. He quickly established himself as an independent thinker addressing the problems posed to Judaism by the challenges of the modern world with critical insight and unwavering intellectual integrity, if not with great theological depth. In a faculty whose other members were immersed in traditional scholarly concerns and who had little interest in the concrete issues of contemporary American-Jewish life, Kaplan was virtually alone in devoting his attention mainly to these, and profoundly influenced several generations of rabbinical students and rabbis. Open to the intellectual currents swirling in the larger American environment in the first half of the twentieth century—the pragmatism of William James and John Dewey, the theological naturalism and humanism of many liberal Protestant theologians, the ideology of cultural pluralism developed by Horace Kallen and others—and molded by the worlds of classical Jewish thought, Haskalah, and Zionism, as well as by the sociological theories of Emile Durkheim and the philosophy of Henri Bergson, he synthesized all of these in his own philosophy of Judaism.

Considering the dominant contemporary interpretations of Judaism, Kaplan found each of them seriously deficient in various respects. Both Orthodoxy and Neo-Orthodoxy, with their supernaturalism and their insistence on the divinely revealed character of the Torah, were clearly unresponsive to the radical challenge of modern science and philosophy. Reform had made a courageous attempt to face these challenges but in the process had reduced Judaism to a religious confession or church and ignored the full-bodied life of the Jewish people. Secularist Zionism, on the other hand, recognized the reality of Jewish peoplehood but minimized the significance of traditional Jewish religious belief and practice. As for Conservatism, it had become the captive of intellectual compromise and timidity and contented itself with serving as a vague middle ground between Orthodoxy and Reform.

[416]

The fundamental fact, from the recognition of which a historically valid and contemporaneously valid understanding of Judaism must derive, Kaplan urged, is that Judaism is not merely a religion but an "evolving religious civilization." That is, it is the way of life of a people which shares not only a common religious faith and cult but also a common language or languages, legal system, customs, literature, and art that have developed over the centuries and are still in the process of evolution. The modern American Jew, Kaplan pointed out, is a dweller in two civilizations, the American and the Jewish, and much of his own effort has been directed to showing that the values of the two civilizations are consistent and complementary.

Nothing was to be gained, according to Kaplan, by ignoring the challenge presented to the classical supernaturalist theology of Judaism by the discoveries of modern science, and he proceeded to reconstruct the major articles of Jewish belief in a way that he believed would render them compatible with scientific and rational thought. God, he maintained, can no longer be conceived as an omnipotent personal being, the Creator, Judge, the Ruler of men; He can only be understood in impersonal terms as the sum of the processes, powers, and agencies in nature and society that promote man's salvation, i.e., his personal and social fulfillment. The Torah cannot be regarded as the product of divine revelation, supernaturally communicated to Israel; it is simply the record of the Jewish people's hard-won historical experience, and its rules and precepts are not God's commandments but folkways or "sancta," hallowed usages which bind the people together and to which it ascribes supreme importance. (Kaplan, unlike most of the reformers, has stressed the high value of the traditional ceremonial practices and urged their continued observance, at the same time that he has advocated the creation of new rituals.) Israel cannot be considered the "chosen people," singled out by God for a supernatural mission and destiny; the Jewish people, like all others, simply has a "vocation," an obligation to enrich the symphony of the world's peoples and cultures by contributing its own distinctive values and ideals to it.

Kaplan's naturalist reformulation of Jewish theology, while repugnant to traditional religious thinkers, proved highly attractive to many rabbis and laymen alike in the Conservative and, to a lesser degree, the Reform camps. It still enjoys considerable popularity, although, as we shall see, its assumptions and conclusions were subjected to intensive criticism and categorically rejected by a number of influential, biblically oriented Jewish theologians who appeared in the period after World War II under the influence of the general movement of religious Existentialism. Less controversial than Kaplan's theology was his practical program for reconstructing American-Jewish life. Although an ardent Zionist, he has always insisted on the possibility and necessity of the creative survival of Jewry in America and elsewhere in the Diaspora. The fundamental unit in the reconstruction of American Jewry, Kaplan contended, should be the "organic community," not the congregation, for Judaism is far more than a religion and there are many Jews who identify themselves strongly with the Jewish people but do not in any way share its religious beliefs or practices. What he had in mind as a general model, by no means satisfactory in all respects, was the traditional community in European-Jewish life or the short-lived Kehillah of New York, in whose establishment he had participated. The all-embracing, democratically ruled "organic community," whose membership he envisaged as consisting of all persons identifying themselves as Jews, would support and coordinate the activities of all the Jewish enterprises conducted within it—religious, cultural, educational, philanthropic, and social. The local community would also join with its counterparts all over the country in organizing and maintaining a strong national Jewish community. It would seem that in the federations and welfare funds, community centers, and community councils that now exist, part of Kaplan's program has already been realized. What is chiefly lacking is the full democracy that he envisioned, as well as support by the community federation or welfare fund of the synagogues; the latter are still totally dependent for their maintenance on the dues and contributions of their own voluntary memberships. In addition, there is hardly as yet an effectively organized national Jewish community in the United States.

For many years Kaplan's influence on American Judaism was intellectual rather than institutional, although he established several agencies, including the Jewish Reconstructionist Foundation, which publishes *The Reconstructionist* magazine, to promote his ideology. In 1945 the Foundation also issued a new Reconstructionist prayer book, which turned out to be quite traditional and departed far less from the classical liturgy than did the Reform movement's *Union Prayer Book*. Publication of the volume so angered the Orthodox "defenders of the faith" that the Union of Orthodox Rabbis solemnly excommunicated Mordecai Kaplan from the Jewish community. The excommunication, vehemently deplored by the Conservative and Reform rabbinates, only served to give greater prominence to Reconstructionism. But Kaplan did not organize a separatist movement with its own synagogues, although a number of congregations began to call themselves Reconstructionist. Only in 1968 did he and his chief disciple and son-in-law, Ira Eisenstein, open the Reconstructionist Rabbinical College in Philadelphia to train rabbis in the spirit of their philosophy of Judaism.

From its inception this philosophy found its major following within the Conservative movement. Beginning in the 1920s and 1930s, Conservatism manifested signs of growing tension between a liberal segment of its rabbinate which wished to formulate explicit principles for the guidance of the movement and forthrightly to revise, within halachic categories, certain aspects of Jewish ritual and law that it believed were clearly outmoded and dysfunctional, and a right-wing group which rejected the formulation of a new program and advocated maintenance of tradition, arguing that in the process of time the Jewish people as a whole would collectively decide what is obsolete or requires alteration. Disagreement over this issue has continued to the present day and still appears far from resolution. The Conservative rabbinate, officially organized since 1919 into the Rabbinical Assembly of America, has throughout its history been largely dominated by the Jewish Theological Seminary faculty. Members of that faculty, with the exception of Mordecai Kaplan and a handful of other figures, have been generally quite traditionalist in their attitude toward Jewish law. During the presidency of Cyrus Adler, who served for twenty-five years after the death of Solomon Schechter until his own death in 1940, and for more than a decade afterward, the leading figure in the Seminary faculty was Dr. Louis Ginzberg (1873–1953), professor of *Talmud*, world-renowned authority on rabbinic literature, and compiler of the classic seven-volume *Legends of the Jews*. [6]

With his commanding influence on the Rabbinical Assembly's Committee on Jewish Law, Ginzberg usually succeeded in restraining the demands of the more liberal members of the Assembly for substantive and far-reaching revisions in the traditional *halachah*. The cause of the traditionalists was strengthened by the accession to the presidency of the Seminary in 1940 of Louis Finkelstein, a distinguished Talmudist and historian, under whose leadership the rabbinical school became even more committed to the preservation of the *halachah*. A number of changes have been officially approved by the Committee on Jewish Law in recent decades, but they have not been of major scope or consequence. Dissatisfied with the resistance to change they encountered in the Seminary and in the Rabbinic Assembly, a good many rabbis and congregational leaders, frequently influenced in their attitudes toward Judaism by the thinking of Mordecai Kaplan, have simply gone their own way and moved their synagogues to a pattern of worship and observance that does not differ greatly from that of right-wing Reform congregations. Remarkably enough, the diversity of ideology and practice within its ranks has not seriously impaired the institutional strength of the Conservative movement.

At the same time that many in Conservatism were calling for a more active adaptation of Jewish law and practice to the conditions of the contemporary world, Reform Judaism, which had in some cases carried such adaptation to the point of virtually de-Judaizing its synagogues as well as the personal religious lives of their members, was moving toward a significant reappropriation of tradition. Under the leadership of Julian Morgenstern, an eminent Bible scholar who was himself a product of a "classical" Reform upbringing, the Hebrew Union College, which he served as president from 1921 to 1947, was strengthened and its faculty augmented by the appointment in the 1930s of a number of renowned refugee scholars whom he rescued and brought over from Europe. Within the Reform congregations, many of which now included in their membership a growing proportion of Jews of east European descent with a lingering nostalgia for the religious customs of their parents and grandparents, a tendency developed to restore some of the ceremonial practices that had been discarded, and a drive appeared to intensify the educational program of their religious schools and to promote the study of Hebrew. These developments were aided to some extent by the influence of some of the immigrants from Nazi Germany who joined Reform congregations and brought with them a pattern of liberal Judaism that was closer to historical tradition than that of American Reform.

The chief factor in the turn of Reform to a greater degree of traditionalism and identification with the larger Jewish community was undoubtedly the changing attitudes within its rabbinate, not a few of whose members had been raised in Orthodox households and given a traditional education in their childhood and youth. For years a segment of the Reform rabbinate with strong Jewish nationalist sympathies had sought vainly to move the Central Conference of American Rabbis away from its official anti-Zionist position. The forces of history—the beginning of Hitler's onslaught against the Jews of Germany in 1933 and the emigration to Palestine of thousands of Jews from that country as well as from Poland and elsewhere in eastern Europe—destroyed attitudes which eloquence and logic had not been able to overcome. In 1935 the Zionist rabbis prevailed on the Conference to adopt a resolution proclaiming its neutrality on the question of a Jewish state. Two years later the Conference adopted a new set of guiding principles to supersede the Pittsburgh Platform, which had served for more than half a century as the quasi-official program of the Reform movement. The new principles, approved at the 1937 convention of the rabbis in Columbus, Ohio, and therefore known as the Columbus Platform, included an explicit approval of Zionism: "In the rehabilitation of Palestine, the land hallowed by memories and hopes, we behold the promise of renewed life for many of our brethren. We affirm the obligation of all Jewry to aid in its upbuilding as a Jewish homeland by endeavoring to make it not only a refuge for the oppressed but also a center of Jewish culture and spiritual life." [7] The Columbus Platform also counterbalanced its assertion that "certain . . . laws have lost their binding force with the passing of the conditions that called them forth" [8] (contrast this mild statement with the aggressive antinomianism of the Pittsburgh Platform, which asserts of the "Mosaic legislation" that "we accept as binding only its moral laws and maintain only such ceremonials as elevate and sanctify our lives, but reject all such as are not adapted to the views and habits of modern civilization") with an acknowledgment of the centrality of the Torah: "As a depository of permanent spiritual ideals, the Torah remains the dynamic source of the life of Israel." [9]

In 1937 the Union of American Hebrew Congregations, the national organization of Reform synagogues, also ratified the already marked trend toward more ceremonial observance by adopting a resolution urging the restoration of traditional customs and symbols, as well as the use in worship of Jewish music sung by Jewish singers and, where feasible, by a cantor. Three years later the Central Conference of American Rabbis published a revised version of the *Union Prayer Book* which clearly reflected a return to tradition; the new edition contained more of the liturgy in Hebrew than its predecessor and included a candle-lighting ceremony and the Kiddush for the eve of the Sabbath. Such changes were regarded by the traditionalists among the rabbis and laity as inadequate and deplored by the substantial minority of "classical" reformers in the movement as a subversion of its fundamental principles. They were only a prelude, however, to the still greater swing toward tradition that was to characterize Reform Judaism in the period after World War II.

We have noted that the Reform rabbinate officially abandoned its erstwhile anti-Zionist position in the mid 1930s. This was only one manifestation of the growing strength of Zionism in the American-Jewish community as a whole at that time. Under the prestigious leadership of Justice Louis D. Brandeis, appointed to the Supreme Court in 1916, the Zionist movement in America had gained significantly in membership and influence during World War I and thereafter until 1921, when Brandeis and his associates withdrew from Zionist activities after their defeat in an internal political dispute. The ensuing decline in popularity of the movement, a decline soon abetted by the preoccupation of American Jewry with the economic problems posed by the Depression, was reversed beginning in the 1930s with the rise of Hitlerism. Zionists began to campaign for increased allocations to Palestine from community welfare fund drives, a move strongly resisted by many of the larger donors, who favored European relief and continued to regard Zionist projects with a certain suspicion. In 1939, under the leadership of Rabbi Abba Hillel Silver, the most eloquent Zionist spokesman of the day, the United Palestine Appeal (UPA) began independent fund raising but quickly reached an agreement with the Joint Distribution Committee and the allied National Refugee Service to establish the United Jewish Appeal (UJA). In the decade that followed the UJA raised over $600,000,000, most of which went to Palestine.

In May 1942, under the impact of the horrors suffered by Jews in Nazi-occupied Europe, news of which was beginning to reach America, and the continued refusal of Great Britain to permit more Jewish refugees to enter Palestine, an extraordinary Zionist conference was convened at the Biltmore Hotel in New York. The conference, whose leaders included Chaim Weizmann, David Ben-Gurion, Stephen S. Wise, and Abba Hillel Silver, adopted the so-called Biltmore Program, demanding termination of the British mandate and establishment of an independent Jewish commonwealth in Palestine. In August 1943 the delegates of the representative American Jewish Conference, which was intended to provide a common voice for the

Jews of America on the issues of peace and postwar reconstruction, assembled. Persuaded by the oratory of Rabbi Silver, the Conference rejected the compromise resolution of the non-Zionist American Jewish Committee calling only for unrestricted Jewish immigration into Palestine and for determination of the country's status later by international agreement, and instead adopted the Biltmore Program. An American Zionist Emergency Council, under Rabbi Stephen S. Wise, carried on a campaign to gain the sympathy of American political and religious leaders for the cause of the Jewish state. In 1944 Rabbi Wise was replaced by Rabbi Silver, who advocated a more militant program of influencing public opinion and placing pressure on the framers of United States foreign policy. Three years later Rabbi Silver was to be the spokesman of the world Zionist movement in advocating the cause of a Jewish state before the United Nations. The overwhelming majority of American Jews supported the creation of a Jewish state, but in 1942 a small group of anti-Zionist Reform rabbis and laymen organized the American Council for Judaism to oppose Jewish nationalism and to maintain the idea that Jews are simply a religious community with a universalist faith, and nothing more. The unrestrained bitterness of the Council's attack on the Zionist movement, as well as on the State of Israel after its proclamation, soon alienated practically all of its rabbinic and many of its lay members, who sadly or indignantly withdrew. The Council still exists, but with a small and constantly declining membership, and its influence on American Judaism has been negligible.

The mood of Jewish life in America underwent profound changes as a result of the crises in the 1930s and 1940s—the Depression and Franklin D. Roosevelt's New Deal, the spread of venomous Jew-hatred in Europe and the powerful manifestation of native forms of anti-Semitism at home, the engulfment of the world in total war, and the Holocaust visited on European Jewry. Long prevalent assumptions and practices were shattered, preparing the way for a restructuring of the Jewish community and the emergence of a new leadership drawn chiefly from Jews of east European origin who were strongly committed to Jewish survival and the preservation of Jewish ethnic values.

Long before the war was over in 1945, many Jews in America had become aware of the atrocities committed against their brethren in Europe by the Nazis, but the full magnitude and unspeakable horror of the tragedy were not to be disclosed until after the guns were silenced. In the years immediately following the end of the war, the American-Jewish community invested immense energy and re- sources in bringing relief to the pitiful survivors of the concentration camps in Europe, and in aiding the struggle for establishment of a Jewish state in Palestine. Fund raising for these causes reached un- precedented levels. Formal identification with Zionism grew dramat- ically; the membership of the Zionist Organization of America, for instance, increased from less than fifty thousand in 1940 to two hundred twenty-five thousand in 1948. American Zionist leaders, foremost among them Abba Hillel Silver, participated in the framing of world Zionist policy and in winning support for establishment of a Jewish commonwealth within the councils of the United Na- tions. Several thousand American-Jewish volunteers served on the "illegal" ships that attempted to smuggle Jewish refugees into Pales- tine past British sentries, and fought in the war of 1948–1949 that followed the proclamation of the State of Israel. To be sure, after peaking in 1947–1950, American Jewry's interest in, and efforts on behalf of, the state leveled off, but these were to be powerfully revived in times of crisis and Israel has continued to be among its central concerns and the major focus of its communal apparatus and activities.

The immediate postwar years also witnessed a great upsurge in religious life in the American-Jewish community, parallel with a similar upsurge in American society at large. This may not have been the authentic revival of religious belief and sentiment that many at the time thought it to be, but it was real enough as a movement of activity and overt identification. We noted the progressive overall decline in the attractiveness of the synagogue in the 1920s and 1930s. This decline was sharply reversed during and immediately after the war. Stimulated by a massive movement of Jews from the crowded and aging city neighborhoods into suburban areas following the war (some cities, such as Cleveland, Detroit, Newark, and Washington saw the overwhelming majority of their Jewish population move to the suburbs), a large number of new synagogues were established and older congregations relocated in the new residential zones. It is estimated that between 1945 and 1952 more than $50,000,000 was spent on synagogue construction, and in the decade that followed twice that amount. Membership rosters swelled as Jewish families that had never before been affiliated with a congregation joined, and the enrollment in religious school classes burgeoned.

The national religious institutions encouraged this growth by rapidly expanding their programs. In the postwar era all of the following substantially enlarged their student bodies: the Jewish Theological Seminary, led by Louis Finkelstein; the Hebrew Union College, which merged with the Jewish Institute of Religion in 1949 and was directed by Nelson Glueck (1900–1971), the distinguished biblical archaeologist who succeeded Julian Morgenstern as president in 1947; and the various Orthodox *yeshivot,* such as the Rabbi Isaac Elchanan Theological Seminary of New York, the Hebrew Theological College of Chicago, the Telshe Yeshivah of Cleveland, and Ner Israel of Baltimore. The national congregational organizations—the United Synagogue, the Union of Orthodox Jewish Congregations, and the Union of American Hebrew Congregations—also intensified their activities and fostered the development of the newly emerging synagogues. Under the leadership of its energetic president, Rabbi Maurice N. Eisendrath, the Reform Union of American Hebrew Congregations became especially concerned with the social and economic issues of the day, and sought to apply Jewish and universal moral values to their solution. As the number of Jews in American colleges and universities increased, the Hillel Foundation movement, which had been inaugurated in 1923 at the University of Illinois and soon obtained the sponsorship of the Order of B'nai Brith for its program of serving the religious, cultural, and social needs of Jewish students, enjoyed substantial growth. Hillel spread to a large number of campuses, first under the guidance of Dr. Abram Leon Sachar, who served as national director from 1933 to 1947, and then of Rabbi Arthur J. Lelyveld, who succeeded Dr. Sachar and served until 1956.

While the Reform and Conservative movements were particularly successful in enlarging their constituencies in the postwar period, attracting many erstwhile Orthodox Jews and children of Orthodox parents, Orthodoxy itself displayed renewed vigor. The graduates of the Rabbi Isaac Elchanan Theological Seminary and other American *yeshivot,* now organized into the Rabbinical Council of America, surpassed in numbers and influence the older, European-trained rabbis banded together in the Agudath Ha-Rabbanim. Under their direction, Orthodoxy divested itself of some of its "siege-mentality" and made concessions to the American environment without sacrificing any of its fundamental principles. Many young and previously indifferent Jews, upon deciding to affirm Judaism, chose Orthodoxy as a more authentic and full-bodied form of the tradition than either Conservatism or Reform. Especially effective in adapting Orthodox synagogue worship to contemporary aesthetic standards, increasing its decorum, and ridding it of debasing commercialism was the Young Israel movement, originally inspired in 1912 by Rabbi Judah Leon Magnes and Professors Israel Friedlander and Mordecai Kaplan of the Jewish Theological Seminary. Young Israel, which broke with its founders and identified itself completely with Orthodoxy in 1922, substantially enlarged the number of synagogues that adhered to its program in the period after World War II and achieved considerable success in promoting a native American traditionalism. While the older, European Orthodoxy continued quixotically to battle against the corrosive influences of the American environment, it obtained a certain accession of strength with the settlement of a number of Ḥasidic groups in New York, most notably the Lubavich Ḥasidim. The charismatic leader of Lubavich, Rabbi Joseph Isaac Schneersohn (1880–1950), came to America in 1940 and soon established a strong center which, in the postwar era, organized intensive missionary activity and a network of day schools throughout the country.

Perhaps the most impressive achievement of Orthodoxy in recent decades has been the establishment of a sizable number of day schools, or *yeshivot ketanot*, formed under the auspices not only of the Lubavich Ḥasidim but of other Orthodox groups as well. While the majority of American-Jewish children have been obtaining only a minimal religious education in Sunday or weekday afternoon schools, a significant minority have been receiving far more intensive training in the day schools, where as much as half of the student's time is devoted to Judaic study. By 1970 there were scores of such schools all over the country, with some eighty thousand children enrolled. Conservative Judaism entered the field belatedly, and Reform has just begun to do so; the number of their schools remains relatively small. With the growth of the day schools, which are receiving increasing financial aid from Jewish federations and welfare funds, the community-supported Talmud Torahs have generally declined in enrollment and influence.

Orthodoxy also produced an outstanding Talmudic scholar and religious philosopher in the person of Rabbi Joseph Dov Soloveitchik, who has for many years been regarded as the outstanding halachic authority in America and the spiritual mentor of most American-trained Orthodox rabbis, to whom he is "the Rav" par excellence. After receiving his doctorate in 1931 at the University of Berlin for a dissertation on the philosophy of Hermann Cohen, Rabbi Soloveitchik emigrated to America in 1932 and became rabbi of the Orthodox community of Boston. In 1941 he succeeded his father as professor of *Talmud* at the Rabbi Isaac Elchanan Theological Seminary. Rabbi Soloveitchik has published very little, exercising his vast influence primarily through his teaching and public lectures. In his major essay "Ish Ha-Halachah" ("The Man of the *Halachah*"), published in 1944, he developed an Existentialist-flavored anthropology. According to Soloveitchik, when man—who is both active and passive, cause and effect, subject and object—assumes the disciplines of the *halachah*, he achieves mastery over his life and its swirling currents. He takes control of his existence and ceases to be dominated by habit and routine. Through halachic observance, which is anything but mechanical, human life is sanctified, and God and man are drawn into a "covenantal community," an intimate and immediate personal relationship.

Although much of the "revival" in American-Jewish religious life in the years after World War II was merely institutional and material, it also had its spiritual aspects. Certainly, many Jews who joined synagogues did so out of a vague feeling that it was the proper and decent thing to do, or under the influence of subtle pressures operative in the larger society, which had come to accord Judaism the status of "the third American religion," along with Protestantism and Catholicism. Moreover, only a relatively small minority attended synagogue services regularly, and fewer still assumed the disciplines of strict Sabbath observance, *Kashrut*, and daily prayer. Nevertheless, many Jews affirmed Judaism out of genuine, even if frequently inchoate and unarticulated, religious yearnings, and others did so in response to the trauma of the Holocaust, determined not to give Hitler ultimate victory insofar as Jews ceased to be Jews simply through apathy and negligence. More than a few of these Jews began to practice at least a few of the traditional religious ceremonies in their homes and to develop an interest in Jewish thought and literature.

❧§❧

This interest was nurtured by the revival of theological thinking in Jewish religious circles, a revival which grappled seriously with the problems of Jewish faith. Theologians had been rare in the

American-Jewish community (Kaufmann Kohler and Mordecai Kaplan were notable exceptions), and theological issues had been spared scant attention by a Jewry whose central concerns were relief of suffering Jews, organization of Jewish communal structures, building of Zion, promotion of Jewish cultural expression, and expansion of Jewish philanthropy. Beginning in the early 1950s, however, a series of works appeared which heralded a new era in American-Jewish religious thought. Most of these were written under the intellectual influence of the three great twentieth-century German-Jewish theologians and philosophers—Franz Rosenzweig, Martin Buber, and Hermann Cohen. In general they represented a movement away from the rationalist, naturalist, pragmatist, and sociological interpretation of Judaism, so sharply exemplified in the thought of Mordecai Kaplan, toward a biblically oriented, existentialist, personalist understanding of Jewish faith. Borrowing some of the characteristic emphases of the general movement of religious Existentialism—that reality is not to be grasped by rational or scientific means alone; that there is a distinction between objective and subjective truth, and that religious truth is a species of the latter; that subjective truth is to be grasped not only with the mind, but with man's whole being; and that such truth is validated and verified only through commitment, decision, and risk—the new generation of American-Jewish theologians sought to affirm biblical faith in the face of the rationalist reformulation of it that Kaplan and like-minded thinkers had attempted.

One of the pioneering works of the new theology was Will Herberg's *Judaism and Modern Man*, published in 1951. In his earlier years Herberg had been active in the Young Communist League and edited Communist Party publications, but he became disenchanted with Marxism and turned to Jewish and Christian thought, studying with the great Protestant theologian Reinhold Niebuhr and reading the works of Buber, Rosenzweig, and Schechter. *Judaism and Modern Man* is essentially the author's personal confession of faith, but it is a faith that is very close to classical biblical-rabbinic faith, and its premises are argued forcefully and eloquently. Against the attempt to reduce God to an idea, or to a power or process, Herberg argued that the true God is the living, personal God of Jewish tradition—the omnipotent Creator, the loving Father, the righteous Judge. Herberg also urged that revelation must be taken seriously, and that at least the moral imperatives of the Bible cannot be reduced to the category of prudential counsel and utilitarian maxims, but must be regarded as absolute divine mandates. He further contended that the mystery of Israel as the supernaturally chosen, covenanted "people of God" is not to be explained away through historicist and sociological reinterpretations, and that the traditional categories of election, covenant, and mission continue to be valid and constitute the only serious foundation for Jewish religious existence.

More influential than Herberg has been Abraham Joshua Heschel (1907–1972), whose philosophy of Judaism represents a synthesis of the intense Hasidic piety in which he was brought up as a child (he was a direct descendant of three of the greatest figures of the Hasidic tradition, Dov Baer of Mezeritz, Abraham Joshua Heschel of Apt, and Levi Yitzhak of Berdichev) and the thought of Martin Buber, with whom he was associated in the 1930s in Berlin and Frankfurt-am-Main. Coming to America in 1940, he served first on the faculty of the Hebrew Union College in Cincinnati and then, in 1945, went to the Jewish Theological Seminary in New York, where he remained until his death. A foremost scholar in Jewish mysticism and medieval Jewish philosophy, Heschel also developed an original philosophy of Judaism in two major works, *Man Is Not Alone* (1951) and *God in Search of Man* (1956), both of which were widely read and admired in Christian as well as Jewish circles.

Like the religious philosophy of Herberg and Buber, Heschel's is radically theocentric, and his God is the living, personal God of the Bible. The major characteristic of this God is His "concern," His passionate interest in, and involvement with, His creatures. The living reality of God, according to Heschel, may be experienced in three ways. His presence may be sensed in the Bible, in sacred deeds, and in the world of nature. For the Jew, the Bible and sacred deeds (or *mitzvot*) provide the classic ways to an encounter with God, but all men may find Him in nature if they do not suppress their capacity for "radical amazement" and cultivate their sense of "the Ineffable." In Heschel's view, the Ineffable, or the inexpressible and irreducible mystery inherent in all things, is the basic source not only of religion but also of poetry and art and even of philosophy. "Without the concept of the Ineffable, it would be impossible to account for the diversity of man's attempts to express or depict reality, for the diversity of philosophies, poetic visions or artistic representations, for the consciousness that we are still at the beginning of our effort to say what we see all about us." [10]

Although Heschel's theology is more impressionistic than systematic, though he relied more on emotive language than on logical analysis in his writing, and though he defended the revealed character of the Torah and the authority of the *halachah* in more or less orthodox fashion, his influence extended far beyond the confines of traditional circles. Not a little of his appeal derived from the fact that he was deeply involved in social issues, playing a prominent role during the 1960s in the civil rights movement in America and in the protest against United States involvement in the war in Vietnam.

Following Herberg and Heschel, a number of younger Jewish theologians appeared, writing in an essentially similar vein. Their common emphasis on the centrality of the covenant in interpreting the divine-human relationship in Judaism and the history of the Jewish people has led some of them to style themselves "covenant theologians." The thought of these men was expressed not only in books but in essays that appeared in the major journals devoted chiefly to discussion of theological issues which were established in the postwar era—*Judaism*, sponsored by the American Jewish Congress; *Tradition*, issued under Orthodox auspices; *Conservative Judaism*, published by the Conservative Rabbinical Assembly; and the *Journal of the Central Conference of American Rabbis*, sponsored by the Reform rabbinate. While interest in these journals and in theology in general has been largely restricted to the rabbinate, it has also spread to a growing, though still small, number of Jewish intellectuals. It is too early to assess the impact of the revival of theological thinking on the religious life of American Jewry, but it may well turn out to be considerable.

☦

The postwar era saw Jews, who had long distinguished themselves in America as doctors, lawyers, scientists, entertainers, musicians, and government servants, attain eminence in new fields as well. Jewish novelists such as Saul Bellow, Bernard Malamud, Edward Wallant, J. D. Salinger, and Norman Mailer, poets such as Delmore Schwartz, Allen Ginsberg, Howard Nemerov, John Hollander, and Karl Shapiro, and critics such as Lionel Trilling, Philip Rahv, Irving Howe, Leslie Fiedler, and Alfred Kazin came to play a commanding role in American literature. Some of them dealt with Jewish themes and stimulated interest in Judaism and the Jewish people in the larger American world. Novels and plays by lesser figures dealing with the Holocaust in Europe, the establishment of the State of Israel, and Jewish life in America were extremely popular among both Jews and non-Jews. For a society increasingly experiencing the mood of alienation, portrayals of the Jew, the classically alienated figure, proved powerfully attractive.

In addition, the faculties of many colleges and universities which had previously been closed to Jews began to welcome them; by the beginning of the 1970s some thirty thousand Jews, comprising perhaps one-tenth of all the college and university teachers in America, were to be found on the campuses of the larger state and privately endowed universities. Jews also made their own institutional contribution to American higher education by opening Brandeis University in Waltham, Massachusetts, in 1948. Under the guidance of Dr. Abram Leon Sachar, who served as president of the nonsectarian university from its inception until 1968, Brandeis, which has received most of its support from Jewish philanthropists, quickly gained recognition as one of the leading institutions of higher learning in the United States.

A highly promising development of the 1950s and 1960s was the establishment of a considerable number of chairs of Jewish Studies at major American universities. To the Nathan Littauer Chair in Jewish Literature and Philosophy, founded at Harvard in 1925 and occupied for many years by the eminent scholar in Jewish philosophy Harry A. Wolfson, and to the Miller Foundation for Jewish History, Literature, and Institutions, endowed at Columbia in 1929 and led by the distinguished historian Salo W. Baron, many others were added elsewhere. These professorships, as well as programs of Jewish studies on scores of campuses, provided students with an opportunity to study Judaica and Hebraica at a high academic level and made Jewish studies a recognized discipline within the university. Thousands of Jewish and non-Jewish students took advantage of the new course offerings.

In the years after the war American Jewry was primarily occupied with providing for the relief and rehabilitation of Jews in Europe, aiding the establishment and development of the State of Israel, and building its own communal institutions and synagogues. Most Jews had been too engrossed in these activities to give any serious thought to the Holocaust or to its meaning for Jews and Judaism, although the memory of it was always in the background. The protracted trial in 1961 of the Nazi mass murderer Adolf Eichmann in Jerusalem stimulated deeper reflection on the tragedy. The sessions of the trial, widely reported on television and in the press and described in numerous books and articles, brought home to many Jews for the first time the full horror of the tragedy. The trial also aroused much discussion about the charges of passivity on the part of the Jews who had been slaughtered, as well as of the complicity of some Jewish officials in the extermination of their brethren. Many young Jews, particularly those who had grown up after the war, were struck with special force by the revelations of the Eichmann trial.

By the early 1960s the growth in synagogue construction and congregational membership had begun to level off. So also had enrollments in religious schools, except for the Orthodox day schools, which continued to expand steadily. A large number of Jews at this time, particularly in the colleges and universities, were caught up in the civil rights struggle, participating in demonstrations and protest marches to dramatize the plight of the black citizens of America. Many young Jews also became part of the so-called hippie movement and joined in the development of the youth counterculture with its new mores and life styles. More than a few young Jews in this era also joined radical movements, the so-called New Left, which condemned the abuses and injustices of American society, denounced the "imperialism" of the United States government and particularly its involvement in Vietnam, and called for world revolution. Among many American Jews, young and old, the State of Israel had become a routine fact and no longer elicited intense concern.

Then, suddenly, the Six Day War in June 1967 and the weeks of crisis preceding it produced an enormous reaction among Jews the world over, including America. Many felt that the very existence of Israel was threatened and were galvanized into action. Thousands of Jewish students attempted to fly to Israel immediately, either to fight or to take over the jobs of Israelis called to military duty. The older generation, including some who had previously been indifferent or negative to Israel, responded with unparalleled contributions of funds to the United Jewish Appeal and purchases of Israel bonds. A few non-Jewish Americans also came forward with offers of aid. The lightning victory of the Israeli armed forces quickly dissipated the deep anxiety of American Jewry and tranformed it into general rejoicing.

The joy, however, was soon clouded by the realization that a good many Americans had transferred their sympathies, in the wake of the Israeli triumph, from Israel to the Arabs. Even when the survival of the Jewish state appeared to hang in the balance, there had been general silence, with few exceptions, on the part of the American clergy, particularly the liberal Protestant clergy, despite the fact that for some years a determined effort had been made, mainly from the Jewish side, to promote mutual understanding through "religious dialogue" between Christians and Jews. Now, as the defeated Arabs became the "underdogs," there were repeated expressions of commiseration for them and condemnations of Israeli "militarism" from these circles. In addition, the New Left, to which a considerable number of young Jews had been drawn, quickly joined militant Third World representatives and black groups in America in championing the Arab cause and denouncing Israel. The professed "anti-Zionism" of this coalition hardly concealed its fundamental anti-Semitism.

The response of the American public as a whole to the bitterly fought "Yom Kippur War" between Israel and the Arab nations, which erupted in October 1973, was generally quite favorable to Israel, and the United States government promptly countered the massive shipment of arms to the Arab countries by the Soviet Union with the dispatch of military supplies to Israel. But even in this situation it was apparent that many Americans were more concerned with the potential inconvenience of an energy shortage that might come in consequence of a reduction in oil shipments to the United States by the Arab nations than with the survival of Israel. The United States government supported Israel in the weeks of battle, but many American Jews wondered how strong the American commitment to Israel and its interests would remain once the United States and the Soviet Union (with which the Jewish Dr. Henry Kissinger, President Nixon's national security adviser and later secretary of state, had for years been energetically seeking a military and political détente) came together to collaborate in efforts toward arranging a peace settlement in the Middle East. Again it seemed to American Jewry that Israel stood virtually alone in a hostile and indifferent world which regarded it as more or less expendable, and that the Jewish state could confidently look to no resources other than its own, aside from the aid of world Jewry, in its struggle for survival. The Day of Atonement War evoked an even more generous outpouring of money and offers of personal service to Israel by American Jews than had the Six Day War. However, in the light of Israel's fearfully high number of casualties, the unexpectedly strong performance of the Arab forces in battle, the inconclusiveness of the war itself (despite Israel's clear military victory), and profound uncertainty as to what the future might hold for Israel, the mood of

American Jewry when hostilities ended was somber rather than jubilant.

In consequence of the aftermath of the Six Day War in 1967, there was a general withdrawal from the New Left and a renewed Jewish self-consciousness, especially among the Jewish university population in America. A considerable number of Jewish college students, although only a small proportion of the total, banded together in newly organized Zionist societies which they styled, in the accepted fashion of the contemporary counterculture, "radical" or "liberation" movements. More than a few left the United States to settle in Israel; between July 1967 and January 1971 over seventeen thousand American Jews, most of them young, emigrated to Israel. Others in recent years have formed *ḥavurot* or Jewish "fellowships" on university campuses and in the larger American cities to live together and share in a common quest for a deeper knowledge of Judaism and intensified self-awareness as Jews. In their new self-affirmation more of the young have turned to a study of Hebrew and even Yiddish. A certain brash assertiveness characterizes some of these student groups; they delight in condemning their elders as "inauthentic" Jews and in excoriating the existing Jewish institutions—community federations, welfare funds, and synagogues—as "irrelevant" and "outmoded." The latter have responded with expressions of concern over the ostensible "revolt" of the young, with commissioning new studies of "Jewish identity" and organizing new "institutes for Jewish living," and with attempts—generally quite successful—to co-opt the dissidents into the "establishment." Some of the leaders of the student "revolt" eagerly solicit the Jewish federations for funds to organize conclaves and print newspapers in which they can denounce federation programs and policies, and the federations gladly comply and in some cases invite the "rebels" to join their boards and committees—a flattering invitation rarely refused.

The continued vulnerability of the State of Israel and the attacks launched on it from certain liberal and radical circles in America; apprehension over the fate of the Jews in the Soviet Union; the anti-Semitism and glorification of violence and revolution expressed by some of the more militant black leaders and their white followers; concern over the future of Jews in the United States, where they have prospered under a system of meritocracy by virtue of their personal achievements, as other minority groups demand a larger representation in all areas of economic and professional life through a quota system based simply on numbers and which, if effected, could be highly detrimental to Jews—all these factors have combined to move American Jewry at least somewhat away from the political liberalism that it long generally espoused as both morally right and best calculated to advance its own welfare. The shift is evidenced in the substantially increased number of American Jews who supported the Republican candidate for the presidency in the elections of 1972, as well as by a growing mood of isolationism and concern for their own group interests. Whether this is an ephemeral or an enduring phenomenon cannot yet be predicted with any certainty, but it seems plausible to suggest that the liberal and universalist thrust of the Jewish tradition will not be permanently deflected within the ranks of American Jewry. Indeed, it may be argued that the recent move of a good many American Jews to the "right" represents not a repudiation of liberal attitudes and values, but an affirmation of them, an attempt to defend them against a New Left, some of whose spokesmen have nothing but contempt for liberalism in the classic sense and prefer pseudomessianic, utopian, revolutionary, and totalitarian visions of social change. It may be that many Jews realize instinctively that in the kind of order projected by the extremist leaders of the New Left, Jewish survival would become highly problematic.

Although a kind of romantic ethnicism, no doubt inspired to some degree by the black revolution, appears recently to have enchanted certain segments of the American-Jewish community, both young and old, it is doubtful that ethnic awareness or "racial pride" alone will contribute significantly to the community's long-range survival and creativity. It seems reasonable to assume that these goals, while aided by ethnic self-consciousness and pride, will be assured only by loyalty to Judaism, by an ongoing commitment to the Jewish religious and cultural tradition and its creative expansion. And although a growing secularism in the larger American society threatens all religious groups, Jews have resisted such threats before and may be expected to do so again.

What appears to be required if American Jewry is to endure in the face of the assimilatory pressures of the larger environment is not only its renewed dedication to Judaism but a certain degree of reordering of priorities in the utilization of its assets. For a long time philanthropy has occupied the most important place on its communal agenda, but philanthropy and "good works," while certainly authentic and major expressions of the Jewish spirit, are not the whole of Judaism; religious faith, practice, and learning—and the institutions that sustain and nourish them—are also indispensable. For many years the security and welfare of the State of Israel have been the chief concern of the organized American-Jewish community. That concern has been right and good, and it must obviously continue and perhaps become even more intense. American Jewry, however, is not a colony of the State of Israel, and cannot, if it wishes to survive, ignore its own vital interests. Enthusiasm for Israel, the "brand plucked from the fire" of the Holocaust, has revitalized the American-Jewish community and served as a powerful bond of union among its members. But many American Jews, carried away by sentiment, have supported the religious, educational, and cultural institutions of Israel with princely generosity while sparing little or nothing of their energy or resources for the advancement of corresponding institutions at home. Such skewed concern serves the long-term interests neither of Israel nor of United States Jewry. There is enough wealth and generosity in the American-Jewish community to provide for the needs of Israel without subjecting American-Jewish religious, cultural, and educational enterprises and organizations to starvation or malnutrition. A balance is clearly required, and it is likely that it will eventually be achieved. In the meantime, as long as the very survival of Israel is threatened, its requirements must obviously be given priority.

The Jews of America constitute the largest, freest, and most prosperous community in the history of the Jewish people. While they have not yet become the most creative, their achievements to date are already more than remarkable. One can safely predict that American Jewry's chapter in the history of Judaism will prove to be one of its most glorious.

CHAPTER

ఆ XVI ౢ

The State of Israel:
Achievements
and Problems

W<small>E HAVE NOTED</small> that the British White Paper of 1939 restricted Jewish immigration into Palestine and proposed to end it entirely within a few years precisely at the time that the situation of the Jews of Europe was becoming desperate in the extreme. His Majesty's government carried out the policy of its White Paper with utmost rigor during the years that Hitler and his henchmen were encompassing the destruction of their six million Jewish victims. But there were Jews in Europe and in the Palestinian *Yishuv* at this time who refused to accept the British decision meekly, and sought to defy it. Those Jewish refugees who could reach the shores of Palestine, and evade British patrols, were spirited into the country "illegally" by members of *kibbutzim* located near the coast in cooperation with the Haganah, the *Yishuv's* self-defense force. Some succeeded but many failed in their desperate attempt to enter Palestine. Shiploads of refugees from central Europe who managed to arrive in Haifa Bay were deported by the British fleet to the island of Mauritius; others were interred in detention camps at Athlit. Of the many tragedies that occurred, one of the worst was that of the *Struma*, an "illegal" immigrant vessel that left Rumania for Palestine late in 1941 carrying seven hundred sixty-nine refugees. The ship reached Istanbul but was turned back when the British mandatory government indicated that it would not permit the refugees to enter Palestine. Turkey would not admit them, and Rumania refused to allow them to return. Shortly afterward, in February 1942, the *Struma* foundered in the Black Sea, and all but one of its passengers and crew were lost. The world at the time took little notice.

During the war years the Jews of Palestine, despite their bitter opposition to the White Paper, vigorously supported British military efforts in the Near East both with thousands of soldiers and with civilian production of war materials. A considerable number of Arab leaders, on the other hand, openly sympathized with the Axis (the Grand Mufti of Jerusalem lived in Berlin as a guest of the Nazis, broadcasting pro-German propaganda to the Moslem world), and the Arab countries did virtually nothing to aid the cause of the Allies. Many Jews naively believed that Jewish loyalty and aid would be rewarded by Great Britain with abrogation of the restrictions on Jewish immigration into Palestine upon cessation of hostilities. Hopes were raised especially at the close of the war when the Conservative Party government of Winston Churchill was replaced with a government of the Labour Party, which, in 1939, had denounced the White Paper as an act of moral treachery. But the Labor government and its intransigent foreign secretary, Ernest Bevin, proved to be far more concerned with placating the Arabs and protecting British military and oil interests in the Near East than with providing a home for the tens of thousands of Jewish "displaced persons" (DPs) and the one hundred thousand "walking dead," survivors of the Nazi concentration camps languishing in temporary centers in the British and American occupied zones of Germany, for most of whom Europe had become a charnel house and who were clamoring for permission to go to Palestine. The restrictions on immigration remained in force, and attempts to evade them were dealt with in the harshest fashion possible.

Bevin's refusal to be moved by the plight of the DPs (he is reported to have said in 1946, "If the Jews, with all their sufferings, want to get too much at the head of the queue, you have the danger of another anti-Semitic reaction through it all" [1]) aroused widespread demands within the *Yishuv* and the world Zionist movement for the immediate establishment of a sovereign Jewish state in Palestine that would control its own immigration. It also provoked a few hundred Jews in Palestine to acts of terrorism. As the British turned back one "illegal" shipload of Jewish refugees after another in 1946 and 1947, members of the Irgun Zevai Leumi (National Military Organization), the military arm of the extremist Revisionist Party, some of whom were embittered recent arrivals from eastern Europe who had seen their own parents, children, husbands, or wives go quietly to be incinerated in Hitler's crematoria, and of the even more extremist Stern Gang, decided that only terror and assassination would change the adamant heart of Whitehall. Irgunists and Sternists set fire to British ammunition and oil dumps, ambushed and gunned down British soldiers, and even blew up the King David Hotel in Jerusalem, indiscriminately destroying scores of British, Jewish, and Arab lives. The majority of Jews in Palestine and throughout the world repudiated these desperate acts, but the attention of the world was called by them to the mounting gravity of the crisis in Palestine.

Far more effective in gaining the sympathy of the world were the widely publicized attempts of the DPs to enter Palestine in defiance of Great Britain and the obdurate refusal of the British authorities to admit them. Between April 1945 and January 1948 there were numerous secret sailings of ships carrying "illegal" refugees (or *maapilim*, as they were called) from Italian, French, and Yugoslavian harbors. The collecting of the DPs from camps in Germany at the ports of embarkation was largely the work of Haganah agents, who also clandestinely arranged for the vessels that would transport their human cargo to the coast of Palestine in the hope of evading the British blockade. Most of these attempts failed and the would-be immigrants were herded into detention camps on Cyprus, but the attempts themselves dramatized the desperation of the DPs. Men and women of goodwill throughout the world were profoundly affected by the newspaper accounts and pictures of the refugee ship *Beauharnais* moving toward British destroyers in Haifa Bay with a banner proclaiming: "We survived Hitler. Death is no stranger to us. Nothing can keep us from our Jewish homeland. The blood be on your heads if you fire on this unarmed ship!" Even more moving was the story of the rickety tub *Exodus-1947*, which sailed across the Mediterranean from France in the summer of 1947 with a cargo of forty-five hundred refugees. When the *Exodus* was boarded by British military personnel on arriving in Palestine territorial waters, its passengers and crew tried to fight off the boarding party in hand-to-hand combat and surrendered only when the British used machine guns and tear gas and threatened to sink the ship with all on board. The enraged foreign secretary of Great Britain then ordered the refugees returned in prison ships to Marseilles, where they adamantly refused to disembark despite all threats and cajolements. After three weeks, the British government made ready forcibly to return the refugees to DP camps in Germany, the land of the recent murderers of their relatives and friends. This time the world, which had been watching the entire drama of the *Exodus* closely for two months, reacted with sympathetic admiration for the courage of the refugees and wholesale disgust at the callousness of the British.

Ultimately the government of Great Britain had to admit that it could no longer cope with the situation in Palestine and communicated to the United Nations its intention to give up the mandate that it had held for a quarter of a century. On November 29, 1947, the General Assembly of the United Nations adopted a resolution calling for a division of the country into independent Arab and Jewish states, with Jerusalem, the site of so many places holy to Jews, Christians, and Moslems, to be under international control.

Although the area assigned to the Jewish state by the United Nations resolution was far smaller than many had hoped, the leaders of the *Yishuv* and the world Zionist movement accepted the resolution and looked forward to its implementation. The leaders of the Arabs in Palestine and the governments of the Arab nations, on the other hand, denounced the partition proposal and proclaimed that they would destroy the Jewish state if it ever came into being. As for the British government, it refused to cooperate with the United Nations in moving in orderly fashion toward partition, insisted that it alone would retain authority in Palestine until the day the mandate came to an end, and proceeded to begin the withdrawal of its officials and troops in such a way as to leave the country in chaos but building up Arab strength for the battle which—it was clear—would come.

On May 14, 1948, the day before the mandate officially terminated and the last British soldiers were preparing to depart, the cabinet of the Provisional Government that had been assembled three weeks earlier by the leader of the Labor Party of the *Yishuv* and prime minister-to-be, David Ben-Gurion, gathered in the art museum of Tel Aviv to proclaim the independence of the Republic of Israel. After surveying the historic events that had led to this moment, the Declaration of Independence proclaimed that Israel's doors would be open to any Jew who wished to settle there, that full political and social equality would be granted to all its citizens regardless of religion, race, or sex, and that freedom of religion, conscience, education, and culture would be guaranteed for all. Realizing full well the imminence of invasion by the armies of the neighboring Arab nations, the authors of the Declaration concluded with a plea for peace:

We extend our hand in peace and neighborliness to all the neighboring States and their peoples, and invite them to co-operate with the independent Jewish nation for the common good of all. The State of Israel is prepared to make its contribution to the progress of the Middle East as a whole. Our call goes out to the Jewish people all over the world to rally to our side in the task of immigration and development, and to stand by us in the great struggle for the fulfillment of the dream of generations for the redemption of Israel. With trust in the Rock of Israel, we set our hand to this Declaration, at this Session of the Provisional State Council, on the soil of the Homeland, in the city of Tel Aviv, on this Sabbath Eve, the fifth day of Iyar, 5708, the fourteenth day of May, 1948.

Within minutes after the news of Israel's Declaration of Independence flashed across the White House teletype, President Harry S. Truman, ignoring the counsels of State Department and other American officials, extended de facto recognition to the new state. Three days later the government of the Soviet Union, which—to general surprise—had supported the Palestine partition resolution in the United Nations, granted de jure recognition. Most other non-Arab nations quickly followed the United States and Russia, only Great Britain grudgingly withholding recognition as long as it could.

During the months between the partition resolution and establishment of the State of Israel, thousands of Arab irregulars, mainly from Syria and Lebanon, had infiltrated into Palestine, laying siege to Jerusalem and attacking Jewish settlements elsewhere. Almost immediately after the Declaration of Independence, an invasion by the armies of Syria, Lebanon, Iraq, Trans-Jordan, and Egypt, equipped with British weaponry and with some units commanded by former British officers, was launched on the new state simultaneously from the north, south, and east. The Israelis, armed with weapons they had either themselves manufactured or smuggled in from Czechoslovakia and a few other countries, fought with the courage and tenacity of men who knew they were engaged in a life-and-death struggle. When the United Nations, after a series of temporary truces, finally arranged an armistice in 1949 on the basis of existing military boundaries, the Arab armies had been decisively defeated and Israel was in control of a territory considerably larger than that envisioned in the U.N. partition resolution, including all of the Negev (except for the Gaza Strip) and the New City of Jerusalem. The eastern sector of Jerusalem, including the Old City and the Hebrew University on Mount Scopus, was in the hands of Trans-Jordan's Arab Legion.

Undoubtedly the greatest tragedy of the war, aside from the bloodshed, was the creation of a body of six hundred fifty thousand civilian Arab refugees who fled from Israel during the hostilities. Prime Minister Ben-Gurion and the Israeli government had made every effort to keep the Palestinian Arabs from leaving the country, assuring them that they would not be harmed. Many thousands remained, but the majority responded to the intensive propaganda of the leaders of the neighboring Arab countries, who warned them to leave their homes for the duration of hostilities and promised that they would return to repossess them and to enjoy the spoils of war as soon as the Jews were destroyed. After the armistice, the Israeli government declined to repatriate the Arabs who had fled. In light of the adamant refusal of the Arab nations to make peace with Israel and their repeated threats that they would fight again and eventually drive the Israelis into the sea, the decision of the government not to readmit a great host of potential "fifth columnists" is understandable. Furthermore, hundreds of thousands of Jewish refugees from Arab countries, most of whom had to abandon their homes and property, were resettled in Israel within a few years. The Israeli government has repeatedly indicated its willingness to compensate the Arab refugees for their property in the framework of a general Middle East peace settlement, but peace has still not been achieved. For their part, the neighboring Arab nations, which could easily have absorbed and resettled the refugees, refused to do so, preferring to utilize them as a pawn in their ongoing struggle against Israel. The result has been that a quarter of a century after their misguided but understandable decision to flee, many of the Palestinian refugees and the children subsequently born to them still live in camps maintained by the United Nations, their bitterness and frustration constantly growing.

After the armistice of 1949 the Arab nations not only refused to enter into a peace treaty with Israel but continued to send terrorists and saboteurs into the country with orders to kill, destroy, and create as much havoc as possible. Despite the urgent need for time to organize its governmental structures soundly, as well as severe economic problems worsened by the ending of trade relations with its neighbors and the need to maintain a sizable military force to defend itself against both infiltrators and threats of renewed aggression, Israel at once opened its gates to all Jews who wished to enter. Even while the War of Liberation was still going on, massive efforts were made to move the survivors of Hitler's concentration camps from Europe to Israel; within a few months after the armistice, the task was practically completed. Beginning in the fall of 1949, virtually all of the fifty thousand threatened members of the ancient Jewish community of Yemen in southwest Arabia were flown to Israel in a series of airlifts which came to be called "Operation Magic Carpet." In May 1950 "Operation Ezra and Nehemiah" was initiated to fly one hundred twenty thousand Jews from Iraq, where their situation had become precarious, to Israel. Most of the members of the long-isolated community of Cochin in southern India were transported to the new Jewish state, as were many Jews from the Moslem nations of North Africa. In the first years of Israel's independence immigrants arrived from practically every country in the world, but particularly from those nations where their freedom and security were seriously threatened, mainly the Moslem lands and eastern Europe. Large numbers came from Poland, Rumania, Hungary, Czechoslovakia, and Bulgaria. Even the Soviet Union permitted handfuls of its Jews to emigrate to Israel at that time.

Within a decade from the time of the Declaration of Independence, the population of Israel had risen from six hundred fifty thousand to nearly two million, of whom 90 percent were Jews. The task of feeding, housing, and providing employment for the immigrants, many of whom were destitute and unskilled, was an enormous burden. To be sure, Israel was aided by generous financial contributions from Jews abroad, as well as by grants and loans from the United States government and by large amounts of money and material from the West German government in reparation for the damage and atrocities inflicted on the Jews of Europe by the Nazis. But the largest part of the burden was shouldered by the citizens of Israel, who accepted crushing taxation and a regimen of severe austerity to make possible the work of *kibbutz galuyot*, the ingathering of the exiles.

Within a comparatively short time the *maabarot*, the temporary tents and huts in which the new immigrants had been lodged, were dismantled. The newcomers were provided with permanent housing and efforts were undertaken to integrate them socially and economically into the life of the country as quickly as possible. The task was made infinitely more difficult by a continuing need for a strong defense posture. Infiltration and sabotage, originating chiefly from the Gaza Strip and Jordan, continued unremittingly, despite reprisals by the Israeli army. Great efforts were made to train and equip a strong army and air force to ward off direct attacks from Israel's hostile Arab neighbors. In late October and early November 1956, Israel launched its Sinai Campaign to break the threat of encirclement by Egypt, Jordan, and Syria, which had joined in a military alliance under the leadership of Egyptian president Gamal Abdel Nasser. The campaign was intended to destroy the concentration of Egyptian armaments which Nasser had been threatening to use against Israel, and to eliminate the bases in the Gaza Strip which were being employed by Arab marauders and saboteurs. Within a matter of days Israeli units had seized almost the entire Sinai Peninsula and the Gaza Strip, taking fifty-six hundred Egyptian prisoners of war and large quantities of armaments which the Soviet Union, now allied with the Arab nations and bitterly anti-Israel, had been supplying to Nasser for months.

Israel's victory alone evoked widespread admiration (once again it was proved that those supposedly cowardly Jews could fight!), but then on November 2 the British and French governments ordered their bombers to attack strategic Egyptian positions before occupying Port Said in an attempt to regain control of the Suez Canal, which Nasser had nationalized. Under intense pressure from the United Nations, where the United States and the Soviet Union collaborated in pushing through a resolution calling for immediate withdrawal of the English, French, and Israeli forces from Egyptian territory, Britain and France abandoned the positions they had occupied. The Israeli evacuation was completed in March 1957, with a withdrawal from the Gaza Strip and Sharm e-Sheikh at the southern tip of the Sinai Peninsula. The Sinai Campaign of 1956 clearly demonstrated Israel's military strength and resulted in the opening of the Gulf of Aqaba to Israeli shipping and, thus, access to the commerce of Asia. President Dwight D. Eisenhower personally assured David Ben-Gurion that United Nations forces would remain in Gaza indefinitely and that the United States would guarantee the freedom and safety of Israeli ships in the Gulf of Aqaba.

The State of Israel

While the morale of the Egyptian army was broken and the prestige of Nasser greatly impaired by the Sinai Campaign, the years that followed did not bring peace or security to Israel. Destructive forays into the country by Arab saboteurs continued, and the Arab governments constantly repeated their irrevocable intention to destroy Israel as soon as they acquired sufficient strength. In 1967 war between Israel and Egypt, Jordan, and Syria again erupted. This war, from June 5 to June 10, which came to be known as the Six Day War, was preceded by many months of extreme tension, produced by sabotage within Israel as well as by border raids, the latter undertaken chiefly by Syria, whose rabid government leaders wished to drag the other Arab nations into renewed hostilities against Israel. In May 1967 Nasser moved the Egyptian army into the Sinai Peninsula and demanded the removal of the United Nations troops from the Gaza Strip; the secretary-general of the United Nations, U Thant, immediately and inexplicably complied. Nasser thereupon blockaded the Straits of Tiran, preventing Israeli ships from entering or leaving the port of Elath, Israel's outlet to the Indian Ocean and Asia. While intense diplomatic activity was being carried on to keep the situation from exploding into war, Nasser ordered more troops and tanks into Sinai, as the other Arab nations coordinated their moves with the Egyptian high command in preparation for a combined attack on Israel.

Amidst the rising war hysteria, the Israeli government decided to strike on June 5. Within a few hours its air force had destroyed more than three hundred Egyptian planes grounded at their bases and also eliminated practically the entire air power of Syria and Jordan. Simultaneously, Israeli infantry and tank battalions attacked Egyptian positions in the Gaza Strip and the Sinai Desert; by June 8 they had reached the banks of the Suez Canal and occupied Sharm e-Sheikh. A few hours before the hostilities began, the prime minister of Israel, Levi Eshkol, had assured King Hussein of Jordan that if his country did not join in the fighting her territory would not be attacked. The Jordanians, however, proceeded to shell Jerusalem and border settlements in Israel. Israeli troops then moved against Jordan and on June 7 occupied Jordanian Jerusalem, including the Old City. The whole area west of the Jordan River, including Bethlehem, Hebron, and Nablus, was occupied by the Israeli army. When Israeli troops reached the Western Wall of the Temple in Jerusalem, from which Jews had been barred by the Jordanians for almost two decades, the chief chaplain of the armed forces, Rabbi Shelomoh

Goren, sounded the shofar amidst scenes of tearful rejoicing. Only after completing its operations on the southern and eastern fronts did the Israeli army move to attack the Syrians entrenched in heavily fortified positions on the Golan Heights overlooking Israeli border settlements, which they had been shelling for many months. After three days of bloody combat, the Golan Heights were occupied and Israel acceded to the demand of the United Nations for a cease-fire.

❦

The stunning victories of the Six Day War brought jubilation to Israel, but sorrow as well. Many were appalled by the amount of both Arab and Jewish blood that had been shed. Even crack commando troopers from the *kibbutzim*, who had borne the brunt of the fighting, reported in interviews shortly after the hostilities ceased their grief and frustration over being compelled once again to go to war, to kill and be killed. How many times again in their lives, they wondered, would they be forced to fight? What had happened to the golden dream of a peaceful and secure Jewish state? [2]

The war itself brought as immediate results a temporary removal of the Arab threat to destroy Israel, a shattering of Arab military strength (which was soon rebuilt by massive shipments of new planes, tanks, and other armaments to Egypt and Syria by the Soviet Union), reopening of the Straits of Tiran to Israeli ships, removal of the constant threat of attack on the Jewish settlements along the Syrian border near the Golan Heights and elsewhere, and acquisition of military boundaries that could be more easily defended. The war also presented Israel with a tremendous problem—a million Arabs in the occupied territories. While Israeli authorities attempted to administer the occupied territories humanely but firmly and to raise the economic level of the Arab residents without interfering excessively with their internal autonomy and traditional way of life, the future of the territories was not decided and continued to present a serious predicament to Israel.

The Soviet Union and the communist regimes of eastern Europe, all of which (with the exception of Rumania) broke off diplomatic relations with Israel in the wake of the war, joined the Arab nations in attempting to nullify Israel's victory. President Charles de Gaulle of France also assumed a strongly anti-Israel position. The government of the United States, however, under the leadership of President Lyndon B. Johnson, did not waver in its support of Israel. For months a heated debate was carried on in the United Nations, and in November 1967 a resolution was finally adopted calling on Israel to withdraw from the territories it had occupied and for the Arab countries to end their state of belligerency with Israel. A variety of diplomatic initiatives were subsequently made, but no progress was achieved in implementing this resolution. Although the government of Israel indicated a willingness to give up much of the territories and to negotiate new boundaries in direct peace talks with the Arab nations, such peace discussions were spurned.

The Six Day War, as we noted in the previous chapter, created an enormous upsurge of concern and feeling for Israel among the Jews of America. Similar upsurges, some of even greater intensity, took place among Jewish communities throughout the world. Financial contributions in unprecedented amounts poured in, and many hundreds of volunteers departed by every available means of transport to Israel to aid in the war effort and to undertake civilian tasks left by Israelis who had been mobilized. Never before had the bond between Israel and world Jewry, which saw the very existence of the state threatened in May and June of 1967, been so deep and powerful.

The Six Day War, however, brought no real peace or relaxation of tensions to Israel. As soon as Egypt regained its military strength, it undertook what Gamal Abdel Nasser called a "war of attrition" against Israel, sending its airplanes and missiles across the Suez Canal to rain destruction and death on military installations in Israeli-held territory. Furthermore, Arab terrorist organizations began to proliferate and grew ever more reckless. Finding themselves virtually powerless to inflict any damage in Israel itself in the face of a government determined not to brook their actions, the terrorists launched a campaign of sabotage and murder on a worldwide scale, hijacking commercial airliners all over Europe and the Middle East and extorting enormous ransoms for their release, attempting to bomb Israeli embassies throughout the world, and gunning down Israeli diplomats and citizens abroad. The height of the atrocities seemed to have been reached with the slaughter of scores of innocent passengers at the Lydda airport in 1972 by some Japanese gunmen enrolled in an Arab terrorist organization, but this catastrophe was soon outshadowed, as far as publicity was concerned, by the kidnapping and brutal murder by another band of Arab terrorists of eleven Israeli athletes at the World Olympic Games in Munich later that year. Some governments murmured their sympathies politely, but little forthright action was taken to stem the tide of terrorism or resist the outrageous demands of its perpetrators. Indeed, in the late summer of 1973, the government of the supposedly sovereign and free state of Austria cravenly acceded to the demands of a handful of Arab terrorists who had hijacked a train, and announced its intention to close the transit camp at Schonau Castle outside Vienna where, over a period of years, tens of thousands of Jews fleeing from the Soviet Union had been housed for the few days necessary to arrange their further transportation by air to Israel.

It was clear to many that the Arab nations were only biding their time and rebuilding their strength for another round with Israel. The fourth Arab-Israeli war—the so-called Yom Kippur, or Day of Atonement, War of October 1973—broke out with unexpected fury precisely at a time when Arab government leaders and diplomats in the United Nations and in the capitals of the world were sounding notes of sweet reason and accommodation on a peace settlement with Israel. Hostilities erupted suddenly on the holiest day of the Jewish year, at a time when many Israelis were at prayer in their synagogues, with an unprecedented massive attack across the Suez Canal in the south by Egyptian air and ground forces and a simultaneous attack across the Golan Heights in the north by the Syrian army and air force. Israeli intelligence apparently had advance information about the massing of enemy forces, but this time, out of overconfidence in its military strength, the government, headed by Mrs. Golda Meir, decided not to mobilize all its forces and attack.

The consequence of this decision was that the defeat of the Egyptian and Syrian forces, quickly joined by Saudi Arabia, Iraq, and Jordan, was by no means achieved in lightninglike fashion, but took three weeks of the bitterest and most intense fighting. The Arab armies and air forces had been equipped for years by the Soviet Union with enormous quantities of its most advanced and lethal planes, tanks, and missiles, and during the war itself the Russians maintained a massive resupply of weapons to their Arab clients. Countering the Soviet government's brutal play for power in the Middle East, the United States government responded after a few days by shipping a large number of planes and other armaments to Israel. From a certain not altogether erroneous perspective, the war in the Middle East might have been regarded as a proving ground for the relative effectiveness of Soviet and United States weapons in a possible future war between the great powers, with Israeli and Arab soldiers serving as surrogates for American and Russian troops.

The State of Israel

When a cease-fire was arranged in the Security Council of the United Nations through Russian-American collaboration after three weeks of bloody battle, Israel had managed not only to repel the Syrian forces from the Golan Heights and to drive many miles into Syria on the road to Damascus, but also to surround completely and entrap the Third Army of Egypt, which had crossed over to the eastern bank of the Suez Canal, and to occupy a considerable area of Egyptian territory on the western side of the canal. But there was no jubilation in Israel over the military victory; the number of men slain, wounded, and captured had run into the thousands, and there was little consolation in the fact that Arab casualties had been three or four times as high.

Furthermore, there was widespread apprehension about the still greater losses and more serious threats to the security of the state that the future might bring. Once more it had become clear that Israel was without friends in the world, except for the United States government and—of course—American and world Jewry, which again responded magnificently with monetary contributions and offers of personal service to replace the reservists called to military duty. Not only did the Arab nations and the Soviet Union, as well as China and the communist regimes of eastern Europe, remain implacably hostile, but most of the countries of the Third World intensified their longstanding animosity toward Israel. In addition, almost all the democracies of western and central Europe—England, France, Germany, Italy, and so on—some of which had formerly been relatively friendly to Israel, responded with deep fear during and after the Yom Kippur War to the threat of a reduction in their oil supplies by the Arab nations, and made it more than obvious that, in their view, the vital interests of Israel were expendable while Arab oil was not. Only the government and people of the Netherlands proclaimed, for a few weeks longer, that they would not abandon their support of Israel in exchange for oil.

As of April 1974 it is not possible to foresee all the enormous pressures that might be brought to bear upon Israel in the negotiations toward a "peace settlement" with the Arab nations. But it seems probable that the nations of the world, including perhaps also the United States, will push Israel very hard toward making concessions that may significantly diminish its strength and security. Nor is it realistic to expect that the Arab nations, although they may agree formally to signing a peace treaty with Israel and officially recognizing its right to exist and its territorial integrity, will really renounce their frequently repeated goal of liquidating, as soon as they have the requisite strength, the Jewish state, which they continue to regard as a foreign, cancerous intrusion in a Middle East that rightfully belongs in its entirety only to them. In any case, there are sufficient grounds for apprehension that the fourth Arab-Israel war will have brought no gains to Israel but only magnified its problems and intensified its isolation in the world.

❧❦❧

Despite having to wage four wars in the first twenty-five years of its existence and to assume the burden of integrating a large number of newcomers (with additional immigration, the Jewish population of the state by 1973 reached almost two million, seven hundred thousand), Israel achieved not only enormous economic progress but also made rapid strides in developing both the quantity and quality of its cultural life. The educational system was greatly expanded, and to the Hebrew University of Jerusalem, which achieved preeminence in a number of disciplines, were added several other promising universities in Tel Aviv, Haifa, and Beersheba. The publication of books and journals in Hebrew, Yiddish, English, and several other languages increased rapidly. In recent years some two thousand volumes, approximately one-fourth of them translations into Hebrew, have been published annually, and Israel now ranks second in the world in number of titles in proportion to the total population. Theater companies, the most distinguished of them the famed *Ha-Bimah*, produce numerous plays by native and foreign dramatists, while the Israel Philharmonic Orchestra continues to enjoy an international reputation, making frequent appearances in Europe and America.

Poetry in Hebrew has flourished in Israel, with such figures as Avraham Shlonsky, Lea Goldberg, Yitzhak Lamdan, Uri Tzevi Greenberg, Nathan Alterman, and Reuven Avinoam (Grossman) among the older generation, and a number of younger poets, including Yehudah Amichai, Abba Kovner, Dalia Ravikovich, and David Rokeah, especially distinguishing themselves. The novel has also been cultivated by such outstanding writers as Asher Barash, Hayyim Hazaz, Jehudah Burla, Moshe Shamir, Aharon Meged, and Avraham Yehoshua. When Shemuel Yosef Agnon received the Nobel prize for literature in 1966, the award was rightly regarded as a recognition by the world of the importance of the new Hebrew literature. Agnon's richly symbolic tales [3] in Hebrew portray Jewish life in Galicia, where he was born in 1888, and in Palestine, where he settled permanently in 1923. His style is unique, blending elements from the Bible and the *Talmud* with modern Hebrew. After the establishment of the state a group of native-born writers emerged on the literary scene, depicting the life and aspirations of Israeli youth. Others have recently turned to more universal themes, and their poems, short stories, novels, and dramas have received wide acclaim.

While the achievements of the State of Israel in the first quarter century of its existence have been highly impressive, many urgent problems remain unresolved. The most pressing and immediate is, of course, the continuing hostility of the Arab nations. In twenty-five years Israel's relationships with the Arab world have, as we have seen, deteriorated rather than improved, and the government and people have had to live in a climate of siege and to maintain a constant state of readiness for war.

It is not likely that this situation will change merely with the signing of a peace treaty. Most of the Arab leaders, both "moderate" and "revolutionary," of the present and recent past have repeatedly declared that the very existence of an independent Jewish state in the Middle East is intolerable to the Arab people; the most that even the moderates have indicated as acceptable in the long run is the existence of a Jewish community in a binational "Palestine" that would be part and parcel of the Arab world. Considerations of international diplomacy and immediate political advantage may dictate official recognition of Israel's sovereignty and territorial integrity, but it would be foolhardy for Israel to assume that this meant a final and definitive renunciation by the Arabs of their professed aim of destroying the Jewish state. Reason and logic may demonstrate that it is to the mutual political and economic advantage of the Arab nations and Israel for the Arabs to give up their bitter hostility to Israel, accept its existence, and join with it in cooperative efforts to develop the region; but it is doubtful that rational considerations will outweigh the fierce pride of the Arabs and their conviction that they are divinely destined to be the sole masters of the Middle East. Thus Israel, it would seem, will have to maintain a constant state of preparedness to ward off repeated blows aimed at its annihilation. Although it wishes nothing more fervently than genuine peace with its neighbors, it must always be ready for war.

The sober fact is that the Arab nations may lose a war against Israel three, four, or a dozen times, and be little the worse off for it, while for Israel no victory can be regarded as definitive and any defeat might well be the last. The grim past, the memory of the Nazi Holocaust, with the reminder that its reenactment is by no means inconceivable, is very much alive in the hearts of the Jews of Israel and has been so since the establishment of the state. That is perhaps the reason for the somberness and melancholy that lie barely hidden beneath the forced gaiety and volubility of so many Israelis.

Most Israelis realize intuitively, as do the majority of their fellow Jews throughout the world, that on the survival of Israel depends, in a very real sense, the entire future of the Jewish people as a whole. Irving Kristol has rightly noted the utterly demoralizing effect that the destruction of Israel might well have on world Jewry:

Should Israel be extinguished in a blood bath, it could be the end of 3,000 years of Jewish history. In the course of World War II, two out of every five Jews on this earth were slaughtered for no other reason than that they were Jews. But that holocaust was in part redeemed—was given some meaning—by the astonishing emergence of the State of Israel, a sudden and unanticipated answer to 2,000 years of daily prayer. If that fantastic dream, now realized, should turn into just another Jewish nightmare, a great many Jews are going to conclude—reluctantly but inevitably—that the burden of Jewish history is just too grievous to bequeath to one's descendants, and they will opt out.[4]

Hence, when the Israelis fight for the security and survival of Israel, they are engaged not only in a struggle for their own lives but for the future of the whole Jewish enterprise.

Assuming, as it must, the present desire of its Arab neighbors to destroy it, Israel will necessarily be and remain—perhaps for a very long time—something of a garrison state. For years it has been such to some extent, but the apprehensions of some critics, both at home and abroad, that it would degenerate into a Middle Eastern Sparta, focusing its energies on the maintenance of military might alone and cultivating the martial virtues at the expense of building a humane society, have not been realized, nor are they likely to be. Nevertheless, the diversion of so much of its resources to the maintenance of a strong defense posture will inevitably affect Israel's capacity for social and cultural progress. It will undoubtedly be able to count on the continued support—financial and moral—of American and world Jewry. But a high price will have to be paid for the fact that not only its security but its very survival continue to be threatened.

Although hopes for attainment by Israel in the near future of an enduring peace with its Arab neighbors may be unrealistic, all possible avenues toward a genuinely lasting settlement must be explored and pursued. The search for abiding peace and, ultimately, even fraternity with its Arab neighbors is for Israel not only a matter of political expediency but a moral task. Israel as a nation came into existence, in considerable measure, under the impetus of a religious, quasi-messianic drive. It was not to be simply another little state glorying in the panoply and power of national sovereignty. Many of the great figures of the Zionist movement firmly believed that the Jewish state would serve as a "light to the nations." The sense of transnational mission and purpose has not been altogether suppressed in contemporary Israel. In recent years, despite little gratitude and much hostility, Israel has generously offered technical and scientific assistance to a number of the new nations of Africa and Asia and provided educational opportunities for a good many students from these countries in its universities and technological institutes. It has also responded with medical missions and other forms of aid whenever large-scale natural disaster has struck in any part of the world. These acts have not been motivated simply by considerations of expediency, to obtain goodwill and political support. Much more can and will be done along these lines by Israel, but her primary goal in the long run must be, unpromising as the prospects may presently appear, a just peace with the Arab states.

Given the present attitude of its neighbors, Israel has no choice but to maintain its military might; any other course would be suicidal. But it hardly seems utopian or naively idealistic to insist that it must, at the same time, investigate and follow all roads possibly leading toward peace and reconciliation that may unpredictably open themselves in the future. In this connection, the simplistic and unreflecting "hawkishness" which appears to be the dominant attitude of the majority of American Jews and American-Jewish organizations when they contemplate the problem of Israel-Arab relationships is hardly helpful. In Israel itself, particularly in its academic community, there are many responsible persons who do not automatically endorse the policies that their government may at any moment choose to adopt, and who call for a more imaginative and energetic approach to the solution of Israel-Arab problems, including the question of the refugees. Such utopianism or idealism, if that is what it be, may prove to be just as necessary and helpful in the long range as the presently justified policy of maintaining military strength and resisting, on the international secne and in the diplomatic arena, all concessions that may diminish the security of the state and its capacity to defend itself.

❦

Another major problem that continues to perplex Israel is the role of religion in the life of the nation. We have noted that some of the early Zionist leaders were thoroughgoing secularists with little interest in, or commitment to, Jewish religious belief or practice. Most of the *halutzim* of the Second and Third Aliyot were, as ideological Marxists and socialists, definitely antireligious and anticlerical. The only form of Judaism they had known in Russia and Poland was a rigid and dogmatic orthodoxy which showed little concern with issues of social justice and confined its interest largely to ritual questions; with such a Judaism they could feel no vital affinity. The *halutzim* who came to Palestine, however, found a considerable number of orthodox Jews already living there, especially in Jerusalem and the three other "holy" cities, and many more followed as the Jewish settlement of the land proceeded. Especially in the 1920s and 1930s a considerable number of traditionalist Jews, fleeing from eastern and central Europe, settled in the country. Most of these were more or less orthodox in belief and practice and looked to the rabbis, especially the chief rabbinate, for guidance. Tension between the religious and secularist groups, though generally muted, was a constant phenomenon during the period of the British mandate.

Intensifying the conflict was the fact that all matters regarding marriage, divorce, family status, and inheritance were under the control of the rabbinate. During its long administration of Palestine the Turkish government had not established any common law governing these areas. Its position was that, as far as these questions were concerned, residents of Palestine should be subject to the religious law of the faith-community to which they belonged. Thus, Moslems were to be governed by Moslem law, Catholics by Catholic canon law, Protestants by their various church rules, and Jews by Talmudic law administered by the chief rabbinate.

When the British took over control of Palestine from Turkey under the League of Nations mandate, they continued the Turkish system. The secularists would have preferred that the system be abandoned; in the plan which they submitted to the mandatory government for the organization of the Jewish community there was no mention of the chief rabbinate. The British authorities, however, regarded the Jews as essentially a religious community and insisted that the chief rabbinate continue as an institution responsible for the administration of religious life and vested with full authority in matters of marriage, divorce, inheritance, and family status. The first elections held in the 1920s for the Rabbinical Council, which appoints the chief rabbi, proved disappointing both to the orthodox and to the nonorthodox and secularists. The latter group realized that their hopes for substantial change in irksome provisions of the *halachah* were not to be fulfilled. The rabbis, for their part, discovered that they would have to get along simply with a majority in the Rabbinical Council. Repeated proposals were made by secularist spokesmen for the removal of jurisdiction over the areas of personal status mentioned above from exclusive control of the chief rabbinate. But the questions which were to disturb Israeli society so frequently after establishment of the state—questions such as the marital disabilities of the *kohen*, or individual of priestly lineage, the *agunah*, or married woman separated from her husband who cannot legally remarry, and *mamzerim*, or bastards—did not come to the fore during the mandatory period.

From 1921 to 1935 Abraham Isaac Kook (1865–1935) served as the first Ashkenazi chief rabbi of Palestine.[5] A highly charismatic personality who enjoyed many warm friendships among the nonorthodox and secularist leaders of the *Yishuv*, as well as a great Talmudic scholar and mystic, Rabbi Kook insisted that even secularist Jews were fulfilling a supremely important *mitzvah* by settling in the Holy Land, and that their dedication to social ideals, which he shared, must be set against their violations of the precepts of *halachah* and their professed atheism or agnosticism. He also hoped that eventually the breach between the secularists and the religious Jews of Palestine would be healed, and all would return to Torah Judaism. In 1924 Rabbi Kook organized a *yeshivah* in Jerusalem which came to be known as Merkaz Ha-Rav and was unique among the Talmudic academies of Palestine in its positive attitude toward Zionism. The chief rabbi's conciliatory attitude toward the secularists and his friendship with nonreligious Zionist leaders angered the ultraorthodox. The outstanding leader of the latter group was Rabbi Joseph Sonnenfeld, a Hungarian-born Talmudist who declined to take any religious responsibility for a secular Jewish society in Palestine and organized a separatist orthodox community in Jerusalem, consisting of Jews who were strictly devoted to the *halachah* and wished to remain uncontaminated by any contact with the non-observant.

When the State of Israel was created in 1948 there was a serious potentiality of overt and even violent conflict between the extremely orthodox Jews, who wished to see all of the *halachah* become the law of the state, and the secularists, most of whom advocated a separation of "church" and "state," along American lines. The impossibility of resolving this conflict totally was one of the major factors in the decision not to attempt to write a constitution for the new nation. To avoid a major confrontation at the time and to mitigate future controversy, Prime Minister David Ben-Gurion and Rabbi Judah Leib Maimon (Fishman), a distinguished leader of the Mizrahi, or religious, Zionists and the first minister of religious affairs in the cabinet of Israel, reached an understanding that the arrangements which had been in effect during the period of the British mandate would continue, with no substantial changes favoring either the religious or the secularist groups. The agreement between the prime minister and Rabbi Maimon has come to be known generally in Israel as the "Status Quo" and is still formally in effect. The "Status Quo" explains some of the seemingly inexplicable phenomena that may be observed in Israel today—the facts, for instance, that public buses make their runs on the Sabbath in Haifa but not in Jerusalem and Tel Aviv, that marriages between Jews performed in Israel must be in accord with *halachah* (there is no civil marriage in the country, and intermarriage is impossible) but civil marriages between Jews performed abroad are generally recognized as valid, and that the telephone system operates on the Sabbath but the postal and telegraph services do not.

The term *dati*, or "religious," as it is used in contemporary Israel, refers generally to those who identify themselves with orthodoxy, a substantial minority consisting of perhaps 40 percent of the total population. The Jews considered "religious," however, include elements that differ considerably from each other—members of orthodox *kibbutzim* who combine socialism and communitarian living with an attempt to follow the *halachah* strictly; the Lubavich, Bratzlav, and other Ḥasidic groups who maintain their own prayer houses and schools; followers of the so-called *gedolei ha-Torah*, the renowned rabbis who came to Palestine from eastern Europe after the rise of

Hitler and who, by reason of their scholarship and stature, have been able to form an ultraorthodox pressure group that has dictated its views even to the chief rabbi; the mass of more or less traditional and observant Jews; and the small number of extremists dwelling largely in the Meah Shearim section of Jerusalem and in Bene Berak who call themselves the *Neturei Karta* (guardians of the city) and simply do not accept the authority of the secular Israeli government, refusing to carry an Israeli identity card, recognize the jurisdiction of the courts, or vote in elections.

While the orthodox groups vary greatly, most of them collaborate as a political bloc through well-organized political parties, notably the National Religious Party and Agudas Yisroel. Because the dominant Mapai (Labor) Party has never had a clear majority in the Kenesset, or parliament, of Israel and has had to resort to forming coalition governments with the support of the religious parties, the religious bloc has gained a considerable amount of political power and won many concessions in exchange for its support of Mapai on foreign and domestic issues.

Despite their present power, many leaders of the religious bloc feel threatened and insecure. They believe there has been a progressive deterioration of the "Status Quo" and that the agreement between Ben-Gurion and Maimon has been repeatedly violated. More planes, ships, and factories are operating on the Sabbath, and the exclusive control of the rabbinate in the area of marriage is threatened by the possibility of legislation making civil marriage ceremonies possible under certain circumstances. A proposal to authorize such ceremonies has been put forward in the Kenesset by secularist members outraged by the actions of the rabbinic authorities in refusing to recognize the validity of conversions to Judaism performed by nonorthodox rabbis and in branding certain persons as *mamzerim* (bastards, or offspring of a union within the biblically prohibited degrees of consanguinity or of a married woman with a man other than her husband) and refusing to allow them to marry anyone but another *mamzer* or a convert. When the new Ashkenazi chief rabbi, Shelomoh Goren, in 1972 manifested a tendency toward a more humane and flexible interpretation of the *halachah* by nullifying a bastardy verdict that had been issued by lower rabbinical courts, he was vitriolically denounced by a number of ultraorthodox rabbis in both Israel and the United States.

While some of the orthodox leaders feel apprehensive about a possible diminution of their present power, many of the nonorthodox and secularists are deeply resentful of what they regard as religious coercion and unwarranted interference with their personal freedoms. Moreover, they are repelled by the dogmatism of the official religious leaders and their isolation from the cultural and intellectual life of the country as a whole. In the synagogues as presently organized they find little to attract them or to engage their ongoing interest. Most of the synagogues are merely prayer houses; where there is preaching and religious instruction, it is generally at a rather banal level. The rabbis, with some notable exceptions, are not intensely concerned with the personal problems of their people; most of them are not in any sense spiritual and intellectual guides, but salaried officials of the government who concern themselves with the administration of *kashrut* and the rabbinic courts.

Many of the secularists and their children have come to identify orthodoxy as it is now constituted in Israel with the whole Diaspora experience, and they repudiate both. *Galut*, all of the eighteen centuries between the end of the Second Jewish Commonwealth and the establishment of the State of Israel, is rejected by a great number of Israelis as a largely meaningless, if not somewhat shameful, interlude in Jewish history. Some, totally ignorant of the religious and intellectual achievements of this era, dismiss them as valueless. Officials of Israel's government educational system (the orthodox have their own separate schools, supported by government funds), with a deeper knowledge of history and a stronger sense of identification with the Jewish people as a whole, decided some years ago to organize special courses in *todaah yehudit*, or "Jewish consciousness," in an effort to prevent the secularist young from becoming completely estranged from the total history of their people and, in consequence, from their fellow Jews in the Diaspora. But the courses met with only limited success, and there is still a good deal of contempt for the Diaspora Jew and little understanding of, or appreciation for, the achievements of the Jews in their history as a people without a land after 70 C.E.

Many, however, among both the young and old, who were previously quite content with secularism and atheism and found sufficient meaning and purpose for their lives in participating in the development of the communitarian *kibbutz* society or in nation building have come to experience a certain spiritual emptiness and dissatisfaction. Once achieved, these enterprises no longer serve as compelling integrative centers for their personal existence. Some are searching for new values and goals, embarking on what can only be described as a fundamentally religious quest, and are turning in the process to a Judaism different from the official version presented by the orthodox spokesmen in Israel today, to see whether they can find in it what they are seeking.

Their quest has been aided to some extent by the recent establishment of a number of nonorthodox religious institutions. The handful of Liberal congregations formed by German immigrants in the 1930s had very little impact, and indeed differed only slightly from the orthodox synagogues, distinguishing themselves mainly by stressing decorum in worship and modern preaching. The newer congregations that have been established since 1958 under the auspices of the World Union for Progressive Judaism have attracted more interest and attention. At present these congregations, although numbering less than ten, already have a few native-born rabbis, some trained at the Hebrew Union College in the United States. The American Conservative movement has also attempted to establish congregations in Israel, and both the Jewish Theological Seminary and the Hebrew Union College have study programs in Jerusalem for their students and alumni.

The progress of the liberal religious movement, still in an incipient stage, has been hampered by the vehement attacks of official orthodoxy, whose leaders have also attempted to prevent the use of public facilities for nontraditional religious services. Furthermore, liberal rabbis have no recognized status (they are not authorized to perform marriages and cannot serve on rabbinic tribunals), and the liberal congregations receive no financial support from the government, as do the official synagogues. Nevertheless, the progressive movement is beginning to show signs of engaging the interest of a significant number of Israelis. Certainly American Reform and Conservatism cannot be simply exported without substantive modification to Israel, with its very different cultural and social environment. However, the new congregations and study and discussion groups that the American movements are sponsoring and stimulating may in time give rise to meaningful forms of religious experience for many who have hitherto had no alternatives other than official orthodoxy or a simplistic atheism and secularism.

It does not appear overoptimistic to hope that eventually Israeli orthodoxy will find ways of adjusting *halachah* to the requirements of modern life, and not resort to the coercive power of the state in an effort to impose a rigid religio-legal system on those who find it unacceptable. Already within orthodox circles there are voices calling for the surrender of coercion and its replacement by persuasion, and for a revival of creative innovation within the framework of tradition. It may also be hoped that the liberal religious forces will become stronger, leading to an engagement with the Jewish religious tradition by a larger segment of the population now estranged from it. A merely secularist nationalism, it seems clear, cannot in the long run prove religiously and morally satisfying. Moreover, it will have to be transcended by the people of Israel in a religious direction if their bonds of brotherhood and cooperation with the Jewish communities of the Diaspora, whose organizing principle is Judaism and not nationalism, are to be permanently maintained at a high and mutually enriching level.

The environment necessary for a great revival of Judaism is already present in Israel. The overwhelming majority of its citizens are Jews, who find there little lure in any competing religious system—unless secularism itself be regarded as such. Many of the fundamental institutions of Judaism have been incorporated into the life of the state; the Sabbath is the official day of rest, and the festivals of the Jewish religious calendar are national holidays. The Bible and other classics of the Jewish spirit are taught in all schools, secular as well as religious, and the language of these classics is more or less known to all. There is widespread fascination with the history of the land and people during the biblical age; indeed, amateur biblical archaeology currently comes close to being a national craze. Under the influence of a new generation of historians at the Hebrew University and elsewhere, popular interest in the biblical period of Jewish history seems likely to expand to encompass the entire career of the Jewish people, which in turn may lead to a renewal of appreciation for the values of Judaism. Furthermore, much of the recent Hebrew literature of Israel is permeated with spiritual yearning and a quest for religious meaning. It cannot be predicted when these factors may combine to inaugurate a new era of unprecedented vitality for Judaism in the Jewish state. "The spirit bloweth where it listeth," but the soil of Israel is prepared.

One of the other major problems toward the solution of which substantial progress has been made, although it is by no means completely resolved, is that of the relationship between the Ashkenazic (or European) and non-Ashkenazic (North African, Iraqi, Yemenite, and other) elements of the population. Citizens of European origin and descent clearly occupy the dominant place in the economic, social, political, and cultural life of the country. They and their forebears have been the architects of the chief institutions of Israel, its social structure and values. The hundreds of thousands of immigrants who came from various Moslem countries in the years immediately after the establishment of the state—many of them illiterate, without marketable skills, and lacking strong communal leadership—found themselves proletarians, not only economically and socially but culturally and politically as well. In general devoutly loyal to their respective versions of the Jewish religious tradition, they also felt themselves disoriented in the modern, secularized society of Israel and under pressure to abandon their own traditions and culture and to adopt those of the dominant European segment of the population. What happened in many cases in the short run, however, was not, as the Europeans expected, an assimilation of their value system, but simply a rejection by the children of the Oriental immigrants of their parents' traditions and the breaking up of the patriarchal family structure that had been the chief source of their cohesiveness and strength.

Tensions between the Ashkenazim and non-Ashkenazim—the two *edot* ("communities") or the "first Israel" and the "second Israel," as they have been called—were exacerbated not only by the cultural gulf between them, but by the sense of victimization through prejudice and discrimination felt by many in the latter group. They complained that the better jobs were being systematically denied to them, that the schooling provided for them was inferior, and that they were economically depressed. With a few notable exceptions, the immigrants from the Islamic countries had no skillful leaders to organize them politically and advocate their interests; the existing political parties, massively dominated by the Europeans, contented themselves with including a few token Oriental candidates in their election lists.

The tensions of the first decade after statehood, which occasionally erupted into small-scale rioting, have been reduced in recent years. Strong efforts have been made by the government of Israel to expand the educational opportunities open to the children of the immigrants from Moslem countries. It has been an arduous struggle and has attained only moderate success, primarily because the Oriental family and home do not provide an atmosphere that is as conducive to study and academic achievement as those of the Europeans, and because the better schools are in the large urban centers while the Oriental communities are concentrated in the newer "development" areas. That considerable progress has been made is attested by the fact that the percentage of students of Afro-Asian origin in Israel's secondary schools increased from 13 percent in 1956 to more than 42 percent in 1970. Special tuition rates and scholarship programs have been instituted under government auspices to encourage Oriental children to continue to higher levels of education. The economic level of the Oriental Jews has also risen steadily but still lags far behind that of the Europeans. Dissatisfaction has clearly not ended in the Oriental community, as evidenced by such phenomena as the surfacing in 1971 and 1972 of the so-called "Black Panthers" demanding a larger share in the nation's resources and wider social and economic opportunities.

The difficulties in the relationships between the two *edot*, or communities, in Israel are not based, as is mistakenly supposed in certain quarters, on racial prejudice, though such prejudice is not entirely absent. Ashkenazim and non-Ashkenazim in Israel share a common national, and also in many cases religious, loyalty. The rate of intermarriage between members of the two groups is growing, but not as fast as some had predicted and hoped; in the late 1960s 17 percent of all Jewish marriages were between partners of European and Afro-Asian origin. Furthermore, there is universal agreement that the divisions between the two communities must be bridged and their full social and economic equality established. The tensions that have arisen derive mainly from the shocks of the sudden encounter between two very different cultures and the necessity for a rapid accommodation between them. Obviously the European culture is the more powerful and dynamic. The problem is whether the non-European Jews can absorb its positive values without altogether losing what is distinctive and valuable in their own cultural heritage—their patriarchal family life, their piety, their strong sense of community and tradition of mutual helpfulness, their folksongs and dances, and their skill in various arts and crafts. Whether this will happen is not presently foreseeable, but the aim to which the people and government of Israel are committed is the fullest possible social and economic integration of the two segments of its society.[6]

❧§❧

While Israel has clearly defined the goal it seeks to achieve in the relationship between the two communities within its own borders, there is far less clarity about the relationship it wishes to have with world Jewry, or the Diaspora. And this poses another of its major unresolved problems, a problem that it shares with world Jewry.

There are a good many Jews in Israel (the late David Ben-Gurion was one of their more moderate spokesmen) who might be described as doctrinaire "negators of the Diaspora" (*sholelei ha-galut*). Their understanding of the goal of Zionism is that it was not merely to build a Jewish state for those Jews who wish or must go to live in it, but for *all* Jews; the Jewish state will solve the "Jewish problem" simply by "liquidating" the Diaspora communities. In the view of the more extreme ideologists of this position, the Jews of the Diaspora are doomed; the fate of the Jews of central and eastern Europe during the Nazi Holocaust is a paradigm of what will eventually happen to all Jewries outside the State of Israel. More moderate exponents of the "negation of the Diaspora" believe that even if the Jewish communities of the world survive physically, they will sooner or later inevitably assimilate to the larger environment and disappear within it. By "assimilation" many of these understand primarily the abandonment of ethnic self-consciousness and sense of nationhood, the surrender of distinctively Jewish languages such as Hebrew and Yiddish, and indifference toward the State of Israel: a Jewish community that would be loyal to Judaism but did not identify itself in ethnic and nationalist terms and that became apathetic toward Israel would, in their view, be assimilated. "Negation of the Diaspora" is by no means a universal or perhaps even a majority attitude in contemporary Israel. However, more than a few have espoused it and drawn the conclusion that it may be appropriate to hasten the "liquidation" of the Diaspora communities by attracting as much of their manpower and resources as possible to Israel before they are destroyed. Oddly, many of the more extreme "negators of the Diaspora" ignore the probability that in a world in which Jewish communities outside of Israel would be annihilated either by anti-Semitism or assimilation, the survival of Israel would also be highly problematic. Needless to say, the overwhelming majority of the Jews of America and other nations categorically reject the "negation of the Diaspora." But so also do many Israeli Jews who experienced in the crises of the Six Day War of 1967 and the Yom Kippur War of 1973 what the loyalty and support of Diaspora Jewries can mean to Israel.

The problem is that the interests of Israel and those of the Diaspora communities, while generally congruent, are not necessarily identical. This is especially the case in regard to the matter of immigration to the Jewish state. Israel's interests demand a continuing high rate of immigration, both because its economy as presently organized will flourish best if there is a constant flow of newcomers into the country, and because increased manpower is required to maintain Israel's military strength in the face of the intransigently hostile Arab nations. It is clear, however, that the interests of the American-Jewish community, for instance, are not served by the immigration of very large numbers of its members to Israel. American Jewry has not been growing in size for many years. Its present birth rate is extremely low, and considerable losses may be sustained in the future through the rising incidence of intermarriage and consequent assimilation. The Jewish community of the United States cannot afford substantial losses of its membership to Israel. A continuous flow of sizable immigration to Israel—something that has not yet taken place, except for an apparently temporary upsurge in the immediate wake of the Six Day War—would inevitably diminish its vitality.

Moreover, it is not at all clear that the weakening of American Jewry and other large Jewries elsewhere in the world will really serve the long-range interests of Israel. The Jewish state has benefited greatly from their financial support and is still in need of it. Furthermore, given the international situation, Israel requires staunch friends and loyal supporters who will advocate its cause abroad, and none can be expected to be more friendly and loyal than Jews. It may well be argued that the interests of both Israel and world Jewry are best advanced by the kind of symbiotic partnership that has prevailed up to the present, in which Israel has provided heightened morale and a deeper sense of unity and purpose to members of the Diaspora communities, while these in turn have provided Israel with financial and political assistance.

The relationship of Israel and world Jewry is complex and will inevitably change, given the vagaries of history and destiny. But the doctrinaire assumption that the Jewish communities of the world may be treated simply as colonies whose human and financial resources are to be systematically depleted in order to strengthen Israel appears to be an unpromising basis on which to build a mutually beneficial relationship. Leaders of the Jewish state will venture to play the role of God in determining the fate of Diaspora communities only at their and its own peril.

The State of Israel

❦

In the twenty-five years of its existence the State of Israel has had an enormous impact on Jews and Judaism throughout the world. Many Jews have come to regard the establishment of the state as at least a partial redemption of the unmitigated tragedy of the Holocaust. It represents, for some who are religiously minded, an assurance that God has not totally withdrawn His presence from the historical arena. This conviction was strengthened in more than a few Jews by the astonishing triumphs of the Six Day War, as well as by the more ambiguous victory of the Yom Kippur War. For many others, the deep anxiety preceding the earlier war and during the latter derived from their feeling that the Holocaust might be repeated, that what had been saved out of it might now be lost. And, indeed, there is no doubt that the destruction of Israel would be a shattering, if not mortal, blow to the Jewish people and to its determination to survive.

Israel has given a sense of dignity and worth to Jews everywhere. Although they may be critical of certain aspects of Israeli life and government policy, they take pride in the remarkable achievements of the Jewish state—its generally successful integration of huge masses of immigrants from a hundred nations and many different languages and cultural traditions, its heroic defense against hostile neighbors, its substantial economic progress, its high level of cultural development, and its steady advance toward building an authentic welfare state. Many have also been inspired by the *kibbutz* experiment which, despite its present decline in popularity among Israelis, has served as a demonstration of the possibility of constructing and maintaining a genuinely equalitarian and cooperative society.

Not only has Israel served to bolster the morale of Jewish communities everywhere, but it has also become the strongest bond uniting their members. Whatever other issues on which Jews may disagree— and their number is legion—there is virtual unanimity on the necessity for protecting the security and promoting the welfare of the Jewish state. Concern and work on its behalf has revitalized Jewries all over the world and infused a new élan into their communal life and institutions.

Israel has not yet solved all of its problems or fulfilled all the hopes that Jews cherish for it, nor in its brief span of life could it have been expected to do so. But the miracle of a Jewish commonwealth rees-

[465]

tablished after a hiatus of almost two millennia and born out of the travail and agony of the greatest tragedy that has ever befallen the Jewish people has already raised Jewish life to a new peak of intensity. The future glories that will emerge from it are still hidden in the womb of time, but that they will be many and great no one can doubt.

NOTES

I Jewish Religious Thought after Maimonides

1. Isaac bar Sheshet, *Responsa* (Constantinople: 1546), 267.
2. Quoted in *Jewish Encyclopedia* (New York: Funk and Wagnalls, 1901), vol. 1, pp. 316–317; cf. Solomon Alami, *Iggeret Ha-Musar* (Vilna: 1878), pp. 44ff.
3. Shemtov ibn Shemtov, *Sefer Ha-Emunot* (Ferrara: 1556), fol. 4a.
4. *Pirkei Avot* 3:19.
5. Albo, *Sefer Ha-Ikkarim*, ed. and trans. Isaac Husik (Philadelphia: Jewish Publication Society, 1929), vol. 1, p. 198.
6. Ibid., vol. 1, p. 158.
7. Ibid., vol. 3, p. 128.
8. Ibid., vol. 3, pp. 147–148.
9. Ibid., vol. 2, p. 98.
10. Ibid., vol. 3, p. 291.
11. Ibid., vol. 4, p. 482.
12. Arama, *Hazut Kashah* (Pressburg: V. Kittseer, 1849), p. 34a.
13. A. Neubauer, ed., *Medieval Jewish Chronicles: Seder Ha-Hachamim Ve-Korot Ha-Yamim* (Oxford: Clarendon Press, 1887), vol. 1, pp. 111–112.
14. Yaabetz, *Or Ha-Hayyim* (Shklov: 1796), p. 12.

II Jewish Mysticism: The Kabbalah

1. *Hagigah* 14b.
2. Gershom Scholem, "Kabbalah," in Cecil Roth, editor-in-chief, *Encyclopedia Judaica* (Jerusalem: 1971), vol. 10, col. 507.
3. Gershom Scholem, *Major Trends in Jewish Mysticism*, 2nd ed. (New York: Schocken Books, 1946), p. 139.
4. *Zohar* (Mantua: 1588) 2, 20a.
5. Quoted in I. Zinberg, *A History of Jewish Literature*, vol. 3: *The Struggle of Mysticism and Tradition Against Philosophical Rationalism*, trans. B. Martin (Cleveland: Press of Case Western Reserve University, 1973), p. 49.
6. *Zohar*, 2, 75a. Quoted in A. J. Heschel, "The Mystical Element in Judaism," in L. Finkelstein, ed., *The Jews: Their History, Culture and Religion*, 3rd ed. (New York: Harper & Row, 1966), vol. 2, p. 935.
7. *Tikkunei Zohar* (Brody: 1883), p. 362.
8. Quoted by J. Abelson in the introduction to *The Zohar*, trans. H. Sperling and M. Simon (London: Soncino Press, 1933), vol. 1, pp. xiii–xiv.
9. Avot 3:1.
10. *Zohar*, 3, 104.
11. Ibid., 2, 97b; 1, 168a.
12. *Iggeret Ha-Kodesh* (Constantinople: 1590), chap. 2.

III Franco-German Judaism in the Middle Ages

1. *Teshuvot Hachmei Tzarefat Ve-Lotir*, 21.
2. Solomon Zeitlin, "Rashi and the Rabbinate," *Jewish Quarterly Review* 31, no. 1 (1941): 58.
3. I. Abrahams, *Hebrew Ethical Wills* (Philadelphia: Jewish Publication Society, 1926), pp. 208–218.
4. Samuel ibn Tibbon, *Maamar Yikkavu Ha-Mayyim* (Pressburg: 1837), p. 173.
5. *Minhat Kenaot* (Pressburg: 1838), p. 94.

Notes
IV Italian Jewry and the Renaissance Era

1. *Tanna De-Ve Eliahu* (Warsaw: 1890), chap. 9.

2. Yehiel ben Yekutiel ben Benjamin Ha-Rofe Anaw, *Maalot Ha-Middot* (Zolkiev: 1806), Introduction.

3. H. Vogelstein and P. Rieger, *Geschichte der Juden in Rom* (Berlin: Mayer und Müller, 1895–1896), vol. 1, p. 277, list by name about twenty such learned copyists.

4. The notion that he was actually a friend of Dante's, as was maintained by a number of nineteenth-century Jewish scholars, has been shown to be without foundation.

5. Joseph Karo, *Shulhan Aruch: Orah Hayyim, Hilchot Shabbat*, 307:16.

6. Immanuel of Rome, *Mahbarot* (Lemberg: M. Wolf, 1870), p. 230.

7. Leone Ebreo, *The Philosophy of Love*, trans. F. Friedberg-Seely and J. H. Barnes (London: Soncino Press, 1937), p. 50.

8. Leo da Modena, *Kol Sachal*, in Isaac Samuel Reggio, ed., *Behinat Ha-Kabbalah* (Gorizia: J. B. Seitz, 1852), p. 62.

9. Ibid., pp. 25–26.

V East European Jewry

1. *Sanhedrin* 17a.

2. Nathan Hannover, *Yeven Metzulah* (Cracow: J. Fischer, 1895), pp. 60–61. For Hannover's description of Jewish religious life in Poland, see A. J. Mesch's translation of his work, *Abyss of Despair* (New York: Bloch Publishing Co., 1950), pp. 110–121.

3. Israel Zinberg, *Die Geshichte fun Literatur bei Yidn* (Buenos Aires: Asoçiaçion Pro Cultura Judia, 1966), vol. 5, p. 66.

4. Moses Isserles, *Torat Ha-Olah* (Prague: 1570), p. 75.

5. Moses Isserles, *Responsa* (Amsterdam: 1711), no. 6.

6. Solomon Luria, *Yam Shel Shelomo: Bava Kamma* (Prague: 1616–1618), chap. 8, no. 58.

7. Isaiah Horowitz, *Shenei Luhot Ha-Berit* (Amsterdam: 1649), p. 181a.

8. For Hannover's complete account of the massacre at Tulchin, see his *Abyss of Despair*, trans. A. J. Mesch (New York: Bloch Publishing Co., 1950), pp. 54–61.

9. Ephraim of Luntschitz, *Ammudei Shesh* (Prague: 1617), chap. 5.

10. Tzevi Hirsch Koidonover, *Kav Ha-Yashar* (Frankfort: 1705), chap. 9.

11. Quoted in I. Zinberg, *Die Geshichte fun Literatur bei Yidn*, vol. 5, pp. 130–131.

12. Quoted in S. Dubnow, *A History of the Jews in Russia and Poland*, trans. Israel Friedlander (Philadelphia: Jewish Publication Society, 1916), vol. 1, p. 210.

VI Two Melancholy Centuries

1. Cecil Roth, *A Short History of the Jewish People*, rev. ed. (Hartford: Hartmore House, Inc., 1969), p. 281.

2. An English translation is to be found in Leo Schwarz, ed., *Memoirs of My People Through a Thousand Years* (New York: Farrar and Rinehart, 1943), pp. 84–94.

3. Baruch Spinoza, Letter to Albert Burgh, in *Works of Spinoza*, trans. R. H. M. Elwes (London: G. Bell and Son, 1883), vol. 2, p. 416.

4. Harry Wolfson, *The Philosophy of Spinoza* (Cambridge: Harvard University Press, 1934).

5. Baruch Spinoza, *Ethics* 1.17.

6. Ibid., 4.54.

7. Ibid., 5.36.

8. The English translation by E. H. Lindo, *The Conciliator of R. Manasseh ben Israel*, has been reissued (New York: Hermon Press, 1972).

9. Menasseh ben Israel, *Nishmat Hayyim* (Leipzig: H. L. Schnaus, 1862), pp. 30, 66.

Notes

10. *The Life of Glückel of Hameln: Written by Herself*, trans. and ed. Beth-Zion Abrahams (New York: Thomas Yoseloff, 1963), pp. 45–46.

VII Ḥasidism

1. S. A. Horodezky, *Leaders of Ḥasidism* (London, "Ha-Sefer" Agency for Literature, 1928), pp. 10–11.

2. This phrase was coined by Martin Buber, perhaps the foremost contemporary interpreter of Ḥasidism, to express his understanding of the central thrust of the movement.

3. Quoted in M. Waxman, *A History of Jewish Literature*, 2nd ed. (New York: Bloch Publishing Co., 1945), vol. 3, pp. 32–33.

4. N. N. Glatzer, ed., *In Time and Eternity* (New York: Schocken Books, 1946), p. 111.

5. Solomon Schechter, "The Chassidim," *Studies in Judaism*, First Series (New York: Jewish Publication Society, 1896), pp. 31–32.

6. Ibid., p. 30.

7. Martin Buber, *Ten Rungs* (New York: Schocken Books, 1947), p. 106.

8. Waxman, *A History of Jewish Literature*, vol. 3, p. 36.

9. Ibid., p. 37.

10. Dov Ber of Meseritz, *Or Ha-Emet* (Husiatyn: 1889), p. 13.

11. Jacob Joseph of Polonnoye, *Toledot Yaakov Yosef* (Korets: 1780), Introduction.

12. Ibid., p. 40.

13. Martin Buber, "On National Education," in *Israel and the World* (New York: Schocken Books, 1948), p. 159.

VIII Into the Modern World

1. For an interesting discussion of these figures, see Selma Stern, *The Court Jew: A Contribution to the History of the Period of Absolutism in Central Europe* (Philadelphia: Jewish Publication Society, 1950).

2. Moses Mendelssohn, *Jerusalem and Other Jewish Writings*, trans. and ed. A. Jospe (New York: Schocken Books, 1969), pp. 114–115.

3. Ibid., p. 117.

4. Heinrich Graetz, *History of the Jews* (Philadelphia: Jewish Publication Society, 1895), vol. 5, p. 335.

5. Mendelssohn, *Jerusalem and Other Jewish Writings*, pp. 18–19.

6. Ibid., p. 44.

7. Ibid., p. 37.

8. Ibid., p. 48.

9. Ibid., p. 97.

10. Ibid., p. 71.

11. Ibid., pp. 98–99.

12. Ibid., p. 102.

13. Ibid., p. 105.

14. Ibid., p. 71.

15. Ibid., p. 104.

16. Quoted in Milton Steinberg, *The Making of the Modern Jew* (Indianapolis: Bobbs Merrill Company, Inc., 1934), pp. 149–150.

17. Marvin Lowenthal, *The Jews of Germany* (Philadelphia: Jewish Publication Society, 1936), p. 231.

IX Haskalah

1. Quoted in Simon Halkin, *Modern Hebrew Literature: Trends and Values* (New York: Schocken Books, 1950), p. 38.

2. "Essay of a plan of reform, with the object of enlightening the Jewish nation in Poland and correcting its customs." The work was published in Warsaw.

3. Quoted in Shalom Spiegel, *Hebrew Reborn* (New York: Macmillan, 1930), pp. 129–130.

Notes

4. Quoted in Lucy S. Dawidowicz, ed., *The Golden Tradition: Jewish Life and Thought in Eastern Europe* (New York: Holt, Rinehart, and Winston, 1967), pp. 24–25.

5. According to Baruch Schick's Hebrew translation of the first part of Euclid's *Elements* (Hague: 1780), Introduction.

6. Ibid.

7. For an account of his life and work, see David Patterson, *Abraham Mapu: The Creator of the Modern Hebrew Novel* (London: East and West Library, 1964).

8. Judah Leib Gordon, *Hakitzah Ammi* ("Awake, My People"), in *Kol Shirei Yehudah Leib Gordon* (Tel Aviv: Devir Publishers, 1929), vol. 1, p. 33.

9. Ibid.

10. Ibid.

11. *Kol Shirei Yehudah Leib Gordon*, vol. 3, p. 175.

12. Dawidowicz, *The Golden Tradition*, p. 135.

13. Ibid., pp. 128–129.

X   New Interpretations of Judaism

1. *Bava Kamma* 113b.

2. *Mishnah: Kiddushin* 1:9.

3. David Philipson, *The Reform Movement in Judaism* (New York: Macmillan, 1907), p. 180, n.1 (quoted from Wilhelm Freund, ed., *Zur Judenfrage in Deutschland* [Breslau: 1843–1844], 2, pp. 165 f.).

4. Z. Frankel, *Prospectus* (Berlin: 1843), pp. 5 f., quoted in W. Gunther Plaut, *The Rise of Reform Judaism* (New York: Union of American Hebrew Congregations, 1963), p. 23.

5. *Literaturblatt des Oreints*, 1842, p. 363.

6. Ibid.

7. Quoted in David Rudavsky, *Emancipation and Adjustment* (New York: Diplomatic Press, Inc., 1967), p. 212.

8. Ibid., pp. 212–213.

9. *Mishnah: Avot* 2:2.

10. I. Grunfeld, ed. and trans., *Judaism Eternal: Selected Essays from the Writings of Rabbi Samson Raphael Hirsch* (London: Soncino Press, 1959), 1, p. 210.

11. S. R. Hirsch, *The Nineteen Letters of Ben Uziel*, trans. Bernard Drachman (New York: Funk and Wagnalls Co., 1899), seventeenth letter, p. 174.

12. Ibid., pp. 66–67.

13. Ibid., p. 167.

14. Ibid., pp. 156–157.

15. S. R. Hirsch, *Horeb*, trans. I. Grunfeld (London: Soncino Press, 1962), vol. 2, p. 461. Dayan Grunfeld notes: "Samson Raphael Hirsch refers here obviously to the famous Talmudical passage in *Kethuboth*, 111, in which Israel is enjoined neither to seek its deliverance from the *Galuth* by force nor to rebel against the nations of the world which treat it with injustice; and the nations are enjoined not to oppress Israel unduly." *Horeb*, Vol. 1, p. 145.

XI   The Science of Judaism and Nineteenth-Century Jewish Philosophy

1. Moses Mendelssohn, *Gesammelte Schriften*, ed. G. B. Mendelssohn (Leipzig: F. A. Brockhaus, 1843–1845), vol. 5, p. 342.

2. Leopold Zunz, *Gesammelte Schriften* (Berlin: L. Gerschel, 1876), vol. 2, p. 158.

3. Nahman Krochmal, *Kitvei Nahman Krochmal*, ed. S. Rawidowicz (Berlin: Verlag "Ajanoth," 1924), p. 167.

4. Solomon Schechter, "Nachman Krochmal," in *Studies in Judaism*, first series (New York: Jewish Publication Society, 1896), pp. 66–67.

5. Quoted in Michael A. Meyer, *The Origins of the Modern Jew* (Detroit: Wayne State University Press, 1967), p. 161.

6. Ibid.

7. Immanuel Kant, *Foundations of the Metaphysics of Morals* (New York: The Library of Liberal Arts, 1959), p. 5.

Notes

XII American Judaism from Its Beginnings to the End of the Nineteenth Century

1. B. A. Elzas, *The Jews of South Carolina* (Philadelphia: 1905), p. 160.
2. *The Israelite* 2, no. 18 (November 9, 1855).
3. *The Occident* 1, no. 12 (March 1849).
4. Quoted by Israel Knox, "Isaac Mayer Wise," in *Great Jewish Personalities in Modern Times*, ed. S. Noveck (Washington, D.C.: B'nai Brith Department of Adult Education, 1960), p. 120.
5. Quoted in B. H. Levy, *Reform Judaism in America* (New York: Bloch Publishing Co., 1933), p. 3.
6. Quoted in N. Glazer, *American Judaism*, 2nd ed. rev. (Chicago: University of Chicago Press, 1972), p. 39.
7. *Protokolle der Rabbiner—Conferenz abgehalten zu Philadelphia, von 3 bis zum 6 November 1869* (New York: 1870).

8. For a full account, see Bernard Martin, "The Religious Philosophy of Emil G. Hirsch," *American Jewish Archives* 4 (1952): 66–82.
9. *Yearbook* of the Central Conference of American Rabbis, vol. 1 (Cincinnati: 1891), pp. 120–122.
10. David Philipson, *My Life as an American Jew* (Cincinnati: J. G. Kidd and Son, 1941), p. 23.
11. *Jewish Theological Seminary Students Annual* (New York: Jewish Theological Seminary Student Association, 1914), p. 17.
12. Glazer, *American Judaism*, pp. 69–70.
13. *Jewish Encyclopedia*, vol. 12 (New York: Funk and Wagnalls Co., 1906), p. 360.
14. Ibid., vol. 1 (New York: Funk and Wagnalls Co., 1901), p. vii.

XIII The Recrudescence of Anti-Semitism and the Rise of Zionism

1. Quoted in Marvin Lowenthal, *The Jews of Germany* (Philadelphia: Jewish Publication Society, 1936), p. 305.
2. Ibid., pp. 305–306.
3. Ibid., pp. 309–310.
4. Ibid., p. 310.
5. Quoted by Paul Massing, *Rehearsal for Destruction* (New York: Harper, 1949), p. 168.
6. Moses Hess, *Rome and Jerusalem*, trans. Meyer Waxman (New York: Bloch Publishing Co., 1918), p. 40.
7. Theodor Herzl, *The Diaries of Theodor Herzl*, trans. H. Zohn (New York: Herzl Press, 1960), vol. 3, p. 1,090.
8. Arthur Hertzberg, ed., *The Zionist Idea*

(Philadelphia: Jewish Publication Society, 1959), p. 111.
9. Ibid., p. 114.
10. Leo Pinsker, *Auto-Emancipation*, trans. D. S. Blondheim (New York: Zionist Organization of America, 1948), pp. 15–16.
11. Ibid., p. 16.
12. Ibid., p. 19.
13. Herzl, *The Diaries of Theodor Herzl*, vol. 2, p. 81.
14. Ibid., vol. 3, p. 1,202.
15. A. D. Gordon: *Selected Essays*, trans. Frances Burnce (New York: Bloch Publishing Co., 1938), p. 13.
16. Ibid.

XIV European Jewry in the Twentieth Century

1. Since Bialik's time the term *Oneg Shabbat* has been broadened to signify any celebration held during the Sabbath.

2. Five volumes, translated by Bernard Martin, have appeared to date: 1, *The Arabic-Spanish Period*; 2, *French and German Jewry in*

the *Middle Ages* and *the Jewish Community of Medieval Italy;* 3, *The Struggle of Mysticism and Tradition Against Philosophical Rationalism* (Cleveland: Press of Case Western Reserve University, 1972); 4, *Italian Jewry in the Renaissance Era;* and 5, *The Jewish Center of Culture in the Ottoman Empire* (New York: Ktav, 1974).

3. Several of Shestov's works have now appeared in English: *Athens and Jerusalem,* trans. Bernard Martin (Athens, Ohio: Ohio University Press, 1966); *Potestas Clavium,* trans. Bernard Martin (Athens, Ohio: Ohio University Press, 1968); *Kierkegaard and the Existential Philosophy,* trans. Elinor Hewett (Athens, Ohio: Ohio University Press, 1969); and *Nietzsche, Dostoevsky and Tolstoy,* trans. Bernard Martin and Spencer Roberts (Athens, Ohio: Ohio University Press, 1970).

4. An English translation by Simon Kaplan has now appeared (New York: Frederick Ungar Publishing Co., 1972).

5. A translation into English by William Hallo was recently published (New York: Holt, Rinehart and Winston, 1971).

6. See Franz Rosenzweig, *On Jewish Learning,* ed. N. N. Glatzer (New York: Schocken Books, 1955).

7. See, e.g., the symposium "The State of Jewish Belief," *Commentary* 42 (August 1966): 71–160.

8. *Tales of the Ḥasidim: The Early Masters* (New York: Schocken Books, 1947), and *Tales of the Ḥasidim: The Later Masters* (New York: Schocken Books, 1948).

9. Two translations into English of *I and Thou* have been published, by Ronald Gregor Smith (Edinburgh: T. and T. Clark, 1937) and by Walter Kaufmann (New York: Charles Scribner's Sons, 1970).

10. Quoted in N. N. Glatzer, ed., *The Judaic Tradition,* rev. ed. (Boston: Beacon Press, 1969), pp. 613–614.

11. Leo Baeck, *The Essence of Judaism,* trans. Irving Howe (New York: Schocken Books, 1948).

12. The work was translated by A. H. Friedlander under the title *This People Israel: The Meaning of Jewish Existence* (New York: Holt, Rinehart and Winston, 1964).

XV Jewish Life and Religious Thought in America in the Twentieth Century

1. Kaufmann Kohler, *Jewish Theology Systematically and Historically Considered* (New York: Macmillan, 1918), p. 6.

2. Ibid., pp. 73–74.

3. Kaufmann Kohler, *Studies, Addresses, and Personal Papers* (New York: Alumni Association of the Hebrew Union College, 1931), pp. 189–190.

4. *The United Synagogue of America, Fourth Annual Report* (New York: The United Synagogue of America, 1917), pp. 9–10.

5. Solomon Schechter, *Studies in Judaism,* first series (Philadelphia: Jewish Publication Society, 1896), pp. xvii–xix.

6. Louis Ginzberg, *Legends of the Jews,* trans. Henrietta Szold (Philadelphia: Jewish Publication Society of America, 1909–1938).

7. W. Gunther Plaut, *The Growth of Reform Judaism* (New York: Union of American Hebrew Congregations, 1965), p. 97.

8. Ibid.

9. Ibid.

10. A. J. Heschel, *Man Is Not Alone* (New York: Farrar, Straus, and Young, 1951), p. 21.

XVI The State of Israel: Achievements and Problems

1. Quoted in H. M. Sachar, *The Course of Modern Jewish History* (Cleveland: World Publishing Co., 1958), p. 464.

2. See M. Barkai, ed., *Written in Battle: The Six-Day War as Told by the Fighters Themselves* (Tel Aviv: Le'dory, 1970).

Notes

3. A number of Agnon's works have appeared in English. Among them are *In the Heart of the Seas*, trans. T. H. Rome (New York: Schocken Books, 1948); *Two Tales: Betrothed* and *Edo and Enam*, trans. W. Lever (New York: Schocken Books, 1966); *A Guest for the Night*, trans. M. Louvish (New York: Schocken Books, 1968); and *Twenty-One Stories*, ed. N. N. Glatzer (New York: Schocken Books, 1970).

4. Irving Kristol, "Notes on the Yom Kippur War," *The Wall Street Journal*, October 18, 1973.

5. For an account of his life and thought, see J. B. Agus, *Banner of Jerusalem: The Life, Times and Thought of Abraham Isaac Kuk, the Late Chief Rabbi of Palestine* (New York: Bloch Publishing Co., 1946).

6. For a discussion of the problem of the two *edot*, see R. Patai, *Israel Between East and West: A Study in Human Relations*, 2nd rev. ed. (Westport, Conn.: Greenwood Publishing Corporation, 1970).

GLOSSARY OF HEBREW AND TECHNICAL TERMS

Acquired intellect: Among the Jewish and Arabic Aristotelians, the new intellect produced in man when he has acquired abstract concepts through the operation of the Active Intellect (see below).

Active intellect: Among the Jewish and Arabic Aristotelians, the universal "Intelligence" which serves to control the motions of the sublunar world and especially to develop the human faculty of reason, which, in the infant, is merely a capacity or potentiality—a "material" intellect.

Aggadah (or Haggadah): The nonlegal part of the postbiblical Oral Torah (see below), consisting of narratives, legends, parables, allegories, poems, prayers, theological and philosophical reflections, and so on. Much of the *Talmud* (see below) is aggadic, and the *midrash* (see below) literature, developed over a period of more than a millennium, consists almost entirely of *Aggadah*. The term *aggadah*, in a singular and restricted sense, refers to a Talmudic story or legend.

Amora: (pl. Amoraim) The title given to the Jewish scholars of Palestine and especially of Babylonia in the third to sixth centuries, whose work and thought is recorded in the *Gemara* (see below) of the *Talmud* (see below).

Anusim: See Marranos.

Ashkenazim: Since the ninth century, a term applied to the German Jews and their descendants, in contrast to the Sephardim (see below). After the Crusades, many Ashkenazic Jews settled in eastern Europe and from there migrated to western Europe and America. In recent centuries they have constituted the overwhelming majority of the world Jewish population.

Baal Shem: (Hebrew, "master of the divine name") The title given to men who, it was believed, could effect miracles by conjuring with the divine name.

[474]

Glossary of Hebrew Terms

Bar Mitzvah: (Hebrew, "one obliged to fulfill the commandment") The ceremony marking the initiation of a boy who has reached the age of thirteen into observance of the commandments of the Torah.

Bet Din: (Hebrew, "house of judgment") A rabbinic court, exercising authority in all fields of Jewish law.

Bet Ha-Midrash: In the Talmudic age, a school for higher rabbinic learning where students assembled for study and discussion as well as prayer. In the post-Talmudic age most synagogues had a Bet Ha-Midrash or were themselves called by the term, insofar as they were places of study.

Blood libel: The charge frequently made in the Middle Ages and later to the effect that Jews murder Christians in order to obtain blood for the Passover *seder* (see below) and other rituals. The first recorded case of such an accusation was in 1144, in connection with a Christian child named William at Norwich in England. Despite the fact that the charge was declared absurd by many Christian scholars and numerous papal edicts, it continued to be made sporadically as late as the twentieth century.

Combinations of letters: A method of exegesis of biblical and other texts through combination and permutation of the constituent letters of their words, practiced by many Kabbalists. It was also believed by some Kabbalists that supernatural and miraculous results could be obtained in practical life by application of this method.

Dayyan: (Hebrew, "judge") A judge of a rabbinical court, qualified to decide not only on ritual questions but on money matters and on problems of civil law.

Derash: Homiletical interpretation of Scripture.

Ein Sof: Literally, "without end" or "infinite." In Kabbalist thought, the undifferentiated unity of the unknown and unknowable God, the *deus absconditus* as He is in His own being before His self-revelation through the *sefirot* (see below).

Gaon: (pl. Geonim) The spiritual and intellectual leaders of Babylonian Jewry in the post-Talmudic period, from the sixth through the eleventh centuries C.E. The head of each of the two major academies of Babylonia, at Sura and Pumbedita, held the title Gaon. The Geonim had considerable secular power as well as religious authority, and their influence extended over virtually all of world Jewry during the larger part of the Geonic age. The title Gaon is occasionally applied in a general honorific sense to an eminent Judaic scholar.

Gemara: The second basic strand of the *Talmud* (see below), consisting of a commentary on, and supplement to, the *Mishnah* (see below).

Gematria: A system of exegesis based on the interpretation of a word or words according to the numerical value of the constituent letters in the Hebrew alphabet.

Genizah: (Hebrew, "hiding") A repository for used or worn-out sacred books and other religious items.

Golem: (Hebrew, "formless mass") An automaton, usually in human form, produced by supernatural means, especially the invocation of secret divine names.

Ḥacham: (Hebrew, "wise man") Originally, an officer of the rabbinic courts in Palestine and Babylonia. Later the term was applied to an officiating rabbi in Sephardic communities.

Halachah: (Hebrew, "law"; derived from the verb *halach*, "to go" or "to follow") The legal part of Talmudic and later Jewish literature, in contrast to *Aggadah*, or *Haggadah* (see above), the nonlegal elements. In the singular, *halachah* means "law" in an abstract sense or, alternatively, a specific rule or regulation; in the plural, *halachot* refers to collections of laws.

Ḥalutz: (pl. Ḥalutzim) A pioneer in Israel, especially one working on the soil.

Ḥasidei Ashkenaz: (Hebrew, "the pietists of Germany") A religious movement in twelfth- and thirteenth-century Germany, emphasizing religious intensity and a high level of morality with mystical overtones.

Haskalah: The movement for disseminating modern European culture among the Jews from about 1750 to 1880. It advocated modernization of Judaism, westernization of traditional Jewish education, and revival of the Hebrew language.

Ḥavurah: (pl. Ḥavurot) A society or fellowship, usually organized to foster specific religious or social purposes.

Ḥazzan: (pl. Ḥazzanim) In recent centuries, the cantor or precentor in the synagogue service.

Ḥeder: (Hebrew, "room") A school for teaching children the fundamentals of Judaism, particularly prevalent in the Jewish communities of eastern Europe.

Ḥerem: Excommunication or official removal from the religious fellowship of the Jewish community.

Glossary of Hebrew Terms

Ḥevlei Ha-Mashiaḥ: The woes and troubles, especially those inflicted on the Jewish people, that were expected to precede the advent of the Messiah.

Ḥiddushim: Glosses and comments on the *Talmud* and subsequent rabbinic codes that seek to derive new legal principles or rules from the implications of the text.

Ḥumash: The Pentateuch, or Five Books of Moses.

Ineffable Name: (YHWH, the Tetragrammaton or *Shem Ha-Meforash*) The particular name of the God of Israel in the Bible. Its original pronunciation is no longer known, although it is generally conjectured to have been Yahweh. By the second century B.C.E. it was no longer pronounced, except by the High Priest on the Day of Atonement, but read as *Adonai*.

Kabbalah: The mystical religious movement in Judaism and/or its literature. The term Kabbalah, which means "tradition," came to be used by the mystics beginning in the twelfth century to signify the alleged continuity of their doctrine from ancient times.

Kahal: Generally, a Jewish congregation. In east European Jewry the term was applied to the organized apparatus of the Jewish community which exercised autonomous powers and collected taxation for the secular government. This apparatus was abolished in the nineteenth century.

Kashrut: The regulations connected with the Jewish dietary laws.

Kavvanah: (pl. Kavvanot; Hebrew, "devotion") The quality of devotion, intention, and spiritual concentration which, according to Jewish teaching, should accompany the fulfillment of religious commandments, especially prayer. *Kavvanah* was particularly stressed by the Kabbalists and the later Ḥasidim, in whose view prayers uttered with *kavvanah* have a direct influence on the supernal worlds. Many Kabbalists believed that *kavvanah* in prayer is effectuated by various combinations of the letters of the Ineffable Name (see above), and such a combination itself came to be called a *kavvanah*.

Kehillah: An organized Jewish community or congregation.

Kelippah: (pl. Kelippot) Literally, "husk" or "shell." A mystical term in Kabbalah, denoting the forces of evil.

Kevutzah: (pl. Kevutzot) A cooperative agricultural commune in Israel, organized on collective principles and working a tract of land that is nationally owned.

Kibbutz: (pl. Kibbutzim) A collective village in Israel, similar to the

Kevutzah (see above), but in some cases including light industry and permitting hired labor.

Kol Nidrei: (Aramaic, "all vows") A liturgical formula for the annulment of vows, prescribed for recitation on the eve of the Day of Atonement.

Ladino: The Judeo-Spanish dialect, based on medieval Castilian, spoken by the Sephardim (see below) of the Mediterranean world and written in Hebrew characters.

Landesmannschaft: A society of persons coming from the same city or region, usually organized for purposes of mutual aid and fostering memories of the former home.

Maaseh Bereshit: Literally, "work of creation." The term refers to the first chapter of Genesis, the exposition of which was one of the primary concerns of early Jewish mysticism.

Maaseh Merkavah: Literally, "work of the chariot." The term refers to the first chapter of Ezekiel, the exposition of which constituted the second basic concern of early Jewish mysticism.

Mahzor: (Hebrew, "cycle") A term commonly used to designate the Festival Prayer Book. At first the *Mahzor* contained prayers for the whole year, including the daily and Sabbath services, but most Ashkenazic *mahzorim* now contain only the festival prayers.

Marranos: (a Spanish term meaning "swine"; in Hebrew, *Anusim*, i.e., those "forced" or "coerced") A term applied in Spain and Portugal to those descendants of baptized Jews who were suspected of continued covert loyalty to Judaism. The class became particularly numerous in Spain after the massacres of 1391 and in Portugal after the forced conversions of 1497. The Marranos achieved high standing socially, economically, and politically, but were frequently persecuted by the Inquisition.

Maskil: (pl. Maskilim) An adherent of Haskalah (see above).

Matzah: (pl. Matzot) The unleavened bread prescribed by Jewish tradition for consumption during the Passover season as a memorial of the bread baked in haste by the Israelites departing from Egypt.

Melamed: (Hebrew, "teacher") A private teacher or the assistant teacher in a heder (see above).

Mezuzah: (pl. Mezuzot) A parchment scroll placed in a container and affixed to the doorposts of rooms occupied by Jews, in fulfillment of an injunction in the sixth chapter of Deuteronomy.

[478]

Midrash: (pl. Midrashim) The discovery of new meanings besides literal ones in the Bible. The term is also used to designate collections of such scriptural exposition. The best-known of the *midrashim* are the *Midrash Rabbah, Tanhuma, Pesikta De-Rav Kahana, Pesikta Rabbati,* and *Yalkut Shimeoni.* In a singular and restricted sense, *midrash* refers to an item of rabbinic exegesis.

Minhag: (pl. Minhagim) A Jewish religious custom or observance. When employed in connection with the liturgy, the term means the prayer customs of a given group, e.g., Ashkenazim, Sephardim, or Italian Jews.

Mishnah: The legal codification containing the core of the post-biblical Oral Torah (see below), compiled and edited by Rabbi Judah Ha-Nasi at the beginning of the third century C.E.

Mitnaggedim: (Hebrew, "opponents") The opponents of the Hasidic movement. The name was applied to them after the issuance of a herem (see above) against the Hasidim by the Gaon of Vilna in 1772.

Mitzvah: (pl. Mitzvot) A positive or negative precept of the Torah. According to the *Talmud,* there are six hundred thirteen *mitzvot* in the Pentateuch, in addition to others ordained by the rabbis.

Mohel: The person performing the ritual circumcision of a Jewish child.

Musar: Traditional Jewish moral literature.

Nagid: (Hebrew, "prince") A title applied in the Middle Ages, especially in Moslem countries, to the Jewish leader recognized by the secular government as the chief of the Jewish community.

Neilah: The closing service of the Day of Atonement at sunset when, according to tradition, the gates of the Temple were closed and the heavenly "gates of judgment" are sealed.

Notrikon: A method of abbreviating Hebrew words and phrases by writing only single letters, usually the initials.

Oral Law: (or Oral Torah) The body of interpretation and analysis of the written law of the Pentateuch created in postexilic Judaism and handed down orally from generation to generation. The Oral Law consists of the *Mishnah* (see above) and the *Gemara* (see above), both of which were combined to form the *Talmud* (see below). Even after the redaction of the *Talmud,* the body of tradition contained in it continued to be known as the Oral Law because its roots were in an oral tradition.

Glossary of Hebrew Terms

Parnass: (from the Hebrew term *parnes,* meaning "to foster" or "to support") A term used to designate the chief synagogue functionary. The *parnass* at first exercised both religious and administrative authority, but since the sixteenth century religious leadership has been the province of the rabbis. The office of *parnass* has generally been elective.

Paytan: A liturgical poet (see *piyyut*).

Peshat: The plain, literal meaning of Scripture.

Pilpul: In Talmudic and rabbinic literature, a clarification of a difficult point. Later the term came to denote a sharp dialectical distinction or, more generally, a certain type of Talmudic study emphasizing dialectical distinctions and introduced into the Talmudic academies of Poland by Jacob Pollak in the sixteenth century. Pejoratively, the term means hair splitting.

Piyyut: (pl. Piyyutim) A Hebrew liturgical poem. The practice of writing such poems began in Palestine probably around the fifth century C.E. and continued throughout the ages, enriching the Jewish prayer book. Perhaps the greatest of the medieval writers of *piyyutim* were Solomon Ibn Gabirol and Moses Ibn Ezra.

Rebbe: Yiddish form of the term rabbi, applied especially to a Hasidic rabbi.

Sanhedrin: A Hebrew word of Greek origin designating, in rabbinic literature, the assembly of seventy-one ordained scholars which served both as the supreme court and the legislature of Judaism in the Talmudic age. The Sanhedrin disappeared before the end of the fourth century C.E.

Seder: (Hebrew, "order") The ritual dinner conducted in the Jewish home on the first night (and outside Israel, the first two nights) of Passover. The story of the Exodus from Egypt is recounted and a number of symbols related to it are included in the ritual.

Sefirah: (pl. Sefirot) A technical term in Kabbalah, employed from the twelfth century on, to denote the ten potencies or emanations through which the Divine manifests itself.

Semichah: (in Hebrew literally, "placing" [of the hands]) The practice of ordination whereby Jewish teachers, beginning in the Talmudic age, conferred on their best pupils the title "rabbi" and authorized them to act as judges and render authoritative decisions in matters of Jewish law and ritual practice.

Sephardim: The term applied to the Jews of Spain (in Hebrew, Se-

Glossary of Hebrew Terms

pharad) and afterward to their descendants, no matter where they lived. The term Sephardim is applied particularly to the Jews exiled from Spain in 1492 who settled all along the North African coast and throughout the Ottoman Empire.

Shechinah: A term used to imply the presence of God in the world, in the midst of Israel, or with individuals. In contrast to the principle of divine transcendence, *Shechinah* represents the principle of divine immanence.

Shema: (Hebrew, "Hear!") The fundamental confession of faith in Judaism proclaiming the unity of God: "Hear, O Israel, the Lord is our God, the Lord is One!" (Deut. 6:4).

Shtadlan: A title applied to a Jewish "lobbyist" skilled in diplomatic negotiations and with access to the seats of power.

Shtetl: A Yiddish term denoting a small town or village (used especially in eastern Europe).

Shtibl: A small prayer house.

Shul: A Yiddish term denoting a synagogue.

Siddur: (Hebrew, "order") Among the Ashkenazim (see above), the book containing the daily and Sabbath prayers.

Takkanah: (pl. Takkanot) A regulation supplementing the law of the Torah.

Tallit: The prayer shawl worn by adult males.

Talmud: The title applied to the two great compilations, distinguished as the *Babylonian Talmud* and the *Palestinian Talmud*, in which the records of academic discussion and of judicial administration of postbiblical Jewish law are assembled. Both *Talmuds* also contain *Aggadah* (see above), or nonlegal material.

Talmud Torah: (Hebrew, "study of the Law") A term applied generally to Jewish religious study. Alternatively, the term denotes a school for Jewish religious study established under community auspices.

Tanna: (pl. Tannaim) A teacher mentioned in the *Mishnah* (see above), or in literature contemporaneous with the *Mishnah*, and living during the first two centuries C.E.

Tefillin: Two black leather boxes fastened to leather straps worn on the arm and head by an adult male Jew, especially during the weekday morning prayer. The boxes contain four portions of the Pentateuch written on parchment.

Tikkun: (or Tikkun Ha-Olam) In Kabbalist thought, the restoration by men of the damage done to the world at the time of creation. *Tikkun*, which is accomplished by observance of the commandments, study of the Torah, and mystical meditation, effects the release of the "holy sparks" from their enslavement in matter and uncleanness.

Torah: In its narrowest meaning, the Pentateuch; in its broader meaning, Torah comprises all the Written and Oral Law. In its widest meaning, Torah signifies every exposition of the Written and Oral Law, including all of Talmudic literature and its commentaries.

Tosafists: The French and German scholars of the twelfth to fourteenth centuries who produced critical and explanatory notes on the *Talmud*.

Tosafot: (Hebrew, "addenda") Critical and explanatory notes on the *Talmud*, written by French and German scholars of the twelfth to fourteenth centuries.

Tzaddik: (Hebrew, "righteous man"; pl. Tzaddikim) A term applied to a person distinguished by his faith and piety. Among the Ḥasidim, *tzaddik* is the term applied to the leader of the Ḥasidic community, who is regarded as an intermediary between God and man and the instrument for bringing divine blessings to men.

Tzimtzum: (Hebrew, "contraction") In the Kabbalah of Rabbi Isaac Luria, the idea that the creation of the material world was effected by a kind of "contraction" or withdrawal of God "from Himself into Himself," thus leaving a vacuum in which creation could then take place through a process of emanation.

Vaad Arba Aratzot: The autonomous central organization of Polish-Lithuanian Jewry, originating in the sixteenth century. The Vaad was dissolved in 1764.

Wissenschaft des Judentums: The critical, scientific inquiry into Jewish history, literature, and religious development inaugurated primarily in Germany in the first half of the nineteenth century.

Yeshivah: (pl. Yeshivot) A traditional Jewish school devoted primarily to study of the *Talmud* (see above) and rabbinic literature.

Yishuv: A term applied to the Jewish settlement or community in Israel.

BIBLIOGRAPHY

I Jewish Religious Thought after Maimonides

For historical background on Jewish life in Christian Spain, which continued to be the major European center of Judaism for almost three centuries after Maimonides, the reader should consult Y. Baer, *A History of the Jews in Christian Spain*, 2 vol. (Philadelphia: Jewish Publication Society, 1960, 1966) and A. Neuman, *The Jews in Spain*, 2 vol. (Philadelphia: Jewish Publication Society, 1942).

Full and detailed summaries of the thought of the most important Jewish philosophers before and after Maimonides, and of Maimonides himself, are given by I. Husik, *A History of Medieval Jewish Philosophy* (Philadelphia: Jewish Publication Society, 1916). A more critical exposition, as well as a discussion of postmedieval Jewish thinkers, is to be found in J. Guttmann, *Philosophies of Judaism* (New York: Holt, Rinehart and Winston, 1964).

Gersonides' *Milḥamot Adonai* (*Wars of the Lord*) has still not been translated into English. Parts I–VI, however, are available in a somewhat unreliable German translation, and there is a good French translation of parts III and IV by C. Touati under the title *Levi ben Gershom: Les Guerres du Seigneur, Livres III et IV* (Paris: Mouton, 1968). On Gersonides as a philosopher and scientist, see N. Adlerblum, *A Study of Gersonides in His Proper Perspective* (New York: Columbia University Press, 1926), and G. Sarton, *Introduction to the History of Science*, vol. 3 (Baltimore: Williams and Wilkins, 1948), pp. 594–607.

An important segment of Hasdai Crescas' *Or Adonai* (*The Light of the Lord*)—part 1 of book 1 and the first twenty chapters of part 2 of book 1—were translated, on the basis of a critical text and with an invaluable introduction and notes, by H. A. Wolfson in his *Crescas' Critique of Aristotle* (Cambridge: Harvard University Press, 1929). The following works in English on Crescas are also important: S. Pines, *Scholasticism after Thomas Aquinas and the Teachings of Hasdai Crescas and His Predecessors* (Jerusalem: Central Press, 1967); D. Neumark, "Crescas and Spinoza," *Yearbook of Central Conference of Ameri-*

[483]

can Rabbis 18 (1908): 277–318; and M. Waxman, *The Philosophy of Don Hasdai Crescas* (New York: Columbia University Press, 1920).

The major work of the last of the significant Spanish-Jewish philosophers, the *Sefer Ha-Ikkarim* (*Book of Principles*) of Joseph Albo, was translated into English, on the basis of a critical text and with an introduction and notes, by I. Husik, 4 vol. (Philadelphia: Jewish Publication Society, 1929–1930). For a discussion of Albo see Husik, "Joseph Albo: The Last of the Jewish Medieval Philosophers," *Proceedings of the American Academy of Jewish Research* (1930), pp. 61–72.

On Isaac Arama, the last of the great preachers of Spanish Jewry, see I. Bettan, *Studies in Jewish Preaching* (Cincinnati: Hebrew Union College Press, 1939) pp. 130–191, and C. Pearl, *The Medieval Jewish Mind: The Religious Philosophy of Isaac Arama* (London: Vallentine, Mitchell, 1971).

On Don Isaac Abravanel and the expulsion of the Jews from Spain, the works by Baer and Neuman mentioned above are illuminating. Also interesting are B. Netanyahu, *Don Isaac Abravanel: Statesman and Philosopher*, 2nd ed. (Philadelphia: Jewish Publication Society, 1968); J. S. Minkin, *Abravanel and the Expulsion of the Jews from Spain* (New York: Behrman's Jewish Book House, 1939); and J. B. Trend and H. M. J. Loewe, eds., *Isaac Abravanel: Six Lectures* (Cambridge: Cambridge University Press, 1937).

II   Jewish Mysticism: The Kabbalah

The literature on Jewish mysticism and the Kabbalah is vast. Undoubtedly the most valuable works on the subject are those of Gershom Scholem, the foremost contemporary scholar in the field. Scholem's superb book-length article, "Kabbalah," in the *Encyclopedia Judaica* (Jerusalem: Keter Publishing House Ltd., 1971), vol. 10, col. 489–651, is one of the finest treatments of the subject available. Also of importance are Scholem's *Major Trends in Jewish Mysticism*, rev. ed. (New York: Schocken Books, 1946), and *On the Kabbalah and Its Symbolism* (New York: Schocken Books, 1965). Other valuable works in English are J. Abelson, *Jewish Mysticism* (London: G. Bell and Sons, Ltd., 1913); A. Franck, *The Kabbalah: The Religious Philosophy of the Hebrews* (New Hyde Park, New York: University Books, 1967); L. Ginzberg, *The Cabala in Jewish Law and Lore* (Philadelphia: Jewish Publication Society, 1955); E. Mueller, *A History of Jewish Mysticism* (Oxford: East and West Library, 1946); A. E. Waite, *The Secret Doc-*

trine in Israel: A Study of the Zohar and Its Connections (New York: Occult Research Press, 1913); and I. Zinberg, *A History of Jewish Literature*, vol. 3: *The Struggle of Mysticism and Tradition Against Philosophical Rationalism*, trans. B. Martin (Cleveland: Press of Case Western Reserve University, 1973). A fascinating book on the practical Kabbalah is J. Trachtenberg, *Jewish Magic and Superstition* (Philadelphia: Jewish Publication Society, 1939).

For an appreciative essay on Naḥmanides see Solomon Schechter, *Studies in Judaism*, 1st ser. (Philadelphia: Jewish Publication Society, 1896), pp. 99–141.

An English translation of the *Zohar* by H. Sperling, M. Simon, and P. Levertoff is available in five volumes (London: Soncino Press, 1931–1934).

A classic essay on the Kabbalists of Safed, especially Isaac Luria, is Solomon Schechter's "Safed in the Sixteenth Century: A City of Legists and Mystics," in his *Studies in Judaism*, 2nd ser. (Philadelphia: Jewish Publication Society, 1908) pp. 202–306.

A very incisive treatment of the Shabbetai Tzevi movement is G. Scholem's "Redemption Through Sin," in his *The Messianic Idea in Judaism and Other Essays* (New York: Schocken Books, 1971). See also his article, "Shabbetai Zevi," *Encyclopedia Judaica* (Jerusalem: 1971), vol. 14, col. 1219–1254. Scholem's two-volume work in Hebrew on Shabbetai Tzevi has been published in English translation under the title *Sabbatai Ṣevi: The Mystical Messiah* (Princeton: Princeton University Press, 1973).

For a discussion of Kabbalah and Kabbalists in the contemporary world, see H. Weiner, *Nine and One Half Mystics: The Kabbalah Today* (New York: Holt, Rinehart and Winston, 1969), and *The Wild Goats of Ein Gedi* (Garden City, N. Y.: Doubleday, 1961).

III   Franco-German Judaism in the Middle Ages

For the early history of the Jews in Germany and France see M. Lowenthal, *The Jews of Germany* (Philadelphia: Jewish Publication Society, 1936); L. I. Rabinowitz, *The Social Life of the Jews of Northern France in the XII-XIV Centuries as Reflected in the Rabbinical Literature of the Period* (London: Edward Goldston, 1938); G. Kisch, *The Jews in Medieval Germany* (Chicago: University of Chicago Press, 1948); and J. R. Marcus, *The Rise and Destiny of the German Jew* (Cincinnati: Union of American Hebrew Congregations, 1934). Histories of sev-

Bibliography

eral of the ancient communities of Germany are included in the "Jewish Communities Series" published by the Jewish Publication Society of America. Among them are: A. Kober, *Cologne* (1940); A. Freimann and F. Kracauer, *Frankfort* (1929); M. Grunwald, *Vienna* (1936); and R. Strauss, *Regensburg and Augsburg* (1939).

An account of the life of the first important teacher of Franco-German Jewry, Rabbenu Gershom, is given by A. Marx in his *Essays in Jewish Biography* (Philadelphia: Jewish Publication Society, 1947), pp. 39–60. The life and work of the great exegete of the Bible and the *Talmud*, Rashi, is described in a number of works. Especially valuable are the *Rashi Anniversary Volume* (Philadelphia: American Academy for Jewish Research, 1941); H. Hailperin, *Rashi and the Christian Scholars* (Pittsburgh: University of Pittsburgh Press, 1963); M. Liber, *Rashi* (Philadelphia: Jewish Publication Society, 1906); and S. M. Blumenfield, *Master of Troyes: A Study of Rashi the Educator* (New York: Behrman House, 1946). The Pentateuch with Rashi's commentary was translated into English and annotated by M. Rosenbaum and A. M. Silbermann, 5 vol. (London: Soncino Press, 1929–1934).

On the Crusades and their effects on the Jews of Europe see S. Runciman, *A History of the Crusades*, 3 vol. (Cambridge: Cambridge University Press, 1951–1954); J. Katz, *Exclusiveness and Tolerance: Studies in Jewish-Gentile Relations in Medieval and Modern Times* (London: Oxford University Press, 1961); and S. Landau, *Christian-Jewish Relations: A New Era in Germany as a Result of the First Crusade* (New York: Pageant Press, 1960).

For the social, communal, and religious life of the medieval Jewish communities, see the work of L. I. Rabinowitz mentioned above; I. Abrahams, *Jewish Life in the Middle Ages* (Philadelphia: Jewish Publication Society, 1920); L. Finkelstein, *Jewish Self-Government in the Middle Ages* (New York: Jewish Theological Seminary of America, 1924); and D. M. Shohet, *The Jewish Court in the Middle Ages* (New York: Commanday-Roth Co., Inc., 1931).

The ethical ideals of the Jews of medieval France and Germany are best reflected in their most famous "morality book," *Sefer Ḥasidim*, which has now appeared in an English translation by S. A. Singer, *Medieval Jewish Mysticism: The Book of the Pious* (Northbrook, Ill.: Whitehall Co., 1972). The moral and religious values of the Jews of this era are also reflected in the collection *Hebrew Ethical Wills*, ed. Israel Abrahams, 2 vol. (Philadelphia: Jewish Publication Society, 1926). See also Solomon Schechter's "Jewish Saints of Me-

Bibliography

dieval Germany," in his *Studies in Judaism*, 3rd ser. (Philadelphia: Jewish Publication Society, 1924), pp. 1–24.

The controversy between the rationalists and orthodox pietists revolving around the works of Maimonides at the end of the twelfth and the first half of the thirteenth centuries is portrayed in D. J. Silver, *Maimonidean Criticism and the Maimonidean Controversy; 1180–1240* (Leiden: Brill, 1965). An older account is J. Sarachek, *Faith and Reason: The Conflict Over the Rationalism of Maimonides* (Williamsport, Pa.: Bayard Press, 1935).

The life and work of Meir of Rothenburg is presented in the exhaustive study of I. A. Agus, *Rabbi Meir of Rothenburg*, 2 vol. (Philadelphia: Dropsie College for Hebrew and Cognate Learning, 1947).

The literature of medieval Franco-German Jewry is discussed in I. Zinberg, *A History of Jewish Literature*, vol. 2: B. Martin, trans., *French and German Jewry in the Early Middle Ages* (Cleveland: Press of Case Western Reserve University, 1972).

IV   Italian Jewry and the Renaissance Era

The outstanding writer in English on the history of the Jews in Italy has been Cecil Roth. Particularly noteworthy are his *History of the Jews of Italy* (Philadelphia: Jewish Publication Society, 1946) and *The Jews in the Renaissance* (Philadelphia: Jewish Publication Society, 1959). H. Vogelstein, *A History of the Jews in Rome* (Philadelphia: Jewish Publication Society, 1940) is based on an excellent older study in German. Also of interest is H. J. Leon, *The Jews of Ancient Rome* (Philadelphia: Jewish Publication Society, 1960). See also Roth's *History of the Jews in Venice* (Philadelphia: Jewish Publication Society, 1930).

Thus far little of the poetry of Immanuel of Rome has been rendered into English, but there is a translation of his *Tophet and Eden* (*Hell and Paradise*) by H. Gollancz (London: University of London Press, 1921). Immanuel is discussed by S. Morais, *Italian Hebrew Literature* (New York: Jewish Theological Seminary of America, 1926), pp. 9–51, and I. Zinberg, *A History of Jewish Literature*, vol. 2: *The Jewish Community of Medieval Italy* (Cleveland: Press of Case Western Reserve University, 1972). The fourth volume of Zinberg's *History*, entitled *Italian Jewry in the Renaissance Era* (New York: Ktav, 1974),

surveys the rich achievements of the Jews of Italy from the fourteenth to the seventeenth centuries.

Judah Abravanel's (Leone Ebreo's) *Dialoghi di Amore* was translated
into English by F. Friedeberg-Seeley and J. H. Barnes under the
title *The Philosophy of Love* (London: Soncino Press, 1937). On Judah
Abravanel and the Renaissance spirit, see J. B. Agus, *The Evolution of
Jewish Thought* (New York: Abelard-Schuman, 1959), pp. 291–299.

The Christian scholars of Kabbalah in Renaissance Italy are discussed by J. L. Blau, *The Christian Interpretation of the Cabala in the
Renaissance* (New York: Columbia University Press, 1944).

Judah Moscato and other renowned preachers in medieval Jewry
are treated in I. Bettan, *Studies in Jewish Preaching* (Cincinnati: Hebrew Union College Press, 1939).

The major work of one of the great Jewish historians of medieval
Italy, Samuel Usque, has been translated from the Portuguese by
M. A. Cohen, *Consolation for the Tribulations of Israel* (Philadelphia:
Jewish Publication Society, 1965). For a discussion of another major
historian of that era, see S. W. Baron, "Azariah de Rossi's Attitude
to Life," in *Israel Abrahams Memorial Volume* (New York: Press of the
Jewish Institute of Religion, 1927), pp. 12–52.

One of the most fascinating figures of Italian-Jewish history is
treated by E. Rivkin in his *Leon da Modena and the Kol Sakhal* (Cincinnati: Hebrew Union College Press, 1952).

V   East European Jewry

The best all-around treatment of the history of the Jews of eastern
Europe is an older work: S. M. Dubnow, *History of the Jews in Russia
and Poland*, 3 vol. (Philadelphia: Jewish Publication Society,
1916–1920). Also of value are M. S. Lew, *The Jews of Poland in the
Sixteenth Century* (London: Edward Goldston, 1943) and B. D.
Weinryb, *The Jews of Poland* (Philadelphia: Jewish Publication Society, 1973). L. Finkelstein, ed., *The Jews: Their History, Culture, and
Religion*, 3rd ed. (New York: Harper & Row, 1966) also contains a
number of valuable articles; among these are I. Halpern, "The Jews
in Eastern Europe from Ancient Times to the Partition of Poland,
1772–1795," pp. 287–320; B. D. Weinryb, "East European Jewry
Since the Partitions of Poland, 1772–1795," pp. 321–375; and A.
Menes, "Patterns of Jewish Scholarship in Eastern Europe," pp.
376–426. A beautifully evocative portrait of the inner life of east Eu-

ropean Jewry, in the form of an elegy over its destruction at the hands of the Nazis, is A. J. Heschel, *The Earth Is the Lord's* (New York: Henry Schuman, 1950).

Readers who wish to delve into the history of the fascinating Khazar kingdom should read D. M. Dunlop, *The History of the Jewish Khazars* (Princeton: Princeton University Press, 1954).

A portrait of one of the great centers of Jewish learning in eastern Europe is presented in I. Cohen, *History of the Jews of Vilna* (Philadelphia: Jewish Publication Society, 1943).

A reliable history of the Jews of Russia in the last two centuries is contained in L. Greenberg, *The Jews in Russia*, 2 vol. (New Haven: Yale University Press, 1944, 1951). Also interesting is I. Levitats, *The Jewish Community in Russia: 1776–1844* (New York: Columbia University Press, 1946).

For a sampling of rabbinic legal thinking in the classical age of Polish Jewry, see S. Hurwitz, *The Responsa of Solomon Luria* (New York: Bloch Publishing Co., 1938).

One of the major contemporary chronicles of the catastrophe of 1648, Nathan Hannover's *Yeven Metzulah*, has been translated into English by A. J. Mesch under the title *Abyss of Despair* (New York: Bloch Publishing Co., 1950).

There are a number of interesting essays on the foremost figure of Polish Jewry, Elijah Gaon: "Rabbi Elijah, Wilna Gaon," in Solomon Schechter, *Studies in Judaism*, 1st ser. (Philadelphia: Jewish Publication Society, 1896) pp. 73–98; "The Gaon, Rabbi Elijah Wilna," in L. Ginzberg, *Students, Scholars and Saints* (Philadelphia: Jewish Publication Society, 1928), pp. 115–124; and "Vilna Gaon" by M. Waxman, in S. Noveck, ed., *Great Jewish Personalities in Ancient and Medieval Times* (Washington, D.C.: B'nai Brith Department of Adult Education, 1959), pp. 313–327.

VI Two Melancholy Centuries

A historical portrait of the Ottoman Empire as a place of refuge for Jews after the expulsion from Spain, and of its most prominent family, is given in Cecil Roth's works, *The House of Nasi: The Duke of Naxos* (Philadelphia: Jewish Publication Society, 1948) and *The House of Nasi: Dona Gracia* (Philadelphia: Jewish Publication Society, 1948). On the Jews of Palestine under Ottoman domination, see I. Ben-Zvi, "Eretz Yisrael under Ottoman Rule," in L. Finkelstein, ed., *The*

Bibliography

Jews: Their History, Culture, and Religion, 3rd ed. (New York: Harper & Row, 1966), vol. 1, pp. 602–689. On the major center in Safed, see Solomon Schechter's "Safed in the Sixteenth Century: A City of Legists and Mystics," in his *Studies in Judaism*, 2nd ser. (Philadelphia: Jewish Publication Society, 1908), pp. 202–306. The literature produced by the Jews of the Ottoman Empire is discussed by I. Zinberg, *A History of Jewish Literature*, vol. 5: *The Jewish Center of Culture in the Ottoman Empire* (New York: Ktav, 1974).

R. J. Z. Werblowsky provides an interesting biography of the author of the *Shulḥan Aruch* in his *Joseph Karo: Lawyer and Mystic* (New York: Oxford University Press, 1962). On Solomon Molcho, see J. H. Greenstone, *The Messiah Idea in Jewish History* (Philadelphia: Jewish Publication Society, 1906), and A. H. Silver, *A History of Messianic Speculation in Israel* (New York: Macmillan, 1927).

For a discussion of Luther, the Protestant Reformation, and the Jews, see H. H. Ben-Sasson, "The Reformation in Contemporary Jewish Eyes," *Proceedings of the Israel Academy of Sciences and Humanities* (1970). See also L. I. Newman, *Jewish Influences on Christian Reform Movements* (New York: Columbia University Press, 1925). Ben-Sasson's study, "Jewish-Christian Disputation in the Setting of Humanism and Reformation in the German Empire," *Harvard Theological Review* 59 (1966): 369–390, is also of importance.

On the Counter Reformation and its effect on Jews, especially the imposition of the compulsory ghetto, see Cecil Roth, *A History of the Jews in Italy* (Philadelphia: Jewish Publication Society, 1946).

On the Marranos who established new Jewish communities in Amsterdam, London, and elsewhere, see Cecil Roth, *A History of the Marranos* (Philadelphia: Jewish Publication Society 1932), and E. Rivkin, "The Rise of Capitalism: The Marranos," in *The Shaping of Jewish History* (New York: Charles Scribner's Sons, 1971), pp. 140–158. On the Jewish community of Amsterdam, see H. Bloom, *The Economic Activities of the Jews of Amsterdam in the Seventeenth and Eighteenth Centuries* (Williamsport, Pa.: Bayard Press, 1937).

The standard work on Menasseh ben Israel is Cecil Roth, *A Life of Menasseh ben Israel* (Philadelphia: Jewish Publication Society, 1934). Another interesting work is L. Wolf, ed., *Menasseh ben Israel's Mission to Oliver Cromwell* (London: Macmillan, 1901), containing pamphlets written by Menasseh regarding the readmission of the Jews to England.

A translation of Uriel Acosta's autobiography, *Exemplar Humanae Vitae*, is contained in L. Schwarz, ed., *Memoirs of My People Through a Thousand Years* (New York: Farrar and Rinehart, 1943).

Bibliography

Perhaps the most convenient introduction to the works of Spinoza for the beginning student is *Spinoza: Selections*, ed. with introduction by J. Wild (New York: Charles Scribner's Sons, 1930). The literature on Spinoza is extensive. Among the best works in English are H. Joachim, *A Study of the Ethics of Spinoza* (Oxford: Clarendon Press, 1901); L. Roth, *Spinoza, Descartes, and Maimonides* (Oxford: Clarendon Press, 1924); L. Roth, *Spinoza* (Boston: Little, Brown and Co., 1929); L. Strauss, *Spinoza's Critique of Religion* (New York: Schocken Books, 1965); and H. A. Wolfson, *The Philosophy of Spinoza*, 2 vol. (Cambridge: Harvard University Press, 1958).

On Shabbetai Tzevi and the cataclysmic messianic movement that he launched, the reader should consult G. Scholem's *The Messianic Idea in Judaism and Other Essays* (New York: Schocken Books, 1971), and the same author's *Sabbatai Ṣevi: The Mystical Messiah* (Princeton: Princeton University Press, 1973).

The *Memoirs* of Glückel of Hameln were translated and edited by M. Lowenthal (New York: Harper and Brothers, 1932) and by B. Z. Abrahams, *The Life of Glückel of Hameln* (New York: Thomas Yoseloff, 1962). See also Solomon Schechter, "The Memoirs of a Jewess of the Seventeenth Century," in his *Studies in Judaism*, 2nd ser. (Philadelphia: Jewish Publication Society, 1908), pp. 126–147.

VII Ḥasidism

On Jacob Frank and the Frankists, see Gershom Scholem's classic essay, "Redemption Through Sin," in his *The Messianic Idea in Judaism and Other Essays* (New York: Schocken Books, 1971), pp. 78–141.

The earliest collection of legends about the founder of Ḥasidism is *Shivḥei Ha-Besht*. This work has now been edited and translated by D. Ben-Amos and J. R. Mintz under the title, *In Praise of the Baal Shem Tov* (Bloomington, Ind.: University of Indiana Press, 1970). Another important work is Martin Buber, *The Legend of the Baal Shem*, trans. Maurice Friedman (New York: Harper, 1955).

Buber is the best known modern expositor of the teachings of Ḥasidism. Among his major works on the subject that have been translated into English are *Ḥasidism*, trans. Greta Hort (New York: Philosophical Library, 1948); *Ḥasidism and Modern Man*, trans. Maurice Friedman (New York: Horizon Press, 1958); and *The Origin and Meaning of Ḥasidism*, trans. Maurice Friedman (New York: Horizon Press, 1960). Buber also wrote an interesting novel on the theme

[491]

Bibliography

of Ḥasidism, *For the Sake of Heaven*, trans. Ludwig Lewisohn (Philadelphia: Jewish Publication Society, 1945).

Among other general works on Ḥasidism are J. S. Minkin, *The Romance of Ḥasidism*, 2nd ed. (New York: Macmillan, 1955); H. M. Rabinowicz, *The World of Ḥasidism* (London: Vallentine, Mitchell, 1970); and Solomon Schechter, "The Chassidim," in his *Studies in Judaism*, 1st ser. (Philadelphia: Jewish Publication Society, 1896), pp. 1–45. An important scholarly article is Gershom Scholem's "Devekuth: Communion with God in Early Ḥasidic Doctrine," *The Review of Religion* 15 (1950): 115–139. Also of great value is I. Zinberg, *A History of Jewish Literature*, vol. 9: B. Martin, trans., *Ḥasidism and Enlightenment* (1780–1820), which will be published soon.

On the role of the *tzaddik* in Ḥasidism see S. H. Dresner, *The Zaddik* (New York: Abelard-Schuman, 1960).

Stories and legends about the great Ḥasidic masters are to be found in Buber's *Tales of the Ḥasidim*, 2 vol. Olga Marx, trans. (New York: Schocken Books, 1947, 1948). The lovely and poetic stories of Rabbi Naḥman of Bratzlav, which represent a landmark in the development of Yiddish literature, are to be found in Buber's *The Tales of Rabbi Naḥman*, trans. Maurice Friedman (New York: Horizon Press, 1956). Another useful collection of Ḥasidic tales and sayings is L. I. Newman, *A Ḥasidic Anthology* (New York: Charles Scribner's Sons, 1934).

The major text of Ḥabad Ḥasidism, the *Tanya* (*Likkutei Amarim*), has been translated by Nissan Mindel (Brooklyn: Kehot, 1965). On Shneour Zalman, see B. Chavel, "Shneour Zalman of Liady," in L. Jung, ed., *Jewish Leaders* (New York: Bloch Publishing Co., 1953) pp. 51–75. A work on Ḥabad Ḥasidism has been written by the present leader of the movement, Rabbi Joseph Schneerson: *Some Aspects of Chabad Chassidism* (Brooklyn: Kehot, 1957). On contemporary Ḥabad Ḥasidism, see also H. Weiner, "The Lubavitcher Movement," *Commentary* 23 (1957): 231–241, 316–327. On another major Ḥasidic group in America, see H. Gersh and S. Miller, "Satmar in Brooklyn," *Commentary* 28 (1959): 389–399.

VIII   Into the Modern World

For a discussion of the factors leading to the emancipation of the Jews in the eighteenth and nineteenth centuries, and for modern Jewish history as a whole, see H. Sachar, *The Course of Modern Jewish History* (Cleveland: World Publishing Co., 1958).

Bibliography

On the era of the Enlightenment in eighteenth-century Europe, the reader might profitably consider I. Berlin, *The Age of Enlightenment* (Boston: Houghton, Mifflin, 1957), and E. Cassirer, *The Philosophy of the Enlightenment* (Boston: Beacon Press, 1955).

On the emancipation of the Jews and its consequences, see S. W. Baron, "The Modern Age," in L. Schwarz, ed., *Great Ages and Ideas of the Jewish People* (New York: Random House, 1956), pp. 315–484. Also of value is D. Rudavsky, *Emancipation and Adjustment* (New York: Diplomatic Press, Inc., 1967). A work of considerable significance is A. Hertzberg, *The French Enlightenment and the Jews* (New York: Columbia University Press, 1968).

Articles that the reader may find of interest include H. Kohn, "The Jew Enters Western Culture," *Menorah Journal* 18 (April 1930): 291–302; I. E. Barzilay, "The Jew in the Literature of the Enlightenment," *Jewish Social Studies* 18 (October 1956): 243–261; S. Posener, "The Social Life of the Jewish Communities in France in the Eighteenth Century," *Jewish Social Studies* 7 (July 1945): 195–232; and G. Karpeles, "Jewish Society in the Time of Mendelssohn," in his *Jewish Literature and Other Essays* (Philadelphia: Jewish Publication Society, 1895).

Moses Mendelssohn's *Jerusalem* and several other Jewish writings have been edited and translated into English by A. Jospe (New York: Schocken Books, 1969). On Mendelssohn, see A. Altman, *Moses Mendelssohn: A Biographical Study* (University, Ala.: University of Alabama Press, 1973); M. Simon, *Moses Mendelssohn: His Life and Times* (London: Jewish Religious Educational Publications, 1953); H. Walter, *Moses Mendelssohn: Critic and Philosopher* (New York: Bloch Publishing Co., 1930); M. A. Meyer, *The Origins of the Modern Jew* (Detroit: Wayne State University Press, 1967), pp. 11–56; and N. Rotenstreich, *Jewish Philosophy in Modern Times* (New York: Holt, Rinehart and Winston, 1968), pp. 6–29. Interesting articles on Mendelssohn are A. Jospe, "Moses Mendelssohn" in S. Noveck, ed., *Great Jewish Personalities of Modern Times* (Washington, D. C.: B'nai Brith Department of Adult Education, 1960); F. A. Levy, "Moses Mendelssohn's Ideals of Religion and Their Relation to Reform Judaism," *Yearbook of the Central Conference of American Rabbis* 39 (1929): 351–367; J. Kopald, "The Friendship of Lessing and Mendelssohn," *Yearbook of the Central Conference of American Rabbis* 39 (1929): 370–387; and W. Rothman, "Mendelssohn's Character and Philosophy of Religion," *Yearbook of the Central Conference of American Rabbis* 39 (1929): 305–347.

On the aftermath of the grant of civic equality to the Jews of

Bibliography

France, see S. Posener, "The Immediate Economic and Social Effect of the Emancipation of the Jews in France," *Jewish Social Studies* 1 (July 1939): 271–326.

IX   Haskalah

The literature of Haskalah is discussed exhaustively in vols. 8–12 of I. Zinberg's *History of Jewish Literature* (New York: Ktav), scheduled for publication in the next two years. Valuable treatments of the Haskalah writers are also to be found in S. Halkin, *Modern Hebrew Literature* (New York: Schocken Books, 1950); S. Spiegel, *Hebrew Reborn* (New York: Macmillan, 1930); N. Slouschz, *The Renascence of Hebrew Literature* (Philadelphia: Jewish Publication Society, 1909); J. Klausner, *A History of Modern Hebrew Literature, 1785–1930* (London: M. L. Cailingold, 1932); J. S. Raisin, *The Haskalah Movement in Russia* (Philadelphia: Jewish Publication Society, 1913); and H. Bavli, "The Modern Renaissance of Hebrew Literature," in L. Finkelstein, ed., *The Jews, Their History, Culture and Religion*, 3rd ed. (New York: Harper & Row, 1966), vol. 2, pp. 893–931.

For individual Haskalah writers, see I. Barzilay, *Shelomo Yehudah Rapoport (Shir) and His Contemporaries* (Tel Aviv: Massada Press, 1969); L. S. Greenberg, *A Critical Investigation of the Works of Rabbi Isaac Baer Levinsohn* (New York: Bloch Publishing Co., 1930); D. Patterson, *Abraham Mapu* (Ithaca, N.Y.: Cornell University Press, 1964); and A. B. Rhine, *Leon Gordon: An Appreciation* (Philadelphia: Jewish Publication Society, 1920).

X   New Interpretations of Judaism

Two informative books dealing with the various new interpretations of Judaism that arose in nineteenth-century Germany are J. L. Blau, *Modern Varieties of Judaism* (New York: Columbia University Press, 1966), and B. Rudavsky, *Emancipation and Adjustment* (New York: Diplomatic Press, 1967).

On Reform Judaism, see D. Philipson, *The Reform Movement in Judaism*, rev. ed. (New York: Ktav, 1967); W. G. Plaut, *The Rise of Reform Judaism* (New York: Union of American Hebrew Congregations, 1963); J. R. Marcus, *Israel Jacobson: The Founder of the Reform Movement in Judaism*, rev. ed. (Cincinnati: Hebrew Union College

Bibliography

Press, 1972); M. A. Meyer, *The Origins of the Modern Jew* (Detroit: Wayne State University Press, 1967); and J. J. Petuchowski, *Prayerbook Reform in Europe* (New York: World Union for Progressive Judaism, 1968).

On Abraham Geiger, the leading theoretician of German Reform Judaism, see Solomon Schechter, *Studies in Judaism*, 3rd ser. (Philadelphia: Jewish Publication Society, 1924), pp. 47–83; J. B. Agus, *Modern Philosophies of Judaism* (New York: Behrman's Jewish Book House, 1941); and M. Weiner, *Abraham Geiger and Liberal Judaism* (Philadelphia: Jewish Publication Society, 1962).

A piece by the leader of the German Positive-Historical school, Zacharias Frankel, "On Changes in Judaism," is to be found in M. Waxman, ed., *Tradition and Change* (New York: Burning Bush Press, 1958). On Frankel, see L. Ginzberg, *Students, Scholars, and Saints* (Philadelphia: Jewish Publication Society, 1928), pp. 195–216, and D. Rudavsky, "The Historical School of Zacharia Frankel," *Jewish Journal of Sociology*, 5 (1963): 224–244.

A considerable number of the works of Samson Raphael Hirsch, the foremost figure of Neo-Orthodoxy in nineteenth-century Germany, have been translated. Among them are *The Nineteen Letters of Ben Uziel*, B. Drachman, trans. (New York: Funk and Wagnalls, 1899); *Horeb*, I. Grunfeld, trans., 2 vol. (London: Soncino Press, 1962); *Introduction to Commentary on the Torah*, J. Breuer, trans. (New York: Feldheim, 1948); *Commentary to the Pentateuch*, I. Levy, trans., 2nd ed. (New York: Feldheim, 1971). The reader may also wish to consult *Judaism Eternal: Selected Essays from the Writings of Rabbi Samson Raphael Hirsch*, 2 vol. (London: Soncino Press, 1956). Essays on Hirsch have been written by M. Heller, "Samson Raphael Hirsch, In Honor of the Centenary of His Birth," *Yearbook of the Central Conference of American Rabbis* 18 (1908): 179–216; E. W. Jelenko, "Samson Raphael Hirsch," in S. Noveck, ed., *Great Jewish Personalities in Modern Times* (Washington, D. C.: B'nai Brith Department of Adult Education, 1960), pp. 69–95; and S. Schwarzschild, "Samson Raphael Hirsch: The Man and His Thought," *Conservative Judaism* 13 (1959): 26–45. Among books on Hirsch are I. Grunfeld, *Three Generations: The Influence of Samson Raphael Hirsch on Jewish Life and Thought* (London: Jewish Post Publications, 1958), and J. Rosenheim, *Samson Raphael Hirsch's Cultural Ideal and Our Times* (London: Shapiro, Vallentine, and Co., 1951).

On Samuel David Luzzatto, see S. Morais, *Italian Hebrew Literature* (New York: Jewish Theological Seminary of America, 1926); N.

Bibliography

Rotenstreich, *Jewish Philosophy in Modern Times* (New York: Holt, Rinehart and Winston, 1968), pp. 30–42; D. Rudavsky, "S. D. Luzzatto's Jewish Nationalism," *Herzl Yearbook* 6 (1964–1965): 9–23; and N. H. Rosenbloom, *Luzzatto's Ethico-Psychological Interpretation of Judaism* (New York: Yeshivah University Press, 1965).

On David Hoffman, one of the great figures of modern orthodoxy in Germany, see L. Ginzberg, *Students, Scholars, and Saints* (Philadelphia: Jewish Publication Society, 1928), pp. 252–262.

XI   The Science of Judaism and Nineteenth-Century Jewish Philosophy

Two valuable articles on the origins of the Science of Judaism are B. Bamberger, "The Beginnings of Modern Jewish Scholarship, *Yearbook of the Central Conference of American Rabbis* 42 (1932): 209–235, and L. Wallach, "The Beginnings of the Science of Judaism in the Nineteenth Century," *Historia Judaica* 8 (April 1946): 33–60. Also important is N. Glatzer, "The Beginnings of Modern Jewish Studies," in A. Altman, ed., *Studies in Nineteenth Century Jewish Intellectual History* (Cambridge: Harvard University Press, 1964).

On Nachman Krochmal as a scholar and a philosopher, see A. I. Katsh, "Nachman Krochmal and the German Idealists," *Jewish Social Studies* 8 (April 1946): 87–102; I. Schorsch, "The Philosophy of History of Nachman Krochmal," *Judaism* 10 (Summer 1961): 237–245; S. Schechter, "Nachman Krochmal and the Perplexities of the Time," in his *Studies in Judaism*, 1st ser. (Philadelphia: Jewish Publication Society, 1896), pp. 46–72; N. Rotenstreich, *Jewish Philosophy in Modern Times* (New York: Holt, Rinehart and Winston, 1968), pp. 136–148; and J. Guttmann, *Philosophies of Judaism* (New York: Holt, Rinehart and Winston, 1964), pp. 321–344.

On S. J. Rapoport, the reader should consult I. Barzilay, *Shelomo Yehudah Rapoport (Shir) and His Contemporaries* (Tel Aviv: Massada Press, 1969).

A good portrait of Leopold Zunz, the foremost nineteenth-century protagonist of the Science of Judaism, emerges from N. N. Glatzer, ed., *Leopold and Adelheid Zunz: An Account in Letters, 1815–1885* (London: East and West Library, 1958). Also valuable is L. Wallach, *Liberty and Letters: The Thoughts of Leopold Zunz* (London: East and West Library, 1959). Worthwhile articles on Zunz include

Bibliography

F. Bamberger, "Zunz's Conception of History," *Proceedings of the American Academy for Jewish Research* 12 (1941): 1–25; G. Karpeles, "Leopold Zunz," in his *Jewish Literature and Other Essays* (Philadelphia: Jewish Publication Society, 1895); M. E. Meyer, "Leopold Zunz and the Scientific Ideal," in his *The Origins of the Modern Jew* (Detroit: Wayne State University Press, 1967): and S. Schechter, "Leopold Zunz," in his *Studies in Judaism*, 3rd ser. (Philadelphia: Jewish Publication Society, 1924).

Noteworthy articles on other major figures of the Science of Judaism in the nineteenth century are S. W. Baron, "I. M. Jost, the Historian," *Proceedings of the American Academy for Jewish Research* 1 (1930): 7–32; M. Weiner, "Abraham Geiger and the Science of Judaism," *Judaism* 2 (January 1953): 41–48; S. B. Freehof, "Moritz Steinschneider," *Yearbook of the Central Conference of American Rabbis* 26 (1916); A. Marx, in his *Essays in Jewish Biography* (Philadelphia: Jewish Publication Society, 1947); and S. W. Baron, in *Alexander Marx Jubilee Volume* (New York: Jewish Theological Seminary of America, 1950).

Unfortunately, very little of the work of the nineteenth-century German-Jewish philosophers has yet appeared in English translation. The major exception is Moritz Lazarus, *The Ethics of Judaism*, 2 vol. (Philadelphia: Jewish Publication Society, 1901). On Lazarus, as well as on Solomon Formstecher, Samuel Hirsch, and Salomon Ludwig Steinheim, see J. B. Agus, *Modern Philosophies of Judaism* (New York: Behrman's Jewish Book House, 1941); J. Guttmann, *Philosophies of Judaism* (New York: Holt, Rinehart and Winston, 1964); and N. B. Rotenstreich, *Jewish Philosophy in Modern Times* (New York: Holt, Rinehart and Winston, 1968). An important article is E. L. Fackenheim, "Samuel Hirsch and Hegel: A Study of Hirsch's *Religionsphilosophie der Juden*," in A. Altmann, ed., *Studies in Nineteenth Century Jewish Intellectual History* (Cambridge: Harvard University Press), pp. 171–201.

XII American Judaism from Its Beginnings to the End of the Nineteenth Century

An extensive literature has been produced on the history of Jews and Judaism in America. The reader will find M. Rischin's *An Inventory of American Jewish History* (Cambridge: Harvard University Press, 1954) an extremely valuable bibliographical essay.

Bibliography

Important documentary histories are S. W. Baron and J. L. Blau, eds., *The Jews of the United States, 1799–1840: A Documentary History*, 3 vols. (New York: Columbia University Press, 1963), and M. U. Schappes, *A Documentary History of the Jews in the United States, 1654–1875*, 3rd ed. (New York: Schocken Books, 1971).

Worthwhile general histories include N. Glazer, *American Judaism*, 2nd ed. (Chicago: University of Chicago Press, 1972); O. Handlin, *Adventure in Freedom* (New York: McGraw-Hill, 1954); R. Learsi, *The Jews in America: A History* (Cleveland: World Publishing Co., 1954); and A. L. Lebeson, *Pilgrim People* (New York: Harper, 1950).

The dean of living American-Jewish historians is Jacob R. Marcus. The reader would do well to consult his works. Among the most important of these are *Colonial American Jews*, 3 vol. (Philadelphia: Jewish Publication Society, 1971); *Early American Jewry*, 2 vol. (Philadelphia: Jewish Publication Society, 1951–1952); *Memoirs of American Jews*, 3 vol. (Philadelphia: Jewish Publication Society, 1955–1956); and *American Jewry: Documents, Eighteenth Century* (Cincinnati: Hebrew Union College Press, 1959).

Other notable books on the early history of the Jews in America are A. L. Lebeson, *Jewish Pioneers of America: 1492–1848* (New York: Brentano's, 1931); L. M. Friedman, *Jewish Pioneers and Patriots* (Philadelphia: Jewish Publication Society, 1942); A. V. Goodman, *American Overture* (Philadelphia: Jewish Publication Society, 1947); and H. B. Grinstein, *The Rise of the Jewish Community in New York, 1654–1860* (Philadelphia: Jewish Publication Society, 1945).

On the history of the German Jews in the United States, see R. Glanz, *The German Jew in America* (Cincinnati: Hebrew Union College Press, 1969).

A valuable and informative overview of the history of Judaism in America is M. Davis, "Jewish Religious Life and Institutions in America: A Historical Study," in L. Finkelstein, ed., *The Jews: Their History, Culture and Religion*, 3rd ed. (New York: Harper & Row, 1966), vol. 1, pp. 488–587.

On the history of Reform Judaism in America, see D. Philipson, *The Reform Movement in Judaism*, rev. ed. (New York: Ktav, 1967); B. Levy, *Reform Judaism in America* (New York: Bloch Publishing Co., 1933); and S. S. Cohon, "Reform Judaism in America," *Judaism* 3 (Fall 1954): 333–353. A valuable source book is W. G. Plaut, *The Growth of Reform Judaism* (New York: Union of American Hebrew Congregations, 1965).

A good many of the books of Isaac Mayer Wise, the builder of

Reform Judaism in America, are still available. Interesting selections will be found in D. Philipson and L. Grossman, eds., *Selected Writings of Isaac M. Wise* (Cincinnati: R. Clarke and Co., 1901). The reader may also wish to peruse Wise's *Reminiscences* (Cincinnati: L. Wise and Co., 1901); *The Essence of Judaism* (Cincinnati: Bloch Publishing Co., 1868); and *Judaism: Its Doctrines and Duties* (Cincinnati: Office of the Israelite, 1872). A number of biographies of Wise have been written, of which the best is J. G. Heller, *Isaac M. Wise: His Life, Work, and Thought* (New York: Union of American Hebrew Congregations, 1964). Others worth consulting are J. H. Gumbiner, *Isaac Mayer Wise: Pioneer of American Judaism* (New York: Union of American Hebrew Congregations, 1959); I. Knox, *Rabbi in America, The Story of Isaac M. Wise* (Boston: Little, Brown, 1957); J. R. Marcus, *The Americanization of Isaac Mayer Wise* (Cincinnati: privately printed, 1931); M. B. May, *Isaac Mayer Wise* (New York: G. P. Putnam's Sons, 1916); and Dena Wilansky, *Sinai to Cincinnati: Isaac M. Wise, Founder of Reform in America* (New York: Renaissance Book Co., 1937).

Insight into the thought of other noted Reform Rabbis in nineteenth-century America will be found in D. Philipson, *Max Lilienthal, American Rabbi: Life and Writings* (New York: Bloch Publishing Co., 1915); K. Kohler, ed., *David Einhorn Memorial Volume* (New York: Bloch Publishing Co., 1911); David Einhorn, *Selected Sermons and Addresses* (New York: Bloch Publishing Co., 1911); and Emil G. Hirsch, *My Religion* (New York: Macmillan, 1925).

On the foremost figure of the Positive-Historical school in nineteenth-century America, see H. Englander, "Isaac Leeser, 1806–1868," *Yearbook of the Central Conference of American Rabbis* 28 (1918): 213–252. The rise of the Positive-Historical school, which later came to call itself Conservative Judaism, is traced in M. Davis, *The Emergence of Conservative Judaism* (Philadelphia: Jewish Publication Society, 1963).

For an account of the immigration of Jews from eastern Europe after 1881, which changed the character of American-Jewish life, see S. Joseph, *Jewish Immigration to the United States, 1881–1910* (New York: Columbia University Press, 1914) and M. Wischnitzer, *To Dwell in Safety: The Story of Jewish Migrations Since 1800* (Philadelphia: Jewish Publication Society, 1948).

On the growth of the largest Jewish community in America and the city that became the center of both the Conservative and Orthodox movements in the nineteenth century, see I. Goldstein, *A Cen-*

tury of Judaism in New York (New York: Congregation B'nai Jeshurun, 1930).

For a biography of the figure who was chiefly responsible for organizing the Jewish Theological Seminary and also participated in the establishment of many other important Jewish institutions in the last decades of the nineteenth century and the first decades of the twentieth, see A. A. Neuman, *Cyrus Adler* (Philadelphia: Jewish Publication Society, 1942).

On Jewish learning in America, see I. Elbogen, *American Jewish Scholarship: A Survey* (New York: American Jewish Committee, 1943).

XIII   The Recrudescence of Anti-Semitism and the Rise of Zionism

On the history of the Jews in Europe during the period when modern racial anti-Semitism emerged and the Zionist movement developed, see H. Sachar, *The Course of Modern Jewish History* (Cleveland: World Publishing Co., 1958) and I. Elbogen, *A Century of Jewish Life: 1840–1940* (Philadelphia: Jewish Publication Society, 1944).

There is an extensive literature on modern anti-Semitism. Among the best treatments are Maurice Samuel, *The Great Hatred* (New York: Alfred A. Knopf, 1940) and K. S. Pinson, ed., *Essays on Anti-Semitism*, new ed. (New York: New York Jewish Social Studies, 1942).

The best introduction to the history of Zionist theory, containing extensive selections from virtually all the important Zionist thinkers of both the nineteenth and twentieth centuries, is Arthur Hertzberg, ed., *The Zionist Idea: A Historical Analysis and Reader* (Philadelphia: Jewish Publication Society, 1959). Other worthwhile histories include I. Cohen, *A Short History of Zionism* (London: Muller, Ltd., 1952); R. Learsi, *Fulfillment: The Epic Story of Zionism* (Cleveland: World Publishing Co., 1951); and W. Z. Laqueur, *A History of Zionism* (New York: Holt, Rinehart and Winston, 1972).

Moses Hess' *Rome and Jerusalem* was translated into English by M. Waxman (New York: Bloch Publishing Co., 1918).

The Diaries of Theodor Herzl were edited and translated by M. Lowenthal (New York: Dial Press, 1956). Herzl's *The Jewish State*, Sylvia d'Avigdor, trans. (New York: American Zionist Emergency Council, 1946) and his *Old-New Land*, Lotta Levensohn, trans. (New

York: Bloch Publishing Co., 1960) are also available in English translation. On Herzl, see A. Bein, *Theodor Herzl: A Biography* (Philadelphia: Jewish Publication Society, 1940); J. DeHaas, *Theodor Herzl: A Biographical Study*, 2 vol. (Chicago: The Leonard Co., 1927); I. Cohen, *Theodor Herzl* (New York: Thomas Yoseloff, 1959); and L. Lipsky, *Herzl, Weizmann, and a Jewish State* (Rehovot: Yad Chaim Weizmann, 1956).

Some of the writings of the great apostle of the "Religion of Labor," A. D. Gordon, are available in his *Selected Essays* (New York: Bloch Publishing Co., 1938). On Gordon, see H. Rose, *The Life and Thought of A. D. Gordon* (New York: Bloch Publishing Co., 1964); N. Rotenstreich, *Jewish Philosophy in Modern Times* (New York: Holt, Rinehart and Winston, 1968); and H. Bergman, *Faith and Reason: An Introduction to Modern Jewish Thought* (Washington, D.C.: B'nai Brith Hillel Foundations, 1961).

A number of Aḥad Ha-Am's essays are to be found in L. Simon, ed., *Aḥad Ha-Am: Essays, Letters, Memoirs* (Oxford: East and West Library, 1946). See also *Aḥad Ha-Am: Selected Essays* (Philadelphia: Jewish Publication Society, 1912) and *Ten Essays on Zionism and Judaism* (London: G. Routledge and Sons, 1922). On Aḥad Ha-Am, see N. Bentwich, *Aḥad Ha-Am and His Philosophy* (Jerusalem: Keren Ha-Yesod, 1927), and L. Simon, *Aḥad Ha-Am: A Biography* (Philadelphia: Jewish Publication Society, 1960).

XIV   European Jewry in the Twentieth Century

For an overview of the history of the Jewish people in the twentieth century, the reader should consult H. Sachar, *The Course of Modern Jewish History* (Cleveland: World Publishing Co., 1958); S. Grayzel, *A History of the Contemporary Jews* (New York: Meridian Books, 1960); and I. Elbogen, *A Century of Jewish Life: 1840–1940* (Philadelphia: Jewish Publication Society, 1944).

For a survey of east European Jewish history in modern times, see B. D. Weinryb, "East European Jewry since the Partitions of Poland, 1772–1795," in L. Finkelstein, ed., *The Jews, Their History, Culture, and Religion*, 3rd ed. (New York: Harper & Row, 1966), vol. 1, pp. 321–375. On the history of the Jews in Russia in modern times, see J. Frumkin *et al.*, eds., *Russian Jewry: 1860–1917* (New York: Thomas Yoseloff, 1966); S. W. Baron, *The Russian Jew under Tsars and Soviets* (New York: Macmillan, 1964); and S. M. Schwartz,

Bibliography

The Jews in the Soviet Union (Syracuse: Syracuse University Press, 1951). The material collected in L. S. Dawidowicz, ed., *The Golden Tradition: Jewish Life and Thought in Eastern Europe* (New York: Holt, Rinehart and Winston, 1967) will give the reader insight into the ideological tendencies prevalent among the Jews of eastern Europe. M. Zborowski and E. Herzog, *Life Is with People: The Jewish Little Town of Eastern Europe* (New York: International Universities Press, 1952) provides a good, if somewhat romanticized, portrait of the east European *shtetl* in the nineteenth and twentieth centuries.

The greatest Jewish poet of modern times was the Russian-born Ḥayyim Naḥman Bialik. His *Complete Poetic Works* were edited by I. Efros (New York: Histadruth Ivrit of America, 1948). A fine sampling of his poetry is to be found in *Selected Poems: Chaim Naḥman Bialik*, with the translations by Maurice Samuel (New York: The New Palestine, 1926).

On Simon Dubnow's "Diaspora Nationalism" and his interpretation of Jewish history, see I. Friedlander, *Dubnow's Theory of Jewish Nationalism* (New York: Maccabean Publishing Co., 1905).

For the development of Yiddish literature in the nineteenth and twentieth centuries, consult Y. Mark, "Yiddish Literature," in L. Finkelstein, ed., *The Jews, Their History, Culture and Religion*, 3rd ed. (New York: Harper & Row, 1966), vol. 2, pp. 1191–1233; A. A. Roback, *The Story of Yiddish Literature* (New York: Yiddish Scientific Institute, 1940); L. Wiener, *History of the Yiddish Literature of the Nineteenth Century* (New York: Charles Scribner's Sons, 1899); and S. Liptzin, *A History of Yiddish Literature* (Middle Village, N.Y.: Jonathan David Publishers, 1972). Particularly illuminating and valuable are two special studies by Maurice Samuel, *The World of Sholem Aleichem* (New York: Alfred A. Knopf, 1943), and *I. L. Peretz: Prince of the Ghetto* (New York: Alfred A. Knopf, 1948). A good deal of the work of the great masters of Yiddish literature has now appeared in translation. An excellent sampling will be found in I. Howe and E. Greenberg, eds., *A Treasury of Yiddish Stories* (New York: Viking Press, 1954), and J. Leftwich, ed., *The Golden Peacock: An Anthology of Yiddish Poetry* (Cambridge: Sci-Art Publishers, 1939).

On Jewish life in Poland after World War I, see J. Apenszlak, *The Black Book of Polish Jewry* (New York: American Federation of Polish Jews, 1943); W. Glicksman, *A Kehillah in Poland During the Inter-War Years* (Philadelphia: M. E. Kalish Folkshul, 1970); and J. Tenenbaum, *In Search of a Lost People* (New York: Beechhurst Press, 1949).

On Judaism in England, see J. Gould and S. Esh, eds., *Jewish Life*

Bibliography

in Modern Britain (London: Routledge and Kegan Paul, 1964); V. D. Lipman, *A Social History of the Jews in England 1850–1950* (London: Watts, 1954); and C. Roth, *A History of the Jews in England* (Oxford: Clarendon Press, 1964).

The best book on German Jewry, but carrying the story only to the beginning of the Nazi era, is M. Lowenthal, *The Jews of Germany* (Philadelphia: Jewish Publication Society, 1936). The reader should also consult J. R. Marcus, *The Rise and Destiny of the German Jew* (Cincinnati: Union of American Hebrew Congregations, 1934); S. Liptzin, *Germany's Stepchildren* (Philadelphia: Jewish Publication Society, 1945); and A. Myerson and I. Goldberg, *The German Jew: His Share in Modern Culture* (New York: Alfred A. Knopf, 1933).

Several of the major figures in the twentieth-century Jewish theological renaissance in Germany—Hermann Cohen, Franz Rosenzweig, and Martin Buber—are discussed in S. H. Bergmann, *Faith and Reason: An Introduction to Modern Jewish Thought* (Washington, D.C.: B'nai Brith Hillel Foundations, 1961); J. B. Agus, *Modern Philosophies of Judaism* (New York: Behrman's Jewish Book House, 1941); and B. Martin, *Great Twentieth Century Jewish Philosophers* (New York: Macmillan, 1970).

Hermann Cohen's *The Religion of Reason out of the Sources of Judaism* has appeared in an English translation by Simon Kaplan (New York: Frederick Ungar, 1972). Selections from his other works may be found in E. Jospe, *Reason and Hope: Selections from the Jewish Writings of Hermann Cohen* (New York: Schocken Books, 1971). On Cohen, see T. Weiss-Rosmarin, *The Religion of Reason: Hermann Cohen's System of Religious Philosophy* (New York: Bloch Publishing Co., 1936); N. Rotenstreich, *Jewish Philosophy in Modern Times* (New York: Holt, Rinehart and Winston, 1968); H. Slonimsky, "Hermann Cohen," in *Historia Judaica* 4 (October 1942): 81–94; and E. L. Fackenheim, *Hermann Cohen—After Fifty Years* (New York: Leo Baeck Institute, 1969).

Franz Rosenzweig's major work, *The Star of Redemption*, has now been translated into English by William Hallo (New York: Holt, Rinehart and Winston, 1971). Selections from a number of Rosenzweig's writings, as well as from his letters, are to be found in N. N. Glatzer, *Franz Rosenzweig: His Life and Thought* (Philadelphia: Jewish Publication Society 1953). Glatzer also edited Rosenzweig's *On Jewish Learning* (New York: Schocken Books, 1955) and *Understanding the Sick and the Healthy* (New York: Noonday Press, 1954). On Rosenzweig, see S. S. Schwarzschild, *Franz Rosenzweig: Guide to Reversioners*

(London: Educational Committee of the Hillel Foundation, 1960).

Well-chosen selections from the works of Martin Buber are available in Will Herberg, ed., *The Writings of Martin Buber* (New York: 1956). Buber's most famous work, *I and Thou*, has been translated by Ronald Gregor Smith, 2nd ed. (New York: 1958) and by Walter Kaufmann (New York: Charles Scribner's Sons, 1970). Among other works of Buber that deal largely with Jewish themes, see *Israel and the World* (New York: Schocken Books, 1948); *Addresses on Judaism*, N. Glatzer, ed. (New York: Schocken Books, 1966); *Ḥasidism and Modern Man*, M. Friedman, trans. (New York: Horizon Press, 1958); and *Moses* (Oxford: East and West Library, 1945). A series of critical and evaluative essays is contained in F. Schilpp and M. Friedman, eds., *The Philosophy of Martin Buber* (La Salle, Ill.: Open Court, 1967). The reader may also wish to consult M. Friedman, *Martin Buber: The Life of Dialogue* (Chicago: University of Chicago Press, 1955); M. L. Diamond, *Martin Buber: Jewish Existentialist* (New York: Oxford University Press, 1960); and E. Simon, "Martin Buber and German Judaism," in *Yearbook of the Leo Baeck Institute* 3, London (1958), pp. 3–39.

Leo Baeck's classic work, *The Essence of Judaism*, is available in English translation by I. Howe (New York: Schocken Books, 1948). So is his major book *This People Israel*, A. Friedlander, trans. (Philadelphia: Jewish Publication Society, 1965), as well as *God and Man in Judaism*, A. K. Dallas, trans. (New York: Union of American Hebrew Congregations, 1958), and *Judaism and Christianity*, W. Kaufmann, trans. (Philadelphia: Jewish Publication Society, 1958). On Baeck, see A. Friedlander, *Leo Baeck: Teacher of Theresienstadt* (New York: Holt, Rinehart and Winston, 1968); M. Grunewald, "Leo Baeck: Witness and Judge," in *Judaism* 6 no. 3 (1957): 195–201; and F. Bamberger, *Leo Baeck: The Man and the Idea* (New York: Leo Baeck Institute, 1958).

The literature on the Holocaust has grown to extensive proportions. For a brief survey of this crowning tragedy in Jewish history, see A. Tartakower, "The Decline of European Jewry: 1933–1953," in L. Finkelstein, ed., *The Jews: Their History, Culture and Religion*, 3rd ed. (New York: Harper & Row, 1966), vol. 1, pp. 427–446. Other works that might be consulted are L. Poliakov, *Harvest of Hate: The Nazi Program for the Destruction of the Jews of Europe* (Syracuse, N.Y.: Syracuse University Press, 1954); G. Reitlinger, *The Final Solution*, 2nd ed. (New York: Thomas Yoseloff, 1968); and R. Hilberg, *The Destruction of the European Jews* (Chicago: Quadrangle

Books, 1961). Much of the poignant literature produced by Jews in Europe during the Holocaust era has now appeared in translation. Outstanding examples of it will be found in A. Friedlander, ed., *Out of the Whirlwind: A Reader of Holocaust Literature* (New York: Union of American Hebrew Congregations, 1968), and J. Glatstein, I. Knox, and S. Margoshes, eds., *An Anthology of Holocaust Literature* (Philadelphia: Jewish Publication Society, 1968). One of the survivors of the Holocaust who has dedicated himself to portraying its tragedy and searching for its meaning is the distinguished novelist and essayist Elie Wiesel; the reader will find his novels and books particularly moving and eloquent. Other important eyewitness accounts are Emmanuel Ringelbaum's *Notes from the Warsaw Ghetto* (New York: McGraw-Hill, 1958) and Chaim Kaplan's *Scroll of Agony* (New York: Macmillan, 1965).

On post-Holocaust European Jewry, consult H. Sachar, *The Course of Modern Jewish History* (Cleveland: World Publishing Co., 1958), and the annual volumes of the *American Jewish Year Book* from 1945 on.

These volumes of the *American Jewish Year Book* also contain articles on the various Jewish communities, all deriving originally from Europe, settled in Australia, Canada, Latin America, and South Africa.

For recent developments among Jews in the Soviet Union see Ben-Ami (A. Eliav), *Between Hammer and Sickle* (Philadelphia: Jewish Publication Society, 1967), and Y. A. Gilboa, *The Black Years of Soviet Jewry* (Boston: Little, Brown, 1971).

XV Jewish Life and Religious Thought in America in the Twentieth Century

For general works on American-Jewish history, see the bibliography to Chapter XII. A particularly important source for American Judaism in the twentieth century is the *American Jewish Year Book*, published annually from 1899. An *Index to the American Jewish Year Book: 1899 to 1949* has been prepared by E. Solis-Cohen (Philadelphia: Jewish Publication Society, 1967).

For an overview of the development of American-Jewish religious life in the twentieth century, see N. Glazer, *American Judaism*, 2nd ed. (Chicago: University of Chicago Press, 1972) and M. Davis, "Jewish Religious Life and Institutions in America: A Historical

Bibliography

Study," in L. Finkelstein, ed., *The Jews: Their History, Culture and Religion*, 3rd ed. (New York: Harper & Row, 1966), vol. 1. pp. 488–587.

On the development of Reform Judaism, see D. Philipson, *The Reform Movement in Judaism*, rev. ed. (New York: Ktav, 1967); B. Levy, *Reform Judaism in America* (New York: Bloch Publishing Co., 1933); W. G. Plaut, *The Growth of Reform Judaism* (New York: Union of American Hebrew Congregations, 1965); and S. S. Cohon, "Reform Judaism in America," *Judaism* 3 (Fall 1954): 333–353.

Kaufmann Kohler's *Jewish Theology* (New York: Macmillan, 1918) still repays study as an example of Reform Jewish thought in its "classical period." Selections from other of Kohler's writings are available in S. S. Cohon, ed., *A Living Faith: Selected Sermons and Addresses from the Literary Remains of Kaufmann Kohler* (Cincinnati: Hebrew Union College Press, 1948). On Kohler, see S. S. Cohon, "Kaufmann Kohler: The Reformer," in *Mordecai Kaplan Jubilee Volume* (New York: Jewish Theological Seminary of America, 1953), and "Kaufmann Kohler," in S. Noveck, ed., *Great Jewish Thinkers of the Twentieth Century* (Washington, D.C.: B'nai Brith Department of Adult Education, 1963).

On the history, ideology, and sociology of the Conservative movement in twentieth-century American Judaism, see M. Sklare, *Conservative Judaism* (Glencoe, Ill.: The Free Press, 1955) and R. Gordis, *Conservative Judaism* (New York: Behrman House, 1945). The nineteenth-century antecedents of the Conservative movement are discussed in M. Davis, *The Emergence of Conservative Judaism* (Philadelphia: Jewish Publication Society, 1963). H. Parzen's *Architects of Conservative Judaism* (New York: Jonathan David Co., 1964) contains popular biographical sketches of a number of important figures in the movement.

A good sampling of the work of the chief architect of twentieth-century American Conservative Judaism is to be found in N. Bentwich, ed., *Solomon Schechter: Selected Writings* (Oxford: East and West Library, 1946). Schechter's *Studies in Judaism*, 3 vol. (Philadelphia: Jewish Publication Society, 1896, 1908, 1924) are models of scholarship and clarity. The reader will also find of interest Schechter's *Some Aspects of Rabbinic Theology* (New York: Macmillan, 1909) and *Seminary Addresses and Other Papers* (Cincinnati: Ark Publishing Co., 1915). On Schechter, see N. Bentwich, *Solomon Schechter: A Biography* (Philadelphia: Jewish Publication Society, 1938) and L. Ginzberg, "Solomon Schechter," in *Students, Scholars, and Saints* (Philadelphia: Jewish Publication Society, 1928), pp. 241–251.

Bibliography

Of considerable interest is the autobiography of Schechter's successor in the leadership of the Conservative movement, Cyrus Adler, *I Have Considered the Days* (Philadelphia: Jewish Publication Society, 1943).

On the growth of contemporary Orthodox Judaism in America see C. S. Liebman, "Orthodoxy in American Jewish Life," in *American Jewish Year Book* 66 (1965), pp. 21–98. For a survey of the history of Yeshiva College, see J. Hartstein, "Yeshiva University: Growth of the Rabbi Isaac Elchanan Theological Seminary," *American Jewish Year Book* 48 (1946–1947), pp. 73–84. On the leader and builder of the Rabbi Isaac Elchanan Theological Seminary and Yeshiva College, see L. Jung, "Bernard Revel," *American Jewish Year Book* 43 (1941), pp. 415–424, and A. Rothkoff, *Bernard Revel: Builder of American Jewish Orthodoxy* (Philadelphia: Jewish Publication Society, 1972).

Mordecai Kaplan's most important works are *Judaism as a Civilization* (New York: Macmillan, 1934); *Judaism in Transition* (New York: Covici, Friede, 1936); *The Meaning of God in Modern Jewish Religion* (New York: Behrman's Jewish Book House, 1937); *The Future of the American Jew* (New York: Macmillan, 1948); and *The Greater Judaism in the Making* (New York: Reconstructionist Press, 1960). For an estimate of Kaplan's impact on American Judaism, see I. Eisenstein and E. Kohn, eds., *Mordecai M. Kaplan: An Evaluation* (New York: Jewish Reconstructionist Foundation, 1952).

On American Jews and Judaism in the period after World War II, the reader might profitably consult two informative sociological works: C. B. Sherman, *The Jew Within American Society: A Study in Ethnic Individuality* (Detroit: Wayne State University Press, 1961) and M. Sklare, ed., *The Jews: Social Patterns of an American Group* (Glencoe, Ill.: The Free Press, 1958). Also of interest is J. Neusner, *American Judaism: Adventure in Modernity* (Englewood Cliffs, N.J.: Prentice-Hall, 1972).

For an account of the life and thought of the outstanding thinker in contemporary Orthodox Judaism in America, see A. Lichtenstein, "Joseph Soloveitchik," in S. Noveck, ed., *Great Jewish Thinkers of the Twentieth Century* (Washington, D.C.: B'nai Brith Department of Adult Education, 1963).

Will Herberg's *Judaism and Modern Man* (New York: Farrar, Straus, and Young, 1951) is of major significance as the work which, in some respects, inaugurated the postwar Jewish theological renaissance in America.

Abraham Joshua Heschel's most important theological works are

Bibliography

Man Is Not Alone (New York: Farrar, Straus, and Young, 1951); *God in Search of Man* (New York: Farrar, Straus, and Cudahy, 1956); *Man's Quest for God* (New York: Charles Scribner's Sons, 1954); and *The Sabbath: Its Meaning for Modern Man* (New York: Farrar, Straus, and Young, 1951).

For a sampling of recent thinking in American Reform Judaism, see B. Martin, ed., *Contemporary Reform Jewish Thought* (Chicago: Quadrangle Books, 1968).

XVI   The State of Israel: Achievements and Problems

On the Zionist movement in the period leading up to the establishment of the State of Israel and on the first years of the new state, see D. Ben-Gurion, *Rebirth and Destiny of Israel* (New York: Philosophical Library, 1954); H. Sacher, *Israel: The Establishment of a State* (London: G. Weidenfeld and Nicolson, 1952); J. C. Hurewitz, *The Struggle for Palestine* (New York: Norton, 1950); N. Bentwich, *Israel Resurgent* (New York: Praeger, 1960); D. R. Elston, *Israel, The Making of a Nation* (London: Anglo-Israel Association, 1963); Chaim Weizmann, *Trial and Error* (New York: Harper & Row, 1949); and O. I. Janowsky, "The Rise of the State of Israel," in L. Finkelstein, ed., *The Jews, Their History, Culture and Religion*, 3rd ed. (New York: Harper & Row, 1966), vol. 1, pp. 696–765.

On the political, diplomatic, and military problems of the State of Israel in the first decades of its existence see Y. Bauer, *Flight and Rescue: Brichah* (New York: Random House, 1970); M. H. Bernstein, *The Politics of Israel: The First Decade of Statehood* (Princeton: Princeton University Press, 1957); T. Draper, *Israel and World Politics: The Roots of the Third Arab-Israeli War* (New York: Viking Press, 1968); L. J. Fein, *Israel: Politics and People* (Boston: Little, Brown, 1968); Y. Freudenheim, *Government in Israel* (Dobbs Ferry, N.Y.: Oceana Publications, 1967); O. I. Janowsky, *Foundations of Israel: The Emergence of a Welfare State* (Princeton: Van Nostrand, 1959); J. M. Landau, *The Arabs in Israel: A Political Study* (London: Oxford University Press, 1969); W. Z. Laqueur, *The Road to War, 1967: The Origins of the Arab-Israel Conflict* (London: G. Weidenfeld and Nicolson, 1968); and N. Safran, *From War to War: The Arab-Israeli Confrontation, 1948–1967* (New York: Pegasus, 1969).

On the Jews of Israel, their backgrounds, social institutions, and cultural and religious life, see J. Badi, *Religion in Israel Today* (New

Bibliography

York: Bookman Associates, 1959); J. S. Bentwich, *Education in Israel* (Philadelphia: Jewish Publication Society, 1965); H. Bavli, *Some Aspects of Modern Hebrew Poetry* (New York: Theodor Herzl Foundation, 1958); S. N. Eisenstadt, *Israeli Society* (New York: Basic Books, 1967); A. Elon, *The Israelis: Founders and Sons* (New York: Holt, Rinehart and Winston, 1971); Georges Friedmann, *The End of the Jewish People?* (Garden City, N.Y.: Doubleday, 1967); J. Matras, *Social Change in Israel* (Chicago: Aldine Publishing Co., 1965); R. Patai, *Israel Between East and West: A Study in Human Relations*, 2nd rev. ed. (Westport, Conn.: Greenwood Publishing Corp., 1970); H. M. Sachar, *Aliyah: The Peoples of Israel* (Cleveland and New York: World Publishing Co., 1961), and *From the Ends of the Earth: The Peoples of Israel* (Cleveland and New York: World Publishing Co., 1964); R. Sanders, *Israel: The View from Masada* (New York: Harper & Row, 1966); M. E. Spiro, *Kibbutz: Venture in Utopia* (Cambridge: Harvard University Press, 1956); R. Wallenrod, *The Literature of Modern Israel* (New York: Abelard-Schuman, 1956); and A. Weingrod, *Israel: Group Relations in a New Society* (New York: Institute of Race Relations, 1965).

INDEX

Index

Index

B'nai B'rith, 411, 425
Board of Deputies of British Jews, 331, 345
Boccaccio, Giovanni, 93
Bodleian Library, Oxford University, 273, 275
Boeckh, August, 265
Bohemia, 79, 81
Boleslav the Pious, King of Poland, 114
Bolshevik Revolution, 353, 355, 360, 361–362
Bomberg, Daniel, 102, 152
Bonnet, Charles, 194
Börne, Ludwig, 208
Borochov, Ber, 339–340, 352
Boston, 296, 306, 395
Brandeis, Louis D., 345, 395, 422
Brandeis University, 431
Brandes, Georg, 361
Bratzlav Ḥasidim, 456
Brazil, 162, 286, 391
Breslau, Menaḥem Mendel, 213
British Columbia, 389
British East Africa, 337
Bruno, Giordano, 97
Buber, Martin, 179–180, 187, 357, 373, 376, 377–379, 402, 428, 429
Buber, Solomon, 377
Buchenwald concentration camp, 371
Büchler, Adolph, 366
Budapest, 383
Buenos Aires, 391, 392, 393
Bulan, 113
Bulgaria, 327, 443
Bulls, papal, 89–90, 152
Bülow, Bernhard von, 337
Bund, 307, 353–354, 355, 358
Burla, Jehudah, 450
Buttenwieser, Moses, 315
Byk, Jacob Samuel, 219
Byzantine Empire, 84, 86, 87

Caesar, Julius, 83, 84, 106
Cagoulards, 371
Cahan, Abraham, 315
Cairo, 367, 402
Callixtus II, Pope, 89–90
Cambridge University, England, 208, 367, 402
Canada, 389
Canadian Jewish Congress, 389
Cantors (*ḥazzanim*), 65
Caracalla, Emperor, 84
Casimir the Great, King of Poland, 114–115
Cassel, David, 238
Castile, 3, 13, 14
Castro, Benedict de, 164
Catalonia, 14, 23
Cavour, Camillo di, 328
Central Conference of American Rabbis, 293, 312, 314, 368, 420–421

Cerf-Berr, Lippmann, 203, 204–205
Chagall, Marc, 369
Chamberlain, Houston Stewart, 322
Chamberlain, Joseph, 337
Chamberlain, Neville, 346
Chamisso, Adelbert von, 139
Chariot-Throne (*maaseh merkavah*), 36, 70, 95
Charlemagne, 55
Charles V, Emperor, 149
Charles X, King of Sweden, 132
Charleston, South Carolina, 287, 289
Chazar kingdom, 113–114
Chekhov, Anton, 361
Chesterton, G. K., 365
Chile, 392
China, 448
Chmielnitzki, Bogdan, 47, 119, 130, 131, 134, 135, 142
Chmielnitzki massacres, 168, 170–171
Chorin, Aaron, 234
Christianity, 24, 56, 110, 158, 232–233, 393, 427; American, 294, 295; conversions to, 7, 15, 16–17, 23, 27, 30, 97, 130, 131, 137, 170, 202, 208–209, 221; Counter Reformation and, 129–130, 151–153; Enlightenment and, 190–191, 192, 194–195; in Italy, 84, 87–88, 89–90, 95, 100, 101, 109; Judaism's theology and, 20, 21, 50, 59, 70, 112, 240–241, 277–278, 280–281, 284, 285, 320, 371, 377, 398; medieval Europe and, 54–55, 62–63, 74, 78; Reformation and, 141, 150; in Spain, 3, 14, 15–17
Christian Socialist Workers Party (Germany), 321
Christina, Queen of Sweden, 162
Churchill, Winston, 438
Cicero, 83, 103, 106
Cincinnati, Ohio, 291, 295, 298
Circumcision, 22, 66, 243, 246, 314
Citizenship rights, 202–207, 319, 362–363
Clemenceau, Georges, 324
Clement of Alexandria, 106
Clement VI, Pope, 8
Clement VII, Pope, 149
Clermont-Tonnerre, Count, 204
Cleveland Conference, 292–293, 298
Cochin Jews, 389, 390, 443
Cohen, Arthur, 331
Cohen, Hermann, 373–375, 427, 428
Cohen, Nehemiah, 48
Collegiants (Mennonite sect), 157
Collegio Rabbinico Italiano, Padua, 259, 260
Colombia, 393
Columbia University, 431
Columbus Platform, 421
Communist Party, 353, 361, 383
Communities (*kehillot*), 64–66, 168, 276–277, 288, 373, 384, 400–401, 418
Community centers, Jewish, 413–415

Index

Index

Index

Index

Index

Index

Index

Index

Index

Index

Index

Index

Index

Index

Zedekiah ben Abraham Anaw, 91, 92
Zeitlin, Joshua, 220
Zeitlin, Solomon, 60, 359
Zerubbabel, 87–88
Zinberg, Israel, 359
Zinoviev, Grigori, 360
Zion College, 297
Zionism, 209, 250, 258, 261, 373, 378, 440, 453, 454; American, 304–305, 313, 395, 397, 399, 401, 404, 405, 409, 410, 416, 418, 421, 422–424, 428, 434; anti-Semitism and, 325–348; English, 366, 367; Haskalah and, 210, 223, 224, 230; Russian, 351, 362
Zionist Congress: First, 333, 336, 337; Sixth, 337–338
Zionist Organization of America, 400, 409, 424
Zohar (Moses de Leon), 33, 37, 39–44, 45, 46, 50, 53, 94, 95, 101, 112, 128, 129, 139, 146
Zola, Emile, 324
Zunz, Leopold, 215, 239, 245–246, 259, 265, 268, 269, 270–274, 275, 404